THE AMERICAN CENTURY

A multimedia collection of primary sources complementing this book is available at www.mesharpe-student.com.

Resources for instructors who adopt this book are available at www.mesharpe-instructor.com.

The American Century
A History of the United States Since the 1890s, 7e

By Walter LaFeber, Richard Polenberg, and Nancy Woloch

Also available in two separate volumes:

The American Century
A History of the United States from 1890 to 1941, 7e

The American Century
A History of the United States Since 1941, 7e

THE AMERICAN CENTURY

A History of the United States Since the 1890s

Seventh Edition

Walter LaFeber, Richard Polenberg, and Nancy Woloch

M.E.Sharpe
Armonk, New York
London, England

The EuroSlavic fonts used to create this work are © 1986–2013 Payne Loving Trust.
EuroSlavic is available from Linguist's Software, Inc.,
www.linguistsoftware.com, P.O. Box 580, Edmonds, WA 98020-0580 USA
tel (425) 775-1130.

Library of Congress Cataloging-in-Publication Data

LaFeber, Walter.
  The American century : a history of the United States since the 1890s / by Walter LaFeber,
Richard Polenberg, and Nancy Woloch. — Seventh Edition. —
     volumes cm
  Includes bibliographical references.
  ISBN 978-0-7656-3483-2 (hardcover : alk. paper)—ISBN 978-0-7656-3484-9 (pbk. : alk. paper)
  1. United States—History—20th century. 2. United States—History—21st century. 3. United
States—Foreign relations—20th century. 4. United States—Foreign relations—21st century.
I. Polenberg, Richard. II. Woloch, Nancy, 1940– III. Title.

E741.L45 2013
973.9—dc23   2013004357

Printed in the United States of America

The paper used in this publication meets the minimum requirements of
American National Standard for Information Sciences
Permanence of Paper for Printed Library Materials,
ANSI Z 39.48-1984.

~

IBT (c)   10   9   8   7   6   5   4   3   2   1
IBT (p)   10   9   8   7   6   5   4   3   2

Contents

List of Maps

Preface

We are most grateful for the response to the first six editions of *The American Century*. That response has confirmed the need for a concise text that is both highly factual and, at appropriate points, interpretive. In this seventh edition, we have adopted suggestions and corrections given to us by instructors and students. We particularly appreciate Sal Barbera's help in the revision of material in Chapter 9.

Necessarily believing that the past does shape the future, and noting how some historians have compared the Gilded Age of the late nineteenth century to the high-tech age of the late twentieth and early twenty-first centuries (both, for example, suffering far-reaching, highly painful economic downturns), we have devoted about as much space to pre-1945 America as to the Cold War years and after. The volume stresses the importance of economic and urban growth, social and political change, civil rights and liberties, and the evolution of the United States into a global superpower; but also, we devote feature sections to art, architecture, baseball, music, dance, theater, football, poetry, photography, sculpture, basketball, computer technology, recreation, and evolving secondary education. Since its inception, this book has given equal attention to U.S. foreign and domestic policies, at points noting how the two are necessarily related. To help students understand that foreign (and often domestic) policy, we include brief analyses of developments elsewhere in the world.

We are especially indebted to the staff of M.E. Sharpe, above all to Steven Drummond, Executive Editor for History, for his encouragement, friendship, unfailing good advice, and awesome patience; and Kimberly Giambattisto and Henrietta Toth for their care and professionalism in handling editorial and other issues that invariably and unexpectedly arise.

THE
AMERICAN
CENTURY

CHAPTER ONE

1890s
The Beginnings of Modern America

Henry Ford in his first model car, completed in 1896. *(AP Photo/Ford Motor Company)*

Modern America emerged during a forty-year crisis that began with the Civil War (1861–1865) and ended with the war against Spain in 1898. The crisis, which recast every part of the nation's life, climaxed in the 1890s. At the Chicago Columbian Exposition of 1893, Americans celebrated their triumphs in industry and technology while, ironically, enduring the nation's worst economic depression. A young historian, Frederick Jackson Turner of the University of Wisconsin, delivered a speech at this world's fair that helped explain the irony. The vast open lands of the West, Turner asserted, had shaped American social and political institutions. According to the 1890 census, however, these lands had finally been settled. Turner concluded: "And now, four centuries from the discovery of America, at the end of a hundred years of life under the Constitution, the frontier has gone, and with its going has closed the first period of American history." Scholars later agreed that Turner overemphasized the importance of the frontier in the shaping of American character, but few, then or since, would deny that a different America was indeed born in the last years of the century. The birth pains were promising—and terrifying.

THE SCULPTOR OF MODERN AMERICA: THE CORPORATION

Between 1860 and 1900 no birth was more notable than that of the modern industrial corporation. Barely conceived of before the Civil War, it quickly came to dominate Americans' lives by determining what they possessed and where they worked and, in general, by producing everything they needed from their baby food to their tombstones.

Before the Civil War, state and national governments had created corporations largely to operate public highways and banks. But shrewd business executives soon realized that merely by obtaining a charter of incorporation from a state government, they suddenly had the right to acquire great sums of capital through sales of stock. At the same time, the liability of each investor was limited to the amount he or she invested. It was like magic. The new creature first appeared to build railroads during the 1850s boom. It was the Civil War, however, that shaped the industrial corporation.

The mammoth armies of the North and South created an immense market that demanded rapid production of goods. Through privately owned corporations, such men as Gustavus F. Swift (meat), Gail Borden (dairy and groceries), and Andrew Carnegie (railways and later steel) got their start by supplying the sinews of war. Equally important, when Southerners deserted Washington in 1861, unopposed Northern politicians were able to whip legislation through Congress to aid their section's factories. Between 1862 and 1865 members of Congress consequently built a tariff wall insulating American producers against foreign competition, passed bank laws to standardize and liberalize the monetary system, and allowed owners to import cheap labor from Europe. Most striking, Congress simply gave away tremendous amounts of land and mineral resources to corporations that were building the transcontinental railway (completed in 1869) and other transportation systems. By the early twentieth century, the government had given private railway builders free land equivalent to the areas of Maine, New Hampshire, Vermont, Massachusetts, Rhode Island, and much of New York. Some of this acreage held rich deposits of coal, lead, and iron ores.

This was hardly "private enterprise." Corporations obtained incalculable favors from government to develop the country's wealth. An intimate, sometimes questionable, relationship developed between business and government. One member of the House of Representatives observed in 1873 that Congress had become like an "auction room where more valuable considerations were disposed of under the speaker's hammer than in any other place on earth." More cynically, one presidential candidate advised another during the 1870s that businessmen wanted "men in office who will not steal but who will not interfere with those who do." The result was historic: in 1850 the laws had shaped the corporation, but by 1900 the corporation shaped the laws.

The railroads even changed how Americans told time. Until the 1880s, the country was a chaos of time zones. Wisconsin alone had thirty-eight such zones. But cross-country travel required a better system, so in 1883 the railroads imposed four time zones on Americans—Eastern, Central, Rocky Mountain, Pacific—and in 1918 Congress finally made this system law. The isolated, rural "island communities" of the 1870s became part of an integrated and more homogeneous America. Small local firms suddenly faced competition from giant producers and either copied or merged with the giants or were wiped out by them.

Inheriting a chaotic and decentralized America, the corporation streamlined and centralized the nation's economic life. It also produced unimagined wealth that marked the beginning of an affluent America. In 1860, 31 million Americans turned out manufactures valued at $2 billion, traveled on 30,000 miles of railroads, and produced little iron or steel. Forty years later, 75 million people produced manufactures worth $11 billion, used 200,000 miles of rails, and overtook Great Britain and Germany to become the world's greatest iron and steel (and soap) producers. The corporation helped create such new cities as Chicago, Atlanta, Kansas City, Minneapolis, and Dallas.

THE NEW TECHNOLOGY: EDISON, ENERGY—AND SECRETARIES

The new corporation was the child of the new machines. For in the late nineteenth century American technology, which had lagged behind British and French technology, suddenly developed and transformed the world with the electric light, typewriter, telephone, thermionic valve (which made possible radio and, later, transistors), automobile, and airplane. All of these discoveries and products appeared in the forty years after the Civil War.

To develop the technology Americans wanted to sell overseas and use in their own homes required two particular ingredients: scientific knowledge and money. The lonely inventor living on a shoestring, whose sudden discovery changed the world, was becoming rare. Thomas Edison's laboratory, which developed the incandescent bulb in 1879, had by 1901 turned into the General Electric Corporation's laboratory employing hundreds of skilled technicians. The garage where Henry Ford tinkered on his first horseless carriage had become a mechanized industrial complex. Only the corporation could provide the range of management skills and the amount of money needed for developing much of the new technology.

But from the start, government at both the state and the national level was also necessarily involved. The 1862 Land Grant College Act had established new universities and poured resources into other schools, which were to "teach such branches of learning as are related to agriculture and the mechanic arts." These schools began producing professional engineers who drove the United States to the forefront of world technology. An American people that too often is thought of as anti-intellectual actually built its twentieth-century civilization on scientific discoveries and technology that demanded the most rigorous intellectual training and application.

The transformation of the business office exemplified the changes. Before 1860 the office usually had a few male employees who, with their pens, handled a wide range of tasks and acted as both managers and secretaries as they tried to work their way up. Men continued to be the managers, but by 1900 the office was a large enterprise with many women who performed specific tasks (such as typing and filing) with such new machines as the typewriter, which appeared in the 1870s. Women left their homes to become wage earners. With no hope of moving up the corporate ladder, they were the new proletariats of American business. The office was becoming routinized, bureaucratized, and—most important—mechanized and corporatized. And so was much of American society.

The creators of this society naturally believed it was the best of worlds. In 1886 Andrew Carnegie looked at his vast, efficient steel empire and observed, "If asked what important law I should change, I must perforce say none: the laws are perfect."

BOOM HIDDEN IN BUST

Not all Americans agreed with Carnegie. During the quarter-century following 1873, the country suffered from increasingly severe periods of economic depression. The 1873 panic was triggered by overexpansion and stock exchange corruption. The economic crisis worsened until labor violence erupted in 1877, 1886, 1892, and then sporadically between 1893 and 1895. Overproduction caused this twenty-five-year crisis. Industries and farms produced so much that markets were glutted, prices fell, and both farmers and laborers suffered. Pig-iron production, for example, doubled between 1873 and 1893, while its price dropped from $50 to $13 a ton. Production of cotton, traditionally the nation's leading export, increased more than 50 percent during these years; Americans eventually produced more cotton than the entire world could consume. Some corporations, like some farmers, could not stand the competition and went bankrupt.

As men such as Carnegie learned that efficiency and cost cutting were necessary for survival, they tended to drive others out of business until such vital industries as sugar refining, oil, steel, and tobacco were dominated by one or two companies. In these fields, competition increasingly disappeared. Prices were then determined not by many sellers in an open marketplace, but by a few corporations based on their own costs and whatever return they thought desirable on their investment. Companies banded together to fix prices in "pools" or formed giant combinations known as "trusts," which destroyed competition. To form a trust a number of corporations would join together, giving a group of trustees the power to set prices for all of them. Thus the corporations fixed prices and cut out competition. Their profits skyrocketed.

But at the very moment competition was vanishing and opportunity narrowing, belief in the self-made man flourished. Business tycoons helped popularize the idea that success came to those who worked hard and saved their money. The view that there was room at the top for all who were virtuous received its most popular formulation in the novels of Horatio Alger. The typical Alger hero, such as "Ragged Dick" or "Mark the Match Boy," began life as a poor orphan. But he was "manly and self-reliant" and through honesty and hard work attained a position of solid respectability with the further assurance that he would "go far." The belief that success resulted from virtue sanctified corporate practices and led Americans to praise entrepreneurial liberty ("free enterprise") as the highest social value.

When state or national legislatures tried to control corporations, the courts often stopped them. Carnegie might have believed the laws were perfect, but the Supreme Court tried to improve on perfection. It did this by radically changing the idea of "due process," a basic tenet of American law. Before the 1880s due process referred to procedure. For example, the Constitution's Fifth Amendment provides that no person can "be deprived of life, liberty, or property, without due process of law," that is, be subjected to arbitrary arrest, unlawful forfeiture of property, and the like. In 1868 the Fourteenth Amendment strengthened this guarantee by providing that no state government can take away individual rights without due process. This amendment was aimed especially at preventing Southern states from depriving black citizens of voting and other rights. The Supreme Court, however, interpreted it in quite another way.

Between 1886 and 1898 the Court ruled on whether the Minnesota and Nebraska legislatures could regulate railroads in those states. The judges held the state laws invalid, not because the legislatures had violated *procedural* due process in passing the regulations, but because in the Court's opinion the laws were unfair *in substance* to the railroads. The Court asserted the right to decide whether the railway rates were reasonable, instead of deciding, as it had in the past, whether the procedures used in passing the laws were constitutional. Judges thus declared that their own views, rather than those of elected officials, should determine the substance of these particular state laws.

This was potentially an explosive situation, for the Court had put itself above elected officials in order to protect private corporations. Justice Stephen J. Field, who served on the Supreme Court from 1863 to 1897, often shaped its view. His beliefs, in turn, had been molded by his experience as an ambitious businessman on the California frontier (where in self-defense he learned the art of shooting to kill without taking the pistol out of his pocket) and from his reading of classical economists who believed an open marketplace existed in which everyone competed equally.

In the *Wabash* case of 1886 the Court struck down an Illinois law regulating railroads that crossed state boundaries. The Court declared that since the railway was in interstate commerce, only Congress could deal with it. This decision forced Congress in 1887 to establish the Interstate Commerce Commission (ICC) to stop such unfair practices as rebates to favored customers. At first the railroads fought the ICC, but shrewd railway lawyers, such as Richard Olney of Boston, adopted different tactics. Olney argued that the ICC was inevitable because public opinion demanded it; therefore, the railroads should simply ensure that their friends controlled the agency. This was one reason why the ICC proved ineffectual; the other was a series of Supreme Court decisions that stripped the ICC of any powers to set fair rates. The same fate paralyzed the Sherman Antitrust Act, passed by Congress in 1890 to outlaw business combinations that tried to monopolize markets or engaged in "restraint of trade" in interstate commerce. The impact of the Sherman act was so pitiful that the spectacular merger and trust movement followed it between 1897 and 1902.

Americans, who have always professed reverence for both efficiency and competition, found by the 1890s that they could not always have both. With the aid of the Supreme Court they chose efficiency. Some critics might tag the corporate leaders of the cut-and-thrust post–Civil War era "Robber Barons." Most Americans, however, were willing to overlook the brutal, often illegal, practices if Rockefeller could deliver cheap, dependable oil for home lamps, or if Cornelius Vanderbilt's New York Central Railroad could reduce the price of bread by cutting transportation costs for flour from $3.45 a barrel in 1865 to only 68 cents in 1885. When writers debated whether Shakespeare or Vanderbilt had contributed more to the human race, Shakespeare inevitably lost.

The Robber Barons corrupted politics, undercut laws, and stifled competition, but many people nevertheless agreed with Carnegie's assessment. "It will be a great mistake for the community to shoot the millionaires," he said, "for they are the bees that make the most honey, and contribute most to the hive even after they have gorged themselves full." For these Americans who questioned whether they should obediently serve such queen bees as Carnegie, alternatives seemed quite limited. The crucial question became: What kind of checks could the society produce to limit the corporation's spreading power? Queen bees, after all, are quite brutal.

THE COLLAPSE OF THE FIRST BARRIER: THE SOUTH, WHITE AND BLACK

Five forces in American society might have made the corporation more responsible: the South, labor unions, protest movements, organized religion, and the political parties. During the 1880s and 1890s each of these either finally accommodated itself to the new industrial America or else was swept aside.

Historically the South had led opposition to the corporation's dominance, for that section had fought for low tariffs, agrarian values, and easy credit. However, Southern resistance halted after the Civil War as Northern capitalists followed Union soldiers into the defeated South, making the area a virtual colony of the North. Spurred by new wealth, cheap labor, and nonexistent taxes, the South doubled the number of its industrial laborers and tripled its investment in manufacturing between 1880 and 1900. By 1900 the region contained half the nation's textile mills. In 1870 one house stood at a rail intersection in Alabama; thirty years later this site, named Birmingham, produced $12 million of manufactures annually and competed with Pittsburgh as leader in world steel production. Yet the South industrialized only as rapidly as the rest of the country. Its spectacular development simply allowed it to keep pace with the North.

Much of the new southern industry, moreover, depended on northern capital. Many southerners, knows as "redeemers," rushed to make their own fortunes by cooperating with the entrepreneurs from above the Mason-Dixon line. The redeemers sacrificed tax income, thereby sacrificing schools and community facilities, in order to induce industry to build in their towns. One redeemer believed that "it were better for the state to burn the schools" than levy heavier taxes on corporations to pay the state debt. The thirteen southern states together had less taxable property than the single state of New York and spent $3 million less each year on education than did New York. In 1890 illiteracy afflicted nearly half of all southerners and more than three-quarters of the section's African-Americans. State universities in the South were nearly bankrupt. In 1890 Harvard alone received more income than all southern colleges combined. The institutions that did thrive, such as Vanderbilt in Tennessee and Johns Hopkins in Maryland, depended on northern funds. Even in higher education, the North colonized the South.

The agrarian South did not disappear, but its character greatly changed. The average farm, approximately 350 acres before the Civil War, shrank to less than half that acreage afterward. Meanwhile the number of farms doubled to over 1 million, one-third of them operated by tenants or sharecroppers for absentee owners. This was hardly an economic base from which the South could challenge the mighty corporation.

Blacks particularly depended on tenant farming or sharecropping. White farm owners preferred former slaves to white workers, for as one owner remarked, "No other laborer [than the Negro] . . . would be as cheerful or so contented on four pounds of meat and a peck of meal a week, in a little cabin 14 by 16 feet with cracks in it large enough to afford free passage to a large sized cat." During the 1890s, however, race relations underwent a transformation. On the farms African-Americans saw that tenant farming renewed their slave ties to the land, now without even the relative security that slaves had possessed. When blacks tried to gain employment in the new factories, bloody clashes with whites resulted.

During the late 1880s radical whites attempted to weld the poor of both races into a class movement that became the Populist Party. But redeemers broke up this coalition with racist attacks that first split apart the whites and then turned them violently against blacks. Racism proved stronger than common economic interests shared by both blacks and whites. Lynchings multiplied until they averaged 188 a year during the 1890s. "The government which had made the Negro a citizen found itself unable to protect him," black antilynching crusader Ida Wells-Barnett claimed in 1895. "The white man's victory became complete by fraud, violence, intimidation, and murder." So-called Jim Crow laws were rushed through state legislatures, segregating schools and transportation into supposed "separate but equal" facilities. In 1896 the Supreme Court upheld such laws in *Plessy v. Ferguson.* The Court brusquely overrode the lone protest of Justice John Marshall Harlan, who argued, "our Constitution is colorblind." By 1900 the illiteracy of African-Americans was six times as great as that of whites.

When the United States declared war against Spain in 1898, many African-Americans insisted they be allowed to fight for the liberation of Cubans and Filipinos from Spanish control. After overcoming considerable white opposition, President William McKinley finally allowed the creation of four black regular regiments and a volunteer force that reached about 10,000 men. The regulars distinguished themselves in Cuba, but when black soldiers returned home they found conditions worse than before. The president would do nothing. The *New York World* published a cartoon showing McKinley studying a map of the Philippines. In the background a figure pulled back a curtain to reveal the murder and lynching of blacks. The caption read: "Civilization Begins at Home."

Most African-American leaders responded to this crisis by accepting the policies of Booker T. Washington, a black educator. Washington advised acceptance of segregation, stressed the need for nonviolent accommodation to white society, and urged blacks to achieve equality ultimately by means of economic gains, particularly through vocational training. "The opportunity to earn a dollar in a factory just now is worth infinitely more than the opportunity to spend a dollar in an opera house," he observed. Washington hoped that self-help measures would eventually tear down most racial barriers. "In all things purely social we can be as separate as the fingers, yet one as the hand in all things essential to mutual progress." In effect Washington promised that African-Americans would constitute a docile labor force. "The Negro is not given to strikes," he noted.

Some black elders dissented. T. Thomas Fortune, a New York editor, founded the Afro-American League in 1890. It protested strenuously against the spread of Jim Crow institutions but died out within a short time. W.E.B. DuBois, who began teaching at Atlanta University in 1897, also criticized the accommodationist doctrine. He asserted that Washington's emphasis on vocational training cheated blacks of the cultural advantages of a liberal education and deprived them of leaders. But the great majority of black clergymen, professionals, and politicians flocked to Washington's side. His popularity grew when such corporate leaders as Carnegie applauded his policies and when President Theodore Roosevelt asked him to dine at the White House—the first black ever invited as a guest to the mansion. The ensuing antiblack uproar ensured that he was also the last of his race invited to the White House by Roosevelt. By the turn of the century it was impossible for either a black movement led by Washington or a South whose industry and culture were largely dependent on northern capital to check the new corporation.

THE COLLAPSE OF THE SECOND BARRIER: LABORERS AND UNIONS

Like the South, the labor movement initially fought the corporation, then accommodated to it. Between 1860 and 1900 the number of industrial workers increased from 2.7 million (or 40 percent of all workers in farms and factories) to 13 million (65 percent). Several union movements attempted to organize laborers after the Civil War but fell victim to racism, the economic depression, and internal political divisions. The continual economic crises after 1873 drove workers to the breaking point, and some organized in small local groups. Nearly 24,000 strikes occurred during the last quarter of the century. Several were especially dangerous.

The general railroad strike of 1877 nearly paralyzed the nation, frightening some Americans into urging a third presidential term for General Ulysses S. Grant because he was the best hope to head off "another French Revolution." Nine years later the Haymarket Riot began when two laborers were killed during a clash with police during a strike in Chicago. At a protest meeting the next night in Haymarket Square, a bomb was thrown. Eight policemen were killed. The bomb thrower was never caught, but amid the hysteria the anarchist movement, which preached individual freedom by abolishing all state controls, was conveniently blamed. Four anarchists were hanged; a fifth committed suicide in his prison cell. The Haymarket became a symbol to critics of the new corporate system. The riot inspired a number of works that fundamentally criticized industrialism, among them Mark Twain's *A Connecticut Yankee in King Arthur's Court* (1889). Twain ends his novel with the freewheeling Yankee entrepreneur using his industrial ingenuity to kill 25,000 people. The image of capitalism did not improve in 1892 when strikers at Carnegie's Homestead works in Pittsburgh were fired on by hired Pinkerton detectives.

The new corporate America was born amid bloodshed and violence. The terrible depression of 1893 to 1896 worsened matters, as labor uprisings threatened to paralyze many cities. The most serious was a strike against the Pullman Company in Chicago. The trouble began when management sliced wages by 25 percent and fired many workers but refused to reduce costs in the model town of Pullman, where most employees lived. The American Railway Union, led by Eugene V. Debs, refused to move Pullman coaches. The railroad owners then declared that they would not run trains without those cars and blamed the union for disrupting transportation. On the advice of Attorney General Richard Olney, President Grover Cleveland obtained an injunction against the strikers and then, over the protest of Illinois governor John P. Altgeld, sent federal troops into the city. The ostensible reason was to keep U.S. mail moving, but the effect was to break the strike for the benefit of a private corporation. In 1894 the Supreme Court upheld this use of a sweeping injunction, and Debs went to jail.

Labor's only major success occurred when Samuel Gompers organized the American Federation of Labor (AFL) in 1886. This union survived the horrors of the 1890s largely because Gompers reached an accommodation with the new corporation. One leader of an earlier, short-lived union had urged his members to become politically active in order to "strangle monopoly." But Gompers refused to identify labor's interests with those of any one political party, choosing instead to work for whichever candidates seemed most friendly at the time. Gompers, moreover, had little desire to "fight monopoly." Instead he tried to counter big corporations with big labor, using union techniques such as strikes and boycotts directly against a particular corporation in order to obtain recognition and benefits. He concentrated on organizing skilled workers along craft lines because he believed that only they could exert much leverage on employers. This policy excluded not only most men in the industrial work-force but almost all women factory workers, who tended to hold unskilled jobs. By 1900 the AFL had organized only 3 percent of the nation's nonfarm employees, but it had established the roots for its twentieth-century triumphs. Gompers survived by accepting the corporation and by accepting as well the antianarchist, antisocialist, and, to some extent, nativist fears of most Americans.

The immigration question proved especially important. Through the mid-nineteenth century the country received over 2 million newcomers each decade, but this number doubled in the 1880s and 1890s. The source of the migration changed from western Europe to eastern and southern Europe, which in turn meant accepting increased numbers of Roman Catholics and Jews. Both old-stock Protestant Americans, who considered the newcomers racially inferior, and segments of organized labor, which disliked the added competition for jobs, favored attempts to restrict immigration. The long-cherished notion that the country could transform immigrants into acceptable citizens through the so-called melting pot of schools and churches began to fade. In 1882 the first exclusion law in American history was passed; it was limited to keeping out Chinese.

THE COLLAPSE OF THE THIRD BARRIER: PROTEST MOVEMENTS

Farmers already knew about the closed frontier. Following the 1873 depression, the great American West changed for them from a promise to a hell. During the next quarter-century, the cost of growing wheat and corn was sometimes considerably more than the price the crops brought on the market. With new machinery and vast lands, farm output soared. Farmers produced so much that they had to rely on exports to other nations to absorb surpluses. But on the world market, Americans had to compete with cheap grains from newly opened fields in Argentina and Russia. Terrible winter storms followed by intense heat and drought during the 1880s left many farmers with no crops at all. Some farmers tried to escape to the growing cities but others tried to fight. They organized such political movements as the Grange, the Greenback Party, and the Populist Party. The Populists hoped to improve the farmer's condition by gaining control of the federal government and then using it to regulate the railroads and trusts, provide more credit, impose graduated income taxes, and clean up corrupt politics. Corporate leaders attacked the Populists, and so did many urban laborers who feared that "farm power" might mean higher bread prices. The Populists' demand for government help led to their being labeled "radical" and "socialist." Such terms were beside the point,

FRANK LLOYD WRIGHT
ARCHITECT OF THE OLD FRONTIER
AND THE NEW CITY

Frank Lloyd Wright and his wife, Olgivanna, reading in the living room at Taliesin, Wisconsin. *(Wisconsin Historical Society)*

"American architecture," a critic acidly observed in 1891, "was the art of covering one thing with another thing to imitate a third thing, which, if genuine, would not be desirable." Houses and office buildings were mere boxes, banks resembled Greek temples, government buildings looked like ancient Rome. There was little that could be called American architecture. Then Frank Lloyd Wright burst upon the scene.

Fallingwater, the famous split-level house designed by architect Frank Lloyd Wright and built in 1936. *(Time & Life Pictures/Getty Images)*

Wright was born in Wisconsin in 1869. His work by twentieth century's turn exemplified key American characteristics. Like the frontier thesis of Frederick Jackson Turner, Wright's genius emphasized the importance of space and the natural frontier environment in American life. "Intimacy with Nature is the great friendship," he insisted, then built structures that followed the land's contours and harmonized with the environment. His houses were not mere boxes ("more of a coffin for the human spirit than an inspiration," he sniffed), but a "prairie architecture" that would not be "on a hill," but "*of* the hill." Inside, room flowed into room, space into space, like the prairies outside, instead of being artificially separated by walls. These were the first ranch houses. In Wright's plans, they were to be wholly American and functional for Americans, much as Greek temples were useful for Greeks, but less so for American business executives.

During the 1890s many Americans became frightened that machines would soon strangle the natural environment. Wright, however, saw no conflict between machines and nature. In building his prairie architecture he was the first designer to use products of the industrial revolution that transformed the nation between 1870 and 1900. He innovated with such new building materials as steel, reinforced concrete, and, later, plastics. Like Carnegie and Rockefeller, moreover, Wright was an ambitious American entrepreneur, and he hated any governmental interference in either his art or his business. "I believe in the capitalist system," he declared. "I only wish I could see it tried some time."

Yet he was too much of an individualist and nonconformist to be accepted by his countrymen. Scandal plagued him, particularly after he left his wife and children to travel in Europe with the wife of one of his clients. For his new love, he built the ultimate prairie-style house, Taliesin, in Wisconsin. In 1914 a crazed servant killed the woman and six others, and then burned Taliesin. Wright rebuilt it, but after the scandal had difficulty obtaining work. Nearly bankrupt in 1929, he was saved by a commission to build the Johnson Wax Company's administration building in Racine, Wisconsin. He then entered his last, greatest period, creating magnificent homes, the entire campus of Florida Southern College, and a radical tubular structure for the Guggenheim Museum in New York City. He rightly considered himself the world's greatest architect, condemning cities that would not take his advice (on Dallas: "Seems to be made of rubber bath-mats"; on Pittsburgh: "Abandon it"). He died at ninety years of age, having completed 700 buildings and while working on plans for a mile-high, 528-floor skyscraper that would reach upward like the great trees of the American West. His epitaph was written by a French newspaper editor: "Nothing was ever more deliberately and more profoundly American than the personality and career of Frank Lloyd Wright."

Web Links

www.delmars.com/wright/index.html
A virtual look at Wright's work with links to collections and resources.

www.FrankLloydWright.org
The site of the Frank Lloyd Wright Foundation, with a tour of Taliesin and lists of sites open to the public.

for corporations had been growing rich from government legislation since the Civil War. The real struggle was over who would use the government.

In 1892 the Populist presidential candidate, James B. Weaver, received more than a million popular, and twenty-two electoral, votes. The party also elected governors in Kansas, North Dakota, and Colorado. Two years later, in the congressional elections, Populist candidates received nearly 1.5 million votes. That was the peak of the party's power. The last hope for a racially tolerant party that could make important changes in industrial America disappeared when William Jennings Bryan and the Democratic Party absorbed most Populists in the 1896 presidential campaign.

Another reform movement more effectively challenged the social values of the new corporation. The women's rights organization began in 1848 at Seneca Falls, New York, when a group of feminists resolved that since "all men and women are created equal" and since men refused women the vote and thus made them "civilly dead," any law that treated women as inferior to men would have "no force or authority." In 1869 Wyoming territory gave women the vote. By the 1870s, moreover, feminist leaders attempted to build on the Seneca Falls declaration by urging massive social change that would go far beyond the vote ("that crumb," as one leader termed it): the reform of divorce laws, an end to job discrimination, legal equality (in many states married women could not testify in court against their husbands or hold title to property), and a marriage institution in which the partners would be more equal.

Every feminist reform seemed to threaten social stability. Critics frequently linked the feminists to anarchists and strikers as threats to social order. Business leaders, even as they transformed the nation, tried to retain the image of tranquil, stable society that rested on the family and on a clear division of labor within the family. The prospect of women voting brought dire predictions of role reversal, domestic disorder, and social anarchy. In an early debate over the suffrage question, one senator charged that if women were given the vote, they would turn society "into a state of war, and make every home a hell on earth."

The woman suffrage movement split into conservative and liberal factions, then reunited into an organization that, led by Susan B. Anthony and later by Carrie Chapman Catt, dropped demands for drastic reforms in order to gain the vote. To accomplish this goal, suffragists shrewdly used the arguments of their male opponents: women were concerned primarily with taking care of the family and consequently should have the vote since their concern for spiritual and traditional values, as opposed to men's money-grubbing, would raise the moral level of politics. But women were also capable of appealing to other prejudices. Suffragists in the South exploited racial fears by asserting that the enfranchisement of white women would ensure white supremacy in the voting booths. Elsewhere, native, white, Protestant women, indignant because they could not vote—whereas male immigrants ultimately could—spoke with disdain of "the ignorant vote." The drive for the franchise thus gained momentum. But in narrowing their program, feminists—like the South, the AFL, and Populists-turned-Democrats—had gone far in accommodating themselves to the America of the industrial corporation. In the end, conflicts in the post–Civil War era revolved not around the question of whether conservatives could carry out a class solution, but around the question of which class would succeed in carrying out a conservative solution.

American socialists never capitulated in quite the same fashion. Neither, however, did they gain many followers. In the United States, unlike England and Germany, no close bonds ever developed between the socialist movement and organized labor. The socialists who achieved the widest recognition sought to modify Marxist ideology by smoothing its rough edges. The Christian Socialists, for example, sharply attacked the new corporate order and the suffering it caused, but called for the creation of a cooperative society in the name of traditional Christian morality. They rejected Marx's materialism and belief in the inevitability of class struggle.

No one carried the attempt to reconcile socialism with American values further than Edward Bellamy, whose best-selling *Looking Backward* (1888) led to the creation of "Nationalist Clubs" across the country. Bellamy's novel described a society in the year 2000 that was organized according to socialist principles, one in which cooperation had replaced competition. But his utopia differed substantially from Marx's. Bellamy did not condone class conflict or assume that the working class was a repository of special virtue. He emphasized change in the United States rather than around the world; he found a place for religious worship in his new order; and he saw the new society developing in a gradual, peaceful way. One character explains: "Evolution, not revolution, orderly and progressive development, not precipitate and hazardous experiment is our true policy . . . prudence and conservatism are called for." This moderate approach helps explain why Bellamy gained such a large following.

THE COLLAPSE OF THE FOURTH BARRIER: CHURCHES

In an earlier America the church had been an outspoken critic of men who sought profit rather than godliness. By the post–Civil War era, however, both Protestant and Roman Catholic leaders in the United States had largely lost their capacity to make fundamental economic or political analyses. "Our churches are largely for the mutual insurance of prosperous families, and not for the upbuilding of the great under-class of humanity," a leading New York City clergyman commented in 1874. Church leaders, moreover, confronted not only the complexities of the new industrialism, but an intellectual revolution that transformed every branch of knowledge.

Discovery of the quantum theory in physics demonstrated that energy is not emitted in predictable, continuous steps, but in unpredictable and interrupted stages. This discovery threatened to replace the ordered seventeenth-century world of Isaac Newton with an uncertain, rapidly changing universe that apparently had few if any absolutes. Sigmund Freud's investigations in Austria revealed new, treacherous depths in the unconscious. Such findings triggered the dilemmas that would characterize, and haunt, twentieth-century thought.

Some church leaders worked to reconcile the new science with their religious beliefs. The most popular response, however, was the new revivalism led by Dwight L. Moody, who condemned outright Charles Darwin's discoveries that species had evolved over the ages and were not created in a particular moment, as the biblical version seemed to indicate. Moody handled such problems by proclaiming that reason was less useful in religion than emotion. His message was particularly well received in college communities. John R. Mott, a Cornell University graduate, responded to the new revivalism by spearheading the spectacular growth of the Young Men's Christian Association. Some churchgoers tended to solve their intellectual confusion through sheer activity.

By 1900 the church had failed utterly to lessen the oppressiveness or the power of rampaging industrialism. Its failure was so marked that new organizations, such as the Salvation Army, had developed to aid the human casualties in the urban slums. By 1902 coal mine owner George F. Baer could oppose strikers with the remark: "The rights and interests of the laboring man will be protected and cared for—not by the labor agitators, but by the Christian men to whom God in his infinite wisdom has given the control of the property interests in this country." Few church leaders disputed Baer. The question thus became: Would these "Christian men" indeed care for—or exploit—their fellow men and women?

THE COLLAPSE OF THE FIFTH BARRIER: THE POLITICAL PARTY SYSTEM

Some scholars believe that the last, best hope to check the corporation's rising power was the political system and particularly the choice it provided voters in the 1896 presidential election. This is doubtful. Given the experiences of the social groups discussed above, the issue had been decided before 1896. The triumph of William McKinley over William Jennings Bryan in that election did no more than confirm a prevailing trend. It also established a political pattern that would govern the United States for nearly forty years.

The roaring depression of 1893 was the destroyer. It struck while a Democratic president, Grover Cleveland, and a Democratic Congress held power. The 1894 elections consequently brought about the largest turnover of congressional strength in the nation's history. The Democrats lost 113 House seats; their Capitol Hill leadership was virtually wiped out. In New England only a lone Democratic congressman survived (John F. Kennedy's grandfather, John "Honey Fitz" Fitzgerald), and even such southern states as Texas and Virginia elected Republicans.

Until this point, voters had been able to separate Democrats from Republicans rather neatly. Democrats preached limited government and noninterference in the affairs of individuals, states, and corporations. The marketplace, not the government, was supposed to encourage or regulate the society. As one Democratic leader proclaimed, "We are never doing as well as when we are doing nothing." The Republicans, on the other hand, urged a more active government and greater centralization of power. They used government to erect protective tariffs, give land to railroads, and make the monetary system more efficient for business. Republicans, however, did not plan to use power to reform or regulate. The corporations, therefore, had nothing to fear from Democrats and much to expect from Republicans.

But after the 1894 disaster, Democrats searched desperately for new blood. They found it when Bryan, a former Nebraska congressman, electrified the party's 1896 national convention with his "Cross of Gold" speech. He urged increased coining of silver (which was cheaper than gold) to create more money and thereby enable farmers and other depression victims to pay their debts. The proposal found no support from leading businessmen. They feared that mixing silver with gold, as Bryan proposed, would so cheapen the nation's currency that the banking and credit system would sink. Nor did urban wage laborers like Bryan's plan, for it could mean they would be paid in cheaper silver dollars and have to pay higher grocery prices.

The Nebraskan also had another major problem. Since the 1840s and 1850s, American politics had been increasingly influenced by close-knit, well-organized ethnic and cultural groups (such as the Germans and Irish) that were concentrated in the cities. These ethnic groups sought to preserve such traditions as beer fests and nonreligious activities on Sunday afternoons. The Democratic Party, with its tolerant view of pluralism and ethnic traditions, offered little interference and these groups had consequently become highly important in the party organization. Bryan was a Democrat, but he represented a largely rural view and constituency, was a "dry" on the burning question of whether alcoholic beverages should be prohibited, and practiced a religious fundamentalism abhorrent to many Roman Catholics and liberal Protestants in the Democratic Party. He argued for an activist government that would move decisively in both the society and the economy.

McKinley, meanwhile, transformed the Republican Party. Republicans had long been friends of business, but since the antislavery crusade of the 1850s they had also become identified with attempts to impose their own moral and political standards on ethnic groups and newly arrived immigrants. When Republicans preached the evils of alcoholic drink and the need to reserve Sunday for nothing but quiet meditation, Irish, German, and Jewish immigrants tended to vote Democratic. As a rising star in the political jungles of Ohio, however, McKinley had learned how to moderate such zeal so that he could win votes from ethnic settlements and "wets" in Cleveland and Cincinnati, as well as from traditional Republican rural areas. During the 1896 campaign he blurred the lines between the parties by welcoming the ethnic Democrats, whom Bryan was driving out, while keeping most traditional Republicans.

The confrontation was one of the most dramatic in the country's political history. An unprecedented number of voters turned out to give McKinley a triumph. His administration raised the tariff and then, with the help of rising prices in 1897 and 1898 caused by new discoveries of gold and increased agricultural exports to Europe, the president killed any hope for modifying the currency by having Congress pass the Gold Standard Act. With these issues decided, Americans began staying away from the polls on Election Day. One-party states became fixtures. Democrats owned the South (especially when African-Americans were kept from voting after the 1890s). Republicans controlled much of the Northeast and Midwest. A new era of American politics began, characterized by a diminished concern for elections, little party competition in many states, and Republican power. The new corporate industrialism had little to fear from Washington.

THE UNITED STATES BECOMES A GREAT WORLD POWER

Not coincidentally, the United States saw its economy mature at the same time that it became a world power. It joined England, France, Germany, and Russia in the great-power class when the Europeans were most imperialistic: between 1870 and 1900 they conquered more than 10 million square miles (one-fifth of the earth's land) and 150 million people. (Imperialism may be defined as one sovereign people subjugating and controlling an alien and formerly sovereign people.) The United States, however, did not join the rush for land. It thus differentiated its empire from that of the Europeans, who sought colonial areas—that is, territory that the Europeans could formally control and populate. After the Civil War, Americans sought empire primarily for trade, not territory, and preferred to allow native inhabitants to rule themselves under informal U.S. protection. This was the Americans' "new empire," as it was termed in the late 1890s.

The old empire, developed between the seventeenth century and the 1850s, had been based on the land conquered by Americans in their march across the continent. This old empire ended with the settlement of the Pacific coast, the close of the frontier, and the consolidation of the continent by the corporation. The last act had been a series of vicious Indian wars that climaxed a determination to drive Native Americans from lands in the Dakotas, Oklahoma, and Wyoming that had been given to them earlier in the century. These lands had been thought barren, but settlers rapidly encroached upon them after the Civil War, whereupon the federal government concocted devices to expel the American Indians. Between 1887 and 1934 they lost to whites about 86 million of their 138 million acres. One Sioux chief asked the obvious: "Why does not the Great Father put his red children on wheels, so he can move them as he will?" When some tribes refused to budge, the U.S. Army struck. "We must act with vindictive earnestness against the Sioux, even to extermination, men, women and children," General William Tecumseh Sherman proclaimed in the late 1860s. Sherman was especially ruthless. He destroyed buffalo herds, and then attacked Indian camps in midwinter so he could burn all provisions and thus cause mass starvation. The tribes were exterminated or reduced to begging. Their great chiefs—Geronimo, Big Foot, and Chief Joseph—died or fled, while Sitting Bull, the famous conqueror of Lieutenant Colonel George Custer's cavalry in 1876, ended as an exhibit in a circus.

Perhaps the ultimate horror occurred at Wounded Knee, South Dakota, in 1890. After troops disarmed cooperative Sioux, someone fired a rifle. The cavalry opened full fire, and then unloaded large cannons, which exploded nearly a shell a second in the defenseless camp. "We tried to run," one Sioux woman recalled, "but they shot us like we were buffalo." At least 150 and perhaps 250 of the original 350 men, women, and children were murdered. The American Indian campaigns sharpened the military's effectiveness. More important, they gave many Americans a rationale for warring against peoples of other colors.

Racism, however, did not trigger American imperialism in 1898. Its taproot lay in the post-1873 depressions and the need to find overseas markets for the overly productive factories and farms. That need became imperative during the strike-ridden days of the mid-1890s, when, in the words of Secretary of State Walter Quintin Gresham, "symptoms of revolution" appeared among unemployed laborers and farmers. Riots and strikes from Brooklyn to Chicago to San Francisco were capped by a march of thousands of unemployed (the so-called Coxey's Army) on Washington, DC, in 1894. The "symptoms" would disappear only with employment, and that required expanded markets. "The prosperity of our people," the secretary of the treasury announced in 1894, "depends largely upon their ability to sell their surplus products in foreign markets at remunerative prices."

The United States exported less than 10 percent of its manufactures and about 18 percent of its farm products, but these figures were misleading. Products that formed the economy's backbone heavily depended on external markets: 70 percent of the cotton crop had to be sold abroad, as did 40 percent of the wheat, 50 percent of the copper, 15 percent of the iron and steel, and even 16 percent of the agricultural equipment. These figures were impressive, but they were also inadequate, for the magnitude of exports did not prevent a quarter-century of depressions. Even greater overseas markets were required. There was, of course, an alternative. Americans could reorient their system, making more equal the distribution of wealth. Business and political leaders, who instead preferred greater production and expanded markets, never seriously considered that alternative. The needed world outlets, however, were coming under the control of the aggressive Europeans. If Americans were to find overseas buyers, they needed the aid of the State Department and perhaps the U.S. Army and Navy. As one prominent Republican observed in 1897, "Diplomacy is the management of international business."

Two business possibilities suddenly opened dramatically, one in Asia, the other in Latin America. In 1895 a surging Japan humiliated China in a brief conflict that revealed the loser to be a paper dragon. The European powers rushed to carve out areas of China exclusively for

President William McKinley, c. 1900. *(Library of Congress)*

their own trade and investment. This flew directly in the face of a half-century of an American policy known as the "open door," whose objective was to trade with a whole, sovereign China. McKinley knew that major American interests were deeply endangered, particularly after iron and textile exporters implored him to stop the European moves. The president's hands were tied, however, by another crisis ninety miles off the Florida coast.

Since 1868 Cubans had revolted against the domination, corruption, and inefficiency of their Spanish rulers. The United States had barely avoided involvement during the 1870s. The conflict simmered down during the next decade, but burst into flames once again in 1895. Under the leadership of José Martí, the Cubans announced the establishment of their own independent government. Several restraints initially kept Americans out of the struggle. For one thing, they feared that intervention might result in their having to annex Cuba, which they wished to avoid because of the racial, constitutional, and political problems that would inevitably arise. As it was, they were experiencing enough difficulty just keeping their own nation together during the 1890s. Moreover, the business community, with which McKinley was in close contact, did not at first want war. The depression at last seemed to be lifting in 1897. Finally seeing the light at the end of a gloomy economic tunnel, businessmen feared that the demands of a war economy would threaten the growing prosperity.

In early 1898, however, both restraints disappeared. The first problem evaporated when Americans began to understand that they did not have to govern a free Cuba. They needed only a veto over certain Cuban actions so that, for example, the island could not fall under British power. The inhabitants could otherwise be allowed to govern themselves. McKinley and Congress devised a classic solution in which the United States would enjoy power over, but have little daily responsibility for, the Cubans.

The second restraint disappeared in March 1898, when the business community and McKinley began to fear that a continuation of the Cuban struggle endangered $50 million worth of American investments on the island. A political threat also existed. If McKinley let Cuba fester and uncertainty continue, Bryan might oust the Republicans in 1900 with the cry of "Free Cuba and Free Silver." "Look out for Mr. Bryan," remarked McKinley's top political adviser, Mark Hanna, in February 1898. But, he was asked, would not the Democrats hesitate before offering the nomination again to Bryan? "Hesitate?" Hanna replied. "Does a dog hesitate for a marriage license?"

In late January 1898 McKinley sent the warship *Maine* to Havana to protect U.S. property. Two weeks later the warship blew up, killing more than 250 Americans. The causes have never been determined, but the nation (although not the president) quickly blamed Spain. War sentiment grew, fueled by an increasing fear that the United States would not be able to protect its growing interests in China until the Cuban problem was solved. On March 25 a close political adviser in New York City cabled McKinley: "Big corporations here now believe we will have war. Believe all would welcome it as relief to suspense." Two days later the president presented an ultimatum to Spain. The Spanish acquiesced to two of his demands by promising to stop their brutalities and to declare an armistice. But they refused McKinley's request that they promise eventual independence to Cuba and allow him to act as a mediator in the negotiations. Any Spanish government that accepted that demand would have immediately fallen from power. On April 11, McKinley asked Congress to declare war. Not for the first or last time, Americans concluded they would have to fight abroad in order to have peace and prosperity at home.

"THAT SPLENDID LITTLE WAR"

It would be one of the weirdest and most significant of wars. The first action occurred not in Cuba, but thousands of miles away in the Spanish-controlled Philippines. Six weeks before declaring war, McKinley had ordered Admiral George Dewey, the American commander in the Pacific, to take the Philippines should war erupt. Dewey's force was not overly imposing. When it left Hong Kong to fight the Spanish fleet, British naval officials remarked that the Americans were "a fine set of fellows, but unhappily we shall never see them again." Dewey, however, easily blockaded, then in less than six hours smashed a decrepit Spanish flotilla, killing or wounding 400, while only a few Americans suffered scratches. The United States suddenly became a major military power in the Far East as the result of Dewey's victory at Manila Bay in May 1898.

The campaigns in Cuba were not as spectacular. The American army numbered only 28,000 regulars before the war, and when augmented with 200,000 volunteers it was short of modern rifles, had inadequate medical supplies, ate food that was unfit for human consumption, and wore uniforms designed for duty in Alaska. The War Department proved so ineffectual that McKinley had to fire his secretary of war amid a national scandal. Americans escaped additional humiliation only because Spain was even more inefficient and corrupt. A broken-down Spanish navy struggled across the Atlantic only to be blockaded in Santiago. American troops overcame the heat and malaria long enough to win the heights overlooking that Cuban city. Theodore Roosevelt, who had the good taste to have his uniform custom-tailored by Brooks Brothers in New York City, led one charge up the heights, thus leading the troops directly into the enemy fire. They were saved only by the inability of the Spanish garrison to hit slowly moving targets. Americans held their precarious position for two days, in part because of the heroism of African-American units. Spain's navy was thus forced out into the harbor and then destroyed easily by the American fleet. Madrid asked for peace.

A war that lasted only three months made the United States a great world power. Roosevelt groused, "there wasn't enough war to go around." Americans now held a commanding position in Asia and the dominant role in the Western Hemisphere. At home they felt only the exhilaration, for they never had to consider curtailment of their individual liberties or rationing of foodstuffs in order to fight the war. Only 500 Americans died in battle, but four times that number fell victim to diseases. It was an unreal war. One reporter noted that as an American warship shelled a Spanish fort in Cuba, the sailors "whispered and chuckled. . . . Meanwhile from below came the strains of the string band playing from the officers' mess. . . . War as it is conducted at this end of the century is civilized." The horrors of 1873 to 1897 were over, with the new corporate system preserved and dramatically expanded by what Secretary of State John Hay called "that splendid little war."

THE PEACE: CLOSING CUBA, OPENING CHINA

McKinley had limited diplomatic objectives. He did not want to copy the Europeans by obtaining a large, expensive, unmanageable colonial empire. After obtaining Cuba, therefore, he allowed the Cubans to write their own constitution but forced them to accept the Platt Amendment passed by the U.S. Congress. This legislation gave the United States the right

Emilio Aguinaldo, commander of Filipino insurgents. *(The Granger Collection, NYC)*

to land troops in Cuba to maintain law and order, limited the amount of debt the island could accumulate, and later made Guantanamo a U.S. naval base. "There is, of course, little or no independence left Cuba under the Platt Amendment," the U.S. commander in Cuba accurately observed. Supposedly independent, the island would actually be controlled and exploited by the United States for sixty years. The president in addition took Puerto Rico from Spain and made it an unorganized territory of the United States.

He also acquired the Philippines, but the Filipinos reacted quite unexpectedly. McKinley had decided that they were unprepared for self-government and that if left to themselves they would be victimized by some European power. He did not want all of the islands, only the magnificent port of Manila, from which American merchants and warships could develop and protect interests in China. Manila, however, would be threatened if the remainder of the islands fell into European hands. McKinley therefore decided reluctantly that he had no alternative but to take all of the Philippines. As he later explained to missionaries who visited the White House, he had constantly prayed about the problem; then one night a voice told him to annex the Philippines for, among other reasons, "we could not turn them over to France or Germany—our commercial rivals in the Orient—that would be bad business and discreditable." Apparently everyone who had endured the post-1873 depressions knew the horrors of "bad business," even ghostly voices. The Filipinos, however, were not impressed. Led by Emilio Aguinaldo, they declared themselves independent and fought 120,000 American troops in a three-year struggle. Some 2,000 Americans and perhaps as many as 200,000 Filipinos died. The United States used increasingly brutal methods to end the insurrection. After some American troops were massacred, one general ordered the killing of every Filipino male over the age of ten. This order never took effect, but lesser barbarities continued until 1902, when Aguinaldo had been captured and resistance finally broken.

At home, anti-imperialist groups, led by conservative businessmen, intellectuals, and some Democrats, organized to blast McKinley's Philippine policy. "G is for guns / That McKinley has sent / To teach Filipinos / What Jesus Christ meant," went one anti-imperialist poem. But despite financing from Andrew Carnegie and literature written by such figures as Mark Twain, these groups received little support. In the election of 1900 Bryan tried briefly to gain the support of the anti-imperialists, but he decided to soft-pedal their cause in order to emphasize again the free-silver issue. Nothing could save either the anti-imperialists or Bryan. McKinley and his vice presidential running mate, Governor Theodore Roosevelt of New York, won a landslide victory larger than the Republican triumph of 1896.

Despite the Philippine bloodshed, the president had scored notable victories, including an end to the depression, solution of the Cuban problem, and establishment of the United States as a great power in Asia. The last was particularly important. Using Dewey's victory as leverage, McKinley moved to stop the carving up of China by the Europeans. Viewed another way, he sought to keep all of China open to American exporters and missionaries. In 1899 and 1900, Secretary of State John Hay issued two "open door" notes asking the other powers to promise that they would keep China open on an equal basis to all outsiders; meanwhile Chinese sovereignty would be recognized in all parts of the empire. The other powers, particularly Russia, grumbled, but Hay publicly announced that everyone had accepted the American position. This was not accurate, for the Russians, and later the Japanese, would not agree that China should become a marketplace open to all. They believed that their proximity to the China market gave them—indeed, required that they have—favored positions for their own economic and political interests. Hay and McKinley nevertheless insisted that American businessmen and missionaries enjoy an open door to compete for Chinese customers and souls on the same terms as anyone else, even Russians and Japanese. American statesmen would hold to that insistence until the 1940s.

The Civil War and the ensuing economic crisis mark the most threatening forty-year era in U.S. history. But McKinley's triumph at the end of the dark years gave Americans new optimism and reaffirmed their traditional belief that the nation had a special mission to perform in the world. The country had not simply survived the terrors of the post-1860 years. It had done great works. Americans had developed the modern corporation, an almost magical instrument for ordering and expanding wealth. With the conquest of Spain and the issuance of the open door notes, the nation stood on the world stage as one of the great global empires. Frederick Jackson Turner had been proven correct: a new period was indeed opening in American history. With the continental frontier apparently closed, Americans were seeking new frontiers.

In September 1901, McKinley explained why to the Pan-American Exposition in Buffalo, New York. The United States possessed "almost appalling" wealth, the president announced, and must therefore move into the world market to trade: "Isolation is no longer possible or desirable." The next day an anarchist shot McKinley. Theodore Roosevelt, a most outspoken expansionist and a student of Turner's theories, moved into the White House.

CHAPTER TWO

1900–1917
The Progressive Era

Suffragists on a picket line in front of the White House. One banner reads, "Mr. President How Long Must Women Wait For Liberty." *(Library of Congress)*

An interest in reform has always characterized American history. What varied over time has been the things people identified as evils, the intellectual justifications and political techniques used to eradicate those evils, the obstacles reformers encountered, and the degree of support those reforms received. Seldom has a larger proportion of the population favored social improvement than during the opening years of the twentieth century, when Americans first tried in a systematic way to control the forces of industrialization and urbanization. Because the United States was becoming a major world power, the successes and failures of the Progressive movement affected not only Americans but also people around the world.

THE REFORM IMPULSE

Although progressivism followed on the heels of the Populist revolt and sometimes echoed certain Populist demands, the two movements differed in important respects. Populism had drawn support primarily from farmers and had always remained a sectional force; progressivism won backing from city dwellers, including the middle classes, and had as wide a following in New York and California as in Kansas and South Carolina. Populists had sought for the most part to improve conditions in the countryside; Progressives devoted considerably more attention to political and social problems in the cities. Precisely because Progressives drew on a wider constituency and were concerned with a broader range of issues, they achieved a measure of influence at the city, state, and national levels that had eluded the Populists.

Progressives did, however, pay a price for this success. So many different people wanting so many disparate things styled themselves "Progressives" that the movement often seemed to lack a clearly defined program. Progressivism attracted surprisingly diverse groups: small businessmen who favored a curb on monopolies, and big businessmen who sought to extend their economic influence and eliminate their competitors; native Americans who feared the influx of eastern European immigrants, and settlement-house workers who appreciated the newcomers' contributions to American culture; southern whites dedicated to the preservation of Jim Crow, and northern blacks just as fully committed to its eradication; social scientists who believed that planning held all the answers to human progress; and prohibitionists who imagined that closing the saloons would usher in a new world.

Yet for all its diversity, there was a distinctly Progressive approach to social problems. Progressives saw industrialization and urbanization as potentially disruptive forces. The burgeoning cities and corporations seemed to endanger social stability and to undermine older ideals of individual initiative and equal opportunity. To restore a sense of order, to impose a reasonable measure of control on the forces transforming American life, Progressives used the power of government in an unprecedented fashion. In some respects the concern with democratizing government through the direct election of senators, the initiative and referendum, and woman suffrage followed logically from this conviction that government had to play an expanded role. Progressives were optimists, activists, and rationalists. They assumed that society was malleable and devoted their energies to molding it in the proper way.

BIG BUSINESS

One major impetus to progressivism was an awareness of the social problems resulting from explosive economic growth. Between 1880 and 1900 the United States took over world leadership in industrial output. Not only did production increase, but also it became concentrated in the hands of relatively few corporations and trusts, which often found it both possible and profitable to control market conditions. The creation of the United States Steel Corporation in 1901 symbolized the growth of industry, its consolidation, and its domination of the market. By purchasing Andrew Carnegie's steel interests, J.P. Morgan established the first billion-dollar corporation and controlled 60 percent of steel output. Yet this was only the most spectacular in a series of mergers that took place at the time. By 1904, 1 percent of American companies produced 38 percent of all manufactured goods.

Recognizing that the existence of mammoth trusts called for a measure of public control, reformers were divided over what course to pursue. Some wished to restore competition by dismantling the trusts, outlawing monopolies, and encouraging small enterprise. Others believed that big business was highly efficient. They saw nothing wrong with trusts so long as the government ensured that the benefits of efficiency were passed on to the public in the form of low prices and that profits were kept within reasonable bounds. Despite sharp differences of opinion on this matter, Progressives agreed on the desirability of bringing private economic power under a larger measure of public control. Most reformers thought that government should regulate railroad rates, lower the protective tariff, and protect consumers from impure or unsafe products. What distinguished Progressives was less their unanimity on a solution to economic problems than their agreement that unruly economic forces required some form of discipline.

Those most directly affected by the growth of industry were factory workers themselves. Efforts to improve their conditions centered on three issues: compensating workers injured on the job, regulating the hours and wages of working women, and restricting child labor. Reformers channeled most of their energies into enacting laws for these purposes at the state level. Not until relatively late in the Progressive Era did they turn to federal legislation, and then they met with only partial success. In 1908 a major obstacle to state regulation crumbled when the Supreme Court, reversing an earlier ruling, held in *Muller v. Oregon* that fixing a ten-hour day for women did not violate the Fourteenth Amendment's guarantee against deprivation of property without due process. Equally important, the Court based its decision on documentary evidence concerning the harmful social effects of long working hours, thereby accepting a key argument of reformers.

CITIES AND SLUMS

The United States became more highly urbanized as it became more highly industrialized. Progressivism represented a response to the city as much as to the corporation. Between 1890 and 1920 the number of people living in cities increased by 300 percent, while the number of rural dwellers increased by only 30 percent. Urban population grew by 11.8 million in the decade after 1900, so that by 1910 more than 44 million Americans—45.7 percent of the total population—lived in areas defined as urban by the Census Bureau. The largest cities grew at a spectacular rate: by 1910, 1.5 million people lived in Philadelphia, 2.1 million in Chicago, and 5 million in New York. Not only did big cities grow bigger, but there were also more of them. In 1860 there were nine cities with a population over 100,000; in 1910 there were fifty. This urban expansion reflected a natural increase in population as well as the effect of both migration from rural areas and immigration from Europe.

Because cities grew so swiftly, contained such a diverse population, and furnished some people with a chance to acquire fabulous wealth, they were plagued by mismanagement. Investigations into municipal government unearthed officials who took bribes or who, for the right price, granted lucrative gas and streetcar franchises to private corporations. Where city government was not corrupt it often seemed archaic, administratively unable to cope with the needs of modern urban life. Above all, there was what Jacob Riis termed "the blight of the tenement": dimly lit, badly ventilated slums, jammed with more people than it seemed they could possibly hold. To Progressives the slum was "the great destroyer of individuality" and as such posed a threat not only to the health of its residents but also to the health of the state. "Democracy was not predicated upon a country made up of tenement dwellers," said one reformer, "nor can it so survive."

Progressive solutions for these problems were as varied as the problems themselves. Some reformers concentrated on modernizing and depoliticizing urban government. They favored extending the merit system, streamlining municipal administration, freeing cities from state control, and transferring powers traditionally exercised by mayors to impartial city managers or commissions. Other Progressives, including mayors Samuel "Golden Rule" Jones of Toledo and Tom Johnson of Cleveland, emphasized the benefits of municipal ownership of public utilities. Many reformers sought to tear down slums by enacting building codes that imposed structural and sanitary safeguards. New York City adopted such a tenement-house law in 1901, and other cities followed suit. Finally, there were those in the city planning movement who wished to create a more rational urban environment.

MORALITY AND DEMOCRACY

Some Progressives wanted to protect Americans not only from the perils of urban and industrial life, but from their own impulses as well. Moral uplift was an important element in reform, and perhaps nothing revealed this relation more clearly than the link between progressivism and Prohibition. Not everyone who supported Prohibition was a Progressive in politics, but a large number of reformers favored a ban on alcohol and, what is more significant, justified their stance on thoroughly Progressive grounds. Starting with the premise that the saloon functioned as the home of the political boss and a breeding ground for corruption, reformers concluded that if they ended the sale of liquor they would take a long step on the road to urban reform. Moreover, many believed that liquor caused workers to squander hard-earned wages and neglect their families. A Boston social worker thought that ignoring Prohibition was like "bailing water out of a tub with the tap turned on; letting the drink custom and the liquor traffic run full blast while we limply stood around and picked up the wreckage." In this view, Prohibition seemed an indispensable weapon in the effort to stamp out poverty.

To achieve any of these goals—business regulation, urban reform, social justice, moral uplift—required, in the view of Progressives, the extension of political democracy. Reformers favored the election of senators directly by the people rather than by state legislatures, and in 1913, after several states had made this change, it was incorporated into the Seventeenth Amendment. Similarly, Progressives endorsed the preferential primary, which gave voters a larger voice in the selection of candidates; most states adopted some variant of this system. Progressives also favored the initiative and referendum. By 1915, twenty-one states had accepted such plans, under which citizens could introduce a measure into the state legislature and vote on it at a general election. Finally, reformers supported woman suffrage, in part because they expected women to vote in behalf of social reform. A litmus-paper test for progressivism might well have involved attitudes toward popular rule.

WOMEN AND THE PROGRESSIVE IMPULSE

If Progressives counted on woman suffrage to provide votes for social reform, they had reason. Middle-class women supported the Progressive agenda. In women's clubs, temperance locals, social settlements, and other reform associations, they strove to foster urban improvement, moral uplift, and social justice. Such activism not only served Progressive ends, but also bolstered the arguments of suffragists, who based their claim to the vote on the good that women would do for society if they were enfranchised.

A great swell of female organization, well under way by the 1890s, laid the groundwork for women's involvement in Progressive reform. The first women's clubs, formed after the Civil War, had been devoted to cultural projects. In 1892, when the National Federation of Women's Clubs began, clubwomen decided to "contemplate our own social order" and steered their attention to urban improvement. Contributing to libraries, settlements, and hospitals, they advocated better city services, protection for women and children in factories, and finally, in 1914, woman suffrage. Members of the militant Women's Christian Temperance Union, meanwhile, followed leader Frances Willard's injunction to "Do everything." In addition to campaigning for Prohibition, they endorsed a gamut of causes—pacifism, labor reform, social purity, and city welfare work. Many temperance workers were also drawn into the suffrage movement.

The city provided a broad arena for women's collective efforts. As the new century began, women created new reform organizations to improve urban life and to serve as bridges between social classes. The National Congress of Mothers (1897) sponsored playgrounds and kindergartens, battled urban problems and promoted "all those characteristics which shall elevate and ennoble." The National Consumers League (1899) sought to curb hours of women wage earners in stores and factories and to ensure the safety and cleanliness of products bought by homemakers. The Women's Trade Union League (1903), whose members included women factory employees as well as their middle-class "allies," hoped to unionize women workers. With major bases in New York and Chicago, the league burst into action. In New York's shirtwaist strike of 1909–1910, when some 30,000 garment workers walked off the job, league members masterminded strike publicity and joined waistmakers on the picket line. They protested the infamous Triangle Fire of 1911, when scores of women garment workers, locked in the upper stories of a shirtwaist factory, were incinerated or leaped to their deaths. Since unionization proved difficult, the league supported the passage of protective laws to ensure women workers a minimum wage, limited working hours, and safer working conditions. Between 1908, when the Supreme Court voiced approval of such laws in *Muller v. Oregon*, and 1917, some twenty states enacted them.

The most significant achievement of Progressive women was undoubtedly the settlement house. In 1889, Jane Addams founded Hull House in Chicago and a group of women college graduates started the College Settlement in New York. By 1900, 100 settlements existed; by 1905, 200; and by 1910, 400. Located in the immigrant ghetto, the settlement house responded to neighborhood needs by providing clubs and social services. It answered what Addams

People lined up to identify the bodies of victims after a fire at the Triangle Shirtwaist Company in New York City that killed 146 workers on March 25, 1911. The disaster drew attention to inadequate fire regulations and poor working conditions in the city's sweatshops. *(Hulton Archive/Getty Images)*

called the "subjective need" of young educated women who wanted to contribute to public life. (Men worked in settlements, too, but they were in a minority.) It gratified, in one settlement worker's words, a "thirst to know how the other half lived." The settlement house also became an urban social science laboratory, investigating local conditions and transforming its findings into legislative proposals. Settlement house residents supported juvenile courts, compulsory education laws, housing laws, factory regulation, and sanitation measures. Finally, the settlement house propelled its leading residents into positions of civic responsibility. Florence Kelley of Hull House moved on to become a state factory inspector, consumer advocate, and lobbyist. Julia Lathrop, another Hull House resident, became the first head of the federal Children's Bureau, founded in 1912.

The suffrage movement capitalized on the activism of urban reformers, labor advocates, and settlement house workers. Hull House leaders such as Lathrop and Kelley spoke at suffrage conventions. Addams, too, served as an officer of the National American Woman Suffrage Association. In her articles and speeches, she argued for the vote by appealing to Progressive sensibilities. The complexity of city government, Addams claimed, demanded "the help of minds accustomed to . . . a responsibility for the cleanliness and comfort of other people." Modern urban problems could not be solved by mere business expertise, she argued, but required "the human welfare point of view." When the Progressive Party first convened in 1912, it endorsed woman suffrage and invited Jane Addams to make a major seconding speech for nominee Theodore Roosevelt. When a "great party" pledged itself to protect children, care for the aged, and promote industrial safety, Addams explained, it was "inevitable that it should appeal to women and seek to draw upon the great reservoir of moral energy so long undesired and unutilized in politics."

The energy generated by Progressive reform pervaded the women's movement and ranged across the political spectrum. In the decade before World War I, women established a peace movement. They joined the campaigns against prostitution and "white slavery." College students formed suffrage societies and social service clubs. Progressive educators sought to reform classroom teaching and to promote vocational education. Through the Young Women's Christian Association, women reformers offered residences and services to young working women. On the left, socialist women contributed to labor reform and suffrage campaigns. Elizabeth Gurley Flynn, an organizer for the Industrial Workers of the World, mobilized workers in the Lawrence, Massachusetts, and Paterson, New Jersey, textile strikes. Anarchist and free speech advocate Emma Goldman toured the nation and voiced her views in *Mother Earth* (1906–1918). Decrying the "conventional lie" of marriage and woman's role as "sex commodity," Goldman defended free love, contraception, and women's emancipation. Public health nurse Margaret Sanger, following Goldman's example, campaigned for sex education, contraception, and other radical causes. Her short-lived periodical, *The Woman Rebel* (1914), where the term "birth control" was first used, brought her a multicount federal indictment for violation of the obscenity laws. Radical efforts were not necessarily appreciated by the Progressive mainstream of the women's movement, which was devoted primarily to woman suffrage and social service, but they contributed to a rising feminist tide.

An influential feminist of the era was Charlotte Perkins Gilman, who was less interested in the vote than in women's emancipation from economic dependency. In *Women and Economics* (1899) and subsequent works, Gilman denounced the home as an archaic institution that imprisoned women, transformed them into nonproductive consumers, and clogged the wheels of progress. "Only as we think, feel, and work outside the home, do we become humanly developed, civilized, and socialized," she wrote in 1903. To foster women's economic independence and liberate women from the home, Gilman proposed large apartment units, collective housekeeping arrangements, and child care facilities. Although her ideas diverged from those of mainstream feminism, which tended to emphasize women's homemaking expertise, Gilman's views won admiration both within the women's movement and outside it. Progressive America was receptive to all facets of reform.

SIN AND SOCIETY: THE MUCKRAKERS

That receptivity, in turn, was fostered by a group of journalists known as muckrakers who set out to document the social costs of urbanization and industrialization. The development of this literature of exposure reflected technological changes in magazine publishing. In the decade of the 1890s new developments in printing and photoengraving made the publication of inexpensive magazines feasible. As the price dropped from 25 or 35 cents to 10 cents, the magazine-reading public tripled and advertising revenue soared. Not only could writers reach a wide audience, but that audience apparently wanted to read about what was wrong with America. Articles of a muckraking nature began to appear, and in 1901 *McClure's* published "In the World of Graft," which exposed the alliance between police and criminals in various cities.

In 1902, *McClure's* circulation was boosted by the start of two major muckraking series, Lincoln Steffens's probe of corruption in municipal government, "The Shame of the Cities," and Ida Tarbell's exposé of the development of John D. Rockefeller's Standard Oil trust. From 1903 to 1912 nearly 2,000 articles in this genre appeared. Virtually no area of American life escaped the muckrakers' attention. They exposed corrupt city officials and U.S. senators who never cast a vote without consulting business interests. They zeroed in on fraudulent business deals. They described what it was like to live in a slum or work in a sweatshop. The muckrakers told of vermin scurrying around the floors of meat packing plants: "The rats were nuisances; the packers would put poisoned bread out for them; they would die, and then rats, bread and meat would go into the hoppers together." They depicted workers horribly maimed when factories failed to install safety devices. They threw a harsh light on those who made a living from gambling, liquor, or, worst of all, the white-slave trade—"the recruiting and sale of young girls of the poorer classes by procurers." The muckrakers taught consumers about food adulteration and dangerous patent medicines.

Behind these journalistic assaults rested characteristically Progressive assumptions. Muckrakers went after the inside scoop. They believed that the truth lay beneath the surface, that things were not what they seemed, that as the historian Richard Hofstadter observed, "reality was the inside story. It was rough and sordid, hidden and neglected." In trying to get to the bottom of things, journalists often sought real-life experiences. Jack London served time in a county penitentiary before he described the brutalizing effects of the prison system. Upton Sinclair worked in the Chicago stockyards before he wrote *The Jungle*. John Spargo recounted his attempt to do a child's work in a coal mine: "I tried to pick out the pieces of slate from the hurrying stream of coal, often missing them; my hands were bruised and cut in a few minutes; I was covered from head to foot with coal dust, and for many hours afterwards I was expectorating some of the small particles of anthracite I had swallowed." Muckrakers usually wrote fact, not fiction; they were concrete; they named names. They spent more time criticizing specific evils than proposing broad solutions.

THE REFORM IDEOLOGY

The muckrakers, by calling attention to social evils, helped create a climate conducive to reform. Similarly, a group of intellectuals, by developing a new approach to economics, law, and history, lowered another barrier to change. This barrier had taken the form of an ideology that rejected state aid for the victims of industrialization and urbanization. Conservatives, following what they believed to be Charles Darwin's path, reasoned that society, like nature, evolved through a struggle that assured the survival of the fittest. In economics conservatives stressed laissez-faire; in law they worshipped precedent; in history they dwelt on the sanctions for private property written into the Constitution. In each instance society was a captive—of natural law, of precedent, of the past. William Graham Sumner, perhaps the most prominent American social Darwinist, summed up this outlook in the title of an essay: "The Absurd Attempt to Make the World Over."

Unlike Sumner, a group of reform-minded economists reasoned that the attempt to make the world over was anything but absurd. Rather, it seemed to them the height of common sense. Richard T. Ely of the University of Wisconsin denied that natural laws governed the workings of the economic system or that laissez-faire was an adequate guide to public policy.

Thorstein Veblen, in *The Theory of the Leisure Class* (1899) and other works, pointed to the inefficient and unproductive aspects of the profit system as well as to the waste involved in conspicuous consumption and conspicuous leisure.

During the Progressive Era the courts often acted as an obstacle to reform. But at the same time men like Oliver Wendell Holmes Jr., who was appointed to the Supreme Court in 1903; Louis D. Brandeis, appointed in 1916; and Roscoe Pound of Harvard Law School, began to transform the law from a bulwark of the status quo into a vehicle for change. Although they would not always be found on the same side of an issue, Holmes and Brandeis shared a similar conception of the relationship of law to society. Holmes believed, "the life of the law has not been logic: it has been experience." If the law was rooted in human history rather than in abstract principles, if people made laws to fulfill their needs, then the law must change as new needs arose. Pound, in "The Need for a Sociological Jurisprudence" (1907), held that law must conform to "the general moral sense" of the community. It could do so by placing a higher value on social justice than on individual property rights.

Once legal scholars had reached this point, it remained only for Progressives to interpret the Constitution itself as the product of particular social interests. A number of historians did so, but none captured more attention than Charles Beard did in *An Economic Interpretation of the Constitution* (1913). Beard shared the Progressive concern with unmasking the "real" forces in history. He attempted to demonstrate that the upper classes, who had not been making out well under the Articles of Confederation, had organized the movement for adoption of the Constitution; that the document lacked widespread popular support; and that "the Constitution was essentially an economic document based on the concept that the fundamental private rights of property are anterior to government and morally beyond the reach of popular majorities." Once Americans realized that the Constitution was a biased document, as one reformer believed, they would not allow it to stand in the way of necessary change.

Muckrakers and intellectuals played the complementary roles of popularizing and rationalizing reform. Both showed less interest in how society was supposed to function than in how it really did. Both sometimes regarded ideology as nothing more than a cloak for economic interest. Journalists and scholars assumed that just as a bad environment made bad citizens, so a good environment could work wonders, for "to up build human character in men you must establish for them the right social relations." While they ranged over the political spectrum— from the socialist Upton Sinclair to the rather conservative Oliver Wendell Holmes—their work resulted in a diagnosis of social problems and a theory of state action that provided the underpinning for progressivism.

NATIVISM VERSUS THE MELTING POT

In their search for social harmony, reformers discovered no greater sources of dissonance than the twin issues of ethnicity and race. Progressivism coincided with a massive wave of immigration. In the twenty-five years before World War I, 18 million immigrants came to the United States, nearly four-fifths of them from Italy, Russia, Poland, Greece, and other countries in southern and eastern Europe. By 1917 one of every three Americans was an immigrant or the child of one. With the nation becoming more urban and industrial, these immigrants, more so than those who had arrived earlier, settled in big cities and took jobs in manufacturing. Some had left Europe to escape political or religious persecution and some

Immigrants on deck of S.S. *America*, c. 1907. *(Library of Congress)*

left to avoid military service, but most were drawn by the magnet of economic opportunity. Industrialists who needed a supply of cheap labor often encouraged migration. Immigrants themselves wrote home urging their friends to join them. One Polish immigrant reported, "Let nobody listen to anybody but only to his relatives whom he has here, in this golden America."

Many Americans, Progressives among them, believed that the new immigrants were racially inferior and therefore incapable of becoming good citizens. In 1910 this view drew support from the report of a commission headed by Senator William T. Dillingham. The commission concluded that people from southern and eastern Europe did not assimilate as well as older immigrant groups, but rather committed more crimes and had a higher incidence of alcoholism and disease. A few Progressives, such as Edward A. Ross, rested their nativism squarely on racial grounds; Ross saw new immigrants as "beaten members of beaten breeds" who "lack the ancestral foundations of American character."

Most Progressives who wished to restrict immigration, however, wanted to do so for reasons of reform rather than of race. A number of reformers believed that immigration injured American workers. Not only did the immigrants depress wages by working for next to nothing, but also they retarded the growth of trade unions. Employers understood all too well that a labor force in constant flux, composed of men and women of different nationalities speaking different languages, could not very easily be organized. Progressives often located the source of poverty in the boatloads of immigrants who, with few skills and little prospect of employment, placed an intolerable strain on existing charities and social services. Reformers also thought that immigrants provided the main prop for boss rule in the cities and believed that without such votes political machines would die a natural death.

Although most Progressives appear to have viewed immigrants as their racial inferiors or as impediments to reform, there were some who took a considerably more tolerant position. Either they expressed confidence in America's capacity to absorb the immigrants, or they invoked the concept of a vast melting pot in which all people contributed something to a novel American type. In addition, the doctrine of cultural pluralism—that each immigrant group should preserve its own heritage—gained a number of converts. Norman Hapgood, Randolph Bourne, and Horace Kallen, among others, envisioned the United States as a world federation in miniature. Asserting that diversity enriched American culture, Kallen held that each immigrant group could preserve its own language, religion, and culture yet share equally in American life. He favored "a democracy of nationalities, cooperating voluntarily and autonomously . . . an orchestration of mankind."

RACISM AND REFORM

Black Americans occupied a more precarious political and economic position than did immigrants, yet attracted even less support from Progressives, few of whom saw any conflict between racial discrimination and social reform. In the South, woman suffragists promised that they would use the vote to maintain white supremacy. In the North, black women sometimes marched in a separate column at the rear of suffrage parades. Settlement houses often set aside segregated facilities, if they provided them at all, for blacks. New York social worker Mary White Ovington attempted but failed to found a settlement house for blacks; in 1911 she published a pioneer study about the problems of New York's black ghetto for the Greenwich Street Settlement. But few settlement workers shared Ovington's interests or sympathies. Most Progressives would surely have agreed with Theodore Roosevelt who, although he opposed the disfranchisement of blacks, held that "as a race and in the mass they are altogether inferior to the whites."

During the Progressive Era most southern blacks lost the right to vote. In the 1890s three states disfranchised blacks. After the Supreme Court ruled in favor of the literacy test in *Williams v. Mississippi* (1898), ten southern states deprived blacks of the franchise. Some set literacy and property qualifications for voting, but added "understanding" and "grandfather" clauses that in effect exempted whites. Persons without property and illiterates could vote if they demonstrated an understanding of the Constitution or if they were the lineal descendants of someone who had voted in 1867. Most southern states enacted poll taxes, which, although

W.E.B. DuBois, arguably the most notable political activist on behalf of African-Americans in the first half of the twentieth century. *(Library of Congress)*

not very high, deterred poor blacks and whites from voting. Poll taxes had to be paid well in advance (usually during the spring when farmers had little spare cash) and were cumulative, so as people fell into arrears it became more difficult to catch up. Finally, the South adopted the white primary. Given Democratic control of southern politics, exclusion from the primaries amounted to virtual exclusion from the political process. These measures had an awesome effect. From 1896 to 1904 the number of black voters in Alabama plunged from 180,000 to 3,000; the number in Louisiana from 130,000 to 5,000. Southern Progressives defended these measures in part on reform grounds: removing Negro voters, they said, would end political corruption and produce good government. Indeed, one way to stop the stealing of ballots, historian C. Vann Woodward has remarked, was to stop people from casting them.

If progressivism could serve as the basis for white supremacy, it also provided W.E.B. DuBois and other black leaders with a model for new strategies of protest. DuBois, who had studied in Berlin and received a doctorate from Harvard, taught at Atlanta University from 1897 to 1910. He served as a spokesman for black intellectuals who rejected Booker T. Washington's program of racial accommodation. DuBois also exhibited a characteristically Progressive faith in the redemptive powers of reason. He assumed that by presenting empirical data about black Americans' condition he could persuade white Americans to eliminate racial injustice. In *The Philadelphia Negro* (1899) and other books, DuBois offered a meticulous examination of the conditions under which blacks lived in the hope that his readers would recognize the need to end discrimination. For DuBois, as for other Progressive intellectuals, research was the first step on the road to reform.

But it was no more than a first step. As early as 1905 DuBois attempted to found an organization devoted to the defense of civil rights. Five years later he succeeded in creating the National Association for the Advancement of Colored People (NAACP), with the goals of abolishing segregation, restoring voting rights to blacks, achieving equal educational facilities, and enforcing the Fourteenth and Fifteenth Amendments. The NAACP had the support of such white reformers as Oswald Garrison Villard, Jane Addams, Lincoln Steffens, John Dewey, and Moorfield Storey, who became its first president. In 1915 the NAACP filed an amicus curiae brief in a Supreme Court test of Oklahoma's "grandfather" clause, which the Court found unconstitutional. With its emphasis on political and legal rights, its belief in educating the public, and its assumption that segregation hindered the free development of the individual, the NAACP accurately reflected the Progressive movement, of which it was part. Perhaps it did so in another way as well: during its first seven years, DuBois was the only black to serve in a policy-making position.

THEODORE ROOSEVELT

Theodore Roosevelt's contribution to Progressivism, one historian has said, was "to infuse reform with respectability." Born in New York to a well-to-do family in 1858, Roosevelt graduated from Harvard in 1880 and then was elected a Republican state assemblyman. A profound personal tragedy struck in 1884 when his wife died of Bright's disease the day after giving birth to a child. Roosevelt sought refuge for a time in the Dakota Badlands, but returned to New York and began his climb up the political ladder. In 1889 he became a member of the Civil Service Commission, in 1895 president of the New York City Police Board, and in 1897 assistant secretary of the Navy. In 1898, after his service with the Rough Riders in Cuba, he was elected governor of New York. Two years later the Republican leaders decided to exile Roosevelt to the vice presidency. Political boss Thomas C. Platt said, "Roosevelt might as well stand under Niagara Falls and try to spit water back as to stop his nomination." Roosevelt complained that he would "a great deal rather be anything, say professor of history, than Vice-President," but, like the good party man he was, he went along. In September 1901, with the assassination of William McKinley, Theodore Roosevelt took over the presidency.

Roosevelt had much in common with the conservatives of his day. He believed in the essential goodness of American institutions, and he hated those who wanted to tear down what had taken so long to construct. He always considered the muckrakers overly concerned with the seamy side of life, and throughout his career he denounced Populists, trade unionists, and socialists who threatened the existing order of things. In the 1890s he had noted, "the sentiment now animating a large proportion of our people can only be suppressed as the Commune in Paris was suppressed, by taking ten or a dozen of their leaders out, standing . . . them against a wall, and shooting them dead." The realities of political life in 1901 nourished his conservative instincts. In the White House only by accident, Roosevelt faced a Republican Party and a Congress dominated by conservatives. Mark Hanna, a powerful party leader and senator from Ohio, warned the new president to "go slow."

What set Roosevelt apart from the stand patters and validated his Progressive credentials was his belief in orderly change. Reform, by perfecting the system, would help to preserve it. "The only true conservative," Roosevelt remarked, "is the man who resolutely sets his face toward the future." Not only did he welcome moderate change, but Roosevelt also thought that the national interest transcended the claims of any particular class, and he assumed that the president had an obligation to act as spokesman for that interest. These beliefs helped shape the response of his administration in four important areas: business, labor, reform legislation, and conservation.

THE SQUARE DEAL Consumer protections, protect middle class

Despite his reputation, Roosevelt never believed in trust-busting. Combination seemed to him a natural process, but one that required federal supervision to protect consumers. Eventually Roosevelt came to a tacit understanding with some of the biggest businessmen: he would not enforce the antitrust law if they would open their books for inspection and keep their dealings aboveboard. But in some cases Roosevelt considered government intervention necessary. During his presidency the Justice Department instituted forty-four antitrust suits, the most famous of which involved the Northern Securities Company. J.P. Morgan had created this $400 million holding company through a merger of important northern railroad lines. In 1902 the Justice Department invoked the Sherman Antitrust Act, claiming that the Morgan firm unfairly restrained trade, and two years later the Supreme Court narrowly upheld the government. The significance of Roosevelt's move lay less in its impact on the railroad—the ruling merely banned one particular holding company—than in its clear assertion of his willingness to act in behalf of the public interest.

Roosevelt's action in the anthracite coal strike illustrated his skill as a mediator. In 1902, 50,000 Pennsylvania miners struck for higher wages, an eight-hour day, and union recognition. Management refused to negotiate. By October, when the fuel shortage threatened homes, hospitals, and schools, Roosevelt called both sides to the White House. Even then the owners refused to talk to the union leaders, whom they considered "outlaws" responsible for "anarchy" in the coalfields. Furious at what he termed their "arrogant stupidity," Roosevelt, without any clear constitutional authority, declared that he would send 10,000 soldiers to the mines, not to break the strike, but to dispossess the operators. The owners quickly agreed to the creation of an arbitration commission, which, in March 1903, proposed a 10 percent increase in wages (and the price of coal) and establishment of an eight- or nine-hour day, but did not recommend union recognition. Roosevelt did not consider himself a champion of labor—on other occasions he used troops against strikers in Colorado, Arizona, and Nevada—but a steward of the national interest. In his successful campaign against the Democrat Alton B. Parker in 1904, Roosevelt said that his mediation in the coal strike had afforded both sides a "square deal."

The Square Deal reached a culmination in Roosevelt's second term with the enactment of three major pieces of legislation. The Pure Food and Drug Act of 1905 made it a crime to sell

BOXING
BLACK CHAMPIONS AND WHITE HOPES

James Jeffries and Jack Johnson at the World Championship battle in Reno, Nevada, on July 4, 1910. *(Library of Congress)*

Boxing, in its modern form, originated in England in the nineteenth century. Efforts to civilize the sport ("All attempts to inflict injury by gouging or tearing the flesh with the fingers or nails, and biting shall be deemed foul.") culminated in 1867, when John Sholto Douglas, the Marquis of Queensberry, proposed new rules. They eliminated "wrestling or hugging," provided for three-minute rounds (rather than rounds lasting until a knockdown), established a sixty-second rest period between rounds, substituted padded gloves for bare fists, barred hitting a man who was down, and warned: "A man hanging on the ropes in a helpless state, with his toes off the ground, shall be considered down." For years, boxing in America was dominated by Irish immigrants, the most famous of whom was John L. Sullivan. But the era of Irish supremacy was interrupted in 1908 when Jack Johnson, a black fighter, won the heavyweight title.

During the seven years he held the championship, Johnson elicited a response from white America that reflected broad currents of racial tension in the Progressive Era. Johnson flouted social conventions, most importantly the injunction against interracial sex. He was often seen with white women, and three of his four wives were white. A black newspaper speculated that his behavior had led directly to the introduction of bills banning interracial

Joe Louis *(AP Photo)*

marriage in several state legislatures. In any event, a search rapidly began for a "white hope" who might defeat Johnson. It soon narrowed to Jim Jeffries, who had retired unbeaten in 1905. The fight was scheduled for July 1912. Jeffries's supporters were confident, believing him superior "in both breeding and education." But Johnson won easily and collected $120,000. An outcry then arose against showing films of the fight, for many believed that youths would be "tainted, corrupted, and brutalized by such scenes." Reformers claimed a victory when Congress made it a federal offense to transport motion pictures of prizefights across state lines.

It was another act of Congress, however, that proved Johnson's undoing. The Mann Act (1910) was aimed at the "white slave trade," that is, at those who transported women across state lines for purposes of prostitution. Given the existing prejudice, Johnson was a natural target. "In Chicago," thundered a southern congressman, "white girls are made the slaves of an African brute." Johnson, who had sent his white girlfriend a railroad ticket, was unfairly convicted of violating the law and in 1913, rather than serve a jail sentence, he fled to Canada and then to Europe. In 1915 he lost the title to Jess Willard in a match fought in Havana, Cuba. In July 1920 Johnson returned home, surrendered, and was sentenced to a year in the penitentiary. After his release he fought exhibition matches, worked in nightclubs, and developed a vaudeville routine. He died in an automobile crash in 1946.

The next black heavyweight champion, Joe Louis, aroused no such bitter antagonism. Louis held the title from 1937 until his retirement in 1949, and his victories became occasions for celebration in black communities. Novelist Richard Wright believed that Louis tapped the deepest springs of rebellion in the black community: "Joe was the concentrated essence of black triumph over white." Yet Louis was at the same time exceedingly popular among whites. He violated no racial taboos and he epitomized good sportsmanship in the ring. In 1938 his crushing first-round defeat of the German fighter Max Schmeling, who supposedly believed in Aryan supremacy, was hailed as a vindication of democracy. When the United States entered World War II, Louis enlisted and was frequently cited as a model of patriotism.

Attitudes toward military service affected the career of another black fighter in a much different way. In 1964 Cassius Clay won the heavyweight championship. He then announced his conversion to the religion of Islam and changed his name to Muhammad Ali. His commitment to black nationalism provoked anger among those who favored integration. Former champion Floyd Patterson challenged Ali ("just so I can bring the championship back to America"), thereby becoming what one critic termed "the first black 'white hope' in boxing history." In 1967, Ali refused induction into the army on the grounds of religious objection. He told reporters, "I ain't got no quarrel with them Viet Cong." Indicted for draft evasion, Ali was stripped of his title and denied a chance to fight until March 1971, when he lost a decision to Joe Frazier. Ali later regained his title, but his most significant victory came in June 1971 when the Supreme Court found that his religious convictions entitled him to a draft exemption.

In Ali's case, as in Jack Johnson's, the heavyweight championship had itself become a focal point of racial tension.

Web Links

www.ibhof.com
The site of the International Boxing Hall of Fame in Canastota, New York.

www.cyberboxingzone.com/boxing/jjohn.htm
Website with many video clips of Johnson's boxing matches.

www.cyberboxingzone.com/boxing/jlouis.htm
The career of Joe Louis.

www.ali.com
The official Muhammad Ali website.

adulterated foods or medicines and provided for the correct labeling of ingredients. The Meat Inspection Act of 1906 led to more effective supervision of slaughterhouses, provided for the dating of canned meat, and prohibited the use of dangerous chemicals or preservatives. The Hepburn Act of 1906 authorized the Interstate Commerce Commission to set aside railroad rates upon the complaint of a shipper and to establish lower rates. The courts would then pass on the "reasonableness" of commission rulings. These new laws, which had attracted public backing as a result of muckraking exposures, broke new ground in regulating business practices.

Perhaps no cause was more closely linked to Roosevelt's name than that of conservation. Unlike aesthetic conservationists who wished to save the forests from commercial exploitation, Roosevelt preferred a utilitarian approach to natural-resource development. Roosevelt favored the commercial use of such resources in a controlled and scientific manner. He popularized conservation through several White House conferences and broadened its definition to include coalfields, mineral lands, and oil reserves as well as forests. And he supported the Newlands Reclamation Act (1902), which enabled the proceeds from the sale of western lands to be used for federal irrigation projects. Under Frederick H. Newell, the Bureau of Reclamation undertook work on twenty-five major projects within a few years. Roosevelt created the Forest Service in the Department of Agriculture and made Gifford Pinchot its chief. He appointed an Inland Waterways Commission, which in 1908 submitted a plan for multipurpose river development. Using executive authority, Roosevelt created five new national parks, established fifty-one wildlife refuges, restricted the uncontrolled development of coalfields and waterpower sites, and added 43 million acres to the national forests.

THE NEW NATIONALISM

During his second term Roosevelt became a more ardent reformer. In his last two years in office, he called for increased federal controls, taxes on income and inheritances, stricter regulation of railroad rates, implementation of the eight-hour day and workmen's compensation, and limitations on the use of injunctions in labor disputes. Roosevelt spoke indignantly about "certain malefactors of great wealth" and condemned the conservatism of the courts. This posture may have reflected Roosevelt's concern over the strength shown at the polls by socialists, his resentment at the effort of businessmen to attribute the economic slump of 1907 to his policies, or his willingness to speak out more boldly since he did not expect to seek renomination. Whatever the reason, Roosevelt had gone far toward embracing the doctrine that came to be known as the "New Nationalism."

That doctrine received its fullest statement in Herbert Croly's *The Promise of American Life* (1909). A prominent Progressive who later helped found the *New Republic*, Croly believed that a "morally and socially desirable distribution of wealth" must replace the "indiscriminate individual scramble for wealth." A Jeffersonian fear of positive government, Croly said, had kept American reformers in a straitjacket. To achieve order and rationality, they must reject laissez-faire in favor of positive action, competition in favor of concentration, and equal rights in favor of aid to the underprivileged. Croly, who regarded labor as another selfish interest group and opposed the common ownership of property, was not a socialist. But he went as far toward accepting the welfare state as any Progressive when he said: "Every popular government should have, after deliberation, the power of taking any action which, in the opinion of a decisive majority of the people, is demanded by the public welfare."

TAFT AND THE INSURGENTS

Theodore Roosevelt groomed William Howard Taft as his successor, and as president, Taft helped win important victories for progressivism. He proved to be a vigorous trust-buster. His attorney general brought twenty-two civil suits, and the courts returned forty-five criminal indictments, for violations of the Sherman Antitrust Act. In 1911, however, the Supreme Court crippled antitrust enforcement by accepting the "rule of reason." Asserting that the Sherman act was not intended to prohibit all combinations in restraint of trade, but only those that were unreasonable, the Court made it virtually impossible to prosecute monopolies successfully. In the field of conservation, Taft continued Roosevelt's program by safeguarding additional forest lands and oil reserves. Taft favored the Mann-Elkins Act (1910), which placed telephone and telegraph companies under the jurisdiction of the Interstate Commerce Commission and authorized it to examine railroad rates on its own initiative. He reformed government administration by creating the Department of Labor, establishing a Children's Bureau, and introducing the eight-hour day for federal employees. Two constitutional amendments ratified in 1913—the Sixteenth Amendment authorizing an income tax and the Seventeenth Amendment providing for the direct election of senators—obtained congressional approval during Taft's years in office.

Despite his record, however, Taft gradually lost the confidence of Progressives. Between 1909 and 1912, Taft's position on three major issues—legislative reform, trade, and conservation—alienated Progressives. In each case Taft sympathized with their position, but his political technique, or lack of one, brought him into the conservative camp.

For many years the Speaker of the House of Representatives had dominated that body. He served as chair of the Rules Committee, made all committee assignments, and granted or withheld recognition during debate. Progressive Republicans disliked this arrangement because they considered the power itself inordinate and believed that the Republican Speaker, Joseph Gurney "Uncle Joe" Cannon of Illinois, used his position to subvert reform. Taft was no admirer of Cannon either, but conservatives threatened to block other legislation if he sided with the insurgents. Taft backed away from the fight and in 1909, when the challenge to Cannon failed, Progressives attributed their defeat in part to Taft's desertion. The revolt later succeeded: in 1910 the Rules Committee was enlarged and the Speaker was removed from it, and in 1911 the Speaker lost the right to make committee assignments. But Taft took none of the credit; instead, insurgents regarded him as an ally of the old guard.

Controversies over the tariff drove yet another wedge between Taft and the reformers, both of whom, ironically, favored downward revision. Their differences first emerged over the Payne-Aldrich Tariff of 1909. The measure effected a modest reduction in the tariff. But it did not go as far as some Progressives would have liked, and they strongly resented Taft's claiming credit for the measure and heralding it as a major reform. Again, in 1911 Taft urged Congress to adopt a reciprocal trade agreement with Canada that would remove tariffs between the two nations. Many midwestern Progressives, who came from dairy and lumber states, feared competition from Canadian imports and opposed this particular form of tariff revision. It passed over their objections, but Canada refused to cooperate and the plan died. Republican insurgents and Democrats then enacted three low-tariff bills. Taft, claiming that they were politically motivated attempts to embarrass him, vetoed the measures.

A bitter dispute over the activities of Secretary of the Interior Richard Ballinger completed the rupture between Taft and the insurgents. In the summer of 1909 Louis Glavis, an investigator for the Interior Department, informed Gifford Pinchot that Ballinger had, shortly before taking office, apparently profited from aiding a Seattle group in its effort to deliver rich Alaskan coalfields to a large business syndicate. Pinchot brought the accusation to Taft who, after listening to both sides and asking Attorney General George W. Wickersham to investigate, exonerated Ballinger and fired Glavis. Pinchot leaked his side of the story to the press and in January 1910 publicly condemned Ballinger. Taft then dismissed Pinchot, the idol of conservationists, from his post as chief of the Forest Service. From January to June 1910, a joint congressional committee conducted an investigation. It found no proof that Ballinger was corrupt, but it turned up a damaging fact: Taft had asked Wickersham to pre-date his report so it would appear that the decision to fire Glavis resulted from it rather than from a preliminary verbal report. A generation of reformers convinced itself that Ballinger and Taft had betrayed the conservation movement.

Dissatisfaction with Taft led Senator Robert M. La Follette of Wisconsin, Governor Hiram Johnson of California, and others to create the National Progressive Republican League in January 1911. Designed to push La Follette's candidacy within the Republican Party, the league ended by endorsing Theodore Roosevelt's candidacy on a third-party ticket. At first it seemed doubtful that Roosevelt would make the race. He had returned from a hunting expedition to Africa in June 1910 with no thought of seeking renomination and with some hope that Taft could heal the wounds in the Republican Party. But in 1911, as his disenchantment with the president grew, Roosevelt changed his mind. Taft's remark that the War of 1812, the Mexican War, and the Spanish-American War "might have been settled without a fight and ought to have been" offended Roosevelt. Taft's decision to bring an antitrust suit against United States Steel for its acquisition of the Tennessee Coal and Iron Company in 1907, a merger to which Roosevelt had tacitly assented, infuriated the former president.

By the time the Republican convention met in June 1912, the two men, once good political friends, had become bitter personal enemies. If Roosevelt, who had done well in the primaries, was the people's choice, Taft was the convention's. His control of the Republican National Committee and of the party machinery in the South assured Taft's renomination on the first ballot. Reformers walked out in disgust, and in August Roosevelt agreed to run as the candidate of a new Progressive Party. His assertion that "every man holds his property subject to the general right of the community to regulate its use to whatever degree the public welfare may require it" summarized the party's platform. His cry to the convention—"We stand at Armageddon and we battle for the Lord"—captured the movement's religious fervor.

WOODROW WILSON

Republican disunity, however, permitted the Democrats to capture the White House for the first time in twenty years. Their candidate, Thomas Woodrow Wilson, was born in Virginia in 1856, the son of a Presbyterian minister. After graduating from Princeton (1879), Wilson studied law at the University of Virginia but gave up his practice for graduate work in political science at Johns Hopkins University. His doctoral dissertation, *Congressional Government*, appeared in 1885. In it Wilson held that American politics, characterized by a powerful but irresponsible Congress and a weak president, was inferior to the cabinet system that linked the interests of the executive and legislative branches. He then taught at Bryn Mawr, Wesleyan, and finally at Princeton, which named him its president in 1902. There, Wilson encouraged the introduction of small seminars and tried unsuccessfully to abolish the exclusive "eating clubs," which he regarded as anti-intellectual. In 1910 the New Jersey Democratic leaders, considering Wilson a safe but attractive figure, invited him to run for the governorship. He did and, to the bosses' dismay, presided over a reform administration, enacting a direct primaries law, a corrupt practices act, and workmen's compensation. In 1912 Wilson won the Democratic presidential nomination on the forty-sixth ballot. That November, with Roosevelt and Taft dividing the normal Republican vote, Wilson, although he received only 41.8 percent of the popular vote, carried forty states and won an overwhelming electoral college victory.

His southern upbringing helped mold Wilson's political outlook. Wilson, whose father had owned slaves and served as a chaplain in the Confederate army, remarked, "The only place in the country, the only place in the world, where nothing has to be explained to me is the South." He later demonstrated his loyalties to section and party by rigidly segregating black and white officeholders in government agencies and by removing southern blacks from federal jobs. Like most white progressives, Wilson saw no contradiction between his political convictions and his racial practices.

In 1912 Wilson campaigned on the slogan of the "New Freedom," which he presented as an alternative to Roosevelt's New Nationalism. The New Freedom, which Wilson worked out in discussions with the prominent Boston attorney Louis D. Brandeis, held that government should intervene in the economy to the extent necessary to restore competition. Unlike Roosevelt, who now viewed antitrust actions as a throwback to the past, Wilson asserted that trusts were inefficient, the product of financial manipulation, and the cause of artificially inflated prices. He would not go on a rampage against trusts but believed that by stripping them of special privileges they would fall of their own weight. Unlike Roosevelt, who favored child-labor legislation and a minimum wage for women, Wilson denounced paternalism. He told a group of workers: "The old adage that God takes care of those who take care of themselves is not gone out of date. No federal legislation can change that thing. The minute you are taken care of by the government you are wards, not independent men." Whereas Roosevelt, in advocating welfare measures, implied that the condition of the poor did not necessarily reflect a failure on their part, Wilson placed the issue squarely on moral grounds: under the rules of free competition an individual's character—as measured by thrift, hard work, ingenuity—would determine the individual's reward.

ENACTING THE NEW FREEDOM

Once elected, Wilson met with remarkable success in enacting his program. This resulted from a receptive legislative climate as well as from his creative use of presidential authority. In 1913 the Democrats controlled both houses of Congress. With Wilson only the second Democrat to occupy the White House since the Civil War, the party was determined to demonstrate its capacity for national leadership. Moreover, presidents usually receive wide support from newly elected congressmen, and of the 290 House Democrats, no fewer than 114 were first-termers. Wilson used every device at his disposal to corral supporters. He conferred regularly with legislative leaders, enforced party discipline by dispensing patronage, stressed loyalty to caucus decisions, and, when he thought it necessary, appealed directly to the people. His strategy reflected his admiration for English government and his belief that the president "must be prime minister, as much concerned with the guidance of legislation as with the just and orderly execution of law." Indeed, it was during Wilson's tenure that, for the first time since Jefferson abandoned the practice, a president delivered his messages to Congress in person.

Within a year and a half of Wilson's inauguration, Congress placed the New Freedom on the statute books. The Underwood Tariff (1913) substantially reduced import duties. During the debate Wilson had publicly denounced the lobbyists who were swarming into Washington to look after their clients' interests. He aroused such a furor that, before voting, senators felt obliged to reveal how the tariff affected their own financial holdings. The act also included the first income tax passed under the Sixteenth Amendment. The tax rose from 1 percent on personal and corporate income over $4,000 to 4 percent on incomes over $100,000. The Federal Reserve Act (1913), which reformed the banking and currency system, resulted in part from a congressional inquiry into the "money trust." The investigation revealed that Morgan and Rockefeller interests held a tight grip on credit institutions. The act provided for a more flexible currency and established a measure of public control over private bankers. It created twelve Federal Reserve Banks that, although privately controlled, also were responsible to a Federal Reserve Board. Finally, the Clayton Antitrust Act (1914) attempted to bolster the faltering attack on monopoly by prohibiting interlocking directorships and other devices that lessened competition. The Clayton act made a gesture toward exempting labor unions, but the wording remained ambiguous enough so that the Supreme Court could later rule certain kinds of strikes and boycotts illegal.

With the passage of this legislation, Wilson considered his work largely done. Convinced that reform had gone far enough, he wanted to go no further. The only important Progressive measure he endorsed in 1915, and grudgingly at that, was the La Follette Seamen's Act. It freed sailors on merchant ships from a contract system that, in practice, amounted to forced labor. In other areas Wilson drew the line. He opposed establishing federally financed credit institutions to provide long-term loans to farmers on the grounds that this would unduly favor one interest group. He continued to regard federal child-labor legislation as unconstitutional, and he refused to support woman suffrage. In February 1915 he nominated five men to serve on a newly created Federal Trade Commission. But Wilson, in the words of a cabinet member, regarded the commission as "a counsellor and friend to the business world" rather than as "a policeman to wield a club over the head of the business community." For the most part his appointees interpreted their task in the same way.

Yet by early 1916 Wilson began to modify his position, and he did so largely because he reassessed the political situation. The Democrats had done poorly in the 1914 elections, losing two dozen seats in the House and giving up the governorships of New York, New Jersey, Illinois, and Pennsylvania. Moreover, the Progressive Party had begun to disintegrate after Roosevelt's defeat. Lacking a formal grass-roots organization, beset by financial problems, torn by dissension over its policy toward business, the party met with disaster in 1914, losing virtually every contest it entered. Ironically, the demise of the Progressive Party, by raising the specter of a unified Republican opposition, helped move Wilson toward an accommodation with the Progressive platform. To win reelection, Wilson knew he must make inroads into Roosevelt's old constituency.

This he attempted to do in a number of ways. In January 1916 Wilson nominated Louis D. Brandeis to the Supreme Court, a move that infuriated conservatives and touched off a bitter four-month struggle for Senate confirmation. Wilson also reversed his position on several issues. He supported the Federal Farm Loan Act (1916), which created twelve regional banks to provide long-term, low-interest loans to farmers. Similarly, in July he asked the Senate to approve a child-labor bill that had already cleared the House. His efforts helped pass the Keating-

Owen Act (1916), which barred the products of firms employing child labor from interstate commerce. (In 1918 Wilson's earlier fears proved correct when the Supreme Court, in *Hammer v. Dagenhart*, found the measure unconstitutional.) Having made overtures to agrarians and social reformers, Wilson turned his attention to labor. He backed the Kern-McGillicuddy Act (1916), which provided workmen's compensation for federal employees. In September, to head off a railroad strike, Wilson urged Congress to pass a law giving the union essentially what it wanted: an eight-hour day for railroad workers in interstate commerce. Congress obliged by passing the Adamson Act (1916). Finally, Wilson moved still closer to the ground Roosevelt had once occupied by supporting the Webb-Pomerene bill (which did not pass until 1918), which exempted the overseas operations of business firms from the antitrust laws.

Wilson's strategy succeeded against a Republican opponent, Charles Evans Hughes, who had compiled a reform record as governor of New York and as a member of the Supreme Court. Campaigning not only on his record of Progressive achievement, but also on a pledge to keep America out of the European war, the president won a narrow victory. Wilson received 9.1 million votes to 8.5 million for Hughes and managed a twenty-three-vote margin in the electoral college. Nearly 3 million more people than in 1912 voted for Wilson, including many farmers, workers, and New Nationalist Progressives who approved of the direction his administration had taken in 1916. Also, the peace issue apparently helped Wilson among German Americans and socialists and among women in the eleven states—particularly California, Washington, and Kansas—that granted them the vote.

Early in 1917, therefore, most Americans expected Wilson's victory to keep the nation at peace and permit completion of the Progressive agenda. Few had any reason to suppose that, within a few months, Wilson would lead the nation into war. Indeed, World War I would expose many of the limitations of progressivism. In retrospect, the reformers' optimism would seem naive, their apparent dedication to serving the general interest merely a rationalization for preserving narrower class interests. Laws regulating morality would seem self-righteous attempts to impose conformity. The Progressive effort to throw the weight of government on the side of the less fortunate would, to a later generation, appear inadequate or paternalistic. Even the struggle for political democracy might be construed as emphasizing form over content. But during the Progressive Era only a handful of critics voiced such doubts. In the years before the war the Progressive faith burned brightly.

CHAPTER THREE

1900–1917

A Progressive Foreign Policy—From Peace to War

Theodore Roosevelt *(center)* inspects the construction of the Panama Canal in 1906.
(Library of Congress)

The ideals and policies that Americans have at home determine their ideals and policies around the globe. Between 1900 and 1917 the Progressive Party exemplified this rule of American history. As Progressives searched desperately for order and stability at home amid the industrial revolution, so overseas they used the new American economic and military power in an attempt to impose order in such areas as China, the Caribbean, Mexico, and western Europe. Many Progressives believed that only in orderly societies could the United States hope to find political cooperation and long-term markets for the glut of goods and capital produced by American corporations. Without such help from foreign friends, unemployment and radical movements could threaten Progressive programs at home.

THEODORE ROOSEVELT

Theodore Roosevelt once remarked that a man's mission in life could be summed up by the admonition to "work, fight, and breed." He did all three rather well. Roosevelt (often called TR, but never Teddy—a name he hated) achieved particular success as a fighter in Cuba in 1898. Those wartime exploits associated his name with militant American expansionism and catapulted him into the vice presidency in 1900. After McKinley's assassination in September 1901, Roosevelt assumed personal control of American foreign policy.

The new president's alternatives were analyzed in an article published by his close friend Brooks Adams in the *Atlantic Monthly* in 1901. Adams observed that since 1860 the Republicans had helped create the nation's great industrial power by passing high tariffs that protected American producers from cheap foreign competition. Now the need was to find world markets for U.S. products. The president, Adams argued, would have to choose one of two paths. He could try to lower the tariff as part of a deal in which other nations would reduce their tariffs on American goods. This policy, however, could result in a violent struggle within the Republican Party between high-tariff and low-tariff advocates. The second alternative was to retain the high tariff, but then (1) to use the powers of the federal government to make American production and transportation so efficient that U.S. products could compete globally regardless of tariff policy, and (2) to develop a great military force, which would assure American producers and investors that their government could protect their interests in such vital potential markets as China, Latin America, and Africa. Unwilling to rock his own political boat and deeply committed to the idea that military force ultimately decided world affairs, Roosevelt enthusiastically chose the second alternative. In this way he hoped to achieve both political peace at home and expansion overseas.

Roosevelt was clear about the tactics for achieving these goals. He extolled the "strenuous life" of the military, continued the rapid building of the battleship fleet, and built an isthmian canal in Panama so that the fleet could more easily shift from the Atlantic to the Pacific theater. To ensure rapid decision making and to protect his foreign policy from what he believed to be the provincialism of American domestic politics, he concentrated the power to make decisions in the White House. This move drained the power from Congress, a body he believed was "not well fitted for the shaping of foreign policy."

In formulating his foreign policy strategies, TR distinguished sharply between friendly and potentially threatening nations. Although he had mistrusted the British during the 1890s, he now understood that they no longer threatened the United States in Latin America and that Great Britain and the United States had similar interests in Asia. Anglo-American cooperation, moreover, fit Roosevelt's views of the superiority of the Anglo-Saxon people, who were, in his eyes, destined to "civilize" the nonindustrialized areas of the world. Another partner would be Japan, which Roosevelt believed shared American open-door policies in Asia. Japan was certainly not Anglo-Saxon, but it was industrialized and efficient and thus, in the words of Captain Alfred Thayer Mahan (one of TR's close friends as well as a leading naval strategist), "Teutonic by adoption." On the other hand, Roosevelt feared Germany and Russia: the former because its rapidly growing navy threatened British dominion in Europe and Africa; the latter because it seemed to endanger Anglo-Japanese-American interests in Asia.

Roosevelt was willing to use the mushrooming American industrial and military power to expand the nation's interest. The president agreed not with Shakespeare's "Twice is he armed that has his quarrel just," but with the version of American humorist Josh Billings: "And four times he who gets his fist in fust."

"I TOOK THE CANAL" . . .

Roosevelt followed Billings's admonition in regard to Latin America. Throughout the late nineteenth century the United States had tried to escape from an 1850 treaty made with Great Britain that pledged each nation to construct an isthmian canal only in cooperation with the other. Beset by problems in Africa and Europe, the British finally agreed to negotiate the point. In the Hay-Pauncefote Treaty of November 1901, Britain gave the United States the power to build and to fortify a canal.

As late as 1902, it seemed that the least expensive passageway could be built in Nicaragua. But a group of lobbyists who had interests in Panama used political pressure and bribes to win congressional support of the Panamanian site then ruled by Colombia. A treaty of January 1903 (the Hay-Herrán pact) gave the United States rights over a six-mile-wide strip in Panama in return for $10 million and a $250,000 annual payment to Colombia. The Colombian senate, however, then demanded $25 million. Roosevelt angrily—and ingeniously—announced that if the Panamanians revolted against Colombia, he would prevent Colombian troops from entering Panama by invoking an 1846 treaty in which the United States had promised Colombia to help keep Panama "free and open." The lobbyists gratefully arranged the revolution in November 1903. TR sent a warship to make sure that Colombia would not interfere. He then recognized the new government, gave it $10 million, and made the new country an American protectorate by guaranteeing its independence. In return, the lobbyists gave him a ten-mile-wide strip across Panama where he could build the canal. Later Roosevelt bragged, "I took the Canal Zone and let Congress debate."

. . . AND ALSO SANTO DOMINGO

Fomenting revolutions was quite out of character for one as strongly antirevolutionary as Roosevelt. More characteristic was his policy in the Caribbean nation of Santo Domingo. The stage was set in 1903 when Great Britain and Germany temporarily landed troops in Venezuela in order to protect the property of their citizens. The resulting uproar in the United States and the threat that in the future such temporary landings might become a permanent occupation led Roosevelt to conclude that he could not allow an open door for European forces in Latin America. The Europeans announced that they did not like sending military personnel to Latin

America, but would have to do so unless the United States policed the region in order to prevent the recurrence of revolutionary disturbances and resulting dangers to foreign investors.

Roosevelt's opportunity soon appeared in Santo Domingo, a country plagued by dictatorial governments as well as by struggles between German and American business interests. The president initially moved into Santo Domingo not to check European threats to American security, but to fight the inroads that German shipping lines were making on American shippers. State Department officials on the scene told Roosevelt that the immediate threat was a revolution that the Germans might use as an excuse to land troops for the enforcement of their business claims.

The president responded by announcing a formula in December 1904 that has become known as the Roosevelt Corollary to the Monroe Doctrine. Any "chronic wrong-doing" might "require intervention by some civilized power," he warned. In the Western Hemisphere the United States would act as this "civilized power" by exercising "international police power" to correct "flagrant cases of such wrong-doing or impotence." In early 1905 Roosevelt displayed American strength by sending warships to Santo Domingo. He then made a pact with that country giving the United States control of the customs houses through which the Dominicans collected most of their revenue. In return Roosevelt promised to use the receipts from the customs to pay off the Dominican debts and the foreigners' claims. Although the American Senate refused to consent to this agreement, Roosevelt enforced it by calling it an "executive agreement" (that is, an agreement that would last at least through his presidency, but not necessarily be binding on the next president). He had again circumvented the constitutional restraints on his actions, and in 1907 the Senate reluctantly ratified the treaty. The president meanwhile kept warships in control of the waters around Santo Domingo. He instructed the naval commander "to stop any revolution." TR hardly solved the Dominican problem. In order to stop recurring revolutions, U.S. troops were periodically stationed in that country through the administrations of the next five American presidents.

The Roosevelt Corollary is important primarily because it committed American power to maintain stability in the Caribbean area. With that commitment, Roosevelt finally destroyed the ideal of the Monroe Doctrine of 1823, which had aimed at preventing outside forces from controlling sovereign nations in Latin America. Contrary to the principles of 1823—and 1776—New World revolutionaries were no longer necessarily allowed to work out their own nations' destinies. Roosevelt best summarized the results when he claimed that the American intervention would free the people of Santo Domingo "from the curse of interminable revolutionary disturbance" and give them "the same chance to move onward which we have already given the people of Cuba."

Cuba, however, was hardly a good example. In 1906 infighting between Cuba's two major political parties threatened to paralyze the island's government. Anti-American factions again surfaced in Havana. Roosevelt thereupon ordered U.S. troops to land and restore a government acceptable to Washington.

ROOSEVELT LOSES HIS BALANCE

Outside the Caribbean, the president faced a tougher job. In Europe and Asia he had to expand American interests not by unilateral military power but by the delicate game of balance-of-power politics.

During 1905, for instance, Germany challenged France's protectorate over Morocco, and the German kaiser asked his good friend Theodore Roosevelt to mediate the crisis. Despite their personal friendship, Roosevelt was alarmed by the rapid rise of German naval power, and he was not anxious to help Germany gain an important foothold in northern Africa. After TR finally arranged a conference at Algeciras, Spain, in January 1906, France's claims were upheld by nearly every European power in attendance. The president meanwhile worked through the two American delegates at the conference to ensure that the United States did not come away empty-handed. He gained a pledge from the powers for an open door in Morocco for American and other interests. After World Wars I and II the State Department used this 1906 pledge as an entering wedge to gain oil and trade concessions in northern Africa for American entrepreneurs.

Roosevelt did not, however, display such sure-footedness in the Far East. The focus in that area was on the struggle between Japan and Russia over the rich and strategic Chinese province of Manchuria. In that confrontation, TR much preferred the Japanese. As for China, the victim in the struggle, he observed that it was able neither to industrialize nor to militarize; when he wished to condemn an incompetent person, Roosevelt would call him "a Chinese." His racism, combined with his Progressive enchantment with efficiency, led him to view the Chinese less as actors on the world scene than as a people to be acted upon.

American missionaries and exporters viewed China from the same perspective. Businessmen particularly were watching the development of China. In 1900 they sent $15 million worth of products to the area; in 1902, $25 million; and by 1905, $53 million. The great China market was apparently being realized at last. Most of these U.S. goods went into Manchuria and northern China, precisely the area over which the Japanese and Russians were struggling. When Japan suddenly struck the Russians with a devastating sneak attack on February 9, 1904, Roosevelt happily wrote to his son that the Japanese were "playing our game."

But as Japan destroyed the Russian fleet, consolidated its control over Korea and Manchuria, then threatened to invade Siberia, the president had second thoughts. Fearing that a precarious Russian-Japanese balance was being replaced by an aggressive Japanese empire, Roosevelt moved to stop the war by calling on the two belligerents to meet at Portsmouth, New Hampshire, in mid-1905. TR was delighted with the conference's work. Japan received control over Korea and in return promised an open door in Manchuria for the United States and the other powers. The Japanese also obtained key Russian bases in Manchuria. The Russians received a badly needed peace.

Japan's promise of the open door, however, soon proved empty. Such major American exporters as Standard Oil, Swift meatpacking, and the British-American Tobacco Company were eventually driven out of Manchuria by Japan. Tokyo's policy was capped in 1907 when Japan and Russia, bloody enemies just twenty-four months before, agreed to divide Manchuria, with the Japanese exploiting the south and the Russians the north. Roosevelt's first attempt to form a profitable partnership with the Japanese had ended badly.

In 1907 another threat arose to endanger TR's dream of Japanese-American cooperation in developing Asia. Since the 1890s the number of Japanese living in California had leaped from 2,000 to nearly 30,000. Many of them were laborers who were willing to work more cheaply than Americans. Threatened by what California's governor, George Pardee, called a "Japanese menace," the state's legislature tried to pass an exclusion bill. Anti-Asian riots erupted. Having just defeated a major white power, Japan was in no mood to back down

Negotiating the Treaty of Portsmouth, 1905. *(Library of Congress)*

before laws that restricted the rights of its citizens to travel, either to Manchuria or to California. Roosevelt temporarily quieted the tumult by working out a deal: California dropped the impending exclusion act and the Japanese promised that they would voluntarily restrict passports issued to laborers wishing to move to the United States.

THE FAILURE OF BIG-STICK DIPLOMACY

Roosevelt's hope that Japan would manhandle Russia in 1904 had produced not an open door but a one-way street for the movement of the Japanese empire. "I am more concerned over this Japanese situation than almost any other," TR admitted privately. So the man who gave his countrymen the phrase "Speak softly and carry a big stick" decided to send sixteen American battleships on a goodwill cruise to the western Pacific. Congress blanched when it heard of the plan, for it feared that Japan would destroy the fleet with a sudden attack like that launched against the Russians in 1904. Some congressional leaders announced that they would not appropriate money to send the fleet. Roosevelt thereupon bellowed that he had enough money to send the ships to Japan; if Congress wished to leave them there it was Congress's responsibility. Again outmaneuvered—even humiliated—by the president, Congress approved the funds. The visit of the Great White Fleet to Japan in 1907 produced effusions of friendship on both sides, but it failed resoundingly to persuade Tokyo officials to retreat in Manchuria.

On the eve of his departure from the presidency, TR made one last attempt to bring the Japanese into line. In the Root-Takahira agreement of November 1908 (negotiated for Roosevelt by his secretary of state, Elihu Root), the United States and Japan reaffirmed their meaningless pledge to maintain the open door, but in the wording of the agreement, Root accepted Japan's control of South Manchuria.

The president's gentle encouragement to Japan in 1904 had resulted in cruel policy dilemmas for Roosevelt. But perhaps the greatest irony of the Russo-Japanese War was that, although American Progressives wanted to avoid revolution at all costs, the conflict ignited the Russian Revolution in 1905. The victory of yellow over white also set off unrest in the French empire in Indochina, helped trigger revolts in Persia and Turkey, and fueled the Chinese revolutionary outbreak of 1911.

Roosevelt never understood that force determines not who is right, but who is strong. He therefore had been initially pleased with the Russo-Japanese War. TR failed to understand how the chaos and disruption of such a conflict could produce the revolutionary outbreaks that he and most Americans so dreaded.

REPLACING BULLETS WITH DOLLARS

Roosevelt's successor, William Howard Taft, was too conservative for most Progressives, but his experience as governor-general in the Philippines and as TR's diplomatic troubleshooter in Cuba and Asia had made him a practitioner of the Progressives' ardent search for order and stability. He had learned from these experiences that military force had only a limited capacity for solving problems. Taft consequently hoped to use America's burgeoning financial power, instead of the army, as his main foreign policy instrument. He could point to the expansion of U.S. overseas investment from about $800 million at the time of the 1898 war to more than $2.5 billion in 1909 as proof that his countrymen were obtaining the power to achieve the economic reordering of the world.

Taft advocated dollar diplomacy, but not because of any special ties to American bankers. He appointed leading New York corporation lawyers Philander C. Knox as secretary of state and Henry Stimson as secretary of war, but Taft also thought "Wall Street, as an aggregation, is the biggest ass that I have ever run across." For this reason, Taft believed that private interests often needed direction from Washington.

REPLACING DOLLARS WITH BULLETS $ → Bullets

Roosevelt's actions in the Caribbean had spread ill will and fear throughout Latin America. Taft wanted a quieter policy, but the full force of dollar diplomacy was quickly made apparent in Nicaragua. That nation, the alternate site for an isthmian canal, was of particular interest to Secretary of State Knox because of his past associations with extensive American mining interests there. Events began to unfold in 1909 when a long-term dictatorship was overthrown by revolutionaries, including numerous Americans. Knox immediately sided with the revolution. He moved in to control the situation by seizing the customs houses, which were the country's main source of revenue. The secretary of state urged the new government to pay off long-standing claims to Great Britain by borrowing large sums from American bankers. When the Nicaraguans balked at Knox's demands, he dispatched a warship. The agreement was then quickly signed. But the fires of Nicaraguan nationalism had been lit, and the American-controlled government could not maintain order. In 1912 Taft took the logical step required by his dollar diplomacy, sending more than 2,000 Marines to protect American lives and property and to prevent European powers from intervening to shield the interests of their own citizens. The U.S. troops remained in Nicaragua for most of the next twenty years.

While the president dispatched troops to Central America, the U.S. Senate also tried to protect American interests in the area. In 1912 the Senate added the so-called Lodge Corollary to the Monroe Doctrine in reaction to the threat of a private Japanese company obtaining land on Magdalena Bay in lower California. (The corollary was proposed by the powerful Republican senator from Massachusetts, Henry Cabot Lodge.) The Lodge resolution stated that no "corporation or association which has such a relation to another government, not American," could obtain strategic areas in the hemisphere. This provision greatly extended the compass of the Monroe Doctrine, which had previously applied only to foreign governments, not to companies. The State Department used the resolution during the next quarter-century to stop the transfer of lands, particularly in Mexico, to Japanese concerns.

CANADA

The giant neighbor to the north could not be dealt with in such summary fashion. Americans and Canadians had last warred against each other in 1814, but during the 1830s, 1860s, and 1870s conflict had threatened over border incidents. Canada was extremely sensitive to growing American power, particularly since discovering that, although it was a member of the British Empire, London officials were anxious to please the United States even when the matter involved conflicting Canadian-American claims. In 1903, for example, Canada had protested Roosevelt's demand that a disputed part of the Alaskan-Canadian boundary be settled in favor of the United States. When both parties agreed to submit the dispute to a jury of "six impartial jurists of repute," Roosevelt loaded the jury with his own type of expansionists and threatened to deploy the army if he did not get his way. The British jurist, casting the deciding vote, ruled in favor of Roosevelt and against the Canadians.

The Canadian government had scarcely recovered from this humiliation when in 1911 it signed a long-sought reciprocity trade agreement with the Taft administration. Canadian officials were initially pleased, believing that the pact opened the mammoth American market to their country's raw material producers. But the agreement could also make these producers an integral part of the U.S. industrial complex, a fact noted publicly when a congressional report in Washington likened the treaty to "another Louisiana Purchase." When the Speaker of the House of Representatives added that it would not be long before the American flag would be flying over all the territory to the North Pole, the ensuing uproar forced the Canadian government to call a national election. A new administration came to power, repudiated the reciprocity pact, and set higher tariffs on U.S. goods. The annexationist movement was dead. During Taft's presidency, dollar diplomacy worked no better in the north than in the south.

CHINA ONCE AGAIN

The results were even worse in China, although in this labyrinth of revolution, power politics, and diplomatic double-dealing, Taft and Knox were not wholly to blame. But they certainly made a bad situation worse.

Railroad control = economic control (Taft)

In late 1909 Knox feared that the Chinese would be unable to prevent Manchuria from being carved into Japanese and Russian protectorates that would exclude American products. Citing the open-door principle and insisting that the United States must share in the investment opportunities, the secretary of state proposed a "neutralization" scheme whereby Americans and Europeans would pool their money to help China buy back the key railroads in Manchuria from the Russians and Japanese. This would effectively "neutralize" the area, reopening it to American traders and investors. But Knox had made a blunder of the first magnitude, for when he tried to push his way into Manchuria, he only further united Russia and Japan against all outsiders. The neutralization plan was stillborn.

Apparently learning nothing from the experience, Knox made a second attempt to retain China as a frontier for Americans. In 1910 he insisted that the United States be allowed to participate in an international banking consortium organized by the British, French, and Germans to build railroads in the province of Hukuang. The Europeans allowed American financiers into the scheme reluctantly, realizing that once outsiders like the Americans entered, Russia and Japan would also demand entrance. This indeed occurred, and the Russians and Japanese proceeded to paralyze the Chinese consortium so it could not endanger their own private spheres of interest.

Now that he was faced with the utter failure of dollar diplomacy in the Far East, the only remaining tactic left to Taft seemed to be the use of American military force to prop open the gates of Manchuria. But the president knew the United States did not have the military power to scare either Russia or Japan. Theodore Roosevelt had finally realized this when he wrote privately to Taft in 1910: "Our vital interest is to keep the Japanese out of [the United States] and at the same time to preserve the good will of Japan." The Japanese, TR continued, must therefore be allowed to exploit Manchuria and Korea unless Taft was prepared to go to war. "I utterly disbelieve in the policy of bluff, . . ." Roosevelt railed, "or in any violation of the old frontier maxim, 'Never draw unless you mean to shoot!'" The mess was left for Woodrow Wilson.

THE ULTIMATE PROGRESSIVE DIPLOMAT

Woodrow Wilson exerted extraordinary influence on twentieth- and early twenty-first-century American foreign policy. Richard Nixon, for example, privately remarked in 1968, "Wilson was our greatest President of this century. . . . Wilson had the greatest vision of America's role." Highly complex, insecure, and driven by ambition, Wilson once recalled that a classmate asked him, "'Why, man, can't you let anything alone?' I said, 'I let everything alone that you can show me is not itself moving in the wrong direction, but I am not going to let those things alone that I see are going downhill.'"

He wanted to move the world uphill—uphill, Wilson believed, to the political and economic systems of the United States. The touchstone of Wilson's dealings with other nations was whether they were moving rapidly enough in the direction of a democratic, capitalist system. "When properly directed," Wilson observed, "there is no people not fitted for self-government." He determined to provide the direction, not merely with self-righteousness, but within a framework in which morality, politics, and economics were closely integrated.

Since his objectives were so exalted, Wilson, like Roosevelt, did not worry often enough about the means he used to achieve them. He even told his closest friend and adviser, Colonel

ASHCANS AND THE ARMORY SHOW

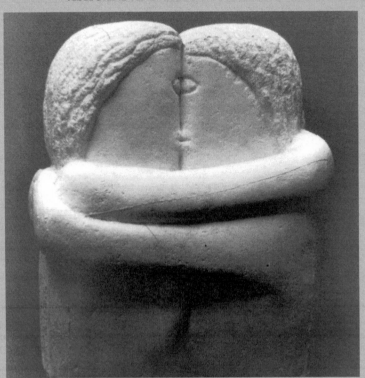

Sculpture of a couple kissing by Constantine Brancusi, exhibited at the
Armory Show of the Association of American Painters and Sculptors in
New York, 1913. *(Library of Congress)*

For nearly a century American artists had painted idealized scenes of canyons, rivers, and
people. The canyons and rivers had become polluted, and the people changed by industrialism, but the painters nevertheless had continued to draw the old, reassuring scenes.

In 1900 a few artists determined to change this. They shared a Progressive faith that by
stripping away corruption and hypocrisy, they could make Americans see clearly and then
save their republic. Some of these artists, such as John Sloan and George Luks, worked as
illustrators or cartoonists for newspapers and so were outside the dominant art traditions
but in positions to witness the social problems. When art organizations refused to show the
works of these new artists, eight of them presented their own exhibition in 1908. As the
titles demonstrated, these works depicted striking new subjects: Sloan's *Sunday, Women
Drying Their Hair* and Luks's *The Wrestlers*. Some critics condemned them for "exhibit-
ing our sores," denounced them as the "Ashcan School," and excluded them from polite
art exhibitions.

Members of the Ashcan School and others excluded by art associations decided to hold
an exhibition at the New York City Armory in 1913. This time they accompanied their work
with recent European paintings by cubists, expressionists, and neo-impressionists. These new
artists included Van Gogh, Cézanne, and Picasso, the fathers of twentieth-century art, whose

The oil painting *Nude Descending a Staircase, No. 2*, by French Dada and surrealist artist Marcel Duchamp. *(Lee Boltin/Time & Life Pictures/Getty Images)*

works often exhibited unrecognizable or weirdly distorted forms and violent, clashing colors. They differed as much from earlier paintings as the New York City tenements differed from the seventeenth-century English countryside. Marcel Duchamp's *Nude Descending a Staircase, No. 2* symbolized the Armory show, for the figure was dynamic and flowing but unrecognizable (newspapers ran "Find the Nude" contests). One critic called it "Explosion in a Shingle Factory."

Theodore Roosevelt stormed through the exhibition, according to a witness, "waving his arms, pointing at pictures and saying 'That's not art! That's not art!'" But he wrote a moderate review for a periodical praising the more traditional American works. That was a misjudgment for the Europeans overpowered the American painters. American audiences were particularly frightened by the European claim that art was not decoration, but a judgment on Western society and especially the fragmentation of the human spirit resulting from the industrial revolution. The artist now claimed total freedom to show this new world. If the machine had created a modern environment and if psychiatrists were discovering hidden motivations, then artists had to be free to show these new worlds in new ways.

Such radical art has never been welcome in traditional societies. Nearly 300,000 Americans saw the 1,300 paintings in New York, Chicago, and Boston, but in Chicago art students burned in effigy the show's organizer as well as a copy of Matisse's *Blue Nude*. The exhibition, however, was applauded by others, especially women, whose own drive for equality made them sensitive to the new art's demands for freedom. The Armory show shocked the United States into twentieth-century culture, while warning of a breakdown in Western culture itself, a breakdown made real in the horrors of World War I.

Web Links

www.artlex.com/ArtLex/a/armoryshow.html
The story of the 1913 Armory Show.

www.marcelduchamp.net
The career of the famous artist.

Edward House, that lying was perhaps justified if it involved a woman's honor or a matter of public policy. Those categories gave Wilson ample room for maneuver. Even as a young professor of political science he had advocated strong presidential rule that would circumvent the often-messy pluralistic politics of the American congressional system. During an explosive crisis with Germany in 1915, he refused to see not only congressmen but also his closest advisers and communed only with himself for several days. Wilson also exemplified how such self-isolation often ends in disaster.

His policies rested on a crucial belief: the world must look to the United States for its example and, in turn, Americans depended on the rest of the world for their survival. Wilson had been deeply affected by the depression and threats of revolution within the United States during the 1890s. He was therefore open to the influence of Frederick Jackson Turner's frontier thesis, which argued that the 1890s crisis could be understood as the terrible result of the closing of America's land frontier. After 400 years, Turner had warned in 1893, the United States had lost that frontier. Wilson, who knew Turner personally, paraphrased the frontier thesis several years later: "The westward march has stopped upon the final slopes of the Pacific; and now the plot thickens." The world market must act as the new frontier for the American system, Wilson warned during the 1912 presidential campaign, or disaster threatened: "Our industries have expanded to such a point that they will burst their jackets if they cannot find free outlets in the markets of the world."

He believed that open markets and capitalism were necessary for democratic political systems. His famous remark "Without freedom of enterprise there can be no freedom whatsoever" applied, in his mind, at home and overseas. So Wilson felt justified in intervening in revolutions in Mexico or Russia because such upheavals threatened to become both antidemocratic and anticapitalist. The meshing of his economic, political, and moral beliefs was perhaps most strikingly phrased by Wilson during his first presidential term:

> Lift your eyes to the horizons of business . . . let your thoughts and your imagination run abroad throughout the whole world, and with the inspiration of the thought that you are Americans and are meant to carry liberty and justice and the principles of humanity wherever you go, go out and sell goods that will make the world more comfortable and more happy, and convert them to the principles of America.

Wilson tied the American need to export its goods, its political system, and its morality in a single package of red, white, and blue.

In encouraging such expansion, he went beyond the acts of previous presidents in two respects. First, he used military force not only to a greater degree, but also in an attempt to reform entire societies (see Marine Corps Progressivism below). Second, he used the powers of the federal government to a greater extent in capturing markets. The Federal Reserve Banking Act of 1913, for example, created new powers that American bankers and industrialists could use in competing for credit and money in foreign money markets. In 1914 Wilson sponsored the creation of a Bureau of Foreign and Domestic Commerce within the Department of Commerce. This bureau sent government agents abroad to be, in the president's words, the "eyes for the whole business community." The Webb-Pomerene Act of 1918 allowed exporters to organize associations for the development of overseas trade, associations that previously had been outlawed by antitrust laws. The Edge Act of 1919 provided similar privileges for American bankers, and for the same reasons.

In all, it was a beautifully integrated program. The key was restoring vitality and competition at home by exporting goods, political ideals, and morality abroad. The government was to play a central role by creating new agencies and laws for the benefit of various exporters. This was hardly traditional "free enterprise" capitalism. And if Progressive agencies did not do the job, there was always the Marine Corps.

THE FAR EASTERN MERRY-GO-ROUND

Shortly after entering the White House, Wilson destroyed the China consortium, which had been established by Taft and Knox, by allowing American bankers to leave the group. This did not signify an American retreat from Asia, however. Realizing that the consortium was useless in maintaining the open door, Wilson attempted to devise an independent, go-it-alone approach to China that would provide American financial support unfettered by any European or Japanese controls. The president believed that this unilateral approach would build China to the point where Japan and Russia could no longer exploit it at will.

Wilson's first attempt at making his progressivism work abroad never had a chance to succeed. The Chinese Revolution, erupting in 1911, wrecked his policies, and the approach collapsed entirely when World War I began in August 1914. Japan took advantage of the European struggle to seize German possessions in China (including the strategic Shantung Peninsula), and then tried to impose the so-called Twenty-one Demands on the Chinese. If China had acquiesced, these demands would have not only consolidated the Japanese hold on Manchuria, but also given Japan economic and political concessions in China proper. Wilson strongly protested the demands, but it was British pressure and Chinese resistance that finally forced the Japanese to retreat. By 1917, as he prepared to go to war in Europe, Wilson had been ineffective in trying to roll back the Japanese.

MARINE CORPS PROGRESSIVISM

The open door was also closing in the Caribbean area, but here it was Wilson and Secretary of State William Jennings Bryan who vigorously excluded European powers. Wilson sought stability and control in the Caribbean, especially after the Panama Canal opened in 1914 and war broke out in Europe.

In 1914, for instance, Bryan signed a treaty with Nicaragua giving the United States rights to a future isthmian canal, bases on the Pacific, and the right to intervene in Nicaragua to protect these new interests. In Santo Domingo, Wilson mistakenly thought he had averted a revolution by holding an election in 1914. When the new government failed to show its friendship by extending financial favors to Americans, however, chaos developed, and Wilson finally sent the Marines in 1916 to control the country. The following year U.S. troops entered Cuba once again, remaining until 1921 in order to protect American-controlled sugar plantations, particularly from attacks by armed Cubans.

But it is Haiti that provides a case study of the tragedy of Wilsonian Progressive diplomacy. Black slaves had successfully revolted against France in 1801, making Haiti the oldest independent nation in the hemisphere except for the United States. In a population of 2 million, the vast majority were small independent farmers and more than 95 percent were illiterate. Politics were controlled by and for the elite. Presidential political life in Haiti was about as

A guide *(right, front)* leads U.S. Marines searching for bandits in Haiti, 1919. *(Time Life/Getty Images)*

violent as in America—between 1862 and 1914 three presidents were assassinated in each nation. Until 1910 the United States had displayed relatively little interest in Haiti. But then the harbor of Môle-Saint-Nicolas became attractive to the growing American navy, and the Banque Nationale (the major financial institution in the country, controlled by French-German interests) fell into the hands of New York City bankers after a slight push by the State Department.

The American bankers next sought to control the customs houses. Since these provided the government's main source of income, however, Haiti refused. The bankers went to Bryan, giving him false information about the impending dangers of revolution and European control if they did not have their way. The secretary of state was hardly capable of making his own estimate. Both he and Wilson were largely ignorant of Latin American affairs, and both shared the racism that had influenced Roosevelt's diplomacy. When a New York banker tried to inform the secretary of state about the language and culture of Haiti, Bryan could only utter with amazement, "Dear me, think of it! Niggers speaking French."

In 1915 the Haitian president was killed by a mob because of his supposed involvement with a mass murder of political opponents. Wilson seized on this disruption as an excuse for landing more than 300 Marines and sailors in Haiti. The Haitian treasury was given to the bankers, while the United States gained control of the customs houses. The State Department succeeded in finding an acceptable president only after promising to use the Marines to protect him from his own countrymen. But still the Haitians fought back with guerrilla warfare in 1915 and again more massively in 1918 and 1919. After Wilson imposed martial law, the American military killed more than 2,000 Haitians while losing sixteen Marines. In several major actions, Americans slaughtered their opponents rather than take prisoners.

Progressive diplomacy succeeded in tearing up Haiti's society by its roots. A 1918 constitution (written largely by Assistant Secretary of the Navy Franklin D. Roosevelt) legalized American economic interests and the military occupation. Years later Americans had difficulty understanding why Haitians were impoverished and endured repressive dictators who received support from Washington. ⟩This is so important

THE FIRST TWENTIETH-CENTURY REVOLUTION: MEXICO ⟩ Failure

Wilson's attempts to apply some of these methods to Mexico ended in failure. In that nation the president encountered his first twentieth-century revolution, one of those upheavals that, because of their turmoil and radical redistribution of power, gravely endangered the American hope for orderly change. American interests in Mexico were large. With the help of dictator Porfirio Díaz, Americans had amassed holdings amounting to between $1 and $2 billion. Most of this investment was in railroads, oil, and mines. In 1911 the aged Díaz surrendered to the superior force of Francisco Madero, who, after threatening foreign economic holdings, was himself overthrown by opposing forces under the control of General Victoriano Huerta. Huerta was strongly supported by the American ambassador in Mexico City. Then, to the horror of the world, Madero was murdered by Huerta's forces.

Entering the White House at this point, Wilson refused to accept Huerta's methods, and his refusal became adamant as it appeared that British oil interests were supporting Huerta. In fact, Wilson would not recognize the new government, thereby marking a historic shift in American recognition policy. Before 1913 the United States had recognized any government that controlled its country and agreed to meet its international obligations. Wilson now insisted that the government also be politically acceptable, that is, that it be elected through democratic procedures. The president threw his support to Venustiano Carranza, a military leader enjoying successes in northern Mexico. Huerta did hold elections in late 1913; not surprisingly, he won the presidency.

Deeply angry, Wilson redoubled his efforts to support Carranza and cut off aid to Huerta. In April 1914, on learning that a German ship was taking supplies to Huerta at Vera Cruz, Wilson landed troops to occupy the port. Mexican cadets opened fire. More than 300 Mexicans and 19 Americans were killed. Wilson's display of force and Carranza's steadily successful military campaigns finally forced Huerta to flee to Europe in August 1914. When Carranza assumed power in Mexico City, however, Wilson discovered that, like his predecessors, the new ruler would make no deals with the United States.

Searching for an alternative to Carranza, Wilson briefly thought that he had found his man in the notorious bandit Pancho Villa. But Carranza succeeded in isolating Villa, and then began preparations for a convention that would issue a revolutionary constitution promising agrarian reform and the placing of all subsoil mineral rights (such as oil and mines) in

Mexican hands. Outmaneuvered by Carranza and spurned by Wilson, Villa retaliated with attacks against American citizens, including killing seventeen Americans in Columbus, New Mexico. In March 1916 Wilson insisted that U.S. troops be allowed into Mexico to capture Villa. Carranza agreed reluctantly and then was horrified to discover that an army of 6,000 troops under the command of General John J. ("Blackjack") Pershing was marching into his country. As the American troops penetrated farther south, Carranza finally tried to stop them with force. Forty Mexicans and twelve Americans lost their lives. Carranza steadily refused to listen to Wilson's demands for new elections and the protection of foreign holdings. The president, moreover, now faced the much greater problem of American involvement in Europe.

In early 1917 the last American troops left Mexico. Carranza issued his constitution several months later. Wilson had utterly failed to control the Mexican revolution.

FIRST PHASE: AMERICAN ENTRY INTO WORLD WAR I

Wilson's immersion in the revolutions of China and Mexico was unfortunate, particularly since he had little experience in foreign policy before becoming president. His policies tended to emerge from an understanding of the marketplace requirements of the American industrial complex and his personal preferences for the order, stability, and gentlemanly processes that he associated with Anglo-Saxon institutions. As a young professor, he had venerated the British political system. When World War I exploded in August 1914, therefore, Wilson asked the impossible even of himself when he pleaded that the American people be "neutral in fact as well as in name" and "impartial in thought as well as in action." Within a year, however, Wilson told Colonel House that he "had never been sure that we ought not to take part in the conflict," especially if Germany appeared to be growing stronger. By that time, the United States was well down the road to war. The American approach to the conflict evolved through three phases.

The first occurred in 1914 and early 1915 when the Allies (Great Britain, France, and Russia) seriously discriminated against American and other neutral shipping by blockading the Central Powers (Germany and Austro-Hungary). The Allies mined shipping routes through the North Sea and forbade neutrals even from trading with other neutrals if the goods traded appeared to be heading ultimately for Germany. After extended negotiations the United States accepted these Allied policies.

Several factors shaped the American surrender. Since 1900 American officials had viewed Germany, and not Great Britain, as the gravest military threat to U.S. interests in the Western Hemisphere. Once war broke out, moreover, London played on such fears by flooding the American press with stories of supposed German atrocities. The effect of this propaganda has probably been overestimated, but it intensified the sympathy most Americans already felt for the British. On the official level, Washington's responses to London were written not by Wilson (who was grieving over the death of his first wife), but by Robert Lansing, counselor to Bryan in the State Department. A former member of the New York City mercantile community, which had strong economic and social ties with Great Britain, Lansing did not even pretend to be neutral. He later bragged that he weighted down the American protests with complex legal language that would prolong the dispute until Americans perceived that "German absolutism was a menace to their liberties and to democratic institutions everywhere. Fortunately this hope and effort were not in vain." But Lansing did not wholly have to fabricate a case for Great Britain. Judged by traditional international law, most of the British actions were not illegal.

Most important, however, the ultimate recourse against the British acts, short of war, would have been an American embargo on exports to Great Britain. This alternative was never seriously considered because, Wilson admitted, an embargo would be "a foolish one as it would restrict our plants." During the summer of 1914 the economy was already depressed. An embargo on exports, even on ammunition and other articles related to war, could gravely affect the American system. When Wilson made this assumption—that is, that the United States had to be able to carry on its large international trade with all the markets the British navy would allow—he had ceased being neutral. The *Literary Digest* phrased this perfectly: "The idea generally held is that we are not our brother's keeper. We can make and sell what any nation wishes to order. . . . If it happens that only certain nations control the Atlantic, . . . that is not our fault or concern."

By early 1915 Great Britain and France were running short of money to pay for these American goods. During the early days of the war Wilson and Bryan had determined that no loans or credits could be issued by American bankers to either side, for "money was the worst of all contraband" in that it determined all other trade. That policy, however, was completely undercut by the president's determination to keep overseas markets open. By late autumn of 1914 the administration agreed to turn its head while U.S. bankers gave both Germany and the Allies credits, that is, money tagged for specific purchases in the United States. A year later, in August 1915, an intense debate within the Wilson cabinet ended in permission for American bankers to float a $500 million loan to the Allies. The lid was completely off. By early 1917 Americans had provided $2.5 billion in credits or loans to the Allies and less than $300 million to the Central Powers. Wilson explained the necessity for this policy in 1916: "There is a moral obligation laid upon us to keep out of this war if possible. But by the same token there is a moral obligation laid upon us to keep free the courses of our commerce and of our finance."

SECOND PHASE: SUBMARINES

Once Wilson accepted the British blockade, another major obstacle to American trade— German submarine warfare—arose. Unable to compete with British surface naval power by February 1915, the Germans launched a submarine campaign that hardly distinguished among armed ships of war, unarmed merchant ships, and transports carrying civilians. Americans found this relatively new kind of warfare full of horrors. They sharply distinguished between British blockades, in which the English could leisurely search suspected merchant ships, and German submarines, which (because their thin plates and light arms rendered them an easy target) could not surface to ask a ship to identify itself or evacuate civilians before sinking it. Nor did the British make Wilson's situation easier when they illegally flew American flags from some of their vessels.

The president warned that he would hold Germany to "strict accountability" for any underwater attacks on American shipping. On May 15, 1915, the British liner *Lusitania* went down with the loss of 1,198 lives, including 128 Americans. Historians later discovered that the ship was carrying a large amount of ammunition from New York to London. Even had that been known at the time (and there is evidence the president did indeed know the *Lusitania* was carrying war materiel), Wilson doubtless would have sent the same strong protest to Berlin. When Germany seemed to snub this note, he sent one that threatened war. Secretary of State

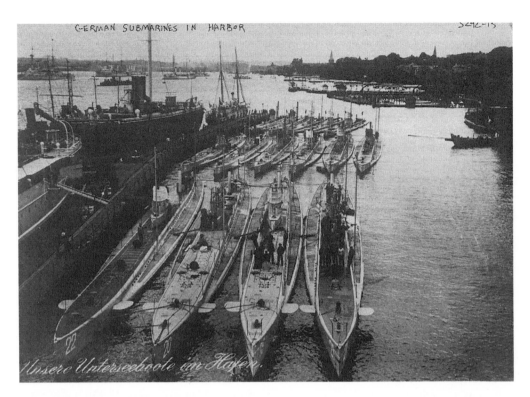

German submarines in harbor, including the U-20 *(front row, second from left),* which sank the *Lusitania. (Library of Congress)*

Bryan resigned over the dispatching of this second note. The secretary of state insisted that if Wilson protested so strongly against submarines, he should also wage a stronger fight against the British blockade, which threatened the Central Powers with starvation. Wilson refused to take that position. A leading Democratic newspaper editor wrote of Bryan's resignation, "Men have been shot and beheaded, even hanged, drawn and quartered, for treason less heinous." Bryan's departure removed the only relatively neutral member of Wilson's cabinet. Lansing became secretary of state.

Although the Germans finally promised not to attack passenger liners, they stepped up their attacks on merchant vessels. In February 1916 many Americans feared that the sinkings would soon pull the United States into war. Congress threatened to pass the McLemore Resolution warning Americans not to travel on belligerent ships, that is, ships owned by nations fighting in the war; but Wilson waged an all-out effort to kill the measure, vowing that he would never "consent to any abridgement of the rights of American citizens in any respect." It was a brave statement, but his refusal to restrict the rights of Americans to trade or travel in wartime meant that he would have to protect those rights.

Then, on March 24, 1916, several Americans suffered injuries when an unarmed French passenger liner, the *Sussex,* was torpedoed. This sinking marked a turning point in Wilson's diplomacy. He demanded that underwater attacks on both passenger and unarmed merchant vessels cease or the United States would have to go to war. Germany responded with the

Suxxex Pledge

so-called *Sussex* pledge: Germany would sink no more such vessels unless adequate search and safety procedures were carried out. But Germany asked that Wilson also issue a strong protest against the British blockade of central Europe. The president ignored the German request. In obtaining the pledge, Wilson believed he had scored a significant diplomatic victory. *10|*

THIRD PHASE: MAKING THE WORLD SAFE ③
FOR DEMOCRACY

After receiving the *Sussex* pledge, Wilson pushed the submarine problem to the background and concentrated on devising a method of intervening in the war. He hoped to act as a mediator trusted by both sides. As early as 1915, he saw himself as the central figure in reconstructing a postwar world in accord with Progressive principles.

During the early months of the war, Colonel House journeyed twice to Europe in attempts to prepare the ground. House got nowhere with the Germans, who clearly perceived the Americans' pro-Allied bias; the British and French refused to cooperate because they believed they could win a military victory. In any event, the Allies' and Central Powers' peace terms were irreconcilable by late 1915. So much blood had already been shed that a compromise peace was not possible. The president's situation worsened in 1916. The British not only refused to ask for his mediation, but angered Americans by further restricting U.S. mail, goods, and passengers that had to travel through the war zones.

In 1916 Wilson started out on a course to try to be more independent of the Allies. He had carefully laid the groundwork the year before with his "preparedness" program that started the construction of new warships and armed additional men. In July 1916 he supported legislation for more warships and submarines. As he told House, "Let us build a navy bigger [than Great Britain's] and do what we please." This remark was not in the same spirit as the slogan "He kept us out of war," which Democrats were then spreading across the country to urge Wilson's reelection. But the president did not care for that slogan. During the presidential campaign he warned that Americans must help in the search for peace, for they could not "any longer remain neutral against any willful disturbance of the peace of the world." Throughout the year he elaborated on his idea, first revealed in May 1916, when he called for a "universal association of nations" that would carry out worldwide progressivism by creating global free trade, freedom of the seas, and stability through territorial guarantees.

Wilson's hope for the postwar world became more urgent in June 1916 when the French, British, and Russians met secretly at the Paris Economic Conference to make plans for economic warfare against the United States. The Allies agreed on schemes for government-subsidized industries that would be able to compete against such American giants as United States Steel and Standard Oil. When Wilson and Lansing learned of these agreements, they drew up their own economic plans, but equally important, the president increasingly feared what might happen to American interests if the Allied nations won a total victory and then dictated a peace without his mediation. Such a victory could produce an overwhelmingly dominant power (such as Great Britain or Russia), which could dictate a peace that threatened American global interests.

But the president was given little choice. A month after his reelection in November 1916, Germany decided to wage all-out submarine warfare, even if such a policy brought the United States into the war. German war aims had escalated during the war until only a quick military

Germany wages all out war

Wilson doesn't declare war for 2 mths

victory could obtain those prizes—neutralization of Belgium, annexation of French territory, naval bases in the Atlantic and Pacific, perhaps even economic reparations from the Allies. The German naval command confidently told the kaiser, "England will lie on the ground in six months, before a single American has set foot on the continent."

Learning of this decision, Wilson went before Congress on January 22, 1917, in a last dramatic attempt to preserve his role as a neutral broker in a postwar peace. He demanded a "peace without victory." The Allies responded with cynicism, and on January 31 German underwater warfare began.

But Wilson, continuing to stall, did not move to declare war for two months. He feared above all that taking the United States into the conflict would guarantee an overwhelming Allied victory, ruin his own hopes of acting as mediator, and ensure the carrying out of the Paris Economic Conference's plans. Wilson worried, moreover, that American entry would decimate the "white civilization" needed to rebuild the postwar world, while allowing a "yellow race—Japan, for instance, in alliance with Russia," to exclude the United States from China. That was an exclusion Wilson swore he would never allow.

The president also encountered determined antiwar opposition led by Republican Progressive senators Robert La Follette of Wisconsin and William Borah of Idaho. Since 1900 a small band of Progressives had vigorously opposed the use of military intervention by Roosevelt, Taft, and Wilson, particularly since foreign involvements could take the nation's attention away from domestic reforms. They now also feared that entry into war could tie Americans into a power structure that would force the United States to support European empires and to fight wars for European, not American, interests.

On March 1, 1917, the antiwar group suffered a severe defeat with the publication of the Zimmermann telegram. British agents had intercepted and given to Wilson a note written by the German foreign minister, Arthur Zimmermann, which proposed to Mexico a Mexican-German alliance. If Mexico cooperated, Germany would help it retrieve the "lost provinces" of Texas, New Mexico, and Arizona, taken from Mexico in the 1840s. Newspapers headlined the telegram, and prowar sentiment flashed to new heights—especially in the Southwest. But despite this sensation, antiwar voices were not stilled. When the president asked Congress in April 1917 for a declaration of war, six senators and fifty representatives voted against entering the conflict, while eighty-two senators and 373 representatives supported Wilson's request. American men and women prepared to fight and die in the first modern global conflict.

As his nation finally entered the struggle, Wilson tried to preserve part of his status as a neutral by designating the United States an "Associated" power rather than a full-fledged Allied partner, but this was equivalent to a hope of losing only part of one's virginity. The president went to war because Germany declared submarine warfare against the United States, but equally important, because American economic requirements developed since 1914 left no alternative but to work with the Allies. Wilson especially believed that only by becoming a belligerent could he force Britain and France to open the world to the stabilizing influences of American progressivism. As he explained privately, he had to participate in the war if he hoped to have a seat at the peace table rather than "shout through a crack in the door." So he asked Americans to go to war to "make the world safe for democracy." Progressive diplomacy had once again ended in the use of military force, this time on a level never before seen in world history. Given the record of 1900 to 1917, too few Americans were asking whether progressivism was safe for the world.

CHAPTER FOUR

1917–1920
The Failure of World War I

American soldiers demonstrating the different types of gas masks worn by *(left to right)* U.S., British, French, and German troops. *(The Granger Collection, NYC)*

When Woodrow Wilson addressed Congress in April 1917, he proclaimed that World War I would be fought for the cause of humanity, not for mere conquest. The president and his supporters justified U.S. intervention on the ground that while Germany stood for reaction, that is, extreme political conservatism, the United States and its allies fought for liberalism. Confident that an American victory would make the world safe for their brand of democracy, Progressives also assumed that at home the war could be conducted in accord with their principles. Progressives had always valued efficiency, harmony, and the search for a "constructive social ideal." Now, many reasoned, wartime mobilization would be entrusted to the very experts in whom they had such confidence. Nagging social conflicts would be swept away in a wave of patriotic unity. The terrible realities of war soon shattered these expectations. Far from making the world safe for anything at all, the war undermined progressivism and unleashed revolutionary forces on an unparalleled scale.

MOBILIZATION AND REFORM

A month after Wilson's war message, Walter Lippmann (an influential Progressive journalist) remarked that the nation stood "at the threshold of a collectivism which is greater than any as yet planned by the Socialist party." In fact, the war did enable Progressives to push through much of their remaining program in the fields of economic policy, moral uplift, and political reform. For a brief, euphoric moment Progressives imagined that the war served their own purposes. "Into a year has been packed the progress of a decade," one reformer exulted in 1918. Only gradually did it become apparent that, whatever the immediate accomplishments, World War I had exacted a frightful toll.

The War Industries Board served as the chief vehicle for directing the production and distribution of war materials. Created in July 1917 and headed after March 1918 by financier Bernard Baruch, the board embodied several features of the business-government partnership envisioned by New Nationalist Progressives. Under Baruch's guidance the board performed a variety of functions: it allocated scarce materials, coordinated purchasing, determined priorities, encouraged the development of new facilities, fixed prices, and occasionally granted exemption from the antitrust laws to promote efficiency. All these functions usually gained the approval of businessmen who cooperated because they respected Baruch (a highly successful Wall Street operator), were given a large role in deciding board policy, and could usually count on making a handsome profit from war orders.

The Wilson administration experimented with new policies to increase wartime food production. Because European nations relied heavily on American wheat and sugar exports, food administrator Herbert Hoover got farmers to bring additional land under cultivation by offering to purchase agricultural commodities at high prices. At the same time Hoover urged consumers to observe "wheatless," "meatless," and "porkless" days, and he also asked grocers to restrict each person's sugar ration to two pounds per month. Hoover ruled that restaurants could not serve bread until after the first course, and he insisted that they serve small cubes of sugar rather than sugar bowls. Posters and billboards appeared everywhere with such slogans as "Food Will Win the War," "Serve Just Enough," and "Use All Left-Overs." Conserving food itself came to be known as "Hooverizing." Meanwhile, food exports nearly tripled during the war.

In two additional areas—fuel and transportation—the Wilson administration assumed far-reaching power. The Fuel Administration under Harry A. Garfield fostered a substantial increase in coal and oil production, in part by increasing the mechanization of mines. When a coal shortage threatened, Garfield ordered many factories producing civilian goods to close down for a few days and to observe subsequent "heatless" days as a conservation measure. In December 1917, faced with a massive transportation tie-up, the administration took over the railroads. William G. McAdoo, who headed the Railroad Administration, proceeded to integrate rail schedules, limit passenger traffic, modernize equipment, and increase the amount of uniform track gauge. Private owners took directions from the Railroad Administration, but received a rental fee that guaranteed them a substantial return on their investment.

Besides encouraging these new techniques of industrial control, the war also paved the way for other reforms that Progressives had been demanding for years. For the first time the government interceded on behalf of trade unions. The War Labor Board supported the right of workers to unionize and bargain collectively, and it succeeded in obtaining the eight-hour day in many places. A newly created U.S. Employment Service helped workers find war jobs. In 1919 the Labor Department established a Women's Bureau to protect the interests of women workers, a major goal of Progressive reformers. The government, in addition, took pioneering steps in the field of social insurance and public housing. The Military and Naval Insurance Act (1917) provided for the retraining of disabled veterans and established a voluntary insurance system under which families of servicemen received federal aid. Finally, a dream of reformers seemed to come true with the initiation of a public housing program for workers who had gone to cities in search of defense jobs in shipyards and munitions plants.

PROHIBITION AND WOMAN SUFFRAGE

Progressives had always exhibited a keen concern with moral questions, and World War I gave the moral uplift forces a golden opportunity. Starting with the premise that men in uniform must be protected against venereal disease, social hygienists, with the support of the War Department, launched a successful campaign to shut down brothels near military bases. They adopted the motto "Men must live straight if they would shoot straight." The government's Committee on Women's Defense Work created a department for "Safeguarding Moral and Spiritual Forces" to preserve American purity. Lecturers from the Young Women's Christian Association traveled across the country, warning young women against the hazards of illicit love, fostering "a higher standard of personal conduct and civil cleanliness," and exhorting their listeners to "Do Your Bit to Keep Him Fit." The obsession with cleanliness was sometimes carried quite far. One crusader noted that a boy who joined the army was "swept into a machine that requires cleanliness first, last, and all the time" and consequently became a person with "clean motives and higher desires."

The forces of moral uplift won by far their most important victory with the enactment of Prohibition. Although prohibitionists had always relied on a variety of medical, moral, and social arguments, the war provided them with just the ammunition they needed. Since the manufacture of beer required barley, temperance became a means of food conservation. Since many brewers were German-Americans, temperance could be equated with Americanism. Since drunkenness lowered the efficiency of defense workers and the potential fighting ability of soldiers, temperance achieved the status of a patriotic necessity. Liquor manufacturers, said William Jennings Bryan, "would, if they could, make drunkards of the entire army and leave us defenseless before a foreign foe." The year 1917 saw a form of creeping prohibitionism.

In May the sale of liquor around military camps was forbidden. In December the alcoholic content of beer was reduced, and Congress passed the Eighteenth Amendment. Even before the amendment was ratified in January 1919, a Prohibition Act (1918) outlawed the sale of all intoxicating beverages. Elated by their success, some reformers believed that World War I might yet make the world safe for teetotalers. A speaker at an Anti-Saloon League Convention proclaimed, "With America leading the way, with faith in Omnipotent God, and bearing with patriotic hands our stainless flag, . . . we will soon . . . bestow upon mankind the priceless gift of world Prohibition."

Finally, the war helped Progressives win the battle for woman suffrage. By the time the United States entered the war, women had gained the vote in eleven states. However, the House had defeated a constitutional amendment that would have given women the vote, and the suffrage movement seemed stalled. A dissident wing, inspired by British suffragists and led by Quaker Alice Paul had broken off to form the Woman's Party. Attacking the party in power, as British suffragists did, the Woman's Party adopted militant tactics such as picketing the White House, to the dismay of other suffragists. But war enabled the suffrage movement to gain the momentum it had sought for half a century. The incongruity of fighting a war for democracy while denying the vote to half the population—at the very time that women were playing an increasingly essential part in industry—suddenly became too painful. Besides, many claimed that women possessed nurturing qualities of tenderness and mercy that a war-ravaged world desperately required. Suffrage leader Carrie Chapman Catt was more pragmatic. In 1917 she announced that she did not know whether the vote was a right, a duty, or a privilege, but "whatever it is, women want it."

In 1917 six states—including New York, the key political battleground where women's suffrage had been rejected in 1915—enfranchised women; in January 1918 the House adopted the suffrage amendment, but the Senate rejected it. By then Woodrow Wilson had finally come over to the side of suffrage. He began to define it as a war measure, "an essential psychological element in the conduct of the war for democracy." For a time southern Democrats, who apparently feared that enfranchising women might set a precedent for protecting the right of blacks to vote, helped block action by the Senate. But in 1919 the Nineteenth Amendment obtained the needed congressional majority in both the House and Senate, and a year later, after ratification by three-fourths of the states, it became law.

PROPAGANDA AND POLITICS

Although the war smoothed the passage of political, moral, and economic reforms long sought by Progressives, it also led to government actions that conflicted sharply with Progressive values. In its search for wartime unity, the Wilson administration conducted a massive propaganda campaign, one designed to inspire rather than to instruct. The Committee on Public Information under George Creel published millions of pamphlets, all hammering home the same message: the forces of a peace-loving democracy were pitted against those of a war-crazed autocracy. The Creel committee recruited 75,000 "Four Minute Men" who, in some 7.5 million speeches at theaters, clubs, and churches, described German atrocities and urged people to buy Liberty Bonds. One pamphlet predicted the consequences of a hypothetical enemy invasion: German soldiers would "pillage and burn," demand huge sums of money, execute anyone who refused to cooperate, and then "look on and laugh" while a priest and a minister were "thrown into a pig-sty."

Supreme Court Justice Oliver Wendell Holmes. *(Library of Congress)*

The war injected into politics new issues that badly shook Wilson's electoral coalition. Because the administration imposed controls on wheat but not on cotton prices, Democrats representing midwestern wheat growers charged that Wilson unfairly favored the South. Democrats from the South and West called for stiffer corporation taxes and complained that the administration, under the influence of the party's eastern wing, was coddling war profiteers. Many southern Democrats opposed Wilson on the issue of conscription. They asserted that volunteers would make better soldiers and that a draft would militarize the nation. Although conscription bills passed in 1917 and 1918, with the result that 24 million men registered and 3 million were drafted (and 1.8 million volunteered), Democrats in Congress were sharply divided.

Not only did the war distort certain Progressive principles and disrupt Wilson's coalition, but also it gradually eroded the reformers' confidence in progress, rationality, and order. With the Western world in flames, with senseless slaughter occurring daily and national passions aroused beyond all reason, it became increasingly difficult to sustain the old faith in the perfectibility of either people or institutions. If this disillusionment were not serious enough, Progressives' confidence in Wilson's policies and in their own ability to control events was badly shaken by the administration's response to wartime dissent and to the Russian Revolution.

CURBING DISSENT: WHY

In November 1917 the motion picture *The Spirit of '76*, which depicted various atrocities committed by British soldiers during the American Revolution, played in Los Angeles. The film was seized and the producer indicted under the Espionage Act, for in 1917 the British were allies. The judge in the case *United States v. The Spirit of '76* sentenced the producer to a $10,000 fine and a ten-year prison term (later commuted to three years). Although extreme, this was not an atypical case. During World War I the government imposed harsh restrictions on the expression of antiwar opinion, and when official action was not swift enough to suit the public, vigilante groups took matters into their own hands. The targets of repression were radicals who opposed the war, pacifists who opposed all wars, and German-Americans and other immigrant groups who were suspected of having a divided allegiance.

The amount of dissent a nation tolerates in wartime is usually proportional to the internal threat it perceives. In 1917 many Americans felt a keen sense of peril from within because of the nation's very heterogeneity. In the preceding twenty-five years nearly 18 million immigrants had come to the United States, most of them from countries involved in the war. One of every three Americans at the time was either an immigrant or the child of an immigrant. Many people, who imagined that the newcomers retained Old World loyalties, feared that entering the war with a divided populace would destroy the bonds of social cohesion. Wilson himself had once warned of the danger that Americans might be divided into "camps of hostile opinion, hot against each other." For those plagued by fears of disunity, the war created a grave threat.

Such fears led to different sorts of defensive reactions. Some Americans tried to extinguish manifestations of German culture: several state legislatures eliminated the "kaiser's tongue" from school curricula, a few universities revoked honorary degrees bestowed in the past on noted Germans, and a town in Oklahoma even burned German-language books as part of a Fourth of July celebration. Others revealed their fears by insisting on a formal observance of patriotic ritual. Mobs often forced people who had criticized the war to buy Liberty Bonds, to sing the national anthem in public, or even to kiss the American flag, presumably with the proper ardor.

For those who were not satisfied with symbolic acts of conformity there remained yet another possibility—joining a patriotic organization. By far the largest was the American Protective League. With a membership that eventually climbed to 250,000, the league pried into people's opinions and checked on who was buying war bonds. To uncover "slackers," the league stopped men on the street and demanded that they produce their draft cards. The league even enjoyed quasi-official status. Its stationery read "Organized With the Approval and Operating Under the Department of Justice of the U.S."; its members received cards identifying them as federal agents; and in May 1918 the attorney general named the league an "Auxiliary to the Justice Department."

In addition to this widespread feeling of insecurity, the behavior of government officials fanned the flames of repression. Woodrow Wilson considered dissent dangerously disruptive, and he regarded the socialist leader Eugene V. Debs and other antiwar spokesmen as little better than traitors. Unable to give personal attention to each civil liberties case, Wilson delegated broad responsibility to members of his cabinet and usually stood by their decisions. Postmaster General Albert Burleson wanted to bar from the mails any publication that criticized the reasons for American entry into the conflict or said anything "to hamper and obstruct the Government in the prosecution of the war." Attorney General Thomas Gregory advised opponents of the war to seek mercy from God "for they need expect none from an outraged people and an avenging government." On occasion Wilson would overrule his subordinates, as when Burleson barred an issue of the liberal journal *The Nation* from the mails. Also, such officials as Secretary of Labor William Wilson and Secretary of War Newton D. Baker held more libertarian views. But usually the Wilson administration cracked down on dissenters with little hesitation.

SOCIALISTS AND PACIFISTS

It could do so in part because of the nature of the opposition to the war. Not only were there relatively few war critics, but also most were socialists, anarchists, or members of the Industrial Workers of the World (IWW), people on the margins of society who had little political or economic weight and therefore made convenient targets. The war, in fact, proved disastrous for the Socialist Party, which had until then achieved a modest degree of success. In 1912 Debs had polled 900,000 votes—6 percent of the total—in the presidential election. Even in 1916 the party received 600,000 votes, elected candidates to office in scores of cities and towns, and reached a wide audience through its press. But when the United States entered the war, the Socialist Party, declaring that the war benefited only the ruling classes, called on American workers to repudiate the government. It branded the declaration of war "a crime against the people of the United States and against the nations of the world. In all modern history there has been no war more unjustifiable."

This posture weakened the socialist movement for several reasons. Although most socialists opposed the war, not all party leaders did. A small but influential segment, including Upton Sinclair, Charles Edward Russell, and Jack London, supported Wilson. Not only did the war split socialists into warring camps, but it linked the party in the public mind with treason and thereby robbed it of a good deal of its respectability. Finally, suppression broke the back of the party in some areas. Socialists found their literature barred from the mails, their headquarters wrecked, and their leaders indicted for sedition.

Like the Socialist Party, the women's movement also divided on the issue of war. Women reformers had long been committed to pacifism. In 1915, a coalition of delegates from women's organizations formed the Woman's Peace Party, led by Jane Addams and Carrie Chapman Catt. Once the United States entered World War I, the party splintered and women's pacifist efforts disintegrated. The woman suffrage movement, which supported the war, took the opportunity to prove its patriotic fervor. Clubwomen similarly joined the war effort by selling war bonds and running canteens. But there were dissidents. Some women socialists maintained their opposition to the war. Members of the Woman's Peace Party continued to demonstrate against "Kaiser Wilson" and, when arrested, went on hunger strikes. Pacifist and feminist Crystal Eastman led a remnant of the Woman's Peace Party that campaigned against American policy.

For pacifists, the war produced a crisis of conscience. In an atmosphere in which an ordinarily tolerant man like attorney Clarence Darrow could remark that "the pacifist speaks with the German accent" and in which conscientious objectors were labeled parasites whose liberties were being preserved by others on the battlefield, it is not surprising that many pacifists recanted. In 1916 the American Peace Society declared that Jesus Christ was a pacifist; in 1917 it backed the war. More than one hundred prominent Quakers announced their "loyalty to the Cause of Civilization, and to the President of the United States."

For those conscientious objectors who stood by their convictions, the government made provisions of a sort. The Selective Service Act of 1917 exempted from combat duty members of recognized religious sects whose teachings forbade participation in war. These men had to register for the draft and accept induction as noncombatants in the medical, engineering, or quartermaster corps. Of the 24 million registrants, 65,000 requested this classification. Only 21,000 were actually inducted, but fewer than 4,000 of them made use of their noncombatant status. The rest apparently took up arms. About 500 men who refused to cooperate in any way, or whose opposition to the war rested on political grounds and did not qualify them for consideration, were sent to jail; the last was not freed until 1933. In all, the number of conscientious objectors never approached the number of draft dodgers, which the War Department estimated at 171,000.

CURBING DISSENT: HOW

The Wilson administration launched a three-pronged assault on dissenters. First, it attempted to deport radical aliens. Existing laws already excluded immigrants who favored the forcible overthrow of the government. Immigration legislation in 1917 and 1918 tightened these provisions and gave the government additional power to deport aliens who advocated the destruction of private property or who belonged to organizations that worked for revolution. No trial was needed. Deportation could be accomplished through an administrative proceeding. Second, the government dispatched troops to break strikes led by the IWW in lumber camps in Washington and in copper mines in Montana. Claiming that the IWW engaged in sabotage and that it instigated strikes not to improve working conditions but to cripple war production, the government threw union leaders into jail and held them for months on the flimsiest of evidence or on no charge at all.

The third and most widely used weapon to curb dissent was prosecution under the Espionage Act (1917) and the Sedition Act (1918). The Espionage Act made it a crime to obstruct military recruitment, and it authorized the postmaster general to deny mailing privileges for any materials he considered treasonous. Under its terms Burleson barred dozens of periodicals, including an issue of *The Masses*, which had a cartoon captioned "Making the World Safe for Capitalism." Eugene Debs was convicted under the Espionage Act for making a speech that condemned the administration's war policies and its violations of civil liberties. When the Supreme Court upheld his conviction, Debs spent two and a half years in jail. His comrade, Kate Richards O'Hare, was indicted for allegedly saying that any man who enlisted in the army "would be used for fertilizer" and that women who allowed their sons to enlist were "nothing more nor less than brood-sows." Although she denied having made the statements, O'Hare, a victim of wartime hysteria, served fourteen months in the penitentiary.

In the spring of 1918, as reports of mob violence against radicals reached Washington, the Wilson administration decided to support a sedition act in the hope that such a measure would calm public apprehension. The Sedition Act made it illegal to "utter, print, write, or publish any disloyal, profane, scurrilous, or abusive language" about the government, the Constitution, the flag, the armed forces, or even the "uniform of the Army or Navy." Ultimately, more than 1,000 persons were convicted under the Espionage and Sedition acts, including more than a hundred members of the IWW who, President Wilson noted privately, "certainly are worthy of being suppressed."

The Supreme Court ultimately approved these wartime prosecutions. In *Schenck v. United States* (1919), a unanimous Court found that a socialist who had mailed circulars to men eligible for the draft, circulars stating that conscription was unconstitutional and should be resisted, had violated the Espionage Act by interfering with the legitimate power of the government to raise an army. Oliver Wendell Holmes Jr., who delivered the opinion, tried to define the boundaries of permissible speech. The question, Holmes said, "is whether the words used are used in such circumstances and are of such a nature as to create a clear and present danger that they will bring about the substantive evils that Congress has a right to prevent. It is a question of proximity and degree." In *Abrams v. United States* (1919), the Court found the Sedition Act constitutional. Jacob Abrams, an anarchist, and several of his friends had distributed leaflets in August 1918 condemning American intervention in Soviet Russia and calling on munitions workers to strike in protest. The government contended that such a strike would also interfere with the conduct of the war against Germany. The Court upheld the convictions, but Holmes now dissented, asserting that "the best test of truth is the power of the thought to get itself accepted in the competition of the market."

The suppression of free speech had both predictable and unforeseen consequences. It seriously weakened the radical movement. Indeed, groups were sometimes singled out not only for their antiwar stand but also precisely because of their radicalism. For example, the war furnished to employers who had always hated the IWW a patriotic pretext for attacking it. But restrictions on civil liberties also dismayed many Progressives who, though they supported the war, believed that the Wilson administration had gone overboard in curbing individual rights. The crusade for conformity also substantiated the argument of intellectuals, like Randolph Bourne, who rejected all along the notion that war could be directed toward humane ends. War was an inexorable situation, Bourne reasoned, in which the government would do anything it thought necessary to achieve victory. Intellectuals who believed that war could be "moulded toward liberal purposes" were therefore deceiving themselves. The attack on civil liberties, as much as anything else, proved Bourne correct.

ANOTHER REVOLUTION

If the war profoundly affected Americans, it was because, as Bourne observed, they expected too much from the conflict, not because—as compared with the other belligerents—they sacrificed too much for it. The growing American disillusionment with Russia was an excellent example. In March 1917 the Russian people, bankrupt and bled to the breaking point, overthrew the hollow, corrupt regime of Czar Nicholas II. The czar was replaced with a liberal republic headed by Prince Georgy Lvov. President Wilson welcomed the new government, particularly after Lvov promised to keep Russia in the war whatever the cost. The change of government confirmed Wilson's faith that democracy, not authoritarianism, would shape the future. By summer 1917, however, the war was still taking its murderous toll of the dispirited, inefficient Russian army. The slow collapse of Lvov's regime allowed a corresponding rise in the power of V.I. Lenin, a communist leader who had recently returned to Russia from Switzerland. Disillusionment with Lvov's inept policies resulted in July in a new, more conservative regime headed by Alexander Kerensky. The Kerensky government refused to listen to Lenin's demands for withdrawing Russia from the war.

Wilson appointed a special commission to visit Russia during the summer. The commission's report was optimistic, a mood not shared by Wilson or by Secretary of State Robert Lansing, who was convinced the Russians were sailing straight into another bloody French Revolution. This view was confirmed on November 7, 1917, when Lenin's Bolsheviks overthrew the Kerensky regime. Wilson's and Lansing's pessimism turned to hatred as Lenin began confiscating private property, radically redistributing political power, proclaiming the need for worldwide revolution, and in March 1918 making peace with Germany. The Bolsheviks "are avowedly opposed to every government on earth," Lansing privately exclaimed. He hoped they would "go to pieces," but doubted this would occur, for "their cry of 'Peace and Land' is popular with the ignorant Russians who have suffered grievously in the past." Wilson's and Lansing's fear of Lenin, however, did not get in the way of their understanding that the Bolsheviks fundamentally challenged Western "political institutions as they now exist . . . based on nationality and private property," in Lansing's words. Lenin threatened Wilson's entire postwar program.

The president's Fourteen Points speech of January 1918, one of the most famous speeches in American history, was Wilson's first response to Lenin. Two motives, the fear of bolshevism and the desire for American postwar economic expansion, explained why the Fourteen Points speech demanded covenants openly arrived at: freedom of the seas in peace and for neutrals in war; the removal of tariffs, trade preferences, and other economic barriers; reduction of armaments; self-determination as a political principle; recognition of a Russia that would be a reasonable neighbor (to Wilson this obviously meant a noncommunist neighbor); and, finally, "a general Association of Nations" that would uphold all these principles.

Not even Wilson's allies would accept the entire program. At the Paris Economic Conference of 1916, for example, they had planned to keep ambitious Americans out of British, French, and Italian markets. Great Britain, France, and czarist Russia, moreover, had signed secret agreements with Japan and Italy that promised territorial gains and economic booty from the war if they maintained a common front against Germany. Wilson knew about these treaties because Lenin had gleefully published them. The president understood that they ran directly against his principle of self-determination. To keep Japan away from China while American attention was on Europe, Wilson had even ignored several of his own points by negotiating a secret deal with Japan in which the United States agreed to recognize Japan's "special" interests in China. Tokyo officials in turn promised not to use the war as a cover for seizing "special rights or privileges in China." The president knew that this pact (the Lansing-Ishii agreement of November 1917) might later be used by Japan to claim special interests in Manchuria, but Wilson believed that at a postwar conference his own moral stature and his nation's mushrooming economic power would overcome the Allied and Japanese plans. The Bolsheviks, however, were another matter.

INTERVENING IN THE RUSSIAN REVOLUTION

Lenin's government seemed to be beyond Wilson's control. As the American humorist Finley Peter Dunne once observed, a revolution could not be bound by the rules of the

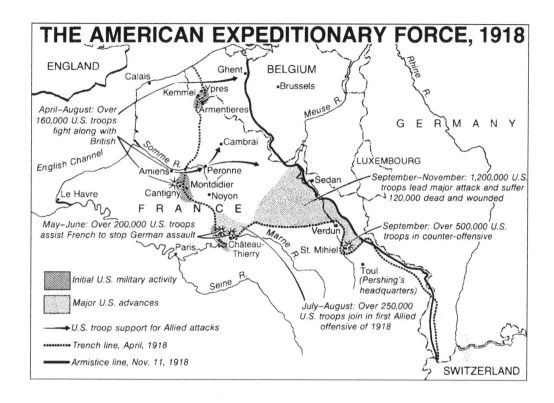

THE AMERICAN EXPEDITIONARY FORCE, 1918

ENGLAND

Calais

Ghent

BELGIUM

•Brussels

Kemmel Ypres

Armentieres

April–August: Over 160,000 U.S. troops fight along with British

Somme R.

•Cambrai

Meuse R.

G E R M A N Y

Rhine R.

LUXEMBOURG

English Channel

Amiens• •Peronne

•Sedan

September–November: 1,200,000 U.S. troops lead major attack and suffer 120,000 dead and wounded

Le Havre

Cantigny Montdidier

•Noyon

F R A N C E

May–June: Over 200,000 U.S. troops assist French to stop German assault

Marne R.

Verdun

September: Over 500,000 U.S. troops in counter-offensive

Paris Château-Thierry

St. Mihiel

Toul (Pershing's headquarters)

Seine R.

July–August: Over 250,000 U.S. troops join in first Allied offensive of 1918

Initial U.S. military activity

Major U.S. advances

➤ U.S. troop support for Allied attacks

•••••• Trench line, April, 1918

━━━ Armistice line, Nov. 11, 1918

SWITZERLAND

game, for it is rebelling against those rules. The president was therefore open to demands by the British and French that he join them in intervening militarily in Russia to overthrow the Bolsheviks and reopen the eastern front. At first Wilson refused, in part because of opposition from young liberals in the State Department who were led by William Bullitt. A handsome, ambitious, aristocratic Philadelphian, Bullitt argued that Leninism could be destroyed only if Wilson moved farther to the left politically and undercut the attractiveness of the Bolshevik program.

The president rejected such advice. In June 1918 he agreed to land Americans at Murmansk in northern Russia. The landing was made in cooperation with French and British troops. The Japanese meanwhile moved into Siberia, threatening to control the vital Trans-Siberian railway system while disguising their takeover as "anti-Bolshevism." In July Wilson sent 10,000 troops to Vladivostok in Siberia, then established an American-controlled group to run the railways. He thus assumed responsibility in that far-off part of the world to stand guard against both Japanese and Bolsheviks. Making the world safe for democracy obviously was becoming a big job.

Wilson publicly justified the intervention in Murmansk on military-strategic grounds, but within days the Allied forces were fighting Bolsheviks, not Germans. The American force remained there, moreover, until June 1919, nearly eight months after the war against Germany ended. The president excused the Vladivostok operation by arguing that he hoped to help some 60,000 Czech soldiers who had been fighting Germany and now apparently wanted to escape through Vladivostok to fight on the western front. When the Americans landed, however, the Czechs were fighting Bolsheviks. The United States protected the rear of the Czech forces and supported White Russian troops that were trying to overthrow Lenin. The American soldiers remained in Siberia until April 1920.

The interventions made little sense in the overall war effort. They were crucial, however, if Wilson hoped to destroy the communist regime and keep Siberia out of Japanese hands. As Secretary of War Newton D. Baker candidly remarked in September 1919, American troops remained in Siberia because withdrawal would leave the area "open to anarchy, bloodshed and Bolshevism." But Wilson failed to overthrow Lenin. He only worsened an already poisonous relationship between Russia and the West. The president fully realized the dilemma. In 1919 he declared that using troops to stop a revolution was "like using a broom to hold back a great ocean." He nonetheless tried to use the broom.

THE YANKS IN EUROPE

A central problem for Wilson was that he had to watch closely not only Germans, Bolsheviks, and Japanese but also his European allies. The political relationship with London and Paris, already strained by the Fourteen Points speech, was not improved by the timing and nature of the American military effort.

No major U.S. force landed in France until eight months after Wilson's war message of April 1917. Not until the spring of 1918 did Americans decisively affect the fighting. But they were then pivotal in turning back a large German offensive just forty miles from Paris. The Americans won a major victory at Château-Thierry, a triumph that Wilson mistakenly thought would put the French in his debt at the postwar peace conference, and then drove the Germans back along the southern front until Berlin asked for peace in November 1918. The war ended on November 11.

The Yanks had arrived none too early, for throughout 1917 and early 1918 the Allies nearly bled themselves to death. In one offensive alone they expended more than a half million lives to move the battle line several miles. An entire generation of Europeans was being exterminated. Nearly 3 million Allied soldiers lost their lives in the war; probably 10 million people in all were slaughtered, but of this number only 52,000 were Americans. These figures help explain why British and French leaders were so driven by hatred for Germany at the Paris peace conference in 1919 and why they scorned Wilson's pleas for moderation. Such feelings, combined with the president's great reluctance to place American troops under European commanders and his refusal to participate fully in several wartime planning conferences, did not augur well for the peace conference. But then the problems Wilson was enduring at home were also ominous for his postwar plans.

1919: RED SCARE

In 1919, as peace came to Europe, industrial warfare flared in the United States. That year more than 4 million workers took part in 3,600 strikes. Most of the walkouts had similar causes. Workers who had won union recognition and improved their working conditions during the war now attempted to solidify or extend those gains. It seemed essential to do so because wages were lagging behind rising prices, and many workers feared that they would lose their jobs as factories converted back to civilian production. Employers, however, wanted to withdraw many of the concessions made during the war; consequently, they often refused even to negotiate. These conflicts took place in the wake of the widespread anxiety aroused by the Russian Revolution. Although only a few strikes were led by radicals and none had radical objectives, employers, hoping to capture public opinion, claimed that labor turmoil posed a revolutionary threat.

Two of these disturbances in particular—the Seattle general strike and the Boston police strike—seemed to endanger law and order. In January 1919, when Seattle shipyard workers struck for higher wages, unions throughout the city voted to walk out in support. Many Americans viewed the general strike, in the words of one presidential adviser, as "the first appearance of the Soviet in this country." The government dispatched the U.S. Marines; the American Federation of Labor (AFL) leadership insisted that Seattle locals return to work; and Seattle's mayor, Ole Hanson, beefed up the police and issued an ultimatum. Under fierce pressure from all sides, the strikers capitulated. Then, in September, policemen in Boston demanded the right to join a union, a right denied them by the police commissioner. A strike followed during which some theft and looting occurred. The reaction was intense. The president branded the strike "a crime against civilization," and Governor Calvin Coolidge of Massachusetts proclaimed that there was "no right to strikes against the public safety by anybody, anywhere, anytime." The city dismissed everyone involved in the strike and recruited an entirely new police force.

In September 1919 the United States also faced the most massive industrial dispute in its history when 350,000 steelworkers left the mills. The men, many of whom still worked twelve hours a day, seven days a week, wanted an AFL union recognized as bargaining agent. The mill owners, for their part, welcomed a showdown over the principle of the open shop. Judge Elbert Gary, the president of United States Steel, accurately reflected the opinion of management when he claimed that most workers were satisfied with their conditions and wanted nothing to do with the union. As in Boston and Seattle, charges of radicalism were hurled at the union leaders. In this case the union gained nothing at all. By January 1920, its resources exhausted by a long and costly struggle, the AFL called off the strike.

In the spring of 1919, a series of bombings and attempted bombings badly frightened the American people. In April a bomb was sent to the mayor of Seattle. Another, mailed to a Georgia politician, exploded, and the maid who opened the package lost both her hands. When the post office intercepted thirty-four identical parcels addressed to J.P. Morgan, John D. Rockefeller, and other prominent business and civic leaders, and all were found to contain bombs, headlines blared: "REDS PLANNED MAY DAY MURDERS." In June bombs went off at about the same time in eight cities, adding to the fear that these acts were the work not of an individual but of a conspiracy. One of the bombs shattered windows in the home of Attorney General A. Mitchell Palmer.

As Americans felt increasingly threatened by signs of violent revolution, they hunted for preventive measures. No fewer than twenty-eight states passed peacetime sedition acts of some sort, under which 1,400 people were arrested and 300 convicted. Legislatures sometimes refused to admit those who held unorthodox views. In November 1919 the House of Representatives refused to seat Milwaukee socialist Victor Berger. When he won reelection, the House again balked at accepting him. In January 1920 the New York State legislature expelled five socialists, although most of them had held office during the war. States tried to uproot subversive influences by investigating public school teachers and requiring them to sign loyalty oaths. Congress further tightened immigration laws in 1920 by providing for the deportation of aliens who merely possessed revolutionary literature.

The Red Scare reached its crescendo with the Palmer raids. Shaken by the bombing attempt on his home, Attorney General Palmer, with the aid of other officials, worked out policies that effectively deprived radical aliens of due process. The Department of Justice launched surprise raids on the headquarters of radical organizations, seized correspondence and membership lists, detained suspects under astronomical bail, and cross-examined witnesses before they could obtain legal advice. Permitting a radical alien to see an attorney before interrogation, J. Edgar Hoover of the Justice Department explained, "defeats the ends of justice." In the first week of January 1920, federal agents, employing these tactics, arrested 3,000 alleged communists in thirty-three cities. Many were imprisoned, although no charges were brought against them; 550 were later deported. Palmer's action violated every civil libertarian principle, but instantly made him a national hero.

The wartime suppression of civil liberties differed in several respects from the postwar Red Scare. In the former, Americans feared subversion, but in the latter, revolution. The target in 1917 was frequently the German-American; the target in 1919 was often organized labor. But in important ways the two episodes resembled each other. Both occurred because society felt threatened from within, both involved legal and extralegal forms of repression, and both exploited anti-immigrant and antiradical sentiments. Each had a crippling effect on the American radical movement, which by 1920 was weak, fragmented, and in disarray. The Palmer raids, no less than wartime intolerance, angered many Progressives, who condemned Wilson for permitting, if not actually encouraging, these excesses. By mid-1920 the Red Scare had run its course. With communism clearly confined to Russia, with labor turmoil and bomb scares at an end, fears began to evaporate. The Wilson administration had won praise for its antiradical stance early in 1920, but had a more difficult time defending its record by the end of the year.

1919: BLACK SCARE

The postwar years were marked not only by labor turmoil but also by intense racial discord. In 1919 lynch mobs murdered seventy-eight African-Americans, at least ten of whom were veterans. From April to October race riots erupted in twenty-five cities, including Washington, DC; Omaha, Nebraska; and Longview, Texas. These riots claimed the lives of 120 people. The worst riot, during what came to be known as the "Red Summer," took place in Chicago; it left 38 dead and 537 injured. In truth, "race riot" was a less accurate term than "race war." Marauding bands of whites and blacks, armed with guns and clubs, roamed the streets and hunted each other down. Racial turbulence, like the Red Scare, had its roots in postwar social and economic dislocations. The war had dramatically altered the position of black Americans and raised their expectations. When those expectations clashed with the ingrained prejudices of whites, the stage was set for the Red Summer.

World War I spurred a mass exodus of blacks from southern farms to northern cities. In 1915 and 1916, floods and boll weevils ravaged crops in the cotton belt and forced many tenant farmers off the land. At about the same time, the war opened magnificent opportunities in the North. The demand for industrial labor seemed insatiable as factories were swamped

BASEBALL
SPORT AND BUSINESS

Babe Ruth and New York Giants manager John McGraw, 1923.
(Library of Congress)

Baseball has long been America's national pastime. It combines raw individual effort with precise team play, compiles masses of figures that enchant statistic-loving Americans, has a long tradition that allows fans to link past heroes to the present, and is played during the school-free, halcyon days of summer. Its complexity even makes it a favorite of intellectuals ("Base-ball is a religion," a distinguished philosopher proclaimed in 1919.).

The game's roots go back to ancient Egypt. Modern American teams appeared in the 1840s, organized—as has been every popular American sport except basketball—by wealthy gentlemen in the Northeast. Baseball was nationally popular by the Civil War. The first professional team, the Cincinnati Red Stockings, was formed in 1869. The National League appeared in 1876, the American League in 1901. World Series competition between the two leagues began two years later. Baseball grew quickly at the twentieth century's turn because of rapid urbanization, new street railways, and, particularly, increased leisure time created by the mechanization of farming and industry.

Equally important, the game was developed by men who viewed it as business, not sport. They organized it along the lines of such corporations as United States Steel. A division of labor existed between management and players, with owners monopolizing the players through a "reserve clause" that made players property of a single club. Owners controlled their market by giving each team absolute rights over its own urban area. Supreme Court rulings meanwhile exempted baseball from antitrust laws (a benefit not even United States Steel received from the courts). Attendance rose dramatically. The value of some clubs multiplied ten times between 1900 and 1918. Then, in 1919, members of the Chicago White Sox (soon tabbed the "Black Sox") were accused of accepting bribes to lose the World Series.

The sport was severely shaken. But four people managed to resurrect baseball so that

Brooklyn Dodgers president Branch Rickey talking to Jackie Robinson. *(National Baseball Hall of Fame Library, Cooperstown, New York)*

it became the rage of sport-minded Americans. Kenesaw Mountain Landis, a tough U.S. district court judge, was brought in as the first commissioner of professional baseball by the frightened owners to clean up the game. He did so brutally, even trying to ban players and owners from attending racetracks (where, Landis believed, lurked shadowy figures who "would sell out the Virgin Mary and their mothers"). He ruled baseball until his death in 1944. The second savior was George Herman ("Babe") Ruth of the Boston Red Sox and New York Yankees. His twenty-nine home runs in 1919 broke an 1884 record and revolutionized baseball by making it a game of exciting power. A son of a Baltimore barkeeper and a hard drinker at age eight, Ruth glamorously flouted Prohibition in the 1920s. He ordered the clubhouse boy to discard all letters except "those with checks or from broads." Landis was the puritanical Calvin Coolidge of baseball while Ruth was Babylonian America having an often illegal and immoral—but wonderful—time.

The third figure was Branch Rickey, a religious, Ohio-born, sharp-eyed lawyer who, as a general manager for several teams, developed the farm system whereby major league clubs developed their own players in minor leagues. This arrangement resembled Standard Oil's system of controlling its profitable product from the oil well to the filling station. The devout Rickey would not play ball on Sunday, but liked the player who "will break both your legs if you happen to be standing in his path to second base." His corporate techniques won championships at St. Louis, Brooklyn, and Pittsburgh. In 1947 he forced reluctant owners to allow him to hire Jackie Robinson, the first African-American to play in the Majors (for the Brooklyn Dodgers). Robinson became baseball's fourth savior.

He was followed by such other black superstars as Willie Mays, Hank Aaron (who broke Ruth's all-time home run record), and Bob Gibson (who struck out more hitters than any other National League pitcher). In 1958 the fabled Brooklyn Dodgers deserted Flatbush and became the Los Angeles Dodgers, making big league baseball a continental sport for the first time. And in the mid-1970s, the courts finally broke the owners' monopoly over their employees. Players with a specific number of years of experience, the courts decided, could test their worth in the open market. Wealthy clubs, such as the New York Yankees, were accused of "buying championships" when they won pennants after paying millions to several such stars. These huge sums were made possible by steadily increasing attendance and lucrative television contracts. The sport prospered, but it had been a close call, for in the 1920s baseball had nearly struck out before Landis, Ruth, Rickey, and Robinson stepped in to save it.

Web Links

www.pbs.org/kenburns/baseball
The public broadcasting system program, with a list of additional websites.

http://blackbaseball.com/
A site that includes a video on the creation of the Negro Leagues.

National Guardsmen are called out to quell race riots in Chicago, July 1919. *(Jun Fujita/Getty Images)*

with military orders, workers left their jobs for the army, and the flow of immigration from Europe came to a virtual halt. Black newspapers, particularly the Chicago *Defender*, encouraged migration by playing up the opportunities available to blacks in the North. Labor agents swept through the South attempting to recruit black workers. Some companies even issued free railroad passes to anyone who promised to work for them. From 1916 to 1918, hundreds of thousands of African-Americans moved north. The black population of Chicago doubled in just four years.

For most, migration had a racial as well as an economic dimension. The letters written by migrants, and their behavior as well, reveal their sense of embarking on a pilgrimage out of bondage and into a promised land. "I am in the darkness of the south," said an Alabama black in explaining his request for train fare to Chicago; "please help me to get out of this low down country [where] i am counted no more thin a dog." A group of blacks from Hattiesburg, Mississippi, on crossing the Ohio River, knelt, prayed, kissed the ground, and sang hymns of deliverance. The North, with its absence of legal segregation, surely afforded some African-Americans an exhilarating sense of freedom. A black carpenter who had moved to Chicago wrote to his brother in Mississippi, "I should have been here 20 years ago. I just begun to feel like a man."

Most blacks genuinely believed that the war would usher in an era of social justice. The National Association for the Advancement of Colored People urged blacks to support the war by enlisting and buying bonds, for then whites could no longer ignore their appeals for equality. A similar conviction led W.E.B. DuBois to advise blacks to "close our ranks shoulder to shoulder with our own white fellow citizens and the allied nations that are fighting for democracy." Several concessions made by the Wilson administration bolstered the prevailing optimism. Although the army remained rigidly segregated, the War Department established an officers' training camp for blacks, created a black combat division, and accepted blacks into medical units. The Railroad Administration, while preserving separate facilities for passengers, paid the same wages to white and black workers and agreed to bargain with a black Pullman union. All this, in the context of 1918, represented progress.

The end of the war, however, disappointed the hopes of DuBois and many others. With the return of millions of veterans, competition for jobs and housing grew fierce. In 1919 African-Americans discovered that many of their wartime gains were vanishing. They were again the last hired and the first fired. They still paid the highest rents for the most squalid dwellings. The Wilson administration no longer showed the slightest interest in them. Disillusionment was profound. For the first time, a number of black spokesmen openly advocated the use of violence for purposes of self-defense. This heightened race consciousness coincided with heightened fears among whites that blacks would drive down property values or, more generally, forget their "proper place."

The race riots occurred against this background of blacks and whites being thrown together in cities, of competition for places to live and work, of increased black militancy and corresponding white anxiety. Though no two riots followed exactly the same pattern, there were some similarities. The riots, which usually broke out during a heat wave when tempers were on edge, were often triggered by rumors of an interracial assault. Once the rioting began, the police seldom acted impartially; rather, they treated blacks more brutally than whites. Both sides committed acts of violence. Usually whites were the aggressors, and blacks defended themselves by trading rifle fire with their foes and making sorties into white neighborhoods. A few riots lasted a long time. It took thirteen days to restore order to Chicago. Invariably the riots left a legacy of bitterness and led not to mutual understanding but to a hardening of racial animosities.

THE ROAD TO PARIS

The class and racial antagonisms in the United States mirrored those of the world community. If Americans had difficulty handling these problems at home, there was little reason to think that they could make the entire world, or even Europe, safe for Progressive democracy. Yet Wilson set out to try.

He immediately ran into a string of disasters. Throughout the war the president had refused to discuss peace terms with the Allies. He feared that such talks could lead to splits that would retard the war effort. He also believed that as the war continued, American economic and military power would give him an increasingly stronger hand. But when he did approach the Allies to discuss the Fourteen Points in late 1918, Wilson discovered that the British refused to negotiate freedom of the seas (a principle that would protect neutrals against the powerful British fleet). The French insisted on destroying German power regardless of Wilsonian

"The Big Four" at the Paris Peace Conference in 1919: David Lloyd George, Vittorio Orlando, Georges Clemenceau, Woodrow Wilson. *(Library of Congress)*

principles. The president's position was weak, for he had refused to recognize neutral rights on the high seas in 1917 and 1918 and had singled out Germany as primarily responsible for starting the war. After all, such policies had been necessary to sustain the American commitment at home.

On the way to Paris Wilson told his advisers that "the United States was the only nation which was absolutely disinterested" in peace making. Allied leaders knew better, and they comprehended how history had shaped the American position as well as their own. Harold Nicolson, a member of the British delegation to Paris and later a distinguished historian, observed that Americans, like Europeans, had used brutal force to conquer territory in the nineteenth century. Then he asked, "Can we wonder that [Europeans] preferred the precisions of their old system to the vague idealism of a new system which America might refuse to apply even to her own continent?" As Europeans such as Nicolson understood, Wilsonian principles were designed to protect American interests.

The president also informed his advisers that, while he embodied the hopes of all progressive peoples, "the leaders of the allies did not really represent their peoples." This was a colossally mistaken belief. David Lloyd George and Georges Clemenceau, the prime ministers of Great Britain and France, respectively, received thumping votes of support at home before the peace conference convened, and both leaders ran on platforms pledging to squeeze every possible pfennig (penny) and acre out of Germany. Wilson, however, in one of the great American political fumbles, had proclaimed in late October 1918 that patriotism required the election of a Democratic Congress. In a congressional election year the Republicans would probably have gained some seats, but they won a major victory by blasting Wilson for questioning their wholehearted support of the war. Republicans even captured the Senate (49 to 47), the body that would have to ratify Wilson's work at Paris.

Nor did the president ease the situation by naming a peace commission that contained not a single important Republican or senator. This bland group was designed to raise few problems for the plans of the delegation's leader, Wilson himself. The president decided that no other person could be entrusted with the mission. He gave his political opponents and those who disliked the Fourteen Points a highly visible figure to attack.

AT PARIS

In the wake of the war's devastation, communist uprisings took place in Germany. A communist government actually controlled Hungary for several months. An American warning that food supplies would be shut off if trouble occurred in part averted threatened left-wing riots in Austria. "We are sitting upon an open powder magazine," Colonel House worried, "and some day a spark may ignite it." By early 1919 Wilson's fear of bolshevism overshadowed his mistrust of the Europeans. He increasingly found himself on their side in a common effort to contain Leninism. He did reject their suggestions that a larger military force be sent to topple the Bolsheviks, but agreed that Lenin should not be invited to Paris. Wilson had decided to use pressure, not negotiation, in handling Lenin.

The president continued to have faith that Leninism could be conquered through a "slow process of reform." Since it was his League of Nations that would carry out the reform, Wilson, over the vigorous objections of the French and British (who wanted first to settle the precise terms for strangling Germany), forced the peace conference to begin in January 1919 with discussions on the League. Within a month the organization was created. The League of Nations consisted of an Assembly containing nearly forty nations (but not revolutionary Mexico, Russia, or Germany); a Council comprising nine nations, with the five permanent seats held by the United States, Great Britain, Japan, France, and Italy; and a Secretariat. Except for procedural matters, most decisions required unanimous consent in the Council.

Article XIV of the Covenant of the League of Nations established the Permanent Court of International Justice, which could decide international cases taken to the Court by the parties involved. Article XVI pledged all members to penalize aggressors by cutting off trade and economic aid. It was Article X, however, that Wilson termed "the heart of the covenant":

> The members of the League undertake to respect and preserve as against external aggression the territorial integrity and existing political independence of all members of the League. In case of any such aggression or in case of any threat or danger of such aggression the Council shall advise upon the means by which this obligation shall be fulfilled.

This wording deserves close study, for in the end Article X contributed to Wilson's doom.

Returning to the United State for a short time in February 1919, Wilson encountered strong opposition to the covenant from Senate Republicans led by Henry Cabot Lodge of Massachusetts. The opponents made public a petition signed by thirty-nine senators condemning the League, six more than the one-third necessary to defeat the pact. This opposition was partly personal. Some Republicans, Lodge and Theodore Roosevelt in particular, hated Wilson, a feeling not lessened by the president's partisan attack on Republicans and his often condescending manner. But his opponents primarily attacked several aspects of the treaty itself. Article X, they feared, committed Americans to uphold the status quo around the world, pledged the United States to preserve British and French imperial interests, and weakened Congress's power to declare war by providing a nearly automatic American commitment to intervene. League opponents also attacked the lack of a provision protecting America's use of the Monroe Doctrine in the Western Hemisphere and the failure to exclude domestic questions (such as tariffs) from League authority.

The president was furious with the Senate. "I am going to resume my study of the dictionary to find adequate terms in which to describe the fatuity of these gentlemen with the poor little minds that never get anywhere," he remarked privately. "I cannot express my contempt for their intelligence." Wilson then made another critical mistake. Returning to Paris, he demanded changes in the covenant—although not in Article X—that would meet some of the Senate's objections. Time that was to have been devoted to carefully drawing up the peace treaty with the Germans was, at the president's insistence, spent on rewriting the covenant. Lloyd George, Clemenceau, and Vittorio Orlando, the Italian leader, knew that they had Wilson at a disadvantage and consequently gave in to some of his requests only after he gave them much of what they wanted in the peace treaty. The president had to surrender parts of his Fourteen Points, particularly those concerning self-determination and territorial settlements.

As one American official later commented, "One came to Paris when hope was riding high, and each day you could see these hopes just—well, you soon detected that it was a great enormous balloon and gradually all the air was coming out of it. . . . Then there was Russia, a vast black cloud that overhung the whole thing." As the conference wore on and revolution threatened Germany, Hungary, and Austria, the key problem was, indeed, how the Soviet Union could be isolated and central Europe, particularly a weakened Germany, protected from the virus of communism. Wilson hoped to rebuild Germany so that it would be strong enough to provide its own immunity. Clemenceau, however, and to a lesser extent Lloyd George, determined that Germany must be stripped so that it could never again launch war. Territory taken from Germany was given to France, Poland, and the new independent state of Czechoslovakia. Millions of Germans were thereby wrenched from their native government and placed within the boundaries of other, weaker nations.

Equally important, Germany was saddled with $33 billion of war reparations that had to be paid out of a decimated economy. The French had actually asked for $200 billion, but Wilson fought Clemenceau and scaled down the French demands. In return, however, the president and Lloyd George signed a security treaty promising France aid if it were attacked by Germany. The plan thus became clear: in order to assist a weakened Germany to withstand the onslaughts of communism sweeping in from the east, the peace conference essentially threw out the principle of self-determination, particularly for Germans, in order to build the newly independent states of Poland, Hungary, and Czechoslovakia, which were to act as buffers, or a cordon sanitaire, between Russia and Germany. In reality, of course, these states were too weak to stand between two potential giants, so France gave territorial guarantees to the eastern Europeans by pledging to assist if they were attacked by a third party.

Self-determination was also sacrificed in the Pacific, where the Chinese province of Shantung, formerly controlled by Germany, was claimed by Japan. Wilson initially fought this transfer, but surrendered when the Japanese threatened to leave the League of Nations unless they received Shantung. The president did prevent Italy from claiming non-Italian territory along the Adriatic Sea, even though Orlando dramatically walked out of the conference in protest. Finally, Wilson accepted a compromise on the question of Germany's former colonies in Africa and the Pacific that, in actuality, gave France, England, and Japan the complete control they demanded in these areas. Germany was never consulted on these terms, but was simply given the hurriedly written treaty in May to sign—or else. The "or else" probably would have been an economic blockade designed to starve the Germans until they did sign. Berlin officials finally accepted the treaty only after bitterly protesting its terms. One war had finally ended.

REJECTION

As Wilson returned to do battle with the Senate, he found three groups preparing to fight the Covenant of the League of Nations and the peace treaty. The first group, centering on Lodge and other conservative Republicans, determined to defeat anything Wilson recommended, but focused its objection on the automatic commitment implied in Article X. A second group comprised such Progressives as Herbert Hoover and Charles Evans Hughes. This group did not personally dislike Wilson (Hoover, indeed, had been one of the president's important advisers at Paris), but attacked Articles X and XVI and was afraid the covenant would endanger Congress's constitutional control over domestic affairs. A third group, led by Progressive Republicans William Borah of Idaho and Hiram Johnson of California, formed the "Irreconcilables," for they refused to agree to American participation in any international organization resembling the League of Nations. Moreover, they blasted Wilson's refusal to deal with Russia as, in Johnson's words, "an exhibition of the crassest stupidity." One common thread united the three groups: all wanted to maintain maximum freedom of action for the United States in the world, particularly so Americans could freely exploit their new economic power without having to worry about political restraints.

Wilson's opponents enjoyed a strong position. With the Republicans in control of the Senate, Lodge became chair of the Foreign Relations Committee, which would first have to act on the covenant and the treaty. As it became clear that Lodge was mustering opposition, the president attempted to pressure the Senate by embarking on an exhausting speaking tour. After thirty-six formal speeches in three weeks, the sixty-three-year-old Wilson suffered the beginnings of a paralytic stroke on September 26. Desperately ill, he nevertheless angrily stuck to his refusal to compromise with the Senate. When the Senate added reservations that modified Article X and condemned Japan's hold on Shantung, Wilson ordered Democratic senators not to vote for the amended covenant. In November 1919 the Senate rejected the League of Nations charter, with reservations, by a vote of 39 to 55. Four months later the charter again fell short of the necessary two-thirds needed for ratification, 49 to 35. Twenty-three Democrats, obeying Wilson's orders, ironically joined the Irreconcilables in defeating American entry into the League.

The president made one final effort during the 1920 presidential campaign. At first Wilson apparently decided to try for an unprecedented third term, but his illness and realistic Democratic political advisers ended that dream. He then declared the election a "solemn ref-

Senator Henry Cabot Lodge, chair of the Senate Foreign Relations Committee. *(Library of Congress)*

erendum" on the League of Nations. The president urged the Democratic ticket of Governor James Cox of Ohio and young Franklin D. Roosevelt of New York to support the covenant strongly. The Democratic ticket equivocated, however, while the Republicans, led by Senator Warren G. Harding of Ohio and Governor Calvin Coolidge of Massachusetts, talked on both sides of the League issue. Harding won overwhelmingly, obtaining 60.3 percent of the popular vote and carrying thirty-seven of the forty-eight states. Foreign policy issues, however, were peripheral. Once elected, Harding clearly stated that he would not push for American association with the League.

Wilson must bear primary responsibility for the American failure to join the League of Nations. His refusal to appoint an important Republican or senator to the delegation, his procedures at Paris, and his unwillingness to compromise with the Senate doomed the covenant. But in the end, American participation might have made little difference anyway. The fundamental problem was not the League of Nations but the ill-constructed peace treaty, which no organization of mere mortals could have saved. The treaty's treatment of Germany territorially and financially sowed the seeds for the terrible economic depression and the rise of Nazism in the 1930s. The exclusion of Russia from the peace conference and the League, and Wilson's announcement in March 1920 that the United States would not even recognize the existence of the Soviet government, piled unreality upon unreality. The failure to handle the problems posed by Germany and Russia set off a right-wing reaction not only in the United States, but also in Italy, France, Germany, and eastern and southern Europe, where the stage rapidly filled with fascists and National Socialists.

"What gave rise to the Russian Revolution?" Wilson finally queried in 1923, one year before his death. "The answer can only be that it was the product of a whole social system. It was not in fact a sudden thing." The same explanation can also be applied to the appearance of right-wing forces in the 1920s and 1930s. For the Paris conference in the end decided not on peace but on vengeance; not on economic justice—for there was little discussion of such issues at Paris—but on a political settlement that would allow economic exploitation; not on an inclusion of all people but on an exclusion of many, particularly revolutionary regimes.

In Paris, William Bullitt best summarized the result after he bitterly resigned from the American delegation. He declared that the peace treaty could result only in "a new century of wars." As he left his hotel, reporters asked Bullitt where he would go. "I am going to lie in the sands of the French Riviera," he replied, "and watch the world go to hell." He went. And it did.

Chapter Five

1920–1929
The New Era

President and Mrs. Coolidge, with their two sons and their pet dog in 1924. *(Library of Congress)*

Progressivism had appealed to many Americans because it promised stability to a nation experiencing rapid change. By 1920, however, the Wilsonian years had linked reform not with orderly change but with war and revolution. Consequently, Americans in the 1920s turned toward leaders who invoked traditional values and played on the widespread nostalgia for a simpler, happier past. But progressivism did not die. If anything, the decade was characterized by a quickening of those forces that were transforming American life—urban and corporate growth, racial and ethnic heterogeneity, concern for social morality, active government, and international involvement. The sharpest conflicts arose not over economic policy or foreign affairs, where something close to a consensus emerged, but over religion, ethnicity, and morality. Then, in 1929, Americans suddenly entered a chamber of economic horrors that transformed them, their world, and their progressivism.

REPUBLICAN POLITICS: HARDING AND COOLIDGE

Benefiting from widespread disillusionment with Wilsonianism, Republican Warren G. Harding won a landslide victory in the 1920 election. A senator from Ohio since 1914 (and the first man ever to move directly from the Senate to the White House), Harding was jovial and expansive, a backslapper who joined as many fraternal lodges as possible. He loved to meet people, had a remarkable memory for faces, and played tennis or golf whenever he could. Harding's chief virtue was that he usually recognized his own limitations; his chief defect was that he believed in rewarding old friends with federal jobs. Many of them abused his trust by swindling the government, and when Harding died in August 1923, scandals were erupting on every side. The director of the Veterans Bureau was convicted of stealing hundreds of millions of dollars, the attorney general resigned when charged with authorizing the sale of alcohol from government warehouses to bootleggers, and the head of the Alien Property Custodian's Office was found guilty of accepting bribes. The most famous scandal centered on allegations that Harding's secretary of the interior, Albert Fall, had leased government oil reserves in Teapot Dome, Wyoming, to private owners in order to line his own pocket. Fall resigned in disgrace and later served a one-year prison sentence.

These revelations, however, did not harm the Republican Party, partly because Harding had not been personally involved in the scandals and partly because his successor, Calvin Coolidge, had a reputation for honesty and frugality. A former governor of Massachusetts, Coolidge was a cold, austere individual whose childhood, according to an admiring biographer, was "simple, wholesome and unfurtive." Miles apart in temperament, Harding and Coolidge nevertheless shared similar social and economic views. Both believed that government should foster business enterprise. This meant a hands-off policy in areas where businessmen wanted freedom of action and intervention in areas where they wanted help. "This is a business country," Coolidge remarked, "and it wants a business government." On the other hand, both presidents regarded intervention on behalf of other interest groups as socially undesirable, financially irresponsible, and morally wrong. The Supreme Court also sanctioned this outlook, which governed Republican policies toward business, labor, agriculture, and public power.

Big business benefited handsomely from Republican rule. In 1922 Congress enacted the Fordney-McCumber Tariff, which raised import duties to their highest level ever. Harding and Coolidge filled federal regulatory agencies with men who considered it their task to assist the business community. One of them was William E. Humphrey. Appointed to the Federal

Trade Commission in 1925, he decided not to prosecute companies that had violated the law so long as they promised to behave in the future. Republicans placed tax policy in the hands of Andrew Mellon, who served as secretary of the Treasury from 1921 to 1932. Mellon, who resigned from the boards of directors of fifty-one corporations on assuming office, feared that if high taxes deprived the businessman of a fair share of his earnings, then "he will no longer exert himself and the country will be deprived of the energy on which its continued greatness depends." Mellon fought long, hard, and successfully to reduce taxes on inheritances, corporate profits, and the well-to-do. By 1926 Congress had cut the tax rate on an income of $1 million from 66 percent to 20 percent.

While business received all kinds of support, organized labor went into eclipse. Union membership fell from 5 million in 1920 to 3.4 million in 1930 for several reasons: unions had no foothold in industries undergoing the most rapid expansion, such as automobiles, rubber, and chemicals; the American Federation of Labor clung to an increasingly obsolete craft structure; employers conducted a vigorous open-shop drive, which included the use of spies and blacklists to block organizers; and several large companies introduced welfare measures—pension, insurance, and stock-sharing plans—that stifled union growth. When walkouts occurred, however, the White House occasionally intervened on the side of management. This happened during the railroad strike of 1922, when Attorney General Harry Daugherty persuaded Harding that the nation faced imminent peril. In Daugherty's view, the workers' support for government control of the railroads "was a conspiracy worthy of Lenin." Daugherty obtained a sweeping court injunction that barred virtually all union activities and proved instrumental in breaking the strike.

Harding and Coolidge rejected any government role in supporting farm prices or in developing power facilities. At the time agricultural interests supported the McNary-Haugen plan, which authorized the government to purchase farm products at prices above those offered in the world market. The government would export the goods at the world market price, therefore taking a loss. Farmers would reimburse the government from the profits they realized on sales to American consumers at inflated domestic prices. Congress defeated this proposal in 1924 and 1926 but passed it in 1927 and 1928, only to have Coolidge veto it as "vicious" and "preposterous" special-interest legislation. Republicans also did their best to extract the government from its involvement in the construction of power facilities in the Tennessee Valley. During World War I the government had built power plants at Muscle Shoals. Harding and Coolidge wished to sell these facilities to private entrepreneurs, but Congress blocked their plans.

During the 1920s the Supreme Court mirrored the social philosophy that reigned in the White House. This was hardly surprising since Harding appointed four judges to the bench, including William Howard Taft, who served as chief justice from 1922 to 1930. In a series of decisions concerning organized labor, the Court ruled that unions engaging in certain types of strikes (such as secondary boycotts) were liable to antitrust prosecution, that strict limits could be placed on picketing outside factory gates, and that court injunctions could be used to enforce contracts in labor disputes. The Supreme Court also struck down key welfare legislation. In *Bailey v. Drexel Furniture Co.* (1922), the justices ruled against a child-labor act passed in 1919 that imposed a 10 percent tax on the profits of firms employing child labor. A majority found that the tax was levied to regulate business practices rather than to produce revenue and therefore was inappropriate. The Court decided in *Adkins v.*

As secretary of commerce, Herbert Hoover had this small radio receiver installed in his home so he could understand complaints received by the department, c. 1925. *(Library of Congress)*

Children's Hospital (1923) that states could not establish minimum wages for women workers. Since women could now vote, they no longer merited special protection. Chief Justice Taft, although generally content with the Court's performance, nevertheless feared for the future. "The only hope we have of keeping a consistent declaration of constitutional law," he noted, "is for us to live as long as we can."

A NEW ORDER: REPUBLICAN ALTERNATIVES TO WILSON'S LEAGUE OF NATIONS

In foreign policy as at home, Harding and Coolidge knew that they could not retreat into isolationism or nostalgia for a pre-1914 world. "There never again will be precisely the old order," Harding declared in 1922. "Indeed, I know of no one who thinks it to be desirable. For out of the old order came the war itself." A new order, constructed and dominated by U.S. economic power, would avert future world wars and revolutions. That power was immense. In 1914 Americans owed the world about $3.5 billion; after they financed the Allies in war, the world suddenly owed the United States $13 billion. Fueled by the new radio, airplane, and especially automobile industries, the booming domestic economy doubled its industrial production between 1921 and 1929. Never had a nation become so rich so fast. That success seemed to confirm superiority in other areas. As the *Ladies' Home Journal* trumpeted, "There is only one first-class civilization in the world today. It is right here in the United States."

The new world order was to rest on certain principles. First, military force was to be reduced everywhere. Money spent on rifles would be better invested in automobiles so standards of living could rise. Second, money and trade would be the dynamics of the new order. Americans naturally wanted to set ground rules that played to their own greatest strength in international affairs. Third, economic activities were to be undertaken primarily by private individuals, not governments. If government directed investment and trade, individual rights could disappear and fascism or socialism result. "Constantly I insisted [in the 1920s] that spiritual and intellectual freedom could not continue to exist without economic freedom," Herbert Hoover recalled. "If one died, all would die."

Government's primary responsibility was to ensure that private investment and trade could flow freely into any market. Unfair monopolies were therefore to be broken up, state-controlled enterprises (as in Russia) undermined. Above all, freedom of enterprise was not to be shackled by such political alliances as provided for in Article X of the Covenant of the League of Nations. In 1928, for example, the French again pressed Washington for a political alliance against a revived Germany. Secretary of State Frank Kellogg quickly transformed the request into a meaningless fifteen-nation agreement in which each signatory renounced war, except, of course, for self-defense. The Kellogg-Briand Pact was later laughed at as nothing more than an "international kiss," but, most important for Americans, it retained their complete freedom of action. The most powerful decision makers in foreign affairs were Secretary of State Charles Evans Hughes and Secretary of Commerce Herbert Hoover. Both had long been identified with Progressive programs. Hoover emphasized that the key to happiness and prosperity was "American individualism," which he defined as "an equality of opportunity." To ensure such opportunity, Hoover, like Wilson, stressed the need for an expanding overseas economy. Hoover also believed that, to exploit global opportunities, American entrepreneurs should combine in global associations so they could both compete with foreign cartels and end cutthroat competition at home. One leading American banker caught this policy exactly: businessmen must stop "scrambling amongst each other for the plums which fall," and learn instead "by cooperative effort to plant more plum trees that we might share the larger yield." Since Hoover defined the national interest as the interest of business, his Commerce Department blazed the way. Particularly active was its Bureau of Foreign and Domestic Commerce, which during the 1920s quadrupled its budget as it established fifty offices around the world to help businessmen plant new "plum trees" in foreign markets. If the Republicans failed, it was because their assumptions were wrong, not because they attempted to retreat into a supposed isolationism.

THE WASHINGTON NAVAL CONFERENCE

The first bold stroke of Republican diplomacy appeared when President Harding asked nine major nations to attend the Washington Naval Conference in November 1921. In a brilliantly conceived scheme, Hughes planned to reduce expenditures on warships drastically, dissolve political alliances dangerous to the United States (particularly the Anglo-Japanese alliance, in existence since 1902), and work out an international agreement to maintain the open door to the fabled China market. The last point was crucial, for since 1914 the Japanese, bolstered by their alliance with Great Britain, had been trying to close the door.

In February 1922 the conference produced three interrelated documents. In the Five-Power Treaty, the United States, Great Britain, Japan, France, and Italy received respective ratios of 5.00 to 5.00 to 3.00 to 1.75 to 1.75 for the size of their battleship fleets. In reality, the ratios gave Japan naval superiority in East Asia. American naval officers strongly protested the arrangement, but Hughes overruled the navy with the argument that the ratios also gave the United States dominance in the Western Hemisphere, and Great Britain and France control in European waters. Such a realistic division of world power satisfied the secretary of state.

More important, in return for naval superiority in East Asia, Hughes extracted from Japan an agreement to a Nine-Power Treaty pledging the maintenance of the open door in China. Clearly the United States was trusting that the Japanese would use their superior power to maintain an open marketplace in China for all nations. Hughes's successes were finally capped by a Four-Power Treaty that destroyed the Anglo-Japanese alliance. It was replaced by an agreement among the United States, Japan, Great Britain, and France in which each pledged to respect the others' possessions in the Pacific and to consult with the other powers in the event of aggression in that area.

These three agreements provided the framework for American diplomacy between 1921 and 1941. They marked a triumph for Hughes, for although Japan enjoyed a strong military position, it had now pledged itself to the open door. Moreover, after American pressure was applied, Japan also agreed to withdraw its troops from Siberia and to surrender Shantung to China.

China attended the conference, complained bitterly about being treated like a bone fought over by dogs, and then was ignored. To Western eyes China was doubly troublesome, for it was not only weak, but also unstable. In May 1919 the revolution led by Sun Yat-sen's Kuomintang party had accelerated. The major powers refused to recognize the revolutionaries. Americans tried to go on with business as usual, but in 1924 the revolution veered leftward as the Kuomintang cooperated with Soviet Russian agents. Effective economic boycotts and bloody personal attacks were launched against foreign missionaries and businessmen. One Chinese leader warned, "The time has come to speak to foreign imperialism in the language it understands." But with Sun's death in 1925, his mantle fell on Chiang Kai-shek. Chiang completed the Kuomintang triumph in 1927, broke with the Soviets, and greatly moderated the revolutionary program. In 1928 he worked out agreements with the United States and Western Europe that restored China's control over its own tariffs. Beyond this, however, Washington would not go. American Marines remained stationed in three Chinese cities to protect property, and six new U.S. gunboats moved to the Yangtze. A stable, wealthy, cooperative Japan, tied to American interests through the strong bonds of money, was a much-preferred partner to a revolutionary, erratic, and poverty-ridden China.

THE NEW ORDER RECONSTRUCTS THE OLD

The Washington Naval Conference also aided American policy in Europe, that most crucial of all diplomatic priorities. Before World War I Europeans had taken half of all American exports. Some European nations had recovered from the war quickly. Italy was a model after 1922, when Benito Mussolini assumed power. Despite his fascism, many Americans admired the dictator for embodying their own supposed traits of efficiency, stability, and masculinity; in the words of former Progressive journalist Ida Tarbell, Mussolini was the "despot with a dimple." Germany, France, and Great Britain, however, recovered more slowly, and U.S. officials became concerned. "The prosperity of the United States largely depends upon the economic settlements which may be made in Europe," Hughes observed in 1921, "and the key to the future is with those who make those settlements."

Again American economic leverage allowed Hughes to shape such settlements. His levers were the flush New York money market and the $11 billion loaned to Europe during and immediately after the war. The Republicans insisted that this money be repaid on American terms, not because their Puritan conscience required it, but because these war debts and the European need for capital provided the United States with great power. Washington's attention centered on Germany, for European (and therefore American) prosperity was impossible without a healthy Germany. That nation had been the industrial hub of the continent before 1914 and promised to be so again if properly reconstructed. Moreover, only a stable Germany could protect Europe against the spread of bolshevism.

Disagreeing strongly with this moderate American approach, France pressed the Germans for high reparations payments until, in 1923, they defaulted. When the French army retaliated by trying to separate the Rhineland from Germany, the German economy went completely out of control. All of Europe was threatened with catastrophe. Hughes coolly stepped into the chaos. He convinced J.P. Morgan and British bankers to lend $200 million to Germany and demanded that Germany be given easier reparation terms. Despite some French objections, the deal was completed at a 1924 conference headed by Chicago banker Charles G. Dawes. The Dawes Plan became the key to rebuilding Europe.

But the results were rather different from what Hughes and Dawes anticipated. When Morgan sold $100 million of securities for the German loan in the United States, the offer was oversubscribed in hours. Americans, rushing to invest in a stabilized Germany, snapped up some 180 bond and stock issues amounting to nearly $2 billion. When some American investors discovered a German hamlet needing $125,000 for a small municipal project, they talked the village leaders into taking a $3 million loan instead. Dollars were not only flowing into increasingly questionable projects, but merely moving in a circular fashion: the United States sent money to Germany, which used it to pay reparations to Great Britain and France, which in turn sent it back to New York for payment of war debts and interest on loans. One broken link and the Western economies could collapse like a row of dominoes.

Between 1925 and 1929, however, those economies looked more like a game of Monopoly. During those four years Americans lent more than $5 billion abroad. By 1928 such giant corporations as Standard Oil of New Jersey, DuPont, Ford, General Motors, and Singer Sewing Machine had invested $3 billion in their own overseas subsidiaries. Americans put another $8 billion into overseas portfolio investments, that is, stocks and bonds of foreign-owned companies. In the Middle East, American capitalists bitterly struggled with the British and French for control over the world's greatest oil reserves. The competition ended in 1928 with the "Red Line" agreement, in which the giant oil companies divided a large Middle Eastern area, marked on a map with a red pencil, among themselves. Even Russia welcomed capital for development projects. Washington, despite its refusal to recognize the Bolsheviks, determined to encourage American businessmen to rush into what Hoover called "an economic vacuum" in order to beat out European entrepreneurs. Hoping that the Soviets could be transformed into capitalists, such American corporations as Ford, Westinghouse, and W. Averell Harriman's mining ventures invested millions of dollars in Lenin's country. In this area, however, Germany had become a foe, not a friend. Not only did it dominate foreign investments in Russia, but in 1922 the two outcasts publicly agreed to cooperate economically. Secretly they helped to rebuild each other's military machine.

Despite the successes in rebuilding Germany, the Middle East, and Russia, Hoover watched the outflow of capital with growing concern. He knew that much of it was going into doubtful enterprises and that other American money, such as that of U.S. bankers helping Japan develop Manchuria, injured American export interests. American bankers were following selfish policies that badly hurt other American businessmen. Manufacturers, for example, hated the bankers not only for helping Japanese industry take over former American markets in Manchuria, but also for investing money in bond issues abroad rather than in industrial export enterprises at home. Virtually uncontrolled, the bankers blithely went on, investing in dubious projects until, like lemmings, they nearly self-destructed in 1929.

THE NEW ORDER IN LATIN AMERICA

American capital was also the key to relations with Latin America. In this region, however, Washington officials were not reluctant to use military force to maintain stability. Latin America had so long been counted a U.S. preserve that when new recruits entered the State Department's Foreign Service School in the mid-1920s, they were told not to expect too much from South Americans: their "Latin temperament" and "racial quality" were weaknesses, although Latin Americans could become "very easy people to deal with if properly managed." A 1924 survey revealed that of the twenty Latin American nations, only six were free of some kind of U.S. "management." The rest were either under the control of the U.S. Marine Corps or had their finances controlled by New York bankers. With stability supposedly assured, investments in Latin America more than doubled to $5.4 billion between 1924 and 1929, at a rate more than twice as great as that in any other part of the world. Much of this investment went into oil exploration and development. The southern part of the hemisphere was to provide raw materials for the industrial progress of the northern part.

U.S. officials tried to make Latin America the showcase of American foreign policy. They believed that through cooperation between government and business, the area could produce prosperity and democracy for its peoples and profits for its developers. Hoover's Commerce Department helped investors by coming up with new approaches for building the infrastructure (highways, communications, and utilities) needed to attract private capital. "The number of rebellions per capita is highest in those republics where the per capita mileage of highways is lowest," a Commerce Department official announced in 1929. "Romance may have been driven out by the concrete mixer, but the mixer has paved the way for law and order and for

Nicaraguan revolutionary General Sandino *(center)* and staff en route to Mexico, 1929. *(Time Life/ Getty Images)*

better understanding, as well as better business among the far-flung provinces of these sparsely populated commonwealths."

Hoover also tried to help by announcing new political policies. After becoming president in 1929, he repudiated the Roosevelt Corollary of 1904–1905 and began pulling U.S. Marines out of Caribbean nations. Problems did exist, however, particularly with revolutionary Mexico. The United States had finally recognized the Mexican government in 1923 but continued to object to the Mexican constitution's Article 27, which provided for national ownership of such subsurface minerals as oil. In 1927 a temporary compromise was finally reached on the oil controversy.

A case study of Republican policy took place in Nicaragua. U.S. Marines had occupied that Central American nation since 1912. Of special importance, Nicaragua was a possible site for an interoceanic canal that could rival the U.S. waterway in Panama. North Americans wanted no such competitor. Once the Marines landed, however, they could not leave: when Nicaraguan leaders cooperated with the United States, they became unpopular with their own people and needed protection. In 1925 President Coolidge nevertheless decided to pull the forces out. Rebellion immediately erupted. Coolidge thereupon sent back the Marines, but now the situation had changed. A guerrilla leader, Augusto Sandino, fought the Marines successfully from 1927 to 1933. He found increasing support from Nicaraguan peasants who had not benefited from the U.S. occupation. The costly war and growing protests in the United States finally led Hoover to pull the troops out in 1933. But he left behind a new diplomatic invention: a U.S.-trained Nicaraguan national guard that could replace the Marines in keeping order. In 1934, the U.S.-picked leader of the National Guard, Anastasio Somoza, arrested Sandino (who had quit fighting after the U.S. troops left) and murdered him in cold blood. Somoza then made himself dictator. He and his sons ruled Nicaragua as their personal plantation until 1979, when they were overthrown by anti-American revolutionaries calling themselves "Sandinistas." Such was the forty-five-year legacy of the Republicans' new order in Nicaragua.

By 1928 hemispheric relationships were becoming badly skewed. The United States had lent $2.5 billion and had increased exports to Latin Americans, but when they tried to pay their debts they ran into American tariff walls that prevented many of their products from entering the United States. As in Europe, United States investors swamped South America with dollars; in 1928 Peru received twice as much in loans as it could legitimately use. Anti-Yankeeism flourished in such conditions. At the 1928 Inter-American Conference, the Latin Americans proposed that no state had the right to intervene in the internal affairs of another. When the United States objected, it was joined by only four countries, three of which were under American control. A year later economic depression struck. Seven revolutions erupted in Latin America between 1929 and 1931. Given its own assumption that a foreign policy's success was measured by the stability it produced, the Latin American policies of the United States lay in shambles.

THE POLITICS OF CULTURAL CONFLICT

Social reformers found that the most pressing domestic issues of the decade were precisely those on which they were most bitterly divided, such as immigration restriction and Prohibition. Cultural issues—those relating to ethnicity, morality, and religion—dominated political discourse because prosperity led to a decline in the relative importance of economic concerns and because the spread of cosmopolitan mores and values troubled many small-town Americans who associated big cities with vice, crime, and immorality. The most controversial of these issues, Prohibition assumed new importance simply because it had become the law of the land and could no longer be ignored. Where one stood on such an issue usually depended on where one's parents had been born, which church one attended (or did not attend), and whether one lived in a village or large city.

Proposals to curb immigration clearly exposed some of these cultural tensions. In 1921, after the arrival of 1.2 million immigrants in just one year, President Harding approved a measure drastically limiting further admission. But this was merely a prelude. In 1924 the National Origins Act sailed through Congress with a huge majority. The act provided for the annual entry until 1927 of only 164,000 European immigrants under a quota system determined by the composition of the U.S. population in 1890. Under this arrangement the combined quotas for Russia and Italy were less than that for Norway; the combined quotas for Poland and Greece were less than that for Sweden. Beginning in 1927 the United States would admit 150,000 European immigrants each year under quotas based on the national origins of the white population in 1920. The measure barred all Japanese, but set no limits on immigration from Canada, Mexico, or South America. The National Origins Act won broad support from Progressives, including senators Hiram Johnson of California and George Norris of Nebraska. But urban reformers, whose constituencies included the ethnic and religious groups under assault, expressed dismay at the bigotry of those who had "a fixed obsession on Anglo-Saxon superiority."

BESSIE SMITH
AND THE BLUES

Bessie Smith, 1936. *(Library of Congress, Carl Van Vechten Collection)*

Thomas A. Edison invented the phonograph in 1877. It did not come into general use, however, until the 1890s, when grooved records replaced cylinders and an inexpensive "gramophone" was developed. The popular demand for recordings soon proved overwhelming. In 1919 more than 2.25 million phonographs were manufactured; two years later, over 100 million records were produced. The first blues recording by a black singer—Mamie Smith's "Crazy Blues"—was released in 1920. It sold extremely well and encouraged record companies to sign other black artists. A large "race market" seemed to exist, particularly among African-Americans who had migrated to northern cities during World War I.

Of all the blues singers in the 1920s, none was more popular than Bessie Smith. Born in Tennessee in 1894, she began working with traveling road shows when she was a teenager. For a time she worked with another famous entertainer, Gertrude ("Ma") Rainey. In 1923 Bessie Smith made her first recording, "Down Hearted Blues." Columbia Records paid her $125 a side for the record, which sold 780,000 copies within six months. (Throughout her association with Columbia, which lasted until 1931, she never received royalties based on sales but instead was paid a flat recording fee.) In 1925 Smith organized a traveling tent show, "Harlem Frolics," which toured in a custom-made, seventy-eight-foot-long railroad car complete with seven staterooms, kitchen, and bath. Audiences acclaimed her performances and her records sold remarkably well.

The blues idiom had several characteristics. The music was intensely personal. Songs dealt with the singers' own experiences—broken love affairs, natural disasters, tragedy, sorrow. Bessie Smith's own life, while often marked by luxury and extravagance, had its full share of such misfortune. The blues appealed mainly to the lower classes, for middle-class blacks, and whites, were often offended by the emphasis on gambling, drugs, and sex, allusions to which were usually disguised. "Bought me a coffeegrinder, got the best one I could find," Smith sang, "So he could grind my coffee, 'cause he has a brand new grind." The blues, finally, was race music. Race records were advertised in separate catalogues and sold in stores in black communities. The first black-owned record company, Black Swan, advertised, "The Only Genuine Colored Record—Others Are Only Passing for Colored." Smith almost always sang before black audiences and was booked in black theaters. Only on rare occasions did she perform for whites.

With the stock market crash of 1929, Smith's career, and those of many other black performers, went into decline. Record sales nose-dived and theater attendance dropped. Increasingly, the radio replaced the phonograph as the chief source of home entertainment. The blues, rough and raw-edged, gave way to the softer sound of "swing." Bessie Smith continued to sing, but she never matched her earlier success. On September 26, 1937, she was fatally injured in an automobile accident outside

American blues singer Ma Rainey, c. 1923. *(Frank Driggs Collection/Getty Images)*

Memphis, Tennessee. A legend quickly arose that she died after being refused admittance to a white hospital. Although unfounded, the legend provided the basis for Edward Albee's play *The Death of Bessie Smith*. Her Philadelphia grave remained unmarked for over thirty years until in 1970 a plaque was placed on the site. Rock singer Janis Joplin donated half the cost, as a tribute to a woman who had exerted so important an influence.

Web Links

www.bluessearchengine.com/bluesartists/s/bessiesmith.html
Biographical information, lyrics, and videos, including a clip from St. Louis Blues.

www.redhotjazz.com/rainey.html
A brief biography and many audio clips of Ma Rainey.

If immigration restriction illustrated the divisions among reformers, the experience of the Progressive Party in 1924 demonstrated their essential weakness. The party was formed by diverse groups uniting out of weakness rather than strength: former Bull Moose Progressives, leaderless since the death of Theodore Roosevelt; socialists, whose movement lay in ruins as a result of the war and the Red Scare; Midwestern farmers, resentful over a sharp decline in agricultural prices; and railroad workers, embittered by the Harding administration's role in breaking their 1922 strike. The Progressive platform called for public ownership of railroads, the dissolution of monopolies, direct election of the president, and a constitutional amendment barring child labor. The party also favored prohibiting the use of injunctions in labor disputes, promoting public works in time of depression, and imposing high taxes on business profits. To the Progressives and their sixty-nine-year-old presidential candidate, Robert M. La Follette of Wisconsin, "that government is deemed best which offers to the many the highest level of average happiness and well-being."

La Follette faced an uphill struggle in his race against Republican Calvin Coolidge and John W. Davis, the conservative lawyer nominated by the Democrats. His opponents, assailing La Follette for having opposed American entry into World War I, branded him a dangerous radical, the candidate of "the Reds, the Pinks, the Blues, and the Yellows." The Progressives, moreover, faced many of the same obstacles that traditionally hamper third parties: lack of funds, absence of grassroots organization, and inability to get on the ballot in every state. Although the American Federation of Labor formally endorsed La Follette's candidacy, labor gave the ticket less support than expected. Similarly, as agricultural prices improved in 1924, farmers' enthusiasm for La Follette waned. In November La Follette obtained 4.8 million votes—under 17 percent of the total—and captured only Wisconsin's thirteen electoral votes. Davis received 8.3 million votes, and Coolidge a whopping 15.7 million. Apparently the Republican slogan—"I like silence and success better than socialism and sovietism"—settled the fate of the reform-minded third party.

During the 1920s a new style of urban reform began to emerge, best symbolized, perhaps, by Democrat Alfred E. Smith and Republican Fiorello H. La Guardia. Both came from New York City. Smith, the son of Irish Catholic immigrants, had worked as a boy in the Fulton Fish Market, served an apprenticeship in Tammany Hall, and then became governor of New York. La Guardia, who represented East Harlem in Congress from 1922 to 1933, was an Italian-Jewish-American Episcopalian who spoke seven languages and whose wife was a German Lutheran. La Guardia, his biographer has commented, "was a balanced ticket all by himself." Smith and La Guardia supported a broad range of social welfare proposals, but were distinctive chiefly for their stand on cultural issues. Both championed the cause of immigrants. Both openly flouted Prohibition. Both served as spokesmen for urban cosmopolitanism in a bitter struggle with rural fundamentalism.

This struggle reached a climax when the Democrats selected Smith as their presidential candidate in 1928. Smith favored such reforms as government development of power facilities, but his contest with Republican Herbert Hoover centered not on economic issues but rather on issues of religion, immigration, Prohibition, and the city. One New England Protestant reformer expressed the sense of cultural cleavage when she wrote in her diary, "My American against Tammany's. Prairie, Plantation and Everlasting Hills against the Sidewalks of New York!" Given the prevailing prosperity, Hoover was probably unbeatable, but his margin of victory demonstrated the pervasiveness of cultural tensions. Smith received only 15 million

Governor Al Smith, giving a speech. *(Library of Congress)*

votes to Hoover's 21.4 million. For the first time since Reconstruction, the Republicans broke the Solid South, capturing Virginia, North Carolina, Texas, Florida, and Tennessee. The only consolation for the Democrats was that Smith did extremely well in the nation's largest cities.

PROHIBITION AND CRIME

Many Americans greeted the advent of Prohibition in January 1920 with unwarranted optimism. Prohibitionists had long promised that, given a change, they would eradicate pauperism and improve the condition of the working class. They had also predicted a sudden reduction in crime since "90 percent of the adult criminals are whisky-made." Closing the saloons, many believed, would improve the nation's physical health and strengthen its moral fiber as well.

Yet not all Americans supported Prohibition, and the distinction often followed religious, ethnic, and geographic lines. Typically, prohibitionists were likely to be Baptists or Methodists rather than Catholics, Jews, Lutherans, or Episcopalians; old-stock Americans rather than first- or second-generation immigrants. They were more likely to live in small towns and in the South or Midwest than in New York, Boston, or Chicago. At the heart of the struggle between wets and drys were contrasting cultural styles.

The Eighteenth Amendment, ratified in January 1919 and ultimately approved by every state except Connecticut, Rhode Island, and New Jersey, contained several glaring loopholes. It did not forbid the consumption of intoxicating beverages—only their sale and manufacture. As a result, those who could afford to store up an adequate supply were not terribly inconvenienced. In deference to property rights, liquor dealers were permitted a full year's grace in which to wind up their business affairs. The amendment also failed to define the word "intoxicating" and to provide any means of enforcement. The Volstead Act (1920) attempted to remedy these deficiencies: it arbitrarily defined as "intoxicating" any beverage with one-half of 1 percent alcoholic content, and it provided rudimentary enforcement machinery.

Yet the task of enforcement proved truly Herculean, particularly in those communities where a majority saw no moral virtue in temperance. There seemed an endless number of ways to evade the law. People smuggled whiskey across the Canadian and Mexican borders, made denatured industrial alcohol palatable by adding chemical ingredients, prepared their own "moonshine" at home in one-gallon stills, falsified druggists' prescriptions, stole liquor reserved for legitimate medicinal and religious purposes in government warehouses, and pumped alcohol back into "near beer" to give it more of a kick. Those administering the law encountered many difficulties. The Prohibition Bureau, understaffed and underpaid, was the target of a series of attempted briberies. Some evidently succeeded, for one of every twelve agents was dismissed for corrupt behavior, and presumably others were never caught. The memoirs of a leading Prohibition agent testified to the laxity of enforcement. He related how long it took to buy a drink on arriving in different cities: Chicago—twenty-one minutes; Atlanta—seventeen minutes; and Pittsburgh—eleven minutes. In New Orleans it took thirty-five seconds: when the agent asked a cab driver where he could find a drink, the driver, offering him a bottle, replied, "Right here."

For all its inadequacies, the law almost certainly cut down on alcohol consumption. But the attempt to enforce a moral code to which many Americans did not adhere led to widespread hypocrisy and disrespect for the law. This problem received formal recognition when the Supreme Court ruled that the government could request income tax returns from bootleggers. The Court found no reason "why the fact that a business is unlawful should exempt it from paying the tax that if lawful it would have to pay."

Prohibition was associated not only with a cavalier attitude toward the law, but also with a more sinister phenomenon: the rise of organized crime. Criminal gangs had existed in the past, but in the 1920s they evidently became larger, wealthier, and more ostentatious. Gangland weddings—and funerals—became occasions for lavish displays of wealth and influence. The 1924 funeral of the Chicago gunman Dion O'Banion featured twenty-six truckloads of flowers, an eight-foot heart of American beauty roses, and 10,000 mourners, among whom were several prominent politicians. Gangs became increasingly efficient and mobile because of the availability of submachine guns and automobiles. And they grew somewhat more centralized, dividing territory in an effort to reduce internecine warfare. Although criminals made money through the control of prostitution, gambling, and racketeering, bootleg liquor provided a chief source of revenue.

By the end of the decade, opponents of Prohibition had begun to win over the public. Once the drys had promised that Prohibition would reduce crime; now the wets held Prohibition responsible for organized crime and pledged that, with repeal, "the immorality of the country, racketeering and bootlegging, will be a thing of the past." Formerly the drys had claimed that Prohibition would eliminate poverty; now the wets asserted that the liquor industry could provide needed jobs and revenue to a nation beginning to experience mass poverty in the Great Depression. Prohibition was repealed in 1933. Yet it failed less because it triggered a crime wave or weakened the economy than because it attempted the impossible: to ban allegedly immoral behavior in the absence of a genuine consensus that the proscribed behavior was, in any real sense, immoral.

THE KU KLUX KLAN

In the years following the Civil War, white southerners had organized the Ku Klux Klan to terrorize blacks and prevent them from voting. This early organization faded with the end of Reconstruction, but in 1915 William J. Simmons, a preacher-turned-salesman, founded a new Klan. In the early 1920s millions of Americans joined the hooded order, although membership probably never exceeded 1.5 million at any time. Yet the new Klan was not simply a reincarnation of the old. The Klan of the 1920s, although strong in the South, was stronger still in Indiana, Illinois, and Ohio. Perhaps three of every five members did not live in the South or Southwest. The new Klan also was less heavily rural, enlisting members in Chicago, Detroit, Atlanta, Denver, and other cities. One of every three Klansmen lived in a city with a population of over 100,000. Finally, the Klan was no longer primarily a white supremacist group. Its chief targets in the 1920s were immigrants and Catholics.

The Klan began its rapid ascent in 1920, when two public relations experts, Edward Y. Clarke and Elizabeth Tyler, made an arrangement with Simmons that turned the Klan into a highly profitable business venture. To sell Klan memberships they recruited a legion of high-powered salesmen, known as Kleagles, and adopted shrewd sales techniques. More than 1,000 organizers set forth in search of recruits, and since each membership cost $10, of which the Kleagle kept $4, the incentive was rather high. Simmons and the other Klan leaders eventually grew wealthy by taking a rake-off on everything from membership fees to the sale of official robes and hoods. With so much at stake, power struggles inevitably occurred. In 1922 the Klan changed hands. Hiram Wesley Evans, a Dallas dentist, ousted Clarke and Tyler and agreed to buy out Simmons, who retained his title but no authority.

The Klan created a world of make-believe by carrying ritual, pageantry, and secrecy to the furthest extreme. Klansmen met in a Klavern, held Klonklaves, carried on Klonversations, and even sang Klodes. They aspired to such high offices as that of Grand Goblin, Grand Dragon, and Exalted Cyclops. They followed a Kalendar in which 1867 was the year 1 and in which awe-inspiring names were assigned to days (dark, deadly, dismal, doleful, desolate, dreadful, desperate), weeks (woeful, weeping, wailing, wonderful, weird), and months (bloody, gloomy, hideous, fearful, furious, alarming, terrible, horrible, mournful, sorrowful, frightful, appalling). Klan members spoke a secret language by forming strange, new words from the first letter of each word in a sentence. Thus "sanbog" meant "strangers are near, be on guard."

Clever organization and secret ritual did not alone account for the Klan's success. The Klan also preached an ideology that appealed to Americans who feared that alien groups were threatening a traditional way of life. Evans asserted that blacks could never "attain the Anglo-Saxon level" and regarded Jews as "alien and inassimilable." The Klan was hysterically anti-Catholic. Members believed in the existence of a papal conspiracy to subvert American liberties and blamed Catholics for the deaths of presidents Lincoln, McKinley, and Harding. Racism, anti-Semitism, and anti-Catholicism were all subsumed under a broader fear of the "mongrelization" of America through immigration. As Simmons put it, "The dangers were in the tremendous influx of foreign immigration, tutored in alien dogmas and alien creeds, slowly pushing the native-born white American population into the center of the country, there to be ultimately overwhelmed and smothered."

Klan activities were a strange mixture of benevolence and terrorism. In some cases the Klan functioned primarily as a fraternal organization. Members patronized each other's businesses, helped out in case of sickness or accident, and contributed to various churches and charities. But the Klan also set itself up as a watchdog of community morals. Klansmen spied on people, reported acts of marital infidelity, attacked "indecent" shows and publications, and promised "to drive the bootleggers forever out of this land and place whiskey-making on a parity with counterfeiting." To uncover every possible scandal, the Klan sometimes tapped telephone wires and intercepted mail at post offices. It punished transgressors by burning crosses outside their homes, ostracizing them, or brutally beating and torturing them. Some victims were immigrants or blacks; others were native white Protestants who failed to measure up to Klan standards.

The Klan acquired formidable political power. It helped elect senators in Oregon, Ohio, Tennessee, and several other states. In Texas it elected a senator, held a majority in the state legislature for a time, and controlled Dallas, Fort Worth, and Wichita Falls. The Indiana Klan, under David Stephenson, built a machine that dominated state politics and placed a functionary in the governor's mansion. The Klan's political goals, aside from power for its own sake, were to prohibit immigration, prevent U.S. entry into the World Court, enforce Prohibition, and weaken parochial schools. The Klan put up its own candidates, endorsed others it considered friendly, and above all sought to prevent the nomination of, or else defeat, candidates (such as Al Smith) who stood for everything it abhorred.

Despite Smith's defeat, the Klan by 1928 had passed its peak. Torn by internal conflicts between Evans and state leaders, placed on the defensive by politicians who considered it a disruptive force, and appeased by the enactment of the National Origins Act, the Klan after 1924 began losing members and influence. Stephenson was arrested for abducting a young woman, sexually molesting her, and refusing to let her visit a doctor after she poisoned herself. Convicted of murder and sentenced to life in the penitentiary, Stephenson opened his private files, which exposed Klan lawlessness. Supposedly created to enforce strict moral codes, the Klan could not survive this scandal or the ensuing revelations. By 1930 the organization was everywhere in shambles.

FUNDAMENTALISM AND THE SCHOOLS

In the summer of 1925 the town of Dayton, Tennessee, witnessed an event that symbolized the decade's cultural conflicts. John Thomas Scopes was put on trial for having violated state law by teaching the theory of evolution in the public schools, but the nation's attention was focused on the lawyers for the two sides. Prosecutor William Jennings Bryan was the most prominent spokesman for the traditional values of rural, Protestant America. Defense attorney Clarence Darrow, by contrast, was a skeptic, a relativist, and an agnostic. There seemed no common ground between them. To fundamentalists, the theory of evolution was a scientific sham whose acceptance would erode the moral underpinnings of society. Evolutionists, on the other hand, placed fundamentalists on a par with those who had once refused to believe that the earth revolved about the sun.

Religious fundamentalists believed in the literal truth of the Bible. The story of Adam and Eve was, in their view, a matter of historical fact. Charles Darwin's theory of evolution, as expounded in his 1859 volume, *The Origin of Species*, contradicted the biblical account of Creation, and was therefore wrong. Fundamentalists sometimes assumed an overt posture of anti-intellectualism, as when Bryan declared it more important to know the hymn "Rock of Ages" than to know the age of rocks. Yet fundamentalists oversimplified Darwin: the theory of natural selection—that evolution occurred through a gradual accretion of useful variations that fit an organism to survive—had by no means been proved. Bryan noted sarcastically that Darwin, in two major books, resorted to the phrase "we may suppose" more than 800 times.

Fundamentalists were disturbed by what they considered a breakdown in moral values, by which they meant everything from "vile and suggestive" motion pictures and dance styles to "unchaperoned automobile riding at night." They attributed this breakdown, at least in part, to the popularity of the theory of evolution. By calling the Scriptures into question, Darwin had undermined Christian faith. By emphasizing man's animal nature, he excused immoral conduct. In addition, reformers understood that conservatives had used Darwin's theory to assert that government assistance to the needy violated the natural law of survival of the fittest. If Darwin was not responsible for the uses to which his theory had been put, the application nevertheless had pernicious results.

Fundamentalist opinion was strongest in the South and Southwest, but hardly dominated those regions. During the 1920s, bills designed to prohibit the teaching of evolution were introduced in twenty state legislatures. The measures always encountered stiff opposition and were usually defeated. Only five states—Oklahoma, Florida, Tennessee, Mississippi, and Arkansas—enacted such bills, and even there they were regarded less as weapons of repression than as symbolic expressions of legislative concern. The Butler bill in Tennessee, which led to the Scopes trial, barred the teaching of "any theory that denies the Story of the Divine Creation of Man as taught in the Bible, and [holds] instead that man has descended from a lower order of animals." The bill passed easily since educators feared that opposing a popular measure might jeopardize state university appropriations. No one took it very seriously. "Probably the law will never be applied," said the governor when signing it.

The law was applied when some acquaintances persuaded Scopes to test it and the American Civil Liberties Union agreed to provide legal counsel. No one had interfered with the way Scopes conducted his high school biology class, but he agreed to the trial as a matter of principle. The chief courtroom drama occurred when Bryan took the witness stand and engaged Darrow in a verbal duel over the literal interpretation of the Bible, the exchange revealing Bryan's limited knowledge of science. The outcome, however, was a foregone conclusion, for Scopes had admitted breaking the law and the judge ruled that evidence supporting the theory of evolution was inadmissible. The jury took nine minutes to find Scopes guilty, and he was fined $100. William Jennings Bryan died five days after the trial ended. Forty-two years later, Tennessee repealed the law.

Marcus Garvey, 1924. *(Library of Congress)*

The furor surrounding the evolution controversy concealed the more subtle pressures exerted on teachers nearly everywhere in the United States. Most Americans believed that the public schools should instill certain values in the young, but usually the sensitive areas involved politics or economics rather than religion. In 1927 Nebraska ruled that its teachers emphasize "honesty, morality, courtesy, obedience to law, respect for the national flag, the constitution, . . . respect for parents and the home, the dignity and necessity of honest labor and other lessons of a steadying influence, which tend to promote and develop an upright and desirable citizenry." School boards commonly established curricula, selected textbooks, and hired teachers with the goal of excluding unpopular ideas. In this sense the antievolution crusade did not represent an entirely atypical effort to restrict what teachers might tell their students even as it expressed the cultural tensions that characterized the 1920s.

THE GARVEY MOVEMENT AND THE "NEW NEGRO"

As cities in America got larger, so too did their black ghettos. The northward migration of African-Americans, stimulated by the war, continued into the 1920s. During the decade New York City's black population climbed from 152,000 to 328,000; Chicago's grew from 109,000 to 233,000. People left the rural South to improve their lives and some undoubtedly succeeded, but large numbers did not. In New York's Harlem and Chicago's South Side, they crowded into grimy tenements for which they paid exorbitant rents. In 1927 an investigator said of Harlem, "the State would not allow cows to live in some of these apartments." Most blacks could find jobs only as menial or unskilled workers and even then took home less pay than their white counterparts. As always, poverty produced chronic ill health; in the mid-1920s the death rate in Harlem was 42 percent higher, and the infant mortality rate 70 percent higher, than elsewhere in the city.

These conditions made possible the spectacular success of Marcus Garvey and his nationalist doctrine. A Jamaican who came to the United States in 1917, Garvey dreamed of "uniting all the Negro peoples of the world into one great body to establish a country and Government absolutely their own." His Universal Negro Improvement Association claimed hundreds of thousands of followers in the early 1920s, most of them uprooted blacks who had left the rural South for the urban North. Garvey appealed to race pride by glorifying blackness. His newspaper, unlike other black journals, did not ordinarily accept advertisements for skin-lightening lotions or hair-straightening formulas. Whites, he claimed, had distorted the black past: "When Europe was inhabited by a race of cannibals, a race of savage naked men, heathens and pagans, Africa was peopled with a race of cultured black men, who were masters in art, science and literature."

The coin of black pride had a reverse side: distrust of whites. In Garvey's view, "potentially every white man is a Klansman." As competition for jobs and resources increased, he reasoned, whites would become ever less tolerant of black success. The goal of integration, therefore, was a delusion, for the white majority would never accord justice to the black minority. Instead, blacks should build their own nation in Africa. Garvey did not expect the emigration of all black Americans, but rather envisioned a dedicated cadre of trained people. When whites saw that blacks were capable of constructing an advanced civilization of their own, they would learn to respect blacks. A powerful African state would drape a protective mantle around blacks wherever they might live.

Garvey's approach to economics was wholly in keeping with the business ethos of the 1920s. He asserted that black workers' only ally was the white capitalist who needed their labor. Blacks should shun white trade unions and, indeed, work for just under union wages because employers would always prefer to hire a white unless there was some incentive to hire a black. In the end, though, blacks could become autonomous only by developing their own business and commercial establishments. Garvey sponsored several such undertakings, but by far the most important was the Black Star Line, a steamship company designed to link the non-Caucasian peoples of the world commercially and to transport repatriates to Africa. It thus united the twin themes of African redemption and black entrepreneurship.

But the Black Star Line was also the immediate cause of Garvey's downfall. The company sold thousands of shares at five dollars each to black investors, but it quickly went bankrupt. Lacking managerial experience, Garvey fell victim to unscrupulous dealers who sold him run-down ships at inflated prices. The vessels constantly broke down and failed to pass inspection. The fiasco led to charges in 1922 that Garvey had used the mails to defraud investors. The government was very happy to prosecute, for it had long regarded Garvey, in the words of a State Department official, as "an undesirable, and indeed a very dangerous, alien" who was organizing "all of the Negroes in the world against the white people." The trial began in May 1923; Garvey, who believed himself the victim of persecution, conducted his own defense. He was found guilty and sentenced to five years in prison. In February 1925, when the courts rejected his appeal, Garvey entered the penitentiary. Late in 1927 President Coolidge commuted his sentence and the government deported him as an undesirable alien.

Most other black leaders, who had always considered Garvey's ideology dangerous and his movement a threat, seemed relieved by the outcome. The National Association for the Advancement of Colored People opposed Garvey because he rejected integration and challenged its authority as spokesman for African-Americans. A. Phillip Randolph and other socialists placed their hopes in an alliance of black and white workers. They resented Garvey's enmity toward unions, emphasis on black enterprise, and insistence that race was more important than class. Yet while Garvey's movement failed, his emphasis on race pride had lasting import. In 1927 the *Amsterdam News* assessed Garvey's influence on blacks this way: "In a world where black is despised, he taught them black is beautiful. He taught them to admire and praise black things and black people."

In this respect, Garveyism had much in common with the "New Negro Renaissance," the name given to the work of black poets, novelists, scholars and artists, most of whom lived in Harlem, all of whom were self-conscious participants in a cultural awakening. The person who did most to publicize the movement was Alaine Locke. A Phi Beta Kappa graduate of Harvard, Locke, in 1907, had been the first black Rhodes scholar at Oxford. He went on to study in Berlin and Paris and then became a professor of philosophy at Howard University. In 1925 he published an anthology, *The New Negro*, with contributions by Langston Hughes, Claude McKay, Jean Toomer, Countee Cullen, and most of the other writers prominently associated with the Harlem renaissance. Locke believed that the race consciousness cultivated by the urban ghetto was largely responsible for the new literary and artistic awakening. "In Harlem," he wrote, "Negro life is seizing upon its first chances for group expression and self-determination."

Most of the writers identified with the New Negro Renaissance shared common concerns. They emphasized the African roots of black culture and conveyed a sense that American blacks were spiritual aliens, cut off from their native land. They emphasized the dignity of the common people and the importance of the folk tradition. Writers began to use the cadences and idioms associated with spirituals and jazz, and Langston Hughes published a book of poems titled *Weary Blues* (1925). There were also denunciations of racial injustice, lynching, and segregation. But for all their bitter indignation, these writers, according to historian John Hope Franklin, "were not revolting so much against the system as they were protesting against the inefficient operation of the system. In this approach they proved to be as characteristically American as any writers of the period."

NEW WOMEN AND THE NEW MORALITY

For women, the decade after World War I was decidedly a new era, though in ways unanticipated by suffragists of the Progressive years. Politically, the decade began on a note of elation. The national committees of political parties welcomed women, women candidates ran for office, and politicians catered to the new "woman's vote." In 1921, Congress passed the Sheppard Towner Act, the first federally funded health care plan, which supported maternal and child care services in rural areas. But women's welcome in politics, like the Sheppard-Towner Act, was short-lived. Since women voters did not seem to vote as a bloc or unite behind women's issues, Congress made no further gestures. As progressivism lost momentum, so did the women's movement that had long been associated with it. A prolonged feud arose over an equal rights amendment (ERA), first proposed by the National Woman's Party in 1923. An ERA, its backers claimed, would "secure for women complete equality under the law and in all human relationships." But most women reformers feared that the amendment would harm working women by vitiating protective laws, and they loudly denounced it. The ERA, charged Florence Kelley, was "a slogan of the insane."

While arguments over the ERA raged, women's organizations failed to mobilize the enthusiasm that once had been generated by the suffrage campaign. Young women of the 1920s seemed to have lost interest in both feminist goals and social causes. "Feminism has become a term of opprobrium to the modern young woman," a 1927 article in *Harper's* claimed. As collective purpose waned, attention turned toward private lives and individuals goals. Some "new women" of the decade directed their attention toward jobs, careers, and self-support. A major achievement, one woman journalist claimed in 1926, was "invading every field that had been held the special province of men." Spectacular breakthroughs, such as former suffragist Amelia Earhart's aviation career, drew the most attention. Less spectacularly, large numbers of women entered the labor force in white-collar jobs, and educated women moved into professional work. In the 1920s, women professionals increased by 50 percent and the number of married women in the workforce rose 30 percent. The new woman of the 1920s wanted marriage and family, *Nation* editor Freda Kirchwey explained, but she also wanted "some way of satisfying her personal ambition."

In popular culture, the new woman of the 1920s sought personal independence, often of a sexual nature. Americans of the 1920s witnessed a transformation in private life, one that had been building up since the turn of the century. The much-heralded "new morality" (a label affixed by its defenders) was part of a long-term revolution, or evolution, in moral values and sexual behavior that rose into view after World War I and thereafter became a national preoccupation. Symptoms of moral change had been visible before the war, when dance crazes first burst into vogue and issues such as venereal disease were discussed in the press. But then sexual emancipation was the province of socialists, radicals, and urban sophisticates. Now it was a far more widespread phenomenon that seemed to take hold of the entire young generation, whose antics and attitudes dominated the press. The young and old were as far apart in point of view, an *Atlantic* editorial observed, "as if they belonged to different races."

Behavior, moreover, changed as dramatically as point of view. "The more sophisticated social life of today," reported Helen and Robert Lynd in their classic study of a Midwestern city, *Middletown* (1928), "has brought with it . . . the apparently increasing relaxation of some of the traditional prohibitions upon the approaches of boys and girls to each other's persons." Such relaxation, they observed, was greatly abetted by the automobile. The media played a role, too. Movies depicted attractive young women bickering over men, transforming their image with flapper wardrobes, and frolicking in novel locales, such as bathtubs. Newspapers featured pictures of beauty contests that catered to the decade's competitive and exhibitionist instincts. Popular magazines offered advice on "How to Keep the Thrill in Marriage," and best sellers like *Flaming Youth* (1923), the tale of an adventurous young home wrecker, promised "the truth, bold, naked, sensational." According to social scientists, middle-class morals were in transition. A pioneer study of the sex lives of 2,200 middle-aged, middle-class women, by social worker Katherine Bement Davis, revealed more sexual activity than readers or surveyor anticipated. Subsequent studies suggested that birth control, though illegal, was widely used, especially among the well off.

The new morality fomented conflict between liberals and traditionalists. In some quarters, any dent in Victorian repression meant a gain for women. "The Myth of the Pure Woman is almost at an end," declared enthusiast C.V. Calverton, once editor of *The Masses*, a prewar radical vanguard. "Women's demands for equal rights have extended to the sexual sphere as well as the social." Judge Ben Lindsey of Denver, who applauded the young generation, proposed a new type of "companionate marriage," which would provide a trial run of compatibility and could easily be terminated by divorce. (The divorce rate in 1930 was twice the pre–World War I rate.) But traditionalists feared social disintegration and suspected that the new morality was no morality at all. Progressive Era feminists sometimes agreed with them. Charlotte Perkins Gilman contended that "indulgence" was not necessarily an improvement over "repression" and voiced considerable disgust at the irresponsibility of young women. "It is sickening," she wrote in 1923, "to see so many of the newly freed abusing that freedom in mere imitation of masculine vice and weakness." Contraception, in particular, was an issue that separated prewar feminists from emancipated new women of the next generation. "Your reform is too narrow to appeal to me and too sordid," suffrage leader Carrie Chapman Catt wrote to birth control pioneer Margaret Sanger in 1920.

As with much else in the 1920s, the new morality was less radical a transformation than either proponents or critics believed. Some observers suggested that release from verbal inhibition gave an impression of greater change than actually occurred. Others pointed out that the new morality changed courtship customs, but did not challenge traditional goals. According to surveys, young women's newly liberated attitudes were wedded to old-fashioned aspirations. Few were willing to sacrifice marriage for career; most hoped, rather, to attain "a richer and fuller life" with "an all-round companion." The 1920s popularized the ideal of romantic, companionate marriage, although not the trial run proposed by Ben Lindsey. Women could find fulfillment in traditional domestic roles, now enlivened by a celebrated sexual dimension. Some feminists objected to the emphasis on domesticity. But *Middletown* readers were more likely to listen to columnist Dorothy Dix, who advised wives to join clubs, cultivate worthwhile connections, and strive for upward mobility. "Woman," said Dix, "makes the family status."

Significantly, the birth control campaign, the most radical of prewar reform movements, adapted swiftly to the conservative tone of the decade. Before the war, when Margaret Sanger began her campaign in the 1914 *Woman Rebel*, birth controllers intended to reach a working-class following, end the production of "slaves to capital," and foster proletarian revolution. Since spreading information about contraception violated federal and state laws, advocates of birth control were inviting trouble. When Sanger opened a Brooklyn clinic in 1916, she and her colleagues were arrested, tried, convicted, and jailed. During the 1920s the laws remained on the books, but the mood of the times—and of the birth control movement—had changed. After the war, Sanger's organization, the American Birth Control League, became a middle-

Margaret Sanger, American birth control activist. *(Library of Congress)*

class reform movement, courting the support of physicians, academics, and eugenicists. Birth control clinics, now run by physicians, multiplied. And the arguments in favor of contraception changed. Birth control would emancipate women, Sanger asserted, as she had before the war; but it would also produce "more children from the fit, less from the unfit." It would eliminate the diseased and degenerate, and rid society of "poverty, mental defects, feeble-mindedness, and other transmissible traits." Capitalizing on its scientific and eugenic thrust, rather than on its radical origins, the birth control movement was able to win the approval of the medical profession and the appreciation of a large segment of middle-class practitioners. A pivot of the new morality, it was able to adjust to conservative times as Progressive Era feminism could not.

Nicola Sacco and Bartolomeo Vanzetti, handcuffed together and under guard, in Massachusetts, 1927. *(AP Photo)*

THE DISCONTENT OF THE INTELLECTUALS

Intellectuals in the Progressive Era had been outraged by economic injustice and political corruption. Intellectuals in the 1920s, however, while by no means apologists for Harding and Coolidge, were more often incensed by the materialism and conformity they found at all levels of society. Where one target had once been the crooked politician, now it was more likely to be the narrow-minded puritan who, unable to enjoy life, wanted to make sure that no one else did either. Formerly, intellectuals had drawn up manifestos for social betterment; in the 1920s they were more acutely conscious of the barriers to change, and some lost interest in politics altogether. Two books published in 1922 illustrate these themes: Sinclair Lewis's *Babbitt* and Walter Lippmann's *Public Opinion.*

Of the writers who satirized the values of the business culture, perhaps none did so more effectively than Sinclair Lewis. In George F. Babbitt, Lewis created a figure that personifies boosterism, complacency, and conformity. A small-town real estate agent, Babbitt is a thoroughgoing materialist whose "symbols of truth and beauty" are mechanical contraptions. He advises his son that "there's a whole lot of valuable time lost even at the U., studying poetry and French and subjects that never brought in anybody a cent." In a speech to his fellow realtors, Babbitt defines "the ideal of American manhood and culture" as "a God-fearing hustling, successful, two-fisted Regular Guy, who belongs to some church with pep and piety to it, who belongs to the Boosters or the Rotarians or the Kiwanis, to the Elks or Moose or Red Men or Knights of Columbus." Vaguely discontented with these values, Babbitt finally rebels against them. But finding "nonconformity" hardly more satisfying, he is disillusioned, and when he is subjected to terrific personal and financial pressure from the community, he gratefully reenters the fold. Lewis's target, therefore, was not Babbitt himself so much as the society that produced him and prevented him from becoming anything else.

Walter Lippmann, meanwhile, expressed profound disillusionment with traditional American political beliefs. Lippmann believed that people think in stereotypes—"for the most part we do not first see, and then define; we define first and then see"—and therefore act irrationally. Democratic theory, he held, had "never seriously faced the problem which arises because the pictures inside people's heads do not automatically correspond with the world outside." Since public affairs are too complex for most people to grasp even if they wanted to, and since most people lack the time and interest to try, it is not reasonable to suppose that voters would instinctively or intuitively make the right choices. Instead, Lippmann called for "an independent, expert organization for making the unseen facts intelligible to those who have to make the decisions." Social scientists, organized in a network of intelligence bureaus, might perform such a function. Social progress, Lippmann argued, depended not on the old Progressive faith in an enlightened citizenry, but rather on the scientific organization of intelligence.

Many intellectuals in the 1920s assumed a coolly detached stance toward public affairs. "It was characteristic of the Jazz Age," said F. Scott Fitzgerald, "that it had no interest in politics at all." But even those who held themselves most aloof were caught up in the Sacco-Vanzetti case. Anarchists Nicola Sacco and Bartolomeo Vanzetti were charged with robbery and murder in 1920, convicted the following year, and sentenced to die. Legal appeals dragged on for six years until, in August 1927, both men were electrocuted. The case stirred immense moral outrage because elementary rules of due process were ignored, the judge, Webster Thayer, was viciously biased, and the Commonwealth of Massachusetts seemed determined to carry out an unjust sentence rather than concede the possibility of error. For a generation of intellectuals, Sacco and Vanzetti came to symbolize all that America was not. In a nation of conformists, they were rebels; in a nation of materialists, they were "the good shoemaker and poor fish peddler." They were, many believed, martyrs crucified by an unfeeling society.

THE END OF THE NEW ORDER: 1929

Unfeeling or not at home, Americans had a strongly held view about how they might save the world. "The work that religion, government, and war have failed in must be done by business," an *Atlantic Monthly* correspondent declared in 1928. "That eternal job of administering the planet must be turned over to the despised business man."

One of these businessmen, not all despised, was the newly elected president. A multimillionaire mining engineer, Herbert Hoover embodied the success stories of the 1920s. His efficiency, realism, and faith in technology were exemplified when he installed the first telephone on the president's desk. (Before that, the chief executive had to use a booth in an adjoining room.) For Hoover, the roots of the system needed no examination. As he told a crowded Stanford stadium in 1928, "We in America today are nearer to the final triumph over poverty than ever before in the history of any land. The poorhouse is vanishing from among us."

The economic triumph of American individualism, moreover, had eradicated the causes of world wars. "It seems to me," Hoover wrote to his secretary of state, Henry Stimson, in 1929, "that there is the most profound outlook for peace today that we have had at any time in the last half century." Most Democrats were forced to agree. When the influential periodical *Foreign Affairs* asked a Republican and a Democrat to discuss their differences on foreign policy in 1928, the Democrat, Franklin D. Roosevelt, could find little of substance wrong with Republican diplomacy.

Hoover and many others fully realized that international stability depended on the strength of the American economy. Since becoming the world's leading creditor during World War I, the United States had dominated the international economy as Great Britain had before 1914. That power increased during the 1920s, as the efficient American system exported ever-larger amounts of goods. When foreign customers tried to repay with their own products, however, they encountered walls erected by the 1922 Fordney-McCumber Tariff, which raised average rates on imports to 33 percent. In 1923, U.S. merchandise exports exceeded imports by $375 million; in 1928, by $1.1 billion. Profiting handsomely, Americans covered the difference by lending their dollars to foreigners for the purchase of U.S. goods and by investing directly in overseas stocks and bonds. The dollar made the world economy go around.

By 1929, however, the dollar had begun staying home. New overseas investment opportunities did not appear, and a glamorous alternative, the New York Stock Exchange, quickly seduced big and small spenders. In 1924 the *New York Times* industrial average of stocks was 106; by 1928, it was 331, and during the summer of 1929, it shot up another 110 points. This wild speculation was fueled by "buying on margin," in which an investor bought stocks for a small down payment while borrowing the remainder at interest rates as high as 10 to 20 percent. The government and the banking community watched happily, even encouraging the speculation since they believed the stock exchange rested on a sound American economy.

But that economy was being eaten away by a rash of illnesses. First, the mass of Americans was too poor to buy the glut of goods being produced. Productivity shot up nearly 50 percent between 1919 and 1929 until the gross national product (the sum of all goods and services produced in the country) reached $104 billion in 1929. But wages did not keep pace. By 1929, 5 percent of the people received one-third of all personal income. As the gap between rich and poor widened, the economy became increasingly unstable. The government refused to consider measures, such as higher income taxes, to make income more equal. Farmers, miners, and textile workers especially suffered. Between 1919 and 1929, farm debt more than doubled. Farmers were further hurt in 1928 and 1929 when their foreign markets, now lacking American dollars, were no longer able to buy large amounts of wheat and cotton. Throughout the decade the rate of bank failures was also high. In truth, stock prices rested not on a strong economy, but on bankers' loans and on holding companies that had gained control of smaller firms through complex stock manipulations and business hocus-pocus. In October 1929 the stock market suddenly stalled. Excited bankers demanded repayment of their loans, forcing borrowers to declare bankruptcy, disappear, or jump from high buildings. A run on stocks began. Within a month after "Black Thursday," October 24, stock prices plummeted 50 percent.

A second illness, the inability of the government to control the economy, became obvious next. Throughout 1927 and 1928, the Federal Reserve System had fueled stock speculation with a low-interest, easy-money policy. When the system tried finally to slow the wild lending, large private banks refused to cooperate. As the stock decline accelerated, 800 banks closed in

1930. The government did little to save the banking system. Unemployment, at 1.5 million in 1929, shot up to 4.2 million in 1930, further cutting purchasing power. The Federal Reserve System then set lending rates at historically low levels so money would be very cheap. But there were no takers, for there appeared to be nowhere to invest the money profitably. As American capitalism crumbled, the government passed the Hawley-Smoot Tariff in 1930. It raised average rates on imports to 40 percent in order to keep out cheap foreign goods.

3

But the tariff starkly revealed the third illness. The world economy could survive only with the aid of either dollars or American markets. Now both disappeared. Without dollars foreigners could neither buy American goods nor repay earlier loans. As their own economies began to collapse, they too sought protection behind tariff walls that kept out American goods. From 1929 to 1933, world trade dropped 40 percent in value, with the leading exporters—Great Britain, Germany, Japan, and the United States—especially hard-hit. A domino effect occurred: the American depression caused foreign economies to decline, and the disappearance of these traditional markets for American products in turn worsened conditions in the United States. Meanwhile, President Hoover announced that the economy was basically sound. A group of Harvard economists declared, "a serious depression . . . is outside the range of possibility."

Actually, the world tottered on the edge of catastrophe. The great British economist John Maynard Keynes held out little hope: "A general breakdown is inevitable," he privately commented. "America will revert to a Texas type of civilization, France and Germany will go to war." Keynes's conclusions were appropriate, for without a healthy international economy the treaty system, so painfully constructed in Washington in 1922 and in Europe between 1924 and 1929, could not survive. The problem was not that Americans had become isolationist during the 1920s. Indeed, the internationalization of the American economic system had been so successful that as the domestic economy slowly sank, it dragged the rest of the world down with it.

CHAPTER SIX

1929–1936

The Depression and the New Deal

An unemployed woman sells apples in New York City, 1929.
(Archive Holding, Inc./Getty Images)

The Great Depression had a cataclysmic effect on all areas of American life. Producing unprecedented suffering, the economic crisis posed a severe challenge to the prevailing view of the social responsibilities of government. Within a few years that view, which sharply limited the role of government, proved a dismal failure. Yet the fear that disillusioned Americans would turn to revolution on the left, or to dictatorship on the right, proved groundless. Most people favored more moderate change, and that is exactly what the New Deal provided. Franklin D. Roosevelt's first administration erected the foundations of a welfare state. New Deal policies concerning business, agriculture, conservation, labor, and welfare, while benefiting certain interest groups considerably more than others, nevertheless enabled the Democrats to fashion a new political coalition that dominated American politics for several decades.

HERBERT HOOVER AND THE DEPRESSION

Perhaps no one had ever assumed the office of president with more prestige, or left it so utterly discredited, as Herbert Hoover. Entering the White House in 1929 as a renowned humanitarian who would lead the nation "to the previously impossible state in which poverty in this country can be put on a purely voluntary basis," Hoover exited four years later with his name a synonym for suffering and hard times. People who spent the night on park benches covered by newspapers said they were sleeping under "Hoover blankets." Those who hitched broken-down cars to mules or horses said they were riding in "Hoover wagons." Men who turned their trouser pockets inside out to show they were empty claimed to be waving "Hoover flags." Hoover had once symbolized the application of scientific intelligence to social problems. By 1932 many considered his refusal to face facts squarely a national scandal.

During the 1920s Hoover had expressed boundless confidence in the potential of American capitalism. In *American Individualism* (1922) he asserted that the American system, by promoting equality of opportunity, permitted the "free rise of ability, character, and intelligence." Yet individualism, he added, by no means required the government to pursue a laissez-faire policy. As secretary of commerce under Harding and Coolidge (a position for which he turned down a $500,000-a-year offer as a mining and metallurgical engineer), Hoover endorsed government intervention in the domestic economy. He favored increased spending for public works to create jobs in periods of distress. He supported a constitutional amendment prohibiting child labor. He also advocated the creation of trade associations. By promulgating voluntary codes of business ethics, approved by the government, these associations would allow businessmen to avoid wasteful competition and to pool technical knowledge without violating the antitrust laws. In 1927, when floods ravaged the Mississippi Valley, Hoover brilliantly mobilized state, local, and private resources to aid the victims. Hoover's supporters in 1928 dubbed him "the Master of Emergencies."

His post-1929 program had five parts. First, Hoover summoned business and labor leaders to the White House in an effort to persuade them to maintain wages, keep up production, and proceed with plant expansion. Second, the president stepped up expenditures for the construction of roads, bridges, and public buildings. Federal aid for highway construction jumped from $105 million to $260 million annually, and the number of workers on such projects increased from 110,000 to 280,000. Third, Hoover signed the Hawley-Smoot Act (1930), which substantially raised tariff rates in the hope of protecting American manufacturers and farmers. Fourth, in June 1931 Hoover declared a moratorium on war debts. Convinced that economic collapse abroad was prolonging the depression in the United States, Hoover sought to improve the ability of European nations to purchase American goods and thereby stimulate domestic output. Fifth, the president somewhat grudgingly accepted direct aid to big business. Early in 1932 Congress created the Reconstruction Finance Corporation (RFC) in order to assist businesses in financial trouble. In Hoover's last year in office, the RFC lent $1.78 billion to 7,400 banks, insurance companies, railroads, and other institutions.

Some of these initiatives helped, but none succeeded in reversing the downturn. The "conferences for continued industrial progress," as they were called, produced little more than empty promises. Most business owners simply could not afford to maintain wages or prices while the economy continued to slide downward. The public works program did some good, but even as the federal government was expanding its program, bankrupt states and municipalities were trimming theirs. Consequently, the total amount spent on such improvements and the total number of men employed declined. The Hawley-Smoot tariff was an unqualified disaster; European countries, selling less to the United States, retaliated by erecting high tariff walls of their own. The debt moratorium had little domestic impact. Eventually it led to what its critics had feared—a decision by France, Great Britain, and most other nations to default on further payments. The RFC, whose activities were confined largely to bailing out large concerns, was said to dispense a "millionaire's dole."

By the end of 1932 Hoover's policy lay in ruins. Every statistic revealed a startling degree of deterioration. From 1929 to 1933, gross national product fell from $104 billion to $74 billion, and national income fell from $88 billion to $40 billion. Almost every day there were more bank failures: 1,350 closed their doors in 1930, followed by 2,293 and 1,453 in the next two years. Stock prices tumbled precipitously. General Motors had sold for a high of 91 in 1929; in January 1933 it sold for 13. In the same period Standard Oil declined from 83 to 30 and United States Steel declined from 261 to 27. Farmers watched in dismay as their income plummeted by 61 percent. A pound of cotton, which had sold for 16 cents in 1929, brought 6 cents in 1932; a bushel of corn, which had sold for 79 cents, brought 31 cents. Only the number of unemployed workers rose steadily. In 1929, 1.5 million workers—3 percent of the labor force—were jobless. By 1933, at least 13 million workers—25 percent of the total—were idle. An average of 75,000 workers lost their jobs every week for three years.

THE BREAKDOWN OF RELIEF

Hoover's unwillingness to provide federal relief for the unemployed clearly revealed the inadequacy of his approach. The United States in the early 1930s had an unwieldy and anachronistic system of administering relief. Existing agencies were equipped to deal on a temporary basis with individual victims of accident or illness, but were not equipped to deal over a period of years with millions of jobless workers. Private charities had small staffs and limited funds; even municipalities often lacked the revenue to make sufficient money available. Only families that had become destitute, that had spent every dime of savings and sold every possession of value, could ordinarily qualify for assistance. Even then, those lucky enough to get on the relief rolls received barely enough for food. Rent, clothing, and medical care—all were considered luxuries.

Despite all this hardship, the president vigorously opposed direct federal relief in any form. To his mind it would open a Pandora's box, for it would cause a sizable increase in taxes, thereby discouraging private investment; lead to an unbalanced budget, thereby sabotaging confidence in the nation's credit; and require a gargantuan bureaucracy, thereby jeopardizing states' rights. Above all, the fearful "dole" would undermine its recipients' moral character, which Hoover took to mean "self-reliance," "sturdiness," and "independence." Yet as the situation worsened, the president was forced to take notice. The agencies he created to deal with the problem, however, illustrated perfectly Hoover's commitment to voluntary, cooperative action and his conviction that government could more properly dispense advice than funds.

In September 1930 Hoover set up the President's Emergency Committee for Employment under Colonel Arthur H. Woods. The committee at first subscribed to the view that relief was a local function, but by April 1931 even Woods recognized the need for federal involvement. When Hoover refused to concur, Woods resigned. In August Hoover created the President's Organization on Unemployment Relief, headed by Walter S. Gifford of American Telephone and Telegraph. Gifford arranged for a series of advertisements designed to stimulate charitable donations. But his group confined itself largely to a cheerleading function; as one member put it, "our job is not to raise funds ourselves." By November Gifford was assuring Hoover that "there is every indication that each state will take care of its own this winter." Two months later, testifying before a Senate committee, Gifford confessed that he did not know how many people were unemployed, how many were receiving relief, or how much money was available to the states to assist the needy.

By late 1932 the rickety relief system was collapsing in many places. Reports from cities across the country told of funds dried up and resources exhausted. Toledo: "There is only a commissary available for most families which is distributing the cheapest grades of food at a cost of six cents per person per day." Chicago: "Some families are being separated, husbands being sent to the men's shelter and wives to the women's shelter." Houston: "Applications are not taken from unemployed Mexican or colored families. They are being asked to shift for themselves." In Philadelphia, families on relief received $4.23 a week; in New York City, $2.39. Tragically, the special precautions taken to aid children revealed how bad things were. The American Friends Service Committee provided free lunches to children in the coal towns of Pennsylvania, West Virginia, and Kentucky. Funds were so limited that the Quakers could distribute meals only to children who were 10 percent underweight. In Oklahoma City, veterans collected discarded food from produce houses and scraps from butcher shops to feed the hungry. "All delicacies (such as figs that had spoiled and canned fruit that had gone a bit sour) were saved for the children."

THE BONUS ARMY

The long years of hardship apparently left many Americans psychologically numb. No matter how bad conditions were throughout the country, many people regarded their inability to find work or support their families as a sign of personal inadequacy. Yet sporadic acts of protest, sometimes accompanied by violence and lawlessness, eventually occurred. The Midwest saw the invention of "penny auctions": when banks foreclosed farmers' mortgages and attempted to auction off their possessions, neighbors appeared, armed with rifles, and no one bid more than a penny. The two most important organized protests occurred in the summer of 1932—the Bonus Army and the Farm Holiday Association.

Soldiers in gas masks advance on Bonus Army demonstrators in Washington, DC, July 1932. The Bonus Marchers were unemployed World War I veterans urging the U.S. government to deliver their promised monetary bonus early. *(Jack Benton/Getty Images)*

The career of the Bonus Expeditionary Force demonstrated that even the most disillusioned Americans continued to seek improvement within the system rather than outside it. The bonus issue had originated in 1924 when Congress, over Coolidge's veto, promised a bonus of several hundred dollars (depending on length of military service) to World War I veterans, but deferred payment until 1945. By 1932, however, many unemployed veterans wanted to be paid immediately, since they considered the money rightfully theirs and desperately needed it. When Congress took up a bill providing immediate payment, veterans converged on Washington to lobby for passage. The veterans aroused considerable sympathy, but the Hoover administration believed the case against them to be overwhelming: payment of the bonus would wreck hopes for a balanced budget, give preferential treatment to veterans over other needy citizens, and entitle those veterans who were well-off to payment at a time of declining tax revenues.

In June 1932 some 22,000 veterans, led by Walter W. Waters of Oregon, streamed into Washington. They set up camp across the Anacostia River by building shanties furnished from garbage dumps. Their wives and children joined many veterans. The chief of police of Washington, Pelham D. Glassford, himself a former army officer, provided some funds and provisions. Although the House passed the bonus bill, the Senate rejected the measure on June 17 by a large margin. Congress adjourned in July after allocating $100,000 to provide loans for marchers who needed carfare to return home. Only 5,160 men took advantage of the offer. The rest, presumably having no home or jobs to return to, remained.

The presence of the Bonus Army embarrassed and frightened the Hoover administration. Hoover refused to meet with a delegation of veterans, assuming that an interview would only dignify their cause, raise false hopes, and bring even more demonstrators to Washington. In addition, the president came to accept the view that communist agitators had infiltrated the ranks of the Bonus Army. Ultimately the government increased its pressure on the veterans, demanding that they leave an abandoned Treasury Department building in downtown Washington in which some were living. The evacuation led to a scuffle with the police in which two veterans were killed, providing a pretext for dispersing the Bonus Army itself. On July 28, 1932, General Douglas MacArthur led cavalry and infantry troops, as well as a mounted machine-gun squadron, down Pennsylvania Avenue. With bayonets and tear gas, the soldiers drove the veterans out of the business district and across the bridge to Anacostia and there set fire to the encampment.

The decision to drive the veterans out of downtown Washington was made by Hoover, Secretary of War Patrick J. Hurley, and the District commissioners, but the decision to pursue them to Anacostia and break up their encampment was MacArthur's alone. Convinced that the Bonus Army was "a bad-looking mob animated by the essence of revolution," MacArthur ignored explicit instructions not to follow the veterans across the Anacostia River. But if Hoover had not ordered this pursuit, he accepted MacArthur's estimate of the revolutionary threat, believed that public opinion would support MacArthur's action, and therefore accepted responsibility for it. To have done otherwise would have required the president to repudiate his chief of staff and side with forces he considered subversive. The president thus not only misunderstood what the Bonus Army represented, but also misjudged public reaction to the government's panicky response.

AGRARIAN PROTEST

Even as the government was driving out the Bonus Army, struggling corn and dairy farmers in Iowa and surrounding states were organizing the Farm Holiday Association. Like the veterans who went to Washington, the farmers wanted Congress to enact special-interest legislation. This took the form of the cost-of-production plan, under which the government would support food prices at a level that would guarantee farmers their operating cost, a 5 percent return on their investment, and a living wage for their operators. The plan would have raised the price of a bushel of oats from 11 to 45 cents, the price of a bushel of corn from 10 to 92 cents. The farmers, however, attempted to generate pressure on Congress not by camping on the Capitol doorstep but by withholding their products from market, hoping thereby to force prices upward.

The Farm Holiday Association began implementing its direct-action plan in August 1932. Despite wide support, the plan proved unworkable. Blockading a few markets could not significantly affect overall supply or price levels. Even if prices rose temporarily, they would drop as soon as farmers resumed normal operations. Nor did all farmers wish to cooperate with the strike. As Farm Holiday Association supporters set up patrols and picket lines, they clashed with farmers seeking to transport their goods to market and with sheriff's deputies attempting

JAMES CAGNEY
AND THE GANGSTER FILM

American actor James Cagney *(left)* plays gangster Tom Powers in the 1931 film *Public Enemy*, directed by William A. Wellman for Warner Brothers. *(Hulton Archive/ Getty Images)*

In the early 1930s many Americans were troubled by the existence of organized crime, and troubled even more by what they considered its source: the widespread disrespect for the law bred by Prohibition and the closing of traditional paths to success because of the Great Depression. The release of *Little Caesar* in 1931 marked the appearance of a new film genre, the gangster film, which reflected these concerns. The picture's box-office success led to the production of fifty other such films within a year.

The most revealing of these was *Public Enemy*, in which James Cagney played the gangster Tommy Powers. Even as a youngster Tommy is tripping little girls on roller skates. As a teenager he falls in with the wrong crowd and becomes a thief and bootlegger (although in Cagney's portrayal a rather jaunty, lovable one). As the archetypal gangster, Tommy Powers scorns traditional values, most of which are embodied in his brother Mike. Tommy Powers cuts through social convention with a scalpel. He sneers at education. When an accomplice asks him to involve Mike in a gangland operation, Tommy replies, "He's too busy going to school. He's learning to be poor." Similarly, Tommy exposes the hypocrisy of war. When Mike returns from military service a hero and accuses his brother of murdering rival bootleggers, Tommy snaps, "You didn't get those medals holding hands with Germans." Tommy refuses to be domesticated. When his mistress, played by Mae Clarke, gently scolds him and says she wishes he would not drink so early in the morning, Tommy mimics her savagely: "I wish, I wish, I wish you was a wishing well. Then maybe you'd dry up!" Mashing a grapefruit in her face, he walks out.

In deference to the Hollywood production code, *Public Enemy* opens by stating that it does not intend to glorify the criminal but rather to "depict an environment." There is also a mandatory unhappy ending, in which a rival gang abducts Tommy Powers from a hospital and deposits his corpse on his mother's doorstep. But despite these concessions to convention, the film's message was plain. Its hero, after all, is a man who thumbs his nose at conventional virtues and follows the one career he finds open to his talents. The film was reassuring in another sense. For while Tommy Powers disregards the laws everyone else supposedly observes, his world had laws of its own. The underworld operated according to a clearly defined code, and gangsters dispensed an informal brand of justice by annihilating one another. Moreover, the world of the criminal was encapsulated. The gangster did not injure law-abiding citizens because he moved in a world separate and distinct from theirs.

FBI head J. Edgar Hoover aiming a Thompson submachine gun, 1925. *(Time & Life Pictures/ Getty Images)*

The image of the police officer in the gangster film was that of a dumb flatfoot, either incompetent or corrupt, or both. Yet with the advent of the welfare state under Franklin D. Roosevelt, crime films changed to reflect the new national mood. As the federal government extended its influence, the image of federal law enforcement was refurbished. Partly because of a massive public relations campaign by Federal Bureau of Investigation (FBI) director J. Edgar Hoover, Americans came to regard federal agents as fearless, intrepid, and incorruptible. The circle was not complete, however, until the release of *G-Men* in 1935, starring none other than James Cagney. In the film Cagney joins the FBI to avenge the gangland slaying of a friend. "'Public Enemy' Becomes Soldier of the Law," read advertisements: "Uncle Sam always gets his man." Now Cagney did his shooting from behind a badge—and, even more significant, it was a federal badge.

Web Links

http://lafenty.hubpages.com/hub/Gangster-Movies-1930s-1940s
Clips from many gangster films including *Public Enemy*.

http://themave.com/Cagney/
A website devoted to James Cagney with a biography and video clips.

to keep the road open. The resulting violence dismayed the movement's leaders, who called off the strike in September. By then attention was shifting to the presidential campaign and the opportunity to elect candidates who might relieve the distress. In November 1932 Herbert Hoover failed to carry a single rural county in his home state of Iowa.

ROOSEVELT AND THE NEW DEAL

To face Hoover in that election the Democrats nominated Franklin Delano Roosevelt, often referred to as FDR. Born in Hyde Park, New York, in 1882, the only child of wealthy parents, Roosevelt entered Groton in 1896 and Harvard in 1900, then attended Columbia Law School. In 1910, having practiced law for a time, he entered politics and was elected to the New York State Senate. He strongly backed Woodrow Wilson, whom he later served as assistant secretary of the navy, and in 1920 he ran for vice president on the Democratic ticket with James M. Cox. In August 1921 Roosevelt, until then a vigorous and athletic man, was struck by poliomyelitis. Years of physical therapy helped somewhat, but his legs remained paralyzed. For the rest of his life he wore steel braces, could walk only with assistance, and had to be lifted into and out of automobiles. While Roosevelt adjusted to permanent paralysis, his wife Eleanor threw her energies into Democratic politics in New York State to keep the Roosevelt name in the public eye. In 1928 he had recuperated sufficiently to run for governor. Although Democratic presidential candidate Al Smith lost New York State, Roosevelt won the governorship by a narrow margin and easily gained reelection two years later. In 1932, recognizing that Hoover's policies had alienated millions and that the name Roosevelt was "still almost as much a Republican name as a Democratic one," he purposely conducted a vague presidential campaign, promising to end hard times without ever explaining how.

Roosevelt entered the White House in March 1933 with several advantages. With 22.8 million votes to Hoover's 15.8 million, Roosevelt could claim an undisputed popular mandate. He also had comfortable majorities with which to work in Congress. Democrats outnumbered Republicans 59 to 36 in the Senate, 313 to 117 in the House. For economic advice Roosevelt could turn to members of his "brain trust," which included Columbia University professors Adolf A. Berle, Rexford G. Tugwell, and Raymond Moley. For political advice the president could rely on Louis Howe—an old friend and supporter—and James A. Farley, whom he made postmaster general. Roosevelt's cabinet contained talented administrators, among them Secretary of the Interior Harold L. Ickes, Secretary of Agriculture Henry A. Wallace, and Secretary of Labor Frances C. Perkins. Above all, Roosevelt took office in the midst of a severe national crisis, one he likened to a war. He could depend, therefore, on an extraordinary amount of cooperation from Congress and the public.

As he entered office, Roosevelt affirmed that the government owed each person the "right to make a comfortable living." This as well as anything else marked the distance between his approach and Hoover's. For New Dealers, the depression had exposed the bankruptcy of the existing order, characterized by what Tugwell termed its "violent contrasts of well-being, its irrational allotments of individual liberty, its unconsidered exploitation of human and natural resources." The New Deal, Berle noted, brought "a tremendous expansion of the area in which . . . government is prepared to accept responsibility." Roosevelt indeed saw no practical alternative. To rehabilitate the private enterprise system, government must rescue its victims. Roosevelt feared that a revolution "could hardly be avoided if another president should fail as Hoover has failed."

Pragmatic in outlook, Roosevelt's followers said they wanted "hard facts," declared it "unwise to lay down too specifically the structure of new things," and even announced that "'truth' is irrelevant as a test of an economic philosophy." They believed in trying something to see if it worked, discarding it if it did not, and then trying something else. This willingness to improvise, surely a source of strength, nevertheless raised certain problems. For one thing, it was not always clear how long a period was needed to judge whether a program was working or what criteria would be used in making that judgment. For another, new programs attracted support from political interests and developed bureaucratic structures that resisted change. Policies, once instituted, proved less adaptable in practice than they seemed in theory.

THE BLUE EAGLE

The keystone of the early New Deal was the National Recovery Administration (NRA), created in June 1933. The NRA, rejecting the model of competition, favored business cooperation in partnership with government. Business executives were permitted to draft codes, subject to presidential approval, that regulated prices and wages and forbade a broad range of competitive practices. Those participating in such agreements were exempted from the antitrust laws. In addition, the NRA supposedly guaranteed labor the right to organize, and it inaugurated a public works program to pump money into the economy. This latter function was performed through the Public Works Administration, which Roosevelt placed under Harold Ickes. To head the NRA, however, Roosevelt chose General Hugh Johnson, who had played an instrumental role in the world war mobilization.

Although Congress clothed the NRA with licensing powers, Johnson, fearing that they might not withstand the scrutiny of the courts, attempted to gain voluntary compliance from business. He marshaled public opinion through parades and publicity, and all who took part displayed the NRA symbol—a blue eagle with the slogan "We Do Our Part." Just as soldiers used certain insignia to distinguish friend from foe, Roosevelt said, so those fighting the depression "must know each other at a glance." "May God have mercy on the man or group of men who attempt to trifle with that bird," proclaimed Johnson. The codes, he explained, resembled the Marquis of Queensberry rules in boxing. "They eliminate eye-gouging and knee-groining and ear-chewing in business. Above the belt any man can be just as rugged and just as individual as he pleases." By the fall of 1933 every major industry had pledged its cooperation.

But in economics, as in the ring, heavyweights enjoyed a distinct advantage. Many corporate leaders had always disliked what they regarded as excessive competition. They saw nothing wrong with fixing prices, so long as they did the fixing. The antitrust laws had presumably blocked such concerted action, but their suspension provided business leaders with a long-awaited opportunity. As things worked out, big business played the dominant role in drawing up the codes. The NRA, in consequence, generally kept production down and prices up. The codes restricted output by limiting factory hours and banning new plant construction. Similarly, the codes set minimum prices, prohibited sales below cost, and restricted combination sales, trade-in allowances, credit terms, and other competitive practices.

These policies caused a good deal of dissatisfaction. Consumers resented an arrangement that hurt their pocketbooks, and many owners of small businesses believed that the codes discriminated in favor of large concerns. Women's organizations, led by the League of Women Voters and the National Consumer's League, protested that one out of four NRA codes discriminated against women by setting lower minimum wages for women than for men. At the same time, labor was becoming increasingly dissatisfied because Section 7(a), which was intended to protect the right to organize, was proving insufficient. While it prohibited employers from interfering with their workers' right to join unions and choose bargaining officials, it did not create adequate enforcement machinery or require employers to bargain in good faith. In 1934 Roosevelt appointed a commission, under Clarence Darrow, that investigated the NRA and submitted a highly critical report. "NRA," said the disaffected, stood for "No Recovery Allowed" or "National Run-Around."

The experiment in industrial planning had mixed results. The NRA apparently brought about a measure of economic improvement and, perhaps as important, established the principle of federal responsibility for working conditions. Yet the agency did not live up to expectations, in part because different groups—consumers and workers, large and small businesses—expected different things of it. There was, in truth, little chance that the NRA could have satisfied all the competing demands made of it. Having relied so heavily on public support at the outset, the NRA found itself in difficulty when enthusiasm waned. In early 1935 the Senate agreed to extend the NRA for one, not two, years. That May, the Supreme Court brought the troubled flight of the blue eagle to an end.

It did so in the "sick chicken" case. The Schechter brothers, who owned a poultry market in Brooklyn, purchased chickens raised in surrounding states, slaughtered them, and sold them to retailers. In October 1934 the firm was found guilty of violating NRA wage and hour provisions and of selling unfit poultry. The case eventually reached the Supreme Court, which handed down a unanimous opinion. Chief Justice Charles Evans Hughes ruled that the depression did not confer upon the government powers it might not otherwise exercise, that an excessive delegation of legislative powers occurred in the code-drafting process, and that the Schechter brothers were involved in intrastate commerce and therefore outside the scope of federal regulation. Hughes admitted that the chickens had crossed state lines but reasoned that they had come to a "permanent rest"—that is, were killed and eaten—within New York. They therefore were no longer part of a flow of interstate commerce. Through an extremely narrow reading of the Constitution, therefore, the Court declared the NRA illegal.

TRIPLE A

The New Deal attempted to aid agriculture by helping farmers pay off their mortgages, encouraging inflation to facilitate the payment of debts, acquiring foreign markets for farm products, and reducing acreage to limit supply. The last, known as the "domestic allotment plan," served as the foundation of the Agricultural Adjustment Administration (AAA or Triple A), which was established in May 1933. Under the plan—which affected wheat, cotton, hogs, tobacco, corn, rice, and milk—farmers signed acreage-reduction contracts. In return for curbing output, they received government subsidies. In some respects the AAA was a counterpart of the NRA, for each involved a planned limitation of production under government auspices.

At the outset, the AAA had to persuade farmers to destroy part of their existing crops. Making agreements to curb future output was relatively simple but did not affect the current harvest. The AAA therefore paid farmers $160 million to destroy one-fourth of their cotton. They plowed up 10 million acres, reducing the crop from 17 to 13 million bales. The administration also induced farmers to slaughter 6 million baby pigs and 200,000 sows. Although farmers received $30 million and relief agencies distributed the pork to needy families, the extermination led to howls of anguish. "To hear them talk," Secretary of Agriculture Wallace said disgustedly, "you would have thought that pigs were raised for pets!" Roosevelt apparently regarded the matter less seriously than did his critics. He inquired jokingly, "Wouldn't birth control be more effective in the long run?"

The AAA helped farmers who owned their own land, but it often hurt those who did not. Of the 2.86 million tenant farmers and sharecroppers, 1.6 million, many of them black, labored in southern cotton fields. The AAA policy of reducing farm acreage obviously reduced the need for farm laborers and consequently led to evictions and unemployment. Those tenants and croppers who remained received little, since payments were made only to landowners. They were supposed to apportion the money fairly among their tenants, but seldom did. The Roosevelt administration, believing that the AAA's success hinged on the cooperation of the owners of big farms, would do nothing to jeopardize that support. As AAA director Chester Davis noted in February 1936, the elevation of sharecroppers "cannot be forced by the Federal Government to proceed much faster than the rate that the Southern opinion and Southern leadership will heartily support. To try to force a faster pace would merely be to insure violent controversy, lack of local cooperation in administration, evasion and ineffectiveness for the plan."

Not everyone shared this outlook. A number of AAA officials, led by General Counsel Jerome Frank, wished to protect the sharecroppers' position by requiring that planters continue to employ the same workers. Frank's dispute with Davis eventually forced Wallace to choose between them. Early in 1935 he "purged" the AAA of Frank and those who wanted to make agricultural policy into a vehicle of reform. In July 1935, however, the administration partially appeased Frank's group by supporting the creation of the Resettlement Administration, which took the first, tentative steps toward helping landless farmers acquire their own land and tools. In some cases dissatisfied tenant farmers took independent action. In mid-1934, black and white sharecroppers in Arkansas organized the Southern Tenant Farmers Union. Too frequently, they complained, Roosevelt "talked like a cropper and acted like a planter." When they sang "We Shall Not Be Moved," they were protesting against a New Deal policy that was driving them from the land they worked but did not own.

Despite these difficulties, by 1936 the AAA had succeeded in raising gross farm income by 50 percent, boosting commodity prices by 66 percent, and reducing farm indebtedness by $1 billion. Then the agency met the same fate as the NRA. In January 1936, in *United States v. Butler*, the Supreme Court struck down the AAA by a vote of 6 to 3. Justice Owen Roberts, delivering the majority opinion, held that benefits paid to farmers for reducing acreage actually imposed a system of agricultural regulation under the guise of appropriations for the general welfare. In effect, Roberts said, Congress could not stipulate how its appropriations were to be used. In a stinging dissent, Justice Harlan Fiske Stone termed this "a tortured construction of the Constitution." He added, "the power to tax and spend includes the power to relieve a nationwide economic maladjustment by conditional gifts of money." This view New Dealers considered axiomatic for the continued functioning of the welfare state.

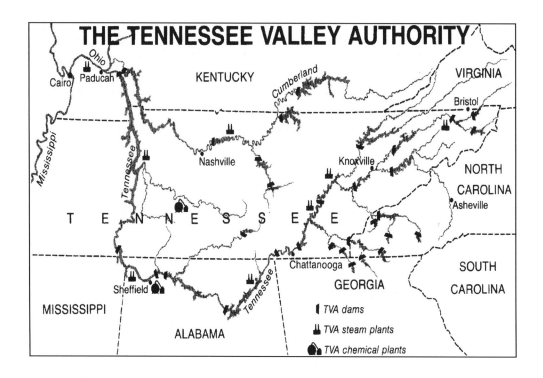

CONSERVATION AND PUBLIC POWER:
THE TENNESSEE VALLEY AUTHORITY

Few causes meant more to Roosevelt than conservation. The existing pool of unemployed young people provided an opportunity to unite the functions of forestry and relief, and this the president proceeded to do in the Civilian Conservation Corps (CCC). Within three months after its creation in April 1933, the CCC had enrolled 250,000 young men in their teens and twenties. The volunteers fought forest fires, built water-storage basins, and reseeded grazing lands. They constructed roads, bridges, and camping facilities. They protected trees against blister rust, bark beetle, and gypsy moths. In three years CCC volunteers planted 570 million trees in the national forests. They also showed farmers how to prevent soil erosion. To conserve wildlife, the agency built refuges, fish-rearing ponds, and animal shelters. In September 1935 the CCC reached a high point with 500,000 volunteers in more than 2,500 camps. The young men received $30 per month, of which $25 went directly to their families as part of a relief program.

New Dealers proposed a still more ambitious plan to transform social and economic conditions in the 40,000-square-mile Tennessee River Valley. There, Roosevelt said shortly before his inauguration, "we have an opportunity of setting an example of planning . . . tying in industry and agriculture and forestry and flood prevention, tying them all into a unified whole." In May 1933 Congress established the Tennessee Valley Authority (TVA), thereby fulfilling—indeed, exceeding—the hopes of such public-power advocates as Senator George

Norris of Nebraska. The TVA promised coordinated, multipurpose development. It not only provided electric power but also prevented soil erosion, helped control floods, allowed for navigation, and experimented with new fertilizers. It meant, Roosevelt said, "national planning for a complete river watershed."

During the 1930s the TVA erected more than twenty dams with a generating capacity of 1 million kilowatts. Consumption of electricity in the region more than doubled. The TVA also cleared a 650-mile channel from Paducah to Knoxville, which greatly stimulated traffic on the river. Inevitably, though, the agency provoked sharp opposition from private electric companies, which took a dim view of government competition. These companies also resented the concept of a federal "yardstick" against which their rates would be measured, arguing, with considerable justice, that TVA costs were not comparable with their own. Wendell Willkie of the Commonwealth and Southern Corporation, a leader of the opposition, branded the TVA "the most useless and unnecessary of all the alphabetical joyrides." Private utilities engaged the TVA in a long series of legal tussles. In February 1936 the agency won breathing room when the Supreme Court, in *Ashwander v. TVA*, upheld the government's right to sell the excess energy generated by Wilson Dam. The Court did not finally resolve the broader constitutional question in favor of the TVA until early 1939.

The TVA accomplished a great deal—as much as, if not more than, any other New Deal program—but it never brought about the "designed and planned social and economic order" for which some had hoped. Spokesmen for the agency advocated what David E. Lilienthal, one of its directors, termed "grass-roots democracy." Lilienthal believed that in assuming broad powers, the federal government must not lose touch with local mores and institutions. This required the "decentralized administration of centralized authority." The policy of encouraging local involvement, while helping to secure support, in effect made the TVA responsive to the largest and most influential interest groups. Its agricultural program, for example, was geared to wealthy farmers rather than to sharecroppers. Those who had the most extravagant expectations were most unhappy at what they viewed as the TVA's capitulation. No less than the NRA and AAA, the TVA often catered to the already powerful.

SOLIDARITY FOREVER?

When Franklin Roosevelt took office, 3 million workers belonged to trade unions, compared with 5 million in 1920. Only one in ten nonfarm workers carried union cards, about the same percentage as in 1910. In the steel, rubber, and automobile industries, unions played virtually no role at all. Thrown on the defensive in the 1920s by the open-shop drive and adverse Supreme Court rulings, labor suffered further losses in the early depression years. Unions found it impossible to keep old members, much less attract new ones, in a shrinking job market. Many workers shied away from union activities for fear of antagonizing employers. After 1933, although the economy slowly revived, the policies adopted by employers and American Federation of Labor (AFL) officials continued to retard unionization.

The techniques employers used to block organizing drives included hiring spies and private policemen, stockpiling small arsenals for use in case of strikes, and recruiting professional strikebreakers. But in the years 1933 to 1935, employers relied chiefly on the company union, which had the advantage of appearing to comply with Section 7(a) of the legislation that created the NRA without actually doing so. These unions, set up and controlled by employers, lacked any semblance of autonomy. Management expected great things of them. A vice president in charge of industrial relations at United States Steel declared that the union he had just organized would lead to "sound and harmonious relationships between men and management," similar to those prevailing "between a man and his wife." Finley Peter Dunne's political cartoon character Mr. Dooley had once said that an employer's ideal union was one with "no strikes, no rules, no contracts, . . . hardly iny wages, an 'dam' few members." Except for the last point, company unions nicely fitted the definition. By 1935 nearly 600 of them existed, with well over 2 million members.

The AFL meanwhile was proving itself unequal to—indeed uninterested in—the task of organizing the unorganized, particularly unskilled workers in mass-production industries. With few exceptions, AFL unions followed craft rather than industrial lines. The AFL adhered to the principle of exclusive jurisdiction under which, for example, its metalworkers' affiliate had a claim on all metalworkers, no matter where they worked or what their preferences. The creation of industrial unions in steel plants or automobile factories could easily demolish these jurisdictional rights. To justify their position, AFL leaders insisted that unskilled workers lacked the leverage to bargain successfully, for if they went on strike, employers could easily replace them. The eventual collapse of such old AFL rivals as the American Railway Union and the Industrial Workers of the World supposedly provided ironclad proof that industrial unionism led up a blind alley.

The Roosevelt administration, unwilling to abandon the NRA concept of a business-government partnership, did little at first to spur union growth. "This is a time for mutual confidence and help," the president said in creating the NRA, but during 1934 capital and labor exhibited little of either. Not only were employers setting up company unions to avoid bargaining in good faith, but labor militancy rose sharply. In 1934, 1.5 million workers went on strike, and industrial violence reached its highest level since 1919. San Francisco longshoremen, Minneapolis truck drivers, Alabama cotton-mill workers—all struck for union recognition and improved conditions, and all clashed with the police or the National Guard. Simultaneously, pressure began to mount in Congress, where Senator Robert F. Wagner of New York drew up a measure to make collective bargaining guarantees meaningful. Roosevelt, claiming that the bill needed more study, succeeded in having it shelved.

With the various strands of his labor policy unraveling, the president finally accepted Wagner's position in the spring of 1935. At the last minute, when the Senate had passed the Wagner Act (1935) and the House was about to do so, Roosevelt endorsed it. The act upheld the right of workers to join unions and created the National Labor Relations Board to conduct shop elections. Most important, the measure substituted the principle of majority rule for that of proportional representation, thereby ensuring that the union winning a majority of votes would represent all the employees. The act prohibited employers from blacklisting workers, refusing to reinstate strikers, engaging in industrial espionage, or setting up company unions. The bill passed by huge margins, in part because many congressmen assumed—mistakenly as it turned out—that the Supreme Court would nullify it.

Enactment of this legislation was like a shot of adrenaline to advocates of industrial unionism. A sizable group within the AFL, led by John L. Lewis of the United Mine Workers, now demanded that the AFL accept industrial unions. Craft unions, Lewis asserted, may have served adequately in the past but were not suited to modern factories, in which technology

Labor leader John L. Lewis, head of the CIO, 1937. *(Library of Congress)*

had erased old craft distinctions. At the AFL convention in September 1935, Lewis presented a plan to allow the chartering of industrial unions. When the delegates rejected his motion by nearly a 2-to-1 margin, Lewis led a walkout. In November Lewis, Sidney Hillman of the Amalgamated Clothing Workers of America, David Dubinsky of the International Ladies Garment Workers Union, and leaders of fledgling unions in the automobile, rubber, and steel industries created what became the Congress of Industrial Organizations (CIO). The AFL demanded the dissolution of the congress and, when it refused, the AFL suspended and later expelled the unions composing the congress. Yet in the long run, the split proved a prelude to success, for it enabled labor to take advantage of the spectacular opportunities for organizing unskilled workers provided by the Wagner Act.

RELIEF AND SECURITY

New Deal policies concerning relief, like those affecting labor, evolved in a halting fashion. This was no fault of Harry Hopkins, who, before Roosevelt brought him to Washington to direct relief efforts, had performed a similar function in New York State. Hopkins's approach diverged sharply from prevailing practice. He believed that all needy persons, the unemployed as well as the chronically unemployable, were entitled to receive relief. He favored raising

Applicants waiting for jobs in front of FERA offices, New Orleans, Louisiana, October 1935. *(Library of Congress)*

standards to furnish such necessities as clothing and medical care. He also believed that payments in cash rather than grocery slips preserved recipients' self-respect. Finally, Hopkins preferred work relief, which made individuals feel like productive members of society, to home relief, which was often degrading. Work relief should, where possible, utilize existing training and skills. Hopkins saw no reason to insist that, as the price of obtaining relief, a teacher or engineer should have to dig ditches.

Hopkins's views regarding eligibility, standards, and programs went far beyond those of the Roosevelt administration and Congress. The first New Deal relief venture—the Federal Emergency Relief Administration (FERA)—showed this clearly. The FERA supervised relief activities from April 1933 to April 1935, except for a six-month period during the winter of 1934. Administration of the program was left largely in state hands. The matching-grants provision had unfortunate consequences. States, hard-pressed to raise the money necessary to obtain such funds, had either to enact sales taxes, which imposed an unfair burden on the poor, or cut other expenditures, such as those for education. If providing outright grants for relief broke sharply with existing practice, echoes of Herbert Hoover's policy lingered on in the decision to leave supervision to the states and in the attempt to squeeze yet more money out of them.

In November 1933, with the unemployed facing a long, cold winter, the administration conceded the FERA's inadequacy and temporarily replaced it with the Civil Works Administration (CWA). The CWA differed from its predecessor in that the federal government administered it and met 90 percent of its cost. The agency also took on some workers who, although unemployed, had not qualified for relief. The CWA offered relatively high wages, paying unskilled workers forty to fifty cents an hour, up to a maximum of thirty hours a week. Within two months the new agency had put 4.2 million men to work repairing streets, laying sewer pipe, building roads, improving schools and playgrounds, and, as critics always pointed out, raking leaves. By the start of 1934, 300,000 women worked for the CWA in sewing, canning, and clerical jobs. Undoubtedly some projects were poorly conceived, but most accomplished useful purposes. Then, in April 1934, the administration, worried by the CWA's high cost and controversial nature, canceled the experiment and reverted to the FERA.

Not until April 1935, when it established the Works Progress Administration (WPA), did the New Deal fashion a workable relief program. The WPA employed only those certified as needing relief, but was federally run, paid good wages, and made room for white-collar and professional workers. At its height, the WPA employed 3 million people a year, and, although starting with an initial appropriation of $4.8 billion, it ultimately spent $10.7 billion over seven years. The WPA included writers' and artists' projects and the Federal Theater Project, which in 1936 employed 12,500 actors who performed before audiences of 350,000 every week. The WPA never helped all the needy, and it was continually fighting off attempts to slice its budget. Yet it embodied many of the principles in which Hopkins believed: decent standards, work relief, and utilization of existing skills.

Roosevelt created the WPA in April, endorsed the Wagner Act in May, and in August 1935 signed a third measure—the Social Security Act—that further institutionalized government responsibility for the disadvantaged. First, the act set up an old-age pension system administered by the federal government and funded by a 1 percent payroll tax. Beginning in 1942 (the date was advanced to 1940), retired workers over sixty-five would receive $10 to $85 a month, depending on the amount that they had contributed. Those who had already retired would receive pensions to which the government would contribute up to $15 a month. Second, the measure provided for a joint federal-state system of unemployment insurance based on employer contributions. Third, the act authorized federal aid for the care of the blind, training for the physically handicapped, and aid to dependent children. Certainly, the Social Security Act had many imperfections: farm workers and domestic servants were excluded from its retirement provisions; state standards for unemployment compensation varied tremendously; and the payroll tax reduced mass purchasing power at the wrong time. Yet the act placed another brick in the arch of the welfare state.

THE NEW DEAL COALITION

Harry Hopkins was once quoted as saying, "We shall tax and tax, and spend and spend, and elect and elect." The remark may have been apocryphal, but it infuriated those who objected to New Deal relief and security policies. Many Republicans asserted, without justification, that Social Security would require federal prying into the private lives of citizens and would force millions of people to submit to fingerprinting or wear dog tags for identification purposes. Many of these same critics argued, with considerably better reason, that Democrats were attempting to extract partisan advantage from federal relief. Officials sometimes dispensed relief in ways calculated to bolster their political position and occasionally pressured WPA workers into voting a certain way. One Democratic leader privately requested the appointment of administrators who favored "using these Democratic projects to make votes for the Democratic Party."

In the 1936 presidential election, when Roosevelt defeated his opponent Alf M. Landon of Kansas, some Republicans blamed the magnitude of their loss on such unfair tactics. Certainly the dimensions of that defeat were stunning. Roosevelt received 27.5 million votes to Landon's 16.7 million and carried every state but Vermont and Maine. The voters sent only ninety Republicans to the House of Representatives and left only sixteen in the Senate, giving the Democrats the largest congressional majorities since the mid-nineteenth century. The vote revealed a sharp split along class lines, with Roosevelt in effect receiving most of his support from the lower classes and Landon receiving most of his from more prosperous groups. Politics had moved full circle from the 1920s, when cultural tensions had overshadowed economic issues. The Roosevelt coalition embraced southern whites and northern blacks, rural dwellers and urban immigrants, middle-class intellectuals and blue-collar workers. In 1936 a person's income and occupation (or lack of one) provided the surest clues to party preference.

The Democratic triumph reflected not illicit pressure exerted on relief recipients, but rather public approval of the programs Roosevelt had instituted. At the time those policies were criticized as inadequate, and in retrospect they may appear even less adequate. In almost every field—business, agriculture, conservation, labor, and relief—the New Deal moved cautiously and catered to more powerful groups at the expense of weaker ones. But this should not obscure the improvements in American life, or the changes in the role of government, that had occurred. In 1936 the clearest point of reference was 1932. The inadequacies of Roosevelt's policies, when compared with those of Hoover, did not seem so great after all.

CHAPTER SEVEN

1933–1941
Hard Times—Politics and Society

The wife of a migratory laborer with three children, near Childress, Texas, 1938. *(Library of Congress)*

Despite his efforts to combat the Great Depression and despite the vote of confidence he received in 1936, President Franklin Roosevelt by no means succeeded in restoring prosperity during his first or, for that matter, his second administration. Millions of Americans who remained poor and insecure concluded that New Deal policies were inadequate. Some turned to socialism or communism, but more supported the proposals of Dr. Francis E. Townsend, Huey Long, and Father Charles E. Coughlin, who promised instant abundance without a radical alteration of the social order. If some complained that the New Deal was proceeding too slowly, conservatives believed it was traveling at breakneck speed. Limited at first to sniping at New Deal policies, Roosevelt's conservative critics launched a massive offensive after 1937. Faced with mounting hostility in Congress and declining public support, New Dealers went on the defensive. By the end of the decade the Roosevelt administration was devoting most of its attention to national defense and foreign policy, not to domestic reform.

THE OLD FOLKS' CRUSADE

In 1935 a California congressman rose in the House of Representatives to reflect on the passing of his mother. "She is the sweetest memory of my life," he said, "and the hands that used to feed me and cool my fevered brow now touch me only in my dreams. But if she were living today, . . . that little frail mother of mine . . . would say, 'Son, you be good to the old folks, and God will bless you.'" In the year 1935 being "good to the old folks" meant one thing: supporting the Townsend Old Age Revolving Pension Plan. Named for its creator, Dr. Francis E. Townsend, the plan gave birth to a movement whose widespread popularity pointed up the deficiencies of the New Deal and influenced the policies of the Roosevelt administration. Better than anything else, the appeal of the Townsend plan illustrated the devastating impact of the depression on the elderly.

For many elderly people the depression was in fact a nightmare. Many who wanted to continue working could not compete with younger workers. Unemployment among those over the age of sixty climbed to 40 percent. Many who had expected to retire on savings found themselves destitute when the banks failed. Others saw their incomes shrivel as the stock market fell and as private pension plans—often poorly conceived and badly financed—collapsed. Of the 7.5 million Americans over the age of sixty-five, fully half could not support themselves. Some were forced to seek assistance from their children who, given the difficult times that everyone faced, were already experiencing hardship. Others had to apply for public charity at the cost of sacrificing their self-respect. Only twenty-eight states provided old-age pensions. For the most part they were sadly inadequate, with monthly payments ranging from $7 to $30. In twenty states no pensions of any kind existed.

All these problems were greatly magnified in California, which, as a haven for retirees, had seen its aged population climb from 200,000 to 366,000 during the 1920s. Five times as many people over the age of sixty-five lived in California as in any other state except Washington. Large numbers of retired men and women, separated from their relatives by hundreds or thousands of miles, had no one to fall back on when the depression hit. California's old-age pension plan was defective by every standard. No elderly person with a legally responsible relative able to provide support could receive aid. To qualify for assistance, an elderly person had to go on the relief rolls, sign a pauper's oath, submit to a "needs" test, and accept a lien on any property so that the state could recover part of the cost of the pension upon the person's death. Then, and only then, were the aged eligible for a sum of $22 a month. The system could hardly have been better calculated to deprive the aged of their dignity.

These conditions help explain the overwhelming response to the Townsend plan. Townsend, who had worked as a ranch hand and traveling salesman before becoming a doctor, had gone to Long Beach after the world war. In 1933, at the age of sixty-six, he presented his "Cure for Depressions." Everyone in the country over the age of sixty would receive $200 a month, on two conditions: that they spend the full amount each month and retire if still employed. This would pump money into the economy, open jobs for younger people, and permit a dignified retirement. The plan would be financed by a national sales tax, later called a transactions tax. Asked why he chose the figure of $200, Townsend explained, "The main reason was so that nobody would come along and offer more." In collaboration with Robert Earl Clements, Townsend set up Old Age Revolving Pensions Ltd. in January 1934. Within two years 7,000 Townsend clubs with about 1.5 million members had sprung up across the country.

The Townsend plan offered a married couple over sixty years of age $4,800 a year, at a time when 87 percent of all American families had annual incomes below $2,500. Yet the plan won support from many who believed in the values of thrift, hard work, and individualism precisely because the plan did not seem at all radical. For example, it did not call for deficit spending. The government would collect in sales taxes what it disbursed, and those taxes would not be levied on the rich but on all consumers. The plan required no bureaucracy other than the Treasury Department to make out the checks and the post office to deliver them. The plan in no way compromised private property rights. Nor did it imply a dole. Rather, Townsend viewed the elderly as "Distributor Custodians," entrusted by society to spend $200 a month wisely. Critics, however, doubted the plan's feasibility, pointing out that it would cost $20 to $24 billion a year (or nearly half the total national income), that it would injure the poor through a regressive sales tax, and that it would require a far-flung bureaucracy to see that recipients spent their allotments.

The Townsend movement nevertheless crystallized popular sentiment for old-age pensions and helped move Congress and the administration to support the Social Security Act of 1935. Townsend condemned that measure because it excluded too many people from coverage and provided inadequate benefits. But, limited as it was, the act eroded Townsend's basis of support. His own plan lost on a voice vote in the House of Representatives. New Dealers responded to Townsend's challenge by attempting to discredit his movement. In the spring of 1936 a Senate committee began investigating the clubs in an effort to prove them a financial fraud. The investigators found that Clements had profited handsomely and that Townsend not only exercised absolute control over the clubs, but privately referred to the members as "old fossils." (When Townsend refused to testify, he was cited for contempt and sentenced to a year in jail; Roosevelt later commuted the sentence because of Townsend's age.) By the summer of 1936 Townsend's estrangement from the New Deal was complete. Certain that "we shall be able to lick the stuffing" out of both major political parties, Townsend prepared to join forces with other foes of the administration.

"SHARE OUR WEALTH"

In 1933 Sinclair Lewis published a novel titled *It Can't Happen Here*, in which a senator named Buzz Windrip established a fascist regime in the United States. One character described

American politician Huey Pierce Long,
c. 1932. *(Hulton Archive/Getty Images)*

Windrip as "a dictator seemingly so different from the fervent Hitler and the gesticulating Fascists . . . a dictator with something of the earthy American sense of humor of a Mark Twain." None doubted that this figure was patterned after Senator Huey Long of Louisiana or that Lewis was asserting that it could indeed happen here. In the highly charged political atmosphere of the 1930s, perhaps no one aroused more intense feelings of love and hatred than did the Louisianan. To his supporters, Long had "changed Louisiana from a hellhole to a paradise. He was emancipator. He brought light." To his critics, Long was an unprincipled demagogue. In the summer of 1932 Franklin Roosevelt privately termed him one of the most dangerous men in America.

Born in 1893, Long as a boy had done odd jobs—driving a bakery wagon, carrying water to construction crews, learning to set type—primarily, it seems, to avoid the drudgery of working on his father's farm. He spent his teens as a traveling salesman and gambler, then borrowed money to attend Tulane Law School, where he crammed a three-year program into eight months and arranged to take a special bar examination. At age twenty-four Long was elected to the Louisiana Public Service Commission and over the next several years gained a reputation for his attacks on the oil and railroad companies that dominated state politics. Although Long cultivated a comical public image, adopting the name "Kingfish" and dubbing his opponents "Turkeyhead" or "Old Trashy Mouth," he was a keenly intelligent man and an astute politician.

In 1928 Long became governor, and even after his election to the Senate two years later he continued to rule Louisiana very much as he pleased. He dominated the legislature, curbed the press, and built a disciplined political machine. When people protested that he was violating the state constitution, Long replied, "I'm the Constitution around here now." Yet for every person who resented Long's dictatorial manner, there were many others who benefited from his reign. He improved the public schools, provided free textbooks, and initiated evening classes for adults; he built new roads, bridges, and highways; he eliminated the poll tax and property taxes on the poor. These reforms broke down the isolation of the rural poor, provided voters with tangible evidence of his accomplishments, and created jobs for political supporters. Unlike most other southern politicians, Long did not appeal to white supremacist sentiment. Once he harshly denounced the leader of the Ku Klux Klan: "When I call him a son of a bitch I am not using profanity, but am referring to the circumstances of his birth."

His advocacy of the "Share Our Wealth" program made Long a figure of national prominence in the 1930s. The government, he insisted, must "limit the size of the big men's fortune and guarantee some minimum to the fortune and comfort of the little man's family." To accomplish this, he proposed limiting individual wealth to $3 to $4 million, providing all citizens with a $5,000 homestead and a guaranteed annual income of $2,500, offering free education through the college level to all whose "mental ability and energy" qualified them, establishing a thirty-hour workweek, and financing generous old-age pensions through taxes on the rich. While this plan would not mean absolute equality, it would remove the most glaring inequalities. "So America would start again with millionaires, but with no multimillionaires or billionaires; we would start with some poor, but they wouldn't be so poor that they wouldn't have the comforts of life." In February 1934, Share Our Wealth clubs began forming; soon there were 27,000 claiming 4.7 million members. The movement's strength centered in Louisiana, Arkansas, and Mississippi.

The Share Our Wealth program went considerably beyond the Townsend plan. Long proposed a more sweeping change in economic relationships and assigned a more prominent role to the federal government than did Townsend. The Louisianan frankly advocated confiscating wealth in order to redistribute income. But in some respects the two resembled each other. Both Long and Townsend were charismatic leaders, both organized clubs that offered members a gratifying sense of personal involvement, and both promised a quick, certain path to good times. In addition, both appealed to those whom the New Deal had helped rather little. Long, who at first supported Roosevelt, broke with him decisively in 1935 on the grounds that the administration was proceeding too cautiously.

Roosevelt considered Long a veritable Pied Piper, leading people astray with spurious and impractical proposals. Nevertheless, in June 1935, the president moved somewhat closer to Long's position by asking Congress to impose high taxes on inherited wealth, corporate profits, and "very great individual incomes." When the president's message was read, Long declared, "I just wish to say 'Amen.'" Roosevelt's recommendations brought anguished cries from the business community, and by the time Congress finished watering it down, the Wealth Tax Act (1935) barely resembled Roosevelt's original proposal, much less Long's. Even as he borrowed a plank from the Share Our Wealth platform, the president attacked Long by denying him federal patronage, by encouraging the Treasury Department to investigate alleged financial wrongdoing in Louisiana, and by permitting his aides to speak their minds. "The

Senator from Louisiana has halitosis of the intellect," said Secretary of the Interior Harold Ickes; "that's presuming Emperor Long has an intellect."

None of this proved very effective. Then, in September 1935, a young doctor, Carl Austin Weiss, assassinated Long and was himself immediately killed by the senator's bodyguards. With its leader gone, the Share Our Wealth movement came under the control of Gerald L.K. Smith, a minister originally hired to organize the clubs. Smith, who had idolized Long (even wearing suits of clothes his mentor had discarded), appealed to similar hopes and exploited similar grievances. Smith cried, "Let's pull down these huge piles of gold until there shall be a real job, not a little old sow-belly, black-eyed pea job, but a real spending-money, beefsteak and gravy, Chevrolet, Ford in the garage, new suit, Thomas Jefferson, Jesus Christ, red, white, and blue job for every man!" By 1936 Smith, like Townsend, was prepared for a head-on clash with the administration. It came with the blessing of the "radio priest," Father Charles E. Coughlin.

THE RADIO PRIEST AND HIS FLOCK

Father Coughlin had been assigned to the parish of Royal Oak, Michigan, in 1926. There he conducted a Sunday-morning radio program, *The Golden Hour of the Little Flower*, which at first consisted of inspirational readings and devotional messages. But in the early 1930s, with the depression worsening, Coughlin turned to economic and social issues. As he did, his audience grew rapidly. Each week more than 10 million listeners tuned in Coughlin's sermons. After every broadcast he received hundreds of thousands of letters and thousands of dollars in contributions. Coughlin enjoyed unusual latitude in his remarks because he had organized his own radio network after a Columbia Broadcasting System attempt to censor him in 1931 and because he had the solid support of his superior, Bishop Michael James Gallagher of Detroit.

Coughlin's position in the Catholic Church went far toward explaining his popularity, but he also set forth economic proposals that, if sometimes vague, proved highly attractive. He wanted to reform the monetary system by increasing the amount of currency in circulation, remonetizing silver, eliminating the Federal Reserve Banks, and replacing interest-bearing government notes with non–interest-bearing ones. He also favored nationalizing "those public necessities which by their very nature are too important to be held in the control of private individuals," providing a "just and living annual wage" for all workers, and imposing heavy taxes on the wealthy. "Modern capitalism as we know it is not worth saving," Coughlin said, but capitalism with its abuses eliminated would be very much worth saving.

In 1933 Coughlin, then a staunch Roosevelt supporter, asserted that "the New Deal is Christ's deal." Yet during the next two years he became disillusioned with the president. Coughlin particularly resented Roosevelt's failure to accept monetary management as the key to recovery, his advocacy of U.S. membership in the World Court, and his opposition to refinancing farm mortgages by issuing millions of dollars in greenbacks. Late in 1934, following the example set by Long and Townsend, Coughlin created the National Union for Social Justice to lobby for his economic program. By mid-1936, having concluded somewhat inconsistently that the New Deal both "protects plutocrats and comforts Communists," Coughlin announced the formation of the Union Party. It quickly gained the support of Townsend and Smith. Coughlin expected the party's nominee—William Lemke of North Dakota—to receive 9 million votes, enough to throw the presidential election into the House of Representatives.

Father Charles Coughlin, advocate of social justice, making an impassioned speech, 1938.
(Time & Life Pictures/Getty Images)

During the campaign Coughlin accused "Franklin double-crossing Roosevelt" of "flirting with Communistic tendencies" and predicted that Roosevelt's reelection would mean "more bullet holes in the White House than you could count with an adding machine." This rhetoric, however, failed to save the Union Party from a humiliating defeat. It received 892,000 votes, fewer than 2 percent of the total. In part this showing resulted from the party's inability to get on the ballot in several important states or to run a full slate of candidates for local office. In addition, Lemke proved a singularly uninspiring figure. Nor could Coughlin, Smith, and Townsend agree on policy and procedure. Expediency had made them allies, but a good deal of rivalry and suspicion remained. Millions of people who were attracted to economic panaceas would not back a hopeless third-party venture. The kind of support Coughlin and the others enjoyed could not be translated into votes on Election Day.

Dismayed by the outcome, Coughlin canceled future radio broadcasts, but his retirement proved brief. By 1938 he was back on the air with sermons that had taken on a distinctly new tone. Coughlin had employed nativist themes in the past, but never so prominently. He insisted that a conspiracy of international Jewish bankers threatened America. His magazine, *Social Justice*, carried the *Protocols of Zion* (a forgery depicting an alleged Jewish conspiracy to take over the world), termed Hitler's Germany "an innocent victim of a sacred war declared against her nine years ago by the Jews," and honored Benito Mussolini as "Man of the Week." In July 1938 Coughlin founded the Christian Front to combat communists and Jews. It prepared a Christian Index listing merchants who had pledged to patronize and employ other Christians as a means of curbing Jewish economic power. Coughlin, who had formerly denounced the anti-Catholic nativism of the Ku Klux Klan, ended by stirring up a vicious anti-Semitism.

THE POPULAR FRONT

During the 1930s the American Communist Party gained a fairly wide influence, certainly wider than its membership (which hovered around 50,000) or its voting strength (which fell from 103,000 in the 1932 presidential election to 80,000 in 1936) would indicate. Party members controlled several large Congress of Industrial Organizations unions, including the United Electrical Workers and the Mine, Mill, and Smelter Workers; held responsible positions in the National Labor Relations Board and other government agencies; and gained a firm footing in the American Labor Party in New York State, as well as in other political organizations. Communist doctrines won a large audience among intellectuals. In 1932, for example, fifty-three prominent writers and artists—including Sherwood Anderson, Erskine Caldwell, John Dos Passos, Sidney Hook, Lincoln Steffens, and Edmund Wilson—endorsed the party's candidates, William Z. Foster and James Ford, explaining, "As responsible intellectual workers we have aligned ourselves with the frankly revolutionary Communist Party, the party of the workers."

Nevertheless, the 1930s hardly deserve to be called "the Red decade." The great majority of Americans remained hostile to communism, and most who joined the movement did so only briefly. The party consisted of a small cadre that remained steadfastly loyal and others who entered and left as through a revolving door. Surely one reason for this was the party's subservience to the Soviet Union. American Communist Party leaders consistently followed policies that conformed to Russian interests, not because they were hired Russian agents but because they believed that the needs of workers in America were identical with those of workers in the Soviet Union. They equated virtue with the Russian system and either rejected or discounted evidence of Stalinist terrorism. With every shift in party doctrine, those who could not adjust departed.

In the early 1930s, seeing themselves as revolutionaries, communists in the United States repudiated halfway measures and called for a dictatorship of the proletariat. They branded Franklin Roosevelt "an abject tool of Wall Street" and condemned the New Deal for striving "to hold the workers in industrial slavery." But in the summer of 1935, the party dramatically modified its approach. By then Stalin had identified Nazi Germany as the greatest potential danger. Accordingly, he urged communists to join liberals and socialists in an antifascist popular front. Communists in the United States worked diligently to soften their image. Their leader, Earl Browder, announced, "Communism is 20th-century Americanism." The party's view of the New Deal underwent a similar transformation. Communists praised Roosevelt as a Progressive and backed almost every one of his proposals.

These popular front tactics exacerbated divisions within the Socialist Party. In 1935 Browder invited socialist leader Norman Thomas to a debate in Madison Square Garden, with the proceeds going to the socialists. When Thomas accepted, old-guard socialists unjustifiably feared that he was ready to collaborate with the communists. By 1936 thousands had deserted the Socialist Party, whose membership dropped below 20,000. Thomas rejected other such overtures and, unlike Browder, kept up a steady attack on the New Deal. Roosevelt, he said, was trying to "cure tuberculosis with cough drops."

To those who urged him to support Roosevelt in the 1936 presidential election, Thomas replied, "The way to get Socialism is to proclaim the Socialist message, not to declare a moratorium on it during an election campaign." But his vote—which fell from 903,000 in 1932 to 187,000 in 1936—indicated that the New Deal had neutralized the Socialist Party's appeal. Thomas confessed as much. "Roosevelt did not carry out the Socialist platform," he declared, "unless he carried it out on a stretcher."

Before the signing of the Nazi-Soviet pact, Roosevelt did not consider domestic communism a major threat. Germany reached that agreement with Russia on August 23, 1939, and went to war with Great Britain and France in September. While the pact remained in force—until June 1941, when Hitler invaded the Soviet Union—communists in the United States completely reversed themselves, scrapping the idea of an antifascist popular front. They opposed American aid to the Allies, claiming that Great Britain and France were imperialist nations. They similarly opposed the buildup of defense industries, on occasion calling strikes to disrupt work in aircraft plants. Communists reverted to denouncing Roosevelt as "the leader and organizer of all reactionary forces in the country." The Communist Party paid a heavy price for this turnabout. Thousands of members, attracted by the popular front ideology, deserted the party in disillusionment. Many liberals who had cooperated with communists considered the party's justification of the Nazi-Soviet pact a symptom of its moral bankruptcy. Finally, the party's stance contributed to a Red Scare that swept the country after 1939.

BLACK AMERICANS AND THE NEW DEAL

"People is hollerin' 'bout hard times, tell me what it all about," wailed a 1937 blues recording; "hard times don't worry me, I was broke when it first started out." In singing the blues, surely, people were laughing to keep from crying. The depression had a devastating impact on African-Americans, even on those who had never shared in the prosperity of the 1920s. Southern black farmers in the early 1930s scraped by on $300 a year. Of those employed in agriculture, four of every five did not own their land but worked as sharecroppers, tenant farmers, or wage hands. Lacking any security, they often lost their homes as hard times settled over the countryside. In the cities conditions were worse. The unemployment rate for blacks was from 30 percent to 60 percent higher than for whites, in part because of bias in hiring, but also because the jobs blacks had held in service occupations were often eliminated. Industries employing large numbers of blacks—such as building construction and bituminous coal—came to a virtual standstill. Desperate whites sometimes resorted to violence to displace blacks. On the Illinois Central Railroad, white firemen terrorized blacks, killing ten of them, to get their jobs. Whites also began taking jobs that blacks had formerly held as elevator operators, hospital attendants, cooks, waiters, bellhops, maids, and chauffeurs.

To people surviving at a subsistence level, the Roosevelt administration offered a ray of hope, primarily in the form of federal relief. Before 1933, localities administering relief often rejected black applicants; but the New Deal reversed this pattern. In 1935 nearly 30 percent of all black families were receiving some form of aid, and in certain cities the figure approached 50 percent. Proportionately, three times as many blacks as whites were on relief. New Deal programs sought to ensure fair treatment. The Works Progress Administration (WPA) enabled hundreds of thousands of African-Americans to weather the depression. Blacks accounted for more than two-thirds of the workers on its rolls in Norfolk, Virginia, where blacks made up less than one-third of the population. The Public Works Administration took a pioneering step by introducing nondiscrimination clauses, under which a contractor had to pay black workers a fixed proportion of the company payroll, based on the number of blacks in the labor force. Although other New Deal agencies often discriminated, on balance blacks received a share of federal assistance in proportion to their numbers, if not their need.

If the Roosevelt administration came to the rescue of jobless blacks, it proved less responsive to demands for legal equality and social justice. Little in Roosevelt's background suggested any such concern. He had served under the segregationist Wilson administration in the archsegregationist Navy Department; he made his second home in Warm Springs, Georgia, and apparently never questioned local mores; he accepted John Nance "Cactus Jack" Garner, a conservative Texan, as his running mate in 1932 and 1936. As president, Roosevelt maintained that economic recovery, not civil rights, would most effectively aid the largest number of blacks. He believed that New Deal legislation would be lost without the support of southern Democrats, who headed important congressional committees, and he recognized that the issue of civil rights for African-Americans was potentially a source of great friction within his party. Committed to a gradualist approach, Roosevelt reasoned that only education would finally eradicate racial prejudice. "We must do this thing stride by stride," he said.

Roosevelt took few such strides, however, during his first and second terms of office. Despite the angry protests of civil rights groups, New Deal programs in the South followed Jim Crow lines. The Tennessee Valley Authority segregated its work crews, hired only unskilled black laborers, and set up a model village that barred blacks. The Civilian Conservation Corps maintained segregated work camps. The National Recovery Administration, which in theory prohibited wage differentials based on race, in practice left loopholes whereby blacks could be paid less. The Agricultural Adjustment Administration's acreage reduction program led to the eviction of thousands of black tenant farmers. The Justice Department refused to prosecute lynchers under a federal kidnapping statute on the grounds that the victims were not taken across state lines for financial gain. Roosevelt branded lynching a "vile form of collective murder," but refused to support an antilynching bill that provided for a federal trial if states failed to prosecute, specified prison terms for members of lynch mobs, and made counties responsible for damages. In 1937, after a mob in Mississippi had set two blacks afire with a blowtorch, the House passed the measure. It was filibustered to death in the Senate in 1938 without protest from the administration.

Given this record, the president won a truly astonishing amount of support from African-Americans. In 1932 nearly three-fourths of them voted Republican; in 1936, more than three-fourths voted Democratic, and the percentage increased in the years that followed. New Deal

Mary McLeod Bethune. *(Library of Congress)*

relief programs—which primarily aided northern and urban blacks, who could vote, rather than southern and rural blacks, who could not—partially, but not fully, explain this shift. Certainly the president benefited when compared with his predecessor, Herbert Hoover, who, unlike Roosevelt, never even verbally condemned lynching. In addition, Roosevelt offered important government positions to such prominent blacks as Mary McLeod Bethune and Robert C. Weaver. Eleanor Roosevelt and other New Dealers spoke up forcibly on the subject of racial injustice. Partly because of his wife's prestige in the black community, Franklin Roosevelt received credit for the New Deal's achievements while escaping blame for its shortcomings.

Developments during the 1930s subjected the National Association for the Advancement of Colored People (NAACP), and the civil rights strategy it advocated, to a severe challenge. The NAACP had assumed that civil rights could be secured by lobbying in Congress and by arguing before the courts. Two events during the 1930s, however, weakened confidence in the possibility of ending Jim Crow through political and constitutional means. The first was the

HALLIE FLANAGAN
AND THE FEDERAL THEATER PROJECT

Hallie Flanagan, director of the WPA Federal Theater Project. *(Library of Congress)*

In 1935, as part of its expanded relief program, the Roosevelt administration initiated various projects to aid unemployed writers, artists, and actors. To head the Federal Theater Project, Harry Hopkins selected Hallie Flanagan, whom he had first met while both were undergraduates at Grinnell College in Iowa. She eventually became director of experimental theater at Vassar College, where she supervised some of the more imaginative productions of the early 1930s.

Under her guidance, the Federal Theater Project employed an average of 10,000 people a year for four years. Many of its plays had a frank social message. The "living newspaper" format, which vividly documented current issues, was well suited for this purpose. *Triple A Plowed Under* (1936) called for a New Deal for farmers, *Power* (1937) advocated a greater measure of consumer control over public utilities, and *One Third of a Nation* (1938) exposed the poverty and filth of big-city slums. Some productions met with huge popular and critical acclaim. A dramatization of Sinclair Lewis's *It Can't Happen Here* played to 275,000 people in four months; it grossed $80,000, even though the average ticket was priced at thirty cents. The Federal Theater provided new opportunities for black performers, who staged a jazz version of *The Mikado* and, under Orson Welles's direction, a version of *Macbeth* set in Haiti during the Napoleonic era.

Throughout its career the Federal Theater faced difficult problems. One concerned the competing demands of relief and art. Some unemployed people who clearly deserved assistance claimed to be "actors" even though they had little talent, and Flanagan sometimes felt obliged to give them jobs. In addition, disputes arose over the nature of the productions. There was built-in tension between the desire to appeal to a mass audience (particularly since public response was a means of justifying further appropriations) and the desire to stage avant-garde works that appealed to the actors' and directors' own aesthetic sensibilities.

There was yet another hard question: as a government agency, funded by the taxpayers,

The WPA Federal Theater Project production of *It Can't Happen Here*, New York, 1935.
(Franklin D. Roosevelt Presidential Library and Museum, Hyde Park, New York)

how far could the Federal Theater legitimately go in advocating controversial views? Some critics denounced it for becoming a "veritable hotbed of un-American activities," and others alleged that its performances were obscene. Hostile congressmen snickered at such titles as *The Bishop Misbehaves* and *Old Captain Romeo's Four Wives*. Of *A New Kind of Love,* one Republican remarked, "I wonder what that can be. It smacks of the Soviets." In 1939, Congress killed the Federal Theater Project. Hallie Flanagan left to become a dean at Smith College.

The federal government did not again undertake a large-scale program of support for the performing arts until 1965, when Congress created the National Endowment for the Arts (NEA). Although it funded many popular programs, the NEA eventually ran into problems not unlike those encountered by the Federal Theater. By the 1990s, conservative congressmen assailed the NEA for funding exhibits by such artists as Andres Serrano and Robert Mapplethorpe, whose work, critics claimed, was "sickeningly violent, sexually explicit, homoerotic, anti-religious and nihilistic." The beleaguered agency sought to appease outraged conservatives without alienating the artists, writers, and photographers it was supposed to encourage. In 1996 Congress cut its funding nearly in half, forcing the agency to scale down its activities.

Web Links

http://memory.loc.gov/ammem/fedtp/ftbrwn00.html
An essay by Lorraine Brown, with links to articles and scripts.

http://memory.loc.gov/ammem/fedtp/fthome.html
Nearly 1,000 slides of posters, sets, and costume designs.

failure of the antilynching bill, which the NAACP had helped draft and to which it devoted a considerable portion of its time, money, and energy from 1935 to 1940. A second event that eroded the gradualist approach was the Supreme Court's decision in *Grovey v. Townsend* (1935). The Court held that the Democratic Party in Texas—and by extension elsewhere in the South—could exclude blacks from membership and thereby bar them from participating in primaries. The white primary did not violate the Fourteenth Amendment, the Court ruled, since the Democratic Party was a voluntary political association whose actions did not involve discrimination by a state. The decision effectively disfranchised blacks since in one-party areas the only meaningful contests occurred in primaries. The closed primary was an even more effective deterrent to voting than the poll tax or the literacy test.

The NAACP above all prized the goal of integration, yet during the 1930s this too came under fire. Led by W.E.B. DuBois, a number of black intellectuals advocated what one termed "the conscious development of nationalistic sentiment." DuBois, whose stand led to his resignation from the NAACP, continued to oppose forced segregation but saw distinct advantages in voluntary segregation. He asserted, "It is the race-conscious black man cooperating together in his own institutions and movements who will eventually emancipate the colored race." In his autobiography, *Dusk of Dawn* (1940), DuBois described his disenchantment with the view that education would wipe out prejudice. Convinced that racism was rooted in the subconscious and reinforced by economic self-interest, DuBois thought it pointless for a black minority to plead for justice from a white majority. Instead, blacks should set up their own institutions—schools, churches, hospitals, theaters—and a largely autonomous economy founded on socialist principles. DuBois's doctrine, although in some respects reminiscent of Marcus Garvey's, appealed to intellectuals rather than the masses, did not contemplate a return to Africa, and combined economic radicalism with racial nationalism.

DuBois's vision of a cooperative commonwealth never approached realization, as indeed it could not, given the lack of economic resources in the black community. The nearest any sizable group of blacks came to attaining perfect security was in the religious "heavens" of George Baker, who went by the name of Father Divine. In 1933 Divine, a preacher in Brooklyn and Long Island for more than a decade, moved to Harlem, where he attracted a huge following. Divine opened heavens—dormitory-like arrangements where his disciples lived and received adequate food and clothing as long as they worshipped their benefactor (and promised to abstain from sexual relations). His followers believed that Divine was God and that he and they were immortal. Those who died or became seriously ill were said to have stopped believing. Divine, the vast majority of whose followers were black but who also appealed to some whites, created a world in which racial conflict, indeed racial differentiation, no longer existed. He referred only to "people of the darker complexion" and "people of the lighter complexion." The names his disciples adopted similarly revealed their search for order and harmony: "Quiet Dove," "Perfect Love," "Sweet Music," and "Keep on Smiling." For thousands of blacks beset by racial, economic, or family troubles, Divine provided a way out, and many remained steadfast in their faith until his death in 1965. During the depression years, when millions followed political messiahs, it was hardly surprising that some turned to a man who claimed he was the True Messiah.

WOMEN AND FAMILIES FACE THE DEPRESSION

"Where the folkways and old patterns of conduct are continued—that it is a man's job to support his family—husbands have been nagged and harassed to desperation," a welfare agency officer reported in 1931. "The degradation, the sheer fear and panic . . . have eaten into men's souls." "I did what I had to do," a housewife recalled of the depression years. "I think hard times is harder on a man." "I was going with someone when the depression hit," an unmarried woman remembered. "Suddenly he was laid off. It hit him like a ton of bricks and he just disappeared." "I feel like I was falling down a long dark shaft that has no end," a teenager told his caseworker. "It is both economically unfair and socially unjust to expect me to continue to support my family."

The depression's impact on family life became a subject of widespread concern. Familiar patterns of courtship and marriage seemed to fall apart. The marriage rate fell in 1929 and did not start to rise until 1934. Often marriages were postponed until hard times had passed or simply never occurred. The divorce rate declined as income fell, but desertion increased. "Mr. Raparka asked [his wife] for money to go to New York in search of a job," sociologist Wight Bakke reported in *Citizens Without Work*. "He has not been heard of since." The birthrate, which had been dropping throughout the 1920s, plunged even further. It fell from 21.3 births per thousand persons in 1930 to 18.4 in 1933. Contraception became more popular, birth control clinics multiplied, and in 1936 a federal court decision made it legal for doctors to distribute contraceptive information and devices, except where prohibited by state law. The demands of the Great Depression appeared to have succeeded where birth control reformers had not.

Case studies revealed that new patterns of domestic life developed within families that had suddenly slipped downward in economic status. In some cases, where relationships had always been stable, families drew into themselves, curtailing outside activities. "Family members have to do things with and for each other," Eleanor Roosevelt wrote in 1933, "and the result is that the clan spirit grows." In other cases, clan spirit disintegrated. When unemployment struck, disconcerting authority shifts often occurred at home. Depression affected male heads of household who lost their jobs. "Working around the house was not all profit to the unemployed man," sociologist Eli Ginzburg reported. "By taking on feminine duties he widened the breach between the old life and the new. His failure was underlined by the transgression of sex boundaries." In study after study, case analysts described the transformation of former "breadwinners" from family head into "just another member of the family." Women seemed less affected when family income dropped, since they retained much the same roles they had held before the Great Depression struck.

In *Middletown* (Muncie, Indiana), sociologists Helen and Robert Lynd reported, unemployed men hung about the street, lost their sense of time, and dawdled helplessly. At home, however, "the women's world remained largely intact and the round of cooking, housecleaning, and mending became if anything more absorbing." Domestic routines took on new significance, especially when family survival depended on housewives' frugality. "Making Do" became an important 1930s adage. Women traded depression recipes, restyled old clothes, took in boarders, ran kitchen beauty parlors, and started other household businesses. Older children sometimes contributed to family income if they could find jobs. But wives were most likely to become the family's major new wage earners.

Women's entry into the depression labor force was hardly popular. Once jobs became scarce, Americans voiced opposition to wives who worked outside the home—and implicitly deprived a male family head of income. Congress prohibited more than one family member from taking a federal service job. State and local governments rejected married women who applied for government posts. In 1931, three out of four school boards refused to hire wives as teachers and many dismissed women teachers who married. The American Federation of Labor urged employers not to hire women who had working husbands. Public opinion surveys, such as the new Gallup poll, echoed such injunctions; respondents declared that wives of employed men should remain at home.

But despite continued pressure against married wage earners, women were less likely to be unemployed than men and were more likely to take jobs for the first time. In the 1930s, the number of workingwomen rose 25 percent, and the majority of new workers were married women, precisely those who were urged to remain at home. One reason for this unexpected development was that opportunities for female employment did not contract as much as those for men. The depression's worst impact was on heavy industry—autos, steel, and mining— where few women were employed. The sectors that employed many women, however, such as sales, service, and clerical work, were less affected and tended to recover more quickly. Most important, men did not seek jobs in what were considered women's fields. The sexual division of labor that usually handicapped women on the labor market suddenly offered a new measure of protection.

Such protection did not extend to black women workers, whose unemployment rates were higher than those of any other group; it did not affect applicants for federal work relief, where male heads of household were favored; and it rarely helped professional women, whose aspirations were now limited. Career ambitions faded, and so did feminist demands for equal rights and equal opportunity. Still, women's employment record reversed the expectations of depression-era Americans. Denunciations of the working wife were counteracted by both family need and, in some cases, new advantages on the employment market. As a result, in the 1930s, women entered the labor force at twice the rate of men.

Women also played new roles in social welfare and political life. During the depression, new welfare agencies opened up at all levels of government and social workers were suddenly in demand. Several women with expertise in social welfare assumed high-level federal government posts. The leading example was Labor Secretary Frances Perkins, the first woman cabinet member, who had a long career in social welfare. Since the Progressive Era, Perkins had worked in settlement houses and for the New York Consumer's League. In 1928, she had been appointed state industrial commissioner by Franklin Roosevelt. As a cabinet member, she did not expect "to gain anything materially," Eleanor Roosevelt explained in 1933, but "to render a public service to . . . the workingmen and women in their families."

Similar experience in social welfare was evident in the careers of almost all the New Deal's high-level women appointees, such as Florence Allen, the first woman appointed to the federal court of appeals; Ellen Woodward, who headed women's work relief projects under the Civil Works Administration; Mary Anderson, head of the federal Women's Bureau; and Mary W. Dewson, head of the Women's Division of the Democratic National Committee and later a member of the Social Security Board. Like Frances Perkins, these new officeholders considered themselves social reformers more than feminists. Eleanor Roosevelt, who campaigned for women's appointments, promoted their careers. "The steady increase of women's influence," she wrote to a friend, "tends to ameliorate bad social conditions." Such influence waned after 1936, when New Deal receptivity to reform dwindled. But the Roosevelt administration had given women more high-level government jobs than had any previous administration. It also propelled into view the most politically sophisticated woman reformer ever to reside in the White House.

During the 1930s, Eleanor Roosevelt capitalized on a decade of experience in Democratic Party campaigns, the League of Women Voters, and other women's organizations, such as the Women's Trade Union League. Increasingly influential in New Deal politics, she became a model of activism. In 1933, she began holding her innovative weekly White House press conferences, limited to women reporters. She also defended the interests of unemployed women, supported the establishment of summer work-relief camps for women, campaigned for the end of Washington's alley slums, worked on the federal homestead program, and aided thousands of correspondents who wrote to her in an unprecedented volume of mail. This pace of activity only increased. As political strategist and presidential adviser, Eleanor Roosevelt helped organize the 1936 campaign, served as a spokeswoman for the disadvantaged, and emerged as a forthright liberal, often taking stands to the left of her husband. By defending black pressure groups, pacifists, and the National Youth Congress, she created her own constituency and simultaneously relieved President Roosevelt of some pressure from the left. Finally, whether visiting coalmines, testifying to Congress about migrant labor, or campaigning against racial discrimination, she was constantly in public view. By the end of the 1930s, through her press conferences, radio talks, and popular syndicated newspaper column, "My Day," Eleanor Roosevelt had become one of the most prominent figures in public life. Although her role was controversial, her causes were ceaselessly publicized by women reporters, who commended her "instinct for civic and social reform" and credited her with "humanizing the New Deal."

THE CONSERVATIVE RESPONSE

There were, of course, many Americans who did not sympathize with the New Deal and who were distinctly unimpressed by either Franklin or Eleanor Roosevelt. The business community constituted one important source of opposition, although sentiment in the business community was never monolithic. Several industrialists endorsed Roosevelt's policies, but organizations such as the National Association of Manufacturers and the Chamber of Commerce consistently fought the New Deal, particularly after 1935. By then, speakers at the association's meetings were talking about the need to rid Washington of "economic crackpots, social reformers, labor demagogues and political racketeers." These critics charged that deficit spending undermined the nation's credit, that the tax on undistributed corporate profits curbed initiative, that the growth of executive power endangered individual liberties, and that the Wagner Act weighted the scales too heavily on labor's side. Roosevelt stirred up class antagonism, business executives complained, by his unfair references to "economic royalists" who sought control of the government for selfish purposes.

The president believed that business critics failed to perceive the true intent, and effect, of his policies. He compared himself to one who jumped off a pier to save a rich gentleman from drowning; at first the gentleman was grateful, but he later complained bitterly that his silk hat was lost. Whether or not the New Deal rescued the capitalist system, it certainly enabled business to make higher profits than it had under Hoover. Despite all the fuss about fiscal irresponsibility, Roosevelt reluctantly turned to deficit spending as a last resort when nothing else seemed to work. Nor did the New Deal redistribute wealth. The share of disposable income held by the rich did not change significantly from 1933 to 1939. Taxes, while higher than in the past, were hardly crushing. Late in the decade they ranged from 4 percent on incomes of $10,000 to 32 percent on incomes of $100,000. "It is the same old story of the failure of those who have property to realize that I am the best friend the profit system ever had, even though I add my denunciation of unconscionable profits," Roosevelt wrote.

In 1934 conservatives created the American Liberty League to mobilize public sentiment against the New Deal. Over the next two years the league enrolled 125,000 members, spent $1 million, and distributed 5 million pieces of literature. In order to appear nonpartisan, it recruited several prominent Democrats. The American Liberty League formulated an essentially conservative indictment of the New Deal. It denounced Roosevelt as a dictator, although it had difficulty deciding whether he more nearly resembled a communist or a fascist. The league held that the welfare state aided the improvident and unfit at the expense of the hardworking and virtuous and was therefore immoral. It exploited popular reverence for the Constitution and the Supreme Court. Roosevelt's sweeping triumph in the 1936 election, however, discredited the league, which had found itself in the position of insisting that the people break sharply with the practices of the past four years and dismantle the welfare state. Roosevelt, by contrast, could promise continuity and stability. Only the initiatives he took in 1937, especially his plan to enlarge the Supreme Court, gave conservatives another chance.

⌈ "COURT PACKING" ⌉

At the time of his second inauguration, Franklin Roosevelt seemed to stand at the pinnacle of his political career. Yet his second term witnessed a sharp decline in New Deal fortunes. In some ways, the very size of his congressional majorities—the House contained 331 Democrats and 90 Republicans, the Senate 76 Democrats and 16 Republicans—encouraged factionalism and discord. Also, relatively large numbers of Democrats were elected in 1936 from safe districts (that is, by a margin of more than 5 percent) and were therefore less responsive to the wishes of party leaders. But Roosevelt's problem stemmed less from the composition of Congress than from what he wanted it to do. This became apparent in February 1937, when he unveiled his plan to reform the Supreme Court. Asserting that the Court carried too heavy a workload, the president proposed to add an additional justice for each one who did not retire at the age of seventy. A maximum of six new positions could be created, and the Court would revert to a smaller size upon the death or retirement of an elderly member.

The president took this stand chiefly because the Court had struck down crucial reform legislation. It had ruled against the National Recovery Administration and the Agricultural Adjustment Administration, and in June 1936, by a narrow 5-to-4 margin, it agreed that a New York minimum-wage law violated the due process clause of the Fourteenth Amendment. Roosevelt believed that the same narrow reasoning would lead the Court to invalidate the Wagner Act and the Social Security Act, both of which were on the docket. It also appeared that federal regulation of wages and hours, another item on the New Deal agenda, would not pass the judges' scrutiny even if Congress approved it. Roosevelt believed that the four conservatives on the Court—Willis Van Devanter, George Sutherland, James McReynolds, and Pierce Butler—were busily reading their own political prejudices into the Constitution under a cloak of judicial impartiality.

The president's decision to make an issue of the justices' ages, when he really objected to their ideology, offended many, including eighty-year-old Justice Louis D. Brandeis. Yet in seeking to enlarge the Court, Roosevelt chose the only course that seemed feasible. He rejected the alternatives—constitutional amendments requiring a two-thirds vote of the Court in order to declare an act unconstitutional, permitting Congress to override Court decisions, or broadening the legislative authority to regulate the economy. Roosevelt knew that three-fourths of the state legislatures would never approve any of these proposals, and certainly not soon enough to help. Besides, in Roosevelt's view the Court, not the Constitution, needed changing.

The proposal triggered the most bitterly fought dispute of Roosevelt's presidency. Advocates said that the Supreme Court was already "packed" with reactionaries who were frustrating the popular desire for social reform as expressed in the election of 1936. There was nothing sacred about the number nine, they continued, for the Court's size had varied in the past. Legislation that affected millions of people should not stand or fall on the whim of a single judge. Opponents responded that the Court, far from obstructing the New Deal, had invalidated only a few measures, and badly drawn ones at that. Roosevelt had never received a mandate to pack the Court, since he had studiously avoided the subject during the campaign. Finally, they pointed out that Roosevelt's plan would set a dangerous precedent. If a liberal president could restructure the Court to suit his fancy today, what would stop a conservative president from doing the same thing tomorrow?

In the spring of 1937 the plan lost whatever momentum it had when the Court—largely because Justice Owen Roberts switched to the liberal side—upheld the Social Security Act and other vital reform measures. In *NLRB v. Jones and Laughlin*, the Court sustained the Wagner Act by a 5-to-4 vote. The majority implicitly overturned earlier decisions by holding that the commerce clause was indeed broad enough to cover federal regulation of manufacturing. In *West Coast Hotel Co. v. Parrish*, again by a one-vote margin, the Court approved state minimum-wage laws. Chief Justice Charles Evans Hughes asserted that "reasonable" regulation, adopted in the interests of the community, by definition fulfilled the Fourteenth Amendment's due process requirements. In May 1937 Justice Van Devanter's resignation gave Roosevelt his first Court appointment. The administration continued to back a compromise permitting the appointment of one additional justice each year for every member who reached the age of seventy-five. This seemed likely to pass because most senators assumed that Roosevelt would nominate their colleague, Majority Leader Joseph Robinson of Arkansas, to fill the first vacancy. In July Robinson died of a heart attack and the Senate quickly defeated the bill.

The Court debacle injured Roosevelt's standing with Congress and the public, although many who would have broken with him for other reasons merely used the episode as a convenient pretext. The struggle over the Court divided the Democratic Party by alienating a number of liberals, aroused widespread distrust of Roosevelt's leadership, and convinced Republicans that their best strategy was to maintain a discreet silence while Democrats battled among themselves. But Roosevelt did not come away empty-handed, for the Supreme Court in 1937 finally put its seal of approval on the New Deal. Roosevelt would appoint five justices during his second term—including Hugo Black, William O. Douglas, and Felix Frankfurter—and after they took their seats, judicial barriers to the welfare state came tumbling down.

THE WANING OF THE NEW DEAL

From Roosevelt's vantage point, administrative reform was hardly less important than judicial reform. In 1936 he had appointed a committee to study administrative management. It reported in January 1937, urging Congress to furnish the president with six assistants, expand the civil service system, improve fiscal management, and establish the National Resources Planning Board as a central agency to coordinate government programs. The committee also suggested creating two new cabinet positions (welfare and public works), changing the name of the Department of the Interior to the Department of Conservation, and giving the president broad authority to transfer agencies, including certain functions of the independent regulatory commissions. In this fashion the committee hoped to find a permanent home for New Deal agencies and provide a suitable administrative apparatus for the welfare state.

But reorganization provoked a storm of opposition when it came before Congress in the spring of 1938. Roosevelt's critics charged that the measure would clamp "one-man rule" on the nation and succeeded in frightening large numbers of people. After squeaking by the Senate, the bill went down to defeat in the House of Representatives when more than a hundred Democrats deserted the president. Congressmen had various reasons for opposing the measure, including a desire to reassert legislative prerogatives, placate pressure groups, and protect their existing channels of access to administrative agencies. The conflict over reorganization resembled the earlier one over the Supreme Court in that both measures failed to elicit support from a sizable constituency, opened Roosevelt to the charge of seeking dictatorial power, divided liberals, and led to stinging presidential defeats. In 1939 Congress passed a mild measure that enabled Roosevelt to establish the Executive Office of the President and to streamline the bureaucracy. But the sweeping changes he favored were not made.

Democratic opposition to Court reform and reorganization crossed sectional lines. But three other measures—relating to housing, wages and hours, and civil rights—divided the Democratic Party into rural and urban, northern and southern factions. The Wagner Housing Act (1937), which authorized expenditures of $500 million to aid the construction of low-cost units, passed only after southerners had extracted concessions limiting the appropriation, the number of dwellings to be built, and the cost per family. The Fair Labor Standards Act (1938) similarly catered to the South, which wished to protect its competitive position as a cheap labor market. The measure regulated child labor and established a minimum wage of forty cents per hour and a forty-hour workweek, but it exempted domestic workers and farm laborers and allowed regional wage differentials. The antilynching bill never had a chance against a Senate filibuster engineered by southern Democrats. Measures that appealed to the New Deal's northern, urban constituency won little support from rural and southern representatives.

The administration's response to the recession of 1937–1938 added to the disenchantment with reform. In the fall of 1937 the economy went into a tailspin. Over the next ten months, millions of people lost their jobs. The slump occurred primarily because the administration, in attempting to balance the budget, had cut expenditures sharply. Yet Roosevelt resisted new deficit spending. Unlike the Keynesians, who favored unbalanced budgets in slack periods, Roosevelt believed pump priming to be appropriate in 1933, "when the water had receded to the bottom of the well," but doubted its worth in 1938, "with the water within 25 or 30 percent of the top." Not until April, when it appeared that economic conditions would ruin the Democrats in the fall elections, did the president listen to advisers who favored additional spending.

He then asked Congress to authorize a $3.75 billion relief appropriation. But the damage had already been done. Those who had lost their jobs or whose businesses had failed blamed the Democrats, not the Republicans, and concluded that the time for further innovation was past.

The president suffered yet another reversal in his attempt to purge the Democratic Party in the 1938 primaries. Roosevelt fought unsuccessfully to unseat Senators Walter George of Georgia, Millard Tydings of Maryland, and Ellison D. "Cotton Ed" Smith of South Carolina. Many southerners appeared to resent the president's intrusion into local affairs, while those benefiting most from New Deal relief programs and presumably most sympathetic to the president—blacks and poor whites—hardly participated in Democratic primaries. Opinion polls indicated that even among the unemployed and those on relief a bare majority disliked the White House's intervention. The purge claimed only one victim. John O'Connor of New York City, chair of the House Rules Committee, was defeated by a local politician friendly to the New Deal. In the November elections Republicans went on to win a smashing victory: they gained eighty-one seats in the House and eight in the Senate. Since all Democratic losses took place in the North and West, southerners emerged in a much stronger position. For the first time, Roosevelt could not form a majority without the help of some Republicans or southern Democrats.

Congress assembled in January 1939 and wasted little time in disposing of the president's program. To demonstrate its resentment at what it judged the attempted politicization of relief, Congress passed the Hatch Act (1939), prohibiting all government employees except a few high-ranking executive branch officials from engaging in political campaigns. The House abruptly cut off funds for the Federal Theater Project, which, because most of its activities centered in a few large cities, was highly vulnerable. The tax on undistributed profits, which the business community bitterly resented, was repealed outright. Congress also refused to increase expenditures for public housing. When the administration requested $3.86 billion for self-liquidating public works projects, the Senate trimmed the amount substantially, and the House voted not even to consider it. Recognizing how far the pendulum had swung, Roosevelt became more cautious. He opposed efforts to expand federal contributions to the Social Security program in order to equalize benefits, disapproved proposals for additional deficit spending, and withheld support from a national health bill that would have provided aid for maternity and child care, hospital construction, and "general programs of medical care."

NATIVISM AND THE APPROACH OF WAR

In the period from 1937 to 1941—years marked first by economic dislocation at home and then by international tension abroad—the United States experienced a sharp upsurge in nativist sentiment. This affected the New Deal because in the minds of some people the Roosevelt administration was playing into the hands of the very groups that seemed to pose the gravest danger—communists, Jews, and labor agitators. Charges that the president had surrounded himself with dangerous advisers and had embraced an alien ideology were by no means new, but after 1937 they were voiced more frequently and accepted more widely. By 1940 the administration itself had grown concerned enough to crack down sharply on suspected subversives. But it did not succeed in quelling popular fears.

In 1937 workers in the Congress of Industrial Organizations adopted radical tactics to gain traditional goals of union recognition and improved conditions. Labor's new weapon,

Members of the nascent United Auto Workers (UAW) union during a sit-down strike in the General Motors Fisher Body Plant in Flint, Michigan. *(Sheldon Dick/Getty Images)*

the sit-down strike, terrified property-conscious Americans. No fewer than 477 such strikes, involving 400,000 workers, took place in 1937, the most important of which was the General Motors sit-down in Flint, Michigan, in January. Most Americans assumed correctly that the union's occupation of a factory violated the law, but concluded erroneously that the automobile workers were inspired by revolutionary intent. Two out of every three people favored outlawing sit-down strikes and employing force against the union. "Armed insurrection—defiance of law, order and duly elected authority is spreading like wildfire," protested one group of citizens. Because Roosevelt refused to call out federal troops to evict the strikers, he was accused of cringing before the forces of anarchy and disorder.

With the outbreak of World War II in September 1939, Roosevelt became worried about the possibility of subversion by fascist agents or by communists (who were then defending the Nazi-Soviet pact). Congress and the administration outdid each other in tracking down potentially disloyal groups. In March 1940, Roosevelt approved the fingerprinting of all aliens applying for visas as temporary visitors, and two months later he authorized the use of wiretaps against anyone "suspected of subversive activities." In June Congress passed the Smith Act, which required aliens to register and made it a crime to conspire to teach or advocate the violent overthrow of the government. Congress also required all political organizations subject to foreign control to register with the attorney general. The government prosecuted

Communist Party leader Earl Browder on the technicality of using a fraudulent passport; he received an unprecedented four-year jail sentence.

At the same time, Roosevelt increasingly shifted his emphasis from domestic reform to foreign policy and national defense. By 1940 his chief legislative goal was to obtain approval for assisting Great Britain and France. This, given isolationist strength in Congress, required the backing of southern Democrats. As one conservative southerner put it, the president had begun "cultivating us in a very nice way." Similarly, Roosevelt's interest in readying plans for economic mobilization in the event of war moved him to mend fences with the business community. In August 1939 he appointed a War Resources Board composed mainly of representatives of big business and headed by Edward Stettinius of United States Steel. Roosevelt, however, came to fear that the board's proposals might dilute his own authority in wartime and did not make them public. In May 1940, when he set up a National Defense Advisory Commission to expedite production, he again turned to Stettinius and to William S. Knudsen of General Motors. By 1940 the process of repairing relations with the business community and southern Democrats alike was well under way.

By 1940 the agenda of American politics had been transformed, with foreign policy replacing reform as the central issue. The presidential campaign that year reflected this change. The international crisis persuaded Roosevelt to seek a third term and gave the Democrats an excuse to nominate him. The Republicans chose Wendell Willkie, who, while a critic of many New Deal policies, accepted much of the welfare state. Moreover, as a spokesman for the internationalist wing of the Republican Party, Willkie endorsed the main outlines of Roosevelt's foreign policy, refusing, for example, to make issues of aid to Great Britain or the peacetime draft. The tense international situation undoubtedly worked to the president's advantage, although Willkie did surprisingly well with 22.3 million votes to Roosevelt's 27.2 million. But during the campaign, Roosevelt made his most famous and, given the events of the following year, his most unfortunate promise: "I shall say it again and again and again: Your boys are not going to be sent into any foreign wars."

CHAPTER EIGHT

1929–1941

The Big Breakdown—
The United States and the World

A small boat rescues a seaman from the USS *West Virginia* at Pearl Harbor, Hawaii, December 7, 1941. *(Library of Congress)*

The Great Depression ripped apart the treaty agreements so carefully built during the 1920s to preserve world peace, for the pacts had utterly depended on a smoothly working economic system. The collapse of 1929 not only destroyed the political arrangements, but it created such chaos and disillusionment that fascists and radical leftists replaced moderate governments in Germany, Spain, and Japan. Extremists did not grasp control in the United States, however. In a remarkable performance, Americans continued their allegiance to the traditional economic-political system, even though it was producing the most miserable and inhumane conditions in the nation's history. Franklin D. Roosevelt's foreign policy mirrored that moderation. But the United States started down the road to Pearl Harbor between 1929 and 1932. FDR was unable to find an exit from that road.

"MAD DOGS" AND ENGLISHMEN:
THE MANCHURIAN CRISIS OF 1931–1932

In June 1931 President Hoover tried to stabilize Western money markets by suggesting a one-year moratorium (postponement) on the collection of reparations from Germany and war debts from France and Great Britain. "Perhaps the most daring statement I ever thought of issuing," as Hoover recalled, was too daring for the French. They insisted on keeping the hatchet of reparations above German heads. When Paris stalled, the president's policy collapsed. In July the German banking system came apart, then Great Britain's economic system went into a tailspin, the French government fell, and panic struck Europe and the United States. In Asia, Japan took its first step toward World War II by invading Manchuria.

The Japanese had been especially hard-hit by the depression. Their economy depended on overseas markets, which by 1931 had largely disappeared. Exports to the vital U.S. market, for example, dropped 30 percent in 1930. Japan's liberal government, like liberal regimes elsewhere, was undercut and then destroyed by the collapse. By early 1931 dynamic political factions led by ambitious militarists demanded that Japan find its salvation not in the sick Western trading community, but in its own empire. Since 1905 Tokyo had controlled and developed South Manchuria. North Manchuria, however, was coming under the domination of Chiang Kai-shek's new regime in China. Chiang and a rapidly multiplying Chinese population even endangered Japanese control of South Manchuria. In September 1931 the Japanese militarists took affairs into their own hands. After a brief skirmish between Chinese and Japanese troops along the South Manchurian railway, Japan's army launched a full-scale invasion of North Manchuria. Tokyo had bloodily repudiated its pledge at the Washington Naval Conference to maintain the open door.

Hoover and Secretary of State Henry Stimson were trapped. Throughout the 1920s America's Far Eastern policy had depended on a cooperative Japan, particularly when the only alternatives as partners were a "revolutionary" China and the Soviet Union. Hoover privately remarked that he had some sympathy for the Japanese, for they faced a "Bolshevist Russia to the north, and a possible Bolshevist China" to the west. Some officials wanted Japan handled gently because it was holding back the Chinese tide. "The Chinese are altogether too cocky," the American ambassador in London told the Japanese ambassador. "What you people need to do is to give them a thoroughly good licking to teach them their place and then they will be willing to talk sense." In December 1931 Japan's militarists overthrew the civilian regime and accelerated the Manchurian offensive; yet nearly a year later Stimson, who knew that "the situation [in Japan] is in the hands of virtually mad dogs," urged a moderate response so that "the little group of militarists" could not "make us a bogey in the whole matter."

During the next ten years the United States single-handedly tried to protect its interests in the Far East. China was undependable, Russia too revolutionary, and Great Britain hesitant and no longer a major Pacific power. The only alternatives were stark: warring against Japan, working out something somehow with Tokyo, or else admitting that the United States had no vital interests in the area. No American president has ever opted for this third alternative. As the Japanese drove deeper into Manchuria in late 1931, Stimson discussed possible economic sanctions (for example, cutting off the considerable American oil and metal exports to Japan), but Hoover refused. The president feared that sanctions would inevitably lead to war. The League of Nations investigated the outbreak, indirectly called Japan the aggressor, refused to recognize Japan's establishment of a Manchukuo puppet state in Manchuria, and then watched hopelessly as Tokyo responded by quitting the League. Stimson refused to work formally with the League. His main effort was to coordinate an Anglo-American reaffirmation of the Nine-Power Treaty backed by an increase of military strength in the Pacific. That policy collapsed when the British decided to work through the League of Nations while privately trying to appease Japan. From 1931 until Pearl Harbor in 1941, Great Britain, whose primary concerns lay in Europe, would support American actions against Japan only if it was certain the United States would accept the possible consequence of war and be willing to fight Japan virtually alone. Otherwise the British were prepared to make deals with the Japanese, and consequently the United States refused in turn to trust the British.

NEW ORDER TO NEW DEAL

Hoover made one final attempt to put the pieces back together. Between 1930 and 1932 nearly every nation withdrew inside itself, erected tariff walls, and attempted to follow autarchic economic policies. In 1930 the United States passed the Hawley-Smoot bill, the highest protective tariff in its history. A more extreme example of autarchy was Britain's construction of the Imperial Preference system in 1932. Through a series of bilateral pacts, the British government and members of the Commonwealth promised to give one another favored trading privileges, thus largely excluding such third parties as the United States from traditional markets in Canada, Australia, and South Africa. The United States bitterly fought such policies, not only because they gravely hurt trade, but also because they injected the government into the realm of private enterprise. In 1932 Hoover counterattacked by proposing an international conference in London that would negotiate war debts, reparations, and disarmament. The president hoped that settlement of the debts could be used to pressure Great Britain and France into accepting liberal trade policies.

Before the conference could convene, however, Franklin D. Roosevelt moved into the White House. When Hoover and Stimson asked Roosevelt to accept their policies in the Far East and the proposed London conference, the new president agreed not to recognize Manchukuo, but absolutely refused to commit himself on economic issues. During his first eight months in office he rejected Hoover's international approach, most dramatically when he destroyed the London conference by refusing to tie American tariff and monetary policy to any international agreement. Believing that the American economy might be able to resurrect itself if it were not tied to a disintegrating world economy, Roosevelt allowed the war-debt issue to die, took the country off the international gold standard, and began tinkering with the dollar to raise its purchasing power. None of these devices sufficiently spurred the economy. "Yes, it is the zero hour in Washington," critic Edmund Wilson observed in early 1934. "The first splendor of the New Deal has faded. . . . The emergency measures which revived our morale have not achieved all that they have promised."

By the spring of 1934 Roosevelt gave up his experiments and returned to Hoover's assumption that recovery required a booming American export trade. Quite clearly the domestic economy would not further improve without measures—some of which smacked too much of socialism for Roosevelt's taste—that would radically change the nature of the system. The president's only alternative therefore was to find help outside the system itself, that is, in the world marketplace.

Two major differences, however, separated Roosevelt's foreign policy from Hoover's. Roosevelt was dealing with a world rapidly compartmentalizing into closed, government-controlled blocs. Japan's Manchukuo and the British Imperial Preference system, for example, were not open to American competition. More ominously, in January 1933 Adolf Hitler assumed power in Germany. Within three years he worked out exclusive, government-controlled trade arrangements in Europe and Latin America that made it difficult for private American traders to compete.

These developments led to the second distinguishing—if not revolutionary —characteristic of New Deal policy: the government had to involve itself directly, for example by giving subsidies to private business that needed help in the marketplace. Hoover had avoided such direct involvement at all costs, fearing that it would change the nature of the system itself. Roosevelt believed that such danger could be averted. Moreover, he had little choice; if Americans were to find economic salvation overseas, they could compete against Germans, Japanese, and British governmental policies only if the U.S. government provided similar aid. That, of course, raised the grave danger that if conflict arose in the marketplace, the governments themselves would become fully involved in the struggle.

The guiding genius behind this policy was Secretary of State Cordell Hull. An ardent Wilsonian and former congressman from Tennessee who prided himself on complete command of the Tennessee mountaineer's earthy vocabulary, Hull was named secretary of state because of his influence on Capitol Hill. He was driven by an obsession to reopen the clogged channels of trade. Only when high tariffs, currency manipulation, and the power of state trading enterprises were obliterated, he believed, could individual freedoms be restored and wars averted. Hull was certain that friction between economic blocs inevitably led to political conflict. He therefore set out to replace such closed blocs with an open, multilateral trading system that had freely convertible currencies (instead of monies manipulated by the state) and that allowed private business concerns to buy and sell anywhere they chose. Hull used this standard of freer trade to judge nearly every diplomatic move he made between 1933 and his retirement in 1944, a standard that led him to condemn Germany in the 1930s, Japan in 1941, and the Soviet Union in 1944. This policy is central to an understanding of why he and Roosevelt came to define these three nations as enemies politically as well as economically.

Between 1934 and 1939 more legislation was enacted in Washington to find markets abroad for American surpluses than in any similar period in the nation's history. Two measures stand out. The Reciprocity Act of 1934 was Hull's pet project. It sharply reversed post-1920 policy

EDWARD R. MURROW
AND THE RADIO

"Radio is a recent innovation that has introduced profound alterations in the outlook and social behavior of men," two noted psychologists concluded in 1935. This dramatic view was accurate, even though commercial radio was just fifteen years old. The first national networks were formed in the mid-1920s by the National Broadcasting Company (NBC) and Columbia Broadcasting System (CBS), breakthroughs that led Secretary of Commerce Herbert Hoover to establish a governmental licensing and regulatory agency in 1927. He was concerned that radio be responsible: "It is inconceivable that we should allow so great a possibility for service, for news, for entertainment . . . to be drowned in advertising chatter." That was a forlorn hope. Radio advertising grew in popularity even during the depression. Albert Lasker, king of the advertising agents, tripled sales of Pepsodent by having the toothpaste sponsor the most popular 1930s program, *Amos 'n' Andy*, in which two white actors impersonated black minstrel-show types. Radio standardized habits of living, speech, and taste in a nation once famous for its distinct regions and diversity.

Edward R. Murrow outside the BBC's Broadcast House, from which Murrow beamed his broadcasts, London, May 1940. *(CBS Photo Archive/Getty Images)*

Until the 1930s radio broadcast little news. NBC did not have a single daily news series. It believed its job was to entertain the entire family while leaving current affairs to newspapers. Franklin D. Roosevelt changed this situation with his "Fireside Chats" in 1933. With a voice perfectly suited for the new medium, his broadcasts were so successful that, in the words of a columnist, "The President has only to look toward a radio to bring Congress to terms."

As Europe moved toward war, news services increased until in 1937 CBS sent twenty-eight-year-old Edward R. Murrow to Europe to establish continent-wide broadcasts. Born in Polecat Creek, North Carolina, he had moved west to study at Washington State College, where the nation's first courses on radio were offered. As Murrow left for Europe, a CBS executive protested, "Broadcasting has no role in international politics," but should limit itself to radioing "the song of a nightingale from Kent, England," a program that had been voted the "most interesting broadcast" of 1932. Murrow destroyed such illusions. CBS's coverage of the 1938 Munich crisis was followed hourly by millions.

Its effect was noticeable a month later when the network produced Orson Welles's ver-

Franklin D. Roosevelt during a fireside chat in Washington, DC, 1935. *(Franklin D. Roosevelt Presidential Library and Museum, Hyde Park, New York)*

sion of *War of the Worlds*, a story of invaders from Mars landing in New Jersey. Welles utilized the news bulletin-spot interview techniques used during the Munich crisis. Within a half-hour after the program began, New Jersey residents filled the highways heading out of the state, two Princeton professors had rushed out to study the invaders, and a Pittsburgh woman, crying "I'd rather die this way than that," was stopped before she could take poison. News broadcasting had come of age.

Murrow built a staff in Europe headed by Eric Sevareid and Howard K. Smith. His most famous programs occurred during Hitler's air blitz of London in 1940 and 1941. His rich, quiet, understated voice began each broadcast with "This—is London." He followed with graphic accounts that tried to "report suffering to people [Americans] who have not suffered" by providing eyewitness testimony of bombing ("that moan of stark terror and suspense cannot be encompassed by words"). Pioneering new uses of the microphone, he once simply put it on a London sidewalk while sirens shrieked, antiaircraft guns fired, and people hurried to shelters. As the foreign policy debate in Washington intensified, Murrow shrewdly helped the pro-interventionist forces by emphasizing Churchill's greatness and England's bravery while reporting British belief that Americans were the last hope for democracy. As American poet Archibald MacLeish wrote of Murrow, "You burned the city of London in our houses and we felt the flames that burned it. You laid the dead of London at our doors and we knew the dead were our dead."

Murrow brought a new dimension to radio, for he used it to educate and mobilize society. Even after his death in 1965, his style and ideals shaped news broadcasting in television as well as radio.

Web Links

CBS News websites devoted to Murrow and his most famous programs—

Person to Person: **www.cbsnews.com/person-to-person/** and
See it Now: **www.cbsnews.com/video/watch/?id=1065699n**.

by giving the president power to reduce or raise tariffs by as much as 50 percent in bargaining with other nations for reciprocal reduction of tariff barriers. The policy also included the unconditional-most-favored-nation principle: trade favors given to one nation would automatically be given to all others that did not discriminate against American trade. That principle made it impossible for two nations to gang up economically against a third. If used successfully, the reciprocity act would be like a giant economic wrecking ball, swinging in all directions to batter down tariff and other state-created barriers that Hull and Roosevelt so hated. Reciprocity pacts with fourteen nations helped accelerate exports between 1934 and 1938 by over $500 million. Imports, however, lagged; this meant that other nations were not selling enough to Americans to obtain the dollars needed to buy increased U.S. exports.

As during 1928 and 1929, therefore, a dollar shortage threatened to stunt the growth of the world, and consequently the American, economy. In 1934 Roosevelt established a government-operated Export-Import Bank through which government credits would be made available to foreign customers so they could purchase U.S. exports. Funds to finance foreign trade would now be provided by the government, not just by the private bankers, who had proven unequal to the job in the 1920s. American tax dollars were lent overseas for the purchase of American goods. These acts creating the reciprocity policy and the Export-Import Bank proved so beneficial that both were renewed and expanded into the twenty-first century.

AREAS OF SPECIAL INTEREST:
LATIN AMERICA AND THE SOVIET UNION

These economic initiatives were aimed at every corner of the world, but the New Deal selected several areas for special attention. Between 1933 and 1938, Roosevelt and Hull devoted great energy to making North and South America "good neighbors," in FDR's words. During those years U.S. imports from Latin America leaped 114 percent to $705 million, while exports to South America rocketed 166 percent to over $640 million. In 1932 the United States accounted for 32 percent of Latin American trade, but after the reciprocity legislation took effect, Americans enjoyed 45 percent in 1938. Politically, Roosevelt continued Hoover's policy of noninterference militarily. A major step occurred at the Montevideo Conference in 1933 when Hull, somewhat against his will, pledged the United States not to carry out further military interventions.

The increased economic leverage was providing Americans with an alternative diplomatic weapon. Cuba provided a classic example. Since 1901 the Platt Amendment had given officials in Washington the right to send troops to Cuba. Control became firmer between 1919 and 1921, when depressed sugar prices ruined plantations and Americans invested heavily in Cuban sugar. Throughout the 1920s a dictator protected these interests, but by 1933 the economy had collapsed and left-wing movements challenged the government. After thirty-five years as an American protectorate, Cuba's trade with the United States had dropped 50 percent since 1929, the island's sugar sold for one-tenth of a cent per pound, and 500,000 of Cuba's 4 million people searched for work. In September 1933 junior army officers under Fulgencio Batista overthrew the government and put a liberal politician into the presidency.

The regime was indeed too liberal for the State Department, which thought it saw communists creeping into power. Hull and Undersecretary of State Sumner Welles, a close friend of Roosevelt, asked him to make a show of force in Havana harbor. The president refused. He had a better alternative. Between 1933 and 1934 FDR and Batista—who desperately needed economic help—agreed to pump life into the Cuban economy by opening the American sugar market to Cuban cane at prices above those in the world market. Other foreign-produced sugar was effectively excluded from the United States. American consumers thus paid extra for their sugar, but Batista lived up to his part of the deal by placing a more conservative president in power in Havana. The policy worked so well that in 1934 Roosevelt felt he could safely repeal all of the Platt Amendment but the part giving the United States the Guantanamo Naval Base. At the same time, Washington also promised to give the Philippines independence in ten years, but again carefully made economic arrangements to protect American interests on the islands.

Roosevelt pursued the same economic approach toward Russia, but with much less success. After frequent consultation with William Bullitt, who had returned from the French Riviera and private life in Philadelphia to advise him, the president recognized the Soviets in November 1933. He had to overcome strong opposition from the American Legion, the Daughters of the American Revolution, Roman Catholic Church leaders, the American Federation of Labor, and, most important, his own State Department. Hull swore that no deals could be made with a state-controlled economy. He also argued that the Bolsheviks would try to interfere in American domestic affairs, as he believed they had in Cuba during the 1933 revolution. Roosevelt did, however, receive strong support from businessmen, who argued that the potentially vast Russian market could help rescue Americans from the depression. Bullitt became the first U.S. ambassador to the Soviet Union.

The Soviets welcomed FDR's initiative, but for very different reasons. They were less interested in trade than in working out a common policy to contain Japan. Since 1931 the Soviets, fearful that Tokyo's militarists would move from Manchuria into Siberia, had desperately searched for friends. One Moscow official remarked that Russia and the United States must join in "breaking [Japan] as between the two arms of a nutcracker."

Within two years after diplomatic relations were resumed, Moscow–Washington relations turned sour. Trade did not prosper because no agreement could be reached on proper credit arrangements. The Soviets became disillusioned when the State Department went out of its way to assure anxious Tokyo officials that recognition was not in any way directed against Japan. Roosevelt and Bullitt plainly informed Russian leader Joseph Stalin they would make no anti-Japanese alliance. Washington preferred to consider a deal with its old friend Japan rather than work with the mysterious, revolutionary Soviets. In 1934 Stalin gave up on the United States. He began negotiating with Japan, joined the League of Nations, and—too late—reversed his attitude toward Hitler (whom Stalin had dismissed as a fool in 1932) in a last-ditch try at working out antifascist alliances with Eastern and Western governments. Russia and the United States continued to go in opposite directions until Hitler startlingly threw them together in 1941.

THE FAILURE OF POLITICAL NEUTRALITY

Between 1933 and 1937 the Japanese carefully refrained from further aggression, but tightened their grip on Manchuria. When Roosevelt attempted to help China in late 1933 with wheat, cotton, and airplanes, Tokyo slammed back with the so-called Amau Statement of 1934, which warned that since foreign aid to China could "acquire political significance," Japan had the right to act unilaterally to maintain "peace and order in Eastern Asia." The State Department again reiterated the Nine-Power Treaty principles for an open door in China, but Japan threw that treaty on the scrap heap by excluding American oil and other interests from Manchuria. By late 1934 Tokyo demanded that the Five-Power Treaty principles be changed to allow Japan parity with the American and British fleets. When this was refused, the Japanese withdrew from the agreement and accelerated the building of their navy and fortifications in the Pacific.

In 1936 Tokyo found new friends. During the previous year Benito Mussolini's Italy had suddenly ravaged the small African nation of Ethiopia. When the League of Nations and the major powers offered little response, Hitler embarked on his own campaign of aggression. The self-proclaimed führer, determined to rectify the 1919 peace conference's dissection of Germany, marched unopposed to reclaim the Rhineland in 1936. During that summer civil war erupted in Spain between the five-year-old republic and the conservative army-church forces led by Francisco Franco. Within a year Hitler and Mussolini funneled vast aid to Franco while the republic obtained major help only from the Soviets. Great Britain and France remained on the sidelines of what they preferred to believe was only a civil war, and the United States followed their example. Franco then overthrew the Spanish Republic and established his own dictatorship. Germany was clearly on the move. In November 1936 the Japanese signed with Hitler the Anti-Comintern Pact, which secretly called for joint consultation if either party were attacked by the Soviets; both parties promised not to make treaties with Russia. Italy joined the pact in 1937. Japan now had friends and security on its Russian flank if it wanted to move into China or areas to the south.

The United States responded to these developments with a series of neutrality laws. A Senate investigation headed by Gerald Nye (Republican of North Dakota) revealed during 1934–1935 that private American bankers had become closely involved with the French and British war efforts during 1915–1917. No evidence demonstrated that President Wilson's policies had been directly shaped by the bankers, but the conclusion was too easily drawn that the United States had been shoved into world war by the profit lust of a few. Congress responded with the 1935 Neutrality Act: when the president declared that war existed, no arms, ammunition, or items of war were to be shipped to any belligerent, and American ships could not transport such supplies to a belligerent. In 1936 Congress passed a second Neutrality Act that prohibited loans to nations involved in war. A year later, in response to the Spanish conflict, other Neutrality Acts forbade Americans from traveling on the vessels of belligerents and applied these various provisions to civil wars.

But one major change appeared in the 1937 legislation. In response to Roosevelt's complaint that the acts tied his hands, and because the damming up of these items threatened vital parts of the country's economy, a "cash-and-carry" provision was added allowing nations to obtain nonmilitary supplies if they paid cash and transported them home in their own ships. Americans, in other words, hoped to avoid wars while making money from them. Obviously the cash-and-carry clause also helped Great Britain and France since in any European war their navies would control the Atlantic. As Japan soon demonstrated, however, the Neutrality Acts were written to prevent the previous war, not the next one.

In July 1937 the Japanese army attacked northern China in an effort to build a buffer area around Japan's puppet state of Manchukuo. The Neutrality Acts were useless, for whereas Americans wanted to help China, the Japanese fleet controlled the western Pacific and hence could take advantage of the cash-and-carry provision. Roosevelt tried to escape from the dilemma by refusing to declare that a war existed in Asia. The neutrality provisions consequently did not take effect. He meanwhile desperately searched for ways to aid China.

On October 5, FDR delivered a "quarantine speech" in Chicago, the center of political isolationism. The president talked vaguely about quarantining aggressor nations, but offered no specific policies. A majority of Americans probably supported Roosevelt's call, but the howls of opposition that arose drove Roosevelt and Hull to disclaim any intention of immediate action.

In December 1937 Japanese planes attacked an American gunboat, the *Panay*, as it stood guard over Standard Oil tankers in China's Yangtze River. Two Americans were killed. Roosevelt strongly protested, and Japan apologized, but the president then tried to take the offensive. In the House he waged a bitter and successful struggle against a constitutional amendment proposed by Louis Ludlow (Democrat of Indiana), which if passed would have required a national referendum before a declaration of war unless the United States itself were attacked. The following month Roosevelt proposed a 20 percent increase in the U.S. naval fleet and began rebuilding Guam and other Pacific bases.

THE FAILURE OF THE NEW DEAL

After these small successes the president had to turn from foreign policy to a crisis at home. In early 1937 he believed that the American economy had recovered sufficiently so that some New Deal measures could be cut back. He especially hoped to balance the budget, a move that would dry up vast federal monies that had been priming the economy. As Secretary of the Treasury Henry Morgenthau phrased it, "This was the moment, it seemed to me, to strip off the bandages, throw away the crutches, and see if American private enterprise could stand on its own feet." Roosevelt pulled government money out too rapidly, however, and like a patient drained of blood, the economy staggered, then collapsed into the most precipitous decline in American history. In nine months industrial production dropped 33 percent, payrolls 35 percent, industrial stock averages 50 percent, profits 78 percent. Only unemployment rose, spiraling upward 23 percent. The domestic New Deal had no other medicines to offer. Roosevelt, one of his cabinet members noted, "did not know which way to turn." But something had to be done rapidly, for the crisis went beyond economics. Harry Hopkins, one of FDR's closest advisers, declared, "This country cannot continue as a democracy with 10 or 12 million people unemployed. It just can't be done."

Roosevelt's massive spending program on the navy and later on a 5,500-plane air force provided one response to the crisis. By 1939 defense spending was putting Americans back to work again, although 10 million remained unemployed as late as January 1940. The full-scale war economy after 1941 would finally solve the terrible economic problems that the New Deal could never sufficiently remedy.

Another response to the crisis was the traditional hope of finding expanded foreign markets for the vast surplus of American goods. China provided the greatest potential market. "Probably never in its history has China offered greater promise for [U.S.] future trade, industry, and general economic progress," a Commerce Department official told a gathering of American businessmen in mid-1937. The Japanese invasion threatened that dream and more: if the Japanese developed a large cotton industry in northern China, then, Secretary of Commerce Daniel C. Roper warned Roosevelt in late 1937, American exports would drop so low as to require "a recharting of the economy of the South and definite Federal production control procedures." Several years later a correspondent of the *New York Times* substituted rubber for cotton, but came up with the same conclusion: "The future of China and the future of the United States in Asia may very well be determined by whether or not those rubber tires that roll on the Chinese roads are made in Akron or in Osaka [Japan]."

Secretary of State Hull was caught in the middle of this maelstrom. In 1936 he had been impressed with the advice from John A. Hobson, the great historian of imperialism, that the "last large possibility of maintaining capitalism lies in the Orient." It was doubtful, Hobson continued, that in exploiting this lush market "the Americans will care to play second fiddle to the Japanese, whose character and behavior are so baffling to the Occidental mind." That advice fitted perfectly with Hull's view that an open-door approach, rather than Japanese exclusiveness, was the only method to develop a healthy global trade, world peace, and the American economy. In November 1938, however, Hull suffered a severe setback when Japan proclaimed a Greater Asia Co-prosperity Sphere, based on anti-bolshevism, which aimed to close off the Far East. It was, Tokyo claimed, an Asian equivalent to the American Monroe Doctrine in the Western Hemisphere. Hull feared that all of Asia would go the way of Manchuria. "In our opinion," he sweepingly declared in late 1938, "an endeavor by any country in any part of the world to establish itself in favor of a preferred [economic] position in another country is incompatible with the maintenance of our own and the establishment of world prosperity." That statement was the cornerstone of American foreign policy.

How to drive Japan from its "preferred position" was the central problem, compounded in early 1939 by statistics showing Japan to be America's third-largest customer. During a severe depression, such trade was not to be lightly discarded for the mere potential of the China market. Japan, moreover, had long been Washington's and London's most dependable ally in the Far East, a bastion against revolution. A war to protect the open door in China, on the other hand, could spawn new revolutions and be bloody as well as long-lasting, particularly if the Japanese and Germans coordinated their efforts. "We would like to help China if we knew how, of course," Secretary of the Interior Harold Ickes summed up the cruel dilemma in late 1938, "without running the risk of our own involvement in war."

Two alternatives emerged. The first, championed by Hull and his State Department advisers, urged continued effort toward a cooperative policy with Japan. Only then, Hull believed, could traditional multilateral cooperation be maintained for propping open the door to Far Eastern markets. He believed that an international trade agreement based on his beloved reciprocity principle would restore economic cooperation and—as Hull's reasoning ran—therefore result in a political agreement. Once brought within such a trade-political network, Japan could find necessary markets peacefully, continue to receive strategic goods from a friendly United States, and quit its evil partnership with Hitler.

A second and quite different answer came from Henry Morgenthau and the Treasury Department. Morgenthau reasoned that Japan's militarists were uncontrollable and too ambitious to settle for a friendly division of the Asian market. He urged direct bilateral aid to help China drive back the invader and bitterly criticized Hull's complicated multilateral, cooperative approach ("while he was discussing it, one country after another goes under").

Roosevelt at first equivocated between the two alternatives but told Morgenthau in late 1938, "Henry, these trade treaties [of Hull's] are just too goddamned slow. The world is marching too fast." The secretary of state's approach was also undercut when Japan insisted that only it and China could settle Chinese affairs; third parties were not wanted. Morgenthau

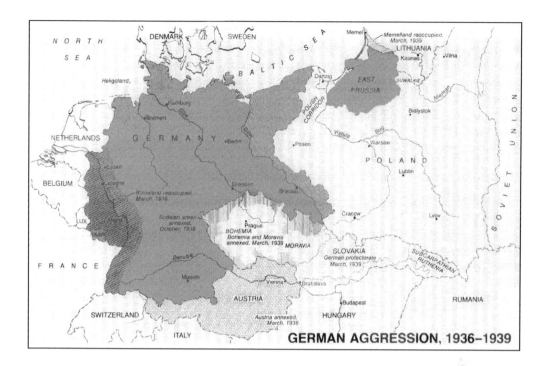

GERMAN AGGRESSION, 1936–1939

won a victory in 1938 when FDR agreed to send a $25 million credit for China's war effort. Then in July 1939 Morgenthau won a major triumph when Hull finally agreed to terminate the 1911 commercial treaty that governed trade with Japan. Roosevelt was so happy with Hull's acquiescence that he blurted out, "Cordell, I feel like kissing you on both cheeks." Morgenthau next pushed for an embargo on oil, but Hull resisted. No more would be done until Hitler had begun World War II.

THE GHOST OF 1919

As European peace disintegrated after 1935, Roosevelt offered only suggestions for disarmament or economic conferences. Not even the British would accept such proposals. The Conservative government of Prime Minister Neville Chamberlain embraced instead the policy of appeasement, a dirty word during the post-1945 era but not in the 1930s, for it meant adjusting the wrongs inflicted on Germany by the 1919 peace conference. In this sense Roosevelt and most Americans were also appeasers. Like Europeans, they were belatedly conscience-stricken by the harsh penalties pressed on Germany and so stood paralyzed as Hitler's armies moved into adjoining territories during the mid-1930s. Also like Chamberlain, Roosevelt believed that compromises could be made with Germany and Italy, especially through the personal, private, and manipulative diplomacy that each leader preferred to more traditional methods.

When the Munich crisis flared in September 1938, Roosevelt encouraged Chamberlain to talk with Hitler. The president refused to take the side of either the German dictator, who demanded annexation of the Czechoslovak Sudetenland area containing several million Germans, or the Czechs (supposedly supported by Britain and France), who did not want to surrender their only defensible frontier area. On September 9, Roosevelt angrily made clear to reporters that Americans had no moral commitment to defend European democracies. Chamberlain finally decided to make a dramatic flight to Munich for talks with Hitler, a decision that resulted in Chamberlain's agreeing that Hitler should have his way. FDR wired the prime minister, "Good man." But a month later Roosevelt confessed to the cabinet his "shame" for supporting the Munich agreement and ordered the acceleration of plans for sending war goods to Great Britain and France.

The president's disillusionment with Hitler also resulted from Nazi activities in Latin America. German businesses, including the powerful Lufthansa airline, scored repeated successes in Latin American markets. An assistant secretary of commerce observed during 1938, "It used to be said that trade follows the flag. Observing world affairs today we might more appropriately say that political ideologies follow trade." As the Germans entered Latin American markets, traditional U.S. markets disappeared, a loss especially felt during the economic crisis of 1938. Roosevelt responded with increased government assistance to American businesses and pushed for a common anti-Axis front. His success was marked in the 1938 Declaration of Lima, when all the nations in the hemisphere agreed to cooperate fully against outside threats. A year later, after war began in Europe, the Americas agreed on the Declaration of Panama, which created a "safety belt" of nearly a thousand miles around the hemisphere in which there were to be no hostile acts by non-American belligerents.

By 1940 the only outstanding hemispheric problem was again the Mexican revolution. In March 1938, Mexico finally nationalized all foreign oil companies. Hull angrily urged quick action against "those Communists down there." The previous U.S. pledges of nonintervention, however, and Roosevelt's fear that a tough policy would turn Mexico toward Japan and Germany, moderated Washington's response. A settlement was finally reached in November 1941, when Mexico agreed to pay $40 million in back claims and establish a committee of experts to settle compensation for the oil companies. In return, the United States helped finance Mexican currency and extended a $30 million Export-Import Bank loan to build a large section of the Pan-American Highway from Mexico into Guatemala. Mexico was restored to the anti-Axis front that the United States was so anxious to forge.

Otherwise appeasement was a disaster. History catches and controls every decade and never more tragically than when the 1919 treaty paralyzed the anti-Hitlerian nations during the 1930s. One nation finally broke away. On August 23, 1939, Stalin signed a nonaggression treaty with Hitler in which they agreed on the division of Poland and the Balkans. Since 1937, Stalin had tried to negotiate a security agreement with France and Great Britain. This had foundered on French and British anticommunist hatred and the refusal of the Poles and Romanians to entrust their existence to Russian hands. Stalin had also carried out a gigantic blood purge of his supposed political enemies. He probably exterminated several million Russians. This brutality turned many Westerners, even Communist Party members, against the Soviets; a typical American magazine account was titled "Stalin, Portrait of a Degenerate," in which he was compared—unfavorably—with the famous Chicago killer Al "Scarface" Capone. Among the victims of the purge were leading Red Army officers. Western officials concluded that in any conflict the weakened Russian forces would be virtually useless. Hitler perceived Russia differently, for a treaty with Stalin would free Germany from the danger of a two-front war. Americans viewed these events incredulously, at first dismissing the Nazi-Soviet pact as a

Secretary of State Cordell Hull, Undersecretary Sumner Welles, and Adolf A. Berle Jr. *(left to right)* going to the White House with the unsigned Neutrality Proclamation in 1939. *(Thomas D. McAvoy/Time & Life Pictures/Getty Images)*

mere "grandstand play" designed by Stalin to frighten the West, then agreeing that there must be no difference after all between communism and fascism.

On September 1, 1939, nine days after the Nazi-Soviet pact was signed, Hitler invaded Poland. Great Britain and France, which had guaranteed Poland's boundaries, declared war on Germany. World War II had begun. After an impassioned congressional debate, Roosevelt won a modification of the Neutrality Acts. The arms embargo was changed to cash-and-carry in order to help the Allies, but loans remained illegal. Unlike Wilson, FDR never asked Americans to be neutral in thought and deed. He did, unfortunately, insist that his policies would keep the United States out of war, even as he was tying the country closer to the Allies.

In November 1939, Russia invaded Finland to obtain strategic areas along the Finnish-Soviet boundary. Despite State Department urgings, Roosevelt refused to break diplomatic relations with Russia, although he placed a voluntary, or "moral," embargo on airplanes and gas ticketed for the Soviets. An important side effect soon appeared. Spurred by war orders, American employment jumped 10 percent in late 1939 as production rose sharply. World War II rescued the economy.

THE TRIALS OF UNNEUTRAL NEUTRALITY

The German blitzkrieg through Poland was followed by a lull, or "sitzkrieg," during winter and early spring of 1939–1940. In May, Hitler suddenly occupied France and the Low Countries. By June, his forces stood triumphant on the English Channel. Only the British remained to face the Nazis. Winston Churchill, who throughout the 1930s had repeatedly condemned appeasement, replaced Chamberlain as prime minister and mobilized Great Britain for a last-ditch fight. In the Pacific, Japan took advantage of the French and Dutch disasters to make demands on French Indochina and the Dutch East Indies. By September the struggle truly became global, for Japan, Germany, and Italy signed a tripartite mutual assistance pact clearly aimed at the United States. Americans now faced the prospect of a two-front war if they went to the rescue of Great Britain.

Roosevelt and his advisers concluded that Germany, not Japan, posed the gravest threat and that Great Britain must have top priority for war supplies. That policy continued to govern American actions until 1945. Protecting Great Britain, however, also meant safeguarding the European colonial empires in South and Southeast Asia, which produced the vital rubber, oil, and metals for the Anglo-American war effort. Japan, therefore, could not be allowed to strike to the south. Roosevelt initially responded by proposing an unbelievable building program to construct 50,000 planes and build over a million tons of ships. In September 1940 he made an executive agreement with Churchill by which fifty U.S. destroyers were sent to Great Britain in return for ninety-nine-year leases on British naval bases in the Western Hemisphere. This act required considerable political courage, for Roosevelt had decided to run for an unprecedented third term and was confronting strong criticism for his earlier aid to Great Britain.

The opposition to FDR's policies was led by the America First group made up of anti–New Deal industrialists (such as Henry Ford and Sterling Morton of Morton Salt), old Progressives (such as Senator Burton K. Wheeler of Nebraska and journalist Oswald Garrison Villard), and public figures who warned of dire military and political consequences should the nation be sucked into the war (such as flying aces Eddie Rickenbacker and Charles A. Lindbergh and historian Charles Beard). On the other side, the Committee to Defend America mobilized pro-Allied sentiment to aid the Allies. The committee vowed that it wanted to stay out of war, but argued that keeping Americans away from the battlefields required sending vast aid to nations resisting fascism. Roosevelt was fortunate in that the 1940 Republican presidential nominee, Wendell Willkie, sympathized with the Committee to Defend America by Aiding the Allies and so refused to condemn the president for helping Great Britain.

During the 1940 campaign FDR stressed that he did not intend to involve the country in war. After the election, however, he stepped up American assistance, often with the public assurance that it would somehow lessen the need for Americans to fight. Roosevelt was trapped. He knew the American system could not long survive in a fascist-dominated world, but he feared making strong public statements because of his estimate of antiwar sentiment, especially on Capitol Hill. When one ardent interventionist urged more action, the president replied, "Whether we like it or not, God and Congress still live." He consequently committed the United States to the Allies while issuing public explanations that fell short of the truth.

Roosevelt moved rapidly in 1941 against the Axis. In March he pushed the Lend-Lease Act through Congress so that the country could be "the arsenal of democracy" and send vast amounts of goods to Great Britain regardless of its inability to pay for the supplies. The act was aimed, he said, at keeping "war away from our country and our people." Senator Wheeler called lend-lease "the New Deal's triple-A foreign policy: it will plow under every fourth American boy." Roosevelt promptly shot back that this was "the rottenest thing that has been said in public life in my generation." But moving supplies to Great Britain through Nazi submarine–infested seas of the North Atlantic soon required the president to send American convoys to protect the supply ships. He ordered such convoying as far as Iceland, despite telling a press conference in late May that he had no plans to permit the U.S. Navy to accompany British vessels. By late summer he secretly ordered American ships to track German submarines and report to British destroyers. When one submarine turned and fired a torpedo at the *Greer*, which had been following the German vessel for three hours, Roosevelt said that the attack was unprovoked and implied that henceforth U.S. ships should feel free to shoot on sight. In November U.S. ships were armed and carrying goods to Great Britain. The nation was all but formally at war.

THE LAST STEP

The formal, constitutional declaration of war ironically resulted from an Asian, not a European, crisis. After Japan threatened Indochina in July 1940, Roosevelt restricted the export of oil, aviation fuel, and scrap metals to Japan. This was a major step, for cutting off Tokyo's main source of these goods could force the Japanese to seize the oil and mineral wealth of South Asia. Yet Tokyo proceeded cautiously. In March 1941 Japan freed itself from the threat of a two-front war by signing a five-year nonaggression treaty with Russia. Hitler was stunned. Great Britain had been tougher than he expected, and he had failed to reach agreement with Stalin on dividing booty in the Balkans, so Hitler had decided to invade Russia. Despite the Tokyo-Moscow pact, the German dictator struck the Soviet Union on June 23 and by early winter had driven to within thirty miles of Moscow. Only the United States remained to keep Japan from taking what it wanted in the Far East.

In July 1941 the Japanese invaded Indochina and Thailand. Roosevelt froze Japanese assets in the United States, thus stopping nearly all trade. Hull had negotiated with Japan throughout mid-1941, but no agreement could be reached on three points: Tokyo's obligations under the Tripartite Pact (Hull demanded that Japan disavow its alliance with Germany); Japanese economic rights in Southeast Asia; and a settlement in China. The secretary of state mumbled to friends that "everything is going hellward," but he refused to give up hope that Japan would be reasonable. Roosevelt supported Hull while restraining cabinet members, such as Morgenthau, who wanted to have a showdown with the Japanese. The president desperately needed time to build American strength in both the Atlantic and the Pacific.

Averting an immediate clash, Hull nevertheless stuck to his demands that Japan get out of China, Indochina, and the Tripartite Pact. The Tokyo government of Fuminaro Konoye, under tremendous pressure from the Japanese military, was reaching the point of no return. American economic pressure was building. Konoye either had to meet Hull's demands and

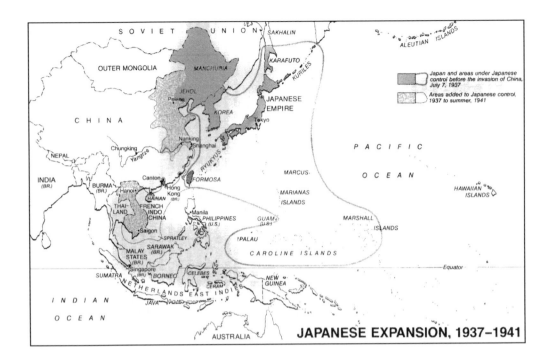

JAPANESE EXPANSION, 1937–1941

restore normal trade with the United States or remove all restraints and conquer the rich resources to the south. In August, Konoye made a final attempt at conciliation by asking Roosevelt to meet him personally to thrash out the problem. FDR was initially attracted, but Hull convinced him the conference would be worthless unless Japan agreed before the meeting to acquiesce to Hull's earlier demands. Konoye naturally refused such preconditions. In early October, Konoye's civilian government was swept aside and replaced by the military regime of General Hideki Tojo.

There was one last effort to avert war. In November the Japanese offered to leave Indochina and implied that they did not feel bound by the Tripartite Pact. In return they demanded vast American economic aid. The United States had cracked the Japanese diplomatic code, so Hull knew that this was the final offer. He rejected it, declaring on November 26 that Japan must in addition evacuate all troops from China and agree to an open-door policy in the Far East. This Japan would not do. The next day Tojo's regime decided to attack the United States on December 7 in a surprise raid on the Pearl Harbor naval base. At no time did the Japanese government harbor any hope of actually conquering the United States. Japan hoped instead that after a large portion of the American fleet was destroyed, Roosevelt would want to avert further conflict and be willing to talk more agreeably about China and trade.

Washington officials knew that Japan was preparing to attack, but they believed that the strike would be against Southeast Asia only. Some, such as Secretary of War Henry Stimson (whom Roosevelt had appointed in 1940 in a bipartisan and pro-Allied gesture), even hoped that the Japanese would attack in the southern Pacific, for the United States would then be justified in declaring war to protect the Philippines. On December 7, 1941, Japan instead struck in the mid-Pacific, crippling American naval forces in a matter of minutes with the worst losses they had ever suffered in a single engagement. More than 3,500 men lost their lives in the attack on Pearl Harbor as six large battleships and numerous auxiliary vessels settled to the bottom of Hawaiian waters.

Pearl Harbor was caught unprepared because of a massive breakdown in military intelligence and communication, not because Roosevelt or Stimson conspired to use the navy as bait so that Japan would attack and thereby enable the administration to take a united country into war. No administration plans to begin a war by losing nearly half its navy. When FDR asked Congress on December 8 to declare war against Japan, he did not think it possible to declare war on Germany, even though Hitler remained the primary objective of American policy. Many Americans, especially in the Midwest, wanted vengeance on Japan but were not yet ready to become embroiled in Europe. Hitler solved Roosevelt's dilemma on December 11 by declaring war on the United States. He did so in part because he had long promised the Japanese to honor their 1940 treaty, but more important because he felt that the United States was already fighting against him without a declaration of war. Hitler's unbounded ego apparently demanded that he, not Roosevelt, take the initiative in the life-and-death struggle.

The breakdown of intelligence at Pearl Harbor was remarkable. Washington's last telegram to the base on December 7 said nothing about a possible attack on Hawaii, went by slow commercial cable after a delay in transmission through military communications, and was finally delivered to authorities by a Japanese-American on a motorbike nearly seven hours after the strike. It was a symbolic end to the decade. The economic system had broken down by 1931, spawning fascism in Japan and Germany. The 1922 Washington Naval Conference Treaty system had consequently broken down, allowing Japan to destroy the open door in Asia. The 1919 peace arrangements had broken down, turning Hitler loose in Europe while Chamberlain and Roosevelt wrung their hands. The American economic system had broken down, leaving the New Deal a failure until it was rescued by war spending. American foreign policy had broken down, leaving Hull uttering platitudes about restoring peace by restoring an international marketplace that had not worked properly since before World War I. The Constitution's checks and balances had broken down, allowing FDR to send Americans to kill and be killed on the high seas eight months before the formal declaration of war while he explained publicly that each step toward war was really a step away from war. After a decade like that, the intelligence breakdown at Pearl Harbor is easier to understand if, like the others, difficult to justify.

Chapter Nine

1941–1947
War and Peace

At Kaiser Shipyards, African-American Eastine Cowner helps construct the Liberty Ship *George Washington Carver*, launched May 7, 1943. *(Library of Congress)*

World War II severely strained American political, economic, and social institutions. The Roosevelt administration had to devise a program that would release the nation's full productive energies and yet restrain rampaging inflationary forces. The government also had to impose restrictions on the daily lives of millions of people without alienating those it depended on for political support. To a large extent Roosevelt found satisfactory solutions to these problems. Americans were united against common enemies that they regarded as the incarnation of evil and were therefore willing to make certain sacrifices. The war, by producing a high level of prosperity, ensured that those sacrifices would not be too painful. Then, in April 1945, Harry S. Truman assumed the presidency, and four months later the war ended. The accumulated pressures of four years suddenly exploded, threatening to make a shambles of Truman's domestic program. Putting the pieces back together again proved an arduous task.

IMAGES OF WAR

In 1942 anthropologist Margaret Mead published *And Keep Your Powder Dry*, a study of the way in which American character and values might shape the future conduct of the war. Americans fought best, Mead observed, when they believed that the other side had wantonly provoked them and left them no alternative to war, and when they thought that the struggle was between antagonists of roughly equal strength. In addition, Americans needed to believe in the justice, indeed selflessness, of their cause. A steady succession of military advances, interrupted only temporarily by setbacks, would bolster these convictions. A protracted series of defeats, on the other hand, would call them into question. "To win this war," she said, "we must feel we are on the side of the Right."

Throughout the war years most people felt precisely that way. The attack on Pearl Harbor, widely viewed as proof of Japanese barbarity, enabled Americans to enter the war with more unity than had seemed possible during the bitter struggle between isolationists and interventionists. Most people believed that the war was being waged for "the right of all men to live in freedom, decency, and security" or, as Vice President Henry A. Wallace put it, to usher in a "century of the common man" in which people around the world would gain political freedom and economic security. One congressman declared, "It is a war of purification in which the forces of Christian peace and freedom and justice and decency and morality are arrayed against the evil pagan forces of strife, injustice, treachery, immorality, and slavery." This was only an extreme statement of a commonly accepted view. "Never in our history," said one observer, "have issues been so clear."

The government did what it could to stimulate a sense of loyalty and unity by channeling civilian energies into war-related tasks. The Office of Civilian Defense organized corps of air-raid wardens, firefighters, auxiliary police, and nurse's aides. The agency maintained that people could, through discipline and self-denial, contribute to an American victory and gave a "V Home Award" as "a badge of honor for those families which have made themselves into a fighting unit on the home front" by conserving food, salvaging vital materials, buying war bonds, and planting victory gardens. Newspaper, magazine, and radio advertisements also attempted to persuade people to get by with less. B.F. Goodrich asked its customers to conserve rubber tires since "Hitler smiles when you waste miles." The government popularized the slogan "Use it up, wear it out, make it do, or do without." The daily use of certain symbols, particularly the ubiquitous "V" for victory, heightened the sense of shared purpose.

So, too, did the image of the enemy that emerged during the war. In the popular mind, Germany, at least since the time of Otto von Bismarck, had acted as an aggressor nation because of the influence of the Prussian military caste. *Life* magazine described those officers: "They despise the world of civilians. They wear monocles to train themselves to control their face muscles. They live and die for war." Adolf Hitler had seized power with an "insane desire to conquer and dominate the whole world" and had pursued a strategy of piecemeal conquest based on "treachery and surprise," with the ultimate goal of conquering the United States. The Japanese were portrayed as a fanatic people, addicted to the practice of emperor worship and unconcerned about the sanctity of human life. Racist stereotypes shaped perceptions of the Japanese. *Time* magazine referred to American soldiers at Iwo Jima as "Rodent Exterminators" and noted, "The ordinary unreasoning Jap is ignorant. Perhaps he is human. Nothing . . . indicates it." Similarly, a float in a patriotic parade "showed a big American eagle leading a flight of bombs down on a herd of yellow rats which were trying to escape in all directions."

THE WAR ECONOMY

The economic problems posed by war differed from those associated with the Great Depression. During the 1930s the Roosevelt administration had attempted to limit productive output, create jobs for the unemployed, and encourage a certain amount of inflation. During the 1940s, however, the government did a sudden turnabout. It endeavored to boost industrial and agricultural production, recruit a sufficient number of workers for defense plants, and hold down wages and prices. The administration sought, wherever possible, to obtain voluntary compliance from businessmen, workers, farmers, and consumers by offering them attractive incentives. But on occasion, when these groups refused to cooperate, the administration resorted to compulsion.

To supply the massive needs of the Allied forces, the government not only induced businesses to expand their facilities and convert them to war production, but also developed new sources of critical raw materials and doled those materials out in a systematic fashion. At the heart of this managerial effort was the War Production Board, which Roosevelt created in January 1942 to exercise general control over the economy. Donald Nelson, formerly an executive with Sears, Roebuck and Company, headed the agency. Nelson wanted "to establish a set of rules under which the game could be played the way industry said it had to play it." In this he echoed the sentiments of Secretary of War Henry L. Stimson, who believed that to carry on a war "you have got to let business make money out of the process or business won't work."

The War Production Board devised various procedures to allow businesses to combine patriotism with high profits. The government underwrote much of the cost of plant expansion by permitting industry to amortize those costs over a short five-year period, thereby lowering taxable income while raising earning capacity. The government also invented the cost-plus-a-fixed-fee contract, which guaranteed the military contractor a profit above his costs and removed almost all element of risk from the acceptance of war orders. Firms that entered into pooling arrangements were granted immunity from the antitrust laws provided they first obtained consent by demonstrating how their activities furthered war needs. These policies proved effective. Industry produced nearly twice as much in 1942 as in 1939. As many new industrial plants were built in three years of war as in the preceding fifteen years. Corporate profits after taxes climbed from $6.4 billion in 1940 to $10.8 billion in 1944.

In three other ways the government stimulated industrial output. To compensate for the loss of 90 percent of America's crude rubber supply when Japan seized the Dutch East Indies and Malaya, a new synthetic-rubber industry was created. The government spent $700 million to construct fifty-one plants, which were leased to rubber companies and operated on a cost-plus-a-management-charge basis. By 1944 annual production of synthetic rubber exceeded 800,000 tons. To eliminate logjams in production caused by shortages of copper, steel, and aluminum (all widely used in the manufacture of airplanes, tanks, and ships), the War Production Board introduced the Controlled Materials Plan. Under it, each agency awarding war contracts, such as the War or the Navy Department, presented its material requirements to the board, which then allotted the agency a fixed quantity of scarce materials for distribution to its prime contractors. To prevent transportation bottlenecks from developing, the government coordinated rail transportation. Unlike the situation in World War I when Washington took over the railroads, a system was devised under which the railroads submitted to central direction, pooled their resources, and streamlined their operations. By voluntarily complying, the railroads avoided nationalization.

The policies adopted in recruiting manpower resembled those applied in mobilizing industry. Again, Roosevelt relied heavily on what he termed "voluntary cooperation." At first the demand for labor was filled from the pool of unemployed workers, augmented by women and teenagers entering the job market. But by the end of 1942, high draft calls and twelve-hour factory shifts had exhausted available reserves. The administration made only a feeble attempt to force workers into war-related jobs, however, and finally had to abandon even that. In January 1943, the War Manpower Commission (WMC) issued a "work or fight" order. It eliminated military deferments for everyone, including fathers with dependent children, who held unessential jobs. But this attempt to substitute occupational for familial responsibility as a criterion for deferment aroused a storm of disapproval in Congress, and in December the order was rescinded.

WOMANPOWER ON THE HOME FRONT

One effective solution to the manpower shortage, as the WMC realized by the end of 1942, was "womanpower." Depletion of the male labor pool, the loss of 16 million workers to the armed services, rapid economic expansion, and heavy investment in war industry—all created unprecedented need and optimal opportunity for women workers. Accordingly, one of the most dramatic changes of the war years was a vast increase in the employment of women. Between 1940 and 1945, some 6 million women joined the labor force, the number of women wage earners increased by over 50 percent, and the proportion of women who worked rose from 27 percent to 37 percent. Before the war ended, more than one-third of civilian workers were women.

Although women's numbers rose in all occupational categories (save domestic service), the surge was greatest in the defense industry, where the employment of women increased by a staggering 460 percent. As the male labor pool dwindled, thousands of women moved into jobs in airplane plants and shipyards, steel mills and ammunition factories. They ran cranes and lathes, repaired aircraft engines, cut sheet metal, mined coal, and made parachutes, gas masks, life rafts, instrument panels, and electrical parts. Employers accepted women workers with reluctance rather than alacrity. As late as the summer of 1942, the War Department

Women's Army Auxiliary Corps. Third Officer Jessie Hogan, who has learned to operate efficiently many types of motor transport vehicles, is now competent to teach WAAC trainees to do likewise. *(Library of Congress)*

urged producers to refrain from a large-scale hiring of women "until all available male labor in the area had first been employed." But by then, few male workers were available. By the war's midpoint, "Rosie the Riveter" had transformed the labor force in defense work and other heavy industry. At seven major aircraft plants, the Women's Bureau reported, women's numbers rose from 143 in mid-1941 to 65,000 by the end of 1942. At automobile plants, now converted to war production, one-fourth of workers were women. In some defense factories, such as Boeing's huge Seattle plant, half the workers were women.

The ramifications of womanpower were far-reaching. States discarded protective laws "for the duration" and working conditions improved. Women flocked to war production zones such as Seattle and Detroit. Occupational mobility increased as well. Women joined the armed services as WACs (Women's Army Corps), WAVEs (Women's Reserve, U.S. Naval Reserve), and members of the Nursing Corps; 1,000 civilian women worked as army pilots, flying noncombat missions. Black women left domestic work for sales and factory jobs, from which they had previously been excluded; older women got work that had been unavailable in peacetime; women professionals found new routes to advancement; and women took half the new government jobs created by war. Salaries rose across the board, most drastically in war production. For former waitresses and salesclerks, defense work meant a doubling of wages. The age of the female workforce rose, as more and more married women took jobs. During the war, three out of four new women workers were wives. For the first time, a majority of the female workforce was married.

The sudden demand for female labor spurred changes in public opinion and government propaganda. In the depression, opinion polls had reflected antipathy to the working wife; now business magazines praised women's skill at precision work and repetitive tasks. Reversing the policies of the 1930s, when women were urged to stay home, the Office of War Information (OWI) and the WMC joined forces to lure women into the defense industry. Wartime advertisements stressed femininity, glamour, patriotism, and personal relationships. Prospective employees learned that war work could save the lives of male relatives. "Her Man Is Out There—Nothing Else Matters," read the caption over a picture of an attractive textile worker, now producing uniforms. The OWI propaganda sought to fuse women's new work roles in heavy industry with familiar domestic images. War workers were reminded that the overhead crane was "just like a gigantic clothes wringer" and that making ammunition was as easy as running a vacuum cleaner.

Women seemed to appreciate new options for high pay more than OWI similes. "The major inducement is money," a housewife wrote to OWI. "Women like to be out taking part in the world," wrote another. But wartime propaganda was intended to minimize the war worker's challenge to traditional roles. Defense work, it stressed, represented only a temporary response to an emergency, rather than a permanent transformation. In general, women seemed to make few permanent gains during the war.

They exerted minimal influence over labor policy; the Women's Advisory Committee to the WMC, formed at the end of 1942, had little leverage. Although the National War Labor Board (NWLB) called for equal pay for equal work, women were often classified as (lower-paid) "helper trainees" or "light" workers. As a result, though all salaries rose, the gap between men's and women's earnings increased. Ambivalence greeted the working mother, "a hazard to the security of the child," according to the Children's Bureau. Concern about high rates of female absenteeism eventually spurred some day-care programs, financed by the Lanham Act of 1941. But only a fraction of working mothers was able to take advantage of them; many remained suspicious of government child care. An additional wartime anxiety was the working woman's impact on family stability. The wartime scarcity of men seemed to encourage hasty courtship, early marriage, and a steep surge in the birthrate. Americans worried about rising divorce rates, juvenile delinquency, illegitimacy, and sexual promiscuity. In war production factories, the government waged special campaigns to curb female "sex delinquency." Most important, new work roles for women *were* only temporary.

In some industries, plans for the demobilization of women workers were under way as early as 1943. At the war's end, the female workforce shrank rapidly. Defense plants closed or converted to civilian production; all industries prepared to make room for returning veterans.

Between layoffs and purges, as in the auto industry, some 4 million women lost jobs between 1944 and 1946. Many war workers expected and accepted such losses; others resented them. "War jobs have uncovered unsuspected abilities in American women," claimed a defense worker who did not want to "return to the kitchen." The public, however, feared that women would replace men in the labor force. Advice literature urged women to relinquish their wartime independence and help returning soldiers adjust to civilian life. Another fear was that women war workers had lost their femininity. "After three months in this land of challenging females," a returning *Stars and Stripes* correspondent wrote, "I feel that I should go back to France."

The wartime demand for womanpower, in the end, had no lasting impact on the labor force. In 1945, as new opportunities vanished, concerns that arose during the war—equal pay and child care—vanished too. Day-care facilities shut down; when a bill for equal pay in private employment was proposed, Congress defeated it. But the war still left economic legacies for women. Economic recovery plus veterans' benefits spurred the rapid growth of the middle class. The expanding postwar economy, like the wartime economy, soon proved receptive to women workers. By the end of the 1940s, women were once again entering the labor force in unprecedented numbers, though now taking more traditional jobs—sales, service, and clerical work. Finally, the war left a legacy of inflation that would eventually legitimize the two-income family and the working wife. It was wartime inflation, indeed, that wiped out the depression. But inflation was also one of Roosevelt's most pressing economic problems.

FIGHTING INFLATION

Booming industrial production and full employment, combined with a high level of federal spending and a scarcity of consumer goods, created huge inflationary pressures. To curb inflation, the administration utilized several weapons: wage ceilings, price controls, rationing, taxation, and bond drives. Everyone agreed on principle on the need to check inflation, but no one wanted to come out on the losing end. The administration therefore had a choice: either freeze economic conditions as they stood at the outbreak of the war, thereby perpetuating certain inequalities, or impose controls selectively, thereby permitting some groups to improve their relative position. The second approach, while perhaps less efficient, was politically more popular and was ultimately adopted.

This was well illustrated by the efforts of the NWLB to halt spiraling wages. In July 1942 the NWLB adopted the "Little Steel" formula, which allowed a 15 percent wage increase to cover the rise in living costs since January 1, 1941. The formula, which applied to all workers, helped those who had not yet benefited from boom conditions. Even labor unions that had already obtained the permissible increase found the formula acceptable. The ruling permitted pay increases through overtime and allowed wage hikes that resulted from the upgrading of job classifications. Moreover, where employers were willing to grant increases—as was often the case, given the labor shortage—they were free to do so. In October 1942 the administration attempted to close this loophole by extending the NWLB's jurisdiction over voluntary wage boosts. When even this proved ineffective, Roosevelt issued a "hold the line" order in April 1943. It prevented revision of the Little Steel formula, but still allowed exceptions in extraordinary cases affecting war production and when exceptions were necessary to correct substandard conditions. By the summer of 1943 the government had largely removed wages from the realm of collective bargaining but had still not brought them under ironclad rules.

Regulating the wages workers earned depended, of course, on controlling the prices they had to pay. In April 1942 the Office of Price Administration (OPA) required all merchants to accept as a ceiling the highest price they had charged that March. This general freeze was difficult to enforce and often unfair, for it failed to control the prices of products whose design or packaging had changed, and it penalized dealers who had not already raised their prices. The cost of living continued to creep upward until April 1943, when Roosevelt's hold-the-line order prevented further inflationary rises. Consumer prices advanced by less than 2 percent during the next two years. To a large extent the success of price control hinged on rationing. The OPA took the initiative by introducing ten major rationing programs in 1942, and others followed later. They served different purposes: gasoline was rationed to conserve automobile tires; coffee, to reduce the burden on ocean transport; and canned food, to save tin. The government could not entirely prevent black-market operations—in 1944 one racketeer was found with counterfeit coupons worth 38,000 gallons of gasoline and 437 pairs of shoes—but rationing ensured a reasonably fair distribution of hard-to-get items, and it protected consumers against inflation.

The Roosevelt administration also reduced inflationary pressure by siphoning off excess purchasing power. Wartime taxes imposed heavy duties on the wealthy. The introduction of the withholding system meant that for the first time in U.S. history virtually all wage earners paid federal income taxes and did so out of current earnings. In addition, Roosevelt launched a campaign to sell war bonds, not through the compulsory plan favored by many of his advisers, but instead through voluntary purchases. Secretary of the Treasury Henry Morgenthau believed that such an undertaking would "make the country war-minded." He recruited advertising men (who invented such slogans as "Back the Attack") and Hollywood entertainers (who put personal possessions up for auction) to aid in the drive. The voluntary program had mixed results as an anti-inflation measure. Seven bond drives netted $135 billion, but large investors bought most of the securities, and the sales of low-denomination bonds were disappointing. Even so, 25 million workers signed up for payroll savings plans, and in 1944 bond purchases absorbed more than 7 percent of personal income after taxes.

DR. NEW DEAL MEETS DR. WIN-THE-WAR

World War II solved some of the most serious dilemmas facing social reformers. It brought about full employment and a higher standard of living. It strengthened trade unions, whose membership climbed from 10.5 to 14.75 million. It pushed farm income to new heights and reduced tenancy as landless farmers found jobs in factories. The war also exerted a modest leveling influence. Between 1939 and 1944, the share of national income held by the wealthiest 5 percent of the American people declined from 23.7 to 16.8 percent. In 1944 Congress passed the GI Bill of Rights, a wide-ranging reform measure providing veterans with generous education benefits, readjustment allowances during the transition to civilian life, and guarantees of mortgage loans. Finally, the war seemed to demonstrate once and for all the efficacy of Keynesian economics. Few doubted that soaring government expenditures had produced the boom. In 1943 one reformer noted, "The honest-minded liberal will admit that the common man is getting a better break than ever he did under the New Deal."

Despite all these gains, the war in many respects weakened social reform by obliging reformers to grant priority to military objectives. Liberals either did not protest or did not protest very loudly when the workday was lengthened to boost industrial output, when rural electrification was curtailed to free copper for the military, and when the antitrust law was shelved to permit greater business efficiency. States frequently diluted their child-labor laws so that fourteen- and fifteen-year-olds could join the workforce and work longer hours. From 1940 to 1944 the number of teenage workers jumped from 1.0 to 2.9 million, and more than 1 million teenagers dropped out of school. In December 1943 Roosevelt declared that "Dr. New Deal" had outlived its usefulness and should give way to "Dr. Win-the-War."

Just as the war shouldered aside reforms, so it provided an excuse to abolish various New Deal relief agencies. During 1942 and 1943 Congress—usually with the consent of the administration—eliminated the Civilian Conservation Corps, the Works Progress Administration, and the National Youth Administration. As a result of job openings in national defense, these agencies' clientele had come increasingly to consist of those last to be hired—blacks, women, and the elderly. Although the agencies tried to justify their continued existence by undertaking projects of military value, they could no longer count on strong backing from Roosevelt. Some reformers urged that the Works Progress Administration be preserved in case it was needed after the war. But in December 1942, asserting that a national work relief program was no longer justified, the president gave it an "honorable discharge."

As military costs escalated, so too did the federal deficit. Congress became more unwilling than ever to appropriate funds for domestic programs not directly related to the war, and Roosevelt, recognizing this, became reluctant to request such funds. When several Senate liberals introduced a plan to extend Social Security coverage, liberalize unemployment insurance benefits, and create a comprehensive health-care program, they failed to gain the backing of the administration and stood no chance of winning a legislative majority. Congress not only refused to broaden Social Security coverage, but also froze the rate of contributions at 1 percent, thereby postponing a small scheduled increase. The same desire to trim nondefense expenditures led Congress to slash the budget of the Farm Security Administration, an important New Deal agency that had helped marginal farmers purchase land and equipment.

If social welfare schemes stood little chance in wartime, proposals to help those on the lower rungs of the ladder stood even less. Although most Americans enjoyed higher incomes than ever before, not everyone was well off. In 1944 a Senate committee reported that 20 million people "dwell constantly in a borderland between subsistence and privation." Ten million workers—one-fourth of those engaged in manufacturing—received less than 60 cents an hour. Yet the administration opposed granting them an across-the-board wage hike because it would increase inflationary pressure. Raising the wages of the lowest paid would send inflationary ripples through the economy, since to preserve wage differentials, adjustments would be made all along the line. The resulting higher prices would eventually rob the worker of any benefit. Roosevelt believed that in wartime the government could do no more than ensure that the poor were "not ground down below the margin of existence."

The war weakened liberalism in one final respect: it raised issues that threatened to rupture the New Deal coalition. Roosevelt had built that coalition—consisting of blue-collar workers, southern white farmers, ethnic and racial minority groups, and portions of the middle class—around economic concerns. So long as recovery remained the chief goal, those disparate groups had a good deal in common. But the war subjected this alliance to severe strain. Three sources of division were potentially most disruptive: heightened sensitivity to racial discrimination made it harder to retain the loyalty of both northern blacks and southern whites; issues concerning foreign policy and civil liberties affected the political sentiments of ethnic groups; and the need to curb strikes and regulate the workforce ran the risk of alienating organized labor.

CIVIL RIGHTS AND THE SOUTH

If the Democratic Party had an Achilles heel, it was the issue of racial justice. During Roosevelt's first two terms the depression had eclipsed racial concerns. New Deal relief programs had proved as attractive to black voters in New York City, Chicago, and Detroit as to white voters in Mississippi, Georgia, and Alabama. But the war spurred blacks to insist more strongly on racial equality. Many African-Americans believed that the policy of accommodation had backfired during World War I and that a militant posture would be most likely to win concessions from the Roosevelt administration. Claiming that only the end of racial oppression would ensure their backing for the war, black leaders undertook a "Double V" campaign, stressing victory in the struggle for equality as well as victory on the battlefield. Yet throughout the war years white southerners clung tenaciously to the doctrine of segregation. The president, inevitably, was caught in the middle.

The war inspired civil rights groups to develop new forms of protest. In the summer of 1941, A. Philip Randolph of the Brotherhood of Sleeping Car Porters called for a march on Washington to protest against discrimination and "shake up white America." He demanded that the president withhold defense contracts from employers who practiced discrimination and abolish segregation in the armed forces and federal agencies. Anxious to have the march canceled, Roosevelt agreed to compromise. On June 25, 1941, he issued Executive Order 8802, which provided that government agencies, job training programs, and defense contractors put an end to discrimination. He also created the Fair Employment Practices Committee (FEPC) to investigate violations. The executive order, although it did not provide for integration of the armed forces, was nevertheless hailed by civil rights workers, who concluded, "we get more when we yell than we do when we plead."

By 1943 Randolph was advocating disciplined acts of civil disobedience, and the newly created Congress on Racial Equality (CORE) took action along those lines. Founded by pacifists, CORE endeavored to apply the same tactics of nonviolent resistance to the cause of racial justice that Gandhi had used in the movement for India's independence. Unlike the March on Washington Movement, CORE was interracial, but it too stressed direct action and concentrated on the economic aspects of racial injustice. In 1943 CORE sit-ins helped eliminate segregation in movie theaters and restaurants in Detroit, Denver, and Chicago. Most civil rights activity during the war, however, was channeled through the National Association for the Advancement of Colored People (NAACP). Relying on the traditional means of protest—exposure, propaganda, political pressure, and legal action—the NAACP greatly expanded its membership and influence.

Most southern whites regarded these signs of increased militancy with mounting apprehension. Committed to the preservation of Jim Crow institutions, whites attempted to explain away any evidence of black dissatisfaction as the product of outside agitation. During the war a tidal wave of rumors swept the South, culminating in the widely held fear that black women would no longer work as domestic servants but were busily forming "Eleanor Clubs" (named after the president's wife), whose goal was "a white woman in every kitchen by 1943." Because southerners played a pivotal role in the Democratic coalition, they warned the president to pay attention to their views or else "witness the annihilation of the Democratic party in this section."

In April 1944 a Supreme Court decision abolishing the white primary added to this unrest. The white primary, which effectively disfranchised blacks in eight southern states, had withstood several court challenges. But in 1941 the Supreme Court decided that primaries were an integral part of the election process, and in 1944, in *Smith v. Allwright*, it ruled that political parties were agents of the state and could not nullify the right to vote by practicing racial discrimination. In an effort to mollify southerners, the chief justice assigned the majority opinion to Stanley Reed of Kentucky. But this did not prevent Democratic politicians or editorial writers in the Deep South from construing the decision as part of a broad campaign "to ram social equality down the throats of the white people of the South." Actually, while the decision enfranchised a number of educated, middle-class blacks in large cities, other obstacles to black voting—such as literacy tests and poll taxes—remained as high as ever.

The career of the FEPC illustrated Roosevelt's difficulties in mediating between the conflicting claims of white southerners and civil rights activists. The FEPC represented an ambitious federal commitment to racial equality, and it succeeded in opening opportunities for some black workers. Yet the agency was hampered by restrictions. Theoretically the FEPC had jurisdiction over firms holding defense contracts, but it could act only when a worker filed a formal complaint (many workers were unaware of their right to do so), and even then it could not require compliance with its orders but had to rely on moral suasion. The FEPC could, as a last resort, request the cancellation of a defense contract. But war production always took priority over fair employment practices. Nor could the FEPC always count on strong presidential backing. When the railroad unions flouted a directive to grant equal rights to blacks, the case went to Roosevelt, who merely appointed an investigating committee that never reported. Southerners in Congress bitterly denounced the FEPC. It lost half its budget in 1945 and dissolved within a year.

Black workers made sizable economic gains during the war, usually because of manpower shortages. As the labor supply dwindled, many of the traditional barriers to black employment fell. Employers began to relax bars to hiring, and unions found it more difficult to maintain restrictive membership policies. Blacks, who accounted for just 3 percent of all war workers in the summer of 1942, made up more than 8 percent three years later. The number of skilled black workers doubled, and even larger gains took place in semiskilled positions. Black people by the hundreds of thousands left the farm for the factory in search of opportunity. The government helped in various ways—by hiring more blacks for federal jobs and employing them in higher classifications, by outlawing wage differentials based on race, and by announcing in November 1943 that it would refuse to certify for collective-bargaining purposes unions that discriminated.

The armed forces offered as much resistance to racial equality as had industry, but once again the pressures of war forced a revision in policy. In 1940 military leaders expressed open disdain for black recruits. Blacks could not enlist in the U.S. Marines or Air Corps. They could join the navy only as messmen. They were accepted in the army but segregated rigidly. The army maintained that "leadership is not yet imbedded in the negro race," that black soldiers were inferior fighters, and that the military should not serve as a laboratory for social experiments. Only when it became evident that the existing system involved an unacceptable waste of manpower was it modified. The navy gradually integrated some of its ships, and the army began the process of desegregating training camps. It also sent black combat units into battle more often, but continued to resist integration in war zones except in extraordinary circumstances. By fall 1944 there were 700,000 blacks in the armed services compared with 97,000 at the outbreak of war.

The wartime upheaval in race relations sometimes triggered deadly riots, especially in overcrowded cities and on army bases. In June 1943 a violent racial clash engulfed Detroit, leaving thirty-four people dead and seven hundred injured. In such cases, civil rights workers and segregationists usually blamed each other for stirring up trouble. Roosevelt, recognizing that he could not satisfy both sides, generally allowed military needs to dictate his civil rights policy. He supported civil rights advances that contributed to the war and opposed those that seemed to interfere with it. The president summed up his own view in December 1943: "I don't think, quite frankly, that we can bring about the millennium at this time."

CULTURAL PLURALISM AND CIVIL LIBERTIES

Just as the issue of race affected Roosevelt's hold on blacks and southerners, so issues concerning foreign policy and civil liberties affected his standing with key ethnic groups. The Democrats had always drawn heavy support from Irish Catholics, Germans, Italians, eastern Europeans, and Jews. New Deal economic programs solidified this support. But in the 1940s the president faced a growing defection by German-Americans, who had grown increasingly isolationist; by Italian-Americans, who feared that harsh terms would be imposed on their homeland; and by Polish-Americans, who feared that Roosevelt would allow Russian control over Eastern Europe after the war. Even more serious, Irish-Americans objected to what they regarded as Roosevelt's subservience to Great Britain and excessive collaboration with Russia. Reports to the White House spoke frequently of ethnic group dissatisfaction, of the "anti-Roosevelt sentiment of the Irish Catholics, Italians, and Germans."

To stem this drift away from the Democratic Party, the president offered assurances that a vindictive peace would not be sought, praised the loyalty of German and Italian citizens, and took pains to build a good civil liberties record. Tolerance toward persons of foreign descent was exhibited in several ways. The government placed relatively few restraints on enemy aliens: they could not travel without permission, were barred from areas near strategic installations, and could not possess arms, shortwave receivers, or maps. As the war progressed, however, restrictions were relaxed. Aliens could work in factories having defense contracts if the aliens first obtained permission, and most applications were approved. U.S. citizens of German and Italian extraction encountered little hostility.

Since the Communist Party supported the government during World War II it did not find its liberties abridged. The government was more interested in curbing the far right than the far left. The administration persuaded the Catholic Church to silence Father Charles Coughlin, whose magazine, in effect, was asserting that Jews and communists had tricked America into entering the war. The Justice Department also indicted twenty-six "native fascists" for engaging "in a mass propaganda campaign spreading hatred against the Jews, prejudice against the Negroes, fear of the communists and distrust of our public officials." After courtroom turmoil marred several trials extending over two years, the case was dropped. In 1942 the Federal Bureau of Investigation captured eight German saboteurs who were planning to dynamite railroad terminals and war plants. Roosevelt denied the saboteurs access to the civil courts and arranged a trial by military commission. The Supreme Court, meeting in special session, decided reluctantly that *Ex parte Milligan*—the case in which the Court had ruled unconstitutional Abraham Lincoln's use of military commissions to try civilians in areas remote from combat—did not apply. Six of the saboteurs were executed and two were given long prison terms.

The government provided conscientious objectors with several alternatives to military service. The Selective Service Act (1940) provided that no one should serve as a combatant who "by reason of religious training and belief, is conscientiously opposed to war in any form." Conscientious objectors usually performed noncombatant duties. Perhaps 25,000 men, most of them Quakers and Mennonites, served in the Army Medical Corps and related branches of the military. Those who objected to military service in any form could do "work of national importance under civilian direction." Some 11,950 men worked in civilian public service camps, where they engaged mainly in forestry and conservation, building roads, clearing trails, fighting forest fires, and digging irrigation ditches. About 500 objectors volunteered to be subjects of medical experiments to find cures for typhus, malaria, and other illnesses. Alternatives to the draft, however, did not satisfy everyone. Those whose conscience did not permit them to register with the Selective Service System, and those whose objection to war rested on political rather than religious grounds, were imprisoned. About 5,500 men went to jail, more than three-fourths of them Jehovah's Witnesses who were denied the ministerial exemptions they sought.

Significantly, the only group of immigrants to lose its rights—Japanese-Americans on the West Coast—was politically powerless. Foreign-born Japanese who had migrated before 1924 were barred from citizenship, and most of their children, although born in the United States and therefore citizens, were too young to vote. Japanese-Americans were vulnerable for other reasons as well. They formed a relatively small group, were concentrated in a few states, were largely confined to nonessential occupations (such as vegetable farming), and could be easily singled out. Powerless and poorly assimilated, Japanese-Americans were considered guilty simply because of their race. During the spring of 1942 more than 110,000 people, two-thirds of them citizens, were herded into relocation centers. There most of them remained until 1945.

The decision to relocate Japanese-Americans reflected racial, military, and political considerations. General John DeWitt, who headed the Western Defense Command, expressed a widely held view that racial attributes made all Japanese a menace. "Racial affinities are not severed by migration," he said. "The Japanese race is an enemy race." Military leaders believed the Japanese-Americans would commit sabotage at the first opportunity. The absence of any such overt acts was merely taken as proof that an "invisible deadline" was drawing near. Although some Americans undoubtedly believed that military necessity justified relocation, others used the argument as a convenient pretext. Nativist groups had long agitated for Japanese exclusion, and some agricultural interests also expected to profit by the removal of Japanese competitors. West Coast congressmen badgered government agencies, urging drastic action. "There's a tremendous volume of public opinion now developing against the Japanese," DeWitt reported in January 1942. He added that this was the opinion of "the best people of California."

Throughout the war the Supreme Court often defended the rights of unpopular groups. It set aside the denaturalization of a German-born citizen charged with continued loyalty to

A Japanese-American family at the Manzanar Relocation Center. *(Library of Congress)*

the Third Reich, it protected a fascist sympathizer who savagely denounced Roosevelt, and it struck down a law compelling schoolchildren to salute the flag. Yet the Supreme Court did not challenge the government's policy toward Japanese-Americans. In June 1943 the Court unanimously held, in the *Hirabayashi* case, that military officials could impose a curfew that applied only to Japanese-American citizens. In time of war, the Court reasoned, "residents having ethnic affiliations with an invading enemy may be a greater source of danger than those of different ancestry." In December 1944, in *Korematsu v. United States*, the Court upheld the exclusion of Japanese-American citizens from the West Coast. One of the three dissenting justices branded the decision a "legalization of racism." At the same time, however, the Court ruled that the government could not hold citizens in relocation centers beyond a reasonable time without evidence of disloyal behavior. The decision, though, was handed down a day after the government had revoked the order banning Japanese-Americans from the coast.

LABOR AND POLITICS

Organized labor was the linchpin of the Democratic coalition. If proof were needed, it was furnished by the 1942 congressional elections. Democrats suffered a severe defeat primarily because many war workers who had moved to new states could not meet residency requirements. The Republicans captured forty-four additional seats in the House of Representatives and nine in the Senate. Roosevelt's policies took account of this dependence on labor. During the war, workers significantly improved their standard of living. Hourly wage rates rose by 24 percent, and weekly earnings (which included overtime) spurted by 70 percent. But as the war progressed, the president was confronted with the politically explosive problem of how to deal with strikes without antagonizing labor.

Late in December 1941 spokespersons for labor and business had agreed to refrain from strikes and lockouts. But the pledge was not legally binding, and workers who suspected that they were being shortchanged ultimately proved willing to violate the agreement. During 1943, 3.1 million workers took part in stoppages compared with fewer than 1 million the year before. The most serious was a strike by 400,000 members of the United Mine Workers under the leadership of John L. Lewis. Dissatisfied with federal wage controls, miners of bituminous coal refused to accept the decisions of the NWLB. The strike caused severe public indignation. By mid-1943 Lewis had apparently become the most hated figure in the United States.

In June 1943 Congress passed the War Labor Disputes Act, making it a crime to encourage strikes in plants taken over by the government, but Roosevelt understood that a harsh response—such as an attempt to draft miners or send them to jail—might easily boomerang. Coal could not be mined without the union's cooperation, and drastic measures would offend most of organized labor. Roosevelt had to avoid taking any step that might cause labor to close ranks behind the coal miners, yet he could not allow so attractive a settlement that other workers would follow the miners to the picket lines. The task, one official noted, was "to isolate Mr. Lewis and his assistants from other more responsible labor leaders."

Pulled in one direction by a desire to appease his labor constituency and pushed in the other by public opinion, the president charted a hazardous course between the two. He had the government take over the coal mines but placed them under Secretary of the Interior Harold Ickes, whose relationship with Lewis was reasonably cordial. He appealed to the miners to return to work but permitted bargaining to proceed even while they stayed off the job. He approved a settlement granting the miners a substantial raise, but which did so through a new system of computing working time that did not technically violate hourly wage ceilings. He vetoed the War Labor Disputes Act, but requested authority to draft strikers (up to the age of sixty-five) as noncombatants. Roosevelt managed to retain the goodwill of most labor leaders, who applauded his veto—which was promptly overridden by Congress—and paid little attention to his alternative proposal.

So successfully did Roosevelt cultivate labor that it provided massive assistance to his 1944 election campaign. Inasmuch as two of every three union members considered themselves Democrats, labor knew that a light turnout, such as had occurred in 1942, would be a disaster. The Congress of Industrial Organizations (CIO), therefore, set up a political action committee that undertook large-scale registration drives and distributed 85 million pieces of campaign literature. On Election Day, committee volunteers made telephone calls reminding union members to vote, provided baby-sitters so that housewives could get to the polls, and arranged transportation for those who needed it. The CIO eventually spent $1.5 million, and labor's total contribution to the Democratic campaign—over $2 million—made up 30 percent of the party's expenditures. Although unions had taken part in past campaigns, never had they done so much for any candidate.

Roosevelt nailed down the labor vote by stressing economic themes. He reminded audiences that the Republicans were the party of Hoovervilles and breadlines, the Democrats the party of collective bargaining and Social Security. Roosevelt endorsed an Economic Bill of Rights, which recognized each person's right to work at a job that would "provide adequate food and clothing and recreation," to live in a decent home, to receive adequate medical care, to obtain a good education, and to be protected against the hazards of sickness, accident, and unemployment. Ironically, Republican candidate Thomas E. Dewey of New York, although critical of Roosevelt's management of the war, endorsed much of the reform program of the New Deal, at least that portion already on the statute books. He supported Social Security, unemployment insurance, relief for the needy, and collective bargaining. Some Democrats dubbed him "Little Sir Echo." The 1944 campaign helped place the welfare state beyond the range of partisan dispute.

Roosevelt, although carrying thirty-six states, won his most slender victory. The president obtained 53.4 percent of the popular vote, compared with 54.7 percent in 1940. He won by a margin of 3.6 million votes as against 5 million in 1940. The key to his win was the labor vote in the big cities. In cities with a population over 100,000, Roosevelt garnered 60.7 percent of the vote. In seven states with enough combined electoral strength to have reversed the outcome—New York, Illinois, Pennsylvania, Michigan, Missouri, Maryland, and New Jersey—his plurality in each state's largest city overcame a Republican majority in the rest of the state. The Democrats picked up twenty-two seats in the House and lost one in the Senate. Without the help of the CIO's political action committee, Roosevelt would not have done so well. That help, in turn, reflected Roosevelt's ability to contend with the potentially disruptive issues posed by the war economy.

WAR AND SOCIAL CHANGE

World War II acted as a catalyst for social change. It increased the power of the federal government and of the presidency in an enduring way. During the war the government employed more people and spent more money than ever before. From 1940 to 1945 the number of civilian employees of the government climbed from 1 million to 3.8 million, and expenditures soared from $9 billion to $98.4 billion. When peace returned, the government reduced its operations, but they remained well above prewar levels. The war also accelerated the growth of executive authority and a corresponding erosion of legislative influence. Congress delegated sweeping powers to the president, who in turn delegated them to administrators in war agencies. The big decisions during the war were usually made by men responsible to the president, not by congressional leaders. The Supreme Court, which had in the past scrutinized such delegations of legislative authority, refused even to review such cases during the war.

War transformed the economic arrangements under which Americans lived. The huge outlay of funds for military purposes (which at the height of the war reached $250 million a day) enormously inflated industrial capacity. Manufacturing output doubled during the war, and gross national product rose from $88.6 billion in 1939 to $198.7 billion five years later. New industries, including synthetic rubber and synthetic fabrics, came into being. But the desire to obtain the greatest output in the shortest time resulted in awarding a predominant share of military contracts to large corporations and fostering the tendency toward business consolidation. Two-thirds of all military contracts went to one hundred firms; nearly one-half went to

MARTHA GRAHAM
AND MODERN DANCE

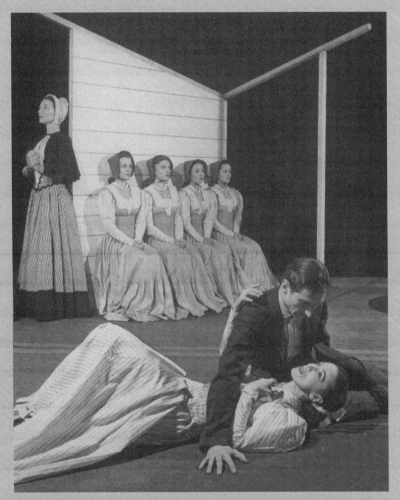

Martha Graham and Erick Hawkins in Aaron Copland's *Appalachian Spring*, 1944. *(Jerry Cooke/Time & Life Pictures/Getty Images)*

In the late 1930s and early 1940s a central theme in the work of writers, artists, photographers, composers, playwrights, filmmakers, and dancers was a fascination with America itself—its history, folklore, heritage, and even geography. Appreciation of the values associated with the American past reached a culmination during World War II when those values seemed to offer a hopeful, decent, and humane alternative to totalitarian doctrine. The success of

Frank Sinatra's "The House I Live In"—and, even more, that of the Broadway musical *Oklahoma!*—attested to the depth of those sentiments. They were also reflected in modern dance, most notably in the work of Martha Graham.

Born in 1894, Martha Graham had spent her youth in California where, in 1916, she began to study dance with Ruth St. Denis and Ted Shawn. She eventually became dissatisfied with the "Denishawn" style, which stressed gossamer motion, oriental pageantry, and silken costumes. Graham was, however, equally dissatisfied with traditional ballet, with its graceful lifts, elegant postures, and classical themes. She sought to develop a new dance vocabulary, in which movement was stark and down-to-earth, the costumes simple and severe. One critic noted, "Her idiom of motion has little of the aerial in it, but there's a lot of rolling on the floor." By 1926 she had moved to New York City, organized her own troupe, and given her first recital.

Graham, who believed that dance should be relevant to contemporary concerns, was by the mid-1930s affirming American values and denouncing fascist brutality. In *Chronicle* (1936), she sympathized with the Loyalist cause in the Spanish Civil War. *American Document* (1938) provided a capsule version of the nation's history—including sections on Puritanism, the Indian, and the Declaration of Independence—ending in what the *New York Times* described as "a final tableau in celebration of democracy." Graham's purpose, noted one critic, was to "bring to bear upon today's perplexities all that was sturdy and upright and liberating in the American dream." Graham used a male dancer, Erick Hawkins, who created something of a sensation by performing bare-chested. She was the first choreographer to utilize a narrator who, by explaining events, made modern dance forms comprehensible to many audiences who had previously found them mystifying.

Graham's celebration of American values reached a peak in the 1944 production of *Appalachian Spring*, which told the story of the marriage of a young couple in rural Pennsylvania in the mid-nineteenth century. The dance was set in a farmyard, the dancers incorporated portions of the Virginia reel, and the music, by Aaron Copland, was based partly on the Shaker hymn "Simple Gifts." *Appalachian Spring* vibrated with a spirit of resilience and optimism.

After the war Graham gradually lost her place as the dominant figure in the world of modern dance, but those who replaced her—Merce Cunningham, Paul Taylor—had been her students. She performed for the last time in 1969 at the age of seventy-five, but remained actively involved in choreography until her death in 1991. Martha Graham's extraordinary career epitomized one of her maxims: "The only freedom in life is that of the discipline one chooses."

Web Links

http://marthagraham.org/downloads/MarthaGraham2005.pdf
The Virginia Arts Festival 2005 website about Graham and her technique.

www.classicalnotes.net/classics/appalachian.html
An essay on Aaron Copland's 'Appalachian Spring' by Peter Gutmann.

Women's Army Auxiliary Corps. Third Officer Jessie Hogan, who has learned to operate efficiently many types of motor transport vehicles, is now competent to teach WAAC trainees to do likewise. *(Library of Congress)*

three dozen corporate giants. From 1941 to 1943, half a million small businesses disappeared. In 1939 firms with more than 10,000 workers employed 13 percent of the manufacturing labor force, but in 1944 they accounted for fully 31 percent. Since army and navy procurement officers awarded war contracts, close ties developed between business and the military. The military-industrial complex reached maturity later, but it had its origins in World War II.

Just as the war modernized and consolidated industry, so it helped create big agriculture and big labor. The farm population declined by 17 percent from 1940 to 1945 as people left the countryside for jobs in factories and shipyards. But farmers' output and productivity climbed sharply as a result of good weather, the increased use of fertilizers, greater mechanization, and the consolidation of small farms into large ones. A million more tractors were in use at the end than at the beginning of the war. Not only did the war hasten the appearance of large-scale, mechanized farming, but it also increased the strength of organized labor. Trade unions attracted millions of members, gained a foothold in new industries, and made collective bargaining accepted practice.

The United States emerged from the war a more highly urban and technological society. The government greatly expanded its role in supporting scientific research and training. Wartime advances in medicine, particularly in the production of penicillin, saved countless lives. Some 12 million men had entered the armed services, and many later received a college education or technical training under the GI Bill of Rights. More than 15 million civilians moved to new homes during the war. Cities with shipyards, aircraft plants, or munitions factories grew at a staggering rate. Six large cities attracted 2 million migrants; California alone received 1.4 million people. As one observer noted, "the whole pattern of our economic and social life is undergoing kaleidoscopic changes, without so much as a bomb being dropped on our shores."

TRUMAN'S TROUBLES: THE POLITICS OF INFLATION

On April 12, 1945, a stunned nation heard that Franklin Roosevelt had suddenly died of a stroke at his retreat in Warm Springs, Georgia. Harry S. Truman, who succeeded to the presidency, was quite unlike his predecessor. Roosevelt had been born to wealth and status on a Hudson River estate; Truman came from a Missouri family in modest circumstances. Roosevelt had attended Groton, Harvard, and Columbia Law School; Truman, upon graduation from high school, worked as a railroad timekeeper, in a newspaper mailroom, as a bank clerk, and on a farm. After a stint in the army during World War I, Truman entered the haberdashery business and then took evening courses for two years at the Kansas City Law School. Later, political boss Tom Pendergast of Kansas City chose him to run for county judge and in 1934 picked him for the U.S. Senate. Roosevelt selected Truman as his running mate in 1944 because Truman was the second choice of each faction in the Democratic Party—labor, city bosses, the South—and the only candidate they all found acceptable. Roosevelt seldom made a rash decision; Truman often acted on impulse. Associates often described Roosevelt as "sphinx-like"; Truman told everyone just what he thought.

Truman, like Roosevelt, had to contend with the problem of inflation, but in a different and less favorable context. Nothing revealed this more clearly than the battle over Truman's attempt to preserve the powerful wartime Office of Price Administration (OPA). The OPA faced criticism from businessmen who wanted to raise prices and, ironically, from consumers who were tired of doing without certain items. In 1946, responding to these pressures, Congress extended the OPA but stripped it of much authority. Truman recognized that if he signed the measure he would be expected to keep prices down even though the OPA would lack the means of doing so. He vetoed the bill; controls expired on July 1, 1946; and prices skyrocketed. The cost-of-living index rose 6 percent in just one month. The administration employed a few stopgap measures to curb inflation but none worked. The consumer price index rose more than twenty-four points from July 1946 to July 1947, compared with less than four points in the preceding year. Prices continued their upward spiral through 1948.

Labor difficulties plagued the Truman administration no less than rising prices. A rash of strikes broke out in 1946 as automobile, steel, electrical, and communications workers walked off their jobs in an effort to win higher wages and consolidate wartime gains. In 1946, 4.6 million workers went on strike, more than ever before in the nation's history. Strikes by railroad workers and coal miners presented especially severe challenges to the administration. In both cases, unions refused to accept arbitrated settlements. Truman, believing that the walkouts jeopardized national security, intervened by taking over the railroads and mines. When the unions persisted, the president was furious. He harshly denounced the railroad workers, called for legislation authorizing him to draft strikers, and spoke of the need to "hang a few traitors and make our own country safe for democracy." He sought and obtained an injunction against the United Mine Workers, which, after the Supreme Court upheld the president, had to pay a stiff fine. Although both disputes were ultimately settled, Truman's proposal to draft strikers and his willingness to use an injunction enraged organized labor.

By November 1946 the various strands in the old New Deal coalition were unraveling, and the Democrats suffered a sharp setback in the congressional elections. Running on the slogan "Had Enough?" the Republicans gained eleven seats in the Senate and fifty-six in the House, thereby capturing control of Congress for the first time since 1928. Democrat J. William Fulbright of Arkansas even suggested that Truman provide what the voters obviously wanted by appointing a Republican as secretary of state (at that time the position that was next in order of presidential succession) and then resigning from office. Truman did nothing of the sort. Instead, by capitalizing on the behavior of the Republican Congress, he began to reconstruct a viable political coalition.

First, Truman made a peace offering to organized labor by vetoing the Taft-Hartley Act in June 1947. Congress had passed the measure in response to postwar labor turmoil and opinion polls showing that two out of three people favored tighter control of union activities. The bill outlawed the closed shop, banned such union activities as secondary boycotts, provided for an eighty-day cooling-off period before calling a strike if the president thought it would cause a national emergency, barred union contributions to political parties, and required labor officials to sign affidavits attesting that they were not subversive. It also permitted states to pass right-to-work laws outlawing the union shop. (In a closed shop, only union members could be hired; in a union shop, anyone hired had to join the union.) Truman declared the act unworkable, unfair, and arbitrary, but a coalition of Republicans and southern Democrats easily overrode his veto. Truman's message nevertheless went far toward mending fences with the labor movement.

Next, Truman appealed to religious and ethnic minorities by urging a liberal entrance policy toward refugees. More than 1.2 million displaced persons, mainly Catholics and Jews from Eastern Europe, were living in camps in American-held zones. Many had been seized by the Germans during the war and used as forced laborers. Others had fled from areas that had fallen under Russian control. Truman admitted 42,000 displaced persons in 1945, and he then urged Congress to revise the immigration laws in order to admit 400,000 displaced persons a year. The old restrictionist argument—that immigrants were dangerous radicals—hardly made sense when applied to people fleeing communist rule. Yet Congress did nothing in 1947. The following year it passed a lukewarm measure admitting 200,000 displaced persons over a two-year period, but excluding most Jews and many Catholics. Terming the bill "flagrantly discriminatory," Truman signed it reluctantly.

Finally Truman attempted to allay any suspicion that his administration was "soft on communism," a theme successfully exploited by Republicans in the 1946 congressional elections. Public opinion polls that year revealed that most Americans considered communism an internal menace. Fear was reinforced when the Canadian government announced that it had broken a

Soviet espionage ring and again when the House Committee on Un-American Activities began a new round of hearings into alleged subversion in government. In 1947 Truman responded. The Justice Department instituted deportation proceedings against aliens with communist affiliations and began drawing up a list of subversive organizations. The administration also introduced a comprehensive loyalty program under which all federal employees would undergo security checks. The program was couched in loose and potentially dangerous language. An employee could be fired if "reasonable grounds exist for belief that the person involved is disloyal." Those grounds included acts of treason or espionage, advocacy of violent revolution, or "membership in, affiliation with or sympathetic association with" any organization on the attorney general's list.

These initiatives were closely related to the deterioration of relations with the Soviet Union. By 1947 Americans came increasingly to accept the view (which they had earlier held during the period of the Nazi-Soviet pact) that Russian communism closely resembled German fascism. Both were characterized by purges, concentration camps, secret police, and one-party rule. Both fomented subversion abroad. Both were aggressive and expansionist. Both understood only one thing: force. "A totalitarian state is no different whether you call it Nazi, Fascist, Communist," Truman told his daughter. "The oligarchy in Russia . . . is a Frankenstein dictatorship worse than any of the others, Hitler included." By 1941 the American people had developed an image of Germany that sustained them through four years of hot war. By 1947 they were developing an image of Russia that would prepare them for four decades of cold war.

CHAPTER TEN

1941–1947
One World Into Two

American soldiers on the deck of a Coast Guard assault transport on the trip across the English Channel. *(AP Photo)*

On the home front Americans were single-minded in their pursuit of victory. On the battlefield they waged campaigns with the same determination. Diplomatically, however, U.S. policies were divided, even contradictory. On the one hand, the Roosevelt administration sought a united world, devoid of exclusive economic or political spheres, in which open access to all areas could be enjoyed by every nation that could compete. This vision was embodied in the Atlantic Charter of 1941. On the other hand, the president had to come to an agreement with his two great allies, Great Britain and Russia, who feared that they had been so weakened by war that they could not compete peacefully against the gigantic American power. The British and Soviets therefore sought their own exclusive spheres of influence. Washington finally made Great Britain abandon its policies of spheres, but could never force Joseph Stalin to do so. In 1945 Roosevelt, then Harry S. Truman, finally opted for an open world and so opposed a Soviet sphere of influence in Eastern Europe. The confrontation thus slowly developed through a series of crises until in 1947 the Truman Doctrine and the Marshall Plan publicly signaled the beginning of nearly a half-century in which the two great powers divided and nearly destroyed the world.

CHURCHILL AND STALIN VERSUS ROOSEVELT

Even before Pearl Harbor, the United States had begun preparing for the postwar peace. The planning took on new urgency on June 23, 1941, when Adolf Hitler suddenly invaded the Soviet Union. Except for a brief honeymoon period in late 1933, Russia and the United States had been opponents since the 1890s. The 1941–1945 alliance provided only a brief interlude in this history of confrontation. Some Americans thought Hitler could quickly defeat the Soviets. Secretary of War Henry Stimson told Roosevelt that Germany might need no longer than one to three months to conquer Russia. Senator Harry S. Truman, Democrat of Missouri, unfortunately made public his hope that Hitler's and Stalin's forces would bleed each other white on the plains of Russia. Roosevelt took a different course. He ordered immediate aid to Stalin and then began a lend-lease program that by 1945 had pumped $11 billion worth of goods into Russia. He managed to do this despite strong anti-Soviet opposition in Congress. FDR and his top advisers hoped that Russia would stop the German armies, and as the summer passed, it seemed that Russia was succeeding. Roosevelt acted on a principle that British prime minister Winston Churchill had declared: he would make a pact with the devil himself if it would help defeat Hitler.

Roosevelt then focused on another danger. After Hitler's invasion of Russia, Churchill and Stalin had exchanged messages that the State Department feared involved deals on postwar boundaries, possibly even a division of Europe into British and Russian spheres. To clarify this explosive problem, Roosevelt and Churchill secretly met off the coast of Newfoundland in August 1941. In the Atlantic Charter issued publicly after the meeting, two key provisions gave the president much of what he demanded. One clause pledged "respect [for] the right of all peoples to choose the form of government under which they will live." These words applied to victims of Germany and Japan, but they could relate to the Baltic States and to areas of Finland and Eastern Europe that the Soviets had claimed since 1939. The phrase could also mean that parts of the British Empire (such as India and Hong Kong) could leave the empire—as Washington had long hoped they would.

Another provision of the charter declared that Churchill and Roosevelt "will endeavor with due respect for their existing obligations, to further the enjoyment of all States, great or small, victor or vanquished, of access, on equal terms, to the trade and to the raw materials of the world which are needed for their economic prosperity." Churchill had strongly objected to this clause. He knew that it aimed at destroying the exclusive British Commonwealth preferential trading system. The prime minister yielded only when the phrase "with due respect for their existing obligations" was added. In February 1942, the United States turned the screws tighter. In return for a long-term lend-lease pledge from FDR, the British had to promise to discuss the dismantling of their Imperial Preference system after the war.

Roosevelt and Secretary of State Cordell Hull were elated. The key to postwar planning lay in Anglo-American cooperation, for before the war these two powers accounted for half the world's trade. Postwar trade would now be conducted on American, not British, terms. As Hull had long believed, moreover, economic success could be quickly translated into a political triumph. In mid-December, British Foreign Secretary Anthony Eden visited Stalin, who immediately demanded Anglo-American agreement to dividing postwar Germany and giving Russia control of the Baltic States and a large slice of eastern Poland. Eden refused, arguing that he would have to clear the matter with Roosevelt. Stalin angrily replied, "I thought the Atlantic Charter was directed against [Hitler and Tojo]. It now looks as if the charter were directed against the U.S.S.R." Eden would not budge, but the following month when Roosevelt asked Russia to agree to the Atlantic Charter, Stalin did so only after adding the formal reservation that "the practical application of these principles will necessarily adapt itself to the circumstances, needs, and historic peculiarities of particular countries." Behind these words lurked the causes of the Cold War: Soviet refusal to allow anyone to claim a right to interfere in Eastern Europe, an area which the Germans had twice used as an avenue to invade Russia during the previous twenty-five years.

ONE WORLD, OR GULLIBLE'S TRAVELS

The central issues of the Cold War were thus in plain view as early as 1942. The question was how Roosevelt and Stalin would deal with them. Washington officials agreed that the most important priority must be a global economic program, resting on Atlantic Charter principles, which would remove the danger of another worldwide depression. Assistant Secretary of State William Clayton put it starkly: if Americans could not be assured of an orderly and secure postwar world, the United States itself would become an "armed camp," living "by ration books for the next century or so." Vice President Henry A. Wallace warned that without comprehensive planning, "a series of economic storms will follow this war. These will take the form of inflation and temporary scarcities, followed by surpluses, crashing prices, unemployment, bankruptcy, and in some cases violent revolution." Wendell Willkie capsulated the solution to such dangers in the title of his best-selling book of 1943, *One World*. Willkie's blasts at exclusive spheres (particularly those in the British Empire) led Churchill sarcastically to suggest that Willkie's book be subtitled "Gullible's Travels." But the phrase "one world" said it all: haunted by the Ghost of Depression Past, Americans determined to find markets for their inevitable postwar surpluses in one world undivided and indivisible.

Of course this goal required, as Hull warned Roosevelt in early 1942, that the United States oppose any "arrangement which would make the Soviet Union the dominating power of Eastern Europe if not the whole continent." The last part of Hull's admonition was crucial. The Eastern European market itself was not of great importance to Americans, but Soviet control would present a grave danger as a precedent. If Stalin succeeded there, he might use his hold over the region as a lever to gain influence in the remainder of Europe. If he did forge a private sphere, moreover, his success might encourage the British to repudiate the Atlantic Charter and reestablish their own spheres. Instead of one world, there would again be, as in the 1930s, a world divided economically and politically. Roosevelt and his countrymen would be back in the dark days of 1938. As Wallace, Clayton, and many others warned, that simply could not be allowed to happen.

In early 1942, Roosevelt began to try to convince the Soviets to work for an open world. In one sense his position was weak, for American military forces were inactive in the European theater and retreating in the Pacific. The Japanese mopped up the Philippines, humiliating and killing thousands of captured Americans by driving them on a horrible "death march" on the Bataan Peninsula. General Douglas MacArthur, U.S. commander in the Pacific, fled the Philippines to establish headquarters in Australia. The Japanese would not be stopped until midyear at the gigantic naval battle of Midway and then in hand-to-hand fighting at Guadalcanal. In Russia, Soviet troops only slowed Hitler's forces, thus adding to Roosevelt's problems—for Stalin pushed hard for Anglo-American armies to open a second front in Western Europe to relieve the German pressure.

Against this background, Soviet Foreign Minister V.M. Molotov arrived in Washington in May 1942. He wanted to discuss postwar boundaries, but Roosevelt avoided embarrassing conversations by suggesting instead that after the war "four policemen" (the United States, the USSR, Great Britain, and China) should patrol the world. Molotov and later Stalin readily agreed, for they believed that as a "policeman" Russia would be able to take what it needed in Eastern Europe. This was not at all what FDR had in mind, but the contradictions in his "four policemen" concept would not be faced for nearly three years. Despite the problems inherent in the idea, Roosevelt wanted to avoid discussing specific postwar settlements. Such a discussion could lead to Soviet-American arguments and disillusionment at home. Moreover, the longer he waited, the more financial and military power the president thought he could bring to bear on Stalin.

A second remark to Molotov had immediate repercussions. Roosevelt promised a second front in Western Europe by late 1942. Molotov and Stalin were elated. They believed that the Soviet people would shortly no longer be alone in engaging Hitler's main forces. But there was no second front in 1942. Churchill killed the plan by refusing to agree that such a campaign could be safely opened so soon.

The prime minister instead urged that Anglo-American forces invade North Africa, where the Nazis and their French collaborators, the Vichy French government, held strategic positions in the Mediterranean. Roosevelt realized that Churchill was advancing this plan in part because North Africa had long been vital to the British and French empires, but he finally acquiesced in order to get American soldiers engaged in the European theater. It almost looked as if Churchill and Roosevelt preferred reclaiming the British and French empires while leaving Stalin alone to endure the full might of Hitler's armies on the European mainland.

1943—TURNING OF THE TIDE

The Grand Alliance of the United States, Great Britain, the Soviet Union, and their allies was thus in trouble by early 1943. Roosevelt tried to repair the damage by asking Stalin and

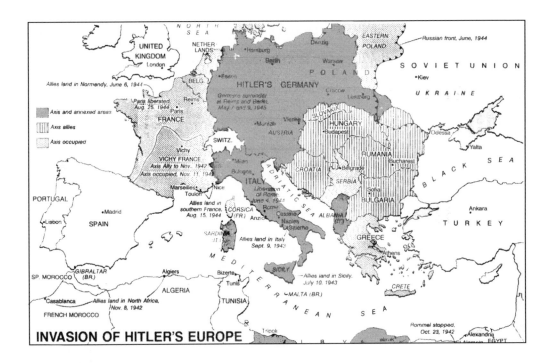

INVASION OF HITLER'S EUROPE

Churchill to meet him at Casablanca in January. Stalin refused, pleading that the climactic struggle at Stalingrad required his constant attention. He asked only that the second front in France be opened immediately. FDR replied that this certainly could be done in 1943. At Casablanca, however, Churchill once more refused. He insisted that since the Allies were not yet militarily prepared, they instead should move from North Africa into Sicily and then Italy. Roosevelt again reluctantly acquiesced, but tried to soften the blow for Stalin by announcing that unlike the case in 1918, when the Germans were not thoroughly defeated, the Allies this time would accept only "unconditional surrender." This sudden announcement was risky, for it threatened to lengthen the war by driving the German people into a last-ditch resistance. Roosevelt and Churchill were willing to take that chance in order to placate Stalin. By insisting on unconditional surrender they assured Russia that although no second front was in sight, they would nevertheless continue the war until a thoroughly defeated Germany would no longer threaten the Soviets.

It was interesting diplomacy, but also increasingly irrelevant. A week after Roosevelt made his pledge, Russian armies stopped the Germans at Stalingrad, capturing hundreds of thousands of Hitler's finest troops. By midsummer the Soviets had regained two-thirds of their lost territory. They had successfully battled 80 percent of Hitler's total force and were now driving it back without the often promised, but never delivered, second front. Stalin's need for his Western allies was still great, but dropping markedly. The military campaigns of 1943 drastically changed the diplomatic relationships between Russia and its two allies.

And so did a political crisis in Italy. After invading that country, the Americans and British refused to allow the Soviets to have any influence in reconstructing the Italian government.

Fearful that Stalin would help Italy's large Communist Party gain power, Churchill argued, "We cannot be put in a position where our two armies [the American and British] are doing all the fighting but Russians have a veto and must be consulted." Roosevelt, agreeing, observed that the Allied military commander, General Dwight D. Eisenhower, must have complete authority. The Russians were thus excluded, but at a cost. For Stalin would repeatedly use the Italian precedent to justify Russian control of Eastern Europe during and after the war. If the Russians were not to have "access" to Italy as the Atlantic Charter seemed to promise, then, Stalin could argue, the charter might as well not apply to Eastern Europe either. He was indeed perfectly willing to accept such a division. Stalin believed that each ally had its own security interests. The question was whether the Americans would accept this splitting of Europe into political spheres or try to have it both ways: exclude the Soviets from Italy but insist that the United States have a voice in Eastern Europe. That key issue was becoming sharper.

Churchill, Roosevelt, and Stalin met together for the first time at Teheran, Iran, in late November 1943 to bind together the splintering alliance. On the surface, discussions went smoothly. The three men established easy personal relationships, doubtlessly helped along by Churchill's and Roosevelt's firm pledges that a second front would be opened in France within six months. Stalin in turn promised he would fight Japan after Hitler's defeat. Roosevelt himself raised the crucial question of Russia's western boundary. He told Stalin that he "did not intend to go to war with the Soviet Union" over Russian absorption of the Baltic States. It was also quickly agreed that the Polish-Russian boundary must be moved westward at the expense of Poland.

But the conference floundered on a pivotal question of the Polish postwar government. Since 1940 a pro-Western Polish government-in-exile had operated in London, while a pro-communist Polish regime worked out of Russia. When the London group refused to accept a new Polish-Russian boundary, Stalin would not recognize the group. The hatred burst into the open in mid-1943, when the bodies of 4,200 Polish soldiers were discovered in Poland's Katyn Forest. The London Poles immediately—and correctly—charged Russia with having slaughtered the men during the fighting in 1940. These charges added a tragic dimension to an already explosive problem. The Big Three (the Soviets, British, and Americans) could not reach agreement on either the composition of a postwar Polish government or a Polish-German boundary. For the next eighteen months the sore of Poland festered, spreading a cancerous infection within the Grand Alliance.

Two acts of wartime diplomacy had now been played. The first had set the theme with the Atlantic Charter and the British and Russian opposition to its principles. The second act, played out in Italy and Teheran, had brought into the open the dilemmas that would wreck the postwar peace. The third act, which in traditional theater resolves the crises of Act II, would occur with the Yalta conference and its aftermath. Instead of resolving the crises, however, Act III was to become a nerve-wracking, multibillion-dollar, forty-year-long ordeal.

ONE WORLD BECOMES TWO: YALTA AND AFTERWARD

On June 6, 1944, Allied troops under the command of General Eisenhower swept ashore on the Normandy beaches in the largest amphibious operation in history. Led by General George Patton's Third Army, the Allied forces broke through German resistance, liberating Paris in

The Big Three: Prime Minister Winston Churchill, President Franklin D. Roosevelt, and Marshal Joseph Stalin at the palace in Yalta. *(Library of Congress)*

late August and crossing into Germany in mid-September. Devastating air raids hit German war industries, while an unsuccessful attempt to assassinate Hitler in July by some of his closest military advisers indicated the extent of the Nazis' internal weakness. Stalin meanwhile launched a major offensive that conquered much of Eastern Europe in 1944.

Churchill now faced a dilemma. The British had important economic and political interests in Hungary, Yugoslavia, and particularly Greece. The Greek situation was especially sensitive, for that nation bordered the eastern Mediterranean (one of the so-called lifelines of the British Empire to Egypt and India). But Churchill's attempt to restore the Greek king's power had produced a civil war in which Greek communists helped the antimonarchical forces. The prime minister flew to Moscow and in a dramatic meeting with Stalin worked out, on a half-sheet of scrap paper, a deal that would give Russia control of Romania and Bulgaria, grant Churchill full power in Greece, and divide Yugoslavia and Hungary equally. Roosevelt warned that he would not be bound by this division. But Churchill went ahead, over strong American objections, to quell the Greek civil war with military force. Stalin kept his part of the bargain by staying out of that situation while clamping firm control over Romania.

As the Big Three made plans for a conference scheduled at the Soviet resort city of Yalta in February 1945, gloom was settling over Washington. It became even gloomier when in

December 1944 the Germans launched a last-ditch counteroffensive that drove a huge bulge into Eisenhower's lines. At Bastogne, Belgium, only heroics by General Patton and a surrounded American force—which refused to surrender—delayed the German onslaught and finally ended the Battle of the Bulge. The rapidly advancing Soviets were meanwhile only fifty miles from Berlin. As Roosevelt sat down at Yalta to reconstruct the world, he held few high cards. He nevertheless managed to work out agreements on four major problems.

First, the Big Three decided to flesh out a postwar United Nations organization. They had concluded in 1944 that the United Nations, like the League of Nations, would have a Security Council dominated by the four great powers (the United States, the USSR, Great Britain, and China), a General Assembly, a Secretariat, and an International Court of Justice. Roosevelt agreed to give the Soviet Union three votes in the General Assembly (in order, so Stalin urged, to offset Great Britain's half-dozen votes of the Commonwealth nations), but only if the United States might, if it wished, also have three votes. Each of the Big Four would have a veto in the Security Council in regard to substantive issues. Roosevelt had maneuvering room here, for both Stalin and the United States insisted on preserving maximum national power through possession of a veto. The United Nations, however, would be able at the most to *maintain* the peace. The question at Yalta was whether the Big Three would be able to *construct* a peace.

A second point of discussion offered some hope, for Roosevelt and Stalin quickly settled questions about the Far East. In return for Russia's promise to fight Japan within three months after Hitler's surrender, FDR secretly agreed that Stalin could have influence in Manchuria, possession of southern Sakhalin and the Kurile Islands (located off the tip of northern Japan), and a lease on the base of Port Arthur. American military advisers, including General MacArthur, had warned the president that Russian warfare against Japan was necessary if he were to avoid the 1 million Allied casualties that would probably result from an invasion of the Japanese home islands. Given such warnings, and the probability that, once in the Pacific war, Stalin would take by force what Roosevelt had already promised, the Yalta agreements on the Pacific were realistic.

A third discussion at Yalta did not end as amicably, for it involved Poland. The Teheran decision on a new Polish-Soviet border was quickly reaffirmed, but again no agreement could be reached on the Polish-German boundary. Stalin wanted that border moved to the Oder and Neisse rivers, so that Poland would incorporate large areas of prewar Germany. Churchill objected: "It would be a pity to stuff the Polish goose so full of German food that it died of indigestion." (Stalin later provided the necessary medicine simply by removing hundreds of thousands of Germans from the area and giving it to Poland. The West would not recognize the boundary until the early 1970s.)

The major argument, however, centered on the composition of the Polish government. In late summer 1944, a new, bloody controversy had further embittered this issue. When Russian troops drove to the outskirts of Warsaw, Poland's capital city, Polish underground fighters attacked the Nazis within the city. The Soviet attack then stalled, in part for military reasons, although Stalin was forthright in calling the anti-Soviet underground "a handful of power-seeking criminals." The Nazis then turned and exterminated the Poles. Stalin would not allow American planes to attempt dropping supplies to the underground fighters until it was too late. In January 1945, after the Soviets had finally captured Warsaw, Stalin moved in his own Polish regime to run the country.

Churchill and Roosevelt protested. They finally obtained Stalin's agreement that the government was to be "more broadly based" and "reorganized with the inclusion of democratic leaders from Poland itself and from Poles abroad." The new government was to hold "free and unfettered elections" as soon as possible on the basis of universal suffrage and a secret ballot. (Such an election was not held.) Shortly after Yalta, Roosevelt and Churchill exchanged angry notes with Stalin over the meaning of "reorganized." Stalin insisted this meant simply adding a few pro-Western Poles to the communist regime in Warsaw. Roosevelt, however, demanded a complete restructuring of the government. He was on weak ground. At Yalta his military chief of staff, Admiral William Leahy, had remarked that the Polish agreement was "so elastic that Russians can stretch it all the way from Yalta to Washington without technically breaking it." Roosevelt understood, but insisted that this was the best he could do. The president made only one other halfhearted effort to straighten out his policies when he asked Churchill and Stalin to sign the Declaration on Liberated Europe, which pledged application of Atlantic Charter principles to liberated countries. Stalin accepted only after inserting an amendment that made the declaration meaningless.

The failure to reach an agreement on Poland made this issue a symbol of the Russian-American conflict. But that struggle increasingly focused on Germany, the fourth question discussed at Yalta. Roosevelt had been torn on this issue. He wavered between punishing the Germans once and for all ("they should be fed three times a day with soup from Army soup kitchens," he commented, and once he even mentioned the possibility of mass castration) or rebuilding Germany under tight controls so it could be the core of a healthy Europe. He finally chose the second alternative under strong pressure from Hull and Stimson. They argued that American prosperity depended on a prosperous Europe, which in turn required a rebuilt Germany. That nation, after all, had been the industrial hub of the continent for nearly a century.

When Stalin at Yalta tried to gain agreement on dismemberment of Germany, Roosevelt and Churchill refused to agree. Stalin then attempted to obtain $20 billion in German reparations (half for the Soviet Union) in order to limit Germany's industry and rebuild Russia. Roosevelt referred this proposal to a study commission with instructions that the $20 billion figure be only a "basis for discussion."

The disagreement over reparations was a clue to the failure of the Yalta Conference. Stalin had two primary objectives: destroying German power so that it never again could threaten Russia, and acquiring great quantities of industrial machinery to reconstruct the Soviets' own war-devastated economy. Large German reparations would help Stalin gain both objectives. When Roosevelt and Churchill refused to agree on reparations, Stalin faced his alternatives: either obtain large loans and credits from the United States to rebuild Russia quickly or impose such absolute control over Eastern Europe (including East Germany) that the region would serve as a Russian-dominated buffer zone between Germany and the Soviet Union and also be forced to surrender its industry for Russia's benefit.

Stalin tested the first alternative several times between 1943 and 1946. The critical moment came in January 1945, when Molotov asked Washington for a $6 billion credit. W. Averell Harriman, the American ambassador in Moscow, advised Roosevelt that the Russians "should be given to understand" that financial aid would "depend upon their behavior in international matters." Harriman's advice was accepted. The United States refused to discuss postwar aid to Russia unless the Soviets essentially opened Eastern Europe as the Atlantic Charter asked. This Stalin refused to do.

Within six weeks after Yalta, an iron curtain descended over parts of Eastern Europe. In Romania, which had been an ally of Hitler, a Soviet official gave the king two hours to establish a government acceptable to the communists, accentuating his demand by slamming the door so hard that the plaster cracked around the door frame. In Poland, Stalin refused to make radical changes in the pro-Russian government. Amid this rapid deterioration, Roosevelt died of a massive stroke on April 12, 1945. His legacy to Vice President Harry S. Truman was not a Grand Alliance but the beginnings of the Cold War, caught perfectly by Roosevelt in a comment made privately during his return from Yalta: "The Atlantic Charter is a beautiful idea." It was nothing more.

THE HOLOCAUST

In February 1945, as the Big Three were concluding their discussions at Yalta, Allied troops reached the Nazi concentration camps and began liberating the survivors. Over the next few months, photographs of the gas chambers and the crematoria at Auschwitz, Buchenwald, Bergen-Belsen, Dachau, Theresienstadt, and other camps were published. The evidence of Hitler's extermination campaign, which claimed the lives of 6 million European Jews, shocked the civilized world. In fact, the U.S. government had known of the Nazis' "final solution" since at least mid-1942. For two years, however, the Roosevelt administration had done virtually nothing to try to stop it.

Many proposals to aid Jews in the concentration camps had been made, but State Department and War Department officials always found reasons why they were "impractical." Some suggested ransoming Jews by offering money or supplies (such as trucks or tractors) in return for their release. However, this suggestion would require negotiating with Nazi leaders and ran an additional risk of strengthening the German war effort, so it was rejected.

The most concrete proposal, made by some Jewish leaders, was that the United States bomb the gas chambers and crematoria at Auschwitz, the scene of mass exterminations of Jews, or at least the railroad lines that were carrying additional victims there. Located in southwestern Poland, Auschwitz was, by the summer of 1944, within easy range of American airplanes. Indeed, the U.S. Air Force was routinely dropping thousands of bombs on industrial sites within a few miles of the camp. In June 1944, a plea to bomb the rail junctions leading to Auschwitz was transmitted to the War Department. Without seriously investigating its merits, the department rejected the idea on the grounds that such a bombing mission was of "very doubtful efficacy" and would divert air support from more crucial operations. The historian David Wyman has concluded that all these explanations were simply excuses: "To the American military, Europe's Jews represented an extraneous problem and an unwanted burden."

By January 1944, even some American officials recognized that the Roosevelt administration's policy was a disgrace. A report prepared for Secretary of the Treasury Henry Morgenthau, "On the Acquiescence of This Government in the Murder of the Jews," charged the State Department not only with a "willful failure to act" but also with "willful attempts to prevent action from being taken to rescue Jews from Hitler." Morgenthau and others took the report to the president, who immediately established the War Refugee Board in order to "rescue the victims of enemy oppression who are in imminent danger of death and otherwise to afford such victims all possible relief and assistance consistent with the successful prosecution of the war." The board worked to evacuate Jews from Axis-occupied territory, set up refugee camps, and send relief supplies to concentration camps. Despite its accomplishments, the War Refugee Board did not receive full cooperation from either the State Department or the War Department and lacked both the funds and the power to save many lives.

The United States was not the only Allied government to fail to act. Great Britain turned down requests from the War Refugee Board for cooperation, as did the Soviet Union. British officials in the air ministry and the foreign office rejected appeals to bomb Auschwitz by saying "this idea would cost British lives and aircraft to no purpose. . . . it is fantastic and should be dropped." Winston Churchill understood more clearly than most Allied leaders the enormity of the Nazi campaign to exterminate European Jews. In July 1944, he commented privately, "There is no doubt that this is probably the greatest and most horrible single crime ever committed in the whole history of the world." But Churchill's government, like Roosevelt's and Stalin's, remained aloof. For all the differences among the three Allied leaders over foreign policy, one thing they agreed on was that action to aid European Jews was not a priority.

TRUMAN

After Roosevelt's death in April 1945, a very different figure entered the scene. Harry Truman had been a Missouri judge, politician, and U.S. senator, but he had no experience in foreign affairs. He entered the White House at precisely the time American policy was hardening against the Soviets. Truman was never confronted with the alternatives that Roosevelt had struggled with between 1942 and Yalta. Truman's temperament was more impulsive and decisive. He disliked delays; the new president preferred to decide on a policy and then make it work. This decisiveness was reinforced by a second characteristic: his jealousy of, and determination to protect, his presidential powers. This jealousy, indeed Truman's enormous personal insecurity during 1945, resulted in part from his realization that he was an accidental president following in the hallowed footsteps of Roosevelt. Truman was adamant in not allowing these circumstances to weaken the presidential powers. This determination easily led him to be as tough as the toughest of his advisers.

Twenty-four hours after entering office and before he was thoroughly briefed on incredibly complex foreign policies, Truman told his secretary of state, "We must stand up to the Russians at this point and not be easy with them." This view was reinforced by advisers (Ambassador to the Soviet Union Averell Harriman, Admiral Leahy, Secretary of the Navy James Forrestal, and Secretary of War Stimson) who harbored deep suspicions about even negotiating with Russia. By late spring Truman was convinced that he might not get "100 percent of what we wanted; but that on important matters . . . we should be able to get 85 percent."

The restraints on the president were few but significant. The Red Army controlled Eastern Europe and had been the first to reach Berlin. Eisenhower's troops might have raced the Soviets to the German capital, but the American commander wisely calculated that it would not be worth the lives lost. The political division of Germany and Berlin for occupation purposes, moreover, had been determined at earlier conferences. The mighty Russian force, astride the eastern half of Europe, was the most formidable barrier conceivable to Truman's hope for realizing "85 percent."

But the president also had problems at home. Between 1940 and 1944, American industrial production rose 90 percent; total production of goods and services jumped 60 percent. Some place had to be found to sell the products of this system or Americans would relive the horrors of the 1930s. Many, particularly those in the business community, believed that the Soviets could become the great market. "Russia will be, if not our biggest, at least our most eager, consumer when the war ends," predicted the president of the U.S. Chamber of Commerce in 1944. Pro-Russian sentiment also had such other roots as propaganda about the valor of "our Russian allies" and movies sentimentalizing the Soviets (for example, *Mission to Moscow*). Truman could not get tough with Stalin until Americans were ready to move straight from hot war against a common enemy to cold war against a former ally. Very few were ready to do that in 1945. The president therefore had to educate the country. He received help from Stalin.

STALIN

The Soviet dictator, in the words of a fellow communist who knew him well, combined "the senselessness of a Caligula with the refinement of a Borgia and the brutality of a Czar Ivan the Terrible." Nevertheless, this observer continued, "Viewed from the standpoint of success and political adroitness, Stalin is hardly surpassed by any statesman of his time." Seizing control after Lenin's death in 1924, Stalin became supreme through blood purges. He brutally collectivized Soviet agriculture, ruthlessly shaped Russia into a growing industrial power, and through luck and skill survived the hatreds of both the Western powers and Germany between 1931 and 1945. The impact of World War II alone was incalculable: more than 20 million Russian dead (600,000 civilians starved to death in the battle of Leningrad alone); thousands of cities and villages decimated; and agriculture and, to a lesser extent, industry destroyed.

In the Soviet mind, East-West animosity was natural, for East was communist, West capitalist, and therefore, according to Leninist teachings, conflict was inevitable. Woodrow Wilson and other Western leaders had earlier made Lenin appear to be a prophet in this respect when they sent troops into Russia. And during the 1930s the Soviets were convinced that the West, particularly at Munich, in 1938, was trying to drive Hitler to war against Russia. These historical events were little emphasized by Americans after 1945, but they were stamped indelibly on the Soviet mind. Stalin determined that history would not repeat itself. So after Truman prevented him from obtaining access to German industrial plants by dividing Germany and, in 1947, integrating western Germany into the U.S. camp, Stalin used the Red Army to dismantle eastern Germany and clamp his control over Eastern Europe. This was hardly classic communist revolution "from the bottom up." Instead, Stalin imposed control from the top down.

But he did so selectively at first. Hungary, Finland, Bulgaria, and Czechoslovakia remained independent to a considerable extent throughout 1946 and 1947. Eastern Europe did not fall behind the iron curtain with one loud clang, but instead disappeared bit by bit as the victim of an escalating Soviet-American argument between 1945 and 1948. Nor did Stalin attempt to overthrow Western European governments during this time. The State Department told Truman in June 1945 that the Russians "are not too greatly concerned about developments in Western Europe so long as the Western European countries do not show signs of ganging up on them." Stalin had broken away decisively from the Marxist-Leninist ideal that world revolution be given top priority. He would settle for "socialism in one zone"—the zone of Eastern Europe, which would protect Russia strategically and help reconstruct it economically. In this zone Stalin tolerated no intervention. After all, Churchill and Roosevelt had tolerated none in their Italian zone. Consequently, when Truman vigorously urged democratic elections in Poland and Romania, Stalin blandly replied, "If a government is not Fascist, a government is democratic."

But on another occasion he was more candid with Truman: "A freely elected government in any of these countries would be anti-Soviet, and that we cannot allow." He would not complain if the West controlled Italy or Latin America, but, Stalin told the president bluntly, he expected Truman to show similar consideration for Soviet interests.

Put simply, Russia's attention focused on Eastern and Central Europe, while America, as a worldwide, expansive economic power, took the entire globe as its province—including the Soviet sphere. For these reasons, the Cold War erupted not over questions in the Americas, Asia, or even Western Europe. It broke out because of American demands in Eastern and Central Europe, that is, in the areas that the Russians were determined to dominate.

POTSDAM: THE TURN IN AMERICAN POLICY

In late April Truman had a stormy session with Molotov over the Polish issue, which produced only more mistrust. In June Stalin inserted several pro-Western Poles into a government that remained staunchly communist. Making the best of a bad situation, Truman recognized the Warsaw regime, hoping that over time he could use American financial aid to change the government's policies. The Big Three then concentrated on the conference in July 1945 at Potsdam (on the outskirts of obliterated Berlin), where, it was hoped, German questions would be handled more satisfactorily than had those concerning Poland.

It was not to be. After acrimonious debates, the two central questions—the German-Polish boundary and reparations—were lumped together and compromised. Stalin and the Poles received permission to govern part of East Germany de facto (although the area was not formally given to Poland). Truman in turn required Stalin to accept a reparations package that gave Russia almost nothing out of the German industrial sectors controlled by the British and American armies. The United States therefore retained the power to reindustrialize West Germany (and in late 1945 and 1946 this was accomplished in rapid steps), but at the price of dividing the country. For if Stalin could not get reparations from the West, he would cordon off and exploit East Germany.

CHINA: ANOTHER REVOLUTION AMID THE COLD WAR

At Potsdam, Truman and Stalin did extend earlier agreements on Asian affairs. The Asia that they discussed, however, was changing radically and rapidly. Japan, which had dominated the area for a half-century, reeled from military defeats. In 1944 American forces had taken Saipan and Guam in bloody fighting, thus providing bases from which the U.S. Air Force devastated Japanese cities. Japan's industrial plants suffered (although not nearly as much as the air force claimed at the time), but the raids proved especially effective as a terror weapon. In a single attack on Tokyo, windswept fires killed more than 80,000 Japanese.

As Japan tottered, American officials hoped that China might replace Japan as the balance-wheel of Asia. Roosevelt pursued this dream, for he clearly realized that if China became dominant in Asia, then it, in turn, would be dependent on American economic and military aid and, he hoped, advice. FDR's schemes went even beyond this. He believed that China and the United States in tandem could dismantle the British and French empires in Asia (including Hong Kong, India, Singapore, Burma, and French Indochina), allow China either to absorb or to police these areas, and then have China and the United States develop them. This vision

MARGARET BOURKE-WHITE
AND PHOTOJOURNALISM

Life photographer Margaret Bourke-White holds an aerial camera in front of a Flying Fortress bomber from which she took combat photographs of the U.S. attack on Tunis, February 1943. *(Margaret Bourke-White/Time & Life Pictures/Getty Images)*

If Edward R. Murrow's radio broadcasts brought the sounds of war to Americans, then Margaret Bourke-White's photographs brought them its awful sights. Bourke-White's career had especially prepared her to document the terrible consequences of modern technology gone berserk. After graduating from Cornell University in 1927, Bourke-White, like many other artists at the time, became fascinated with the aesthetic of the machine. She photographed industrial plants and equipment because she thought them "sincere and unadorned in their beauty." In 1930, when Henry Luce began publishing *Fortune* magazine—which believed that "any modern estheticism must embrace the machine"—he invited Bourke-White to serve as associate editor and photographer. Not only did she photograph examples of American technology, she also documented military rearmament in Germany and the construction of huge dams and bridges in Russia.

By the mid-1930s Bourke-White had shifted her focus from the triumph of industry to the human anguish it produced. She began to photograph the Great Depression's impact on America: the dust bowl, with its parched land and skeletons of dead animals; southern prisons, with their potbellied guards and black chain gangs; tenant farms, with their tarpaper shacks and emaciated children. She published many of these photographs in *You Have Seen Their Faces* (1937), with commentary by Erskine Caldwell (to whom she was married for three years). Bourke-White was not associated with the Farm Security Administration, which accumulated 200,000 photographs of rural America, but was, in the words of her biographer, "virtually a one-woman FSA photographic project." When Luce introduced *Life* magazine in 1936, Bourke-White became a major contributor. She was instrumental in the development of photojournalism—structured photo-essays that told a logically ordered story.

During World War II, Bourke-White was at the height of her creative power. As an accredited

Joseph Stalin smiling for Margaret Bourke-White, Moscow, 1941. *(Margaret Bourke-White/Time & Life Pictures/Getty Images)*

U.S. Air Force photographer, she observed the assembling of airplane squadrons in England, flew with bombing missions over Africa, and documented American army operations in Italy. Accompanying General George Patton in his final drive along the Rhine, she photographed the survivors of the concentration camp at Buchenwald and the charred corpses at the Leipzig-Mochau labor camp. When Patton ordered 2,000 German civilians to walk through Buchenwald, Bourke-White photographed them averting their eyes from the piles of dead bodies. She also photographed Nazi officials who, fearing Allied retribution, had committed suicide along with their wives and children. Her account of these experiences appeared in *Dear Fatherland, Rest Quietly* (1946).

After the war Bourke-White photographed people and events in India and South Africa, and, when the Korean War began, she returned to the battlefield. She was one of the first to appreciate the possibilities for aerial photography provided by the newly developed helicopter. Then, during the 1950s, Bourke-White was stricken with Parkinson's disease, an illness that gradually deprived her of the ability to hold a camera steady. She believed the disease had been triggered by the hardships she had experienced in Korea, but added, "If I had been in a position to make a choice between getting my photographs in the fog, rain and wild mountains of Korea set against the risks involved, I would still choose to get my story—Parkinson's or no Parkinson's." She battled the disease valiantly—a struggle she described in *Portrait of Myself* (1963)—until her death in 1971.

A Polish concentration camp survivor weeps near the charred corpse of a friend, burned to death by flamethrowers while trying to escape. *(Margaret Bourke-White/Time & Life Pictures/Getty Images)*

Web Links

www.smartwomeninvest.com/peoplepics.htm
A gallery of Bourke-White's photographs and a biographical essay.

www.life.com/gallery/27312/image/53374056/wwii-buchenwald#index/0
Her photographs of the Buchenwald concentration camp.

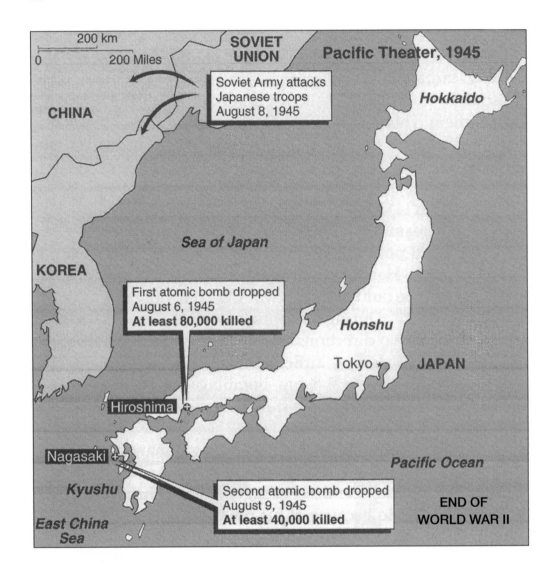

explains why throughout 1943 and 1944 Roosevelt refused to agree that after the war France should be allowed to reenter Indochina. The president hoped that this region—comprising Vietnam, Cambodia, and Laos—would become a United Nations trusteeship under the day-to-day control of China.

In mid-1944 Roosevelt's dream collapsed when a crisis ripped apart Sino-American relations. The focal point was Chiang Kai-shek, China's leader and the pivot for Roosevelt's plans. Harry Hopkins, Roosevelt's closest adviser, had commented that China could be one of the postwar Big Four, but only "if things go well with Chiang Kai-shek." During the spring of 1944 Chiang's government was gravely beset. The Japanese launched an attack on south China in an attempt to destroy airfields from which American planes (including the famed

A mother and child sit on the ground amid rubble and burnt trees in Hiroshima, December 1945. *(Alfred Eisenstaedt/Time & Life Pictures/Getty Images)*

"Flying Tigers") were bombing Japan's bases. FDR pleaded with Chiang to throw his armies and American-supplied equipment fully into the battle, but Chiang stalled.

Roosevelt then urged him to name the American commander in China, General Joseph Stilwell, as head of the Chinese armies. Chiang and Stilwell had never gotten along; "Vinegar Joe" condescendingly called Chiang "Peanut" because of his bald head, but also because of his refusal to fight the Japanese. Chiang interpreted FDR's request as an insult and seized the opportunity to throw Stilwell out of the country in September 1944. Roosevelt lost his illusions about China. At Yalta and Potsdam, Americans and Russians settled Asian problems without bothering to consult with the Chinese.

Chiang refused to fight the Japanese because he was saving his troops for a struggle to the death with the Chinese communists. Since 1927 this battle had raged, primarily in the north, where Mao Zedong's communist armies had taken refuge after their famous "long march" to escape Chiang's wrath in the mid-1930s. By 1944 Mao had consolidated and expanded his power by gaining support among the peasants (by 1945 he controlled one-quarter of China's population) and effectively fighting guerrilla wars against both Chiang and the Japanese.

THE BOMB

Throughout World War II, Stalin recognized Chiang's regime as the official government of China. After a private lunch with Stalin, moreover, Truman told his advisers that he had "clinched" the Russian acceptance of an open door in Manchuria. In return, the president reaffirmed the promises of Far Eastern territory made by Roosevelt to Stalin at Yalta. Truman was elated, but not satisfied. By dropping an atomic bomb on Japan on August 6 and again on August 9, he tried to end the war as soon as possible—that is, before American troops had to die in an invasion of the Japanese home islands and preferably before Russian troops were able to gain control of large chunks of Japanese-occupied territory.

The terrible weapon that Truman now held before the world had resulted from a series of breakthroughs in physics during the interwar era. In 1939 Albert Einstein, the greatest and best known of the physicists, wrote a simple one-page letter to Roosevelt urging him to begin developing an atomic bomb. Fearful that Hitler might produce one first, Roosevelt poured $2 billion into the secret Manhattan Project to create the bomb. (The fears were fortunately misplaced; German scientists ran into numerous dead ends and received little understanding from Hitler.) From the beginning, the bomb was built to be used only under American control, even though British and Canadian scientists provided crucial help. At no time did FDR ever seriously consider sharing the secret of the bomb with Stalin. The president considered it a diplomatic as well as a military weapon. Truman fully accepted Roosevelt's policies. Scientists from the University of Chicago suggested to Truman that demonstrating the bomb in an uninhabited area would be considerably more humane than devastating a city and might convince the Japanese to surrender. But the president sided with his Scientific Advisory Panel, which rejected the suggestion on the grounds that the bomb might not work properly and, if it did, it should be used for maximum military effect. Besides, only two bombs could be built by August to use in the war.

In mid-July 1945, the bomb was successfully tested in the New Mexico desert for the first time. Truman was at Potsdam having difficulty with Stalin, but was greatly "pepped up" by news of the test. The president now assumed an even tougher position with the Soviets. The Americans, as Churchill privately remarked at Potsdam, "do not at the present time desire Russian participation in the war against Japan." The Big Three urged Japan to surrender unconditionally, including the abdication of the emperor Hirohito, or face "utter devastation." The Japanese government refused the ultimatum. On August 6 a U.S. Air Force plane called the *Enola Gay* dropped an atomic bomb on Hiroshima, obliterating the city and killing, searing, and infecting with deadly radiation more than 100,000 people. Two days later Russia declared war against Japan and invaded Manchuria. On August 9 a second bomb destroyed

Nagasaki. Secretary of War Stimson now pushed Truman to accept a Japanese surrender that would keep the emperor in place, but without his traditional powers. Secretary of State James Byrnes, however, warned that if Truman did so the American people would "crucify" him. An unsure president hesitated while U.S. bombers killed thousands of Japanese civilians in heavy conventional air attacks between August 10 and 14. The militarists held out, but on August 14–15, Hirohito took the unusual step of overruling the government and accepting surrender if the terms did not completely destroy his role in Japanese society. Truman now accepted the condition. World War II was over.

The atomic bomb had helped end one conflict, and throughout the summer of 1945 Truman, Stimson, and other top officials discussed how it might be used as a negotiating weapon against Russia to preclude a third world war. In June, according to Stimson's diary, he and the president had talked of possible concessions that the bomb might bring from Russia. Truman "mentioned the same things that I was thinking of, namely the settlement of the Polish, Rumanian, Yugoslavian, and Manchurian problems."

By September, however, Stimson had changed his mind. He warned the president that if the United States refused to cooperate with the Russians in controlling the bomb, but merely talked to them while "having this weapon ostentatiously on our hip, their suspicions and their distrust of our purposes and motives will increase." Truman refused either to negotiate with Stalin about the bomb or to use the bomb as an explicit threat against the Soviets. Perhaps he felt that he did not have to, for Stalin well knew that the president had used the bomb without hesitation against the Japanese.

BACK TO THE 1920s

To drive home his concern over postwar Asia, Truman ordered American planes and troops to help Chiang's forces reach Manchuria ahead of Mao's communist troops. By the end of 1945, 110,000 American soldiers were in China, many of them in the north. But their help was of no avail. Chiang was unable to consolidate his power, the Russians remained in Manchuria until they took out $2 billion worth of plant and equipment, and American officials failed to work out an agreement between Chiang and Mao.

Truman now turned to General George Marshall, the man primarily responsible for planning and coordinating the entire American military effort during the war. Marshall hoped to find a third faction in China that was "liberal" and middle-of-the-road, then construct a political solution embracing Mao's communists, Chiang's nationalists, and the third group. He hoped that after a period of time Chiang would be able to absorb the third group and subordinate the communists. During the spring of 1946 Marshall nearly pulled off the miracle, but by summer civil war had reopened.

China was too polarized between reactionaries and communists to develop any third force. Chiang cared no more for Marshall's telling him—the leader of China—how to run the country than he had for Roosevelt's advice. Marshall reported home that he was confronted by "the incompetence, inefficiency, and stubbornness of the Central government—qualities which made it very difficult to help them." Chiang and Mao, moreover, hated each other. When skirmishes erupted between their forces, Chiang decided that, with his superiority in men (two to one over Mao's) and firepower (nearly three to one), he could destroy the communists militarily, despite Marshall's warning not to try to settle the problem on the battlefield. After initial defeats, the communists inflicted a series of losses on the nationalists in mid-1947. Truman privately berated Chiang, but stuck with him as Mao's forces won victory after victory. Admiral Leahy explained the cruel dilemma: "If we break with [Chiang's] Central Government the result will be that we will have no friends in either of the Chinese factions and no friends in China."

Chiang was past help. In 1947 Washington officials seized the only alternative. They assumed that if Mao won, China would be too chaotic to govern and the Soviets too poor to provide major help. The United States decided to leave a situation it could not control. Truman instead turned to Japan to create once again the stability in Asia that Chiang could not provide. During 1947 and 1948 the American occupation authorities lifted Japanese industrial and political controls. Stalin did not relish the idea of a revived Japan, but he had nothing to say about it, for the United States had frozen Russia completely out of the Japanese occupation. Japan was on the road back. Truman's approach to Asia smacked of the American policy at the Washington Naval Conference of 1921–1922. And it fit in perfectly with the new American approaches in Europe.

NEW SCIENCE—NEW DANGERS

World War II produced advances in technology that not only caused the greatest slaughter in history but, ironically, saved millions of lives and made life more decent for millions of others. Much of the new technology, such as the atomic bomb and the increased size and firepower of air force bombers, aimed at greater and more efficient killing. But the famous aviator Charles Lindbergh, for example, quietly conducted dangerous experiments with new fuel mixtures that eventually doubled the range of warplanes and, later, commercial airliners. Engineers also developed jet propulsion to drive planes not with the old, complex, and less efficient piston engines, but with a great jet of air created by a gas turbine. Before the war, German and British scientists had raced to see who would build the first jet plane. The Germans won one week before World War II erupted, but they could not get planes into operation until 1944. Then American engineers took over. They and the British built jet airliners that, after several disasters, resulted in the Boeing 707. This airplane revolutionized transoceanic flights when it appeared in 1958. Airtime between New York and London was cut in half, to only six hours. A new phrase, "the jet set," described the wealthy who flew around the world as easily as their grandparents had traveled from New York to Chicago.

Other than atomic energy, no discovery proved more important than penicillin. This miracle drug was first glimpsed in 1889, when European scientists discovered "good" bacteria that killed "bad," life-threatening bacteria. In 1928 a British scientist, Alexander Fleming, accidentally discovered a broth on which mold *(Penicillium notatum)* grew. This mold possessed powers to kill bacteria without harming the body's healthy cells. A decade later Americans finally appeared in the story. Only their huge chemical companies had the resources required to develop penicillin. By 1944 these companies produced enough of the drug to reduce the danger of infection in all Allied battle casualties. By 1950, the companies exported enough to meet world demand. The breakthroughs in developing penicillin and sulfa drugs radically changed worldwide health care. Half the drugs used in 1947 had been unknown in 1937.

DDT (dichloro-diphenyl-trichloroethane) became a miracle worker in destroying deadly insects. During World War I, many people had died of typhus (carried by lice). But when a typhus epidemic appeared in Italy during late 1943, Allied physicians quickly stopped it by spraying DDT on 70,000 people in a single day. One expert, Trevor I. Williams, estimates that within the following twenty-five years about 1.5 billion people were for the first time in history free of the dangers of malaria because DDT destroyed the deadly mosquito carrying the disease. A Swiss scientist had discovered DDT's powers in 1939 as he worked in the new field of synthesizing chemical agents (the same field that during the 1920s and 1930s had produced the first plastics, synthetic rubber, nylon, and rayon). Again, U.S. plants refined the European discovery, and then mass-produced the insecticide for the world's health and America's wealth.

But there was a flip side. As penicillin and DDT extended life expectancy and reduced infant deaths, world population increased until observers feared that starvation, even political revolution, would result from overcrowding. Others worried that these scientific miracles saved lives only by altering nature's order. For example, animals that fed on mosquito larvae could be endangered when DDT destroyed the larvae. Traces of the deadly drug began to appear in foods eaten by humans. The new sciences of atomic physics, synthetic chemistry, and drugs altered the world by helping the Allies win World War II and by improving living standards, but they also raised new possibilities of destruction.

CRISES IN THE MEDITERRANEAN—AND AT HOME

There was no peace at the end of World War II. Instead of a world based on the principles of the Atlantic Charter, Americans witnessed the failure of a settlement in Europe, the refusal of Russia to leave Austria (on the grounds that it was a conquered, not a liberated, state), and Soviet rejection of a plan to control atomic energy on American terms. In February 1946, Stalin warned the Russians that because of outside (that is, U.S.) threats they would have to revert to rigid state control and make additional sacrifices under new five-year plans. He was tightly closing off the Soviet Union and its sphere in Eastern Europe.

Washington buzzed with ominous rumors that Stalin's speech was the "declaration of World War III," since the world could not exist "half free and half slave" any more than it had in the 1930s. In March, former prime minister Churchill traveled to Truman's home state of Missouri to announce that "an iron curtain has descended across the continent" of Europe. He pleaded for a joint Anglo-American atomic force to confront the Soviets, especially since "God has willed" that Anglo-Saxons, not communists or fascists, should first have the bomb. Stalin, in reply, compared Churchill's "racial theory" with Hitler's and called the former British leader a warmonger. For his part, Truman had no intention of tying American power to a declining Great Britain, but he believed, like Churchill, that the Soviets respected only superior strength.

The first test came in Iran during March 1946. During the war the United States, Great Britain, and Russia had occupied Iran to assure a route for the delivery of supplies to the Soviets. The Big Three agreed to leave six months after the war ended. But in February 1946, Russia refused to evacuate its troops. Moscow officials claimed that under Western pressure the Iranians were not honoring earlier agreements with the Soviets on oil and security along the Iranian-Russian border. The United States swiftly reacted. It first took the issue to the United Nations. Then, as Stalin moved reinforcements toward the border, Secretary of State Byrnes issued a warning to stop the troop movement or the United States would take countermeasures. The Russians stopped, settled directly with Iran (on Iranian terms), and withdrew their forces.

Truman had won a significant victory. But the Russians continued to press for advantages and additional security around their southwestern borders. The Soviets especially pushed Turkey for a new treaty on the Dardanelles, the vital passage between the Black Sea and the Mediterranean. With American encouragement, including the beefing up of the U.S. fleet in the Mediterranean, Turkey refused to negotiate. In Greece, the civil war against the British-supported king picked up steam as Yugoslavia's communist regime funneled aid to the revolutionaries. The Cold War had expanded from Central Europe into the eastern Mediterranean.

In February 1947, world history took a historic turn. The British suddenly informed the State Department that they could no longer afford to support the antirevolutionary forces in Greece. Decimated by two world wars, Great Britain's economy was suffering through one of the coldest and most destructive winters in history. The British Empire was approaching its end. The question became whether the United States would assume the British role. This question was actually academic, for in Iran and Turkey the United States had already taken the lead.

Here was Truman's chance to create a long-term anti-Soviet policy. Equally important, Washington officials needed to mobilize the United States for an all-out Cold War effort. This became urgent as they realized that such an effort would cost large sums of money, but that Congress was considerably more interested in budget balancing and tax cutting than in another expensive overseas commitment. Somehow, the American people's benign view of world affairs had to be transformed and brought into accord with the tough policies that Washington had actually been following since at least early 1945.

"SCARING HELL" OUT OF THE AMERICAN PEOPLE

Truman encouraged the American people, in four stages during late 1946 and early 1947, to commit themselves to an anticommunist crusade. The first stage occurred in September 1946, when Secretary of Commerce Henry Wallace publicly attacked American policies for alienating the Soviets. He urged a more conciliatory approach along economic lines that would open Russia to American goods. Wallace advocated much the same policy that Hull and others had pushed during the war. That approach, however, had not worked. Truman and Byrnes had moved to the next step: political and military confrontation. When Byrnes demanded Wallace's resignation, Truman fired his secretary of commerce. Some pro-Wallace support appeared, but of greater significance was the number of former New Dealers (led by a new organization called Americans for Democratic Action) who attacked Wallace as naive about Stalin and the communist threat.

The second stage of intensified anticommunism occurred during the 1946 congressional elections. The Republicans scored a stunning victory by capturing both houses of Congress for the first time since 1928. Truman was humiliated; one poll showed his support, which had stood at 87 percent of the electorate in 1945, sinking to only 32 percent. The president, however, turned the defeat to his own advantage. Many of the newly elected Republican senators had advocated tax cuts but had also taken a tough line against subversives at home and abroad. They said they wanted to fight communism—but not spend money. Since Canada had just uncovered a spy ring that had apparently been sending atomic secrets to Russia, attacking subversives promised rich political rewards. Leading members of the Senate's new "Class of '46," including Joseph McCarthy of Wisconsin, John Bricker of Ohio, William Jenner of Indiana, and William Knowland of California, exemplified this Republican line.

Truman tried to take over their position by proposing a government loyalty program under executive control that would ferret out subversives in Washington. The president was taking the lead in the hunt for communists.

The third stage of Truman's program was magnificently handled by Undersecretary of State Dean Acheson when, in a private session, he told the congressional leadership that "like apples in a barrel infected by one rotten one, the corruption of Greece would infect Iran and all to the east." The eastern Mediterranean region, Egypt, and then Europe would be next, as the dominoes would inevitably fall. Believing personally that "we were met at Armageddon," Acheson eloquently concluded, "the Soviet Union [is] playing one of the greatest gambles in history at minimal cost. . . . We and we alone [are] in a position to break up the play." After a stunned silence, the key Republican senator on foreign policy issues, Arthur Vandenberg of Michigan, admitted that he had been persuaded. But he warned Truman and Acheson that they would have to "scare hell" out of the American people if they hoped to get necessary public and financial support for their new foreign policies.

Truman did just that with two speeches in the fourth stage of his program. The first address, at Baylor University in Texas on March 6, 1947, provided the classic explanation of why Americans must embark on a new crusade. "Peace, freedom, and world trade are inseparable," Truman began. "Our foreign relations, political and economic, are indivisible." Then: "We must not go through the [nineteen] thirties again." Freedom of worship and freedom of speech are related to freedom of enterprise, for the first two "have been most frequently enjoyed in those societies" hospitable to free enterprise. And "least conducive to freedom of enterprise" was government intervention. Yet, the president warned bluntly, unless the world marketplaces were quickly reconstructed and opened, even the U.S. government would soon have to step in to control American society in order to allocate goods and resources. Such government intervention "is not the way to peace," Truman concluded. The president's meaning was clear: his administration defined the state-controlled Russian economy as the deadly enemy of American prosperity, and he would do everything possible to save the world on this side of the iron curtain for the American form of "freedom of enterprise." If Americans did not join him, they risked losing all their most precious freedoms.

Six days later he issued the call to action with the "Truman Doctrine" speech before a joint session of Congress. To make the case as forcefully as possible, the president presented a world divided simply between "free peoples" and areas where "the will of a minority [is] forcibly imposed upon a majority." He included Greece and Turkey in the first group, but warned that unless Congress immediately appropriated $400 million for their aid, those two nations would slide into the second. Only the United States could now save the free world: "If we falter in our leadership, we may endanger the peace of the world—and we shall surely endanger the welfare of our own nation."

The speech "scared hell" out of many people. Ohio Senator and the Republican leader Robert Taft disliked it because "I do not want war with Russia." Doubts existed even within the State Department. Some officials had argued that Turkey, which had been pro-Hitler and was not democratic, hardly ranked as a "free people." It shared, moreover, a very sensitive boundary with Russia. Truman nevertheless decided to use the opportunity in Greece to send arms to Turkey. "Turkey was slipped into the oven with Greece because that seemed to be the surest way to cook a tough bird," as one official observed.

George C. Marshall *(left)* chatting with Vyacheslav M. Molotov. *(Thomas D. McAvoy/Time & Life Pictures/Getty Images)*

More generally, the speech was notable because it defined the communist threat as ideological and therefore asked Americans to commit themselves against that threat globally. This request has been the most explosive part of the Truman Doctrine, for once the threat was defined ideologically, Americans had to be ready to intervene anywhere in the world where that threat was perceived, regardless of whether the area in question was in fact directly threatened by Russia or, later, China. Soon presidents could use the doctrine as a rationale for American military intervention in Vietnam as well as in Europe.

It was "the most fundamental thing that has been presented to Congress in my time," Vandenberg rightly observed, so Congress wanted to examine Truman's proposal carefully. The president had defined the issue, created a growing consensus, and outflanked congressional opponents. One Truman supporter in Congress chuckled at the trap the president had sprung on Republicans who wanted to fight communism, but not spend money: "Course they don't want to be smoked out. . . . They don't like Communism, but still they don't want to do anything to stop it. But they are all put on the spot now and they all have to come clean." The $400 million was soon appropriated, allowing American military advisers and equipment to aid the Greek government. The revolution finally subsided, however, only after Yugoslavia defected from the Russian bloc in 1948 and quit sending aid to the Greek rebels.

AVOIDING THE 1930s: THE MARSHALL PLAN

Aid to Greece and Turkey was only a bandage on a large, festering wound that cut to the heart itself, the economy of Western Europe. Confronted with deteriorating economies, the Europeans were responding as Truman feared they would. A British Labour government, for example, nationalized leading industries, while in Italy and France large communist and radical socialist factions gained strength. The American economy maintained its pace, but primarily because of a booming $15 billion in exports during 1946. If Europe could not continue to take its share of these exports, the United States would, in the president's words, "go through the thirties again."

The key to the problem was the lack of dollars that Europeans had to spend for American goods. Moreover, they could derive little from their war-ruined economies to sell to the United States in order to acquire dollars. Great Britain, France, Italy, and the Benelux countries immediately needed about $5 billion if they hoped to buy goods from the United States to maintain a minimum standard of living.

In June 1947, the United States announced its plan to save itself and Western Europe. Newly appointed secretary of state George Marshall offered massive economic aid but attached two conditions. First, the initiative in formulating a long-term program would have to come from the Europeans. Second, the program would have to be cooperative and open. This second requirement worked against Russian participation, for although the Soviets attended the first planning session in Paris, they quickly repudiated the Marshall Plan when they saw that they would have to accept American conditions, including the disclosure of Russian economic information. The Soviets claimed that the Truman Doctrine and the Marshall Plan had now divided the world into "two camps." To solidify their own camp, they announced a "Molotov Plan" to provide economic links for their East European empire.

The Western Europeans finally asked for $29 billion, but the United States cut this to $17 billion for four years, with $5 billion the first year. The figures are revealing, for they show that the decision to give aid was not based merely on anticommunism. More immediately, officials planned to provide the $5 billion they had long before calculated as the amount needed to keep American exports to Europe at necessary levels. When the aid was distributed, moreover, it went not primarily to Italy or France, where the Communist Party threat was greatest, but to Great Britain and Germany, the potential industrial powerhouses for Europe. The Marshall Plan was publicly explained as part of the fight against communism. But the plan also worked to avert a repeat of the 1930s by rebuilding the great market for American products and molding Western Europe into a long-term partner.

The United States had emerged from World War II as the greatest power in world history. Its remarkable economic prowess, monopoly of atomic energy, and success as the world's oldest republic seemed to indicate that Americans were truly embarked on an "American Century," as *Life* magazine proclaimed in 1941. But by 1947 the Truman administration had shifted from trying to create a free world (particularly in China and Eastern Europe) to rebuilding nations this side of the iron curtain. The Marshall Plan seemed an intelligent, manageable, and limited plan for maintaining "freedom of enterprise" in the West. On the other hand, the Truman Doctrine proposed worldwide ideological and even military warfare. Truman had beautifully built a public consensus around both.

It now remained to be seen which road Americans would choose: the path that was more modest and whose terminus could be clearly seen, or the one that required commitment without an apparent limit on dollars, energy, and perhaps even lives. As the ancient Greeks understood, the essence of human tragedy is choice.

CHAPTER ELEVEN

1947–1952
The America of the Cold War

General Douglas MacArthur in Manila, Philippine Islands, 1945. *(Library of Congress)*

Two events in March 1947—the announcement of the Truman Doctrine and the institution of a federal loyalty program—set the tone for American foreign and domestic affairs in the early Cold War era. President Truman, who won reelection in 1948, managed to turn Cold War tensions to his own advantage when he helped create the North Atlantic Treaty Organization in 1949. With the outbreak of the Korean War in June 1950, however, the Truman administration became a victim of its own policies. In the president's view the North Korean attack closely resembled the fascist aggression of the 1930s, but he found that waging a long, limited war imposed strains on society quite unlike those of World War II. Those strains—political, economic, social, and military—nourished a mood of hysteria in which the Truman administration could itself be charged, by Senator Joseph McCarthy and others, with being "soft on communism" at home and overseas. It seemed odd for the globe's greatest superpower to be so insecure.

THE PHYSIQUE OF A SUPERPOWER:
THE AMERICAN ECONOMY

By the late 1940s, as the battlefields cooled, the war dead were buried, and the world faced the unknown nuclear age, Americans were the richest people on the globe—indeed, the richest in recorded history. In merely five years after 1940, their gross national product (GNP, the sum of all goods and services they produced) doubled from $100 billion to $200 billion. With 6 percent of the world's population, the United States produced 50 percent of the world's goods. In 1946, the average American received $1,262 in annual income, compared with $653 in Great Britain and $45 in India. Half the world's population clustered around India's level.

Several reasons explained this remarkable superiority. Two former competitors, Western Europe and Japan, had been largely destroyed by war. In the poorest nations, moreover, population increased faster than wealth. One United Nations (UN) expert believed "that the average and median standard of living of the world as a whole is actually lower today than in 1913."

The United States, however, was so rich and efficient that after a century of declining birthrates, it had a "baby boom" between 1946 and 1960 but still created ever-greater wealth. The immediate basis of the wealth was an economic empire developed during World War II. The government played a key role in the empire's creation. Of some $25 billion worth of new and expanded factories built during the war, the government built three-quarters. Most of this wealth resulted from government spending for the military effort. During the conflict itself, Americans enjoyed good incomes but had many fewer civilian goods available to buy. The results became clear in 1946. First, Americans had a huge $140 billion savings pool to spend when goods again became available in the stores (triple the savings in 1940); and second, war taxes and the general prosperity had redistributed incomes for the only time since 1900. The rich got relatively poorer; the poor richer between 1941 and 1945. Before the great crash of 1929, less than one-third of Americans qualified as "middle-class" (that is, received incomes of $3,000 to $10,000). After the war nearly two-thirds qualified. This meant that the demand for automobiles and new homes would be deep and widespread.

Even as government peacetime spending dropped from $79.7 billion in 1946 to $55 billion in 1948 (due mostly to defense cuts), spending doubled on education (to $7.7 billion) and on highways ($3 billion). These figures included local, state, and national government expenditures. After the Korean War began in 1950, national government expenditures shot up, mostly on the military side, from $70 billion in 1950 to $151 billion in 1960. In addition, the GI Bill of Rights, passed by Congress in 1944, gave veterans money for attending school, starting businesses, and buying houses. In 1946 Congress also passed an employment act that pledged in general terms to use government powers to keep unemployment low (about 6 percent seemed to be maximum). The act also created the President's Council of Economic Advisers to help ensure that full employment measures would be followed. From now on, the American economic machine would have the government's hand near the steering wheel and its feet near the brake or accelerator, as the need arose.

Business and labor made the most of this help. For example, in the synthetic-rubber industry, government built expensive plants, and then leased them to businesses during the war for $1 a year. As production rose, Americans had their own rubber supply, instead of depending on Asian or African producers, for the postwar automobile boom. The all-important rate of U.S. productivity (the amount of goods a worker produced each hour) had long led the world. During the war the productivity rate of American workers rose at about 7 percent annually, but after 1945 jumped to nearly 10 percent a year—the result of new technology and capital expenditures. Despite the economic expansion, the number of factory workers actually dropped in the late 1940s and early 1950s by about 4 percent, while new entrants into the labor market moved into the expanding service and clerical sectors that oversaw the more efficient industrial complex.

A stunning example of this new technology was the chemical industry. Virtually unknown in 1920, it had since expanded three times faster than the rest of industry. As *Life* magazine bragged in 1953, "the $9 billion-a-year chemical industry has transformed American life. It has scrubbed the modern world with detergents, doctored it with synthetic drugs, dressed it in synthetic textiles, cushioned it with synthetic rubber, and adorned it from head to toe with gaudy plastics." Another example could be found in the rich farmlands. During the war agricultural income rocketed from $4 billion in 1940 to $12.3 billion in 1945, but acreage harvested rose only 4 percent. Not more land but new machinery and fertilizers made American farms the world's breadbasket. In 1947 one in six families lived on a farm; three decades later only one in twenty-six would do so, although an amazingly successful U.S. agriculture increased crop and livestock production nearly six times during those years.

After the war, much of the noncommunist world depended for survival on U.S. producers, but those producers also depended on the world. The nation's exports and imports amounted to only about 8 percent of its GNP, but that figure—between $12 and $20 billion—placed Americans behind only the British as the world's greatest traders. Exports of oil, iron and steel, and food were critical for U.S. prosperity. When America's best customers in war-devastated Western Europe lacked dollars to pay for these exports, the Truman administration created the Marshall Plan to pump billions of dollars quickly into Europe so it could purchase U.S. goods. After the Marshall Plan ended in 1952, foreign aid nevertheless continued. In all, between 1945 and 1970 the U.S. government sent $125 billion overseas; most of it was used to help foreigners buy American goods. Europeans received more than one-third of the figure, Asians about one-fifth, and Latin Americans only one-twelfth.

U.S. private firms meanwhile profited from investing directly in this reviving global economy. Between 1945 and 1950 they increased their overseas investment by 33 percent, to nearly $16 billion. Ten giant companies led the drive, with Standard Oil of New Jersey (later Exxon) in front. Standard Oil put about $1 billion into Venezuelan and Middle East oil development. Coca-Cola expanded so rapidly that, as one observer noted in 1950, "The Communists have made a propaganda point of the 'Coca-colonization' of the world. This has not stopped the wine-drinking Italians, among others, from taking heartily to Cokes" and enjoying wages from a bottling industry "worth several thousand jobs." *Fortune* magazine even bragged about "the spectacular export of American ideas to foreign minds." *Reader's Digest*, it pointed out, "is now printed in eleven languages, manufactured in fourteen foreign countries, sold in sixty-one." New York City, the world's money center, helped finance this expansion. U.S. banks had ninety-five branches overseas in 1950 and 536 in 1970.

Seldom in their history had Americans enjoyed such a chance to get rich. In early 1950, their steel industry worked at 98 percent of capacity, back orders for refrigerators were the largest on record, and the Christmas shopping weeks of 1949 had been the biggest in retailing history. Henry Luce, who had coined the phrase "the American Century" in his *Life* magazine in 1941, asked in 1950 why the world should—and would—be led by U.S. business: "First [,] . . . American business" produces "more food, more houses, more doctors, . . . more amusements" than any other nation. Second, it *"has* licked the most serious problem of the economic cycle, namely, real want in the midst of plenty." Luce believed there might be economic downturns, but "the needy will be taken care of; they will be the first charge on the economy." In the American Century, the new superpower would not only do well, but also do good.

CRISIS DIPLOMACY: 1947–1948

But Americans could do little good in Eastern Europe. Undersecretary of State Dean Acheson later observed that by 1948 the Truman administration had concluded that negotiations with Russia were useless, for "the world of the last half of the twentieth century was, and would continue to be, a divided world. The [decision] was to make the free—that is, the non-Communist-dominated—part of that divided world as secure and flourishing as possible." In 1947 Acheson wrote that because negotiations were not successful, "we must use to an increasing extent our second instrument of foreign policy, namely economic power," to protect the free world. The Marshall Plan indicated how the nation's tremendous economic strength would be used to create a postwar world on American terms. As Truman liked to put it, he was "tired of babying the Soviets."

The Republican-controlled Congress passed the $400 million Truman Doctrine appropriations for Greece and Turkey, but proved extremely reluctant to legislate the nearly $12 billion, four-year program that Truman was asking for the Marshall Plan. Secretary of State George Marshall and other officials warned that without the plan the American economy would lose its European markets, and then shrivel. This decline, Marshall predicted, "would drive us to increased measures of government control." Such threats did not move Congress, because it believed that lowering taxes and encouraging private investment to go overseas would do the job. Congress refused to budge. Then came Czechoslovakia.

Although the Czechs had survived as an independent people in 1945, their geographic position (bordering on both Russia and West Germany) forced them to be cautiously neutral in 1946. The Czech Communist Party's power grew steadily, however, and by 1947 American diplomats had given up hope of bringing the nation into the West's camp. No one was prepared, though, for the sudden demand by Czech communists, in March 1948, for key government posts nor for the threat that this demand would be enforced by the Russian Red Army, then camped on the border. The government surrendered. Foreign Minister Jan Masaryk, long a hero in the West because of his opposition to Nazism, fell to his death from an upper-story window. The communists claimed that he had committed suicide. Truman and many other Americans believed that the Czech leader had been murdered. Whatever the cause, Russia was tightening its grip in response to the challenge of the Truman Doctrine and the Marshall Plan. Romania fell under complete communist control in February; Czechoslovakia followed; then noncommunist leaders in Bulgaria, Hungary, and Poland either disappeared or fled to the West.

Truman, comparing these events to those that had triggered world war in 1939, rapidly moved to a tougher military position, which had long been urged by Secretary of the Navy James Forrestal and other officials. Forrestal was the most fervent anticommunist of the president's close advisers. He became especially powerful in mid-1947, when Truman named him the first secretary of defense. In the new position Forrestal was head of all the military services, now centralized in the Department of Defense. A former investment banker, Forrestal had entered government service early in World War II and soon issued scathing warnings about postwar cooperation with Stalin. As he wrote to a friend in 1944, "Whenever any American suggests that we act in accordance with the needs of our own security he is apt to be called a goddamned fascist or imperialist, while if Uncle Joe [Stalin] suggests that he needs the Baltic Provinces, half of Poland, all of Bessarabia and access to the Mediterranean, all hands agree that he is a fine, frank, candid and generally delightful fellow who is very easy to deal with because he is so explicit in what he wants."

Events after 1945 strengthened Forrestal's fears. He concluded that the United States and Russia would conflict politically, militarily, ideologically, and spiritually around the globe. To support this conclusion, he arranged for American diplomat George Kennan to return from the U.S. Embassy in Moscow in order to work out a long analysis of Soviet intentions that supported Forrestal's suspicions. Published in mid-1947 under the mysterious pseudonym of "Mr. X," Kennan's "The Sources of Soviet Conduct" concluded that two factors—communist revolutionary beliefs and Stalin's need to create an external enemy as an excuse for tightening his dictatorship over the Russian people—made Russia like a "toy automobile" that, when wound up, would move inexorably onward until it struck a superior force.

Some Americans disputed this view. Walter Lippmann, the nation's most respected journalist, argued that traditional national interests, not a vague revolutionary mentality or Stalin's personal needs, governed Soviet policy. Therefore, Lippmann concluded, sincere negotiations could end the Cold War by reconciling Russian and American national interests. Forrestal, however, found Kennan's analysis exactly suited to his own views and urged Truman to build the worldwide counterforce needed to stop the toy automobile. With the fall of Czechoslovakia, the president publicly advocated Forrestal's arguments.

On March 17, 1948, just seven days after Masaryk's death, Truman appeared before Congress to deliver a tough speech that urged restoration of selective service, universal military training for all young men (long a pet Forrestal project), and immediate passage of the Marshall Plan. A frightened Congress rushed the Marshall Plan through, though moving more slowly on the draft and rejecting universal military training. But the president had gained a triumph and, as in the case of the Truman Doctrine, had done so by frightening Congress, this time with claims that Stalin had monstrously subjugated another nation without any provocation from the United States. Americans were being conditioned to respond instantly whenever

DR. KINSEY
AND SEX RESEARCH

Dr. Alfred Kinsey, sexual behavior researcher, conducting an interview in his office at the Institute for Sex Research, 1948. *(Wallace Kirland/Time & Life Pictures/Getty Images)*

In 1938 Alfred C. Kinsey began offering a course on marriage at Indiana University. Trained at Harvard as a zoologist, a specialist in the behavior of the gall wasp, Kinsey had been teaching biology at Indiana for nearly two decades without causing a ripple. This abruptly changed when he introduced his new course. Dismayed at the lack of scientific evidence concerning human sexual behavior, Kinsey set out to compensate by taking the sexual case histories of any one willing to cooperate. Assembling these data with the same compulsive care he had once devoted to collecting gall wasps, Kinsey soon found that people were volunteering information faster than he could transcribe it. By January 1948, when *Sexual Behavior in the Human Male* appeared, Kinsey's staff had accumulated more than 5,000 case histories.

Viewing himself as a scientist, Kinsey attempted to exclude all moral judgments from his work. He trained interviewers to ask direct questions, since "evasive terms invite dishonest answers." One of his associates recalled, "We also never asked *whether* a subject had ever engaged in a particular activity, we assumed that everyone had engaged in everything, and so we began by asking *when* he had first done it." Kinsey presented his findings in cold, clinical language: 86 percent of American males had engaged in premarital sexual intercourse, 37 percent had on some occasion engaged in homosexual activity to the point of orgasm, and 40 percent had carried on extramarital affairs. Kinsey concluded that existing laws were violently at odds with prevailing practices; indeed, more than nine of every ten American men at some time in their lives engaged in some form of sexual activity punishable as a crime. The book, in many respects, was a resounding plea to end hypocrisy by bringing public moral codes into line with private behavior.

Most psychologists and sociologists hailed the report. One writer even claimed that Kinsey had done for sex "what Columbus did for geography." But many people criticized Kinsey's methodology, pointing out that his statistical sample was drawn too heavily from underworld characters (because it was easy to obtain their case histories) and that his interview technique did not allow for faulty recall. Others believed that Kinsey took an overly mechanistic approach. Yet the book proved amazingly popular. It went through six printings in ten days, sold 100,000 copies in three months, and remained on the best-seller list for twenty-seven weeks.

In 1953, Kinsey published a sequel, *Sexual Behavior in the Human Female*. He claimed that since "the anatomic structures which are most essential to sexual response and orgasm are nearly identical in the human female and male," any dissimilarity in response reflected psychological and hormonal rather than physiological differences. Kinsey also reported "a marked, positive correlation between experience in orgasm obtained from premarital coitus, and the capacity to reach orgasm after marriage," and he found that women took part in premarital and extramarital affairs more often than was commonly supposed. The second report triggered even sharper criticism than the first, partly because of the double standard concerning sexual behavior but also because of growing conformity in the nation. One congressman denounced the book as "the insult of the century against our mothers, wives, daughters and sisters," and a clergyman feared it "will in time contribute inevitably toward Communism."

In 1954, frightened by this public outcry, the Rockefeller Foundation (under its new president Dean Rusk) cut off support for the Kinsey Institute. The man who had no difficulty probing the most intimate details of a person's behavior was virtually incapable of asking wealthy individuals for money. Bitter and disillusioned, Kinsey died in 1956 at the age of sixty. His work, however, paved the way for many other sex researchers, most notably William H. Masters and Virginia E. Johnson. Their books, *Human Sexual Response* (1966) and *Human Sexual Inadequacy* (1970), reported the results of laboratory experiments that measured the physiological changes in the human body during all phases of sexual stimulation. Yet their volumes, which also made the best-seller lists, caused little commotion, partly because Kinsey's pioneering work had, in the intervening years, made sex research respectable.

Doctors Virginia Johnson and William Masters, 1966. *(Leonard Mccombe/Time & Life Pictures/Getty Images)*

Web Links

www.kinseyinstitute.org/
The Kinsey Institute's website.

www.youtube.com/kinseyinstitute
A site with many video clips discussing the work of the Kinsey Institute.

Truman rang out the Forrestal-Kennan version of Soviet policy. And Stalin was giving Truman ample opportunity to do so.

STALIN'S RESPONSE: THE BERLIN BLOCKADE

The Marshall Plan aimed at rapidly rebuilding Western Europe for two purposes: to make it a market for American farms and factories and to erect a bastion against Soviet expansion. To accomplish these objectives, the reconstruction of West Germany was necessary, for Germany had been the industrial core of Europe. Unless West Germany was rebuilt, there was little chance Western Europe could recover. The West Germans, however, suffered from inflation in early 1948, primarily because they had printed paper money in such volume that the currency had become almost worthless. In the weeks following the Czech crisis, the United States decided to cure West Germany's economic ills with drastic surgery. The Truman administration pushed for a currency reform program that would replace the bad money with new, better-supported bills. Despite the Soviets' objection that this had not been discussed with them, the program went ahead without their approval. Then in June 1948 the Western allies asked West Germany to form a federal republic, that is, an independent nation comprised of the American, British, and French occupation zones. The new nation, which would include West Berlin (located deep within the Soviet zone), would be rebuilt and closely tied to the West through the Marshall Plan.

These moves directly threatened Stalin's plans to keep Germany so weak that it could never again threaten Russia. At the same time, he was challenged from within the Soviet bloc itself. Yugoslavia's communist leader, Josip Broz (Marshal Tito), broke with Stalin, rooted out Russian attempts to assassinate him, and declared Yugoslavia a communist but independent state. Tito had complete control of the nation, and his army was strong enough to make Russian troops pay dearly if they attempted to invade. "Titoism" became a new, hopeful sign to the West. The United States soon sent aid to Yugoslavia.

Confronted with these threats in Germany and Yugoslavia, Stalin retaliated by trying to squeeze the West out of Berlin, thus removing that listening post within the Russian zone and weakening the entire Western position in Europe. In 1945 the Allies had made only oral agreements about the right to use railroads and highways through the Soviet zone to reach West Berlin. On June 24, 1948, the Russians stopped all surface traffic into West Berlin. The city stood isolated.

Truman correctly viewed Stalin's action as a challenge to American policy toward all of Germany. The president had three alternatives: pull out; use force to open access to Berlin, perhaps starting World War III in the process; or fly over the blockaded routes with supplies. Truman never seriously considered the first point. When the question arose in a cabinet meeting, he interrupted to say, "There [is] no discussion on that point, we [are] going to stay, period." But he wanted no war and so followed the last alternative. The 2.5 million West Berliners required 4,000 tons of food and fuel every day. With a massive airlift that landed a plane almost every minute of the day and night in the small West Berlin airport, the West soon delivered more than 12,000 tons each day. More than 300 pilots flew through impossible conditions, with some losing their lives in crashes during bad weather, in order to carry out Operation Vittles. West Berlin held on, and in the early summer of 1949 Stalin agreed to lift some of the road blockades.

The Berlin Airlift, 1948. *(Walter Sanders/Life Magazine/Time & Life Pictures/Getty Images)*

Truman's tough responses to the Greek, Czech, and Berlin crises won support at home. So also did his foreign policy in the Middle East. Since 1945 hundreds of thousands of Jews, many of them survivors of Nazi concentration camps that had become slaughterhouses, flooded into Palestine. For many decades Palestine had been British controlled, but since 1917, British officials had intimated that someday the territory could become the homeland that Jews had sought for centuries. As the Jews moved into Palestine, they met bitter resistance from Arabs already settled on the land. After a bloody conflict with Arab forces, the Jews proclaimed their new nation on May 14, 1948.

Fifteen minutes after the announcement, Truman recognized the new state of Israel. He did so over vigorous opposition from cabinet advisers (particularly Forrestal and Marshall) who feared that recognition would turn the rich oil-producing Arab states against Washington. British prime minister Clement Attlee and other Western Europeans, who were utterly

Henry A. Wallace giving a speech before a large crowd in Charlotte, North Carolina, August 31, 1948. Boos and heckling drowned out most of his address, but he continued through to the end. *(Bill Chaplis/AP Photo)*

dependent on Arab oil, also opposed Truman's action. Nevertheless, the president supported Israel because of his great admiration for what the Jews had accomplished in Palestine, but his recognition also ensured Jewish political support in the 1948 presidential election. Attlee later observed, "There's no Arab vote in America, but there's a very heavy Jewish vote and the Americans are always having elections."

Whatever Truman's motivation, his handling of foreign crises during 1947 and 1948 accelerated his triumphant run for the White House. In Europe Stalin had been especially helpful in this regard. Truman's closest political adviser told him that there was "considerable political advantage to the administration in the battle with the Kremlin."

COLD WAR POLITICS: THE 1948 ELECTION

In 1948 Truman's Fair Deal program combined two features: promises to bolster American defenses against the perceived communist menace and an expansion of New Deal benefits. On the domestic front, he appealed for civil rights legislation, federal aid to education, national medical insurance, power development in river valleys, increases in unemployment compensation and the minimum wage, higher taxes on corporations, and lower taxes on just about everyone else. Truman did not expect the Republican Congress to enact these measures, but he recognized that, in the words of one adviser, recommendations "must be tailored for the voter, not the Congressman." On the other hand, the Truman administration stepped up its attack on suspected subversives. Early in 1948 the Justice Department arrested a dozen aliens who belonged to the Communist Party and instituted deportation proceedings against them. The attorney general also drew up a list of subversive organizations. These groups had no opportunity to contest their listing, and most of them then experienced difficulty in renting meeting halls and recruiting members.

Yet despite Truman's brand of liberal anticommunism, Democratic prospects in 1948 appeared bleak. The Republicans had captured Congress in 1946, and in the past when the party out of power had won control of Congress in an off-year election—Republicans in 1894, Democrats in 1910, Republicans in 1918, Democrats in 1930—it had gone on to victory in the next presidential election. Even worse, the Democratic Party seemed to be coming apart. Henry Wallace was leading a defection on the left into the Progressive Party, and Strom Thurmond was leading a defection on the right into the States' Rights Democratic Party.

Wallace had announced his willingness to run on an independent ticket in December 1947. In the year since he had left the cabinet, his differences with Truman had sharpened. Wallace considered the president too cautious in defending the civil liberties of radicals and the civil rights of blacks. But the major source of disagreement concerned foreign policy. Truman regarded the Soviet Union as inherently aggressive, but Wallace believed that Soviet moves often came in response to an American military buildup. Truman condemned Soviet control of Eastern Europe, but Wallace held that Stalin had legitimate reasons for establishing a political sphere of influence in that area, provided that such a sphere remained open to American trade and investment. Wallace maintained that the American plan for controlling atomic energy was bound to be unacceptable to the Russians. He criticized the Marshall Plan for turning Western Europe into a "vast military camp" and believed that universal military training would persuade people of the inevitability of war. Fearing that "we are whipping up another holy war against Russia," Wallace accepted the Progressive Party nomination in the summer of 1948.

But his candidacy, itself a product of the Cold War, soon became a casualty of that conflict. Wallace was widely denounced as a communist dupe, in part because American communists backed his candidacy, in part because he refused to repudiate their support, and in part because his views concerning the Soviet Union often coincided with the Communist Party line. Americans for Democratic Action, an organization of anticommunist liberals, claimed that the Progressive Party represented "a corruption of American liberalism" for it had "lined up unashamedly with the force of Soviet totalitarianism." Wallace, a devout man who never subscribed to the communist position, failed to repudiate communist backing, although to have done so might well have helped his candidacy. He probably believed that the number of votes to be gained was not worth the price—that is, his repudiation of communist support would contribute to what he considered anticommunist hysteria.

Even had a majority of Americans not come to believe that communists ran the Progressive Party, events in Europe—particularly the coup in Czechoslovakia and the Berlin crisis—would surely have undercut Wallace's candidacy. As it was, the Progressives suffered a disastrous defeat. Wallace received only 1.1 million votes, or 2.4 percent of the total. The party received no electoral votes and elected only one member, Vito Marcantonio of New York City, to the House of Representatives. Wallace made his best showing in New York, where he obtained 8 percent of the vote, and in California, where he received 5 percent. Nor did the Progressives have the murderous impact on the Democrats that had been predicted. Although Wallace garnered enough Democratic votes to deprive Truman of three states—New York, Michigan, and Maryland—his candidacy also acted as a lightning rod for anticommunist sentiment. Wallace, not Truman, became the target, with the result that the Democrats could solidify their hold on voters, particularly ideologically conservative but staunchly Democratic Irish Catholics, who were motivated by such sentiment.

Just as the Progressive Party hurt Truman in some respects and helped him in others, the States' Rights Democratic Party cost Truman electoral support in the South but strengthened his position with black voters in the North. The States' Rights Party was created when the Democratic convention narrowly adopted a civil rights plank calling on Congress to support the president in guaranteeing blacks political and economic equality. A number of southern delegates stormed out, called a convention in Birmingham, Alabama, and nominated J. Strom Thurmond, governor of South Carolina, for the presidency.

The "Dixiecrats" bitterly criticized every attempt by the federal government to ensure racial justice. "We stand for the segregation of the races and the racial integrity of each race," they proclaimed. Proposals to outlaw the poll tax, to permit federal trials of lynch-mob participants, to provide economic opportunity for African-Americans—all were said to violate states' rights. Attempting to turn Cold War rhetoric back on the Truman administration, Dixiecrats denounced the Fair Deal for its "totalitarian" features. Although the party gained support chiefly for its stand on race, it also attracted southern conservatives who had held a grudge against the welfare state since the late 1930s but had lacked a political vehicle for expressing their displeasure.

Dixiecrats and Progressives stood at opposite poles on the issue of civil rights. Wallace was assailed by southern whites for his vigorous advocacy of racial equality and his refusal to speak before segregated audiences. Nevertheless, the two parties faced problems that were in some respects analogous. Just as Wallace failed to win the backing of most liberals, so Thurmond found that many southern politicians, even those who shared his outlook, would not risk forfeiting their patronage and seniority by abandoning the Democratic Party. Both candidates found the electorate enormously reluctant to "waste" a vote on a third party. Progressives and Dixiecrats wanted to bring the Democratic Party around to their way of thinking, but their withdrawals proved only that the Democrats could win without them. Thurmond, like Wallace, polled 1.1 million votes, or 2.4 percent of the total. He carried four states (Mississippi, South Carolina, Louisiana, and Alabama), but by freeing the Democrats from the stigma of southern racism he also simplified Truman's task of appealing to black voters. Blacks provided the Democrats' margin of victory in the crucial states of California, Illinois, and Ohio.

At the Republican nominating convention, delegates were confident of victory. But the Republican candidate, Thomas E. Dewey—who, according to one observer, sought the presidency "with the humorless calculation of a Certified Public Accountant in pursuit of the Holy Grail"—hardly ran an effective campaign. Dewey often spoke in generalities, emphasizing national unity and avoiding harsh personal attacks. He did so for several reasons: his sharp criticism of Roosevelt in 1944 had not paid off; public opinion polls all declared him an easy winner if he did not alienate voters already committed to the Republicans; and growing international tensions meant that voters might resent sharp attacks on Truman. Confident of victory, Dewey spent much time campaigning for other Republican candidates in states that were not crucial to his own election.

The same polls that convinced Dewey to pull his punches persuaded Truman to wage a bare-knuckled campaign. The Democrats emphasized welfare state liberalism but also exploited anticommunism. Truman endeavored to resurrect the Roosevelt coalition by promising to extend the Fair Deal and by charging that Dewey's election would usher in a depression as surely as did Herbert Hoover's. Truman peppered his speeches with references to "Republican gluttons of privilege," "bloodsuckers with offices on Wall Street," who had "stuck a pitch fork in the farmer's back" and had "begun to nail the American consumer to the wall with spikes of greed." Truman not only denounced the Progressive Party as a communist front, but also claimed that communists supported the Republican Party "because they think that its reactionary policies will lead to the confusion and strife on which communism thrives." Truman's strategy paid rich dividends in November 1948. He received 24.1 million votes to Dewey's 22 million. The Democrats, by picking up seventy-five seats in the House of Representatives and nine in the Senate, regained control of Congress. Having successfully navigated the rapids of Cold War electoral politics, it remained for Truman to guide his Fair Deal program through Congress.

THE FAIR DEAL: CIVIL RIGHTS

What Truman managed to do, however, was to extend and codify New Deal measures already on the statute books. Congress accepted his recommendations to expand three programs, all sorely in need of modernization: Social Security benefits, considerably increased, were extended to 10 million people; the minimum wage was raised from forty cents to seventy-five cents an hour; and the federal housing program was further developed. The National Housing Act (1949), a modest measure calling for the construction of 810,000 low-cost units over a six-year period, won bipartisan support in the Senate. Where the New Deal had been innovative, the Fair Deal was more often imitative.

But Congress rebuffed Truman when he attempted to go beyond New Deal initiatives in agricultural policy, federal aid to education, health insurance, and civil rights. In 1949 Truman proposed the Brannan plan for agriculture, named after Secretary of Agriculture Charles Brannan from Colorado. This plan would have substituted an "income support standard" for the concept of farm parity and would have limited the payments available to large, corporate farmers. When organized farm groups denounced the plan, Congress defeated it. The president's $300 million aid-to-education bill was strangled in the House Committee on Education and Labor, whose members were hopelessly divided on the issue of aid to parochial schools. Similarly, Truman's program for health insurance and medical care never got to the floor of Congress. Although the plan allowed patients to choose their own physician and hospital, leaving physicians free to participate or not, it was widely and inaccurately condemned as socialized medicine. Fair Deal programs stood no chance when they antagonized entrenched interest groups, offended influential congressmen, or could be labeled communistic.

Of all these Fair Deal setbacks, however, none was more revealing than the defeat of civil rights. That Harry Truman should have been the first president to support such legislation was surely ironic. Although Missouri was one of the slave states that did not secede from the Union in 1861, Confederate sentiment was strong, and Truman's family had favored the southern cause. Truman described his mother as an "unreconstructed rebel" who, when visiting her son at the White House, warned that if he put her up in the room with Lincoln's bed, "I'll sleep on the floor." Truman observed, "She was just the same Mama she had always been." Yet as senator from Missouri and as president, Truman strongly supported civil rights measures.

This position reflected not only his own convictions, but also his recognition of the importance of the black vote. Large numbers of blacks had migrated north and west during World War II. Strategically located in such states as Illinois and California, they exerted more political leverage than ever before. In 1948, Truman received close to 70 percent of the black vote in large cities. His pluralities in the black wards of Los Angeles, Chicago, and Cleveland enabled him to carry California, Illinois, and Ohio. In addition, Cold War requirements influenced Truman's policies. Since Soviet propagandists never failed to exploit racial discrimination in the United States, Truman argued that such discrimination alienated millions in Africa and Asia. The achievement of racial justice, therefore, could strengthen American diplomacy.

The administration took action on a number of fronts. First, the president appointed a Civil Rights Commission whose report, in October 1947, called for an end to segregation in every area of American life and recommended that steps be taken to implement political, economic, and social equality. Truman endorsed the report, although his own legislative proposals did not go nearly so far. Second, Truman issued executive orders in July 1948 designed to end discrimination in government hiring and to eliminate segregation in the armed forces. Third, the Department of Justice filed briefs in support of groups challenging the legality of segregated housing, education, and transportation. In October 1949 one such brief argued, "'separate but equal' is a constitutional anachronism which no longer deserves a place in our law." Finally, Truman asked Congress to pass legislation creating a Civil Rights Division in the Department of Justice with authority to protect the right to vote, providing harsh penalties for members of lynch mobs, abolishing the poll tax in federal elections, and setting up a permanent Fair Employment Practices Committee with the power to prevent discriminatory hiring. Southern Democrats, however, defeated this legislative package.

The Supreme Court proved more responsive to demands for racial justice than did Congress. In *Shelley v. Kraemer* (1948), the Court held that state courts could not enforce restrictive housing covenants. These covenants, under which a group of homeowners agreed not to sell or lease property to non-Caucasians, played an important part in maintaining residential segregation. If a non-Caucasian family—black, Asian, or American Indian—moved into a home in a restricted area, a state court would issue an injunction requiring the family to leave. Those who favored covenants reasoned that homeowners had the right to protect their neighborhood against "elements distasteful to them" and that covenants, as private agreements, did not violate the Fourteenth Amendment's ban on discrimination. The National Association for the Advancement of Colored People (NAACP), which argued the other side, held that court enforcement of the covenants constituted state action within the meaning of the Fourteenth Amendment. In May 1948 the Supreme Court, by a 6-to-0 vote, accepted the NAACP's reasoning. The decision allowed homeowners to make covenants but not to seek injunctions to enforce them. The ruling by no means removed all the obstacles to integrated housing, but it removed one of them.

If the restrictive covenant decision vindicated the NAACP, A. Philip Randolph's campaign against segregation in the armed forces proved the worth of a more militant approach. In 1948

Randolph demanded integration of the military, first through legislation and after that failed, through an executive order. Insisting that blacks would not fight for democracy abroad if they did not enjoy it at home, Randolph threatened a massive civil disobedience campaign: "I personally pledge myself to openly counsel, aid and abet youth, both white and Negro, to quarantine any Jim Crow conscription system." Asked if this did not border on treason, Randolph replied, "We are serving a higher law than the law which applies to the act of treason." On July 26, 1948, after protracted negotiations with Randolph, the president issued Executive Order 9981, asserting that equality of treatment and opportunity for all members of the armed services would be affected "as rapidly as possible." Randolph expressed satisfaction, and Truman later set up a committee to implement the new policy. The navy and air force quickly agreed to integrate. The army, however, raised one objection after another until in January 1950 it finally accepted a plan of gradual integration. The plan suddenly moved into high gear when American soldiers landed in South Korea.

NATO: MULTIPURPOSE MILITARISM

In early 1949, fresh from his triumphs over the Republicans at the ballot box and over the Russians in West Berlin, Harry Truman was at the peak of his powers. Some leading senators even believed that the Cold War had been "won." But Truman determined to march on, using these victories to consolidate American power in Western Europe. In early 1949, after close consultation with Senate leaders, the president asked for a military alliance between the United States and Western Europe. Called the North Atlantic Treaty Organization (NATO), it became the first United States political tie with Europeans since 1778, when a treaty with France enabled the American revolutionaries to survive.

Truman urged this major break with the American past for several reasons. American officials worried that the Marshall Plan was not working as effectively as they had hoped because of widespread fear among Europeans, and among American investors, that Russia could swarm over Western Europe at will. Such fears were much overdrawn. Half the transportation of the standing Russian army was still supplied by horses. U.S. experts concluded that Stalin would not chance a major war for at least fifteen years. Truman's new secretary of state, Dean Acheson, nevertheless observed that "economic measures alone are not enough," for their success depended "upon the people being inspired by a sense of security." One would not work without the other. Not for the first or last time in their history, Americans had to make a military commitment in order to gain economic benefits.

But NATO also vastly increased American leverage in Western Europe. The European armies required American supplies, and the United States would be in a position to exact political and economic concessions in return for providing the supplies. The European armies, moreover, were ultimately dependent on the American atomic bomb. As Truman's closest military adviser noted, in case of war with Russia, U.S. plans were "completely dependent upon full use of atomic bombs for success." Again, the United States held the high card and could ask Europeans to cooperate with its policies in return for atomic protection.

Secretary of State Acheson eloquently took the lead in urging the new policies. He became Truman's chief foreign policy advocate. Acheson took over that role from Forrestal, who had resigned from the Defense Department and then committed suicide after his fears and suspicions about communism deepened until he became mentally ill. The son of an Episcopal

President Harry S Truman *(center)* with Dean Acheson and George Marshall, December 1950. *(Truman Presidential Museum and Library)*

minister and a graduate of Yale, the elegant, mustachioed, subtle, and brilliant Acheson was a conservative who believed that the American future depended on close cooperation with Europe. To build this community, Acheson determined to deal with Russia only on American terms, which, given Stalin's views, meant not dealing with Russia at all. Acheson similarly dismissed public opinion at home: "If you truly had a democracy and did what the people wanted," he later declared, "you'd go wrong every time." His only allegiance was to Truman, a man completely different in appearance, background, and nearly every other respect except their common mistrust of Stalin and their mutual desire to increase presidential power. An associate of Acheson recalled that the secretary once looked over a speech drafted for Truman, then "said with that magnificent manner of his: 'You can't ask the President of the United States to utter this crap.'" Demanding a typewriter, Acheson pecked out his own draft of the speech. It was clear who made foreign policy in Washington. When the bubble burst, Acheson would be a highly visible target for his enemies.

THE BURSTING OF THE BUBBLE: 1949–1950

Creating NATO marked the high point of American postwar policy. In April 1949 twelve nations (United States, Canada, Great Britain, France, Italy, the Netherlands, Belgium, Norway,

Denmark, Iceland, Portugal, and Luxembourg) pledged that each would consider an attack on one as an attack on all and that each would respond as it deemed necessary, including the possible use of force. But within six months a series of events rocked the Truman administration.

Overseas the Soviets exploded an atomic bomb and China fell to the communist forces of Mao Zedong. American officials knew that the Russians would develop an atomic bomb soon, but few expected it this early. Similarly, the fall of nationalist leader Chiang Kai-shek in China had been expected, but the actual communist proclamation of victory shocked Americans. Acheson correctly argued that the United States had no power to stop the Chinese communists unless millions of Americans were sent to fight, and this not even the most vocal supporters of Chiang Kai-shek were willing to urge. The only hope had been Chiang himself, but despite American advice and $2 billion of aid between 1945 and 1949, his regime had become so corrupt and inefficient that it could not save itself. As Acheson phrased it, Chiang's armies "did not have to be defeated; they disintegrated." The fact remained that the globe's two largest nations were communist and one of them had the atomic bomb. Senate Republican leader Arthur Vandenberg said it best: "This is now a different world."

Truman also faced dangerous conditions at home. The American postwar depression, which many prophesied and everyone feared, seemed to be approaching. The unemployment figure of 1.9 million in 1948 shot up to 4.7 million, or 7.6 percent of the labor force, by early 1950. The Marshall Plan helped keep the economy buoyant, for almost every dollar appropriated by Congress had to be spent by Europeans in the United States for American goods. (This would be the case with nearly every dollar of the $125 billion Congress appropriated for "foreign aid" during the next quarter-century.) The Marshall Plan, however, would last only a few more years. When Congress stopped spending these monies—that is, when Americans had to return to a peacetime economy with more "free enterprise" and less government spending—the nation could find itself in conditions resembling those of the 1930s. Republican congressional leaders who had followed Truman in a bipartisan spirit began to have second thoughts. The administration became a growing target for political attacks.

As the nation settled down into a winter of deep discontent, Truman and Acheson prepared to counterattack. The president ordered a top-secret review of U.S. policy. The review, completed in April 1950, was termed "NSC-68" (National Security Council Paper No. 68). This document set American Cold War policy for the next twenty years. It assumed that only the United States could save Western Europe and Japan, which, along with North America, constituted the globe's great industrial centers. The United States would have to take the lead in reorganizing the "free world," while simply letting its friends follow (much as satellites revolve around a primary planet, as NSC-68 phrased it). According to NSC-68, reorganization meant militarization, and that, in turn, meant that the United States would soon have to accept a $50 billion defense expenditure instead of the $13 billion Truman had budgeted for 1950. Such spending would of course also pump up the deflating domestic economy.

Even as Truman planned a massive escalation of military strength, he and Acheson responded cautiously to developments in Asia. In January 1950 the President's military advisers concluded that the island of Formosa (to which the Chiang regime had fled) would shortly fall to Mao's troops, and the United States should not lift a finger. Acheson clearly was flirting with the idea of recognizing the Chinese communists. The flirtation cooled only after the Chinese seized U.S. property, mistreated American citizens, and signed a friendship pact with Stalin in February 1950.

At the same time, Acheson took steps to ensure that Japan would replace China as the American outpost in Asia. As early as 1947, when Washington officials saw the hollowness of Chiang's regime, they had encouraged Japan to rebuild more rapidly than the 1945 surrender terms allowed. Following this lead, U.S. businesses trooped into the promising Japanese market, increasing their investment from $96 million in 1946 to nearly $500 million in 1949. With Japan recovering and an independent government at work in Tokyo in 1949, the question became how the United States could be assured that Japan would stay on Washington's side for the indefinite future. This question became pressing when China fell to communism. Japan had looked to China for decades as a market and source of raw materials. If something were not done, the Japanese might well fall into the Chinese communist orbit.

Acheson's answer was a NATO-like device: the United States and Japan would sign a treaty ending American occupation, but allowing U.S. military bases to remain. While the Japanese themselves would not possess a large military establishment, their islands would become an American outpost on Russia's Asian rim. Stalin did not care for this solution. As early as 1947 the Soviets had warned against any "intention to restore the economy of Germany and Japan on the old [pre-1939] basis provided it is subordinated to interests of American capital." Acheson had done much more, making Japan both a major economic and a military base for the United States. Faced with NATO to the west and long-term American military bases on his eastern flank, Stalin decided to act.

KOREA: JUNE 1950

His opportunity lay in Korea. In 1945 that nation had been divided between American and Russian forces along its thirty-eighth parallel in order to facilitate the surrender of Japanese troops. After the surrender, however, neither power would leave. Korea was of immense significance: whoever controlled it also controlled strategic entrances to Japan, China, and the Soviet Union. Russian troops finally retreated in early 1949, but left behind a communist North Korean government possessing a strong, Soviet-equipped army. The United States exited from South Korea several months later; it left behind strongman Syngman Rhee and an army useful primarily for eliminating Rhee's domestic political opponents.

Acheson believed that Rhee's troops and the American presence in Japan could protect South Korea. On January 12, 1950, the secretary of state, speaking at the National Press Club in Washington, defined the U.S. defense perimeter in the Pacific as running from the Aleutians through Japan to the Philippines. That was the same defensive line that General Douglas MacArthur, the U.S. supreme commander in Japan, had agreed to in 1949. Acheson carefully added, however, that any aggression against Korea would be opposed by the United Nations. That statement alone, however, did not frighten Stalin, who had little to lose and much to gain by such aggression. His North Korean allies were eager to attack southward to reunite their country. A successful invasion could endanger Acheson's attempt to rebuild Japan. It would also show Mao, who increasingly disagreed with Stalin over the Sino-Russian boundary lines and economic problems, that Russia remained the dominant communist power. Stalin could accomplish all this, moreover, without any direct Soviet involvement in the attack. In the spring of 1950 he flashed the green light to the North Koreans, while sending them supplies and advisers. But he also warned that if they got into trouble, he would not help. Stalin was not going to start World War III over South Korea. He wanted only Asians and Americans killed.

On June 25 North Korean troops moved across the thirty-eighth parallel. A surprised Truman quickly responded. On June 27 he sent in American air and naval forces. When these proved insufficient and South Korea faced certain defeat, he ordered U.S. combat troops into battle. Meanwhile Acheson obtained the support of the United Nations. On June 27 the UN resolved that its members should help repel the aggressors so that "peace and security" could return to the area. Angry over the American refusal to allow the Chinese communists into the world organization, the Russians had been boycotting UN sessions and were not present when Acheson rushed the resolution through. The struggle against North Korea was to be fought by a UN army under General MacArthur's command.

In reality, the United States actually controlled operations through MacArthur, and the UN simply followed Truman's lead. Americans contributed 86 percent of the naval power, more than 90 percent of the air support, and, along with the South Koreans, nearly all the combat troops. The president made these drastic decisions, moreover, without going before Congress to ask for a declaration of war, as the Constitution required. He termed the struggle a "police action," not a war, hoping that this description of the bloodshed would limit the conflict before it expanded with atomic weapons and Russian participation. The president merely consulted and informed congressional leaders, of whom only Senator Robert Taft, the Ohio Republican, raised major objections. This procedure was clearly unconstitutional and later, when the war went badly, proved to be a political error as well, for it left Truman exposed to bitter partisan attack. The president's decision, moreover, set a precedent for the later Kennedy-Johnson-Nixon commitment of American troops to Vietnam, a commitment again taken without a congressional declaration of war.

CHANGING "CONTAINMENT" TO "LIBERATION": THE UNITED STATES ON THE OFFENSIVE

Truman and Acheson used the Korean War as an opportunity to take the initiative against communism not only in Asia but in Europe, too. The remainder of 1950 was the most active and crucial months in the Cold War. Several motivations shaped the new approach. The war gave Acheson a perfect opportunity to build the great military bastions in Asia and Europe that he had long desired. After all, he could argue, if the communists struck in Korea, they might strike anywhere. In a larger sense, the war was the chance to put the global ideas of NSC-68 into effect. Driving back communism would also silence growing criticism at home. These critics, whom Acheson acidly called "primitives" and "animals," attacked the administration for merely containing, instead of eliminating, communism. Truman and Acheson used the Korean War as a springboard to launch a worldwide diplomatic offensive.

In Asia this offensive included the first full-fledged American support to Chiang Kai-shek's rump regime on Formosa. Truman sent the Seventh Fleet to protect Chiang and signed large-scale economic and military aid pacts. By August 1950, the United States had bedded down with Chiang to establish a new American military outpost on Formosa. In Southeast Asia, Acheson had agreed to help France reimpose its control over the Indochinese peoples in May, a month before Korea erupted. By midsummer the United States sent large military assistance and a military mission to aid the French. Here lay the beginning of the American involvement in Vietnam. Acheson also hurried plans to sign the Japanese security treaty, over strong objections from the Soviets and also from such friends as Australia and New Zealand, who feared the threat of a revived Japan.

The secretary of state similarly took the diplomatic offensive in Europe. He used the Korean crisis as the opportunity to achieve goals that had been impossible to gain earlier because of opposition from allies and Congress. Above all, Acheson determined to lock West Germany firmly to the West by rearming it and integrating the new German forces into NATO. France and England voiced strong opposition to any revival of German militarism, but Acheson refused to listen. Simultaneously, Truman, again without consulting Congress, tied the United States closer to Western Europe by stationing American troops on European soil. Both moves were completed despite strong congressional opposition. In 1949 Acheson had told Congress, "We are very clear that the disarmament and demilitarization of Germany must be complete and absolute." At the same time, he had guaranteed that there would be no Americans assigned to NATO duty without the assent of Congress. The shifting Cold War, especially the new Soviet atomic bomb, changed Acheson's mind. The U.S. commitment to Europe was fixed for the rest of the twentieth century, and well into the twenty-first. Truman meanwhile increased defense spending until in 1952 it reached $50 billion, the figure envisioned by NSC-68.

Finally, Truman and Acheson decided not only to stop the North Koreans, but also to drive them back until all Korea was liberated. Such a triumph would teach Stalin a lesson, silence the critics at home, ensure Japan's position, and put the United States on the border of communist China itself. In July and August the tragic decision was taken to cross the thirty-eighth parallel. In September, General MacArthur made a brilliant landing at Inchon, trapping thousands of communist troops. By late October, the UN forces were marching through North Korea toward the Yalu River, which separates Korea from China. At this point the Chinese issued blunt warnings that UN troops should not approach the Yalu. Acheson was not concerned. "Everything in the world" was done to assure China that its interests were not endangered, he later observed. "And I should suppose there is no country in the world which has been more outstanding in developing the theory of brotherly development of border waters [like the Yalu] than the United States."

This was an absurd statement. Such "brotherly development" of the Yalu, with U.S. troops on China's borders, was precisely what Mao determined to prevent. Moreover, Stalin urged Mao to fight the Americans. It was to the Soviet interest that Americans and Chinese kill as many of each other as possible. Mao knew of Stalin's duplicity, knew (correctly, as it turned out) that Stalin would send too little help, and knew that fighting the world's greatest power could perhaps destroy his Chinese Revolution. Nevertheless, after he spent days agonizing over the decision, in late November Mao's armies swarmed southward across the Yalu. Large units of American and South Korean troops were surrounded, killed, or left to freeze to death in a bitter winter. By late December the UN forces had fled south across the thirty-eighth parallel before MacArthur could counterattack. The war then turned into a bloody stalemate. More than 140,000 Americans and more than 1 million South Koreans were killed or wounded. Most of the casualties were suffered after Truman ordered UN forces to liberate North Korea.

The casualties were only part of the high price Americans paid for the administration's 1950 diplomatic offensive. The immense and rapidly mounting war expenditures skewed the nation's economy, producing inflation and labor unrest. A renewed military-industrial alliance fattened on the defense budget, further distorted the economy while wasting irreplaceable resources. Abroad, Americans discovered that their friends held serious doubts about U.S. stability. These allies found German rearmament so repugnant that it would be delayed for four years. Others feared a revived Japan. Some refused to follow Acheson's policy of aiding

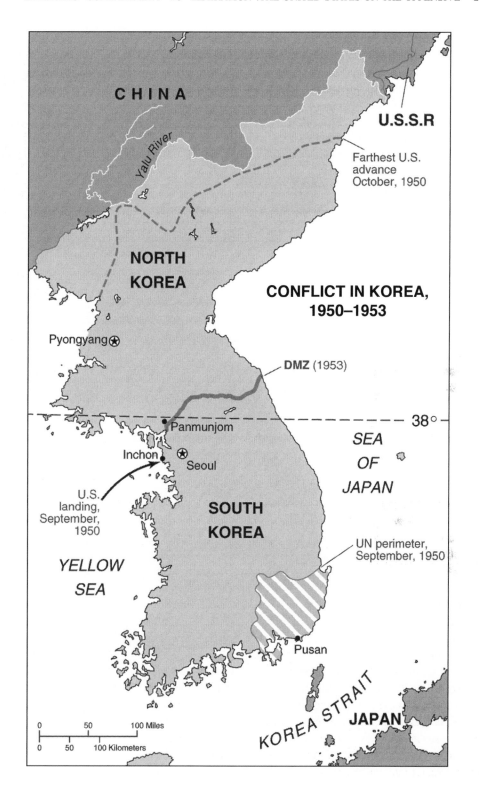

French colonialism in Southeast Asia. All were concerned about how the United States might use its massive power, particularly its atomic weapons.

The Truman administration was also on the defensive at home. Despite the president's assurance that communism could be contained and even driven back, communism had survived, and large numbers of American boys were being slaughtered in Korea. The administration and indeed the entire liberal tradition it claimed to represent were embattled. The struggle at home reached a peak in early 1951, when the president, in his words, reached "a parting of the way with the big man in Asia."

TRUMAN AND MacARTHUR

In April 1951, for the first time in twenty years, baseball fans booed the president of the United States when he threw out the ball to open the Washington Senators' season. A few days before, Truman had relieved General Douglas MacArthur of his command of UN forces in Korea. That action released a tidal wave of sympathy for the general, who, on his return to the United States, received a hero's welcome. When MacArthur concluded a speech to Congress by quoting an old army ballad—"old soldiers never die, they just fade away"—and then added, "like the old soldier of that ballad, I now close my military career and just fade away, an old soldier who tried to do his duty as God gave him the light to see that duty," it seemed as if the applause would never end. The Truman administration, however, regarded MacArthur as an ambitious and dangerous man, one who wanted to subvert civilian control of policy making and plunge the United States into nuclear war.

The basis of the conflict between Truman and MacArthur had existed in 1950, but was concealed because American forces had been successful until late in the year, and the administration, in deciding to cross the thirty-eighth parallel, in effect had endorsed MacArthur's goal of eliminating the communist government in North Korea. Once Chinese forces intervened, however, the options available to the United States narrowed considerably: it could either accept a stalemate or risk nuclear war. Truman chose the first alternative and MacArthur the second. The two men, therefore, rapidly moved toward a showdown. In January 1951 MacArthur demanded permission to blockade China, bomb military and industrial targets across the Yalu River, use Chinese nationalist troops in Korea, and allow Chiang Kai-shek to attack the Chinese mainland. When Truman rejected all these demands, MacArthur took matters into his own hands. In March he publicly threatened to destroy China if it did not concede defeat, and he stated that there was no substitute for victory. Truman then recalled him.

MacArthur not only repudiated the very concept of limited war, but also disagreed with the administration's strategic priorities. As commander of U.S. forces in the Pacific during World War II, MacArthur had declared, "Europe is a dying system. It is worn out and run down." But the Truman administration regarded Europe, not Asia, as the key to containment. Provoking a war with China, as MacArthur seemed ready to do, would antagonize the nations of Western Europe and jeopardize the NATO alliance. By funneling American forces to the Pacific, such a conflict would weaken European defenses. When General Omar N. Bradley, speaking for the Joint Chiefs of Staff, asserted that an attack on China would involve the United States in "the wrong war, in the wrong place, at the wrong time, and with the wrong enemy," he left little doubt as to what he considered the right war, the right place, the right time, and the right enemy: a war waged to defend Western Europe against Soviet domination.

That General Bradley defended the Truman administration was of crucial significance. The conflict between Truman and MacArthur, often interpreted as one between civilian and military interests, actually involved sharp disagreement within the military. The Joint Chiefs of Staff fully endorsed Truman's decision to recall MacArthur. So, too, did General George Marshall, who served as secretary of state (1947–1949) and secretary of defense (1950–1951). "The S.O.B. should have been fired two years ago," Marshall commented. On the other hand, almost all the field commanders in Korea backed MacArthur. (The lone exception was General Matthew Ridgeway, and Truman selected him to replace MacArthur.) The military establishment's support of the president's Korean policy helped him ride out the storm created by MacArthur's dismissal.

LIMITED WAR AT HOME

The Korean War did not require the same level of economic regulation as World War II did. Since military operations occurred on a limited scale, the armed forces absorbed a relatively small proportion of industrial output and consumer goods were plentiful. Inflationary pressures, strong during the first nine months of war, subsided in the spring of 1951. World War II had produced gargantuan deficits, but the government showed a budgetary surplus in 1951 and 1952. Even so, the administration took a number of steps to control inflation and encourage production. The president established the Office of Defense Mobilization, issued an order designed to hold the line on prices and wages, and took possession of the railroads when workers threatened to strike for higher wages. Truman bitterly assailed the union leaders for acting "like a bunch of Russians," but the workers eventually won most of their demands, and the government returned the lines to private owners.

The Supreme Court's response to the president's seizure of the steel mills illustrated the problems encountered in regulating the economy during a limited war. In March 1952 a federal wage panel concluded that steelworkers deserved a raise, but the companies refused to grant the increase unless the administration approved a sizable price increase. When the administration refused, the steel firms rejected a wage hike and the union called a strike. Truman could have invoked the Taft-Hartley Act and ordered an eighty-day cooling-off period, but he did not want to use the law against workers with a legitimate grievance or risk alienating organized labor. Instead he seized the steel mills, citing as justification the existence of a national emergency, the importance of steel production in wartime, and his implied powers as commander in chief. The case rapidly moved to the Supreme Court, which, in *Youngstown Sheet and Tube Co. v. Sawyer* (1952), ruled against the president by a 6-to-3 margin. The majority held that the president had no constitutional authority to order the seizure and that in bypassing the Taft-Hartley Act he had ignored "the clear will of Congress." Truman then returned the steel mills to their owners and, when the union struck, refused to intervene. The strike lasted nearly two months and ended with the workers obtaining their raise and the administration reluctantly granting the steel companies their price increase.

Despite the limited nature of the mobilization, the Korean War greatly bolstered the American economy. Expenditures for purchasing armaments and other equipment, constructing bases, and meeting military payrolls rose sharply, from slightly more than $13 billion in the year ending June 1950 to slightly under $60 billion in the year ending June

1953. Although the percentage of GNP devoted to national security never approached the World War II level (43.1 percent), it nevertheless rose from 6.4 percent in 1950 to 14.1 percent in 1953. As government spending created millions of new jobs, unemployment dropped to its lowest level in years. Federal expenditures, together with special tax incentives, encouraged industries to expand their productive facilities. From 1950 to 1954, steel capacity increased by 24 percent, electrical generating capacity by 50 percent, and aluminum capacity by 100 percent. Finally, the government began to stockpile petroleum, chemicals, and scarce metals to protect itself against shortages in the event of a long war. By 1954 it had acquired more than $4 billion worth of critical materials.

The Korean War also led to a doubling of the size of the armed forces and, more important, to the construction of the hydrogen bomb. Truman had authorized development of the hydrogen (or "super") bomb in January 1950, but little progress was made in the next six months, and doubts about the bomb's feasibility persisted. The outbreak of the Korean War removed several obstacles to its completion. The national emergency convinced a number of scientists who had refused to work on thermonuclear weapons to put aside their moral qualms and also made it possible to justify testing within the continental United States for the first time since 1945. The war allowed Truman to pump billions of dollars into the bomb project; the Atomic Energy Commission eventually employed 150,000 people. Tests in May 1951 proved the technical feasibility of a thermonuclear weapon. Finally, the first hydrogen bomb was detonated over the Pacific on November 1, 1952, its 10.4-megaton explosion obliterating the uninhabited island of Elugelab. Russia, which produced its atomic bomb four years after the United States used its bombs, obtained a hydrogen bomb only one year after the U.S. test of the "super."

If the Korean War had the effect of accelerating the development of bombs and weapons, it had a similar effect in desegregating the armed services. By mid-1950 the navy and air force had taken long strides toward desegregation, but the army, although it had yielded to administration pressure to abolish racial quotas on enlistments, still maintained separate black and white units. Yet segregation led to a wasteful duplication of facilities and an inefficient use of personnel. Moreover, the tendency to assign black units to noncombatant duties meant that whites suffered a disproportionate share of casualties. When white troops experienced heavy losses in the early days of the war, field commanders in Korea broke with existing policy and used black soldiers as replacements. In March 1951 the Pentagon announced the integration of all training facilities in the United States. A few months later the army received a preliminary report from a team of social scientists emphasizing the advantage of integration and denying that it would damage morale. The army then announced that it would integrate its forces in Korea and the Far East. Later it extended this policy to troops stationed in Europe. By the end of the Korean War, nearly all black soldiers were serving in integrated army units.

CIVIL LIBERTIES UNDER SIEGE

The Korean conflict intensified the growing fear of communist subversion, a fear that partly fed on the actions of the House Committee on Un-American Activities. In 1947 the committee sought to prove that communists had infiltrated the motion picture industry. Several writers and producers who refused to answer questions concerning their political affiliations were jailed for contempt, and Hollywood adopted a blacklist barring the employment of anyone who failed to cooperate with congressional investigators. In 1948 the committee stalked bigger game: Alger Hiss, president of the Carnegie Endowment for International Peace, who was charged with perjury for denying that, while working for the State Department in the late 1930s, he had given classified papers to a Communist Party member for transmittal to the Soviet Union. After his first trial resulted in a hung jury, Hiss was convicted of perjury in January 1950. By 1949 the committee was looking into espionage by scientists who had allegedly passed secret information about the atomic bomb to Russia. The Korean War, coming on the heels of this fear of subversion, had a chilling effect on civil liberties. That effect could be measured by the behavior of Congress, the president, and the courts.

Three months after American troops landed in Korea, Congress passed sweeping legislation to curb subversive activities in the United States. The Internal Security Act (1950) made it unlawful to conspire to perform any act that would "substantially contribute" to establishing a totalitarian dictatorship in the United States. The measure required members of communist organizations to register with the attorney general, barred them from employment in national defense, and denied them the right to obtain passports. The act imposed stringent controls on immigrants, aliens, and naturalized citizens. It blocked the entry of those who had belonged to totalitarian organizations, provided for the deportation of suspected alien subversives, and permitted the government to revoke the naturalization of those who joined a subversive group within five years of acquiring citizenship. Finally, the act authorized the president, in the event of war or invasion, to detain persons if there were "reasonable grounds" to believe that they might conspire to commit espionage or sabotage. On September 22, 1950, Truman vetoed the bill, but Congress very easily overrode the veto.

The president's veto of the Internal Security Act did not prevent him from narrowing the rights of government employees under the federal loyalty program. At its inception in March 1947 this program provided for dismissal from federal employment in cases where "reasonable grounds exist for belief that the person involved is disloyal." But the Loyalty Review Board, which supervised the program, found it difficult to discover such evidence. In April 1951 Truman issued a new executive order providing for dismissal from federal employment in cases where "there is a reasonable doubt as to the loyalty of the person involved." In effect, the burden of proof now fell on employees who, to keep their jobs, had to dispel all doubts. Since those doubts might rest on nothing more substantial than associating with persons considered to be communists, attending meetings to raise money for suspect causes, or even subscribing to radical publications, the burden was a heavy one.

At the same time that the new loyalty program went into effect, a jury in New York found Ethel and Julius Rosenberg guilty of conspiring to commit espionage. Documents made public only in the 1990s showed that a top-secret U.S. intelligence operation, named "Venona," had cracked the most sensitive Soviet codes. Venona code-breakers concluded from their reading of Soviet cables that communist agents were working in sensitive U.S. projects. Julius Rosenberg was among the first to be identified. The Rosenbergs were charged with having plotted to arrange for the transfer of atomic secrets to the Soviet Union during World War II. Ethel Rosenberg's brother, who had worked as a machinist on the Manhattan Project, testified that he had transmitted such information and received cash payments; the alleged courier supported this account. The defense denied everything, insisting that the entire story was a fabrication. On April 5, 1951, in handing down a death sentence, Judge Irving Kaufman attempted to tie the case to the Korean War. By helping Russia obtain the atomic bomb, he asserted, the couple had caused "the Communist aggression in Korea, with the resultant casualties exceeding fifty thousand." Appeals dragged through the courts for two agonizing years, with the Rosenbergs protesting their innocence to the end, although their sentence would have been commuted to life imprisonment had they confessed. They were electrocuted on June 19, 1953. Even many who considered them guilty regarded the sentence as barbaric.

In June 1951 the Supreme Court moved with the prevailing tide by upholding the constitutionality of the Smith Act. Passed in 1940, the act made it a crime to conspire to teach or advocate the forcible overthrow of the government. In 1949 Eugene Dennis and ten other communist leaders had been found guilty of violating the act, and the following year a court of appeals sustained their convictions. In *Dennis v. United States* (1951), the Supreme Court approved the Smith Act by a 6-to-2 vote. Chief Justice Fred M. Vinson wrote the majority opinion. To prove the American communists presented a clear and present danger to the United States, Vinson pointed to the formation of a "highly organized conspiracy" with "rigidly disciplined members," the "inflammable nature of world conditions," and the "touch-and-go nature of our relations" with Russia. Justices Hugo Black and William O. Douglas dissented. Affirming the value of free speech, Douglas denied that American communists, whom he termed "miserable merchants of unwanted ideas," posed an immediate threat. The Dennis decision cleared the way for the prosecution of other communist leaders. Nearly one hundred of them were indicted in the early 1950s.

The Internal Security Act, the revamped loyalty program, the trials of alleged spies, and the Smith Act prosecution—all trespassed to some extent on civil liberties. Of these measures, Truman's loyalty program undoubtedly affected the largest number of people. Yet of the 4.7 million jobholders and applicants who underwent rigid loyalty checks by 1952, only about 10,000 failed to gain clearance. Most of them quietly resigned or withdrew their applications; only 560 people were actually fired or denied a job on the grounds of security. The Korean War's impact on civil liberties, however, would not stop at this point. With the emergence of Senator Joseph McCarthy, open season was declared on liberals. The Truman administration itself became the quarry.

McCARTHYISM

Joseph McCarthy, elected to the Senate as a Republican from Wisconsin in 1946, had a meteoric career in the early 1950s. Although he first achieved notoriety for a speech he gave at Wheeling, West Virginia, a few months before the Korean War broke out, and although he remained a powerful political force for some time after the war ended, McCarthy's appeal derived largely from his success in exploiting the frustrations involved in waging a limited war. McCarthy declared at Wheeling that the United States, at the end of World War II, had been the most powerful nation in the world, but by 1950 it had "retreated from victory" and found itself in a "position of impotency." One thing alone, McCarthy said, was responsible: "the traitorous actions" of high government officials in the Roosevelt and Truman administrations. This explanation, as deceptive as it was simple, set the tone for all that McCarthy did and for much of what went by the name of "McCarthyism."

There was nothing new in the charge that communists had infiltrated government. What distinguished McCarthy was his assertion that the most eminent and reputable Democrats were serving the communist cause by waging a "caricature of a war" in Korea. To McCarthy, Secretary of State Dean Acheson was the "Red Dean of the State Department," "the elegant and alien Acheson—Russian as to heart, British as to manner." Similarly, the Wisconsin senator believed that General George Marshall had been hoodwinked into aiding "a great conspiracy, a conspiracy on a scale so immense as to dwarf any previous such venture in the history of man." Democratic governor Adlai E. Stevenson of Illinois "endorsed and could continue the suicidal Kremlin-directed policies of the nation."

McCarthyism meant more than wild attacks on the Truman administration. It also signified a climate of all-embracing conformity. Many people became afraid to voice unpopular views or even to express controversial opinions. The drive to conform was sometimes carried to ludicrous lengths. One state required professional boxers and wrestlers to take a noncommunist oath before entering the ring. Efforts were made in Indianapolis, Indiana, to remove such "controversial" works as *Robin Hood* (whose indiscretion was stealing from the rich and giving to the poor) from public school libraries. Names themselves often took on great significance: the Cincinnati Reds were solemnly renamed the "Redlegs," and a face powder known as "Russian Sable" was marketed as "Dark Dark." Not everyone surrendered to this mood, but pressures for ideological conformity in America have seldom been stronger than during the early 1950s.

McCarthyism was also closely identified with the use of heavy-handed tactics. McCarthy presented himself as a rough-and-tumble fighter; his supporters affectionately termed him "Jolting Joe" and "The Wisconsin Walloper." Never far from the surface was the suggestion that the Truman administration was infested with moral, as well as ideological, perverts. The senator, wrote one admirer, "learned that the State Department was literally crawling with so called 'men' who wore red neckties and sometimes women's clothes—who wanted other men for lovers instead of women." McCarthy's allusions to homosexuality among government employees were hardly more circumspect. He referred to "those Communists and queers" in the State Department who wrote "perfumed notes." McCarthy insisted that the war against communism must be fought with brass knuckles, not kid gloves. The tactics he employed— from the juggling of statistics concerning the number of alleged security risks in the State Department to the browbeating of witnesses—seemed entirely legitimate to his followers.

Support for McCarthy closely followed political, religious, and occupational lines. The senator won more backing from Republican than from Democratic voters, more from Catholics than from Jews, more from Baptists and Lutherans than from Congregationalists and Episcopalians, and more from blue-collar workers than from white-collar professionals. McCarthy also exploited his position in the Senate. Even though some Republican senators found his methods abhorrent, few dared to criticize him openly because they either feared antagonizing him or recognized his partisan value. Moreover, the Senate customarily permits its members broad latitude, relying on tradition and unwritten rules to ensure discretion. McCarthy also manipulated the mass media with great success. He developed techniques for monopolizing headlines that kept his name before the public even when his allegations had no substance.

That McCarthy could have charged the Democrats with treason and that anyone could have taken those charges seriously seems, in retrospect, incredible. In the years from 1947 to 1952 the Truman administration had built up Western European economic and military strength through the Marshall Plan and NATO, faced down the Russians in Berlin, taken stern measures against radicals at home, developed the hydrogen bomb, and fought a war against

Senator Joseph McCarthy and Roy Cohn, 1953. *(Wisconsin Historical Society)*

communists in Korea. Nevertheless, Truman erred in supposing that the American people would be willing to make the terrible sacrifices war required without being convinced that the government was doing everything in its power to win that war. In the past, although war had sometimes been used as an instrument of diplomacy, it had always been presented as a crusade: to free Cuba in 1898, to make the world safe for democracy in 1917, to establish the four freedoms in 1941. When McCarthy asserted that the United States was "engaged in a final, all-out battle between communistic atheism and Christianity," when MacArthur claimed that "there is no substitute for victory," they were speaking the kind of language Americans had customarily spoken when waging war. If Truman was correct in believing that in the nuclear age only limited war was feasible, his opponents were surely correct in recognizing that limited war provided them an unequaled political opportunity. They would make the most of that opportunity in the 1952 election.

CHAPTER TWELVE

1952–1957
Eisenhower and the American Consensus

Aerial view of rows of nearly identical houses in suburban dreamland as envisioned by builder William Levitt. *(Joseph Schersche/Time & Life Pictures/Getty Images)*

Dwight David Eisenhower, reared on the Kansas frontier and the plains of West Point Military Academy, became famous as the commander of Allied forces in Western Europe during World War II. In 1952, campaigning for the presidency as a spokesman for traditional American values, he offered reassurance and hope to a people soured by the trials of the Cold War. Within two years of his election, the Korean War had ended and Joseph McCarthy had fallen from power. Americans then settled down to enjoy the piping prosperity that they believed they so richly deserved. It was, one critic observed, a classic case of "the bland leading the bland." Yet appearances deceived, for beneath a placid surface society was in ferment. At home, pressures were building that later would produce the massive civil rights movement. Abroad, the United States approached the Suez crisis of 1956, a turning point of the Cold War. Not even the smiling, waving golfer in the White House was always what he seemed. Widely perceived as passive and even deferential, Eisenhower, behind the scenes, employed presidential power in an energetic and assertive fashion.

THE SUBURBAN SOCIETY

The most distinctive demographic development in the United States at mid-century was the expansion of the suburbs. During the 1950s, the population of "standard metropolitan statistical areas"—defined by the Census Bureau as places containing a city with at least 50,000 inhabitants—jumped from 95 to 120 million. That growth took place primarily in the suburbs. Central cities grew by 11 percent, from 54 million to 60 million, while suburbs grew by 46 percent, from 41 million to 60 million. Much of the urban growth in the South and West, however, occurred through the extension of cities' boundaries to incorporate suburban tracts instead of through an increase in the existing population. In the North and Midwest this kind of expansion was uncommon. From 1950 to 1960, fourteen of the fifteen largest cities in the nation experienced a population decline even as their suburbs underwent a population explosion: New York City's suburbs grew by 58 percent, Chicago's by 101 percent, Detroit's by 131 percent, and Cleveland's by 94 percent.

Suburban development depended, in the first instance, on the expansion of the automobile industry and the construction of new highways. The postwar years were boom years for American car manufacturers. Passenger car output rocketed from 2 million in 1946 to 8 million in 1955, and registrations jumped from 25 million in 1945 to 51 million in 1955. For nearly all suburbanites, the automobile was a necessity; indeed, by 1960, nearly one-fifth of suburban families owned two cars. At the same time, states and municipalities built or improved many thousands of miles of new roads. The federal government made an essential contribution. The Interstate Highway Act of 1956 provided for the construction of 41,000 miles of express highways at a cost of more than $100 billion. The new roads made it easier to commute and made it more feasible than before to commute over much longer distances.

The government aided suburban growth in other ways as well. The Veterans Administration offered to insure the mortgages of former servicemen on highly advantageous terms. More than 3.75 million veterans bought homes under Veterans Administration programs that, typically, required only a token down payment and provided long-term, low-interest mortgages. The Federal Housing Administration also insured millions of mortgages, giving preference, in all instances, to buyers of single-family, detached dwellings. Those who wanted to buy a new home in the suburbs could therefore count on a much more favorable response from federal agencies than those who wished to purchase an older home in the city. Government programs tipped the balance in favor of middle-income buyers, those looking at homes in the $7,000 to $10,000 range, and those seeking a suburban location.

The burgeoning suburbs began to lure commerce and industry from the cities. The trend toward plant relocation meant that employment in trade and manufacturing declined in the nation's largest cities and rose dramatically in the suburbs. The appearance of giant shopping centers also heralded the economic transformation of suburbia. At the end of World War II there were only eight shopping centers; by 1960 the number had risen to 3,840. In a three-month period in 1957, no fewer than seventeen regional shopping centers opened for business, leading one observer to note, "at times it seemed they must be coming off a hidden assembly line."

The migration from cities to suburbs was predominantly a migration of whites; black Americans characteristically moved from farms to cities. In the decade of the 1950s, the twelve largest central cities lost 3.6 million whites and gained 4.5 million nonwhites. By 1960 more than half the black population, but only one-third of the white population, resided in central cities. In the suburbs, however, whites outnumbered blacks by a ratio of more than 35 to 1. The number of blacks residing in the suburbs did increase, from 1 million in 1950 to 1.7 million in 1960, but most of that increase occurred in older, all-black communities. Few blacks bought homes in the new, postwar suburban tracts. Either they could not afford the price or they were excluded by real estate brokers who would not show them homes, bank officers who would not grant them mortgages, or suburban zoning ordinances that artificially boosted home construction costs in order to restrict entry.

The word "suburbia" brought to mind images of small children, and with good reason. The 1950s saw an unusually high marriage rate and a truly extraordinary increase in the birthrate. The postwar "baby boom" crested in 1957, when the fertility rate reached the highest level since the government first began to compile statistics in 1917. At the rate prevailing in 1957, 1,000 women could be expected to give birth to 3,767 children. At the same time, improvements in medical care led to a steady increase in life expectancy. In 1954, for the first time in American history, life expectancy for white men and women reached seventy years. (Black men and women could expect to live an average of sixty-four years.) The rapid increase in the over-sixty-five age bracket led one enterprising publisher to market a magazine designed exclusively for those preparing to retire. During the 1950s the population of the United States increased from 152.3 to 180.6 million. That represented an annual growth of 1.7 percent, the highest rate of change in four decades. Far from worrying about scarcity or overpopulation, most Americans confidently assumed that growth would trigger further economic expansion. As one business periodical happily proclaimed: "More People: It Means New Trade, Good Times."

DOMESTIC IDEALS IN POSTWAR AMERICA

"No job is more exacting, more necessary, or more rewarding than that of housewife and mother," journalist Agnes Meyer wrote in the *Atlantic* in 1950, and the decade that followed seemed to support her claim. Affluence and suburbanization shaped the aspirations of postwar women. When pollsters George Gallup and Evan Hill surveyed the views of "The American Woman" for the *Saturday Evening Post* in 1962, they had reason to conclude, after 2,300 interviews, that "few people are as happy as a housewife." "The suburban housewife was the

A scene from a Levittown home. *(Joseph Schersche/Time & Life Pictures/Getty Images)*

dream image of the young American woman," Betty Friedan would write in 1963. As wife, mother, homemaker, and consumer, "she had found true feminine fulfillment."

The domestic ideals that flourished in the 1950s reflected a surge of postwar upward mobility and the prevalent national mood, a turning away from public affairs toward private goals and family life. "Togetherness," a *McCall's* slogan of 1954, meant early marriages, large families, and "sharing a common experience." The accompanying article described a young suburban couple that "centered their lives almost completely around their children and their home," while the father served as "a link with the outside world." The homemaker's role, though limited, according to the press was essential. Her presence in the household provided security for other family members in an unstable world. "Two World Wars and a depression have uprooted family life and created a nationwide turmoil," Meyer told her *Atlantic* readers. "The mounting divorce rate, the appalling number of youthful crimes, the deliberate neglect of children in many homes, and the looseness of sexual morality among young and old—these are only some of the inescapable signs of a decaying moral structure in areas for which women have a prime responsibility."

When questioned about their aspirations in moving to the suburbs, women in New Jersey's Levittown cited personal, material goals—privacy, freedom, comfort, roominess, quality of life, and a chance to enjoy a "normal family role, being a homemaker." They also looked forward to "furnishing and decorating the home." If women's roles as consumers increased in the postwar decade, this was hardly a surprise after the deprivations of the 1930s and the scarcities of the war years. In the 1950s, the median family income almost doubled. Stores now promoted electrical appliances, from electric mixers to dishwashers, that had been unavailable during the war and a gamut of new products from aluminum foil to room deodorants. Postwar consumerism was abetted by an eightfold expansion of consumer credit and by advertisers' ingenuity in tapping the growing household market, where women made three out of four family purchases. "It's nice to be modern," a young housewife noted in a postwar survey of women's attitudes toward electric appliances. "It's like running a factory in which you have the latest machinery."

While higher incomes provided a dramatic rise in living standards, the baby boom evoked new interest in child rearing. Dr. Benjamin Spock's *Baby and Child Care* (1946) achieved extraordinary success. No child-rearing manual had ever been published at so propitious a time; in the late 1940s and 1950s, Dr. Spock's book sold over a million copies a year. Though widespread in appeal, Dr. Spock's message was directed toward the new suburban family, in which each child could be expected to have its own room and mothers could be expected to devote themselves to full-time child care. Parents appreciated Dr. Spock's upbeat tone and down-to-earth manner. "You make me feel as if I were a sensible person," one mother wrote. Most of the voluminous correspondence Dr. Spock received also managed to re-create his cheerful tone, even when children refused to eat vegetables or speak in sentences, or got caught in pieces of household machinery. But parents were often unable to meet the demands of "permissive" child rearing. Some letters were from physicians too busy with their practices to pay attention to their own children, from parents who accused themselves of "selfishness," from couples who found child care "an unbearable drain," and from guilt-ridden mothers who reproached themselves. "I know that a lot of my problem is personal," one mother wrote.

Although early marriage, "togetherness," and child rearing appeared to dominate women's lives in the 1950s, the decade also witnessed other developments. Higher education expanded after World War II. Between 1940 and 1960, the percentage of college-age Americans who went to college more than doubled. The proportion of women attending college fell during the late 1940s, when the GI Bill sent millions of veterans back to school, but the educational gender gap was only temporary; during the 1950s, women began to catch up in percentages. Going to college, now a middle-class perquisite, seemed to have no noticeable impact on the domestic goals of most women college students in the postwar era. "The average college girl views her future through a wedding band," the *New York Times* reported. But colleges remained relative enclaves of equality, and they also prepared thousands of alumnae for eventual entry into the labor market.

The decade of domesticity, paradoxically, was one in which the contemporary female workforce took shape. Between 1940 and 1960, the number of women in the workforce doubled. By 1952, 2 million more women than during World War II were at work. The postwar woman worker, moreover, was likely to be married, middle-class, and middle-aged; in the 1950s, women from middle-class families entered the labor market at a higher rate than any other segment of the population. As second incomes were now needed to maintain middle-class family status in an inflationary economy, wives, not older children, became the major supplementary wage earners. The needs of the labor market also changed. Economic expansion increased the demand for low-paid, qualified workers in service jobs, sales jobs, and especially office jobs. Elementary school teachers were needed to accommodate the baby boom population. The pool of young, single women, usually the mainstay of the female labor force, had diminished, due to low birthrates in the 1920s and 1930s. Postwar employers therefore turned to the older, married white-collar worker. By the early 1960s, one worker in three was a woman, one out of three married women worked, and three out of five women workers were married. Significantly, during the 1950s, women's numbers rose more than 40 percent in many occupations, from professional work to clerical work. Equally significant, as a government commission concluded, "Most jobs that women hold are in the low-paid category." Postwar women provided an inexpensive and available new labor pool.

The contradictions between domestic ideals and women's new roles in the labor force would not emerge until the mid-1960s. In the meantime, most Americans, women included, were relieved to be done with the war and the depression and looked forward to enjoying the benefits of the 1950s—security, prosperity, and unprecedented social mobility.

THE MOOD OF THE 1950s

During the 1950s, many social critics diagnosed American society as suffering from a terminal case of conformity. The suburbs, they claimed, best illustrated the symptoms. In *The Organization Man* (1956), William F. Whyte described an emerging group of Americans, primarily middle-class junior executives, who accepted "a belief in 'belongingness' as the ultimate need of the individual." Organization men and women, Whyte reasoned, found their natural habitat in the new suburbia, with its emphasis on participation in community affairs, sociability for its own sake, and conformity to group values. Whyte concluded that the organization man "is not only other-directed" but "is articulating a philosophy which tells him it is the right way to be." David Riesman had first discussed the concept of "other-direction" in *The Lonely Crowd* (1950), one of the most influential books ever written by an American sociologist. Riesman argued that Americans were in the process of moving from an inner-directed to an other-directed society, one in which the peer group replaced parents as the dominant source of authority and in which those who failed to conform experienced anxiety rather than guilt. If the typical nineteenth-century American had a system of values implanted early in life that thereafter acted as a psychological gyroscope, then twentieth-century Americans had built-in radar systems tuned to the sounds around them.

As sociologists found evidence of conformity in the American present, historians discovered evidence of consensus in the nation's past. Many historians in the 1950s minimized conflict and emphasized continuity. David Potter's *People of Plenty* (1954) held that material abundance—the product of "human ingenuity, human initiative, human adaptability, and human enterprise"—had shaped American character. Potter admitted the existence of some inequality (although the word "poverty" did not appear in his index), but noted that social inequality violated the nation's most cherished ideals. He concluded that "in every aspect of material plenty America possesses unprecedented riches and . . . these are very widely distributed." Another historian, Daniel Boorstin, asserted that Americans had always shown a lack of interest in ideology. They had been concerned, rather, with finding practical solutions to everyday problems. That, to Boorstin, constituted "the genius of American politics." In the view of these historians, the American past was as free of doctrinal clashes as of widespread suffering or sharp class rivalry.

Boorstin believed that this historical tradition fitted Americans "to understand the meaning of conservatism." During the 1950s a group of self-styled "new conservatives" attempted to clarify that meaning. They reiterated the importance of religion, tradition, hierarchy, property rights, and the organic conception of society. They continued in varying degrees to oppose the expansion of the welfare state, which they thought rested on the dangerous premise that "justice is identical with equality." If anything identified the new conservatives, it was their assault on "relativism," that is, on the unwillingness of society to uphold correct moral values and stamp out evil ones. This idea was carried furthest, perhaps, in William F. Buckley's *God and Man at Yale* (1951). Buckley, then a recent Yale graduate, condemned the university for hiring professors who caused students to doubt Christianity and the virtues of free enterprise. Buckley claimed that a private university had the duty to inculcate the values held by its financial backers. Professors who did not wish to teach those values, of course, had the right to seek employment elsewhere. The book went through five printings in the first six months of publication.

REPUBLICANS ON THE POTOMAC

In Dwight Eisenhower the American people found a figure who perfectly suited their mood. In the 1952 campaign Eisenhower exploited the issues identified by the formula "K_1C_2"—Korea, communism, and corruption. Of the three, Korea was the most critical. By the fall of 1952 slightly more than half the electorate regarded the war—or, more accurately, how it might be ended—as the single most important issue. Democratic candidate Adlai E. Stevenson of Illinois fully endorsed Truman's war policies, even suggesting that the nation brace itself for years of additional sacrifice. "The ordeal of the twentieth century is far from over," Stevenson said in accepting the nomination. Eisenhower, who also had backed the decision to wage a limited war in Korea, nevertheless seemed to offer a way out of the quagmire. Two weeks before the election he said, "I shall go to Korea," and though he did not say what he would do when he got there, his pledge, coming from a man identified with victory in World War II, was a masterful stroke. Popularly regarded as the candidate best able to end the war, Eisenhower was politically irresistible. It was appropriate that the last word of his last campaign address was "peace."

The two other issues also worked to Eisenhower's benefit. Republican charges that the Truman administration was infested with communists and that Stevenson was himself dangerously "soft" came not only from Joseph McCarthy but also from Eisenhower's running mate. Richard Nixon spoke of "Adlai the Appeaser," who lacked "backbone training" because he was a "Ph.D. graduate of Dean Acheson's cowardly college of Communist containment." Stevenson was vulnerable because he had once given a deposition attesting to Alger Hiss's good reputation. As governor of Illinois, moreover, he had courageously vetoed a bill requiring loyalty oaths of all state employees.

The issue of corruption also plagued the Democrats. In its last years the Truman administration was plagued by scandals, many of them involving moneymaking schemes or influence peddling by the president's cronies. Promising to "drive the crooks and the Communists from their seats of power," Eisenhower embarked on a moral crusade for decent government. Electing a Democrat to replace Truman, an Indiana Republican suggested, would be equivalent to "putting a new pin on a soiled diaper." On the eve of his inauguration one supporter told Eisenhower, "for the first time in many years the country feels clean again."

What was striking about the election was not so much the magnitude of Eisenhower's victory—he received 55 percent of the vote and carried thirty-nine states—as the high level of voter interest. In 1948 only 51.5 percent of those eligible had voted, but in 1952 the turnout was 62.7 percent. Eisenhower broke through traditional Democratic strongholds, winning nearly half the popular vote in the South (doing particularly well in the cities) and carrying Virginia, Florida, Texas, and Tennessee. Stevenson's reluctance to campaign on the old New Deal slogans and Eisenhower's reputation as a liberal Republican combined to mute economic issues. The Republicans, therefore, did better than they had expected in working-class wards. Whether because of his promise to end the war, his crusade for clean government, or his reputation as a family man (in contrast to the divorced Stevenson), Eisenhower was even more popular among women (58.5 percent) than men (52.5 percent). Most significant of all was his showing among the middle class in the burgeoning suburbs. Stevenson captured New York City, Chicago, Cleveland, and Boston, but in each case Eisenhower won the surrounding suburbs by even larger pluralities, thereby offsetting the Democrats' advantage. These expanding areas also had exceedingly high turnout rates.

Critics of Eisenhower interpreted the 1952 election as a popularity contest involving no real issues beyond Ike's famous grin and twinkling blue eyes. They were mistaken. So, too, were those who saw him as a babe in the woods who did not understand politics or the use of power. If Eisenhower seemed to remain above political battles it was because he recognized that his reputation for nonpartisanship was an important political asset. As one adviser explained to him, "The people want another George Washington. They really think of you as a modern George Washington." If Eisenhower urged his program on congressional Republicans cautiously, it was because he knew that his party was torn between a liberal and conservative wing. He wanted to heal rather than widen the rift. If Eisenhower adopted a more restrained view of presidential authority than his Democratic predecessors, it was because of his belief in the separation of powers and his distaste for emotionally charged disputes. None of this, however, prevented him from manipulating his powers to influence legislation or from using patronage to reward loyal followers. He also fashioned an orderly administrative system based on a clear chain of command.

The new president was determined to reverse the direction taken by the New Deal and Fair Deal or, in his words, to remove "the Left-Wingish, pinkish influence in our life." Referring to the Tennessee Valley Authority, which symbolized such intervention in the economy, Eisenhower once blurted out, "By God, if ever we could do it, before we leave here, I'd like to see us *sell* the whole thing, but I suppose we can't go that far." The president demonstrated his economic orthodoxy by removing the moderate wage and price controls Truman had instituted and by closing down many small, federally operated services that appeared to compete with private business. In addition, Eisenhower cut the government payroll by 200,000 workers and trimmed federal spending by 10 percent—or $6 billion—in his first year. In 1954 Congress enacted an administration measure lowering price supports for farm products.

His position on natural resource development clearly revealed Eisenhower's desire to limit federal involvement. The president consistently favored private rather than public development of hydroelectric power plants. He reversed Truman's decision to proceed with federal construction of such a plant in Hell's Canyon, Idaho, licensed a private firm to build the dams, and threatened to veto any legislation looking toward federal development. Eisenhower opposed the Tennessee Valley Authority's request to build a new plant to furnish power for the Atomic Energy Commission. The commission instead awarded the contract to a private concern known as Dixon-Yates. When a 1955 congressional investigation revealed that the consultant who advised the commission to accept this arrangement was connected with an investment firm that marketed Dixon-Yates securities, a scandal erupted and Eisenhower had to cancel the contract. Finally, the president favored granting the states control of offshore oil deposits within their historic boundaries (usually a distance of three miles). Truman had twice vetoed such legislation on the grounds that tidelands oil belonged to the federal government. In May 1953, much to the delight of Texas, California, and Louisiana, Eisenhower signed the Submerged Lands Act, turning these rights over to the states.

Despite Eisenhower's inclination, he in fact presided over a further enlargement of the welfare state. The Social Security system was expanded to include more workers, to increase benefits, and to lower the age of eligibility for old-age pensions. In 1954 an additional 4 million workers were brought under the unemployment insurance program. In 1955 Congress raised the minimum wage from seventy-five cents to a dollar an hour (although Eisenhower had favored a ninety-cent limit). The administration supported, unsuccessfully, a modest program to provide $200 million over three years to assist school construction in impoverished districts. The president also won authorization for building an additional 35,000 public housing units. Finally, the Interstate Highway Act (1956) provided for the construction of a modern interstate highway system. In urging its enactment, Eisenhower pointed out that new roads could reduce traffic accidents, relieve the massive congestion sure to develop as automobile use increased, and provide for quick evacuation "in case of an atomic attack on our key cities."

In expanding government benefits the Eisenhower administration was responding, in part, to congressional pressure. Although the Republicans won a slim victory in Congress in 1952 (they controlled the Senate by one vote and the House by ten), the Democrats recaptured control of both houses in 1954 and retained it throughout the remainder of Eisenhower's presidency. The administration was also taking account of economic realities. Sharp recessions in 1954 and 1958 led the president to abandon his budget-balancing efforts and to accelerate spending. The government therefore ran a deficit in five of his eight years in office. The people had not elected Eisenhower to dismantle the welfare state, the president's brother observed. Conveying the results of a public opinion poll, Milton Eisenhower said, "Please note the 'new conservatism' really means that we should keep what we have, catch our breath for a while, and improve administration; it does not mean moving backward." In the main, that was the prescription the Eisenhower administration followed.

THE WANING OF McCARTHYISM

The president was as determined to step up the campaign against internal subversion as he was to curb the expansion of the welfare state. Eisenhower succeeded in toughening the government loyalty program. He turned responsibility for loyalty investigations over to departmental

Atomic scientist J. Robert Oppenheimer, 1954. *(Ed Westcott/Courtesy of the U.S. Department of Energy)*

security officers who evaluated all employees and submitted reports to each department head for action. The administration also introduced stricter standards for measuring loyalty. The old criteria—reasonable grounds for believing an employee disloyal (1947) or reasonable doubt as to an employee's loyalty (1951)—no longer sufficed. As of 1953 the government would dismiss any "security risk," which meant that it would seek information concerning "any behavior, activities, or associations which tend to show that the individual is not reliable or trustworthy." Partly to appease right-wing Republicans, the State Department appointed an ardent McCarthyite, Scott McLeod, as security officer. Within a year, McLeod had ousted 484 persons, including several career officials whose only crime had been to tell the truth about the relative strength of the communist and nationalist forces in China in the 1940s.

Perhaps the most famous alleged "security risk" was Dr. J. Robert Oppenheimer, who had headed the project to develop the atomic bomb during World War II. A man of profound intellect who exerted a charismatic hold on his fellow physicists, Oppenheimer had associated with left-wing causes and individuals during the late 1930s. The government compiled a massive dossier on him during the war but knew him to be loyal, considered him indispensable, and regarded his activities as merely indiscreet. Disturbed by the nuclear arms race, Oppenheimer unsuccessfully opposed the decision to proceed with a hydrogen bomb in 1949. By 1953 he was head of Princeton's Institute for Advanced Study, retaining only a consultant's contract with the Atomic Energy Commission. When his old dossier was dragged out, Eisenhower directed that a "blank wall" be erected between Oppenheimer and sensitive material. When Oppenheimer refused to resign his contract, a hearing was held in the spring of 1954 that deteriorated into a judicial farce. A special panel found, by a vote of 2 to 1, that reinstating Oppenheimer's clearance would be inconsistent with national security. The Atomic Energy Commission upheld the ruling because Oppenheimer's association with radicals had exceeded the "tolerable limits of prudence and self-restraint," because his attitude toward the hydrogen bomb was "disturbing," and because of fundamental defects in his "character." Nine years later the government implicitly conceded the injustice by presenting the Fermi Award for distinguished contributions to American science to Oppenheimer at a White House ceremony.

Congress, too, joined the continuing hunt for domestic radicals in 1954 by passing the Communist Control Act, which required communist-infiltrated (as well as communist and communist-dominated) organizations to register with the attorney general. The act asserted that the Communist Party was an "agency of a hostile foreign power," an "instrumentality of a conspiracy to overthrow the Government." Declaring that the Communist Party's very existence constituted a "clear, present and continuing danger," the act stripped the party of the privileges political groups usually enjoyed. The act passed the Senate with but one dissenting vote. The measure was seldom invoked, although it once served to deny a communist candidate a place on the ballot in a New Jersey election.

The new security program, the Oppenheimer case, and the mood in Congress all revealed the persistence of anticommunism. But by 1954 the worst of the hysteria was beginning to fade, and with it ebbed the power of Joseph McCarthy. Eisenhower, who strongly disapproved of McCarthy's tactics, had been reluctant to challenge the junior senator from Wisconsin but confessed that "at times one feels almost like hanging his head in shame when he reads some of the unreasoned, vicious outbursts of demagoguery that appear in our public prints." Then, in 1954, McCarthy crossed swords with two institutions—the U.S. Army and the Senate—that proved too powerful for him.

The army seemed a most unlikely target, but McCarthy accused it of promoting and giving an honorable discharge to a dentist who, in filling out loyalty forms, had refused to answer questions about his political affiliations. The senator warned Secretary of the Army Robert Stevens, "I am going to kick the brains out of anyone who protects Communists!" The army retorted that McCarthy had tried to pull strings to obtain preferential treatment for a recently inducted member of his staff. Stevens and McCarthy then lumbered toward a showdown. Congressional hearings into the controversy began before a nationwide television audience in April 1954 and continued for two months. Toward the end, enraged by the attempt of attorney Joseph Welch to poke fun at his allegations, McCarthy savagely attacked a lawyer employed by Welch's law firm for having once belonged to a left-wing organization. Welch then berated McCarthy: "Have you no sense of decency, sir, at long last? Have you left no sense of decency?" That the congressional committee found some of the army's allegations well founded was less important than that many Americans, offended by McCarthy's tactics, had begun to ask the same question.

By hurling wild accusations, McCarthy managed to alienate almost all Senate Democrats and a considerable number of Republicans. "The hard fact is that those who wear the label—Democrat—wear with it the stain of an historic betrayal," he thundered in 1954. McCarthy called Republican senator Ralph Flanders "senile. I think they should get a man with a net and take him to a good quiet place." In June 1954 Flanders introduced a motion to censure McCarthy. It was referred to a special committee that in September recommended censuring McCarthy for showing contempt for the Senate by refusing to testify before a subcommittee investigating the use of campaign funds in 1952. In December, with the midterm elections safely past, the Senate censured by vote of 67 to 22, with Democrats voting unanimously for censure and Republicans dividing evenly. Terming the action a "lynch party," McCarthy apologized to the people for having supported Eisenhower two years earlier. McCarthy retained his committee assignments, but suffered a great loss of prestige. His popularity continued to diminish until his death three years later.

Eisenhower made his most significant contribution to civil liberties through his Supreme Court appointments. His choice of Earl Warren to replace Fred Vinson as chief justice in September 1953 was especially important. In 1956 Warren delivered an opinion in which the Court ruled that the federal Smith Act preempted the field of sedition, thereby rendering state sedition laws invalid. The Court upheld a lower-court decision that overturned the conviction of a communist sentenced to twenty years in prison for having violated a Pennsylvania ordinance. A year later the Court dealt a crippling blow to the Smith Act in *Yates v. United States* (1957). John Marshall Harlan, another Eisenhower appointee, ruled for the majority that the Smith Act's injunction against conspiring to advocate the forcible overthrow of the government applied to the advocacy of concrete actions but not abstract principles. If one did not call for direct revolutionary acts, one could lawfully urge the overthrow of the government. The *Yates* decision rendered further prosecutions under the Smith Act all but impossible.

DESEGREGATION AND THE SOUTH

If the Supreme Court took a leading role in defending civil liberties, it came close to revolutionizing patterns of race relations. On May 17, 1954, in *Brown v. Board of Education*, the Court unanimously overturned the "separate but equal" doctrine. That doctrine, first elaborated in *Plessy v. Ferguson* (1896), had allowed states to provide racially segregated facilities as long as they were of the same quality. It provided the legal foundation for the intricate Jim Crow system in the South, which covered everything from separate schools, hospitals, and railroad cars to separate football fields, drinking fountains, and restrooms. By 1950, the Court had supported the right of African-Americans to attend white universities and law schools, but on the grounds that those facilities could not be duplicated. In the *Brown* decision, however, the Court met the issue squarely, holding that separate public schools were inherently unequal and therefore unconstitutional. Unanimity was possible only because of the influence of Chief Justice Earl Warren. One member of the Court admitted that had the decision come a year earlier, four justices would have dissented and the majority would have written separate opinions. That, he believed, "would have been catastrophic," for only a unanimous decision stood much chance of winning public approval.

To achieve unanimity, however, Warren avoided claiming that the framers of the Fourteenth Amendment had intended to bar segregated schools, for the evidence was at best "inconclusive." Instead, the Court relied on the work of sociologists and psychologists. Even though the buildings might be of similar quality, Warren asserted, racially segregated schools had a harmful effect on black children by creating "a feeling of inferiority as to their status in the community that may affect their hearts and minds in a way unlikely ever to be undone." In asserting that this conclusion was "amply supported by modern authority," the Court relied largely on studies that indicated black children often placed a higher value on white skin color than on black, thereby revealing what one psychologist termed "basic feelings of inferiority, conflict, confusion in the self-image, resentment, hostility toward himself, hostility toward whites." The Court's reliance on evidence of this kind led such critics as Senator Sam J. Ervin of North Carolina to claim that the justices had "substituted their personal political and social ideas for the established law of the land."

Recognizing that its decision required a monumental change in southern life and was sure to provoke intense opposition, the Supreme Court decided to allow ample time for implementation. In May 1955, in a second school decision, it asked local federal courts to determine the pace of desegregation. Insisting only that a "prompt and reasonable start" be made and that desegregation proceed "with all deliberate speed," the Court acknowledged that it would take time to iron out problems relating to administration, school size, transportation, and personnel. A "declaration of unconstitutionality is not a wand by which these transformations can be accomplished," one justice noted privately. The Court, fearing that the inability to enforce a decision would discredit the judicial process, was as committed to gradualism as to integration.

Public opinion polls indicated that most white southerners—perhaps more than 80 percent—opposed the *Brown* ruling. In March 1956, 101 of the 128 southern senators and congressmen echoed this sentiment by signing a "Southern manifesto" that blasted the Supreme Court. This much the Court may have anticipated, but no one was prepared for the wave of massive resistance that followed. In states of the Deep South, "White Citizens' Councils" were formed that applied economic pressure on blacks (and white businessmen) who were known to favor integration. In addition, measures of "interposition" were adopted whereby the states placed their authority behind local school board officials who defied federal court orders. Various states hounded the National Association for the Advancement of Colored People (NAACP) by demanding its membership lists, using such membership as a basis for dismissal from state employment, and making it a crime to incite a disturbance by attacking local segregation ordinances. In some cases, rock-throwing mobs prevented black children from attending classes with whites.

Of all the techniques of evasion and defiance, none was more effective than the pupil placement laws. Enacted in many states after 1954, these laws provided for the assignment of students on an individual basis. The criteria established by Georgia were typical. They permitted school boards to consider "the psychological qualification of the pupil for the type of teaching and associations involved," "the psychological effect upon the pupil of attendance at a particular school," "the ability to accept or conform to new and different educational environments," "the morals, conduct, health, and personal standards of the pupil," and "mental energy and ability." The result was that black and white children were invariably assigned to different schools. In 1958 the Supreme Court accepted the constitutionality of such laws. Consequently, ten years after the *Brown* ruling, the vast majority of black children in the South still attended segregated schools.

Rosa Parks *(center)* rides on a newly integrated bus after the Supreme Court ruling ending the successful 381-day boycott of segregated buses in Montgomery, Alabama. *(Don Cravens/Time & Life Pictures/Getty Images)*

Nevertheless, the forces unleashed by the Supreme Court inspired southern blacks to adopt a more militant posture. In December 1955 blacks in Montgomery, Alabama, began a boycott of city buses to protest Jim Crow seating practices that required blacks to vacate seats and move to the rear to make room for whites who had boarded after them. The boycott began when seamstress Rosa Parks, a long-time NAACP member and well-known member of Montgomery's black community, was arrested for refusing a bus driver's request to vacate her seat for a white male passenger. The protesters demanded courteous treatment by bus drivers, employment of black drivers in black districts, and seating on a first-come, first-served basis with "Negroes seated from the back of the bus toward the front, [and] whites seated from the front toward the back."

The boycott's leader was twenty-seven-year-old Martin Luther King Jr., who, after having received a divinity degree and a doctorate in theology from Boston University, had become pastor of the Dexter Avenue Baptist Church. King considered his task "combining the militant and the moderate." He preached a philosophy of nonviolent resistance: "We must meet the forces of hate with the power of love; we must meet physical force with soul force." By arranging car and taxi pools and sometimes walking long distances, Montgomery's blacks made the boycott effective. They also adhered to King's teachings even when whites retaliated with mass arrests and intimidation. The movement finally achieved victory in May 1956, when a district court ruled segregation on the city buses illegal, and when the Supreme Court

JACK KEROUAC
AND THE BEAT GENERATION

American Beat writers Jack Kerouac (left) and Allen Ginsberg, 1959. *(John Cohen/Getty Images)*

Jack Kerouac's novel *On the Road* was published in 1957 and instantly became a best seller. It had taken Kerouac six years to find a publisher, but that was hardly surprising since the manuscript, in its original form, violated all literary conventions. Typed as an unbroken, seldom-punctuated, single-spaced paragraph, on a 250-foot roll of shelf paper (the last six feet of which were rewritten when a pet cocker spaniel chewed them up), the novel appeared only after the publisher had heavily edited it. Centering on a series of cross-country automobile trips taken by Kerouac and his friends in the late 1940s, the novel popularized the lifestyle associated with the major figures in the Beat movement. The fictional characters—Sal Paradise, Dean Moriarty, Carlo Marx, and Old Bull Lee—had real-life counterparts in Kerouac, Neal Cassady, Allen Ginsberg, and William Burroughs.

Beat writers, rejecting socially prescribed roles and socially approved forms of behavior, exhibited more contempt than pity for the "square" world, for "the middle-class non-identity which usually finds its perfect expression . . . in rows of well-to-do houses with lawns and television sets in each living room with everybody looking at the same thing and thinking the same thing at the same time." The Beats most admired those who in their view were the least tied down by obligations to career or country—the poets, the hoodlums, the junkies, the hoboes, the jazz musicians, and the blacks. Those groups, generally regarded as among the most deprived in the nation, were from the Beat perspective among the most fortunate: free to take life as it came, to act with abandon, to appreciate the intensity of each experience, to "dig everything."

Though Beat writings contained a critique of conformity, technology, and mechanization, Beat writers shared no single political outlook. Allen Ginsberg (whose poem *Howl* began "I saw the best minds of my generation destroyed by madness, starving hysterical naked / dragging themselves through the negro streets at dawn looking for an angry fix") offered a thoroughly radical indictment of American society, its anticommunist paranoia, and its reliance on nuclear weapons. Yet William Burroughs, the author of another Beat classic, *Naked Lunch* (1959), believed that "increased government control leads to a totalitarian state." What united the Beats was a conviction that politics held few answers to life's most crucial problems. Those problems required personal rather than social solutions. The characteristic Beat stance was political disengagement.

Beat authors received much acclaim in the 1950s (a reviewer in the *New York Times* hailed publication of *On the Road* as a "historic occasion"), but they more commonly encountered hostility. *Time* magazine, denouncing the Beats as "disorganization" men concerned only with self-gratification, labeled Ginsberg "the discount-house Whitman of the Beat Generation." Another reviewer, in a blistering assault on "the Know-Nothing Bohemians," remarked on Kerouac's "simple inability to say anything in words." The Customs Bureau seized copies of *Howl*, attempting to repress it on the grounds of obscenity. In 1957, however, a judge in San Francisco cleared the poem of those charges. William Burroughs spent years in self-imposed exile to avoid indictment for drug possession, and Neal Cassady went to jail in 1958 for marijuana possession. Kerouac, a victim of alcoholism, died at the age of forty-seven in 1969. He had been too ill in his final years to realize that the cultural rebellion then sweeping across the nation owed much to the Beat generation.

Web Links

www.dharmabeat.com/links.html
A website with links not only to material about Kerouac but also to information about Allen Ginsberg, Neal Cassady, and William Burroughs.

www.beatmuseum.org/index.html
The American Museum of Beat Art site which includes a list of "beat films."

affirmed the ruling six months later. After another flurry of violence, beatings, and bombings, desegregation was carried out. In 1957 King established the Southern Christian Leadership Conference, which served thereafter as his organizational base.

Turmoil in the South ultimately had repercussions in Washington. Eisenhower personally regretted the 1954 desegregation ruling, believing that law could not alter age-old customs overnight and that, in his words, "we can't demand perfection in these moral questions." The president also opposed federal infringement on states' rights. Yet in the District of Columbia, where the states' rights problem did not arise, Eisenhower moved swiftly to comply with court orders. His administration ended segregation in Washington's restaurants, hotels, theaters, and public schools. Although Eisenhower approached the matter of legislation gingerly, he eventually concurred with Attorney General Herbert Brownell, who favored legislative action. In 1957 Congress passed the first civil rights act in eighty-two years, empowering the Justice Department to seek injunctions against interference with the right to vote and creating the Commission on Civil Rights to investigate such occurrences. Although clothed only with fact-finding powers, the commission viewed its chief task as "restoring the franchise to all American citizens."

The Eisenhower administration faced its most explosive civil rights crisis in Little Rock, Arkansas. Desegregation of Central High School was scheduled to begin in September 1957. But many whites wished to obstruct the plan, and the state's ambitious governor, Orville Faubus, believed that supporting desegregation would mean political suicide. To avert violence when school opened, Faubus sent the National Guard to Little Rock with instructions to prevent integration. Turning back nine black students who sought admission, the guardsmen maintained segregation for nearly three weeks until a federal judge ordered them to desist. When Faubus removed the troops, a furious mob overwhelmed the police who tried to protect the black students. With the level of tension rising by the hour, the mayor appealed to Eisenhower, who responded by sending federal troops to uphold the court order. The president told one unhappy southern senator, "failure to act in such a case would be tantamount to acquiescence in anarchy and the dissolution of the union." Troops patrolled the high school for months, but the controversy over desegregation convulsed the city for two more years.

ACHESON TO DULLES

As massive change began at home, so similar rumbles began to shake a world supposedly divided rigidly into only "two camps" of capitalism and communism. Secretary of State John Foster Dulles had difficulty comprehending the rumbles partly because of his own unbending anticommunist views. The deeply religious son of a Presbyterian minister, Dulles hated atheistic communism. As the senior partner of a powerful New York law firm, Dulles had formed ties during the interwar period with Western nations that were staunchly anti-Soviet. His diplomatic experience, reaching back to 1919, and his religious beliefs led Eisenhower to remark, "To me he is like a patriarch out of the Old Testament."

Several other convictions were perhaps most important in shaping Dulles's policies. He had served under Dean Acheson, notably as the negotiator for the Japanese security treaty. If anything, Dulles believed Acheson had not been tough enough, certainly not anticommunist enough publicly to quiet such critics as Joseph McCarthy. Dulles therefore proclaimed in 1952 that his policies would aim at "peaceful liberation" of communist areas, not mere containment. This

An atomic mushroom-shaped cloud rises above the ground during U.S. atom bomb tests at Yucca Flat, Nevada, 1952. Over 2,000 marines took part in the tests. *(National Nuclear Security Administration/Nevada Site Office)*

meant no negotiations with the Soviets. Even after Stalin's death in March 1953 and Winston Churchill's public plea for a summit conference to reduce Cold War tensions, Dulles assured Americans that he would continue to fight rather than negotiate. Churchill disgustedly remarked that Dulles was "the only bull I know who carried his china shop with him." The secretary's belief that he had to appease McCarthy and other congressmen also resulted in a purge of Foreign Service officers that crippled the American diplomatic corps for the next decade.

Finally, Dulles assumed that for economic and strategic reasons, the United States had to intensify Acheson's drive to integrate the free world within a system controlled by Americans. Dulles constantly worried that communists would gain control of such third-world areas as Southeast Asia and the Middle East, with their rich raw materials, and thus slowly be able to strangle the U.S. economy.

Despite Dulles's fears, American policies were usually restrained because Eisenhower kept firm control of the State Department. The president once remarked, "There's only one man I know who has seen more of the world and talked with more people and knows more than [Dulles] does—and that's me." Eisenhower rejected Dulles's advice to end the Korean conflict "by giving the Chinese one hell of a licking." Instead, the president, knowing military victory impossible, obtained an armistice in mid-1953 by using a combination of diplomacy and military threat (including the deployment of atomic-tipped missiles in Korea) when China and North Korea refused to make peace. Eisenhower's primary concern was to balance the budget and thereby, he believed, invigorate the economy. He cut Truman's military budget, especially the expensive ground combat forces. Informing his cabinet, "peace rests squarely on, among other things, productivity," the president emphasized that "unless we can put things in the hands of people who are starving to death we can never lick communism." His concern heightened when in the mid-1950s Russia's economy grew at the rate of 7 percent annually while America's economy increased at about half that figure.

Dulles's diplomacy therefore had to rely not on conventional ground troops, but rather on nuclear "massive retaliation," or, as he defined it, the ability "to retaliate instantly against open aggression by Red Armies . . . by means of our own choosing." Dulles and new military strategists, such as thirty-year-old Henry Kissinger of Harvard, declared that atomic weapons could be refined so that they could be effectively used in conventional wars. Cheaper than troops, such weapons could give the country "more bang for a buck." Meanwhile, Dulles flew around the globe establishing new alliances with nations on the communist borders. These countries, especially those in the Middle East (where the Central Treaty Organization, or CENTO, was formed) and in Southeast Asia (where the Southeast Asia Treaty Organization, or SEATO, developed), would, he hoped, provide military personnel while the United States would provide atomic support if necessary.

To establish these policies, Eisenhower worked effectively with Congress. Yet the new president fought back hard and successfully in 1954 when conservatives, led by Republican senator John Bricker of Ohio, tried to pass the "Bricker amendment" to the Constitution. This proposal was intended to give Congress additional power over the president's constitutional right to make treaties. It especially struck at executive agreements (those made by the president with a foreign power which would be binding only for the president's term in office, but which usually remained in effect much longer—as had Roosevelt's executive agreements at Yalta). Eisenhower refused to compromise his power. Overcoming strong southern Democratic and Republican support for the amendment, he narrowly defeated it in the Senate.

CRISES IN A THIRD CAMP: IRAN, GUATEMALA, AND SOUTHEAST ASIA

Fate tricked Eisenhower and Dulles. They were prepared to deal with Stalinist Russia, but Stalin died in March 1953. The new Soviet leadership, soon headed by Nikita Khrushchev, changed some policies, concentrated on internal development, and made overtures to Yugoslavia's Josip Broz Tito and China's Mao Zedong—leaders whom Stalin had angered with his ironfisted methods. Eisenhower and Dulles had also planned to concentrate on European affairs, the area they knew best. In 1954 the secretary of state and British officials finally pressured France to agree to German rearmament and membership in the North Atlantic Treaty Organization (NATO). The following year Dulles could claim a victory for "liberation" as Soviet troops finally left Austria after the Austrians promised they would not join any anti-Soviet alliance. Washington's European policies seemed firmly in place.

But American energies soon had to switch to the newly emerging nations. The focal point of the Cold War was changing. Dulles understood the importance of this "third camp." "To oppose nationalism is counterproductive," he declared. He worked to remove British and French colonialism from the Middle East, Africa, and Asia before the foreign domination triggered further radical nationalism. But he also expected the new nations to be pro-American and anticommunist: hence his famous remark that "neutrality . . . is an immoral and short-sighted conception." Fearing that Khrushchev's growing economic and ideological power might woo the third world to the Soviets, Dulles grimly warned NATO leaders of the possible consequences: "The world ratio as between Communist dominated peoples and free peoples would change from a ratio of two-to-one in favor of freedom to a ratio of one-to-three against freedom." "That," the secretary of state emphasized, "would be an almost intolerable ratio, given the industrialized nature of the Atlantic community and its dependence upon broad markets and access to raw materials."

Within eighteen months after entering office, Eisenhower scored two triumphs in the third world. In Iran, a nationalist government under Mohammad Mossadegh in 1951 had taken over the nation's rich oil wells from British companies that had long profited from them. Mossadegh's action set a dangerous precedent, for the Middle East held nearly 90 percent of all noncommunist oil reserves, and his success could lead to similar seizures elsewhere. In 1953 the U.S. Central Intelligence Agency worked with Iranian army officers to overthrow Mossadegh, give full powers to the friendly shah of Iran, and restore the oil wells to the private companies. But henceforth the British oil firms had to share the profits with American companies.

Eisenhower performed an encore in Latin America. Since 1947 the United States had kept its southern neighbors in line by military aid, channeled through the Rio Pact of 1947 (a hemispheric military alliance that was a precursor of NATO), and the establishment of the Organization of American States (OAS) in 1948. In the OAS Charter, each nation promised not to intervene in the others' internal affairs, to consult frequently, and to resolve disputes peacefully. The United States, however, refused to give economic aid that the Latin Americans desperately needed, particularly when their raw materials dropped steeply in price during the mid-1950s.

Guatemalan officials took matters into their own hands. In this desperately poor nation, roughly the size of Tennessee, a 1944 revolution had weakened the dictatorial rule of a few wealthy Guatemalans who had long dominated affairs. During 1953 Colonel Jacobo Arbenz Guzman accelerated the reform, seizing vast properties held by the American-owned United Fruit Company. Dulles demanded prompt payment for the property. Guatemala was obviously unable to pay immediately. In May 1954, as U.S. threats grew more ominous, the Arbenz government received a shipment of arms from the communist bloc. Dulles responded swiftly by arming an anti-Arbenz force that had gathered in neighboring Honduras. In June this unit of Guatemalans marched into their country, overthrew Arbenz with the crucial help of U.S. intelligence agents and airplanes, and restored United Fruit's property. Dulles lied in publicly disclaiming any connection with the coup. He had little choice, for the United States had broken its own OAS pledge not to intervene in another nation's internal affairs. When Arbenz tried to obtain a hearing at the United Nations, Dulles blocked it. The United States had overthrown a constitutional government. Guerrilla warfare soon erupted again in Guatemala, but Eisenhower and Dulles believed that they had saved the hemisphere from communism.

The administration's next crisis was quite different. It occurred in Southeast Asia and required the delicate operation of removing French colonialism from Indochina (Cambodia, Laos, and Vietnam) while preventing Ho Chi Minh, the most powerful and famous Vietnamese leader—who was both nationalist and communist—from taking control in Vietnam. Since 1950 American aid to France had multiplied until by 1953 it accounted for 80 percent of the French war budget for Indochina. France nevertheless suffered defeat after defeat at the hands of Ho's troops. In early 1954 the French made a catastrophic blunder by committing main forces to the indefensible area of Dien Bien Phu. Paris appealed for help. Dulles wanted to intervene, as did Vice President Richard Nixon, and the administration even discussed the use of atomic weapons. Eisenhower's military sense stopped what could have been a tragedy. He refused to intervene with conventional forces unless congressional leaders approved and Great Britain agreed to join the effort. Neither would go along. The opposition of the Senate Democratic leader, Lyndon Johnson of Texas, was especially strong.

The defeated French then met with Ho's government and other interested nations at Geneva, Switzerland. Two agreements emerged in July 1954. The first, signed only by France and Ho's regime, worked out a cease-fire arrangement. To carry out this agreement, a temporary dividing line was drawn across Vietnam at the seventeenth parallel. The second document, the "Final Declaration," provided for reuniting the country under procedures that were to climax with elections in 1956. The document further stated that the seventeenth parallel line "is provisional and should in no way be interpreted as a political or territorial boundary." The United States would not directly endorse this agreement. Ho could obviously win the election (Eisenhower later estimated Ho would have received 80 percent of the vote), and Dulles did not want to be a party to a pact giving Vietnam to a communist regime. Instead, Eisenhower brought in Ngo Dinh Diem, a Vietnamese better known in the United States than in Vietnam, to head a new South Vietnamese government. Diem had been living in a Roman Catholic seminary in New York. Dulles and Diem readily agreed that no national elections should be held. American aid rapidly flowed to Diem, and the United States now replaced France as the key foreign power in Southeast Asia.

The American commitment was neither accidental nor abrupt. The State Department had concluded in 1951 that Indochina had to be controlled for its "much-needed rice, rubber, and tin" and because its fall "would be taken by many as a sign that the force of communism is irresistible." A secret U.S. National Security Council paper in 1952 reiterated these points, adding that the loss of Southeast Asia would "make it extremely difficult to prevent Japan's eventual accommodation to Communism." Japan, which was the centerpiece of American policies in Asia, required Southeast Asia's markets and raw materials. Eisenhower publicly warned in 1954 that if Vietnam fell, the rest of noncommunist Asia could follow like a "fallen domino."

In late 1954 Dulles tried to keep the dominoes in place by establishing SEATO. The signatories (United States, France, Great Britain, Australia, New Zealand, the Philippines, Thailand, and Pakistan) promised to "consult immediately" if aggression occurred in the area. It was a weak alliance, made weaker by India's, Indonesia's, and Burma's refusal to join,

John Foster Dulles and Dwight D. Eisenhower. *(Dwight D. Eisenhower Library)*

but it would provide a major pretext for the American involvement in Vietnam during the 1960s. The Senate overwhelmingly ratified the SEATO pact. Meanwhile, when communist China threatened small islands around Formosa, which China claimed were rightfully its own, Eisenhower warned that any move would be countered by the U.S. fleet. The president was even prepared to use nuclear weapons against China if it attacked the offshore islands. Dulles and Chiang Kai-shek, the Chinese nationalist leader living in exile on Formosa (or Taiwan), then worked out a military alliance that assured long-term American support. To show its enthusiasm for these measures, the Senate vastly increased presidential powers by passing the Formosa Resolution. This resolution gave Eisenhower the right to respond to a crisis in regard to Formosa without consulting Congress. To fight the Cold War more effectively, the Senate was surrendering its constitutional power to declare war.

THE TURN: SUEZ AND HUNGARY, 1956

Centralized presidential power had dangerous implications, particularly if it could be used irresponsibly in a world made up not simply of two camps, but rather of "gray areas," as the nations that disavowed both camps came to be known. The rapid emergence of such gray areas caused two momentous crises in 1956.

The first occurred early in the year when Nikita Khrushchev launched an attack against the ghost of Joseph Stalin by condemning him as a repressive ruler and military blunderer.

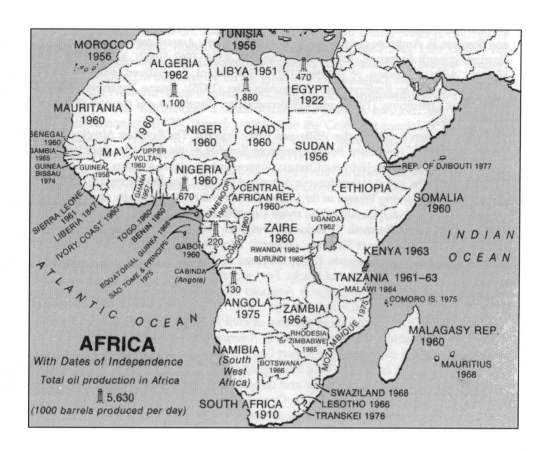

MOROCCO
1956

ALGERIA
1962

TUNISIA
1956

LIBYA 1951

470

EGYPT
1922

1,880

1,100

MAURITANIA
1960

SENEGAL
1960

GAMBIA
1965

GUINEA
BISSAU
1974

MALI
1960

GUINEA
1958

UPPER
VOLTA
1960

GHANA
1957

NIGER
1960

CHAD
1960

SUDAN
1956

REP. OF DJIBOUTI 1977

NIGERIA
1960

1,670

CENTRAL
AFRICAN REP.
1960

ETHIOPIA

SOMALIA
1960

SIERRA LEONE
1961

LIBERIA 1847

IVORY COAST 1960

TOGO 1960

BENIN 1960

EQUATORIAL GUINEA 1968

SAO TOME & PRINCIPE
1975

GABON
1960

CAMEROON
1960

CONGO 1960

220

ZAIRE
1960

RWANDA 1962

BURUNDI 1962

UGANDA
1962

KENYA 1963

INDIAN

OCEAN

CABINDA
(Angola)

130

ANGOLA
1975

ZAMBIA
1964

TANZANIA 1961–63

MALAWI 1964

COMORO IS. 1975

MOZAMBIQUE 1975

MALAGASY REP.
1960

ATLANTIC OCEAN

AFRICA

With Dates of Independence

Total oil production in Africa

5,630

(1000 barrels produced per day)

NAMIBIA
(South
West
Africa)

RHODESIA
or ZIMBABWE
1965

BOTSWANA
1966

MAURITIUS
1968

SWAZILAND 1968

SOUTH AFRICA
1910

LESOTHO 1966

TRANSKEI 1976

Khrushchev hoped to consolidate his own power, remove Stalinists who opposed him, and gain room to carry out his own policies. The results, however, were quite different. Soviet-controlled nations of Eastern Europe seized on Khrushchev's remarks as an opportunity for throwing off Stalinist policies and seeking their own nationalistic goals. Riots occurred in Hungary and Poland as crowds demanded the removal of Stalinist leaders. In early autumn, a confused Khrushchev bent to some demands, but the dissolution of the Soviet bloc continued.

Meanwhile the United States was also clashing with several of its client states. In 1952 the British had been forced by Egyptian nationalism to surrender their long hold on that country. Two years later, the government of General Abdul Nasser demanded that Britain turn over the vital Suez Canal to Egypt. Nasser also planned to build the Aswan dam on the Nile River to provide badly needed electric power. Hoping to pull Nasser closer to the West, Dulles offered to help fund the dam. But Egypt then made an arms agreement with the Soviet bloc and recognized communist China. Dulles retracted his offer, punishing Nasser before the world for dallying with the communists. The Egyptian leader retaliated by seizing the Suez Canal from the British in July 1956 so he could use the canal tolls to build the dam himself.

Dulles rushed across the Atlantic to work out a compromise. His effort was destroyed when the British and French made a final dramatic effort in late October to revive their dying imperial dreams by sending military forces into the Suez. They were joined by Israel, which hoped to improve the dangerously insecure borders it had lived with since 1948. Dulles and Eisenhower were aghast. They feared that the conflict would turn the Arabs against the West, lead to seizure of the vast Western-controlled oil resources in the area, and give Khrushchev the chance to inject Russian power into the Mediterranean theater. The United States turned quickly against its own allies. Eisenhower demanded an immediate withdrawal by Anglo-French-Israeli forces and turned off the flow of oil to England and France until they pulled back. Deserted by the Americans, the Europeans retreated, followed by the Israelis.

Khrushchev seized this opportunity to dispatch the Red Army and execution squads to stamp out the anti-Stalinist uprisings in Hungary. Order was reimposed in Eastern Europe. The United States offered no aid to the Hungarian resistance—so ended Dulles's vaunted policy of "peaceful liberation." Russia then offered Nasser funds and experts to build the Aswan dam. The Soviets were indeed a new presence in the Mediterranean. Equally important, Nasser had successfully defied one of the two superpowers, and the Poles, Hungarians, British, and French had vividly demonstrated that the world was no longer composed of two monolithic camps. The second Eisenhower administration would take office in a radically altered world.

Chapter Thirteen

1957–1963
New Frontiers at Home and Abroad

President and Mrs. Kennedy in a motorcade, May 1961. *(Abbie Rowe, National Park Service/John F. Kennedy Presidential Library and Museum, Boston)*

The Suez and Hungarian crises of 1956 created a different Cold War. The crises demonstrated that the two great powers no longer monopolized global affairs and especially could no longer control the newly emerging areas. Confronted with this different world, American policy makers could respond in one of two ways: either continue to focus on Europe and relationships with Russia or begin to concentrate attention on such less industrialized areas as the Middle East, Africa, Vietnam, and Latin America. The Eisenhower administration chose the first alternative; the Kennedy administration, the second. President Kennedy's fateful choice determined the nation's foreign policy for the next ten years. And like the 1950s crises in foreign affairs, so too would domestic decisions of the Eisenhower years reshape the future choices in domestic politics. The Supreme Court ruling of 1954 outlawing school segregation, for example, provided a legal foundation for the massive civil rights movement of the early 1960s. Both abroad and at home Americans faced a transformed and increasingly rebellious world.

AFTER SUEZ: EUROPE

The most dramatic international event in the late 1950s was the Russian-American confrontation over Berlin, a city that had long symbolized the hostility between East and West. Situated inside communist-controlled East Germany, Berlin had been divided into Russian and Western sectors since 1945. As Soviet leader Nikita Khrushchev bluntly remarked, West Berlin was a "bone in my throat," for it served as a display of Western wealth and power as well as a listening post deep within the Soviet empire.

In 1958 Khrushchev decided to dislodge the bone. He believed that the launching of Sputnik in late 1957 gave him a military advantage. Projecting this earth satellite into the upper atmosphere demonstrated that the Soviet missile capability was greater than the American. Moreover, in early 1958 Western Europe, with American encouragement, created a large economic "Common Market" (the European Economic Community) by agreeing gradually to abolish tariffs and other restrictions on trade. The European Economic Community included France, Italy, Belgium, the Netherlands, Luxembourg, and—most crucial to Khrushchev— West Germany. With this decision, the Europeans had tied West Germany more firmly within the Western economic camp. Faced with a rejuvenated West Germany—always a fearful sight to Russians—and believing that his new missile capacity gave him the necessary diplomatic leverage, Khrushchev struck at the Western powers by demanding in November 1958 that they surrender control of West Berlin. Eisenhower and the European leaders firmly rejected the demand.

Khrushchev then backed off. He proposed that visits be exchanged with Eisenhower for personal discussions. The United States eagerly accepted, particularly because a visit would allow the president to see previously closed areas of Russia and spread the Eisenhower charm. "The name Eisenhower meant so much" to the Russians, one State Department official noted. "I mean, you could send [Vice President] Nixon over, but the average Ivan wouldn't know who the hell he was. But Eisenhower meant something. It was victory. It was World War II and all that." Khrushchev arrived in the United States in mid-1959, visiting American farms and a movie set of *Can-Can* (whose uninhibited dancing girls appalled him), and discussing foreign policy with the president. Eisenhower, however, was never to see Moscow. He had planned to do so after a summit conference in early 1960 in Paris. But before world leaders could fly to the French capital, Khrushchev angrily announced that the Soviets had shot

CENTRAL AND SOUTH AMERICA
IN THE 1954–1970 ERA

UNITED STATES

CUBA
Batista overthrown 1959
Attempted anti-Castro invasion 1961
Soviet military aid, U.S. quarantine 1962

Miami

BAHAMAS
(Br.)

DOMINICAN REP.
U.S. broke diplomatic ties 1960
Trujillo assassinated 1961
Diplomatic ties restored 1962
U.S. and O.A.S. intervention 1965

MEXICO

Havana

Mexico City•

BR. HONDURAS

JAMAICA

HAITI

GUATEMALA
Arbenz overthrown 1954
Castillo Armas assassinated 1957

HONDURAS
Diaz overthrown 1956

BARBADOS
Pérez Jiménez overthrown 1958
Anti-Nixon riots 1958

NICARAGUA

Canal Zone

TRINIDAD AND TOBAGO

EL SALVADOR

COSTA RICA

PANAMA
Anti-U.S. riots 1959

Caracas

VENEZUELA

GUYANA

SURINAM *(Neth.)*
FR. GUIANA

Rojas Pinilla forced out 1957

•Bogota

COLOMBIA

PACIFIC

OCEAN

EQUADOR Quito•

PERU

B R A Z I L

Anti-Nixon riots 1958
Military coup 1962
Military coup 1968

•Lima

BOLIVIA
La Paz•

•Brasília

Average annual per capita income
late 1960's

Argentina	$800
Barbados	428
Bolivia	165
Brazil	350
Chile	465
Colombia	262
Costa Rica	380
Cuba	310
Dominican Rep.	212
Ecuador	183
El Salvador	245
Guatemala	264
Guyana	250
Haiti	75
Honduras	209
Jamaica	431
Mexico	600
Nicaragua	347
Panama	477
Paraguay	192
Peru	241
Trinidad & Tobago	515
Uruguay	537
Venezuela	902

PARAGUAY
Asuncion•

Rio de Janeiro

Salvador
Allende
elected 1970

CHILE

Santiago•

Buenos Aires•

ARGENTINA

URUGUAY
Montevideo•

Punta del Este Conferences
1961, 1962

ATLANTIC

OCEAN

▨	Under $200
▧	$200-399
▨	$400-599
▨	Over $600

down an American spy plane, a U-2, which had been taking aerial photographs more than a thousand miles inside Russia.

At first Washington denied involvement. Khrushchev then produced evidence that the denials were lies, and Eisenhower hastily assumed full responsibility for sending the plane over Russia. The Soviet leader heatedly refused to talk with the president. The summit was over before it had begun. The United States was embarrassed, but it is probable that neither Khrushchev nor Eisenhower had originally wanted to go to Paris, for neither side was willing to budge on the key Berlin question. Of special significance, U-2 planes had been flying over Russia for four years. They brought back information that convinced Washington officials that despite Khrushchev's bragging about his missiles, he did not have missile superiority or even military equality with the United States.

AFTER SUEZ: NEWLY EMERGING AREAS

Berlin captured world attention, but the effects of the 1956 crises were already working profound changes elsewhere. For the Suez episode had demonstrated new and unexpected features of the Cold War. The old bipolar globe—the world divided and controlled by the two superpowers—was disappearing. This disappearance was hastened, as China and the Soviet Union became enemies in 1960 because of differences over communist ideology and their 1,200-mile common boundary.

The effects of these changes were especially noticeable in the newly independent nations in Asia and Africa, which had recently freed themselves from European colonialism. The leaders of these countries often refused to join either the Soviet or the American side. They instead tried to play Washington off against Moscow in order to acquire badly needed economic help from both camps.

Eisenhower and Dulles feared that the new nations would be unstable, anti-Western, and, therefore, procommunist. As Dulles once blurted out, neutrality was "immoral." These changes in turn could threaten the supply of oil that Europe and the United States required from the Middle East. The results could be disastrous. "In my view," Dulles remarked in early 1957, "we are in a war situation right now." Consequently, in the spring of that year Congress passed a resolution proposed by Eisenhower that allowed him to commit American power to stop "overt armed aggression" by communists in the Middle East if a nation in the area asked for such help. This "Eisenhower Doctrine" was unfortunate. It angered some Middle Eastern nations, divided others, and forced some to choose between East and West, something they did not want to do.

The doctrine, moreover, was largely irrelevant. The area was threatened not by overt communist invasion but by intense internal nationalism, which the proclamation did not cover. Yet when the monarchy in Iraq was suddenly overthrown by an internal coup led by non-communist nationalists in 1958, the government of neighboring Lebanon asked for American protection. No "overt" communist threat was apparent; indeed, Eisenhower knew that the Lebanese president needed help against *internal*, not external, opposition. Eisenhower nevertheless immediately landed 14,000 American troops in Lebanon to display U.S. muscle. The bikini-clad bathers on the shore scarcely moved as the Marines waded in, and the effect on Iraq was equally slight. Despite the Eisenhower Doctrine and the Lebanon landings, Middle Eastern nationalism continued to flourish and unsettle the area. As the Suez crisis had demonstrated, foreign troops only worsened the situation. The world could not be rolled back to the pre-1956 years.

THE GOOD NEIGHBOR AND A CHANGING NEIGHBORHOOD

Nationalism also threatened American policies in Latin America, where the United States had seemed to have sure control. By 1955 U.S. firms produced 10 percent of Latin America's products and 30 percent of its export goods (and in such nations as Venezuela and Cuba U.S.-owned companies controlled two or three times that percentage), invested more than $3 billion directly, and dominated the continent's great oil and mineral resources. That domination, however, had brought no prosperity to most Latin Americans. With little industrialization, the area depended on world market prices for its oil and other raw materials, but most of these prices declined in the late 1950s. Foreign investment worsened this drain of money, for Americans took more profits out of Latin America than they put back in. This economic trap was aggravated by the highest population growth rate in the world.

Washington officials understood this, but since 1947 had poured their resources into Europe while taking Latin America for granted. During these years Belgium and Luxembourg alone received three times more economic aid than the twenty Latin American nations combined. More than two-thirds of the aid that did go south was for military purposes, not economic growth. The political results were all too obvious: instability, frequent changes of government, repressive right-wing dictatorships, and a heightened anti-American nationalism among intellectuals and jailed politicians. Between 1930 and 1965, 106 illegal and often bloody changes of government occurred throughout the continent.

Latin America differed fundamentally from Africa or Southeast Asia, for it had been free of direct colonial control for more than a century and was politically more experienced. Latin Americans thus could not solve their problems by throwing off foreign rulers as Egyptians, Vietnamese, and others were doing, for there was no such formal colonialism in the area. Instead, they had to control and develop their internal resources, that is, loosen the economic grip that the United States held on their countries. The question was whether Washington would help or hinder that aspiration. In early 1958 a high State Department official was asked whether he thought there was much anti-Yankee feeling among Latin Americans. "No sir, I do not," he promptly replied.

Two months later Vice President Nixon traveled south. From Uruguay to Venezuela crowds hurled eggs and stones at his car, nearly tipping it over in Caracas, Venezuela. Eisenhower ordered a thousand Marines to prepare to rescue Nixon, who escaped to Washington before the troops were dispatched. The outburst shocked the United States. The president ordered a review of Latin American policies. But this was too little and too late to prevent anti-American nationalists from working fundamental, revolutionary changes.

It was, for example, too late to insulate Cuba from such a revolution. This was striking, for nowhere had U.S. control been so complete. Americans controlled 80 percent of the island's utilities and 90 percent of the mines, ranches, and oil; owned half the great sugar crop; and surrounded Cuba with military might. The island had one of the highest per capita income figures in the Southern Hemisphere, but the wealth fell into the hands of foreign investors and a few Cubans, while the mass of the people suffered in poverty. In 1952 Fulgencio Batista overthrew a moderately liberal regime and created a military dictatorship. He received support

Cuban revolutionary Fidel Castro giving a speech in Cuba, 1959. *(Library of Congress)*

from highly unlikely bedfellows—the U.S. military (which helped train and equip Batista's forces) and a well-behaved Communist Party, which sought to survive by whipping up local support for the dictator. The U.S. Air Force pinned the Legion of Merit on Batista's breast and praised him as "a great president."

Most Cubans did not share that sentiment. In 1953 a young, middle-class lawyer (unemployed, as were most Cuban lawyers) started a revolt. Fidel Castro was captured and imprisoned, but by 1957 he was again free. Collecting a force of peasants and middle-class Cubans, he successfully resisted the police units sent out to destroy the guerrillas. The communists refused to cooperate with Castro until late 1958, when Batista was preparing to escape with millions from the Cuban treasury for a luxurious exile in Spain. On January 1, 1959, Castro marched triumphantly into Havana. Washington officials, an authoritative journalist reported, generally agreed "there was no dominant Communist influence. . . . One official went so far as to say that there was very little trace of Communism in the movement."

As Castro moved to change the distribution of wealth, and especially of land ownership, his relationships with the communists and the United States altered. The communists provided disciplined organization and an ideology, which Castro required. When the Cuban leader visited the United States, Eisenhower left Washington to go golfing. There was little to talk about. Castro insisted that American companies and landholdings be placed in Cuban hands. He could not pay for these without borrowing money from abroad and again becoming indebted to foreigners. As the *New York Times* editorialized in mid-1960, "So long as Cuba is in the throes of a social revolution directed by her present leaders, she is going to be in conflict with the United States. We think it is wrong, but it is a fact of life. The revolution harms American interests in Cuba and in Latin America generally." Castro turned to the Soviet Union for credits, machinery, and military equipment. Eisenhower first cut back Cuban sugar imports, then authorized the secret training of 1,400 anti-Castro Cubans by the Central Intelligence Agency, although the president never did decide when—or even whether—they might be used. Assuming that Castro was "beyond redemption," as a State Department official commented, the United States and Cuba broke diplomatic relations in January 1961.

THE EISENHOWER LEGACY AND THE NEW FRONTIER

Eisenhower presided during a decade that many Americans would later recall with nostalgia. The generation that came of age during the 1950s seemed quiet, apolitical, and more concerned about personal security than international crises. It would later be tagged as "the generation that never showed up." This was how Eisenhower wanted it. Despite provocations in Korea, the Middle East, and Berlin greater than those that later faced Presidents Kennedy and Johnson, Eisenhower, unlike his successors, did not involve the country in war. His use of power was restrained. He frequently remarked that he had seen enough war. Moreover, Eisenhower cared more about balancing the budget and strengthening the American economy than he did about creating a great military force that might intervene at will in the post-1956 world.

He did not disavow anticommunist policies, but neither did he think that those policies were worth undermining the American economic, political, and even educational systems. Between 1950 and 1960, for example, such leading universities as Harvard, Chicago, Columbia, Pennsylvania, California, and Johns Hopkins had obtained large amounts of money, both from such private foundations as Ford and Carnegie and from the federal government, to establish defense-policy centers. Instead of questioning governmental power, many American intellectuals were justifying that power. With this in mind, Eisenhower issued a warning in his farewell address of January 1961. He spoke of "the prospect of domination of the nation's scholars by Federal employment, project allocations, and the power of money." Eisenhower believed that two "threats, new in kind or degree," had appeared:

> This conjunction of an immense military establishment and a large arms industry is new in American experience. The total influence—economic, political, and even spiritual—is felt in every city, every state house, and every office of the federal government. . . . In the councils of government, we must guard against the acquisition of unwarranted influence, whether

sought or unsought, by the military-industrial complex. The potential for the disastrous rise of misplaced power exists and will persist.

In part this warning expressed Eisenhower's fear that the incoming Kennedy administration would try to control world affairs by spending even greater sums on arms. His fear was well founded. In accepting the Democratic presidential nomination in 1960, John F. Kennedy called not for caution, but for "sacrifices" on "the New Frontier." He spoke in Los Angeles in late afternoon as the sun went down on what had been the last of the old American frontier territory. The New Frontier, Kennedy declared, "sums up not what I intend to offer the American people but what I intend to ask of them. It appeals to their pride, not to their pocketbook; it holds out the promise of more sacrifice instead of more security."

This call to action was most eloquently stated in Kennedy's inaugural speech of January 1961. In sharp contrast to Eisenhower's farewell address, Kennedy proclaimed: "Let every nation know, whether it wishes us well or ill, that we shall pay any price, bear any burden, meet any hardship, support any friend, oppose any foe to assure the survival and the success of liberty. . . . And so, my fellow Americans, ask not what your country can do for you; ask what you can do for your country."

JOHN F. KENNEDY

In April 1960 Richard E. Neustadt, a political scientist at Columbia University, published *Presidential Power.* Neustadt believed that a strong president "contributes to the energy of government and to the viability of public policy." He attempted, therefore, to show how a chief executive could exercise power effectively. "The Sixties, it appears, will be a fighting time," Neustadt predicted. "It follows that our need will be the greater for a Presidential expert in the Presidency." Shortly after the book appeared, John F. Kennedy, the Democratic nominee for president, recruited Neustadt as an adviser. In truth, the two men held similar views. Kennedy thought that the president "must serve as a catalyst, an energizer, the defender of the public good and the public interest." He must "place himself in the very thick of the fight," for he was "the vital center of action in our whole scheme of government."

"Energy," "fight," "vitality," "public interest"—the words were temperamentally congenial to Kennedy. But while he was president his approach to domestic policies could more accurately be described by a different vocabulary: "caution," "prudence," "compromise," "interest group." Kennedy believed that politics was the art of the possible, that politicians were most likely to succeed if they dealt with concrete rather than abstract issues, and that a give-and-take process in resolving those issues was not only inevitable but also desirable. For a president to safeguard the national interest translated, in the pluralist world of American politics, into arranging mutually acceptable trade-offs between such competing interest groups as business and labor, farmers and consumers, blacks and whites. "Politics and legislation," Kennedy once said, "are not matters for inflexible principles or unattainable ideals."

Kennedy was elected to the House of Representatives in 1946, to the Senate in 1952, and, at the age of forty-three, to the presidency. His rise to political eminence was so swift and his personal qualities were so attractive that his virtues were exaggerated by the public, by the media, and especially by his inner circle of friends and admirers. A vigorous man who enjoyed sailing and other sports, Kennedy felt it necessary to deny that he suffered from Addison's disease (an adrenal insufficiency requiring cortisone treatments) so as not to jeopardize his career. In World War II Kennedy had been a naval officer who courageously rescued members of his crew after their PT boat had been sunk in the South Pacific. Although he was widely regarded as a hero, Kennedy's poor seamanship was partly responsible for the disaster. A person of impressive intellect, Kennedy was awarded a Pulitzer Prize in 1957 for *Profiles in Courage*, a book written primarily by an aide. The truth about these incidents, however, was not widely known or accepted until after Kennedy's death.

CONGRESS AND THE NEW FRONTIER

Unlike Franklin D. Roosevelt and Dwight D. Eisenhower, Kennedy did not take office with a resounding popular mandate. He barely edged out Richard Nixon, winning by the smallest margin of any president in the twentieth century. Kennedy, who received 49.7 percent of the popular vote to his opponent's 49.6 percent, actually carried fewer states than did Nixon. Although Kennedy secured a 303-to-219 majority in the electoral college, had 4,500 people in Illinois and 28,000 people in Texas voted Republican instead of Democratic, Nixon would have emerged the victor in the electoral college. President by a razor-thin margin, Kennedy was not in a position to make demands on Congress.

Nor could Kennedy turn for support to first-term congressmen carried into office on his coattails. In 1960 Kennedy invariably trailed the Democratic ticket; furthermore, his party lost twenty-two seats in the House and two in the Senate. Although the Democrats maintained comfortable majorities in both houses of Congress, those majorities were deceptive, consisting largely of southerners who regarded many New Frontier programs with distaste. The seniority system gave southern Democrats representing rural constituencies control of key committees. Kennedy barely won a bitterly contested struggle to liberalize the Rules Committee by enlarging its membership, and then only because he had the backing of Speaker Sam Rayburn of Texas.

In some respects religion acted as another constraint on the president. Kennedy's Catholicism had played an important role in the 1960 election. Many Protestants bolted the Democratic Party, but Kennedy received 80 percent of the Catholic vote (rather than the 63 percent a Democrat could ordinarily expect). Overall, the religious issue appears to have cost Kennedy votes. However, his loss of support occurred primarily in the South, where the Democrats could afford it; meanwhile he gained support in such critical states as Illinois and Michigan. As the first Catholic president, Kennedy leaned over backward to dispel any suspicion that he was under church influence. He did not favor sending an American ambassador to the Vatican, and he similarly opposed "unconstitutional aid to parochial schools." It was easier to prove that a Catholic could be elected president than to convince skeptics that a Catholic president could be scrupulously fair.

The conflict over federal aid to education illustrated Kennedy's difficulties with Congress. Early in 1961 Kennedy proposed spending $2.3 billion over three years to build new schools and to raise teachers' salaries. The wealthiest states would receive $15 per child; the poorest, nearly twice that amount. A separate program to aid college students would bring the package to $5.6 billion. But federal aid to education raised the divisive issue of aid to parochial schools. Kennedy declared that the Constitution prohibited such aid, but the Catholic Church replied that the Constitution did not prohibit long-term, low-interest loans to help such schools

DAVID SMITH
THE MACHINE SHOP AND SCULPTURE

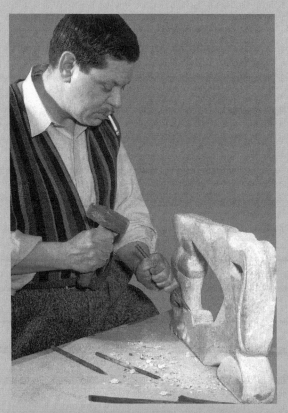

David Smith, 1942. *(David Smith miscellaneous papers, [ca. 1940]–1964, Archives of American Art, Smithsonian Institution)*

David Smith transformed twentieth-century sculpture by combining the American machine shop with radical versions of modern art. Reaching the peak of his powers between 1958 and 1965, Smith exemplified the new American leadership in world art at precisely the same time John F. Kennedy proclaimed in his inaugural address that a "new generation" of Americans would assume world political leadership.

Smith learned about machines in Decatur, Indiana, where he was born in 1906. One of his ancestors had been a frontier blacksmith. Leaving home at sixteen, Smith enrolled briefly at Ohio State and Notre Dame before learning to weld in the Studebaker automotive works in South Bend, Indiana. He then traveled to New York City, encountering the work of leading European artists who were fleeing Nazism to live in the United States. As these émigrés helped make New York City the center of the art world, Smith lived among them. He began as a painter, and then moved into "constructivism," whereby objects other than paint (for example, bits of newspaper, glass, or metal) were placed on the picture to change it from a painting to a construction. At that point, Smith recalled, "I was then a sculptor."

During the 1930s, as many artists protested the drift toward war, Smith became politically involved and saw Nazism up close in 1935–1936 during a stay in Europe. He expressed his vision in fifteen horror-filled, yet magnificently designed "Medals for Dishonor." These depicted scenes of such "dishonors" as *War-Exempt Sons of the Rich*, *Munitions-Makers*, and *Elements Which Cause Prostitution*. In the 1940s his work became increasingly abstract, and for the first time he combined painting with sculpture so that the colors seemed to change the form of his pieces. One critic called some of his work "a graceful abstract drawing that has leaped off the page into three-dimensional life."

Smith was soon exploring all forms, from overpowering mono-liths to light, lyrical creations that, although made from heavy steel, seemed to float in air. His greatest work was done at his studio on the shore of Lake George in upper New York State, where he could display his works outdoors, the only place he thought large enough for them. Here he extended and transformed European art styles, particularly cubism, which drew natural sub-jects in simplified lines and basic geometric shapes, usually to show the subject simultaneously from several points of view. In 1958 he began his spectacular *Cubi* series, shaping great slabs of stainless steel in pure geometric construction and then polishing and arranging them so their three dimensions reflected changing sunlight—sometimes with dazzling intensity, sometimes with a delicacy that one critic called "purely optical poetry." In these new forms, Smith expressed the es-sence of cubism. He indeed worked with steel, he declared, because it was at once "so beautiful" and "also brutal: the rapist, the murderer, and the death-dealing giants are also its offspring." In *Cubi* he brought the beauty and brutality into one.

Cubi XII, a nine-foot stainless steel sculpture by David Smith. *(Gjon Mili/Time & Life Pictures/Getty Images)*

A burly man who lived life to the full, Smith had by the 1960s not only created an American sculpture, but shaped world art as well. Yet in 1965 he could declare, "I'm 20 years behind my vision." In the spring of that year he was killed in an automobile crash.

Web Links

www.theartstory.org/artist-smith-david.htm
A biographical essay with links to resources and exhibitions.

www.davidsmithestate.org/
Includes not only images of Smith's work, but also some of his writings and speeches.

improve their facilities. An arrangement was seemingly worked out restricting the federal aid bill to public schools, but attaching an amendment to the National Defense and Education Act authorizing loans to parochial schools for expanding their mathematics, science, and language facilities. At the last minute, a northern Catholic Democrat on the Rules Committee, fearing that Congress would renege on aid to religious schools, joined Republicans and southern Democrats to oppose the education bill. In July 1961 the president watched helplessly as the Rules Committee, by a one-vote margin, buried the measure.

A second New Frontier proposal—Medicare—met a similar fate. In February 1961 Kennedy asked Congress to extend Social Security benefits to people over the age of sixty-five to cover hospital and nursing home costs. This would be financed by a small increase in the Social Security tax. The president pointed out that the elderly had, on the average, half the income of people under sixty-five but medical expenses that were twice as high. Kennedy insisted that his plan, which would not cover surgical expenses or physicians' fees, ensured "absolute freedom" in the choice of a doctor and hospital. The American Medical Association, however, viewed Medicare as a giant step toward socialized medicine. Physicians foresaw a "bureaucratic task force" invading "the privacy of the examination room." The twenty-five-member House Ways and Means Committee was the real hurdle. Its chairman, Wilbur Mills of Arkansas, opposed the plan, as did ten Republicans and six southern Democrats. They easily bottled up the bill. In July 1962 the Senate defeated the measure by a vote of 52 to 48, with twenty-one Democrats opposing the administration.

THE NEW ECONOMICS

Yet the picture of a stodgy, conservative Congress frustrating the hopes of an energetic, liberal president is accurate only in part. Kennedy set certain domestic priorities, and in the process he often sacrificed reform programs. This was true even in the case of Medicare, for Kennedy, recognizing that he needed Wilbur Mills's support for tax reform and trade expansion, did not press the Ways and Means Committee too hard. Moreover, to attract southern Democratic support for economic proposals, Kennedy postponed introducing civil rights legislation for as long as possible. He always put first things first, and in his view what came first was the economy. In January 1961 the nation was in the throes of a recession: unemployment stood at 5.4 million, more than 6 percent of the labor force. Kennedy's goal was to stimulate economic growth and reduce unemployment while at the same time balancing the budget and preventing inflation.

The administration applied a number of remedies to the sluggish economy. To aid jobless workers, Kennedy extracted from Congress, though usually in a diluted form, legislation that increased unemployment compensation, created retraining programs, and provided for public works in depressed areas. Congress also raised the minimum wage from $1.00 to $1.25 an hour and brought an additional 3.6 million workers under the law's protection. To stimulate business expansion, Congress granted a 7 percent tax credit to firms investing in new equipment. Kennedy attached the greatest significance to the Trade Expansion Act (1962). This facilitated the export of American goods to the European Common Market by authorizing the president to arrange mutual tariff reductions and, in some cases, to eliminate tariffs completely.

The keys to curbing inflation were labor's willingness to limit wage demands to an amount justified by gains in productivity and industry's corresponding readiness to keep prices down.

Early in 1962 Kennedy helped persuade the steelworkers to accept a noninflationary wage settlement. Then, in April, United States Steel announced a price hike of $6 a ton, and other steel companies immediately followed suit. Furious at what he termed this "utter contempt for the public interest," Kennedy mustered every ounce of executive authority to salvage his economic program. He pressured smaller steel companies into holding the price line, threatened to take government contracts away from the offending concerns, and hinted that the Justice Department would determine whether the price increases violated the antitrust laws. Faced with massive presidential and public pressure, United States Steel backed down and rescinded the increase.

Kennedy's stance earned him the lasting resentment of the business community. Yet the New Frontier was hardly hostile to business. Not only did Kennedy's tax and trade policies favor business interests, but the administration also sponsored a plan that conceded a dominant interest in the newly developed communications satellite to the American Telephone and Telegraph Company. (The satellite, launched into outer space, relayed television and radio signals around the world.) In addition to this, during his first eighteen months in office Kennedy worked hard to achieve a balanced budget. So orthodox did the New Frontier's fiscal program appear that journalist Walter Lippmann commented, "It's like the Eisenhower administration 30 years younger."

Not until late 1962 did Kennedy endorse the planned use of budget deficits as the only certain means of spurring further economic growth. In January 1963 the president called for a $13.5 billion reduction in corporate and personal taxes over three years even though this would produce a deficit. Kennedy's plan, while thoroughly Keynesian in its assumptions, did not satisfy all liberals. John Kenneth Galbraith, the Harvard economist whom Kennedy had appointed ambassador to India, believed that "money from tax reduction goes into the pockets of those who need it least; lower tax revenues will become a ceiling on spending." Galbraith wished to create a deficit by expanding programs to aid the needy rather than by cutting taxes. On the other hand, Kennedy's proposal shocked conservatives. Dwight Eisenhower offered a homely bit of economic wisdom: "Spending for spending's sake is patently a false theory. No family, no business, no nation can spend itself into prosperity."

Unfortunately for Kennedy, more congressmen, and particularly more members of the House Ways and Means Committee, preferred Eisenhower's brand of economics to Galbraith's. Once again, as in the case of Medicare and federal aid to education, a House committee blocked consideration of a key New Frontier proposal. But by 1963 Kennedy had somewhat lowered his sights, at least with respect to domestic matters. The exercise of power proved a sobering experience. Although he never repudiated his activist view of the presidency, Kennedy came to see the office in terms of its limitations as well as its opportunities. "The problems are more difficult than I had imagined they were," he conceded. "Every President must endure a gap between what he would like and what is possible."

KENNEDY AND CIVIL RIGHTS

The same practical considerations that modified Kennedy's view of presidential authority also affected his stand on civil rights. In 1960 Kennedy declared that the president should throw the full moral weight of his office behind the effort to end racial discrimination. "If the President does not himself wage the struggle for equal rights—if he stands above the battle—then the battle will inevitably be lost." Once in office, however, Kennedy found himself torn between the claims of white southerners, whose support he needed, and the pressure applied by an increasingly militant civil rights movement. Not until 1963 did Kennedy cease standing above the battle, and he then acted only after segregationist resistance to demands for racial equality provoked massive turmoil.

Unlike Eisenhower, Kennedy relied heavily on the black vote. In the 1960 campaign he expressed agreement with the Supreme Court ruling on desegregation, but perhaps nothing did more to solidify his support among blacks than his intervention on behalf of Dr. Martin Luther King Jr. Late in October a Georgia judge jailed King for taking part in a protest demonstration. In a well-publicized move, Kennedy telephoned King's wife, both to express his concern and to offer assurances regarding her husband's safety. The next day, Robert F. Kennedy, the candidate's brother, helped arrange King's release on bail. John Kennedy's phone call, a symbolic act at best, nevertheless had the right personal touch. When Nixon remained silent, the Democrats printed 2 million copies of a pamphlet titled *No-Comment Nixon Versus a Candidate with a Heart, Senator Kennedy*. In 1960 black voters provided Kennedy's margin of victory in Texas, Illinois, New Jersey, and Michigan. Had only white people voted, Nixon would have received 52 percent of the vote and gone to the White House.

Kennedy understood this, yet he placed civil rights lower on his legislative agenda than other New Frontier measures. To introduce a civil rights bill, Kennedy believed, would alienate southerners, split the Democratic Party, snarl Congress in a filibuster, and dissipate administration energies. He considered the chance of passage too slim to justify these risks. So the president turned instead to other techniques. He issued an executive order designed to pressure federal agencies and government contractors into hiring more black workers. In addition, Kennedy sought to achieve through litigation what he doubted was possible through legislation. Under Attorney General Robert F. Kennedy, the Justice Department attempted to speed the pace of school desegregation by entering court cases on the side of those challenging separate facilities. The policy had some success. In Eisenhower's last three years, 49 school districts had begun the process of desegregation. In Kennedy's three years, 183 did so.

In the eyes of New Frontiersmen, the franchise held the key to racial equality. Litigation to win the vote seemed crucial, for if blacks attained political strength commensurate with their numbers, politicians would accord them justice and the Jim Crow system would topple. Many states in the Deep South systematically excluded African-Americans from the polls. In Mississippi, where blacks constituted more than 40 percent of the population, they made up less than 4 percent of the eligible voters. To attack this system, the Justice Department utilized the Civil Rights Act of 1957, which authorized the department to seek injunctions against interference with the right to vote. The Eisenhower administration had brought only ten suits under the act. The Kennedy administration filed forty-five such suits.

Yet the reliance on litigation had two fatal defects. First, it assumed a degree of judicial impartiality that did not exist. A number of judges in southern district courts held harshly segregationist views and stymied moves toward integration. Judge Harold Cox, a Kennedy appointee, could find no pattern of discrimination in Clarke County, Mississippi, although only one black person, a high school principal, had succeeded in registering to vote in thirty years. Even where successful, litigation was a glacial process, and this proved to be a third source of weakness. Many blacks were no longer willing to let the law run its course. They insisted that equality was a moral as well as a legal issue. By taking direct action to end segregation, they forced Kennedy to choose sides.

The first such case involved the "freedom rides." In May 1961 white and black students boarded buses in Washington with plans to travel through the Deep South, desegregating depots as they went. Angry mobs met the buses, though, and attacked the riders with chains and rocks. The president finally sent five hundred marshals to Montgomery, Alabama, to prevent further violence. Kennedy then asked the Interstate Commerce Commission to ban segregation at all bus and train stations. In November 1961 such an edict took effect, although some southern communities continued to evade it. The Justice Department also persuaded airlines to desegregate their terminals. The freedom riders had, in effect, created the conditions under which Kennedy was willing to use executive authority on behalf of civil rights.

Kennedy's hand was forced a second time in September 1962, when James Meredith tried to integrate the University of Mississippi law school. The controversy originated when a U.S. court of appeals, finding that the university had rejected Meredith solely on the basis of race, ordered his admission. After a segregationist judge stayed the ruling, Supreme Court justice Hugo Black ordered its enforcement. Meredith flew to Oxford, Mississippi, in a federal plane and was escorted to the campus by federal marshals. Governor Ross Barnett tried to convince Robert Kennedy that southern sentiment would never tolerate the integration of Ole Miss. Barnett claimed, "We never have trouble with our people, but the NAACP, they want to stir up trouble down here." The attorney general responded, "If we don't follow the order of the federal court, we don't have anything in the United States." In the end, white students and outside troublemakers, massed behind Confederate battle flags, attacked the federal marshals. A fifteen-hour riot ensued in which two men were killed and the campus was shrouded in tear gas. The president dispatched thousands of federal troops to restore order, to protect Meredith's right to attend class, and to demonstrate that, in Robert Kennedy's words, only the rule of law permitted a nation "to avoid anarchy and disorder and tremendous distress."

The nine months following the Mississippi crisis saw the administration move haltingly toward an affirmative civil rights posture. In November 1962 the president issued a long-awaited executive order banning segregation in all new housing subsidized by the federal government. In February 1963 Kennedy introduced a civil rights bill designed to prevent biased registrars from using spurious tests to deprive blacks of the vote. The bill provided that the completion of six grades of public school would automatically constitute proof of literacy. Yet civil rights activists now considered these steps inadequate. They pointed out that the executive order did not affect housing that was already built or that would be privately financed. They noted that Kennedy, while favoring a civil rights bill, refused to support an effort to amend the Senate rules to prevent a southern filibuster. Assessing Kennedy's record in March 1963, Martin Luther King Jr. found that the administration had settled for "tokenism." Nearly a decade after the Supreme Court's *Brown v. Board of Education* decision, only 7 percent of black children in the South attended classes with white children, and 2,000 districts remained segregated. King concluded: "The administration sought to demonstrate to Negroes that it has concern for them, while at the same time it has striven to avoid inflaming the opposition."

In the spring of 1963 civil rights demonstrations in Birmingham, Alabama, made further fence straddling impossible. Black leaders in the city—where African-Americans constituted 40 percent of the population—launched a drive to end segregation in stores and to pressure businesses to hire black sales and clerical help. Adhering to King's philosophy that "you

A. Philip Randolph stands before the Lincoln Memorial during the 1963 March on Washington. *(New York World-Telegram and the Sun Newspaper Photograph Collection, Library of Congress)*

can struggle without hating; you can fight war without violence," blacks engaged in protest marches, sit-ins, and even kneel-ins at white churches on Good Friday. The city government reacted savagely. Police Commissioner Eugene "Bull" Connor met the marchers, many of them schoolchildren, with fire hoses and snarling police dogs and threw thousands into jail. The mayor, who had lost the previous election but was contesting the result in court, said of Robert Kennedy: "I hope that every drop of blood that's spilled he tastes in his throat, and I hope he chokes on it." In May, riots and bombings rocked the city. The following month, with the crisis in Birmingham still unresolved, Governor George C. Wallace challenged an attempt by two black students to integrate the University of Alabama. To safeguard their entrance, the president federalized the National Guard.

In June 1963, President Kennedy, responding directly to these events in Alabama, endorsed a sweeping civil rights bill. It would outlaw segregation in hotels, restaurants, theaters, and other public places; permit the Justice Department to file suits for school desegregation; prohibit discrimination in state programs receiving federal aid; and remove racial barriers to employment and trade-union membership. "We are confronted primarily with a moral issue," the president asserted. The demand for racial justice had grown so loud, the "fires of frustration and discord" had begun to burn so brightly, that government could no longer stand aside. Indeed, the government must prove that revolutionary changes in race relations could occur in a "peaceful and constructive" way.

Even as Kennedy came to support civil rights, his administration decided to wiretap King's home and office. J. Edgar Hoover, director of the Federal Bureau of Investigation, who was convinced that King was associating with communists, put unrelenting pressure on Attorney General Robert Kennedy to use wiretaps. In October 1963, he authorized the use of taps. Ironically, the administration's new identification with the civil rights movement was partially responsible for the invasion of King's civil liberties. Robert Kennedy evidently believed that if communists were involved in the civil rights movement and if King's opponents publicized that fact, then the president himself could be discredited. While they never accepted Hoover's view that King was under communist influence, the Kennedys fully accepted the Cold War view that communism was a menace at home as well as abroad. This was clearly illustrated when John Kennedy, justifying the use of federal authority to support the movement for racial equality, noted, "Today we are committed to a worldwide struggle to promote and protect the rights of all who wish to be free. And when Americans are sent to Vietnam or West Berlin we do not ask for whites only."

THE WORLDWIDE NEW FRONTIER

The problems afflicting Americans at home deeply influenced Kennedy's foreign policies. His diplomacy assumed a united home front that would unquestioningly support the president in Asia as it had in Europe and that would see racism and poverty at home as less important than using national resources to fight communism overseas. Kennedy, like most of his generation, was the product of World War II and the Cold War. As a young congressman, he had attacked Truman for "losing" China, refused as a senator to take a public position on Senator Joseph McCarthy's vicious attacks, and in 1956 justified American support to Ngo Dinh Diem's autocratic regime in South Vietnam. By 1960 Kennedy had focused on the newly emerging areas as the key to victory in the Cold War. The new president believed that Americans must confront communism everywhere. "What is at stake in the election of 1960 is the preservation of freedom all around the globe," he proclaimed during the campaign, and he made this the central theme of his administration's foreign policy.

That remark seemed to make little-known countries in Southeast Asia, for example, as important to American interests as Western Europe. But as Kennedy saw it, the global battle would be to the finish. In a speech in May 1961 he was specific: "The great battleground for the defense and expansion of freedom today is the whole southern half of the globe—Asia, Latin America, Africa, and the Middle East—the lands of the rising peoples." His famous inaugural address was a trumpet call to that battle. It was also a speech that never mentioned domestic problems. Those could be assumed as secondary to the "historic mission" of America abroad. Nor did Kennedy set any limits on that mission. "I don't believe that there is anything this country cannot do," he declared during his television debates with Vice President Nixon in 1960.

A strong presidency was required to carry out the mission, one even stronger than that developed by Roosevelt, Truman, and Eisenhower. Kennedy proclaimed that the president "must be prepared to exercise the fullest powers of his office—all that are specified and some that are not." He even believed that the office not only spoke for all Americans, but also represented "all of the people around the world who want to live in freedom." Kennedy established a separate foreign affairs group in the White House under his national security adviser, McGeorge Bundy, former dean at Harvard University. Bundy would be followed by Walt W. Rostow and then in 1969 by Henry Kissinger. All three used their office to drain power from the Department of State and congressional foreign affairs committees. In diplomacy, the president had become a virtual king—only more so, for he was an elected king, complete with increasingly important White House advisers who did not have to be responsible to Congress or to anyone but the president.

ICBMs AND GREEN BERETS

As commander in chief, Kennedy had at his disposal the most powerful military force in history. During the campaign he had charged Eisenhower with allowing a "missile gap" to develop in favor of the Soviets. Having seen the U-2 and other intelligence reports, Eisenhower knew that there was no gap. Although Kennedy also soon learned this, he refused to believe that American power was sufficient. Without evidence of Russian intentions, the new president assumed that Khrushchev would try to build new missiles as rapidly as possible. The Soviets had in fact decided to move slowly in this area, but Kennedy nevertheless accelerated American missile building. Khrushchev interpreted this to mean the Americans wanted a first-strike capability (that is, forces sufficient to wipe out Russia in one strike without fear of a return salvo), so he ordered a step-up of Russian production and began nuclear testing at an increased rate. The most expensive arms race in history had begun, with China and France rushing to build their own nuclear weapons. Secretary of Defense Robert McNamara later believed that the Kennedy decision was "not justified" but was "necessitated by a lack of accurate information." By 1964 the U.S. force of 750 intercontinental ballistic missiles (ICBMs) was four times greater than that of the Soviets.

Kennedy, however, determined that since nuclear weapons would be of little use in the jungles and hamlets of the newly emerging areas, he would also need a buildup of conventional forces. Eisenhower, the foremost American military figure of the post-1950 era, believed that such power would be too expensive and ineffective. But Kennedy assumed that it was crucial if the new nations were to be saved from communism. He increased the number of conventional army troops, created the Special Forces (and suggested the special headgear of "Green Berets," by which they would be known) to fight guerrilla wars, and spent billions increasing the nation's helicopter and weapon capacity for fighting in the third world. The Kennedy administration indeed tended to define the world primarily in military terms. Rostow told Special Forces troops in mid-1961, "I salute you, as I would a group of doctors, teachers, economic planners, agricultural experts, civil servants, or others who are now leading the way in fashioning the new nations."

THE NEW FRONTIER CONTAINED: 1961–1962

Kennedy had determined on these policies before entering office, but in early January 1961 Khrushchev delivered a speech that spurred on the new president. The Soviet leader declared that revolutions, such as the "national liberation war" in Vietnam, were "not only admissible but inevitable." He asserted that the communists did not have to start such wars, for nationalists within each country would fight to drive out imperialism. Communists would, however, "fully support" such conflicts. Khrushchev then focused, perhaps unfortunately, on Cuba by saying that Castro's victory was a herald of what was to come.

Kennedy interpreted this speech as a direct challenge. One reaction was to announce with great publicity the Alliance for Progress. Over a ten-year period the Alliance was to use $100 billion of U.S. and Latin American funds to develop and stabilize the southern continent, that is, to prevent any more Castros from appearing. The Alliance quickly encountered innumerable problems. In Washington these included bureaucratic mix-ups, lack of funds, and the growing involvement in Vietnam, which absorbed money and attention. In Latin America there were few funds, mistrust of Yankees, entrenched interests refusing to budge, and disputes between nations. Worst of all, the rich in Latin America used the money to make themselves richer and the poor poorer. The gap between rich and poor widened. Political crises followed. In Central America, for example, only one revolutionary band existed in 1960. But after ten years of the Alliance for Progress, revolutions threatened El Salvador, Nicaragua, and Guatemala.

A serious blow struck the Alliance's dream at the beginning, when Kennedy agreed to allow the Cuban exile force, with American air cover, to invade Cuba at the Bay of Pigs in April 1961 in an attempt to overthrow Castro. It was a disaster from the start. Afraid that the aircraft would too deeply involve the United States, Kennedy recalled them at the last minute, leaving the small exile army at the mercy of Castro's planes and tanks. The invaders were either killed or captured. Washington had assumed that the invasion would trigger a massive uprising against Castro, but Cubans instead rallied to his side. By supporting the exiles, Kennedy had broken numerous American pledges not to use force in inter-American affairs. The invasion marked a terrible start for the Alliance for Progress and Kennedy's struggle to win over the newly emerging peoples. But it redoubled his determination. He secretly ordered an immediate review of policy in other areas and soon sent 500 more special "advisers" to Vietnam. Publicly, he tried to rebuild American prestige by announcing that the country would develop the missile and technological power to land a man on the moon within the decade. (Eight years and $24 billion later, Neil Armstrong walked on the moon, but by 1969 riots at home and interventions in newly emerging areas had gone far toward destroying that prestige.)

In June 1961 Kennedy and Khrushchev met in Vienna. They worked out a cease-fire for one part of Indochina (Laos) but engaged in a heated debate on "wars of liberation." Khrushchev's next move, however, was not to support such wars, but to resolve the Berlin question. Russia had become deeply embarrassed as thousands of East Germans fled the communist zone to find new homes in the West. Announcing that this outward flow of talent would have to stop, Khrushchev demanded an immediate Berlin settlement. Kennedy responded by adding $3 billion more to the defense budget, calling up some national reserve units to prepare for battle, and warning Americans to begin building civil-defense shelters. This last idea was questionable. There was no way to protect even half the population from being killed in a nuclear war; but Kennedy had at least replied to Khrushchev. As Russian and American tanks faced each other in Berlin, the Russians brutally solved the problem in August 1961 by building high concrete walls along the East German borders and ordering guards to shoot anyone who tried to escape.

THE BRINK: THE CUBAN MISSILE CRISIS

The dangers of the Berlin confrontation paled in comparison with the threat of nuclear war that seemed about to happen during the Cuban missile crisis of October 1962. On October 14, a high-flying U-2 plane took pictures of Soviet medium- and long-range ground-to-ground missiles being emplaced in Cuba. President Kennedy summoned a special fourteen-member executive committee (the "ExCom") to meet secretly and advise him on a response.

Khrushchev had begun sending the missiles to Cuba during the spring of 1962 for three reasons. First, since the disaster at the Bay of Pigs, U.S. officials had made plans to overthrow Castro. The plans, code-named Operation Mongoose, proposed covert actions and apparently discussed using American mob figures to kill the Cuban leader with poison pills or explosives. Part of the plans called for a U.S. invasion of Cuba, if necessary, to finish the job. Khrushchev pledged that the Soviets would protect Cuba from such an invasion. Second, Americans enjoyed an overwhelming superiority over the Russians in deliverable nuclear warheads and bombs. Top Washington officials not only publicly discussed this superiority, but also noted that their most awesome nuclear weapon, the ICBM, would double in number during 1963. Khrushchev planned to set up his own missiles in Cuba to partially offset the American superiority. Third, Kennedy had deployed fifteen Jupiter (intermediate-range) missiles in Turkey. They were within easy range of key Soviet cities. As the Jupiters became operational in 1962, Khrushchev came under heavy pressure from the Soviet military to respond. He thus not only sent his missiles to Cuba, but also accompanied them with 42,000 Soviet troops and technicians who were in Cuba when the crisis erupted.

On October 22, 1962, after six days of top-secret ExCom discussions, Kennedy dramatically demanded in a nationwide television speech that the Soviet missiles be immediately removed. He announced that a U.S. naval blockade around Cuba would search Soviet ships carrying missiles and prevent them from reaching Havana. The president warned that if any missile were fired from Cuba, the United States would respond—by attacking the Soviet Union. American forces went on full alert. Airborne U.S. bombers were filled with fuel and nuclear weapons. Khrushchev, however, never put his strategic forces in high-readiness alert. He did not want to test the superior U.S. conventional or nuclear forces in combat. Nevertheless, for six days the Soviet leader refused to remove his missiles from Cuba. As the crisis heated up, the ExCom split. Some members urged Kennedy to stay with the blockade. Others wanted a "surgical strike" on the missiles, which would doubtless have killed Russian advisers. Others urged a full-scale conventional attack to remove both the missiles and Castro. Attorney General Robert Kennedy later wrote that this was "probably the brightest kind of group that you could get together," but "if six of them had been President . . . I think the world might have been blown up."

Just hours before the U.S. attack was planned, a U-2 plane was shot down over Cuba by a Soviet officer who acted without Moscow's instructions. The plane's pilot was killed. Khrushchev later claimed that Castro demanded, "We should launch a preemptive strike against the United States." The Soviet leader turned down the demand. Fighting reportedly broke out between Cubans and Russians over who would control the missile sites. In this super-heated atmosphere, a deal emerged by October 26–27. Khrushchev agreed to remove the missiles. "We're eyeball to eyeball, and I think the other fellow just blinked," Secretary of State Dean Rusk remarked. In turn, Kennedy publicly pledged not to invade Cuba, and his brother privately informed the Soviets that the United States would pull the Jupiter missiles out of Turkey. Indeed, Kennedy was ready to offer further concessions to Khrushchev to avoid a nuclear showdown.

The crisis was over. As Rusk noted to another ExCom member, "We have a considerable victory. You and I are still alive." The reverberations of the crisis were nevertheless felt long after. Kennedy emerged as a hero for apparently facing down Khrushchev, although some critics suggested that the president overreacted, and did so not because of a military threat but for political reasons at home. He could not suffer another Bay of Pigs or Berlin setback, this argument went, particularly after Republicans had warned weeks before about the missiles being shipped into Cuba. The Soviets, moreover, had lied to Kennedy about their plans for putting in the missiles; this deception, together with the U.S. public's belief that the missiles threatened the nation with extinction, forced Kennedy to act or else, his brother Robert warned, he would be impeached. Whatever their motivations, Khrushchev and Kennedy decided to install a "hotline" telephone between Washington and Moscow so that future crises could be handled more intelligently. In 1963 they negotiated a path-breaking nuclear test-ban treaty prohibiting aboveground testing. This treaty stopped further creation of deadly radiation that was building in the earth's atmosphere from earlier tests, but it did not stop all testing. The bombs were taken underground, and more nuclear tests were conducted during the next ten years than had occurred during the previous ten. Another by-product of the crisis occurred in Southeast Asia, and it was not as constructive.

VIETNAM

American involvement in Vietnam had begun between 1950 and 1954. Kennedy transformed that involvement. When he became president, 675 American military advisers helped the South Vietnam government of Ngo Dinh Diem; the number had been determined by the 1954 Geneva agreements. When Kennedy was assassinated in late 1963, 17,000 American troops were in South Vietnam.

Kennedy's commitment is easily understood. He had repeatedly declared that the Cold War would be determined in the newly emerging areas, and Washington officials saw Vietnam as the key to the Asian struggle. A worse place for such a commitment could hardly be imagined, for Americans and Vietnamese lived in worlds so totally different that each easily misunderstood the other. In *Fire in the Lake*, a history of the Vietnam War, Frances FitzGerald noted, "There was no more correspondence between the two worlds than that between the atmosphere of the earth and that of the sea."

Americans thought in terms of expansion, open spaces, limitless advance, and reliance on technology. They preferred to stress the future rather than think about their past, especially if that history showed their limitations, as it often did. They liked a society that was mobile, competitive, and individualistic. But Vietnamese life depended on self-contained villages that had remained little changed for centuries. The Vietnamese considered individualism destructive to the integrated, settled, rural life that centered on the family and the memories of ancestors. Habits were carefully handed down through generations, and when Vietnamese elders died they were often buried in the rice field to help provide sustenance for their grandchildren. More than 80 percent of the Vietnamese were Buddhists, and their religion was tightly integrated with their everyday life.

Changes could be radical as long as the village life retained its wholeness. For this reason, the Vietnamese could accept the revolutionary doctrines of communist leader Ho Chi Minh, for he carefully worked with the villages to drive out French colonialism between 1946 and 1954. The communists later used the same tactic against the Americans. The United States, on the other hand, fought communist successes in the villages by destroying the villages. In so doing, Americans destroyed the very foundation of the society they thought they were saving.

The people of Southeast Asia had long dealt with foreign invaders. For more than a thousand years China had controlled much of the area, but in the eleventh century CE the Chinese were driven out. During the next 800 years vigorous societies developed in present-day Vietnam, Laos, Cambodia, and Thailand, while the peoples continued to repulse Chinese attempts to control the area. In the nineteenth century France established a colonial empire over Cambodia, Laos, and Vietnam. During the 1920s a strong nationalist movement under Ho Chi Minh developed. His great opportunity appeared when Japan defeated and humiliated the French between 1940 and 1945. With American help, French power reappeared in 1946. Ho believed that a settlement could be worked out and preferred dealing with France than with closer, more threatening neighbors: "It is better to smell the French dung for a while than eat China's all our lives." The settlement, however, broke down in late 1946, and war ensued until Ho's victory in 1954.

The Geneva agreements of 1954 temporarily divided the country along the seventeenth parallel until elections could be held in 1956. Historically, South Vietnam had not been a separate nation. But with American support, South Vietnamese president Diem, who had been installed in Saigon during late 1954 with Washington's aid, refused to hold the elections. He knew that his own weakness in the south, Ho's reputation as a nationalist, and Ho's iron hand in the north would result in a lopsided victory for the communists. Believing that American support made his own position secure, Diem cut back drastically on promised-land reforms. He concentrated power within his own family. That family was Roman Catholic, a religion adopted by only 10 percent of the Vietnamese. Elections were rigged and the South Vietnamese constitution forgotten.

Civil war finally erupted against Diem in 1958. In March 1960 the National Liberation Front was organized by communists to lead the rebellion. Guerrilla warfare accelerated. In the fall of 1960 Diem's own army tried to overthrow his government but failed. As Diem approached the brink, he called for help. Kennedy responded.

THE NEW FRONTIER IN VIETNAM: 1961–1963

The United States tried to build a nation where none had existed by supporting a ruler who was under attack by his own people. Kennedy nevertheless thought the effort necessary. Secretary of State Dean Rusk fully supported the policy. Rusk had been an army officer in Asia from 1944 to 1945 and assistant secretary of state for Far Eastern affairs during the Korean War. He fervently believed that the 1960s would test whether Americans could contain communism in Asia as they had in Europe.

In the Department of Defense, Secretary Robert McNamara quickly built the armed force needed by Kennedy and Rusk. A brilliant product of the Harvard Business School and former president of the Ford Motor Company, McNamara used computer and other new quantitative techniques to build and demonstrate the superiority of American power. "Every quantitative measurement we have shows we're winning this war," he declared in 1962. But in Vietnam, numbers could be misleading, for the war involved a struggle in the villages that required political and cultural judgments. McNamara's computers could not make such judgments.

As a consequence, Kennedy continued to try to prop up Diem even as Diem's support was dwindling. In 1961–1962, 10,000 Americans departed for Vietnam. Kennedy made the commitment even though he fully realized it was nothing more than a start. He compared aid-

(Left to right) General Maxwell D. Taylor, General Paul D. Harkins, and Secretary of Defense Robert S. McNamara. *(James Burke/Time & Life Pictures/Getty Images)*

ing Diem with being an alcoholic: "The effect [of one drink] wears off and you have to take another." Diem saw clearly what was happening. The weaker he became, the more he could expect Kennedy's help. Diem could consequently pay little attention to American advice. Meanwhile Diem's generals dreamed up statistics to feed McNamara's computers, and the computers told McNamara and Kennedy what they wanted to hear.

After the Cuban missile crisis, Kennedy's determination increased. He believed that the crisis had forced Khrushchev to retreat in the world struggle but that Russia's place would be taken by Mao Zedong's China. Mao, the president privately believed, was the true revolutionary, and when China developed nuclear weapons, that country would be the great threat to world stability. It was only a short step for Kennedy to conclude that since Vietnam bordered on China, and since Mao aided Ho Chi Minh, the Vietnamese struggle would decide whether

Chinese communism would triumph in the newly emerging nations. All of Kennedy's assumptions were doubtful: Ho and the Vietnamese feared China and did not want to get too close to Mao; Chinese communism had little to do with Vietnamese communism, which was highly nationalistic; and above all, Vietnamese nationalism, not communism, was the main fuel for the war against Diem. As nationalists, the Vietnamese were determined to be free of all foreigners, whether French, American, or Chinese. But Kennedy, who too easily defined the world as simply "half slave and half free," seemed unable to understand these differences.

Despite Washington's help, Diem's forces lost ground in 1962. Kennedy was reluctant to admit this publicly, but Americans learned of Diem's setbacks through American newspaper correspondents in Vietnam. Washington officials tried to silence these reports. Kennedy even privately suggested to the owner of the *New York Times* that he give a "vacation" to one reporter who was telling the story accurately, but not the way Kennedy wanted it reported. To the publisher's credit, he rejected the president's advice.

The turning point came in mid-1963. Buddhist leaders celebrated Buddha's 2,587th birthday with flags and religious demonstrations. Fearful that such demonstrations could explode into massive political opposition to his regime, Diem had banned such displays. He ordered his troops to fire on the Buddhist leaders. Anti-Diem forces immediately rallied to the Buddhists, and civil war threatened within the principal cities. Several Buddhists responded by publicly burning themselves to death, an act that the government ridiculed as a "barbecue show." The deaths, however, dramatized the growing opposition. Kennedy decided to move.

In late August, American officials told South Vietnamese military leaders that there would be no objection if Diem were deposed. On November 1 the South Vietnamese president and his brother were captured and shot by army leaders. Although they had not known about, and indeed had disapproved of, the assassination, American officials had encouraged Diem's overthrow. In doing so, they had again demonstrated their deep involvement in the Vietnamese conflict and their determination to "save" the country even if this required helping overthrow the government. The Kennedy administration was now fully committed to the war and to a new government. What the president would have done next is unknown. On November 22, 1963, while on a political junket to Dallas, Texas, John F. Kennedy also fell victim to an assassin's bullet.

A later government investigation headed by Chief Justice Earl Warren of the Supreme Court concluded that the murderer was probably Lee Harvey Oswald, young, embittered, and, it seems, especially angered by Kennedy's anti-Castro policies. But Oswald never told his story, for shortly after his arrest he was shot—on national television and while surrounded by police guards—by a small-time nightclub owner, Jack Ruby. In the following years many self-appointed investigators produced evidence suggesting that Oswald was innocent, or that he was only one of several killers, or that he was the front man for a powerful secret group still at large. Loving mysteries of this kind, especially when it involved a glamorous president, Americans debated at length the circumstances of the tragedy. While they focused on Dallas and the shattered dreams of the Kennedy promise, a new tragedy was growing 12,000 miles away that would destroy more than 58,000 American lives.

Chapter Fourteen

1963–1968
The Great Society and Vietnam

Martin Luther King Jr., 1966. *(AFP/Getty Images)*

John Kennedy bequeathed to Lyndon Baines Johnson (often referred to as "LBJ") a legacy of social reform at home and military interventionism in Vietnam. That turned out to be a highly explosive mixture. Johnson, who wanted to be regarded as "president of all the people," also wanted to achieve a consensus in favor of his Great Society programs. But while he succeeded in implementing those programs in the fields of civil rights, education, and welfare, his escalation of the war in Vietnam led to unprecedented tensions and divisions. The consequences were disastrous. The war undermined social reform, stimulated the growth of irresponsible presidential power, triggered ruinous inflation, eroded fundamental civil liberties, and strained crucial diplomatic alliances. The war led, finally, to violence at home, which, if not so destructive as the violence in Vietnam, was a political turning point. It forced Johnson to withdraw from the presidential race in 1968 and paved the way for the victory of Richard M. Nixon.

THE 1964 ELECTION

Lyndon Johnson knew as much about the exercise of political power as any American in the post-1945 era. He had grown up in central Texas, learning state and national politics during the New Deal era from such masters as fellow Texan Sam Rayburn, Speaker of the House of Representatives. During the 1950s, when Johnson became leader of the Senate Democratic majority, he often gathered votes by subjecting fellow senators to intense, person-to-person harangues. Such encounters became known as the "treatment"; it was described by one victim as "a great overpowering thunderstorm that consumed you as it closed in around you." When he moved into the White House, Johnson was perfectly prepared to use the vast powers of the executive branch. "When we made mistakes, I believe we erred because we tried to do too much too soon and never because we stayed away from challenge," he later wrote. "If the Presidency can be said to have been employed and to have been enjoyed, I had employed it to the utmost, and I had enjoyed it to the limit."

In the 1964 presidential campaign Johnson ran against Republican nominee Barry Goldwater, a conservative senator from Arizona. Goldwater never had a chance. Johnson had been masterful in ensuring continuity of government after Kennedy's murder. The Republicans' choice of Goldwater reflected a persistent belief in the existence of a "hidden vote," that is, a truly conservative vote that the Republican Party could never obtain so long as it nominated liberal candidates. Goldwater made few concessions to Republican liberals, but he made an explicit overture to those on the right when, in accepting the nomination, he declared, "Extremism in the defense of liberty is no vice; moderation in the pursuit of justice is no virtue."

Goldwater voiced several themes during the campaign. "The moral fiber of the American people is beset by rot and decay," he asserted. He traced this largely to the "political daddyism" of Lyndon Johnson and other politicians whose only concern was "the morality of get, the morality of grab." Goldwater noted ominously, "You will search in vain for *any reference* to God or religion in the Democratic platform." The Republican candidate promised to apply a carving knife to welfare state programs, thereby seeming to be cautious and negative while the Texan was pushing the country forward. "I just want to tell you this," Johnson told a cheering crowd during the campaign, "we're in favor of a lot of things and we're against mighty few."

Goldwater then made the mistake of asserting that the Democrats had dallied in Southeast Asia instead of winning a total victory. He further suggested that such a triumph would be hastened if military commanders in the field, rather than the president, had the final word in

Activists marching from Selma to Montgomery, Alabama, to protest discriminatory voting practices, 1965. *(Library of Congress)*

using nuclear weapons. Johnson effectively seized on these remarks to score Goldwater for being irresponsible and bloodthirsty. As for Vietnam, "We don't want our American boys to do the fighting for Asian boys," Johnson announced on September 25, 1964. "We don't want to get involved in a nation with 700 million people [Red China] and get tied down in a land war in Asia."

It was, therefore, as easy for the Democrats to argue that Goldwater would propel the nation into an all-out war in Vietnam as it was to portray him as an extremist on domestic issues. Johnson humiliated his opponent in the election, winning 61.1 percent of the popular vote and carrying forty-four states to Goldwater's six. One of every five people who had voted Republican in 1960 switched to the Democrats in 1964. When asked why, many said of Goldwater, "He's too radical for me." Prospects for the Johnson administration could hardly have been more promising.

LYNDON JOHNSON AND THE GREAT SOCIETY

Lyndon Johnson had greater success than any president since Franklin Roosevelt in putting across his legislative program. After his sweeping triumph in 1964, Johnson could work with comfortable Democratic majorities in Congress. The Democrats—with majorities of 294 to 140 in the House and 68 to 32 in the Senate—enjoyed their largest margin of control since 1937, the year Johnson entered Congress. The seventy-one freshman Democrats in the House, many of whom owed their election to the Johnson landslide, vied with one another in their willingness to cooperate with the White House. Then too, Johnson's southern background and reputation as a moderate allowed him to enact far-reaching programs without losing his broad popular backing. Those programs often broke sharply with prevailing practice. The Revenue Act (1964) cut taxes by a whopping $11.5 billion even while the government was operating at a deficit. Advocates of an expansionary fiscal policy predicted correctly that the resulting boost in purchasing power would spur economic growth. The Housing Act (1965) provided rent supplements for low-income families displaced by urban renewal or otherwise unable to find suitable public housing. The government would subsidize that portion of their rent that exceeded 25 percent of their income. In 1965, too, Congress renovated the immigration laws, removing quotas based on race or national origin that had existed in some form for more than fifty years. The Great Society, however, channeled most of its energies into four other areas: the war on poverty, aid to education, medical care, and civil rights.

In January 1964 Johnson called for an "unconditional war on poverty," and later that year Congress approved the Economic Opportunity Act as the chief weapon in that war. The measure created the Office of Economic Opportunity (OEO), which sought to provide education, vocational training, and job experience for impoverished youth. The OEO also sponsored community action programs with a view toward improving employment opportunities, health care, housing, and education in poor neighborhoods. These programs were supposed to elicit "the maximum feasible participation of residents of the areas and members of the groups served." The OEO, which spent $750 million in 1965 and $1.5 billion in 1966, succeeded in reducing poverty but not in eliminating it. Government statistics indicated that 15.4 percent of the American people lived in poverty in 1966, compared with 22.1 percent in 1959. Funds for the OEO were always inadequate, and powerful local interests, anxious to get their hands on antipoverty money and patronage, often gained control of the community programs and used them for their own advancement.

The war on poverty was closely linked with federal aid to education. In the past such legislation had bogged down over the issue of assisting religious schools, but in 1965 the Johnson administration discovered an antipoverty rationale for school aid programs. The Elementary and Secondary Education Act (1965), which Congress passed in much the same form as Johnson requested, provided funds to local school districts according to a formula involving the number of children from low-income families in the county. The act also appropriated funds for the purchase of textbooks and other instructional materials that could be used by private as well as by public schools. Under this legislation, U.S. Office of Education expenditures soared from under $50 million in 1960 to $5.6 billion in 1973. Congress also followed Johnson's recommendation in approving the Higher Education Act (1965), which provided college scholarships for needy students, subsidized interest costs on loans to college students, and helped fund classroom construction.

In the case of health insurance, as in that of federal aid to education, Johnson enacted a program first proposed by Harry Truman twenty years earlier. To appease those who saw the specter of socialized medicine in any national plan, the administration tied health care to the existing Social Security system and allowed participating physicians to charge their "usual and customary fees" if these were reasonable. Moreover, it limited coverage to the poor and elderly, who were least able to afford medical care and least likely to be protected by private insurance plans. Medicare provided benefits covering approximately 80 percent of hospital expenses for all persons over age sixty-five. Medicaid provided assistance in meeting doctors' bills for poor people, regardless of age, who qualified for public assistance. By July 1967, at the end of its first year of operation, 17.7 million of 19 million elderly Americans had enrolled in Medicare, one in five had entered a hospital under the law, and 12 million had used it to defray medical expenses.

Civil rights legislation rounded out the Great Society agenda. Early in 1964 the Senate passed a civil rights bill already approved by the House. The act, which grew out of John F. Kennedy's recommendations, barred discrimination on the basis of race in all public accommodations. These included restaurants, gas stations, places of entertainment, and hotels (except for private residences renting fewer than five rooms for overnight lodging). Almost all such enterprises were held to affect interstate commerce—a gas station, for example, if its customers drove across state lines. The act also authorized the Justice Department to bring suit against state facilities, such as parks and auditoriums, which remained segregated. Finally, the act included an equal opportunity clause making it unlawful for firms with more than twenty-five employees to discriminate in hiring on the grounds of race, religion, sex, or national origin.

The measure also included provisions to safeguard the right to vote, but these were soon superseded by the Voting Rights Act (1965) that the president urged Congress to enact after violence erupted in Alabama. Early in 1965 Dr. Martin Luther King Jr. led a demonstration in the town of Selma, in a county where more than 15,000 blacks were eligible to vote but only 335 had been able to register. When state troopers attacked King's followers and extremists murdered a civil rights worker, Congress responded with a drastic measure. It affected counties that prescribed literacy or other tests for voting and contained a substantial nonwhite population, but in which relatively few blacks actually cast ballots. In those counties, located primarily but not exclusively in South Carolina, Georgia, Mississippi, Alabama, and Louisiana, the right to vote would no longer depend on literacy or character fitness. The only valid criteria would be age, residence, and citizenship. The attorney general could appoint federal examiners to register voters, and the states, if they wished to protest, would have to appeal to a federal court in Washington, DC.

Lyndon Johnson never passed up a chance to point out the historical significance of his legislation. To sign the education bill he traveled to the one-room schoolhouse he had attended as a child and asked his former teacher, seventy-two-year-old "Miss Katie," to sit beside him. He journeyed to Independence, Missouri, to present the pen used to sign the Medicare bill to Harry Truman. He signed the Voting Rights Act in the same room that Lincoln had used more than one hundred years before to free the slaves conscripted into the Confederate army. Similarly, Johnson used grandiose terms in defining his objectives. He proclaimed that the Great Society "rests on abundance and liberty for all. It demands an end to poverty and racial injustice." Despite its impressive accomplishments, few would claim that the Great Society achieved that much.

THE WARREN COURT: JUDICIAL ACTIVISM

In seeking new remedies for the nation's problems, the president and Congress were joined by the third branch of government. Far from inhibiting reform, as it had often done in the past, the Supreme Court acted as a catalyst for social change. Of the justices most closely identified with the new activism, two—Hugo Black and William O. Douglas—had been appointed by Roosevelt; two others—Earl Warren and William Brennan—had been named by Eisenhower. John Kennedy's appointment of Arthur Goldberg in 1962 further tipped the scales toward judicial activism. Goldberg replaced Felix Frankfurter, who had long been the most articulate spokesman for the theory of judicial restraint. Frankfurter believed that judges must guard against the temptation to write their own biases into law and that society must not expect the Supreme Court to solve all its problems. After his retirement the Court moved boldly into areas it had once avoided.

Following the path it had charted in the school desegregation decision of 1954, the Court threw its weight behind the civil rights movement. In 1963 the Court was forced to rule on cases stemming from a refusal to seat blacks at lunch counters. It found that local ordinances upholding segregation in private business establishments were unconstitutional, for they involved state action within the meaning of the Fourteenth Amendment.

In *Cox v. Louisiana* (1964) the Court reversed the conviction of black demonstrators in Baton Rouge who had refused to disperse when so ordered by the police. The justices decided that breach-of-the-peace laws could not serve as a pretext for preventing peaceable speech and assembly. The Court quickly sanctioned the civil rights acts of 1964 and 1965. It also ruled that delays in school desegregation were "no longer tolerable," and in *Loving v. Virginia* (1967) it struck down a state law barring marriage between persons of different races.

Religious dissenters, no less than civil rights workers, received new forms of legal protection. In the early 1960s, twelve states required Bible reading in public schools, and thirty others encouraged such exercises. Children in New York State recited a nonsectarian prayer: "Almighty God, we acknowledge our dependence upon Thee, and we beg Thy blessings upon us, our parents, our teachers and our country." A state court saw no objection to this, but the Supreme Court, in *Engel v. Vitale* (1962), ruled the New York prayer unconstitutional on the grounds that it was a religious activity that placed an "indirect coercive pressure upon religious minorities." Then, in 1963, the Court took up the case of Edward Schempp, a Unitarian, whose children attended a school in which biblical passages were read over the loudspeaker and students recited the Lord's Prayer. Those who did not wish to participate could wait outside the classroom. Schempp argued that this arrangement would penalize his children and make them feel like "oddballs." The Supreme Court agreed: "Through the mechanism of the State, all of the people are being required to finance a religious exercise that only some of the people want and that violates the sensibilities of others." The justices ruled that public schools could not show the slightest preference for any particular religion.

Nowhere did the Court break more decisively with the past than in the area of obscenity. In the mid-1950s, explicit sexual references in books, magazines, and motion pictures were illegal, and even such classics as D.H. Lawrence's *Lady Chatterley's Lover* were proscribed. The Supreme Court began to loosen these restraints in *Roth v. United States* (1957). Although ruling that obscenity did not deserve constitutional protection, the Court nevertheless felt it necessary to propose a test of obscenity, which became "whether to the average person applying contemporary community standards, the dominant theme of the material taken as a whole appeals to prurient interest." Thus began years of controversy over the meaning of such terms as "prurience." In 1961 the Court decided that a magazine could indeed appeal to prurient interest so long as it did not reveal "patent offensiveness." The justices went a step further in *Jacobellis v. Ohio* (1963), asserting that "material dealing with sex in a manner that advocates ideas . . . or has literary or scientific or artistic value or any other forms of social

Earl Warren, governor of California, 1942–1952, and then the chief
justice of the U.S. Supreme Court, 1953–1969. *(Library of Congress)*

importance may not be branded as obscenity and denied the constitutional protection." In
1966 the Court extended such protection to *Fanny Hill*, an eighteenth-century novel usually
considered pornographic. A book could not be banned unless "it is found to be utterly without
redeeming social value." Under that standard, nearly all restrictions on the right of an adult
to obtain sexually explicit material vanished.

This expansion of individual freedoms also characterized other areas of Court action. Three
classic decisions revolutionized criminal justice procedures. In *Gideon v. Wainwright* (1963)
the Court decided that an indigent person charged with a felony was entitled to representation
by a state-appointed attorney, although Florida law provided legal aid only for capital offenses.
In *Escobedo v. Illinois* (1964) the Court ruled in favor of a man who, when interrogated on a
murder charge, was not informed of his right to remain silent or permitted to see an attorney.
Five justices believed that when the police centered their investigation on one individual and

sought to extract a confession, they must allow the suspect to see a lawyer. Four members of the Court dissented. A similarly close and bitter division prevailed in *Miranda v. Arizona* (1966), which involved a man who, after a two-hour interrogation, had confessed to charges of kidnapping and rape. The majority of the Court held that a confession could not be introduced as evidence unless the defendant had been informed at the outset of the interrogative process that he could see an attorney or remain silent and that any information he provided would be used against him. The burden of proof was placed on the prosecution to show that a defendant knowingly waived the privilege against self-incrimination and the right to counsel. Four dissenting judges gravely warned that the ruling "will return a killer, a rapist or other criminal to the streets . . . to repeat his crime whenever it pleases him."

Judicial activism reached a culmination in decisions concerning legislative reapportionment. The Court in the past had skirted this issue, reasoning that if district lines were drawn unfairly, citizens should seek political, not judicial, redress. But in *Baker v. Carr* (1962) the Court entered the "political thicket." The case involved a resident of Memphis, Tennessee, who complained that because of malapportionment his vote for a member of the state legislature was worth less than the vote of a rural resident. The Supreme Court agreed that reapportionment was a proper question for judicial determination. Federal district judges were to set guidelines, and in 1963 the Supreme Court provided a clue as to what those guidelines should be. Justice Douglas explained that political equality "can mean only one thing, one person, one vote." The Court applied this doctrine in *Reynolds v. Sims* (1964). Chief Justice Warren, speaking for the majority, said that just as a state could not give a citizen two votes, so it could not permit any person's vote to count twice as much as anyone else's. Both houses of state legislatures had to be apportioned based on population. Substantial equality, if not mathematical precision, was needed in determining the size of districts. Within a few years, the great majority of states had reapportioned their legislatures to conform to these rulings.

Most of the Warren Court's decisions sparked bitter controversy, and efforts were made to overturn certain rulings, particularly those concerning reapportionment and school prayer. In 1964 the House of Representatives passed a bill denying federal courts jurisdiction over apportionment, but the Senate refused to concur. A constitutional amendment that would have permitted the states to apportion one house of their legislatures on some basis other than population (if approved by voters in a referendum) passed the Senate in 1965 and 1966, but each time fell short of obtaining the required two-thirds majority. Similarly, in 1966 the Senate approved an amendment allowing voluntary participation in prayer in the public schools, but again by less than a two-thirds vote. Critics complained that the Supreme Court had become "a general haven for reform movements." There was, however, no minimizing the social and political impact of its rulings.

ORIGINS OF THE NEW FEMINISM

Nor could Americans underestimate the revival of feminism, inspired in part by Betty Friedan's *The Feminine Mystique*, published in 1963. The book indicted the "housewife-heroine" of the 1950s. After World War II, Friedan contended, women had been told that "they could desire no greater destiny than to glory in their own femininity," to seek fulfillment as wives and mothers. Instilled by women's magazines, the feminine mystique found support from psychologists, advertisers, and educators, who dissuaded college women from seeking careers.

Although the feminine mystique seemed to promise a safe, secure existence, Friedan argued, it actually confined women to the home, "a comfortable concentration camp," produced feelings of emptiness, and deprived women of a sense of individualism. To escape the mystique, she concluded, women had to develop "new life plans," establish independent careers, and pursue "goals that will permit them to find their own identity."

Friedan's best seller evoked response from appreciative readers. "I and other women knew we were not alone," one woman wrote. "It struck at the very center of my being," wrote another. Friedan had not intended to create a new feminist movement in 1963; the publication of her book, in fact, did not immediately do so. But the civil rights struggle of the early 1960s provided another catalyst for feminist revival. Civil rights advocates created a climate of protest, demonstrated confrontation tactics, put forth egalitarian arguments, and set a precedent for ending discrimination under law. Finally, and seemingly by accident, the Civil Rights Act of 1964 propelled a new women's movement into existence.

During congressional debate over Title VII of the civil rights bill, which prohibited discrimination in employment on grounds of race, a Virginia representative proposed an amendment that would prohibit such discrimination on grounds of sex as well. His goal was to discredit the bill, bar its passage, and ridicule its supporters. But once the new law passed, with its controversial amendment intact, the sex discrimination clause had an unexpected impact. When complaints about sex discrimination, sent to the Equal Employment Opportunity Commission, received little attention, a small group of women's rights advocates—including Betty Friedan—urged the commission to act on women's grievances. As success seemed unlikely without public support, the new group took action. In 1966, twenty-eight women's rights supporters created the National Organization for Women (NOW) "to bring American women into full participation in the mainstream of American society NOW."

NOW's first effort was to provide the new feminist movement with an agenda. In its manifesto, NOW demanded "a truly equal partnership of the sexes, as part of the worldwide revolution of human rights." Denouncing pay disparities, employment inequities, and educational discrimination, NOW called for new types of social roles. "We reject the current assumption that a man must carry the whole burden of supporting himself, his wife, and family . . . or that marriage, home, and family are primarily woman's world and responsibility," NOW stated. While proposing a new relationship between men and women, NOW stopped short of an attack on marriage. "We believe that a true partnership between the sexes demands a different concept of marriage, an equitable sharing of the responsibilities of home and children, and of the economic burden of their support." Under the leadership of Betty Friedan, its first president, NOW became a national political pressure group, with many local chapters. Its members sought to end sexual inequity through legislation and court decisions. They lobbied, demonstrated, filed class-action suits to end discrimination in hiring and promotion, and insisted that newspapers stop publishing separate want ads for males and females.

Too radical for some, NOW proved too conservative for others. A younger, more radical feminist wing, emerging from the ranks of civil rights activists, soon affected NOW's campaign. In the early 1960s, hundreds of college students had participated in voter registration drives in the South. During these campaigns, young women developed a new consciousness of sex discrimination: "Assumptions of male supremacy are as . . . crippling to the woman as assumptions of white supremacy are to the Negro," one civil rights worker concluded. Similar objections to male dominance were voiced by young women who moved on to New Left

American feminist and author Betty Friedan, a founding member of NOW and the author of *The Feminine Mystique*, 1970. *(B. Friedan/MPI/Getty Images)*

community organizing projects outside the South (see "The New Left and the Counterculture," page 404). By 1967 radical women had developed their own brand of attack. To radical feminists, women constituted "an oppressed class. Our oppression is total, affecting every facet of our lives. . . . We identify the enemy as man." The radical agenda diverged from that of NOW. "The institution of marriage is the chief vehicle for the perpetuation of the oppression of women," the radicals contended. The radical feminist technique of "consciousness-raising" was also innovative. It consisted of small discussion groups in which women reconsidered their personal experiences as political phenomena. Out of consciousness-raising emerged the distinctive aims of radical feminism: "women's liberation" and the eradication of "sexism." Ending sexism, like ending racism, meant changing attitudes, behavior, relationships, and institutions. The goal was fundamental social change, or "revolution."

Structureless, with no headquarters, organization, or officers, women's liberation was again a contrast to NOW. "It's not a movement, it's a state of mind," one advocate explained. But the new state of mind seemed contagious, notably among educated, younger women. In the late 1960s, women's liberation created a ferment of activity. Some radical feminists staged confrontations to gain media attention by crowning a sheep at the 1968 Miss America Pageant or invading an all-male bar in New York City. Others started health collectives, day care centers, and abortion counseling services. Still others published "position papers" and promoted consciousness-raising. While women's liberation campaigns were diffuse, NOW's goals became more specific. By 1968, the core of NOW's legislative agenda was complete. NOW supported passage of an equal rights amendment, a cause that had languished for several decades; demanded repeal of state laws that prevented women from having abortions; and urged the creation of government-funded day care programs to ease the burden on working mothers.

The two feminist wings were apparently much at odds. Reform-minded NOW viewed liberationists as a lunatic fringe; radical feminists denounced NOW members as bourgeois conservatives. But the postures of the two wings were in fact complementary, as feminist successes in the early 1970s were to prove.

BLACK POWER AND URBAN RIOTS

The differences between radicals and reformers evident in the feminist movement were also increasingly apparent in the civil rights movement. The reformist approach, with its stress on nonviolent protest as a means and integration as an end, reached its zenith with the passage of the civil rights acts of 1964 and 1965. But the middle and late 1960s saw the emergence of many black leaders who repudiated integration and nonviolence in favor of separatism and self-defense. The result was a fragmentation of the protest movement.

The "black power" slogan was coined by Stokely Carmichael, who had for several years worked with the Student Nonviolent Coordinating Committee (SNCC). This organization had helped organize the sit-ins and freedom rides. At first it endorsed Martin Luther King Jr.'s approach, but in the mid-1960s many members of SNCC grew disenchanted with the existing civil rights program. They felt betrayed in 1964 when the Democratic convention refused to provide adequate representation for the Freedom Democratic Party, which they had founded in Mississippi as an alternative to the lily-white state organization. SNCC workers found that turning the other cheek often caused them to become enraged. Consequently, they became more receptive to the arguments of militant leaders like Black Muslim Malcolm X, who advised, "If someone puts a hand on you, send him to the cemetery." In June 1966, during a demonstration in Mississippi, Carmichael shouted: "Black Power! It's time we stand up and take over! Take over! Move on over, or we'll move on over you!"

In the following months Carmichael explained his viewpoint. Instead of seeking alliances with white liberals, who, he asserted, wished to perpetuate paternalistic control, blacks should do things for themselves. Instead of adopting nonviolent methods, "black people should and must fight back." Instead of demanding integration, which Carmichael considered "a subterfuge for the maintenance of white supremacy," blacks should develop their own cultural identity, purge their communities of outside control, and thereby achieve self-determination. Black power looked toward the welding of blacks into a cohesive voting bloc capable of controlling political organizations inside the ghetto and creating autonomous parties in the South. It meant establishing self-sufficient business and consumer cooperatives and taking over public schools in black communities. "We don't need white liberals," Carmichael told a sympathetic convention of the Congress on Racial Equality (CORE). "We have to make integration irrelevant."

Not surprisingly, the sharpest critics of this doctrine were themselves veterans of the civil rights crusade. Roy Wilkins of the National Association for the Advancement of Colored People (NAACP) branded black power "the father of hatred and the mother of violence." Bayard Rustin, an associate of King, pointed out that blacks, as a minority, could not hope to achieve anything

Soldiers standing guard after riots in Washington, DC, April 1968. *(Library of Congress)*

of substance without allies, particularly in the labor movement, among ethnic groups, and among poor whites. The organizations that endorsed black power—such as SNCC and CORE—were primarily composed of young people who disliked compromise, distrusted whites, and wanted fast results. Those that supported integration—such as the NAACP—believed that compromise was necessary, hoped to convert whites, and did not expect overnight triumphs. When black power advocates excluded NAACP field secretary Charles Evers from a rally in Jackson, Mississippi, he replied, "I'll be here when they're all gone."

Black power advocates rejected nonviolence as well as integration. This justification of self-defense frightened many whites, but what frightened them even more was a series of explosions that rocked black ghettos across the land. From 1964 to 1968 the United States experienced the most protracted period of domestic unrest since the Civil War. In 1964 blacks rioted in the Harlem and Bedford-Stuyvesant sections of New York City. A year later the Watts district in Los Angeles came to resemble a disaster area after a week-long riot left thirty-four dead, more than a thousand injured, and hundreds of buildings in ashes. To restore order, 15,000 National Guardsmen were sent to the city. In 1966 more than two dozen major riots occurred, most of them marked by looting, firebombs, and sniper fire. A study group concluded that the year's events "made it appear that domestic turmoil had become part of the American scene." Dozens of riots flared in black ghettos in 1967. In Newark, police and guardsmen fired 13,326 rounds of ammunition in three days. In Detroit, forty-three people were killed and 7,200 arrested; the city was thrown into chaos. The assassination of Martin

Luther King Jr. in April 1968 led to the very thing the martyred civil rights leader most abhorred: race riots broke out in Chicago, Washington, and other cities.

The National Advisory Commission on Civil Disorders, which was appointed by the president in 1967 and headed by Otto Kerner, found that the country was increasingly divided "into two societies: one, largely Negro and poor, located in the central cities; the other, predominantly white and affluent, located in the suburbs and in outlying areas." It was this very division that the Kerner Commission, in its February 1968 report, blamed for the outbreaks. The commission viewed the riots as a protest against conditions in the ghetto, and the ghetto as a product of white racism. The commission pointed out that 16 to 20 percent of black city dwellers lived in "squalor and deprivation" and that 40 percent of the nation's nonwhite residents had incomes below the poverty line ($3,335 for an urban family of four). It further noted that a black man was two times as likely to be unemployed as a white man and three times as likely to be working in a low-paid or unskilled job.

A far simpler explanation for the riots, although a much less well-founded one, appealed to officials in the Federal Bureau of Investigation (FBI). Long suspicious of the civil rights movement, FBI director J. Edgar Hoover now attributed the racial violence chiefly to "the exhortations of 'Black Power' advocates" who had transformed "volatile situations . . . into violent outbreaks." Accordingly, Hoover stepped up his agency's surveillance of black communities and its efforts to disrupt nationalist groups and such militant organizations as the Black Panthers. By mid-1968, the FBI's "Ghetto Informant Program" employed about 3,250 agents, and its new "Rabble Rouser Index" listed "individuals who have demonstrated a potential for fomenting racial discord."

The FBI and the Kerner Commission represented two very different approaches to the problems of racism and violence. The first emphasized surveillance of alleged agitators; the second emphasized massive government programs to improve conditions in the ghettos. By 1968, white Americans increasingly were leaning toward Hoover's approach, rather than Kerner's, partly because of a backlash against the urban riots but also because of the domestic costs of Lyndon Johnson's foreign policy.

THE GLOBAL BACKGROUND TO VIETNAM

During his 1964 campaign against Barry Goldwater, Johnson had promised to pursue peace in Vietnam, but had also threatened wider war. In August, just as the campaign was accelerating, he announced that two American destroyers had been attacked in international waters (the Gulf of Tonkin) by North Vietnamese torpedo boats. "The attacks were unprovoked," Johnson claimed. He ordered air strikes against North Vietnam's naval base, and then urged Congress to pass a broad resolution giving him the authority to "take all necessary measures to repel any armed attack against the forces of the United States and to prevent further aggression." (It was later discovered that the White House had drawn up this resolution and the list of bombing targets two months before.) Democrats Wayne Morse of Oregon and Ernest Gruening of Alaska opposed the resolution. They argued that the circumstances of the attack were not clear. It seemed weird, they declared, that several small boats would challenge the strength of the U.S. Navy. They also believed such broad powers should not be given to the president. The House nevertheless overwhelmingly passed the Gulf of Tonkin Resolution 416 to 0; the Senate 88 to 2.

Four years later Secretary of Defense Robert McNamara admitted that the American people had been misled in 1964. He revealed that the American destroyers had been accompanying South Vietnamese ships and commandos that were attacking North Vietnamese bases. Shortly after the engagement, moreover, the North Vietnamese had approached the United States for peace discussions. Fearful that the South Vietnamese government was too weak even to negotiate with North Vietnam, Johnson had rejected the approach and again withheld the information from the American people.

The truth arrived much too late. Congress gave Johnson a blank check in 1964, and then allowed him to cash it over and over again in the following years as he escalated the fighting into a full-scale conventional conflict without asking for a formal declaration of war from the legislative branch. That vital congressional restraint upon the wielding of incalculable power by a single man had disappeared. The president drew decision making increasingly into his own hands until the fundamental choices in Vietnam—choices that would ultimately lead to hundreds of thousands of deaths—were made by four men in a regularly scheduled Tuesday luncheon group: Johnson, McNamara, Secretary of State Dean Rusk, and the president's national security adviser, McGeorge Bundy (replaced in 1966 by Walt Whitman Rostow).

This imperial presidential power was exercised in a rapidly changing world. In the Soviet Union Nikita Khrushchev was forced from office in October 1964, victimized by his ineptness during the Cuban missile crisis and, more important, by his bungling of the Russian economy. He was replaced by two men, Aleksei Kosygin and Leonid Brezhnev, both of whom had risen to power under Stalin. They aimed at two objectives. First, they determined to mobilize Soviet society for rapid economic advances. This determination and their apprenticeship under Stalin led the two leaders to ruthlessly squash any internal opposition. Dissident Soviet intellectuals, particularly Jews, were harassed, imprisoned, or declared insane. Second, the Soviets vowed to keep Chinese power contained. The two leading communist nations were deeply divided over ideology and, more important, over clashing national interests. By 1965 fighting between Chinese and Soviet troops had erupted along a 1,200-mile frontier. When Kosygin visited Chinese leader Mao Zedong in 1965, Mao said that differences between the two nations were so profound that they would last for 10,000 years. When Kosygin protested, Mao agreed to make it only 9,000 years.

These disagreements gave the Johnson administration an opportunity to reduce Cold War tensions by improving relations between the two superpowers. The Russians needed American economic aid and would welcome any easing of relations in Europe, for then they could concentrate on their more dangerous enemy in China. East-West trade did improve. Moscow and Washington, moreover, agreed in a nonproliferation treaty that they would work to prevent the spread of nuclear weapons. But no major initiative to end the Cold War occurred. American officials were too preoccupied with Vietnam. They insisted, moreover, that the Soviets were not truly mellowing. Secretary of State Rusk warned that while Americans had come to see Khrushchev as "an affable old grandfather, he was 68 and a half when he put missiles in Cuba." Rusk's fears seemed verified in August 1968, when Soviet troops suddenly marched into their satellite state of Czechoslovakia to destroy a new regime that, while remaining communist, was nevertheless becoming more liberal and pro-Western.

As the two great powers struggled to keep the status quo, much of the rest of the world struggled to simply survive. In 1965 the North Atlantic nations (United States, Canada, and Western Europe) accounted for only 20 percent of the world's population but 70 percent of

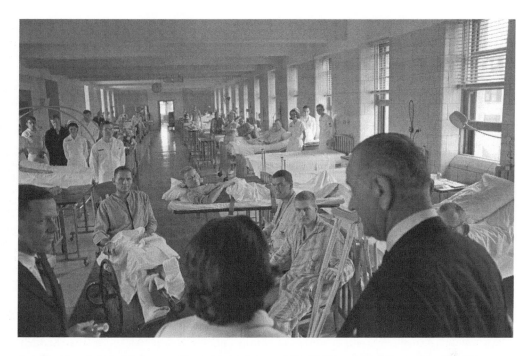

President Lyndon B. Johnson and Lady Bird Johnson visit with injured servicemen returned from Vietnam, 1965. *(Yoichi R. Okamoto, LBJ Presidential Library)*

its income. The United States *added* as much to its income each year as Latin America had in total income, and twice as much as the total income received by Africans. Lyndon Johnson's childhood and his memories of the 1930s depression made him aware of this unequal distribution of the world's wealth. When mass starvation threatened India between 1965 and 1967, he mobilized 600 ships to dispatch one-fifth of the gigantic American grain crop. In one especially revealing remark the president warned Americans "there are 3 billion people in the world and we have only 200 million of them. We are outnumbered 15 to 1. If might did make right they would sweep over the United States and take what we have. We have what they want."

Foreign economic-aid programs had failed to work miracles in the newly emerging nations and were increasingly unpopular in Congress. Special commissions assigned to investigate the problem reported to Johnson that because government programs had failed, he should encourage private investment in Latin America, Asia, and Africa. That approach, however, was hollow. Private investors preferred to operate in a secure, expanding Europe rather than in the chaotic third world. When they did go into the newly emerging nations, their primary investment went into oil, minerals, and other raw materials, thereby further unbalancing economies that were already overly dependent on the ups and downs of world prices for a single product. United Nations studies revealed in the mid-1960s that peoples in the newly emerging areas were closer to starvation than they had been before World War II. Their real income had shrunk so that it actually bought fewer goods than it had ten years earlier.

LATIN AMERICA AND AFRICA

Latin America provided a case study of Johnson's response to these problems. U.S. business had invested $15 billion directly into American-owned firms in these southern nations by 1965. These firms accounted for one-third of Latin America's industrial and mining output, one-third of its exports, and one-fifth of its taxes. The investors, however, were taking more out of Latin America than they were putting in. Between 1965 and 1970 the southern continent sent more money back to U.S. investors than it received in every year but 1967. In 1969 the gap amounted to more than $500 million. While money for future development disappeared back into the United States, the population of Latin America increased by 3 percent a year, one of the largest rates of increase in the world.

President Johnson had few remedies for these predicaments. Kennedy's Alliance for Progress was nearly dead, the victim of too little support in both North and Latin America. And while Johnson was devoting nearly all of his attention in foreign affairs to Vietnam, private interests lobbied in Congress to profit at Latin America's expense. For example, economic aid was given only when the recipient nation promised to spend it on American goods, regardless of the cost. Thus Bolivia had to spend U.S. funds to buy American-made ore carts for its vast mines even though the carts cost three times more than Belgian-made carts.

Increasing political tension resulted. The Alliance for Progress tried to build a new middle class, for such a class, in South as well as in North America, would be least likely to be revolutionary. But the middle classes were actually losing ground in Latin America by the 1960s, as their incomes were eaten by out-of-control inflation. "It is significant," a United Nations report observed, "that groups falling within the narrower definitions of the middle classes, such as bank employees and school teachers, have been among the most frequent and militant participants in strikes in recent years." Revolution grew more likely. To stop any possibility of radical change, military governments rose to power in Brazil, Bolivia, Guatemala, and Ecuador. Latin America was being torn apart.

Lyndon Johnson responded forcefully to a rebellion in the Caribbean nation of Santo Domingo. In 1961 the thirty-year dictatorship of Rafael Trujillo ended with his assassination. Three years of confusion followed until the army took control. In April 1965, however, a strange combination of liberals, radicals, and low-ranking army officers tried to replace the military rulers with a more liberal government. As the military regime crumbled, it pleaded for help from President Johnson and used the bait that supporters of Fidel Castro were gaining power. Johnson immediately dispatched 22,800 American troops to put down the rebellion. At first the president said he only wanted to ensure the safety of American citizens. It soon became clear that he intended to use force to establish a stable, pro-American government. He did this even though the United States had signed the Charter of the Organization of American States (1948), which said in part, "No state or group of states has the right to intervene, directly or indirectly, for any reason whatever, in the internal or external affairs of any other state." The administration proclaimed that the troops had prevented "the Communists . . . from taking over."

No one, however, has ever been able to demonstrate that either communists or Castroites were important in any way in the uprising. But that did not prevent the president from announcing the "Johnson Doctrine": the United States would use force, if necessary, anywhere in the hemisphere to prevent communist governments from coming to power. The Latin Americans did not appreciate this reappearance of Theodore Roosevelt's and Woodrow Wilson's gunboat diplomacy. "It is fall here," one reporter wrote from South America, "and U.S. flags as well as leaves are being burned."

American policies in Africa (especially in those nations south of the Sahara Desert) were not dissimilar. Between 1945 and 1970 more than forty African nations gained independence as the old European colonial empires disappeared. Few of the new governments had the economic or political experience to hold together national, freely elected regimes. For its part, the United States provided little help. In 1965 American development aid amounted to $200 million spread among thirty-three nations. One country received $50,000. Eight countries fell to army coups between 1964 and 1966 as parts of the continent seemed headed toward tribal warfare. American investment meanwhile centered on two white-dominated governments, South Africa and Southern Rhodesia. In addition, South Africa received military aid because of its strategic location at the tip of the continent. Both nations appeared prosperous and stable, but appearances were at the expense of the black population, which constituted the overwhelming majority in both countries. The blacks were victimized by apartheid, a white-controlled system that, through legislation and violence, brutally segregated and exploited the blacks.

The Johnson administration intervened directly in the former Belgian Congo. That area of 17 million blacks had suddenly become free in 1960 despite the lack of any preparation by the former Belgian rulers. Civil war erupted, but the United Nations, with American and Russian support, stabilized the area. By 1964 the United States was the dominant foreign power in the Congo, and the vast copper and diamond mines again produced their riches. Then nationalist revolts began, with rebels massacring thousands of blacks and whites. Despite help from the Central Intelligence Agency, the Congolese government could not quell the rebellion. The United States staged a paratroop strike to free a number of hostages, including sixteen Americans, whom the insurgents had threatened to kill, and by late 1965 the situation was quieted.

VIETNAM ABROAD

The president's responses in Santo Domingo and the Congo differed only in degree from those in Vietnam. In each case the United States chose armed might as a solution for the problems that generated nationalist revolts. Johnson's preoccupation with force led humorist Art Buchwald to claim that the president wanted to alert two airborne divisions, four Marine brigades, and the Atlantic fleet—before proclaiming Mother's Day.

The Gulf of Tonkin incidents in August 1964 were followed by five months of little fighting, but the Johnson administration was exceptionally busy. The murder of President Diem in 1963 had created political chaos. Vietnamese regimes changed so frequently that Johnson twice felt that he had to reject North Vietnamese peace overtures for fear that the American-supported regime in Saigon lacked the strength to negotiate an acceptable peace. These peace feelers from the communists were kept secret from the American people.

On February 5, 1965 (two days after the final American rejection of the second North Vietnamese peace approach), the communists killed seven Americans at a base in Pleiku. The president immediately ordered bombing of North Vietnam in carefully selected attacks aimed at cutting off supplies flowing south to the communist National Liberation Front (NLF) of South Vietnam. As for supplies coming from the north, a careful study by the Department of State, written to justify the bombings, actually revealed that of 15,000 weapons taken from communist soldiers, fewer than 200 were made in communist factories. The remainder had been captured from South Vietnamese troops, the study concluded.

The U.S. escalation, therefore, was aimed less at stopping North Vietnamese intervention in South Vietnam (for in February 1965 that intervention was not significant) than at propping up the U.S.-created Saigon regimes, which seemed incapable of defending themselves in the civil war. In March the escalation took a drastic turn. Johnson sent in Marine battalions. He thus started a buildup of American troops who were to participate directly in the combat rather than merely be "advisers" to South Vietnamese soldiers. During the summer of 1965, over 100,000 more Americans poured into the country. The president tried to cover these actions by declaring that the troops would secure only American and South Vietnamese bases. In a speech in April 1965, he had announced that he would enter "unconditional discussion" with North Vietnam but that the communists would have to begin the discussions by accepting the fact of an independent South Vietnam, something the North Vietnamese would never accept.

With few pauses, American bombing continued for seven years. More bombs were dropped on Vietnam than on Germany, Japan, and their Axis allies combined during World War II. The bombing had little military effect. By 1966, eleven tough regiments of North Vietnamese troops were in South Vietnam to fight 200,000 Americans and 550,000 South Vietnamese. The Russians and Chinese supplied ever-larger amounts of goods to the communists. Most ominous of all, the North Vietnamese, who historically had fought and feared the Chinese, were necessarily moving closer to Beijing in order to receive aid. American policy, aimed at blocking the influence of China, seemed to be producing the opposite result.

By April 1966, more Americans than South Vietnamese were being killed in action. In July the number of American dead reached 4,440, more than the number killed in the American Revolution and ten times the number who died in the Spanish-American War. The results were discouraging. The South Vietnamese controlled less than 25 percent of their own 12,000 hamlets. But a stable government was finally established in Saigon by the army. Its leaders were Major General Nguyen Van Thieu as head of the regime and, as premier, Nguyen Cao Ky, a swashbuckling air force officer who had fought with the French against the Vietnamese nationalists and who had been overheard expressing admiration for Adolf Hitler.

The new regime failed to reverse the course of the war. Lieutenant Colonel John Vann, perhaps the most perceptive American adviser to serve in Vietnam, put his finger on one fundamental problem: "This is a political war and it calls for discrimination in killing. The best weapon for killing would be a knife, but I'm afraid we can't do it that way. The worst is an airplane. The next worse is artillery." Americans were not prepared either politically or militarily to fight such a war. They wanted to resort to their unimaginably powerful technology to blow up enemy troops from the air or engage them in massive ground battles. The communists actually had little to blow up (except their ports, where the presence of Russian ships made attacks dangerous), and they refused to stand still in large groups as targets for U.S. artillery. The war was confusing and frustrating in Vietnam and, increasingly, at home. In 1966 Johnson blurted out the problem: "Most people wish we weren't there; most people wish we didn't have a war; most people don't want to escalate it, and most people don't want to get out."

VIETNAM IN THE WHITE HOUSE

Yet the president insisted on remaining in the war. Escalating troop strength to 485,000 by 1968, he committed the country to the longest and most tragic of all its wars to that time. He did so, he believed, for some sound reasons based on his understanding of history.

First, he believed that South Vietnam was the test of whether the United States could prevent communism—particularly the Chinese brand, which resulted from peasant revolution—from controlling all of Asia. After a fact-finding journey to Vietnam in 1961, Johnson had reported to President Kennedy that since "there is no alternative to United States leadership in Southeast Asia," Americans must make a "fundamental decision whether we are to attempt to meet the challenge of Communist expansion now in Southeast Asia by a major effort . . . or throw in the towel." He never changed that view. Nor did he ever doubt that the civil war was caused not by Vietnamese nationalism, but by Vietnamese who were part of a worldwide communist movement inspired by China. The Chinese were his primary concern: "Communist China apparently desires the war to continue whatever the cost to their [*sic*] Allies," the president remarked on May 13, 1965. "Their target is not merely South Vietnam. It is Asia."

Second, Johnson believed that he was carrying on an essential American policy, for he was stopping communism in Asia just as President Truman had contained the Russians in Europe. He did not wish to repeat the mistake made at Munich in 1938, when Great Britain and France allowed Hitler to take Czechoslovakia and open the way for World War II. Johnson and Secretary Rusk directly compared Munich and Vietnam, a comparison that would have resulted in an instant "failure" for any college student who tried to make it in a history class. But neither Johnson nor any of his close advisers suggested that economic and political conditions in Asia differed fundamentally from those in Europe or that the United States enjoyed strong allies in Europe (allies tied together by language, culture, and wealth) whereas no such friends existed in Asia. Instead, the president attacked critics who pointed out these vital differences by calling them "special pleaders who counsel retreat in Vietnam."

Third, Johnson claimed that he was defending commitments in Vietnam made by Eisenhower and Kennedy. His relationship with Kennedy's ghost, however, involved both love and hate. He publicly pledged to carry out the late president's policies, but privately Johnson never forgave Kennedy for keeping him in the background between 1961 and 1963. He especially grew bitter as many of Kennedy's former aides quit the foundering Johnson administration to protest against the war they had helped begin. When once reminded of a Kennedy policy, Johnson barked, "The touch football crowd [The Kennedys and their friends had loved to play football.] isn't making decisions around here anymore." But the Texan was equally determined not to give up where Kennedy had taken the stand. He would maintain the hallowed commitment and also show the Kennedyites.

Fourth, the president believed that the commitment was consistent with American interests at home as well as abroad. He emphasized "one overriding rule: . . . that our foreign policy must always be an extension of this nation's domestic policy." This "rule" had an ironic, bitter ring in the 1960s, for the fire, rioting, and violence that ripped American cities between 1965 and 1968 mirrored the much greater destruction inflicted on Vietnam. Johnson was not, of course, referring to *that* mirror, but was pointing to the New Deal tradition, which shaped his political outlook. The New Deal had used government action in an attempt to improve living conditions for poor Americans. As president, Johnson announced a "Great Society" program

CHILD CARE
DR. SPOCK AND THE PEACE MOVEMENT

Dr. Benjamin Spock talks to a mother holding a baby, 1955. *(Pictorial Parade/Getty Images)*

Benjamin Spock was born in 1903. He graduated from Yale University, cast his first vote for Calvin Coolidge in 1924, attended Columbia University's medical school, and in 1929 began practicing pediatrics in New York City. At the time, the most popular child-raising manual was John Watson's *The Psychological Care of Infant and Child* (1928). Watson believed that not every action was a response to a stimulus. The chief danger facing children was that they would be smothered by parental love and, consequently, become dependent rather than self-reliant. Warning against the "dangers lurking in the mother's kiss," Watson asserted that cuddling a child would lead to "invalidism," the inability to cope with the harsh realities of life. Children should be treated as though they were young adults. Watson left a professorship at Johns Hopkins to become vice president of an advertising agency, where he applied his theory to the task of finding the right stimuli to induce consumers to respond to his clients' products.

In the 1930s and 1940s the study of child development was revolutionized by Dr. Arnold Gesell, who attempted to establish scientific norms for each stage of mental and physical growth. But it was Dr. Spock who popularized the new approach. His *Pocket Book of Baby and Child Care* (1946), written while he was serving in the U.S. Naval Reserve, contradicted Watson. Spock advised parents to relax, use their common sense, trust their own judgment, and "be flexible and adjust to the baby's needs and happiness. Don't be afraid to love him and enjoy him. Every baby needs to be smiled at, talked to, played with, fondled—gently and lovingly—just as much as he needs vitamins and calories. That's what will make him a person who loves people and enjoys life." Spock, however, did not advocate total permissiveness. "Parents can't feel right toward their children in the long run unless they can make them behave reasonably, and children can't be happy unless they are behaving reasonably."

By 1963 Spock's book was selling about a million copies a year. Spock's career took him to the Mayo Clinic in Minnesota, the medical school at the University of Pittsburgh, and Western Reserve University in Cleveland. Gradually, he turned to political action. In 1960 he supported John F. Kennedy, and in 1962, when

Dr. Benjamin Spock speaks at an antiwar rally, 1967. *(Time Life Pictures/Getty Images)*

the president resumed nuclear testing in response to Russian tests, Spock joined the peace movement. In 1964 he campaigned for Lyndon Johnson, but then became a sharp critic of the war in Vietnam. In 1967 Spock and 28,000 other people signed "A Call to Resist Illegitimate Authority," which branded the war in Vietnam illegal and unconstitutional, supported those who opposed the draft, and called on Americans to join in "this confrontation with immoral authority." Early in 1968 Spock and four other antiwar activists were indicted for conspiring to counsel violation of the Selective Service Act.

The trial, which took place in Boston, lasted nearly a month. Spock took the witness stand to explain why he opposed the war in Vietnam. "I believed that we were destroying a country that had never intended us any harm. . . . What is the use of physicians like myself trying to help parents to bring up children, healthy and happy, to have them killed in such numbers for a cause that is ignoble?" Four of the defendants, including Spock, were found guilty, fined, and sentenced to two-year prison terms. But in July 1969 a U.S. court of appeals reversed the convictions on the grounds that the judge's instructions to the jury were improper. The charges against Dr. Spock were dropped. He responded, "I shall redouble my efforts to free the hundreds of young men who are now serving time for resisting the war."

Web Links

www.drspock.com/
A website for parents.

www.youtube.com/watch?v=GF20rgdd0RI
A 1982 video in which Dr. Spock talks about baby and child care.

to modernize and complete the New Deal. He believed that in a world made smaller by technology, Americans had to help others if they hoped to improve their own society. He proposed an Asian Development Bank and a vast plan to enrich the Mekong Valley in Southeast Asia, much as the New Deal had built the Tennessee Valley Authority. Only the communists stood in the way. To eliminate them, however, became so costly that by 1966 Johnson was forced to cut back his Great Society at home. "Because of Vietnam," he finally admitted, "we cannot do all that we should, or all that we would like to do" in the United States.

Fifth, economic bonds between the United States and Vietnam developed, but quite differently than the administration had planned. The money pumped into the military buildup brought a rosy glow to the American economy. One economic expert concluded that American defense expenditures supported 95 percent of the employment in aircraft and missile industries, 60 percent in shipbuilding, and 40 percent in radio and communications. Including 3 million in the armed services, nearly 7 million Americans were dependent on the Defense Department budget, and Vietnam expenditures constituted an increasingly larger proportion of that budget. When peace rumors circulated in 1965 and 1966, the New York Stock Exchange was hit with heavy losses as investors rushed to cash in their securities before prices dropped. One broker believed that "a genuine peace offer" would "knock the market out of bed." After all, he observed, the government had scheduled a $60 billion defense budget on the assumption that the war would continue. In Vietnam itself, American oil companies and banks led the way, investing to benefit from the war and particularly from the gigantic reconstruction effort that would follow. The American business community did not turn against the war until after 1967, when the conflict began to weaken rather than accelerate the economy.

Sixth, Johnson believed that he possessed the presidential power required to realize his objectives. By the mid-1960s the presidency dominated the nation in a manner undreamed of by the Founders. The Constitution's framers had feared unchecked power, and with Congress's abdication of responsibility in the Gulf of Tonkin Resolution, the president's power in foreign affairs had few limits. As journalist James Reston observed, "Something important has happened in America since Woodrow Wilson went to his grave" believing that a president's foreign policy could be paralyzed by Congress. Johnson was the first president in the nation's history to enter war with a great army prepared to fight. Indeed, it was too easy to order this remarkable striking force halfway around the world.

Finally, the president had strong public support from 1964 to 1966. In December 1965, as he rapidly escalated the conflict, public opinion polls indicated that 58 percent of the American people believed that increased bombing was the way to peace, and 82 percent agreed that U.S. troops would have to remain in Vietnam until the communists agreed to terms. One-third of those having an opinion thought nuclear weapons should be used if they would shorten the war. (Such an opinion allowed Johnson, who opposed using nuclear weapons, to appear as a moderate as he escalated the conventional war.) Support came from all sectors. Some 477,000 students in 322 colleges gave their written commitment to the president's policies in 1966. The American Federation of Labor's national convention pledged "unstinting support" for all measures necessary "to halt Communist aggression" and bring peace to Vietnam. When antiwar spectators got in a shouting match with union delegates, union leader George Meany ordered that "those kookies" be thrown out of the hall. The president of the 250,000-member U.S. Jaycees—formerly the Junior Chamber of Commerce—announced a program to expose "leftists" and "peace advocates," adding that the Jaycees would work closely with the FBI.

A critical newspaper suggested that the Jaycees might better sponsor discussions of the Bill of Rights.

VIETNAM AT HOME

By 1965 important segments of public opinion were beginning to change, and this change was partly inspired by intellectuals—historians, political scientists, and sociologists—who raised fundamental questions about the administration's war policy. Naturally, the questioning was loudest on college campuses, especially at "teach-ins" that began at the University of Michigan in March 1965 and then had spectacular success at other universities. But the administration refused to take its critics seriously. Although many were specialists in Asian and international affairs, Rusk disparaged their credentials by remarking, "That a man knows everything there is to know about enzymes doesn't mean that he knows very much about Vietnam." Johnson simply recruited advisers from among like-minded scholars. One was Walt Rostow, a vocal advocate of "staying the course." Rostow, the president said, was "going to be *my* goddamned intellectual."

Yet as the war continued to escalate, so, too, did opposition to it. By 1967 and 1968 it began to seem as if American society was on the edge of a breakdown. The president implored U.S. troops to "hang the coonskin on the wall." In Vietnam, when an army chaplain was asked to pray for a victory, he is supposed to have pleaded, "Oh, Lord, give us the wisdom to find the bastards and the strength to pile it on." After U.S. soldiers devastated a village allegedly controlled by the NLF, an American officer blurted out, "It became necessary to destroy the town in order to save it." At home, protesters chanted, "Hey, hey, LBJ, how many kids did you kill today?" as they tried to disrupt draft boards and block troop trains. One person burned himself to death at the door of the Pentagon. Students publicly set fire to their draft cards even after Congress passed a law imposing a $10,000 fine or five years in jail for such an act. Colleges were disrupted as students occupied buildings and sometimes battled police summoned to evict them.

Soon the disenchantment approached the White House itself. Senator J. William Fulbright, Democrat of Arkansas and chair of the powerful Senate Foreign Relations Committee, had long been a close friend of Johnson's, but turned against him after discovering that the president had lied about the Gulf of Tonkin affair and the supposed role of communists in the Santo Domingo intervention. Even more ominous, Secretary of Defense Robert McNamara began doubting. The president depended on him more than on any other man in the government. In August 1967, McNamara publicly called the bombing campaign a failure. Three months later Johnson sent him off to become president of the World Bank, a position that McNamara held with great distinction through the next decade.

The closest American allies also fell away. Western Europeans enjoyed prosperity and new political cohesion from their European Economic Community (EEC). When it accepted Great Britain as a member in 1970, the EEC joined the United States, the Soviet Union, and Japan as the world's great economic powers. The Europeans viewed the Vietnam War as a terrible mistake, for it forced Johnson to neglect vital ties with the Atlantic nations and severely weakened the American economy, the EEC's main overseas customer. Not even the British would help in Vietnam. Frustrated and angered, Secretary of State Dean Rusk exploded to a British journalist, "All we needed [from you in Vietnam] was one regiment. . . . But you

Refugees returning to Hue after American troops and their South Vietnamese allies recaptured the city, 1968. *(Central Press/Getty Images)*

wouldn't. Well, don't expect us to save you again. They can invade Sussex and we wouldn't do a damned thing about it." With few friends at home and even fewer overseas, Johnson observed that he was "in the position of a jackrabbit in a hailstorm, hunkered up and taking it."

THE NEW LEFT AND THE COUNTERCULTURE

The war in Vietnam inspired a broad indictment of American society by New Left radicals and by those who considered themselves part of the "counterculture." The merging of the two streams of criticism—one chiefly political and the other cultural—meant that each tended to reinforce the other. Each also found its natural constituency among the nation's youths, particularly those attending college. By 1968, close to half of all young men and women between the ages of eighteen and twenty-one were college students. The size of the student population, its mobility, leisure time, and sense of generational cohesion all contributed to the currents of political and cultural protest.

New Left groups in the 1960s held disparate views and were often torn by bitter factional discord. Yet most radicals agreed with the findings of sociologist C. Wright Mills, who argued that American society was governed by a "power elite" made up of businessmen, military officials, and political leaders, "an elite whose power probably exceeds that of any small group of men in world history." Moreover, radicals believed that domestic reforms only siphoned off discontent and thereby propped up an immoral social system. Tom Hayden, a founder of Students for a Democratic Society (SDS), argued that many reforms were "illusory or token serving chiefly to sharpen the capacity of the system for manipulation and oppression." Finally, radicals argued that the responsibility for American involvement in Vietnam rested with liberals like John F. Kennedy and Lyndon Johnson. "Think of the men who now engineer that war—those who study the maps, give the commands, push the buttons, and tally the dead," said Carl Oglesby, another SDS leader, "They are not moral monsters. They are all honorable men. They are all liberals."

Members of the New Left, centered in the universities, naturally focused much of their attention close to home. They criticized the impersonal quality of education in "multiversities," the restriction on political activity, the retention of outdated requirements, and the absence of relevant courses. Denouncing the alleged complicity of the universities in the development of weapons systems and counterinsurgency plans, radicals charged that institutions of higher learning were not engaged in an objective search for truth but rather were molding students to fit appropriate slots in the worlds of business, politics, and the military. Since, in their view, existing scholarship was committed to preserving the status quo, radicals called for a new scholarship frankly committed to changing things for the better.

The New Left did not succeed in winning over large segments of the public or even a majority of college students. As their frustration mounted, some radicals turned to violence. The career of SDS illustrated this transformation. At its founding in 1962, SDS asserted, "We find violence to be abhorrent because it requires generally the transformation of the target, be it a human being or a community of people, into a depersonalized object of hate." But by 1969, members of an SDS faction known as the "Weathermen" had concluded that it was necessary to disrupt American society. A few hundred young people descended on Chicago and stormed through the city, smashing windows. While only a few people engaged in such activities or justified them, much of the public came to associate radicalism with social disorder.

The public also associated radicalism with a related development: the rise of a counterculture. The counterculture had a distinctive look—love beads, sandals, jeans, and long hair—and an equally distinctive sound—"acid rock" as performed by Jimi Hendrix, the Grateful Dead, and the Jefferson Airplane. Even more than clothing or musical styles, the counterculture was defined by a freer code of sexual behavior, the use of hallucinogenic drugs, and an interest in mystical experiences. Theodore Roszak, whose *The Making of a Counter Culture* (1968) not only chronicled but also justified the new developments, favored replacing an older "cerebral mode of consciousness" with "non-intellective consciousness." Roszak denied that reality consisted only of what objective consciousness could describe. He favored "a naive openness to experience" and a recognition that the warmly visionary could reveal as much as the coldly rational.

For all the differences between the New Left and the counterculture, each, in its own way, represented a challenge to the supremacy of cherished assumptions. The New Left denied that politics always required a willingness to compromise and that moral issues had no place in politics. Instead, radicals made "non-negotiable demands" and posed issues in stark, right-versus-wrong terms. Similarly, the counterculture rejected technological progress and personal achievement, offering as alternatives a return to the land or simply "dropping out." The two movements therefore intersected in important ways, and both political and cultural radicals believed that what was wrong with America was most clearly revealed by its waging of an immoral war in Vietnam.

THE 1968 ELECTION

Throughout 1967, American military commanders confidently predicted victory in that war, but the bombing had not prevented the North Vietnamese from doubling their army in South Vietnam to 475,000 between 1965 and 1967. The buildup on both sides had changed a civil war within South Vietnam in 1960 to a war between the United States and North Vietnam in 1967. In early February 1968, during the Tet Lunar New Year holiday, the communists launched a devastating attack that resulted in the seizure of vital portions of South Vietnam; they even threatened the supposedly impregnable U.S. Embassy in Saigon. Because large numbers of communists were killed in the offensive, the Johnson administration claimed victory. But the American generals then stunned Johnson by requesting another 206,000 more troops to continue the war.

The president ordered an in-depth analysis of the war by experts in and out of government. They bluntly informed Johnson that he was "being led down the garden path" by the American military in Vietnam. This news was coupled with returns from the first Democratic presidential primary in New Hampshire, where Johnson barely defeated antiwar critic Senator Eugene McCarthy of Minnesota, who received a surprising 42 percent of the vote. In late March, the president dramatically announced on television that he was cutting back bombing to get North Vietnam to the peace table and, in order to concentrate on obtaining peace, he would not run for reelection in 1968.

In April 1968 Martin Luther King's assassination set off riots in many cities, including Washington, DC, where smoke from burning buildings floated over the White House. Two months later, presidential candidate Robert Kennedy, Democratic senator from New York and younger brother of the president assassinated just five years before, was murdered in Los Angeles. A climax to the violence occurred with the Democratic National Convention in Chicago during August, when police and U.S. Army troops used tear gas to control antiwar demonstrators. Johnson could send a half-million troops to Vietnam, but could not attend his own party's nominating convention. Through the smoke and the suffocating sweet smell of tear gas, Vice President Hubert Humphrey was named as the Democratic nominee and Senator Edmund Muskie of Maine as the vice presidential candidate.

Richard Nixon and Spiro Agnew, governor of Maryland, headed the Republican ticket. Nixon had risen from the political dead after his loss to John Kennedy in the 1960 election and then another defeat in the California governor's race in 1962. Over the next six years he traveled widely to cement his ties with grassroots Republicans and was in the forefront of those who attacked Johnson for not ending the Vietnam War on American terms. Nixon, however, emphasized law-and-order themes during the 1968 campaign while de-emphasizing the war by saying only that he had "a plan" for stopping it. Agnew was more direct, blasting Humphrey for being "soft on inflation, soft on communism, and soft on law and order."

The presence on the ballot of Governor George C. Wallace of Alabama did much to shape the outcome of the election. Formerly a Democrat, Wallace broke with the party in 1968 to run on the American Independent ticket. He adopted a hard-line anticommunist foreign policy, even selecting retired army general Curtis E. LeMay (who spoke of bombing North Vietnam "back to the Stone Age") as his running mate. Wallace appealed to normally Democratic voters, especially in the South, who were dismayed by the breakdown of law and order and by antiwar demonstrations but were not prepared to vote Republican. Wallace received 9.9 million votes, or 13.5 percent of the total. So Richard Nixon, with only 43.4 percent of the popular vote, eked out a victory over Hubert Humphrey by a 1 percent margin.

Although the war in Vietnam was not the only issue in 1968, it had nevertheless altered the course of American politics. In 1964 the voters had given Lyndon Johnson a dual mandate: for reform and for peace. Johnson had fulfilled the first part of the mandate, but not the second. By 1968 the war had made the return of the Republicans possible, and even the reforms so important to Johnson were placed in jeopardy.

CHAPTER FIFTEEN

1969–1975

The Imperial Presidency and Watergate

April 6, 1973: Two amputees take part in a parade through Times Square in New York City to celebrate the end of fighting by U.S. troops in the Vietnam War. *(Peter Keegan/Keystone/Getty Images)*

Richard Nixon narrowly won the 1968 election by promising to restore law and order and to end a frustrating, unpopular war. He did neither, but nevertheless managed to attract broad new political support by adopting policies he had spent a lifetime denouncing and by exploiting ugly social divisions. In the war, he reduced American casualties through "Vietnamization." By 1972 these tactics had been so successful that Nixon gained reelection by an overwhelming margin. His victory promised still further enlargement of an already bloated executive authority; indeed, a cartoon appeared with the purple-robed figure of "King Richard." But even more swiftly than Nixon had donned the robes of the imperial presidency, they were stripped from his shoulders. The Watergate scandal erupted, leading not only to Nixon's own downfall but also to a widespread crisis of confidence in government. Polls showed that more people than ever before believed "there is something deeply wrong with America."

THE NIXON FOREIGN POLICIES

The new president appointed Henry Kissinger, a professor of international relations at Harvard, as his national security adviser. The two men privately formulated their own foreign policy, neglecting Congress and the State Department, and in many instances not even bothering to keep these two bodies informed. Kissinger believed such secrecy necessary in order to carry out plans quickly and effectively. Nixon agreed, for he cared relatively little about domestic affairs (once remarking that the nation did not need a president to handle internal matters), but deeply involved himself in foreign policies. He also harbored a strong desire to have a private, shielded presidency. Before some of his most momentous decisions, Nixon would isolate himself for long periods, talking with no one.

The president slowly changed the emphases of American foreign policy. He reduced the commitment in Vietnam (and showed little interest in newly emerging areas, such as Latin America and Africa), while opening new relationships with Russia and China. Nixon thus responded to the new post-1956 world by de-emphasizing the Kennedy-Johnson policies in the volatile southern half of the globe and working instead for a settlement with the two giant communist powers. Nixon understood that the world contained not two great powers but more important in his words, "five economic superpowers"—the United States, Russia, Japan, China, and the European Economic Community. Because the first two balanced each other militarily, these five powers "will determine the economic future, and because economic power will be the key to other kinds of power," they will determine "the future of the world in other ways in the last third of this century." Russia and China, moreover, were enemies. As Kissinger noted, "The deepest international conflict in the world today is not between us and the Soviet Union but between the Soviet Union and Communist China."

All this was not new. It had been apparent since 1960, but Nixon was the first president to act upon it. He understood that this five-power world opened a marvelous opportunity for the United States to play the other four powers against one another. Nixon could use new American technology (such as computers) and agricultural products, which both communist nations badly needed, to strengthen political ties and gain access for American business executives to the vast Chinese and Russian markets. Finally, if such ties were made, he hoped the United States could trade its products for Russian and Chinese help in stopping the Vietnam War so that American troops could be withdrawn on honorable terms. Nixon's plans were imaginative and sweeping.

He understood, above all, that the United States had overreached itself during the 1960s with commitments that had already led to violence, economic inflation, and the political demise of President Lyndon Johnson. Thus the new president began by announcing a "Nixon Doctrine" in 1969 that pledged continued economic aid to allies in Asia and elsewhere, but added that these allies should no longer count on the presence of American troops. He also announced that he would end the draft within two years. American troop strength would be reduced systematically in Vietnam while the South Vietnamese received more military equipment so that they could fight their own wars. This policy became known as "Vietnamization."

THE NIXON FAILURES: 1970–1971

Vietnamization, however, was failing by early 1970. As American troops left, the South Vietnamese proved incapable of driving out communist forces. Using bases in neighboring Cambodia, a supposedly neutral state, the North Vietnamese and the communist National Liberation Front of South Vietnam threatened to bring down the Saigon government. Nixon responded with heavy bombing of the Cambodian bases, but kept the raids secret from everyone except a few top officials in Washington and, of course, the Cambodians and Vietnamese. On April 30, 1970, after a conservative, pro-U.S. government suddenly came to power in Cambodia, the president announced that American and South Vietnamese troops were temporarily invading Cambodia to destroy the communist bases. Having promised to end the war, Nixon was now actually expanding it into neighboring areas. Worse, the American troops did not succeed in destroying the bases, for after they retreated, the communists simply moved back in and then threatened to overthrow the Cambodian government itself.

The effect on the American people was electric. College campuses, including many that had remained quiet during the 1960s, erupted into antiwar violence. The nation was shaken when four students were shot to death by Ohio National Guard forces during an antiwar demonstration at Kent State University. Polls showed that half the American people disbelieved Nixon's announcement that the invasion would shorten the war. A lack of confidence in the new president's foreign policy seemed to be developing rapidly. Henry Kissinger privately shuddered at the possible consequences, for he believed that the antiwar demonstrations were not just against Vietnam policies, but

> against authority of any kind, not just the authority of this President, but also the authority of any President. . . . If confidence in him and in all institutions is systematically destroyed, we will turn into a group that has nothing left but a physical test of strength and the only outcome of this is Caesarism.
>
> The very people who shout "Power to the People" are not going to be the people who will take over this country if it turns into a test of strength. Upper middle-class college kids will not take this country over. Some more primitive and elemental forces will do that.

But demonstrations continued, and an angry Senate finally repealed the Gulf of Tonkin Resolution (see page 319). The president, however, claimed that he could continue to fight in Southeast Asia, regardless of what Congress did, in order to protect American troops already in Vietnam.

Dr. Robert Goddard with an early space rocket. *(National Aeronautics and Space Administration)*

The president further widened the war in February 1971 by invading communist bases in Laos. This time, however, South Vietnamese rather than American troops went in; the foray was to be a test of Vietnamization. The South Vietnamese troops flunked the test. Meeting tough resistance, they scattered and ran. By mid-1971 the communists controlled more of Laos than ever before.

The failure of Vietnamization was one of two early crises to confront Nixon. The other was a baffling economy—baffling in that it was by far the world's greatest. In 1970 it had passed the trillion-dollar level in annual gross national product (that is, the total product of all goods and services produced in the nation). But it also suffered from inflation that made American goods more expensive and hence less competitive on the international market. American products lost ground to such cheaply produced Japanese and German products as the Datsun and Volkswagen automobiles.

In 1971, for the first time since 1893, the United States suffered an overall deficit trade balance. It paid out more money to satisfy its international debts ($45.5 billion) than it received from exports and services abroad ($42.8 billion). The world's greatest economy was sick. In August 1971 President Nixon attempted to supply a remedy by devaluing the dollar, that is, reducing each dollar's worth in gold, which is the leading international exchange standard. This act cheapened the dollar and thus made American goods cheaper and easier to purchase internationally. By early 1973 the inflation and deficits continued, so the president again devalued the dollar. American exports picked up, but inflation was not halted.

RACING TO THE MOON

Amid the gloom caused by Vietnam and the economy, the human race realized an age-old dream by sending astronauts safely to the moon and back in July 1969. That venture, the "great leap for mankind" that Neil Armstrong announced when he made the first human imprint on the moon's surface, will doubtless be remembered longer, and be of greater historical importance, than the crises that vexed the earthbound that year.

In a strict sense, space flight developed during the American Century but was the child of both Russian and American scientific breakthroughs. In 1903 a Russian, K.E. Tsiolkovsky, began making basic discoveries (including the idea for a multistage rocket, in which one stage propelled the vehicle and was then discarded as another stage took over to boost the rocket). Between 1919 and 1943, a scientist at Clark University in Massachusetts, R.H. Goddard, improved on Tsiolkovsky's findings and made many of his own, especially in fuels. Goddard worked virtually alone and received little long-term support. Not even the U.S. military supported him during the 1930s because his small rockets seemed unable to carry payloads (such as explosives) of more than several pounds. Goddard, quietly experimenting at Clark or in the New Mexico desert, nevertheless developed automatic steering systems, self-cooling combustion chambers, and other discoveries that led to over 200 patents in his name.

In the 1930s and 1940s the lone figure making basic findings on barebones budgets suddenly gave way to a mammoth wartime rocket project in Germany that employed 20,000 people. By 1944 that program produced V-2 rockets that killed thousands in Great Britain. It also produced scientists who were secretly spirited out of Germany by the victors to shape the American and Russian space programs. By 1957 the Soviets had moved ahead by launching Sputnik, the first artificial satellite to spin into space. They also sent the first human in a rocket beyond the earth's atmosphere. The Cold War now replaced Goddard's personal curiosity as the driving force in the exploration of space. In 1961 the United States began to catch up when Alan Shepard became the first American to travel into space. The following year John Glenn became a national hero by becoming the first American to orbit the earth. President John Kennedy committed the nation to be the first to land on the moon. The $24 billion Apollo project climaxed in 1969 when Armstrong planted the Stars and Stripes on the lunar surface, an event whose miraculousness was matched by the magic of the cameras that televised the event back to earth. The Soviets meanwhile suffered fatal accidents in 1967 and 1971, and then gave up their race to the moon to concentrate on learning how to live in space for long periods. Tsiolkovsky and Goddard had anticipated traveling into the new frontier of space, but not the incredible cost and deadly military competition that now resulted from their pioneering research.

President Richard Nixon *(second from right)* conferring with Chairman Mao Zedong *(center)* as Zhou Enlai *(left)*, Henry Kissinger *(right)*, and an interpreter look on during a historic meeting on February 21, 1972. *(Time Life Pictures/National Archives/Getty Images)*

THE NIXON SUCCESSES: 1971–1972

A year before the 1972 presidential election, Nixon's misfortunes in Vietnam and with the economy hurt his chances for reelection. Any president, however, can use his control of foreign policy to make dramatic headlines and some political gains if he has made adequate preparation and has a sense of timing. No one knew this better than Nixon.

In August 1971 he announced that he would become the first president to travel to China. Chairman Mao Zedong in Beijing had happily cooperated, for he hoped to use his new friendship with the United States as a weapon against his major enemy, Russia, which was massing troops along the Sino-Russian border. In an instant, twenty-two years of Sino-American enmity began to dissolve. Americans who had vocally denounced Red China for years could say little, for Richard Nixon had long been among the most vocal of those critics. Nor was there an outcry when, over U.S. objections, the People's Republic of China replaced Chiang Kai-shek's Taiwan government as the representative of China in the United Nations. In February 1972 Nixon dominated the television screens as he exchanged toasts with Chinese leaders. Americans overwhelmingly applauded his effort to ease tensions.

The president then parlayed the journey into an even greater gain. By pitting the two enemies, Russia and China, against each other for American favors and by sending badly needed American wheat to both, Nixon freed his hand to deal with North Vietnam without fear that the two great communist powers might intervene. Since 1969 he had searched for an agreement with the North Vietnamese and hoped to reach one before the 1972 election, but none had been concluded. In April 1972 the North Vietnamese launched an offensive against the weakened American and South Vietnamese forces. Nixon responded with the heaviest bombing of the war, the bombing of Hanoi, North Vietnam's capital, and then mined North Vietnamese harbors. The mining, which endangered Russian ships using the harbors, was such a threatening move that Lyndon Johnson had flatly refused to do it. But now the Russians and Chinese made no active response.

Indeed, as the mines were being sown, the Russians welcomed Nixon in Moscow as the first American president to make the journey to the Soviet Union. In the Strategic Arms Limitation Talks (SALT I), U.S. and Soviet leaders signed an important pact limiting the number of defensive missiles each nation could possess. They also agreed to a five-year freeze on testing and deploying intercontinental missiles. Putting multiple warheads (multiple independent reentry vehicles, or MIRVs) on the missiles, however, was not prohibited. Both nations promised that SALT I was only the first of several treaties that would reduce the number of nuclear weapons. The treaties would come none too soon, for the nuclear stockpile in the world amounted to the equivalent of fifteen tons of TNT for every man, woman, and child on earth, and the stockpile was growing steadily.

In early 1972 a majority of Americans had disliked Nixon's Vietnam policies. After he mined and bombed North Vietnam, however, and then flew to China and Russia, the nation approved his policies by a ratio of 2 to 1. The president had used foreign policy much as a film director uses music to build emotions to a pitch during a movie. "A lot of things are coming together at a point," said Nixon's right-hand man John Ehrlichman with a smile just before the 1972 election. "And it is a point, frankly, which we selected as a target time as a matter of enlightened self-interest."

RICHARD NIXON AND THE NEW MAJORITY

When he took office, Richard Nixon recognized that the 1968 election left him in a precarious political position. His 43.4 percent of the vote was the smallest winning share since 1912. For the first time since Zachary Taylor's election in 1848, a first-term president failed to carry a majority in either house of Congress. The Democrats retained an edge of 58 to 42 in the Senate and 243 to 192 in the House. To ensure his reelection, Nixon, without alienating the Republican faithful, had to do several things: reassure blue-collar workers that Republicans would not dismantle the welfare state or create economic hardship; exploit social issues that could appeal to ethnic voters; and demonstrate to whites in the South and in the suburbs that he opposed forced integration.

In the realm of economics, the search for a new majority required considerable ideological flexibility. Nixon, an economic conservative who had always advocated a balanced budget, soon approached the problem of unemployment as if he were a liberal Democrat. Unemployment stood at 3.5 percent in December 1969, but it rose sharply to 6.2 percent in the next year. That represented the highest level of joblessness in a decade. To deal with it, the president resorted to planned budget deficits, which, he hoped, would create new jobs by pumping money into the economy. Early in 1971 he presented a "full-employment budget," one that would be balanced if the economy were operating at full tilt but that under existing circumstances would produce a $23 billion deficit. In January Nixon asserted, "I am now a Keynesian in economics." This, one observer noted, was "a little like a Christian crusader saying, 'All things considered, I think Mohammed was right.'"

Similarly, Nixon moved to an acceptance of economic controls to curb inflation. In 1969, he still opposed controls, but by 1971, as the rate of inflation rose to 5 percent, the nation experienced a trade deficit, and the stock market tumbled, Nixon reversed field. In August he imposed a ninety-day freeze on wages, prices, and rents. The president later experimented with mandatory wage and price controls but then abandoned them in favor of voluntary compliance. Nixon always approached controls hesitantly, emphasizing the need for cooperation from business and labor. But the controls, however cautious, restrained inflation during 1972 and temporarily defused it as a political issue.

Nixon campaigned in 1968 against the Great Society's "welfare mess." Yet his own welfare proposals looked toward reform of the system. The Family Assistance Plan, which he proposed in 1969, would have provided a minimum income of $1,600 a year for a family of four, which, together with food stamps, would have meant an income of $2,460. This was more than welfare systems provided in twenty states. The plan also offered income supplements for the working poor in order to reduce welfare rolls by making it more profitable to hold a job than to receive public assistance. To qualify, however, heads of households (except for the infirm and mothers with small children) would have to register for job training and accept "suitable jobs." This provision, Nixon said, would restore the incentive to work and identify welfare chiselers. The House enacted a version of the measure, but it died in the Senate Finance Committee. In 1970, however, the administration succeeded in federalizing the food-stamp program. National criteria for eligibility were established, based on the cost of a nutritionally adequate diet, and benefits were adjusted automatically to take account of inflation.

THE "SOCIAL ISSUE" AND THE SUPREME COURT

Nixon's economic policies were not entirely successful in checking inflation or reducing unemployment, but they preserved a level of prosperity through 1972 that enabled him to attract blue-collar support. Beyond this, however, the administration brilliantly exploited the "social issue"—fears that stemmed from a rising crime rate, the widespread use of drugs, increasingly permissive attitudes toward sex, and growing disdain for patriotic values. The president played on these fears, which cut across usual party lines, in everything from wearing an American flag in his lapel to denouncing the "Spock-marked" generation. Vice President Spiro Agnew did the same in his attack on student protesters (an "impudent corps of snobs") and their "effete . . . hand-wringing, sniveling" apologists.

Three issues particularly aided Nixon among working-class Catholics. The president firmly endorsed federal aid to parochial schools. He also entered an explosive controversy over liberalization of the New York State abortion law, which the Catholic Church bitterly opposed. He told Terence Cardinal Cooke in May 1972, "I would personally like to associate myself with the convictions you deeply feel and eloquently express." In 1970 the Commission on Obscenity and Pornography, all but one of whose members had been appointed by Lyndon Johnson, recommended that all laws "prohibiting the sale, exhibition, or distribution of sexual materials to consenting adults should be repealed." The president repudiated the commission, and Agnew thundered, "As long as Richard Nixon is President, Main Street is not going to turn into Smut Alley."

The social issue also encompassed racial fears. The president, who had received no more than 5 percent of the black vote in 1968, had a mixed civil rights record. The administration supported the "Philadelphia plan" to eliminate discrimination on federal construction projects by establishing a quota system under which trade unions had to accept a certain number of black youths as apprentices and guarantee them union membership at the end of a training period. The plan was upheld in the courts; but implementing school desegregation was a different story. The Justice Department favored the postponement of desegregation plans in communities where strong local opposition existed. In October 1969, however, the Supreme Court upset the administration's strategy. In *Alexander v. Holmes County Board of Education* the Court declared unanimously that "deliberate speed" no longer sufficed; school desegregation must begin "at once."

Given existing patterns of residential segregation, this decision merely raised a more difficult question: Should children be bused to schools far from their homes to achieve racial balance in the schools? There was no more highly charged issue in the early 1970s. Public opinion polls indicated that 78 percent of the people opposed the idea of busing. In some places, attempts to introduce such plans led to violence, disorder, and school boycotts. Maintenance of the "neighborhood school" became a central concern, particularly in the South, in the suburbs, and in ethnic enclaves in large cities. Many people had moved to the suburbs to be in better school districts. Now they faced the prospect of sending their children back into the inner cities every morning. Yet busing plans met with the approval of the Supreme Court in April 1971. In *Swann v. Charlotte-Mecklenburg Board of Education* the justices found that busing, even if awkward or inconvenient, was an acceptable means of integrating "schools that are substantially disproportionate in their racial composition."

The issue was tailor-made for a president intent on currying favor with southern whites, suburbanites, and uneasy ethnic groups. Nixon at the same time reflected the nation's mood and contributed to its intransigence. In March 1970 he called for an "open society" that "does not have to be homogeneous, or even fully integrated. There is room in it for communities. . . . It is natural and right that we have Italian or Negro or Norwegian neighborhoods." He disagreed with those who said, "The only way to bring about social justice is to integrate all schools now, everywhere, no matter what the cost in the disruption of education." The president reiterated his stand during the next two years and even urged Congress to impose a moratorium on the issuance of busing orders by federal courts.

Nixon also sought to use Supreme Court appointments as part of a broader political strategy. Having pledged in 1968 to appoint strict constructionists as a way of reversing the Court's activism, Nixon had the unusual opportunity of choosing four members in his first term. Late in 1969 he nominated Clement Haynsworth of South Carolina. Opposition to Haynsworth quickly developed when the Senate discovered that he had once acted as a judge in a case that could possibly have served his own interests. The Senate rejected the nomination by a vote of 55 to 45, with seventeen Republicans deserting the president. Nixon next submitted the name of G. Harrold Carswell of Florida. A new storm arose, primarily because an extraordinarily high number of Carswell's decisions had been reversed by higher courts. He appeared to lack any intellectual distinction, as even a supporter, Senator Roman Hruska of Nebraska, conceded: "Even if he were mediocre, there are lots of mediocre judges and people and lawyers. They are entitled to a little representation, aren't they? . . . We can't have all Brandeises and Frankfurters and Cardozos and stuff like that there." The legal profession, regarding the appointment as an insult, lobbied against it, and in April 1970 the Senate turned it down. Seeking to squeeze the last ounce of political advantage from the situation, Nixon said that Carswell's rejection was an act of "regional discrimination" against the South.

Ultimately Nixon appointed Harry Blackmun of Minnesota to the vacancy. The three other appointees were Lewis F. Powell, William Rehnquist, and Chief Justice Warren E. Burger. In many respects the Court veered in a more conservative direction. It ruled more frequently in behalf of the prosecution in criminal trials, declaring that a defendant who disrupted a trial by disorderly behavior could, after a warning, be removed from the courtroom or even bound and gagged. It also held that a confession extracted by unconstitutional means did not

Supreme Court Justice Harry A. Blackmun. *(Library of Congress)*

automatically invalidate a conviction if other evidence of guilt existed. The Court also made it easier for prosecutors to establish the admissibility of contested confessions. In *Miller v. California* (1973) the Court widened the grounds for ruling books and films obscene and expanded communities' power to ban offensive material. In 1973 the Court found that schools could be financed by property taxes even though disparities resulted, for, as Justice Powell said, "at least where wealth is involved, the equal protection clause does not require absolute equality or precisely equal advantages."

Yet the Court by no means pursued a course entirely to the president's liking. In cases involving school desegregation and busing, even some of Nixon's appointees disappointed him. In *Furman v. Georgia* (1972) the Court held, by a vote of 5 to 4, that the death penalty as then prescribed was imposed unfairly. It fell most heavily on the poor and violated the constitutional injunction against cruel and unusual punishment. Many states then attempted to make the death penalty mandatory for certain offenses, but the Court had greatly aided opponents of capital punishment. In 1970, in *Welsh v. United States,* the Court ruled that a man, whose opposition to military service was rooted in a deeply held moral or ethical conviction, rather than in religious belief, could qualify for conscientious objector status. Finally, the Court upheld civil liberties in two landmark decisions. In 1971 it ruled that the government could not prevent the publication of the "Pentagon Papers," a secret, multivolume collection of key U.S. government documents on the war that covered the years 1945 to 1968. On June 19, 1972, the Court rejected the attorney general's claim that the government had the right to use wiretapping against alleged subversives or domestic radicals without first obtaining a court order. Justice Powell said, "The price of lawful public dissent must not be a dread of subjection to an unchecked surveillance power." The decision, ironically, was handed down two days after burglars working for the president's reelection were arrested as they tried to place wiretaps in Democratic national headquarters at Washington's Watergate Apartments.

THE IMPACT OF THE WOMEN'S MOVEMENT

On August 26, 1970, thousands of women across the nation celebrated the fiftieth anniversary of the ratification of woman suffrage with parades, demonstrations, and a triumphal march down New York's Fifth Avenue. The celebration marked a peak in feminist mobilization. Every national television network and major publication at the start of the 1970s devoted time and space to the women's movement. The media focused on spokespersons such as Gloria Steinem, who had just founded *Ms.* magazine; the National Organization for Women's Betty Friedan; and New York representative Bella Abzug, who won three terms in Congress starting in 1971. A galaxy of women's liberationists spoke out: "What goes largely unexamined in our social order . . . is the birthright priority whereby males rule females," charged Kate Millett in *Sexual Politics* (1969). "Every avenue of power . . . is entirely in male hands."

But even the most extreme of liberationist visions served a political purpose: they made demands for simple equity seem more acceptable by comparison. Or, as a suffragist once told Charlotte Perkins Gilman early in the century, "What you ask [social and economic equality] is so much worse than what we ask, that they will grant our demands in order to escape yours." Rapid acceptance of more moderate proposals constituted the feminist "revolution" of the early 1970s.

The symbol of feminist success was congressional adoption of the equal rights amendment (ERA), which stated, "equality of rights under the law shall not be abridged by the United States or by any state on account of sex." The amendment prohibited sex discrimination by the government, its agencies and officers, and all institutions closely tied to the government, such as federal contractors. An ERA had been favorably reported by the Senate Judiciary Committee since 1964, but it had then been opposed by the labor movement, the Women's Bureau, and major women's organizations, such as the League of Women Voters, all of which viewed it as a threat to protective laws. By 1970, federal courts were invalidating such laws as discriminatory to women, and the ERA's longtime foes changed their minds. The House approved the amendment in 1971 and by the Senate in 1972, and it was ratified by twenty-eight states within a year. Feminists now had every hope that it would be ratified by the required thirty-eight states within seven years.

Not only did Congress endorse the ERA by wide margins, but between 1971 and 1974 enacted an unparalleled number of laws promoting sex equity. (The only precedent was the Equal Pay Act of 1963, enacted before the resurgence of feminism.) In the early 1970s Con-

Members of the National Women's Political Caucus: *(seated from left)* Gloria Steinem, Rep. Shirley Chisholm, and Betty Friedan; *(standing)* Rep. Bella Abzug. *(Charles Gorry/AP Photos)*

gress barred sex discrimination in medical training programs, enabled middle-class families to claim tax deductions for child care if both spouses worked, and extended the benefits of married women in federal service jobs. It prohibited creditors from discriminating on the basis of sex, extended the Equal Pay Act by the Educational Amendments Act, and passed the Women's Educational Equity Act, which supported training and counseling for women. The only major setback came in 1972, when President Nixon vetoed the Comprehensive Child Development bill, which would have provided a national network of day care centers—and also would have required far more federal funding than any other equity measure. The president denounced the bill's "family-weakening implications."

A series of executive orders and labor department directives complemented congressional efforts. In some cases, civil rights measures were extended to include women. In 1967, for instance, President Johnson had extended an executive order prohibiting racial discrimination by federal contractors to prevent sex discrimination as well. The order had far-flung ramifications. By 1970, the Labor Department issued affirmative action guidelines to all federal contractors (such as universities) to ensure nondiscriminatory hiring. The same year, after a class-action suit by the Women's Equity Action League, colleges and universities had to turn personnel files over to the government so that the schools' efforts at nondiscrimination could be validated. Feminist demands for equal opportunity rapidly had a widespread impact.

Federal court decisions, meanwhile, imposed equity in other ways. Lower courts voided protective laws, challenged sex labeling of jobs (such as "stewardess"), and reaffirmed the principle of equal pay for equal work. In 1972, a sex discrimination suit against American Telephone and Telegraph was settled out of court with a multi-million-dollar payment to women workers (such as operators who had been kept out of better-paying jobs as linemen). The settlement suggested that the average working woman, usually underrepresented in feminist organizations, might have much to gain from the women's movement.

The Supreme Court did its part as well. In the early 1970s, the Court invalidated a state law giving preference to men as executors of wills, banned references to sex in want ads, and equalized benefits for members of the armed services. The Supreme Court's major decision was on abortion. State abortion laws, in effect since the late nineteenth century, had barred abortion in all cases except to preserve a pregnant woman's life. In the 1960s a movement grew to liberalize abortion laws by permitting abortion in other cases, such as rape and incest. By 1972, sixteen states had liberalized their laws. But feminists demanded repeal of all legal limits on abortion. In 1973, in *Roe v. Wade,* the Supreme Court declared state abortion laws unconstitutional on the grounds that they invaded the right of privacy. As legal abortion became available, maternal deaths from illegal abortions dwindled. The Supreme Court's decision had a more far-reaching effect than any other item on the feminist agenda.

While Congress, the courts, and the executive branch transformed feminist demands into federal policy, the women's movement achieved other changes. Public opinion polls reported shifts in attitudes among women and men, from disapproval of the movement to increase women's rights in the late 1960s to support in the early 1970s. Educational changes multiplied. Publishers revised textbooks to eliminate sexual stereotypes; school boards revised curricula so boys and girls would not be segregated in shop and cooking classes; women's studies programs multiplied, reaching 500 colleges by 1974; and all-male colleges rushed to welcome women (though often for financial, not feminist, reasons). Meanwhile, a vocational revolution began as all-male or mostly male job classifications broke down. Women became real estate agents, insurance adjusters, bus drivers, and bartenders; their numbers rose as lawyers, judges, physicians, engineers, executives, ministers, and television anchorpersons. Most significantly, they moved into the labor force at unprecedented rates. The new entrants were mainly married women, especially those with young children at home.

The widespread impact of the women's movement in the early 1970s sparked a bitter debate. A conservative backlash against women's liberation erupted. Working-class women and black women sometimes thought that feminist ideology reflected white middle-class biases. A grassroots middle-class aversion was visible as well, along with concern about whether women were acting in their own interest. "Most just trade the drudgery of housewifery for the drudgery of an office job," one woman wrote to *Time* in 1970. "Already women have more legal freedom than they know what to do with," wrote another. By the end of the 1970s opponents of abortion rights and the ERA would make their voices heard in public debates.

NATIVE AMERICANS AND WOUNDED KNEE II

Of all American minorities, Native Americans suffered most during the 1960s and 1970s. Their population grew at four times the national rate, reaching 792,000 in 1970, but life expectancy was only forty-six years (compared with the national average of sixty-nine). Infant mortality rates were the nation's highest, and the suicide rate was double the country's average. Reservations lacked industry and good schools. Unemployment rates above 50 percent were not uncommon. A startling 50 percent of Native Americans on reservations, and even 20 percent of those in cities, lived below the poverty level in the late 1970s.

Indian leaders tried to deal with this tragedy, but they were divided between young and old, between those living in urban areas and on reservations, and between tribes. The Kennedy, Johnson, and Nixon administrations attempted to return policy to Indian officials. However, this did little to dampen the anger of the many Native Americans who joined militant youth groups (patterned on the black organizations of the 1960s) and, in 1968, formed the urban-based American Indian Movement (AIM). Until 1973, few whites seemed to care.

Then came the second episode of Wounded Knee (for the first, see Chapter One). Wounded Knee is a town in the Oglala Sioux Reservation of South Dakota. The reservation, twice the size of Delaware, contained 3 million acres of which one-third was owned by whites, one-third leased by the Sioux to white cattlemen, and one-third used by the Sioux themselves. Seventy percent of the teachers on the reservation were white. Pine Ridge, the capital, was "a motley collection of shacks and houses of varying degrees of decrepitude," according to one reporter, with "a fine, tan, gritty dust . . . coating everything and getting into mouths and lungs, contributing to the hacking cough that people seem to develop rapidly here."

The reservation contained some of the nation's worst poverty: Half the families were on welfare and a moccasin factory served as the main industry. Most of the employed were mixbloods (Native Americans having both Native American and white ancestry), who controlled the reservation and worked in patronage jobs handed out by Washington officials. Full-blooded Native Americans lived in rural shacks where they tried to save themselves and their culture. The school dropout rate was 81 percent. Alcoholism was rampant among adult males. Considerable tension divided whites and Native Americans. When Raymond Yellow Thunder visited nearby Gordon, Nebraska, in 1972, he was beaten and murdered. Two white attackers were released without bail and charged only with second-degree manslaughter. Not wanting to cause further problems with the whites, neither Bureau of Indian Affairs officials nor the Sioux mixbloods controlling the reservation pushed for an investigation of the murder.

But, led by women, an angry group of Sioux repudiated their leaders, whom they considered corrupt and the puppets of white government officials, and asked for help from AIM. In February 1973 some 200 AIM members and their supporters occupied Wounded Knee. They demanded that the government honor 371 treaties it had broken and insisted that the reservation's regime be radically changed. U.S. forces encircled the area, partly to keep the two Native American factions from attacking each other, but also to block the entry of food into the town. The siege lasted seventy-one days. When AIM tried to move in reinforcements, government gunfire killed one Native American and wounded another. AIM and the Washington officials finally agreed to lift the siege and reexamine treaty obligation. The government, however, did little except bring suit against AIM leaders and sympathizers.

"Wounded Knee II" symbolized the tragedy of the Native American. Indeed, a white backlash erupted in the late 1970s. The backlash was notable in Congress, which had obtained almost dictatorial power over Native American affairs. White congressmen, many from Western states, proposed bills based on a ruthless policy of "termination"—that is, ending federal protection, revoking treaties, and opening Native American lands to the highest bidders. One embittered Native American spokesperson believed that "it all has to do with natural resources," for Congress wanted to "open up Indian lands to energy development interests, ranchers, and commercial fishermen." Tragically, little changed at Wounded Knee itself. One frustrated government official cried, "Damn it, there are no winners." But there were. Elsewhere new, younger Indian leaders, inspired by the confrontation, became more active.

Leaders of the American Indian Movement (AIM) *(left to right)* Dennis Banks, Russell Means, and an unidentified third man give a press conference to demand increased federal financial aid for the town of Wounded Knee, South Dakota, March 16, 1973. *(Agence France Presse/Getty Images)*

They successfully exerted pressure to obtain a new self-governing act that empowered Native Americans themselves. They also instituted lawsuits to obtain economic rights, not least the rights in some states to build enormously profitable gambling casinos. Wounded Knee II, like its 1890 predecessor, marked a turning point in Native American–white relations.

THE ELECTION OF 1972

By 1972 President Nixon had taken great strides toward constructing what he called a "new majority." The Democrats tried to counter by nominating George McGovern of South Dakota for president. After the upheaval at the 1968 Chicago convention, the Democrats had thoroughly revised their delegate selection procedures. In an attempt to open the party to groups that had been excluded, those procedures were democratized and rules were adopted requiring that delegations "reasonably" reflect the proportion of women, blacks, and other minorities in the population. The result was a convention unlike any seen before. Those groups with ample time, energy, and ideological fervor—such as upper-middle-class activists in the antiwar, women's liberation, and civil rights movements—enjoyed greater representation than ever before. By contrast, the traditional power brokers—trade-union leaders, big-city mayors, and southern bosses—enjoyed less.

McGovern's difficulties were compounded when it was learned that his running mate, Thomas Eagleton of Missouri, had some history of mental illness. After days of hesitation, which apparently convinced some voters that he lacked decisiveness, McGovern replaced Eagleton with Sargent Shriver, who had formerly headed the war on poverty. But McGovern's chief problem was that the Republicans succeeded in centering attention on the "social issue" and branding him a radical who favored "the far-out goals of the far left." The code words in 1972 were amnesty, acid, and abortion, and it made little difference that McGovern, a much-decorated bomber pilot in World War II, favored only the first, and then only with reservations. Condemning American involvement in the Vietnam War as immoral, he urged amnesty when the war ended for those who had fled the country to avoid the draft. McGovern did not favor legalized abortion or the use of drugs, but many Americans believed that he did or that, in any event, his supporters did. Nixon's margin of victory was decisive: 47 million votes (to McGovern's 29 million), 61.3 percent of the total vote, and a 520-to-17 electoral college majority. One Democratic campaign worker sighed, "I felt like the recreation director on the *Titanic.*"

WATERGATE AND THE PRESIDENCY

Since the era of Franklin Roosevelt, Americans had looked to the president for leadership in solving the nation's social and economic problems, in part because an increasingly complex society seemed to require centralized direction. More important, presidential authority was pumped up by thirty years of international crises. Throughout the Cold War, presidents exercised powers once reserved for use in full-scale war, for many citizens believed the executive needed a free hand to respond quickly and energetically to foreign threats. Richard Nixon carried the strong presidency to its furthest point in peacetime. Americans were belatedly learning a lesson taught more than 140 years earlier by Alexis de Tocqueville, a perceptive French visitor, in *Democracy in America*:

> No protracted war can fail to endanger the freedom of a democratic country. . . . War does not always give over democratic communities to military government, but it must invariably and immeasurably increase the powers of civil government; it must almost compulsorily concentrate the direction of all men and the management of all things in the hands of the administration. If it leads not to despotism by sudden violence, it prepares men for it more gently by their habits. All those who seek to destroy the liberties of a democratic nation ought to know that war is the surest and shortest means to accomplish it.

Tocqueville recognized that foreign and domestic policies intertwine and shape each other.

The president and the nation learned this truth the hard way. In June 1972 five men connected to the Committee to Re-elect the President were caught trying to burglarize Democratic Party headquarters in Washington's Watergate Apartments. Dismissing the break-in as a "bizarre incident," the president insisted that the White House was not involved. But in

FOOTBALL AND POLITICS

The Four Horsemen of Notre Dame: the famous backfield of 1924. *(Notre Dame/Getty Images)* or *(Hulton Archive/Getty Images)*

The game began in eleventh-century England, when players representing towns pushed animal skulls, and later cow bladders, between villages that stood for "goals." King Henry II outlawed the sport in the twelfth century because its popularity interfered with archery practice needed to defend the kingdom. Reborn 400 years later on playing fields, it became the British sport of rugby and then caught on in the United States. The first college football game was won by Rutgers' six goals to Princeton's four in 1869.

Within twenty years coaches were selecting the best players on "All America" lists. Through the mid-1890s only one non-British name appeared on such lists, but Irish, Jewish, and finally Polish and Hungarian players were honored after 1900 as the new immigration from Europe created an increasingly pluralistic society. The ethnic divisions led to rules that all could understand. Thus, instead of having wild scrambles (as in rugby), the game of football was controlled by having fixed scrimmage lines. Football was nevertheless brutal.

The bloody Stanford-California game of 1904 was followed by riots in San Francisco. Even Theodore Roosevelt, who prided himself on the "strenuous life," finally ordered that football be civilized or, he thundered, it would be ended by presidential proclamation.

So the forward pass was legalized in 1906 to open and speed up the game. This weapon was used by an unknown Notre Dame team to upset mighty Army in 1913. Thus began the Notre Dame football tradition, for the school soon attracted the athletic sons of Roman Catholic immigrants. Colleges began recruiting players in 1915. The sport entered glory days in the 1920s and professional teams appeared. The most renowned coach was Notre Dame's Knute Rockne, who believed that "After the Church, football is the best thing we have." His backfields moved in precise formations like the mass-production assembly lines that Americans so admired. But Americans who preached the virtues of rugged individualism could proudly point to the exploits of Red Grange ("the Galloping Ghost") of Illinois teams in the 1920s, Charlie ("Choo-Choo") Justice of North Carolina squads in the 1940s, and in the 1960s, Joe Willie ("Broadway Joe") Namath of Alabama.

Football's popularity reached new highs in the 1970s. Its quick action and pageantry suited color television screens. Television in turn provided immense wealth ($13.5 million in 1973 for college games alone) for football teams and such $250,000-a-year quarterbacks as Namath. (By the 1990s, quarterback Joe Montana of San Francisco earned more than $3 million a year.) In the 1970s George Allen of the Washington Redskins symbolized the tough, disciplined life with his eighteen-hour-a-day attention to detail and his remark, "Losing is like death. If you don't win you're dead and you don't know it." Allen's good friend, President Richard Nixon, was the nation's leading fan. "The President thinks football is a way of life," Allen observed. "He is a competitor." The game provided the language for politics and diplomacy. The American bombing of North Vietnam in late 1972 was code-named Operation Linebacker, and Nixon's code name was Quarterback. Conversely, such metaphors of war as the "blitz" and the "bomb" were applied to the gridiron.

A University of Oklahoma athletic director declared, "We teach a philosophy, we teach a skill, and we danged sure also teach a little bit of religion. And we teach discipline. This is one of the last areas where true discipline is taught, where love for the American flag and respect for the American President is taught, through discipline." Critics, however, deplored football's commercialism and its use as an example for fighting the Cold War. Former star Dave Meggysey quit the game, claiming that he had illegally received money for playing in college and had been treated as an animal by professional coaches and owners. "Politics and pro football," Meggysey declared, "are the most grotesque extremes in the theatric of a dying empire." In the 1970s football nevertheless seemed to be replacing baseball as the so-called national pastime.

Web Links

www.profootballhof.com/history/
The website of the Pro Football Hall of Fame in Canton, Ohio.

http://homepages.cae.wisc.edu/~dwilson/rfsc/history/
Links to a great many websites relating to college football.

May 1973 a Senate investigation of Watergate uncovered a cesspool of illegal administration activities. Key White House aides were implicated in an attempt to cover up the burglary, and several admitted their guilt. Other revelations indicated that Nixon's campaign staff had illegally accepted large donations from corporations and individuals. In some instances the administration had apparently given the contributors political favors in return. In October 1973, with evidence accumulating that he had accepted payoffs from building contractors, Spiro Agnew resigned as vice president. The Justice Department permitted him to plead guilty to a charge of tax evasion. He was fined and sentenced to three years of unsupervised probation. The president named Gerald Ford, a leader of the House of Representatives from Michigan, to replace Agnew.

Nixon desperately tried to halt the rising tide of criticism, but his efforts were complicated by the discovery that an intricate recording system had for years been tape-recording almost all his White House conversations. Nixon refused to surrender these tapes to Congress. He claimed that to do so would cripple the president's authority and violate the constitutional principle of separation of powers. When subpoenas were issued, he released a few tapes. But investigators found that several contained gaps at crucial points, gaps that could not, despite the president's claims, have been caused by accident. To prove that he was, in his words, "not a crook," Nixon authorized publication of his personal tax returns. These showed that in 1970 and 1971, claiming deductions of dubious legality, he had paid a federal tax of about $800 annually on a salary of $200,000. Nixon had, moreover, paid no state income taxes since 1969 although he was a legal resident of California.

An audit of his tax returns by a congressional committee found that the president had improperly taken a $428,000 charitable deduction for donating his vice presidential papers to the National Archives, had incorrectly written off business expenses, and had failed to declare $92,298 worth of improvements made at his homes in San Clemente and Key Biscayne that were "undertaken primarily for the president's personal benefit." In April 1974, Nixon agreed to pay $444,000 in back taxes and $32,000 in interest.

The effect of these disclosures on the presidency was stunning. For years Congress had endured insults from the Nixon administration. When some members of Congress protested the continued bombing of Cambodia and North Vietnam, for example, a State Department official cynically told them that the "justification" was "the reelection of President Nixon." One newspaper observed, "by that theory he could level Boston." But the Nixon administration's arrogance, Watergate cover-up, and other illegal activities soon led the Senate and House to strike back.

They passed a landmark measure that limited presidential power to make war without Congress's assent. The War Powers Act of 1973 provided that (1) "in every possible instance" the president must consult with Congress before ordering U.S. troops into any hostilities overseas; (2) whenever the president dispatched troops to foreign lands, he must, within forty-eight hours, send a full explanation to Congress; and (3) the president must begin to withdraw the troops within sixty days unless Congress had given him specific authority to maintain them abroad.

To no one's surprise, Nixon vetoed the act. He argued that such a bill would have dangerously tied the president's hands during the Berlin confrontation of 1961 and the Cuban missile crisis of 1962. Liberals opposed the bill for opposite reasons. They claimed it gave the president power to wage war on his own for sixty days without having to obtain congressional approval. Congress, however, believed that it had found a useful middle ground and that the measure would at least prevent future Vietnam-type interventions. The necessary two-thirds of the House and Senate voted to override Nixon's veto. That vote marked an important reversal in the thirty-year enlargement of presidential power.

Watergate not only weakened Nixon's standing with Congress, but also destroyed his ability to lead the Republican Party. By 1974 even those who had stood by Nixon were shocked by each fresh disclosure. One senator said that it was like waiting for the other shoe to drop, except "I don't know how many shoes there are to fall. I feel like I've been dealing with a centipede this past year." One poll found that only 24 percent of the voters classified themselves as Republicans, the smallest percentage identified with any major party in the twentieth century. The Democrats virtually swept the 1974 congressional elections, including such traditional Republican seats as one in Michigan that the Democrats had not held since 1932.

Watergate altered the American political landscape and undermined presidential power. In the late 1960s a majority of Americans had identified the groups dangerous to society as atheists, black militants, student demonstrators, prostitutes, and homosexuals. But by late 1973, none of these groups was considered harmful by a majority of people. Instead, the groups considered dangerous were people who hired political spies, generals who conducted secret bombing raids, politicians who engaged in wiretapping, business executives who made illegal campaign contributions, and politicians who attempted to use federal investigatory agencies for partisan purposes.

THE LOSS OF CIVIL LIBERTIES

While the Watergate scandal was unfolding, the American people learned that, for more than a decade, the federal government had been systematically violating their constitutional rights. First exposed by the *New York Times* in 1974 and then confirmed over the next two years by the reports of a House committee chaired by Democrat Otis Pike from New York, a Senate committee headed by Democrat Frank Church from Idaho, and a special committee under Vice President Nelson Rockefeller, those violations had begun even before the United States entered the war in Vietnam. But that war, and especially the turmoil and dissent accompanying it, had led the Central Intelligence Agency (CIA), the Federal Bureau of Investigation (FBI), and other agencies to mount aggressive campaigns against civil liberties and to conceal their actions from Congress, the courts, and the people.

Nothing better illustrated the government's behavior than the CIA program known as Operation CHAOS. Although the CIA was prohibited by law from spying on American citizens, the agency had begun to do so in the 1950s. In the summer of 1967, with antiwar demonstrations reaching a crescendo and President Johnson convinced that the demonstrators were being funded by foreign powers, the CIA stepped up its activities. Although it discovered no foreign involvement, the agency nevertheless accelerated its campaign at President Nixon's behest in 1969. By 1974 the CIA had compiled dossiers on 7,200 American citizens, stored the names of 300,000 individuals and groups in a computerized index file, opened 215,000 first-class letters, placed wiretaps on telephones, installed bugging devices in people's homes, and burglarized the offices of dissident groups. Speaking of the mail-opening program, one CIA official admitted, "This thing is illegal as hell." Not to be outdone by the CIA, the FBI remodeled its own counterintelligence program, COINTELPRO, and began to shift its attention to black militants, the New Left, and the antiwar movement. A House committee summarized some of the results of the FBI program: "Careers were ruined, friendships severed, reputations sullied, businesses bankrupted and, in some cases, lives endangered."

Two actions demonstrated Richard Nixon's own cavalier disregard for civil liberties. In May 1969, furious that news of the "secret" bombing of Cambodia had leaked to the press, the Nixon administration placed wiretaps on a number of government officials and newspaper reporters. For nearly two years the Justice Department monitored their phone calls, although, as the president later conceded privately, the transcripts produced no evidence of subversion. In July 1970 Tom C. Huston, a presidential aide, concocted a plan designed at once to expand and centralize the government's counterintelligence operations. Proposing that surreptitious entry be used to obtain information, Huston admitted, "Use of this technique is clearly illegal: it amounts to burglary." The president approved these recommendations, but when FBI director J. Edgar Hoover objected (primarily, it seems, because he feared their implementation would reduce the FBI's role), Nixon rescinded his approval.

The administration's contempt for civil liberties was again evident a year later. In June 1971 Dr. Daniel Ellsberg, a former Pentagon expert on Vietnam, made public the secret "Pentagon Papers," which documented American policy in Indochina between 1945 and 1968. The administration first attempted to block their publication in newspapers, but the Supreme Court ruled against prior restraint by a 6-to-3 vote. A majority of the justices found that the government had failed to prove that release of the documents would "inevitably, directly and immediately" injure the nation. Indeed, Nixon never believed that the documents jeopardized the nation's security, although he did fear their release might set a dangerous precedent. Ellsberg was then indicted for stealing government property.

At the same time the White House created a "plumbers" group of secret agents to "stop security leaks and to investigate other sensitive security matters." One of the group's first tasks was to discredit Ellsberg, a goal that, in turn, seemed to require a covert operation. The plumbers believed that damning evidence might be found in the office files of a Los Angeles psychiatrist whom Ellsberg had been consulting. The president's chief domestic adviser, John Ehrlichman, approved a burglary of the office as long as "it is not traceable." In September 1971 the plumbers broke into the psychiatrist's office, but failed to turn up evidence that would, in their words, "nail the guy cold." "All evidence we find with regard to the conspiracy," Nixon told his closest aides, "is going to be leaked, to columnists and the rest. And we'll kill these sons of bitches."

Daniel Ellsberg's trial for espionage and the theft of government property was held in 1973. The government's behavior during the trial was consistent with its previous behavior. While the trial was in progress, Ehrlichman offered the directorship of the FBI to the presiding judge, Matthew Byrne. The offer, if not actually improper, was surely irregular. Having grudgingly confessed that it had masterminded a burglary of Ellsberg's psychiatrist's office, the administration then urged Judge Byrne—unsuccessfully—not to make the information public. Finally, the government did not reveal, until ordered to do so by the judge, that the wiretaps it had installed on officials in 1969 had inadvertently picked up some of Ellsberg's conversations. Furious at this behavior, Judge Byrne declared a mistrial and dismissed the charges against Ellsberg. He noted that the circumstances in the case offended "a sense of justice." That judgment was equally applicable to CHAOS, to COINTELPRO, to wiretapping, to the Huston plan, and, as the Watergate investigation had already begun to reveal, to a much broader range of White House activities.

IMPEACHMENT: THE PRESIDENCY FROM NIXON TO FORD

In late 1973 the House of Representatives ordered its Judiciary Committee to determine whether Nixon had committed impeachable offenses, defined by the Constitution as "Treason, Bribery, or other high Crimes and Misdemeanors." By July 1974, the committee had assembled a massive amount of evidence that seemed damning to the president's case. On July 24 the Supreme Court unanimously ordered the president to surrender sixty-four tapes to John Sirica, judge of the district court in the District of Columbia where the Watergate trial was held. After listening to the tapes, Sirica could give all relevant portions to special Watergate prosecutor Leon Jaworski, who could then turn them over to Congress. The president thus had to retreat from his claim of executive privilege for all his documents. For the first time, however, the Supreme Court also ruled that the president had the right to withhold information on the grounds of executive privilege when the information concerned military or diplomatic matters. Since the tapes in dispute did not cover such national security issues, Nixon had to surrender them so the courts could base their decisions on all possible evidence.

One week later, John Ehrlichman, who as the president's chief domestic affairs adviser had held great power, was found guilty of directing the break-in at the office of Daniel Ellsberg's psychiatrist. Ehrlichman was also found guilty of lying to investigators about his role in the crime. He received a sentence of twenty months to five years in prison. Four of Nixon's cabinet officials, his two top White House assistants, and former Vice President Agnew had now been named in criminal cases. In all, thirty-eight officials associated with the Nixon administration had either pleaded guilty to or been indicted for crimes. American history offered no parallel.

On July 30 the House Judiciary Committee completed six days of public debate by recommending that the full House of Representatives approve three articles of impeachment. The first article accused the president of lying about, and trying to conceal, the role of his White House staff in the Watergate break-in. The second article alleged that Nixon had violated the constitutional rights of citizens by placing unlawful wiretaps on telephones and by using the FBI, CIA, and Internal Revenue Service to harass his political opponents. The third article declared that the president had refused to comply with congressional subpoenas for documents and taped conversations. Two other articles, one condemning Nixon's secret bombing of Cambodia during 1969 and 1970 and another accusing him of income tax evasion and of using government monies for private gain, were rejected by the committee as inadequate reasons for impeachment.

The Judiciary Committee reached its decision after long, bitter debate and intense soul-searching. Republicans and southern Democrats were especially uncomfortable as evidence against the president accumulated. But as a leading conservative from Alabama commented: "And . . . what if we fail to impeach? Do we ingrain forever in the very fabric of our Constitution a standard of conduct in our highest office that at the least is deplorable and at the worst is impeachable?" In the end, as many as seven Republicans and all twenty-one Democrats on the Judiciary Committee voted for at least one of the articles. The committee's debate, which attracted a huge television and radio audience, had an immense political impact.

No one any longer doubted that the House would vote to impeach the president by a wide margin. Nixon's last hope lay in the Senate, but that hope quickly died. On August 5 he released the transcripts of three conversations he had held with his chief White House assistant, H.R. Haldeman, a few days after the June 1972 Watergate break-in. These tapes showed that Nixon had raised the possibility of getting the CIA to order the FBI to halt its investigation of the burglary. "Don't go any further into this case period!" was the language the president proposed. The president also conceded that he had kept this information from his own lawyers and from the impeachment inquiry. Granting that he had committed a "serious act of omission" and that impeachment in the House was "virtually a foregone conclusion," Nixon insisted that his behavior did not warrant a conviction in the Senate.

But the disclosure that he had obstructed justice and withheld the truth provided the "smoking pistol" for which many congressmen were searching. And the fingerprints were unmistakably clear. Support for the president evaporated overnight. Republicans began a stampede for resignation or impeachment. The mood in the White House became desperate. According to investigative reporters, Nixon began to roam the mansion at night, communing with the portraits of past presidents and at one point summoning Henry Kissinger to kneel with him in prayer. White House aides feared that if they pressured him to quit, Nixon might respond irrationally. Top civilian officials in the Pentagon carefully monitored all orders from the president to the military.

Finally, on the night of August 7, Nixon met with two conservative Arizona Republicans, Senator Barry Goldwater and Representative John Rhodes, the House minority leader. They reported that the Senate would surely vote to convict. Even the ten Republican members of the Judiciary Committee who had defended the president a few days earlier had reversed their positions. One member reportedly asked if the committee could reconvene so he could change his vote, but he was informed, "the train had left the station." Its destination became known on August 9, 1974, when for the first time in history an American president resigned his office. Vice President Gerald Ford, whom Nixon had appointed to replace Agnew, became chief executive.

Within a month, Ford unilaterally used his new power to protect Nixon from criminal prosecution. On September 8, 1974, the president said that he was pardoning Nixon for all federal crimes he "committed or may have committed" during his years in the White House. Ford's announcement set off a storm of protest since it precluded a trial and thereby undercut proper legal processes. Two years later, the pardon became an important reason why many Americans preferred Jimmy Carter instead of Ford in the presidential election. The ghost of Richard Nixon continued to stalk the corridors of American politics.

HENRY KISSINGER: FOREIGN POLICY FROM NIXON TO FORD

One official, however, emerged from the morass of Watergate with an enhanced reputation. In 1973, after having served as the president's national security adviser, Henry Kissinger became secretary of state. That same year he finally succeeded in negotiating a Vietnam cease-fire with his North Vietnamese counterpart, Le Duc Tho. The two men were rewarded with the 1973 Nobel Peace Prize. Tho refused his share, correctly asserting that war between North and South Vietnam continued. The American troops left, however, and Kissinger accepted his share of the prize. "Half a prize for half a peace seems just about right," one journalist observed.

Kissinger followed the cease-fire with equally successful (from his and Nixon's view), if less publicized, diplomacy in Chile. Since 1970 President Salvador Allende had turned Chile toward a nationalist, independent course and attempted to gain his nation's economic

Senator Sam Ervin listening to testimony during the Watergate hearings. *(Gjon Mili/ Time Life Pictures/Getty Images)*

independence—and distribute its wealth more equitably—by seizing property owned by North American corporations and wealthy Chileans. Kissinger and Nixon secretly moved to undermine the new regime. By 1973 Allende's government suffered severely not only from its own economic errors, but also from a cutoff of the U.S. aid on which Chile had long depended. Kissinger meanwhile strengthened Washington's ties with the Chilean army. In September 1973 the army struck. Overthrowing Allende, who died in the struggle, the army ended all attempts at reform, established a military regime, and then tortured and murdered thousands of political prisoners. Both North and South Americans were alarmed by Chile's new course, but Kissinger and Nixon were pleased that they had played a major part in overthrowing a government they had always mistrusted and feared.

Turning from Chile with satisfaction (and from Vietnam with obvious relief) Kissinger pledged his full attention to renewing frayed ties with Western Europe. This important relationship had deteriorated politically and economically. The Nixon administration placed first priority on détente with Russia and China. The policy worked well (Soviet premier Brezhnev was so pleased that he embarrassed Kissinger by kissing him full on the mouth when they met), but relations with the Atlantic partners suffered, for they feared the superpowers might be making deals that did not consider Europeans' interests.

Before Kissinger could move to repair the Atlantic alliance, however, war in the Middle East wrecked his plans. The roots of the conflict went back to 1967 when the Egyptians had blockaded several ports that were crucial for Israel's security. On June 5, 1967, the Israelis suddenly retaliated. In the Six-Day War, they humiliated the Egyptians and their Arab allies

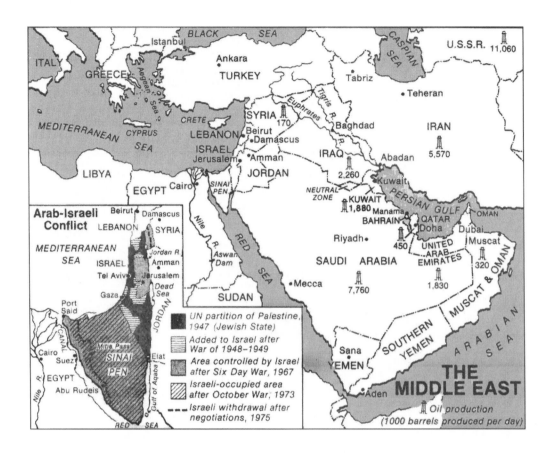

by seizing the prized city of Jerusalem (the world home of three great religious faiths—Islam, Judaism, and Christianity), sweeping across the Sinai Desert to the Suez Canal, and wiping out large portions of the Egyptian and Syrian armies. The Arabs refused to discuss peace until Israel returned the conquered areas. The Israelis rejected this demand, claiming that the new boundaries were necessary for their security.

Re-equipped with massive Soviet aid, the Egyptians and Syrians suddenly attacked Israel in October 1973. The Egyptian army redeemed itself. Israel staved off a major setback only with a brilliant crossing of the Suez that enveloped large numbers of Egyptian troops and placed Israeli forces in Egypt itself. Kissinger flew to the Middle East five times in six months and, aided by cooperation from the Soviets (who feared that a prolonged war would result in Egyptian defeat), brought about direct Egyptian-Israeli talks, the first since Israel was founded in 1948. A temporary settlement provided for mutual troop withdrawal and creation of a buffer zone in the Sinai Peninsula.

Although major problems remained unresolved in the Middle East, the Egyptian-Israeli disengagement gave Kissinger cause for satisfaction. The same could not be said for developments in Southeast Asia. After pulling out its combat troops, the United States actually cut aid to the Saigon government in 1974. During the spring of 1975, the North Vietnamese communists launched an all-out offensive. The beleaguered Saigon regime, riddled with corruption and deserted slowly by Washington, asked desperately for American help. Investigation revealed that two years before, Nixon had secretly assured the South Vietnamese that in such a situation the United States would use its great power to protect them: "You can count on us," the president had told them. But in April 1975, Nixon was retired in disgrace at San Clemente, California. Across the Pacific, television cameras recorded the sordid images of U.S. officials shoving aside former Vietnamese allies so the Americans could escape by helicopter just moments before the communists seized Saigon. The long U.S. war in Southeast Asia was finally over.

Chapter Sixteen

1976–1984
New Directions

Young urban professionals in the 1980s. *(Lambert/Getty Images)*

Vietnam and Watergate continued to influence American life long after the last soldier had returned home and the last conspirator from the Nixon administration had gone to jail. It was only logical, in the aftermath of Watergate, that successful politicians would be those who had no connection with the Washington establishment. Neither Jimmy Carter nor Ronald Reagan had held federal office, elective or appointive, before being elected president. Politics became the art of running against the government. Winning elections became the art of selling a candidate's personal integrity to the voters. It was equally logical, in the aftermath of Vietnam, that an assertive foreign policy, a promise to make America strong again, would exert a strong appeal. Although the policies that Carter and Reagan adopted differed in important respects, the differences concerned the speed at which the nation was moving more than the direction in which it was going: toward a dousing of social reform at home and a rekindling of Cold War hostilities abroad.

JIMMY CARTER AND THE "NEW REALITIES"

In 1971, when he became governor of Georgia, Jimmy Carter regarded the presidency with "reverence." Then he had an opportunity to meet the men—Nixon and McGovern, Humphrey and Muskie, Reagan and Rockefeller—who had been contesting for the office over the years and, as Carter recalled, "I lost my feeling of awe about presidents." In early 1973, undaunted by the label applied to him by journalists—"Jimmy Who?"—Carter set out to win the Democratic nomination. By 1976, with his only political experience one term in the Georgia Senate and one term as the state's governor, Carter recognized that the Watergate backlash might do wonders for his candidacy. He portrayed himself as an outsider who never had been involved in corrupt Washington politics. To voters fed up with deception in high places, he promised, "I will never lie to you."

In his speech accepting the Democratic nomination in June 1976, Carter placed himself squarely within the party's reform tradition. Calling for "an end to discrimination because of race and sex," he said, "Too many have had to suffer at the hands of a political and economic elite who have shaped decisions and never had to account for mistakes or suffer from injustice." Pledging support for a revamping of the income tax structure, he lashed out at the "unholy, self-perpetuating alliance . . . between money and politics." Urging enactment of new welfare programs, including a "nationwide comprehensive health program for all our people," Carter insisted that the "poor, the weak, the aged, the afflicted must be treated with respect and compassion and with love." Although he also warned that government could not solve every problem, most of his listeners detected strong populist overtones in the speech.

Many things helped Carter in the campaign, not the least President Gerald Ford's reputation as a bumbler. Ford tripped down some steps on a state occasion, cut himself diving into the White House swimming pool, and bumped his head boarding a helicopter. Adapting Lyndon Johnson's cruel remark that Ford had played too much football without a helmet, newsmen made it crueler still: "He can't even play president without a helmet." Nor did Ford's choice of Senator Robert Dole of Kansas as his running mate help the Republicans. In a televised debate with his Democratic counterpart, Senator Walter Mondale of Minnesota, Dole charged that World War I, World War II, and Korea were "all Democrat wars." Such remarks angered Democratic moderates whom the Republicans badly needed on Election Day. Finally, Ford's own statement during a debate with Carter that, partly due to Republican policies, "There is no Soviet domination of Eastern Europe," cost the president crucial support from Poles, Czechs, and other Americans of Eastern European origin.

Yet the electorate, or at least the 54 percent that bothered to vote, responded to more than mishaps, mudslinging, and miscues. Ford did best among the affluent and the comfortable; Carter, among the poor and disadvantaged. The vote, pollsters found, "fractured to a marked degree along the fault line separating the haves and the have-nots." Carter won about 55 percent of the Catholic and Jewish vote, but more than 90 percent of the black vote. The Georgian carried ten of the eleven southern states (all except Virginia); in seven of the ten, black voters provided his margin of victory. With a total of 40.8 million votes to Ford's 39.1 million, Carter emerged with a 297-to-241 victory in the electoral college.

Expectations that Jimmy Carter would preside over a new era of reform were short-lived. Within a year or two disgruntled liberals were complaining that Carter was the most conservative Democratic president since Grover Cleveland. Liberals centered their fire on three aspects of the president's legislative program. They claimed that his energy bill, enacted in 1978 after a fierce congressional struggle, benefited the oil companies by deregulating natural gas prices; that his tax reform measure, approved in 1977, failed to close loopholes enjoyed by the wealthy and offered little relief to middle-income individuals; and that his medical care proposals fell far short of the comprehensive health programs supported by Democratic senator Edward Kennedy of Massachusetts. By 1978 Kennedy had begun to complain that the administration was sacrificing the needs of "the poor, the black, the sick, the young, the cities and the unemployed."

Carter's policies undoubtedly reflected his own managerial outlook, his tendency to convert social problems into engineering problems and to seek technical solutions for them. Moreover, Carter found it necessary to placate members of Congress, especially the chairs of powerful committees. Demanding modifications in the energy and tax proposals, these Democratic leaders forced Carter to retreat or even surrender. The president could no longer invoke party discipline against Democrats who increasingly divided along geographic ("sun belt" versus "snow belt") and ideological lines. As the party system fragmented, congressional defiance of the White House became more common. In the late 1970s power shifted dramatically up Pennsylvania Avenue to Capitol Hill.

As presidential influence over—and party discipline in—Congress declined, pressure groups rushed to fill the vacuum. The groups included trade associations (such as the American Medical Association and the National Education Association), corporations, labor unions, and single-issue interest groups (antiabortion and anti-gun-control advocates, for example). They cemented their power by giving lavishly to congressional campaigns. Not surprisingly, Congress passed laws encouraging such gifts. Labor unions had long been allowed to contribute to campaigns, but corporations had not—until, that is, new laws in the 1970s permitted them to set up political action committees (PACs) to support sympathetic politicians. The PACs transformed political fund-raising, especially since the unions' political power seemed to be fading. By 1978 a top adviser to Carter mourned, "We have a fragmented, Balkanized society," with each special economic group "interested in only one domestic program"—its own.

More than anything else, however, the nagging problem of inflation limited Carter's freedom of action. To fight inflation, he believed, it was essential to reduce the federal budget deficit; but since the president also wanted to increase spending for national defense, he recommended a moderate reduction in social welfare expenditures. Carter's proposed budget for 1980, therefore, elicited anger from liberals and cautious approval from conservatives. In January 1979 Carter's chief domestic policy adviser, Stuart E. Eizenstat, explained that the president's scaled-down domestic agenda reflected the "new realities" of the late 1970s. Those "unhappier realities" included "high inflation coupled with high unemployment, and widespread public cynicism toward the government." Such realities—combined with Carter's own managerial disposition, the erosion of presidential power, and the growing influence of interest groups—constituted the legacy of the 1970s, a legacy that would shape politics in the 1980s.

CARTER'S FOREIGN POLICY: CONFUSION . . .

Americans had to deal not only with a fragmented society at home, but also with a fragmented world abroad. They faced complex problems in the newly emerging nations that had little to do with Soviet communism. Dealing with these problems frustrated Americans, who prefer their foreign relations to resemble a baseball game—to be of short duration with clearly identified opponents and a definite winner: themselves. Foreign policy refuses to be so simple.

Jimmy Carter came to power with little knowledge of foreign policy. His colorful younger brother, Billy, was astonished at Jimmy's ambition to lead the world's greatest power: "My mother joined the Peace Corps when she was 70, my sister Gloria is a motorcycle racer, my other sister, Ruth, is a Holy Roller preacher, and my brother thinks he is going to be President of the United States! I'm the only normal one in the family."

The new president tried to make up for his inexperience by appointing Cyrus Vance (a New York lawyer) as secretary of state and Zbigniew Brzezinski (a Columbia University expert on Eastern Europe) as National Security Council adviser. Both had extensive experience in foreign policy, but they offered Carter conflicting advice. Vance hoped to be patient and conciliatory in strengthening relations with Russia. He wanted to deal with crises in the third world not by blaming them on the Soviets, but by treating them as problems of new, ambitious nationalisms. Vance received support from Andrew Young, Carter's ambassador to the United Nations. A well-known black leader, Young believed that African problems, for example, should be dealt with by Africans; neither of the two superpowers had the understanding or power to control such affairs. (Young's approach helped resolve several African crises, especially in removing obstacles so the former British colony of Rhodesia could become the black-governed nation of Zimbabwe.) Brzezinski, on the other hand, viewed the world largely in terms of the U.S.-Soviet conflict. He saw a grim Russian face behind upheavals in third world countries and increasingly urged a tough military line toward the Soviets.

Carter had to choose between the Vance-Young and Brzezinski views. The president was not well equipped for the task. Trained as an engineer at the U.S. Naval Academy, he remained, in the words of close observers, "an engineer, a manager," and a "problem-solving president" who might know "how every single engine or pump works," but had little sense of the larger structure within which machinery had to function. He had no consistent larger view of world affairs. In 1973 Brzezinski had brought Carter into the new Trilateral Commission for an education in foreign policy. Brzezinski and New York banker David Rockefeller had formed the commission to coordinate policies among Japan, the United States, and Western Europe so these industrial powers could deal with the sudden economic and third world crises of the 1970s. By 1980, indeed, the Western alliance would be in its worst shape since 1945.

Camp David Summit, September 12, 1978: Israeli prime minister Menachem Begin *(left)*, U.S. president Jimmy Carter, and Egyptian president Anwar Sadat. *(Keystone/Getty Images)*

Once in office in early 1977, Carter determined to restore U.S. authority abroad (and reinvigorate Americans' faith in their own values at home) by emphasizing his support of human rights. Those rights were to include personal freedom from torture and imprisonment for political reasons. Such rights, Carter declared, were "the soul of our foreign policy." He soon learned, however, that he could not practice what he preached. Some of the world's worst violators of human rights (South Korea, Argentina, Guatemala, Nicaragua, Iran) were also important allies of the United States. He therefore did little to pressure the Korean or Iranian governments. When he criticized Argentina and Guatemala, they refused to cooperate any longer with U.S. military programs. The president's policy was both needed and decent (and ultimately helped return Argentina to democratic government in 1984), but even his advisers admitted that the policy had never been thought through, never reconciled with the major security needs of U.S. foreign policy.

Carter's relations with the Soviets meanwhile steadily declined. Talks aimed at slowing the runaway arms race nearly collapsed. In October 1977 one breakthrough seemed to occur when the two superpowers agreed to work for peace in the explosive Middle East. But the possibility of a larger Russian presence frightened both Egyptians and Israelis. A firestorm of objections from U.S. friends of Israel forced Carter (in Brzezinski's words) to "walk away" from the deal. Soviet leader Leonid Brezhnev was outraged, but Carter managed to score a major victory in 1979 when he mediated the Camp David accords between Egypt's leader, Anwar Sadat, and Israeli prime minister Menachem Begin. The agreement, reached at the presidential retreat in the Maryland mountains, marked the first peace treaty between Egypt and Israel after three decades of war. Begin also pledged to return to Egypt the large Sinai area that Israel had seized in 1967. No deal, however, could be reached on the festering question of other areas claimed by both Israeli settlers and hundreds of thousands of Palestinians.

The Soviets perhaps became most disturbed when the United States announced in 1978 that it would begin formal diplomatic relations with China. The Chinese needed U.S. arms to protect the long border they shared with the Soviet Union and claimed they wanted $100 billion of outside investment to develop their economy in the 1980s. Carter was happy to open China to U.S. investors, but he severely limited any military aid out of fear of possible Russian reaction. Superpower relations further soured during 1978–1979 when Soviet officials and 13,000 Cuban troops appeared in Ethiopia to help that East African nation in a war begun by neighboring Somalia. The region was strategically located along the oil shipping lanes of the Middle East (see map, Chapter 12, page 281). The United States consequently quickly sent aid to the Somalis.

Against this ominous background, Carter and Brezhnev met in Vienna in 1979 to negotiate the second Strategic Arms Limitations Talks (SALT II). Under the agreement, each side was to have no more than 2,400 nuclear missile launchers (with that number reduced to 2,250 in eighteen months). Not more than 1,320 of the launchers were to be "MIRVed"—that is, have as many as ten multiple-independent-reentry-vehicle nuclear bombs that could be separated in midflight and hit individual targets. Congressional critics claimed that SALT II favored the Russians, whose nuclear force was composed of large, single-head missiles, and hurt the U.S. force, which depended more on MIRVs and other new-technology weapons. These critics vowed to kill the treaty when it came before the Senate for ratification.

Carter had not been effective in dealing with Congress. Since the early 1970s, moreover, the two legislative bodies had become fragmented. House and Senate leaders could no longer deliver votes for Carter as, for example, Senator Lyndon Johnson had delivered support for Eisenhower's policies in the 1950s. The Georgian had also spent much of his political capital in pushing through two treaties in 1978 that would give the Panama Canal to the Panamanians in the year 2000. The Panamanians had often rioted against the U.S.-built and -controlled Canal Zone, which had split their country since 1903. U.S. military officials worried that the waterway could not be protected against future rioting. The final treaties gave the North Americans special privileges (including the right to intervene militarily to keep the canal open). But led by conservative senators and former California governor Ronald Reagan, opponents fought the pacts until the treaties were ratified in the Senate with only a single vote to spare.

. . . TO COLD WAR

As SALT II came before the Senate, a series of events suddenly erupted that—like rapid machine gun fire—destroyed both Carter's presidency and his hope of thawing the Cold War. The blasts occurred in Iran, Central America, and Afghanistan.

In late 1978 a revolution led by Islamic religious leaders undermined the Iranian government of Shah Riza Pahlevi. The shah was Washington's closest military ally in the Middle

East. He had used his immense oil wealth to purchase billions of dollars in U.S. arms. But he had also tried to modernize his nation too rapidly. When conservative opposition appeared, especially among college-age Iranians as well as the Muslim leaders, the shah imprisoned and killed many of his critics. As the crisis grew, Carter's advisers again split: Vance wanted to talk with the shah's opposition, but Brzezinski considered even the use of U.S. troops to keep the shah in power. While Americans debated, the shah was toppled from his famous Peacock Throne in early 1979. Ayatollah Ruhollah Khomeini, the eighty-year-old Islamic leader, took control.

More shocks quickly followed. The disruption of Iranian oil exports gave the Organization of Petroleum Exporting Countries (OPEC; the organization of Arab and other oil producers) a chance to raise prices by 50 percent. The price rise drove up inflation in the United States until it skyrocketed from the dangerous 7 percent annual increase between 1974 and 1978 to more than 13 percent in 1979. Alarmed Americans watched 30 billion of their dollars flow to oil producers instead of being used to pay for higher food and housing costs. (A second cause of the disastrous U.S. trade balance was the $7 billion Americans illegally spent to import cocaine.)

Nor could Carter prevent the overthrow of another U.S. friend, Anastasio Somoza, the dictator of Nicaragua. The revolutionary Sandinista Front had been fighting Somoza since the early 1960s. Named after Augusto Sandino, the guerrilla fighter who forced U.S. Marines to stop occupying Nicaragua in 1933, the Sandinistas disliked and feared the United States. Carter (as had many presidents before him) supported Somoza, but also pushed the dictator to pursue human rights principles. That policy undercut Somoza, whose authority increasingly depended on brutality. Carter finally tried to intervene so the Sandinistas could not gain power. When not a single Latin American nation would join Carter, his efforts failed and the Sandinistas marched into the capital, Managua, in July 1979. By 1980 the new government carried on most of its trade with the United States, but increasingly dealt with Castro's Cuba to obtain educational, medical, and military help. The revolution, moreover, threatened to spread to help left-wing forces in neighboring El Salvador, but the rebels' "final offensive" was turned back by the U.S.-supplied Salvadoran army in January 1981.

The setbacks in Iran and Nicaragua were disasters for Carter. Worse, however, lay ahead. In October 1979 he decided to allow the shah, suffering from cancer, to enter the United States for medical treatment. Infuriated Iranian mobs, encouraged by Khomeini, stormed the U.S. Embassy in Teheran on November 4 and seized sixty-nine American diplomats. Fifty-three of them were finally held as hostages; the rest were freed. The crisis dominated American television screens (the popular American Broadcasting Company's late-night news show *Nightline* was born during the crisis). Unable to deal with Khomeini, Carter watched his own popularity sink to new lows. In April 1980, as the presidential election campaign intensified, Carter ordered a secret rescue mission. But several of the U.S. helicopters crashed in an Iranian desert, killing eight American soldiers. Vance resigned after the president overruled his opposition to the mission. (Only after months of secret talks and U.S. economic pressure were the hostages released in January 1981.)

While Americans were preoccupied with the Iranian crisis, the Soviet Union invaded its southern neighbor Afghanistan in late December 1979. It marked the first time in the post–1945 era that Russian troops had launched an invasion outside their East European bloc. Afghanistan was a strategic gateway into both the Soviets' southern borders and the Middle East oil fields. During 1978–1979 the pro-Russian Afghan government had become wobbly. Moscow officials feared that Khomeini's Islamic fanaticism (which condemned communism as much as U.S. capitalism) would spread over Afghanistan. Therefore they dispatched 80,000 troops to take control. Poorly armed Afghan guerrillas fought back with surprising effectiveness. The Soviets found themselves trapped in a long, bloody struggle. A stunned Carter, who in 1977 had declared his policies would not be shaped by "the inordinate fear of Communism," had now become consumed by the fear. He sent arms to the Afghan rebels and then stopped shipment of 17 million tons of U.S. wheat promised to the Soviets. The Russians badly needed the grain because of their own failed agricultural system, but they quickly obtained supplies elsewhere, especially from Argentina and Canada. American farmers bitterly attacked Carter for the loss of the Russian market, and George Shultz (Nixon's former secretary of the treasury) condemned the president for turning vital trade "on and off like a light switch."

The White House then dramatically announced the "Carter Doctrine": the United States would, if necessary, unilaterally use force to prevent any further Russian encroachment in the Middle East or Southwest Asia. He backed up his doctrine with a military budget (which he had promised in 1976 to cut by $5 billion) that now rose $20 billion to a record peacetime high of $106 billion. Carter thus prepared the way for Ronald Reagan's massive military buildup in the 1980s. But the Georgian also prepared the way for Reagan's 1980 election triumph with his ineffectual responses to the crisis of SALT II (which died without a vote in the Senate), economic problems, the overthrow of Somoza and the shah, and the Soviet invasion of Afghanistan. *Business Week* caught the nation's mood: "The country is entering the decade of the 1980s as a wounded, demoralized colossus."

POLITICAL EVANGELICALISM AND THE MORAL MAJORITY

American politics in the 1980s were influenced not only by these reversals, but also by the impact of evangelical Christianity. The word "evangelical" derives from the Greek for "good news," and evangelicals devoted themselves to spreading the good news that Jesus had come into the world to save sinners and make them whole. Emphasizing the responsibility of each person, evangelicals believed that an individual could be redeemed only by being "born again"—that is, by confessing sins, accepting a resurrected Jesus as a personal savior, and leading a new life. In 1966 Jimmy Carter was born again after listening to a sermon titled, "If you were arrested for being a Christian, would there be any evidence to convict you?" Although he was already a Sunday school teacher and a deacon in his church, Carter decided, "If arrested and charged with being a committed follower of God, I could probably talk my way out of it! It was a sobering thought." Carter then began to search "for a closer relationship with God," to devote himself to religious concerns, and to witness publicly. His election gave born-again Christianity wider visibility and recognition.

Pollster George Gallup Jr. termed 1976 "the year of the evangelical," and the late 1970s and early 1980s saw a burgeoning of the movement. Books by evangelical authors became best sellers. Billy Graham's *How To Be Born Again* (1977) had an initial printing of 800,000 copies, the largest for any hardcover book ever published, and another 500,000 copies were soon needed. One million schoolchildren were soon attending 5,000 Christian elementary and high schools where subjects were taught from an evangelical perspective. By 1978 some 1,300 radio stations—one out of every seven in the country—were Christian-owned and -operated, and one new such station was being added every week. But television, not radio, became the chief medium for spreading the message. Pat Robertson's *700 Club*—aired on his Christian Broadcasting Network from Virginia Beach, Virginia—was a pioneering venture. One of the regulars on the show, Jim Bakker, eventually decided to create his own program—*The PTL Club*, the initials standing for "Praise the Lord." Bakker's program combined sermons, inspirational conversation, faith healing, speaking in tongues, and entertainment. The new "electronic church" and the "televangelists" had many critics in the mainstream religious community, but by 1978 Robertson was receiving $30 million a year in contributions, and Bakker, at $25 million, was not far behind.

The new evangelicalism was characterized by social conservatism and political activism. Born-again Christians attacked "secular humanism," by which they meant the view that all truths were relative, all moral values situational, and all ethical judgments tentative. They supported the "right-to-life" movement, which condemned legalized abortion. They opposed the equal rights amendment (ERA) and other feminist demands. They attacked court decisions that they claimed legalized pornography. They blasted the gay rights movement on the grounds that homosexuality was sinful. Other demands focused on the public schools. Evangelicals favored reintroducing prayer, teaching "scientific creationism" as an alternative to the theory of evolution, and imposing strict discipline on students. To a considerable extent, they attributed permissiveness and moral decay to the behavior of politicians who were insensitive to family values.

It was, then, only a short step to full-fledged political action. Many politicians recognized the truly awesome potential of the movement, with its loyal television audience and appealingly simple message, but none more clearly than the Reverend Jerry Falwell. He had his own television program, *The Old Time Gospel Hour*, which raised more money each year than Robertson's or Bakker's. In July 1979 Falwell founded the Moral Majority and within two years was claiming 4 million members. Combining old-time religion with the most sophisticated computer technology, Falwell not only targeted potential contributors but also evaluated candidates for office on the basis of their votes on such issues as the ERA, federal funding for abortions, and school prayer. In 1980, after developing a "hit list" of liberal senators and congressmen, the Moral Majority mailed more than a billion pieces of literature to selected voters. "What can you do from the pulpit?" Falwell asked. "You can register people to vote. You can explain the issues to them. And you can endorse candidates, right there in church on Sunday morning."

In 1980 there was never any doubt which presidential candidate Falwell or most other evangelicals would endorse. Democrat Jimmy Carter, Republican Ronald Reagan, and independent John Anderson were all born-again Christians (as was one voter in every three), but Carter's brand of evangelicalism, and Anderson's, were distinctly too liberal for the Moral Majority. Ronald Reagan said that he deplored the "wave of humanism and hedonism in the land. I think there is a hunger in this land for a spiritual revival, a return to a belief in moral absolutes." He was talking Jerry Falwell's language. As the Republicans looked for a presidential candidate in 1980, Falwell let it be known he would support Reagan "even if he has the devil running with him." To consolidate his hold on the religious right, Reagan appointed the first executive director of the Moral Majority as his campaign's religious adviser.

Evangelicals were fond of quoting a verse from the Book of Proverbs: "Righteousness exalteth a nation; but sin is a reproach to any people." Righteousness and sin, however, could be defined in different ways. Evangelicalism could be—and, for a minority of believers, was—hospitable to ideals of reform, social justice, and disarmament. There were born-again Christians who asserted that Scripture "is clearly and emphatically on the side of the poor, the exploited and the victimized," who spoke out against nuclear proliferation and pledged themselves "to non-cooperation with our country's preparation for nuclear war. On all levels—research, development, testing, production, deployment, and actual use of nuclear weapons—we commit ourselves to resist in the name of Jesus Christ." Yet as the Reagan era dawned, the majority of evangelicals had lined up solidly behind a conservative social agenda and a president committed to cutting social welfare expenditures and building up the military. In the 1980 election, Ronald Reagan received 51 percent of the popular vote, but 63 percent of the votes of white born-again Christians.

THE REAGAN REDIRECTION

The contours of Regan's victory were also shaped by the large number of eligible voters who did not bother to vote. The turnout—52 percent—was the lowest in a presidential election since 1948. As a group, those who actually voted were older, whiter, and wealthier than the eligible voters, since young, black, and poor people have the lowest turnout rates. This worked to Reagan's advantage. He was supported by 55 percent of voters who were forty-five or older, by 55 percent of voters who were white, and by 63 percent of voters earning over $50,000 a year. The outcome was widely construed as a mandate for conservatism because of Reagan's electoral college margin (489 to 49) and his party's congressional gains. Republicans took control of the Senate for the first time since 1954.

An avowed conservative, Ronald Reagan for much of his life had been a staunch liberal. In 1932, at the age of twenty-one, he had supported Franklin D. Roosevelt, and he remained a Democrat, actively involved in liberal causes, through the 1940s. Reagan described himself then as a "very emotional New Dealer" and a "near hopeless, hemophilic liberal." But by 1947 he feared that communists were attempting to infiltrate the motion picture industry and that liberals were ignoring the danger. "Light was dawning in some obscure region of my head," Reagan wrote in his autobiography, *Where's the Rest of Me?* (1965). He began to move to the right, a move sharply accelerated by his marriage in 1952 to Nancy Davis, herself a dedicated conservative. During the 1950s and 1960s, as a popular speaker for General Electric, Reagan asserted that the welfare state was "the most dangerous enemy ever known to man." In 1962 he formally changed his party affiliation, and in 1964 endorsed the presidential candidacy of Barry Goldwater, who, he later said, "was possibly a little ahead of his time." Elected governor of California in 1966 and then reelected in a landslide, Reagan sought the Republican presidential nomination in 1968 and 1976 and finally obtained it in 1980.

Reagan's critics, before his election and after, disparaged his abilities by poking fun at his alleged shallowness, superficiality, and inattention to detail. "You can wade through Ronald Reagan's deepest thoughts and not get your ankles wet," said one pundit; Reagan was "the president with the seven-minute attention span," said another. Yet it was all too easy to underrate his political ability. Reagan understood that the public cared less whether a president had

President Ronald Reagan riding his horse El Alamein at Rancho
Del Cielo, 1983. *(Ronald Reagan Library)*

all the facts at his fingertips than whether an administration had an overall sense of direction.
He used television more successfully than any of his predecessors to convey his message to
the public. He recognized the importance of finding talented administrators and of delegating
authority to them. He knew which voters had elected him and what he had to do (and what
he did not have to do) to be reelected.

In 1980 the presidency was widely thought to have entered its "postimperial" phase: Gerald
Ford claimed it was "imperiled, not imperial," and Walter Mondale called it "the fire hydrant
of the nation." Reagan set out to refurbish executive authority, and to a considerable extent he
succeeded by reasserting influence over Congress, centralizing the budget-making process,
curbing the bureaucracy, and, according to pollsters, persuading most Americans that he had
"strong qualities of leadership." The expansion of executive authority, however, was designed
to curtail rather than expand the scope of government. Federal programs to combat poverty,

to advance civil rights, to protect the environment, and to safeguard consumers were so well entrenched after years of steady growth that it would take an activist in the White House to trim them back. As an Urban Institute study put it, "Reagan found it necessary to adopt the approach of Wilson and Roosevelt in order to pursue the objectives of Coolidge and Harding."

In truth, Reagan endeavored to reverse the direction that social policy had taken ever since the New Deal, but especially since the Great Society. The Reagan administration announced that it was prepared to slice federal welfare spending and adopt "supply-side economics." Supply siders held that the government could stimulate business growth, create new jobs, and ensure widespread prosperity by giving everyone greater incentives—by rewarding entrepreneurial risk taking, by increasing opportunities for profit making, by enlarging take-home pay—in short, by expanding the supply of goods, which would then create a greater demand for them. The centerpiece of supply-side economics was, from a political standpoint, almost too good to be true: a whopping tax cut.

In 1981 the administration won congressional approval for just such a massive tax cut, providing for across-the-board reduction of 5 percent the first year and an additional 10 percent in each of the succeeding two years. The measure was undeniably popular. In a nationwide television address, Reagan asked viewers: "Are you entitled to the fruits of your own labor or does government have some presumptive right to spend and spend and spend?" Public pressure on Congress became irresistible, and as it appeared a bill would, in fact, pass, a multitude of interests clamored for special breaks: accelerated depreciation, lucrative write-offs, near-elimination of the estate tax. An exasperated Democrat finally announced, "the auction is over." But Reagan's own budget chief, David Stockman, offered the most candid description of what had happened: "Do you realize the greed that came to the forefront? The hogs were really feeding. The greed level, the level of opportunism, just got out of control."

Tax reduction benefited all taxpayers, but not equally. The Treasury Department's estimates showed that, over the three years, 9 percent of the total relief would go to those earning under $15,000 and 36 percent to those earning more than $50,000. There were 162,000 families with incomes of $200,000 or more; their taxes were cut by $3.6 billion. There were 31.7 million families who earned $15,000 or less; they realized a saving of $2.9 billion. The administration's overall policies reflected a similar distribution of benefits. Real disposable family income (adjusted for taxes and inflation) fell in 1981 and 1982, then rose in 1983 and 1984 until it was, on the average, 3.5 percent higher than in 1980. But averages could be deceiving. Over the four-year period, the real disposable income of the poorest fifth of American families declined by nearly 8 percent, while that of the middle fifth rose by about 1 percent and that of the wealthiest fifth jumped by almost 9 percent. The Reagan administration presided over a major redistribution of income away from the poor and toward the rich.

Many economists had predicted that a tax cut coupled with increased outlays for defense would produce record deficits. The predictions soon came true. As military spending soared (from $133 billion to $246 billion) and annual budget deficits approached $200 billion, the total national debt, which stood at $800 billion in fiscal year 1981, grew to $1.5 trillion in fiscal year 1985. Nearly as much debt accumulated in Reagan's first administration as in the nation's entire history prior to his election. As the administration understood, such deficits threatened to produce sky-high interest rates and eventually retard economic growth. As some scholars pointed out, however, those deficits were also "a means of advancing the Reagan revolution." A colossal national debt—by 1985 one dollar in every seven spent by the federal government went to pay interest on that debt—created permanent pressure to reduce federal spending for social programs.

One of Reagan's purposes was to cut taxes even if it meant creating deficits; a second was to curb inflation even if it meant temporarily increasing unemployment. The inflation rate in 1980, more than 12 percent, had proven politically fatal for Jimmy Carter. Like Carter, Reagan knew that the surest way to reduce inflation was to permit unemployment to rise, but unlike his predecessor he was willing to do it. The unemployment rate was about 7 percent in November 1980; two years later it was 10.8 percent, the highest level since the late 1930s. Not only were 12 million people jobless, but also 1.6 million were too discouraged to look for work and 6.5 million were working fewer hours a week than they wanted. "The current recession," Reagan's top economic adviser at the time commented, "is an unavoidable cost of slowing inflation." The inflation rate indeed fell to about 4 percent in 1983 and 1984, and as the recession ended the unemployment rate returned to about the level it had been under Carter.

A third objective of the Reagan administration was to cut welfare spending even if such cuts increased the number of people who lived in poverty. The president proposed reducing social programs by a considerably larger margin than Congress would approve. He asked Congress to appropriate $75 billion less for these purposes over a four-year period than would have been spent at prevailing levels; this would have amounted to a 17 percent reduction. Congress grudgingly granted a little more than half of what the president wanted, agreeing to a cutback of $38 billion, or 9 percent. Significantly, the administration requested the most draconian reductions—totaling 28 percent—in programs that directly benefited the poor, such as food stamps, Aid to Families with Dependent Children, school lunches, housing assistance, and Medicaid. The administration sought only an 11 percent reduction in Social Security, Medicare, and unemployment insurance, many of whose beneficiaries were not poor. When Ronald Reagan took office, 11.7 percent of Americans had incomes that placed them below the poverty level. The figure had remained steady for about a decade, but by 1982 it rose to 15 percent, the highest since Lyndon Johnson had launched the war on poverty.

THE POOR AND THE YUPPIES

The antipoverty crusade had been inspired, in part, by the appearance of Michael Harrington's *The Other America* in 1962. Harrington's *The New American Poverty,* published in 1984, met a chillier response. Harrington pointed out that government social programs primarily aided those who were not poor rather than those who were. The chief beneficiaries were not welfare recipients but rather the aged, who were entitled to Medicare and Social Security. Harrington described the new poor—the "uprooted" and the "superfluous," the homeless men and women sleeping in doorways, the deinstitutionalized mental patients roaming the streets aimlessly, the black teenagers facing unemployment, the illegal aliens toiling in sweatshops, and the Native Americans, "the poorest of the poor in a land that was once their own."

Harrington also said that it was the young in particular who "need a vision that transcends the mindless hedonism of so much of contemporary life." But according to *Newsweek* magazine, which dubbed 1984 "the year of the Yuppie," a new class of young urban professionals could not get enough of hedonism, mindless or otherwise. Yuppies were characterized by their age (which ranged from the early twenties to late thirties), their income (which began at $40,000 but seemed not to have an upper limit), and their occupations (which cut across the

A homeless woman with her daughter on a street in San Diego, California. *(Bushnell/Soifer/Stone/ Getty Images)*

professional and managerial worlds), but especially by their concern with their own "lives, careers, apartments and dinners," and by their willingness to "define themselves by what they own." They joined expensive fitness clubs, exchanged business cards at "networking" parties, shopped at gourmet food stores, wore designer-label clothing, and lived, when they could, in newly "gentrified" districts. *Newsweek* concluded that millions of Yuppies, who were generally conservative on economic issues but liberal on social issues, voted for Ronald Reagan in 1984.

In 1984 Reagan not only captured a large share of the Yuppie vote but also consolidated his hold on a very different constituency: evangelical Christians. The president, who had brought into existence virtually all of his economic policies, had instituted virtually none of the Moral Majority's social program. Reagan first deferred congressional consideration of antiabortion and school prayer proposals so his tax and budget policies could be enacted. By 1983, when the administration got around to supporting the measures, it could not muster the necessary support in Congress. In March 1984 the Senate turned down a constitutional amendment permitting voluntary individual or group prayer in the public schools. The vote, fifty-six in favor and forty-four opposed, fell eleven short of the needed two-thirds majority; of the opponents, twenty-six were Democrats and eighteen were Republicans. One Reagan aide, when asked what the administration planned to give the Moral Majority, replied "symbolism." The president granted a White House audience to right-to-life marchers, supported tax-exempt status for Christian schools that barred blacks, pronounced 1983 "the year of the Bible," and endorsed the entire evangelical platform. In the 1984 election, exit polls indicated, Reagan was the choice of 80 percent of white born-again Christians.

AFFIRMATIVE ACTION AND UNDOCUMENTED ALIENS: DILEMMAS OF RACE AND ETHNICITY

The problems of "affirmative action" and "undocumented aliens," which plagued Ronald Reagan's administration as they had Jimmy Carter's, were in a sense legacies of the 1960s. The Civil Rights Act of 1964 had barred discrimination on the basis of race or sex, and the Equal Employment Opportunity Commission thereafter instituted policies to ensure that all federal contractors, city and state governments, and colleges and universities established goals or timetables for the hiring and promotion of members of minority groups. The purpose was to remedy years of discrimination by acting affirmatively in behalf of blacks, women, Hispanics, Native Americans, and Asian Americans, but the method sparked bitter controversy. Similarly, the Immigration Reform Act of 1965 had abolished the discriminatory policy of admitting people on the basis of their national origins, but established, for the first time, numerical limits on immigration from nations in the Western Hemisphere. As population pressures mounted in Mexico, Central America, and South America, millions of illegal or undocumented aliens entered the United States. Their presence posed a dilemma that was as much political as it was legal.

Carter approached the problem of affirmative action cautiously because the issue was one on which Democrats sharply disagreed. Civil rights organizations viewed all-out support for affirmative action, including the setting of "quotas," as a litmus-paper test of an administration's commitment to racial justice, but such quotas offended other important elements in the Democratic coalition, especially labor unions, whose members felt threatened, and Jews, who historically had been victimized by quotas. These differences were evident in 1977 when the administration decided to file a brief in the case of Allan Bakke, who was challenging "race conscious" admissions policies at the medical school of the University of California at Davis. The Department of Justice first circulated a brief that defended the principle of affirmative action but opposed actual quotas. When civil rights leaders and the Black Congressional Caucus protested strongly, the department prepared a new statement that omitted any condemnation of quotas.

In June 1978 the Supreme Court handed down its ruling in the Bakke case. Bakke, having twice been turned down by the medical school at Davis, in 1973 and 1974, had appealed to the courts to gain admission. At the time the school reserved sixteen of one hundred places in its entering class for "disadvantaged students"—blacks, Chicanos, Native Americans, and Asian Americans. Bakke had a better academic record than all of those admitted under this minority quota, and so he claimed he had been denied the equal protection of the law. By a 5-to-4 margin the Supreme Court ruled in his favor: the use of an "explicit racial classification," in situations where no former discriminatory behavior had been demonstrated, violated the Fourteenth Amendment. At the same time, however, the Court approved, by another 5-to-4 vote, programs that used race as "simply one element in the admissions process." Justifying such "race conscious programs," Justice Harry A. Blackmun said, "In order to get beyond racism, we must first take account of race."

The Reagan administration took a much dimmer view of affirmative action programs than had the Carter administration. Reagan called quotas "reverse discrimination," a "federal distortion of the principle of equal rights." When the Detroit and the New Orleans police departments established quotas for promoting blacks, the administration interceded to overturn

U.S. agents arrest illegal Mexican immigrants. *(Stege Northup/Time Life Pictures/Getty Images)*

the agreements, which had been entered into voluntarily. This opposition to affirmative action had much to do with the widespread perception among blacks that the Reagan administration was hostile to their best interests. Blacks, who had given Reagan only 11 percent of their votes in 1980, gave him a minuscule 9 percent in 1984.

The Supreme Court also began to edge away even from its very limited endorsement of affirmative action in the Bakke case. In 1980 the Memphis fire department had agreed to fill one-half of all new vacancies with blacks (and upgrade many black employees), but in 1981, city agencies, facing financial difficulties, were forced to cut back. To preserve seniority rights, the fire department began laying off the recently hired blacks. Black firefighters obtained an injunction to stop the department from implementing this policy, the union fought back, and the Supreme Court, in June 1984, ruled that the injunction had been improperly granted. A six-member majority declared that it was not permissible to give preferential treatment to black firefighters who had not themselves been discriminated against. The Court declared that Congress had not intended, in passing the Civil Rights Act of 1964, to set racial quotas.

Patterns of discrimination—less familiar, perhaps, but no easier to erase—also affected millions of undocumented aliens. Calculations of the number of people who were, by the mid-1980s, living and working in the United States illegally varied widely, but the lowest figure anyone cited was 4 million, and some observers thought 6 million or 8 million was a better estimate. The Census Bureau indicated that 45 percent of the undocumented aliens came from Mexico, 17 percent from countries of Central and South America, and the remainder from Asia, Africa, and Europe. Most of the illegal aliens worked at hot, dirty jobs

THE COMPUTER REVOLUTION
AFTER FOUR CENTURIES OF EVOLUTION

Computer, 1985. *(Roger Viollet Collection/Getty Images)*

Time magazine annually chooses a "Man of the Year" or "Woman of the Year." Winston Churchill, Adolf Hitler, Queen Elizabeth II of England, and the astronauts have been acclaimed. In 1983, however, an object—the computer—won for the first time. As *Time* explained, the computer had revolutionized American life for it "can send letters at the speed of light, diagnose a sick poodle . . . test recipes for beer," and be used by the rock group Earth, Wind, and Fire to explode smoke bombs at precise moments in concert. A California high school programmed a computer that at 5:15 PM each day phoned the parents of absent students. The truancy rate in the school dropped 64 percent in one year.

The machine's effect on the exchange of information—especially the printing of newspapers, the publishing of books, and the writing of college term papers and laboratory reports—had no parallel since Gutenberg first used movable type in Germany during the 1450s. More than half of all employed Americans in the 1980s made their living not by making products but by exchanging information. This rapidly growing part of the workforce depended on computers whose disk memory was small enough to be carried in a handbag

ENIAC at the University of Pennsylvania, 1946. *(AP Photo)*

but contained the equivalent of more than a thousand books. With lightning speed, the machine carried out its two basic functions: computing numbers and storing and retrieving information.

Most Americans encountered the computer in the 1970s and 1980s, but some of its basic principles date back to the seventeenth century, when the great French philosopher Pascal devised the first machine that could multiply as well as add. At about the same time a mathematician, John Napier, invented logarithms that allowed complex figures to be adapted easily to computing machines. The next key step occurred two centuries later when an eccentric British inventor, Charles Babbage (who also devised the speedometer) spent forty years building a huge, incredibly complicated machine that contained nearly all the main features of the modern computer. It could even be programmed.

Americans then stepped in to make the Pascal-Babbage inventions more practical. Herman Hollerith was an engineer working with the U.S. census of 1880 when he borrowed Babbage's device of putting information on punched cards and then retrieving it with spring-loaded pins that corresponded to the holes of the cards holding the information wanted. The 1890 census results were consequently tabulated in one-third the time spent on the 1880 survey. Hollerith quit his government job to build a fortune with his now-famous punch-card system. In 1924, during this first great era of American corporate development and mergers (1890s through the 1920s), Hollerith's Tabulating Machine Company became International Business Machines (IBM).

Within a decade, IBM dominated the business machine industry. Over the next sixty years it became the most glamorous and successful of American corporations. But IBM's initial successes came from fast-talking salesmen, not technical breakthroughs. Important scientific innovations began in the 1940s and were spurred on by U.S. military needs in the early Cold War years. Scientists at the University of Pennsylvania built the ENIAC, whose thirty tons, 18,000 vacuum tubes, and 6,000 switches performed 5,000 computations a second to target artillery fire. Sperry-Rand Corporation's UNIVAC of 1951 pioneered modern programming by using magnetic tapes instead of punched cards. UNIVAC helped make computers famous by accurately predicting Dwight Eisenhower's triumph in the 1952 presidential election.

American scientists were now making breathtaking discoveries. In 1947 researchers at Bell Telephone Laboratories had developed the transistor. This device used semiconducting materials (silicon, for example) to control electrical currents, and it did so more rapidly, cheaply, and with cooler temperatures than could vacuum tubes. Within a decade transistors were being printed on silicon pieces to become microchips, or integrated circuits for computers. In the early 1970s engineers succeeded in putting the machine's entire processing unit on a single silicon chip. The chip thus became a microprocessor. As one observer summarized the change in computer technology by the 1980s, "if the automobile business had developed like the computer business, a Rolls-Royce would now cost $2.75 and run 3 million miles on a gallon of gas."

In the early 1980s small, pioneering businesses, led by Apple and Hewlett-Packard—and joined later by IBM—developed desktop-size computers that cost under $1,000 and could be used in the home or office. The American industrial revolution had thus come full circle. The individual artisan in an eighteenth-century cottage had become the centralized giant corporation producing iron, steel, and automobiles in the early 1900s. But now, as the twentieth century came to a close, the "electronic cottage," as futurist Alvin Toffler called it, created vast new possibilities for decentralization and individual enterprise.

Web Links

www.computerhistory.org/timeline/?category=cmptr
Includes a timeline of computer history, beginning in 1939.

www.microsoft.com/presspass/exec/billg/
Everything you ever wanted to know about Bill Gates.

Supreme Court Justice
Sandra Day O'Connor.
(Library of Congress)

for minimum or below-minimum wages, doing the kind of work for the kind of pay that American citizens would not do. The states with large numbers of illegal aliens—California, Texas, Florida—were those with low rates of unemployment. Although undocumented aliens paid Social Security taxes, income taxes, and sales taxes, they were not eligible for food stamps, Aid to Families with Dependent Children, Medicaid, or school lunch programs. They often did not make use of social services for which they were eligible for fear of being discovered and deported.

As public awareness of the problem increased, Carter and Reagan appointed special commissions to devise a solution. The commissions made three recommendations: "amnesty" for illegal aliens who had resided continuously in the United States for a certain period; stiff sanctions for employers who knowingly hired illegal aliens; and a system of national identification to permit employers to distinguish between citizens and others. These proposals formed the basis of the Simpson-Mazzoli bill, a bipartisan measure. In 1986 Congress finally enacted a modified version of Simpson-Mazzoli that provided amnesty to undocumented aliens who could prove they had entered the United States before 1982; the law also penalized employers who hired illegal aliens.

In the meantime, one of the most crucial rights enjoyed by illegal aliens—the right of their children to attend the public schools—was preserved by the narrowest of margins. In June 1982, by a vote of 5 to 4, the Supreme Court declared that a Texas ordinance that denied funding for the education of children who had entered the country illegally violated the equal protection clause of the Fourteenth Amendment. To deny these children a public education, the majority said, deprived them of "the ability to live within the structure of our civic institutions" and "does not comport with fundamental conceptions of justice." Chief Justice Warren Burger wrote the minority opinion and was joined by Justice O'Connor. Burger conceded that the Texas statute was wrongheaded, even harmful. But he warned, "The Constitution does not provide a cure for every social ill, nor does it bestow judges with a mandate to try to remedy every social problem."

THE FEMINIZATION OF POVERTY, THE ERA, AND THE GENDER GAP

In the fifteen years since the rebirth of feminism, many changes had reshaped women's lives. In 1960, 35 percent of American women were in the labor force; by 1980, over half were wage earners. In the past, only a minority of married women worked outside the home, and they tended to enter the job market after their children were grown. By 1980, three out of every five married women with school-age children had joined the workforce, as had half of married women with children under six. Women's private lives had also changed. In 1960, less than one-third of women aged 20 to 24 were unmarried; by 1980, half were unmarried. Prospects for motherhood shifted too. In 1960, just after the peak of the baby boom, a woman might expect to have 3.61 children; by 1980, only 1.86, less than the number needed for a no-growth population rate. Finally, family life became less stable. Between 1960 and 1980, the divorce rate doubled. In the 1970s, the number of families headed by women steadily rose, as did the number of women living alone.

Some statistics suggested clear advances. By 1980, for instance, women constituted a majority of the college population; they entered prestigious professions and profitable vocations. Record numbers ran for public office, and many won, especially on the state and local levels. But other developments were less auspicious, such as the rapid rise of the female-headed family (a family headed by a single mother) and the consequent "feminization of poverty." By 1980, two out of three female-headed families received child welfare, and two-thirds of the long-term poor were women. In some instances, marital breakdown caused a drop in female living standards. According to one study of the early 1980s, divorce could mean "financial catastrophe" for women. Births to never-married mothers led even more directly to the feminization of poverty. In the 1970s, the number of families headed by unwed mothers increased more than 400 percent. Half of all out-of-wedlock births were to teenagers. Although the rate of births to single women rose most rapidly among whites, it was highest among blacks. At the start of the 1980s, over half of all black children were born to unwed mothers. Almost half of black families with children were headed by women, compared with 21 percent of such families in 1960.

The major issues of the women's movement reflected concern over women's family roles. In the late 1970s, an antifeminist backlash gained momentum. The "Stop ERA" campaign, led by Phyllis Schlafly, lobbied in state legislatures to prevent ratification of the ERA; the deadline had been extended by Congress until June 1982. Schlafly argued that the ERA would cause "radical loosening of the legal bonds that keep the family together." The National Organization for Women (NOW) contended that the ratification battle was a referendum over sex discrimination. When the amendment failed, three votes short of ratification, Schlafly claimed that feminists had "shot themselves in the foot"; NOW vowed to continue the campaign. One factor that abetted the ERA's failure was the difficulty of the amending process. Another was ambivalence among women. Even among sympathizers, some doubted that the ERA would have a significant impact, or could not judge what that impact might be. A third factor was the conflict between polarized, politicized groups of women. Foes believed that the ERA disparaged women's traditional roles and devalued their lives. Advocates never heeded such objections, not did they assuage their opponents' suspicion that legal equality might exact a price. Despite the ERA's widespread support, conflict among women affected state legislators, who controlled the ratification procedure.

The ERA was not the sole source of controversy. The right-to-life movement that began in the 1970s advocated a constitutional amendment that would reverse federal policy and prohibit all abortions. Life, it contended, began at conception. In June 1983 the Senate defeated the antiabortion amendment and the Supreme Court confirmed women's constitutional right to abortion by upsetting city ordinances that limited access to it. But right-to-life advocates, continuing their campaign, evoked strong sentiments. Feminist issues became an enduring and controversial part of the political agenda.

According to opinion polls of the early 1980s, a majority of both men and women supported the ERA and abortion rights. But a gender gap had developed on other issues. It first appeared in the 1980 presidential election, when women provided a far larger proportion of the Carter vote (58 percent) than the Reagan vote (49 percent). Subsequent opinion polls suggested that more women than men favored Democratic candidates and Democratic policies on employment, inflation control, and staying out of war. Pollsters also discovered that the greatest contributors to the gender gap were wage-earning women and women under forty-five, two categories of voters that were expected to grow. As the election of 1984 approached, Democratic presidential candidates tried to capitalize on the new trends in voting behavior.

NEW DIRECTIONS IN U.S. FOREIGN POLICY, OR THE GREAT DEBATE OVER THE USE OF FORCE

"When we move from domestic affairs," Reagan proclaimed to the roaring 1980 Republican Party convention that nominated him, "we see an equally sorry chapter in the record" of Jimmy Carter. The Californian then ticked off Carter's failures: a Soviet military presence in Cuba; the Soviet Union's invasion of Afghanistan; American defense strength "at its lowest ebb in a generation, while the Soviet Union is vastly outspending us"; and the holding of "more than 50" American hostages in Iran, "a dictatorial foreign power that holds us up to ridicule before the world." On his inauguration day Reagan was able to welcome home the hostages, who had been freed by Carter's last-minute diplomacy. But the other problems remained. None was more important to Reagan than building up tremendous military strength and then demonstrating that the "Vietnam syndrome"—American reluctance to use military force because of the Vietnam debacle—no longer existed.

The new president used his communication skills honed as a movie actor to convince Americans to follow his foreign policies. "The White House always seemed like a set," Reagan's speechwriter, Peggy Noonan, recalled. "I wasn't surprised when I heard what Reagan said twenty years earlier, when he was asked, 'What kind of governor will you be?' He answered, 'I don't know, I've never played a governor.'" Reagan did know the kind of president he wanted to be in foreign affairs and successfully talked Congress into "rearming America" (as he misleadingly called it) by raising defense spending until it would amount to $1.5 trillion over the next five years (1981–1986). Unlike earlier presidents (especially Eisenhower), Reagan had little experience with the military. He had spent World War II living in Hollywood making army-training films. From then until 1980 he had shown little interest in military affairs. He nevertheless decided that spending on arms was to be the cornerstone of his foreign policy. In early 1982, he signed a directive, National Security Decision Directive 32 (NSDD 32), instructing military leaders to build forces so they could prevail either in a prolonged global conflict with conventional weapons or in a nuclear war.

The president's plans quickly ran into obstacles. His advisers could not come up with a coherent foreign policy that could justify and wisely use such huge amounts of money. For example, the president pledged to fight for freedom everywhere, but no one (including Reagan) argued that U.S. troops should actually fight in communist Vietnam again or in Afghanistan. Another obstacle was that as many as 70 percent of Americans who were asked disagreed with the president's belief that Vietnam had been "a noble cause." They wanted no more Vietnams; instead, they wanted what one public opinion expert described as "win quickly or get out." Any kind of protracted war (as suggested in NSDD 32) would not sit well with most Americans. That sentiment soon combined with another problem for Reagan. Huge government deficits in 1984 and 1985, caused in part by the military spending, led many members of Congress to question the arms budgets. By the mid-1980s Congress had cut Reagan's defense-budget growth rate to the level proposed by Jimmy Carter in 1980 when he actually began the arms buildup.

Reagan and Carter also had something else in common: each president's closest advisers bitterly differed with each other over policy. Reagan's secretary of defense, Caspar "Cap" Weinberger, led the drive for huge military budgets. Much of the money was spent on overpriced items that enriched defense contractors. Weinberger soon "became a captive of his generals and admirals," recalled Larry Speakes, the White House press secretary, "and it was while Weinberger was in charge that we had . . . $640 toilet seats and $7,400 coffee brewers for air force planes." But the secretary of defense was reluctant to use the military force he created. In late 1984 Weinberger delivered a remarkable speech that declared U.S. troops would not be sent to war unless certain conditions existed. It was the first time in history that a Washington official publicly told potential enemies the exact conditions that had to be met before Americans would fight. Two of his conditions were shaped by the Vietnam experience: strong support from the U.S. public for any fighting, and assurance that military commanders in the field would be allowed to "win" wars.

On the other hand, Reagan's two secretaries of state, Alexander Haig (1981–June 1982) and George Shultz (July 1982–1989), were more willing to use force. Shultz's first experience in the use of force, however, was a disaster. In 1982 Israel's armies struck at their leading enemy, the Palestinian Liberation Front, which had bases in neighboring Lebanon. Lebanese groups armed by Syria (which was supplied by the Soviets) struck back and bogged down the Israeli troops. Shultz proposed a peace plan and sent 1,500 U.S. troops as part of a multination force to pacify the area. The Israelis left Lebanon, but U.S. forces then tried to separate warring Christian and Muslim armies. Encamped in an indefensible position in the Lebanese capital of Beirut, the troops became the target of snipers and terrorists. In late 1983, a Muslim terrorist drove a truck full of explosives into a U.S. Army barracks and killed 241 American soldiers. Reagan quickly declared that the troops would remain because pulling them out would amount to a "surrender" to the pro-Soviet, Syrian-Lebanese groups. But as more Americans died, his policy became unpopular, the 1984 election approached, and Reagan reversed himself. The troops came home.

The president had learned a lesson about American public opinion. In October 1983, within days after the tragic American deaths in Lebanon, Reagan and Shultz decided to invade the tiny Caribbean island of Grenada. A pro-Cuban government whose radical wing had executed its opponents controlled the island. Reagan announced that he invaded to protect the safety of American citizens on the island and at the request of worried neighboring states. Weinberger's Pentagon had opposed the hurried invasion, and the operation nearly turned into a disaster. Forty-five Grenadans, eighteen Americans, and twenty-four Cuban technicians were killed in the fighting before the tiny island (the size of the District of Columbia) was pacified after nearly ten days of shooting. Reagan, however, scored a major political victory at home. He demonstrated he was not afraid to use force, and he kept the public happy by observing the rule "win quickly or get out."

CENTRAL AMERICA

Reagan and Shultz learned from their quite different experiences in Lebanon and Grenada. Determined to fight revolutionaries, the two officials understood that the fight had to be waged cheaply, especially in terms of U.S. lives and money. Believing that pro-Soviet revolutionaries controlled Nicaragua and threatened to control El Salvador, Reagan and Shultz tried to reimpose U.S. power over Central America by using proxy armies, that is, native troops supplied and trained by the United States. This approach, however, inflamed North American opinion in a way unmatched since the explosive Vietnam debate a decade earlier.

Reagan had bitterly attacked the Sandinista government in Nicaragua for its Cuban ties, aid to Salvadoran leftists, and reluctance to hold elections. Unwilling to accept a political settlement and refusing to work with democratic nations in the region that criticized his military approach, Reagan chose to try to overthrow the Sandinistas with force. Working through the Central Intelligence Agency (CIA), he armed a force of anti-Sandinista Nicaraguans (soon known as Contras) that by 1985 numbered 10,000 troops. This force used U.S.-created camps in Florida for training (an act that was illegal under U.S. law) and bases in Honduras for attacks on Nicaragua.

The Contras, however, were so ineffective that the CIA decided to take direct charge. It led attacks deep into Nicaragua, flew air missions, and then aided in mining Nicaraguan harbors. The mining proved to be a mistake. Neutral ships suffered damages, and in 1984 an outraged U.S. Congress, reflecting strong public opinion, stopped all government aid to the Contras. The aid, however, was replaced by more than $5 million of supplies sent by private American groups. The CIA also continued to be active in the region. The Sandinistas meanwhile conducted an election in late 1984 that consolidated their hold on the country, although the vote also brought a strong opposition minority group into the government.

Perhaps more important, Reagan's military policies produced results opposite from those he intended. To meet the U.S. pressure, the Sandinistas doubled their army to 50,000 regular troops, armed over 100,000 civilians to fight invaders, tightened their control over the country, and moved closer to Cuba and the communist bloc for help. More than 4,000 lives were lost in the fighting. As the war intensified, so did the U.S. debate over Reagan's policy, especially as the president suddenly shut off U.S. trade with Nicaragua in 1985 in an effort to bring down that nation's economy.

Washington officials claimed greater success in El Salvador, but that claim was also challenged. The smallest country in the region, El Salvador suffered one of the widest gaps between the few rich (the so-called forty families) and the millions of poor. In 1979 some army officers tried to stop a spreading revolution by seizing power and promising reforms. But little happened. Instead the army split between right-wing leaders, who frequently murdered civilians whom they suspected of "liberal" tendencies, and the moderates, who became politically isolated. By 1984 the right-wing "death squads" had killed 40,000 civilians. The terror only strengthened the revolutionaries who controlled much of the eastern part of El Salvador, but it sickened U.S. public opinion.

To check the revolution, Washington officials began a massive training program for Salvadoran troops (including instruction on treating civilians more humanely). Reagan also picked José Napoleón Duarte, a U.S.-educated politician, to create a government that could effectively wage war but also impress North Americans with its moderation. In 1984 Duarte won the presidency in an election heavily influenced by millions of dollars sent into El Salvador by the Reagan administration.

Many critics disagreed with that policy. They claimed (correctly, as it turned out) that no military victory was in sight and that the Reagan administration, in both Nicaragua and El Salvador, was willing to "fight to the last Central American" while understanding that U.S. troops could not be directly used. The wars meanwhile devastated the already poor countries. El Salvador was completely dependent on U.S aid for its survival. One of every seven Salvadorans fled to the United States, the overwhelming majority illegally. When the Reagan administration cracked down and tried to return some of these Salvadorans to their own country, U.S. church leaders began a "sanctuary movement" that defied Reagan on the grounds that the Salvadorans' return to their homeland meant their death. Washington officials responded with a number of arrests, including the imprisonment of priests and nuns. But the sanctuary movement nevertheless spread—along with the instability, poverty, terror, and revolution in Central America.

NEGOTIATING WITH THE "EVIL EMPIRE"

Reagan had a simple explanation for his Central American, and indeed global, problems. "The Soviet Union underlies all the unrest that is going on," he declared in 1980. By 1983 he was denouncing the Soviets as "the evil empire" with which diplomatic talks were of little use. Moscow officials, he claimed, "reserve unto themselves the right to commit any crime, to lie, to cheat." The Soviets responded in kind. Their policies, moreover, became more unpredictable, even threatening, when death struck their aged leadership. Three different men headed the Soviet government between 1982 and 1984. In September 1983, the Soviets shot down a civilian South Korean airliner that had wandered 350 miles off its route over highly sensitive Russian strategic bases. One U.S. congressman was among the 269 people who perished. Relations between the two superpowers sank to the lowest level since the worst days of the Cold War in the early 1950s.

As Reagan accelerated his military buildup, he also moved to quiet his critics by agreeing to talk with the Soviets about limiting the number of nuclear missiles. The talks continued until 1983, when the Russians walked out because the United States began placing new intermediate-range missiles in Western Europe.

President Reagan was remarkably ignorant of basic facts about the arms race. (He wrongly believed, for example, that the Soviet SS-19 missile was larger than the SS-18 because, as he pointed out, 19 is larger than 18.) In truth, he cared less about an arms treaty than about his military buildup, which, he hoped, would force the Soviets to accept his terms. But as he approached his reelection campaign in 1984, polls revealed that Reagan's popularity was weakest on arms issues. Voters' fear that the president might be trigger-happy was reinforced when word leaked that he had signed a secret executive document that specified how to carry on a protracted nuclear war. Democratic Party leaders joined a "nuclear freeze" movement that aimed at freezing the present number of missiles of both the superpowers until a treaty could be negotiated. To undercut these threats to both his arms buildup and his reelection plans, Reagan suddenly softened his anti-Soviet rhetoric and pledged new arms talks.

Most dramatically, he announced on national television in mid-1983 that more military spending could lead to scientific breakthroughs that might produce a foolproof defense against a missile attack. He urged Congress to begin a multi-billion-dollar program to develop this Strategic Defense Initiative (SDI; or "Star Wars," as his critics quickly labeled it) so that someday Americans could shoot down incoming Soviet missiles while they were still out in space far above the earth. Reagan's plans called for technology that, one expert predicted, would require eight times the new discoveries that first sent astronauts to the moon. (The moon, moreover, had not put up any resistance; the Soviets would certainly try to counter each American discovery with new weapons of their own.) SDI, even if developed, could not protect Americans against new Soviet cruise missiles that delivered nuclear bombs in the atmosphere—that is, below the proposed SDI system. Reagan, it was discovered, had not consulted closely with his top military and scientific advisers before making his speech. He had been heavily influenced instead by Edward Teller, a superhawk among scientists, who had helped develop the hydrogen bomb in the early 1950s and was a model for the war-crazed central character in the popular 1964 movie, *Dr. Strangelove or: How I Learned to Stop Worrying and Love the Bomb.*

Aside from the invasion of Grenada, the president could claim no major foreign policy victories. But American voters did not notice or did not care. As usual, they voted on the bases of their pocketbooks and their personal liking of the president. Reagan scored heavily on both counts. Helping to open the 1984 Summer Olympic Games in Los Angeles, he became a glamorous television image as hundreds of thousands of spectators waved American flags and proclaimed "We're Number One." Perhaps the former actor had not known how to play a governor in the 1960s, but he certainly knew how to play the president in the 1980s.

THE 1984 ELECTION

Hoping to counter the president's popularity, the Democrats at their 1984 convention nominated former Vice President Walter Mondale, and he chose New York representative Geraldine Ferraro as his running mate. Describing herself as a "housewife from Queens," Ferraro had spent three terms in the House and served as head of the 1984 Democratic Platform Committee. A combination of circumstances led to her candidacy. First, there were no self-evident competing choices for the vice presidential spot. In addition, Mondale was under pressure from NOW, which had supported him early on (and some of whose members briefly threatened to withdraw their support were a woman not chosen). Betty Friedan argued that selecting a woman would represent a commitment to expansion of opportunity for all, a theme Mondale wished to stress. Among women candidates, Ferraro appeared to be the most promising because of her potential appeal to an ethnic vote—Catholic, Italian-American, and working-class—as well as to other traditional Democrats. The daughter of immigrants, she had worked her way up in the world as teacher, lawyer, and public prosecutor. Ferraro also had much support from important politicians. Finally, the Mondale camp felt that a bold, unconventional step was needed both to energize the campaign and to prove that the candidate could take strong, decisive action.

Ferraro's historic nomination generated widespread enthusiasm and drew an outpouring of volunteers. Republicans criticized the nomination as tokenism. No sooner had the campaign started than a furor erupted over whether Ferraro would reveal the entirety of her family finances beyond the income tax statements required by law. To do so, as the press demanded, meant a public airing of her husband's finances, a possible source of irregularities, as well as her own. No comparable concern over a spouse's finances had arisen before a woman candidate ran for vice president. Ferraro finally released the information demanded by the press and acted with aplomb. But the controversy hurt the Democratic campaign.

When votes were counted, the gender gap—the Democrats' edge among woman—seemed to have vanished. Reagan won 57 percent of the women's vote, as opposed to 42 percent for Mondale. (The male vote was 61 percent to 37 percent.) All nine women challengers for Senate seats lost, as did thirty-nine of forty-one women challengers for House seats. Recriminations about the women's vote were rampant in the Democratic camp. Feminists were "remote from the women's vote," a top Democratic consultant charged. "These people can't deliver their sisters." With an eighteen-point gap between the candidates, Democratic women pointed out, the gender gap could not be expected to have had much impact. "We didn't invent defeat," said Ann Lewis, political director of the Democratic National Committee. "White men have been losing elections for years."

The campaign waged by the Democrats shows the extent to which Ronald Reagan had altered the political agenda. Mondale represented a traditional brand of Democratic liberalism, but his speech accepting the nomination called for a well-managed, not merely a well-meaning, government; a president who could say no to special-interest groups; a strong military posture with no major cuts in defense spending; policies to ensure private-sector, not public-sector, economic growth; and the maintenance of family values. "I will cut the deficit by two-thirds," the liberal Democrat promised; "we must cut spending and pay as we go." Mondale did attack Reagan for pandering to the rich and powerful, but the Democrat said little or nothing about social welfare, racial justice, or immigration reform. In November, Reagan captured 59 percent of the popular vote and carried forty-nine of fifty states. Ronald Reagan had established the terms of political debate for the 1980s as surely as Franklin Roosevelt had for the 1930s.

CHAPTER SEVENTEEN

1985–1992
The End of the Cold War

After the Gulf War, 1991. *(Per-Anders Pettersson/Photonica World/Getty Images)*

After Ronald Reagan's sweeping victory in 1984, one of his most vigorous critics, House Speaker Thomas "Tip" O'Neill, told him, "I've never seen a man more popular than you are with the American people." Reagan maintained that popularity throughout his second term, even though he failed to effect promised changes in social, judicial, and environmental policies and also failed to find solutions for growing budget deficits, declining American productivity, and a widening gap between rich and poor. The president even managed to emerge largely unscathed from "Irangate" and a savings-and-loan scandal. But as domestic difficulties mounted, relationships with the Soviet Union dramatically improved. It was left to Reagan's successor, George Bush, to discover that the end of the Cold War did not mean an end to foreign policy difficulties, or even an end to the threat of war—or war itself.

THE ROARING EIGHTIES

Having triumphed in one of the largest political landslides in the nation's history, Ronald Reagan began his second term as "Ronald II"—a smiling monarch who watched contentedly as his country seemed to grow richer amid the greatest economic boom of the post–World War II years. A combination of massive tax cuts and growing government deficits fueled the boom. In 1980 his political opponent, George H.W. Bush, had ridiculed Reagan's promise to cut taxes (and thus reduce government income) while boosting military spending and at the same time balancing the budget. Bush called this plan "voodoo economics." He nevertheless gladly joined up as Reagan's vice president and shared the glory of the Reaganomics boom. The U.S. gross national product (GNP) mushroomed to $5 trillion, nearly twice the size of either the Soviet or the Japanese economies.

Some Americans grew very rich. In 1982 there were thirteen billionaires; by 1988, at least fifty-one. Additional long-distance telephone area codes had to be devised for the Atlantic and Pacific oceans because of the many phone-equipped private yachts. New cultural heroes included multimillionaire basketball, football, and baseball players (some baseball pitchers averaged a $10,000 income for each inning they worked); New York real estate tycoon Donald Trump; and Wall Street wizards Michael Milken and Ivan Boesky. The world's most widely watched television program was *Dallas*, which told lurid stories about superrich and superdevious Texas oil families. *Falcon Crest*, starring Reagan's ex-wife Jane Wyman, did the same for the California superrich. New law school graduates worked long hours but enjoyed $50,000 to $75,000 or more in annual income at Wall Street firms. As the New York Stock Exchange's equities soared to all-time high prices in early 1987, one broker was stupefied: "It's unbelievable the amount of money that is out there."

For various reasons, however, the economy's health was less rosy than it appeared. First, Reaganomics, especially the tax laws of 1981 and 1986, badly skewed income distribution. In 1979, the average corporation's top executive made twenty-nine times the income of the average manufacturing worker; by 1988 it was ninety-three times. The richest 2.5 million Americans enjoyed a spectacular 75 percent increase in their income during the 1980s. By 1990 they had nearly as much income as the 100 million Americans who had the lowest incomes.

By the end of the Reagan years, 31.5 million people, or about 12 percent of the population, lived at the poverty level. (The U.S. government defined that level as below a $9,885 annual income for a family of three.) The percentage was higher than at any time in the 1970s. Blacks and other minorities especially suffered. Over 9 million African-Americans, or 2 million more than in 1978, lived at or below poverty levels despite the economic boom. Unemployment among blacks hovered around 15 percent, twice that among whites. Among inner-city young black adults, the rate soared to 50 percent. American children also suffered amid the boom. By 1990 almost 20 percent of them lived in poverty, but for black children the figure skyrocketed to 45 percent. It was the worst record among industrialized Western nations. Critics doubted whether many of these children could escape poverty through education. Many inner-city schools were battlegrounds. In the drug-soaked schools of Washington, DC, within sight of the nation's Capitol, thirteen-year-olds came to class armed with automatic weapons. The United States meanwhile ranked fourteenth out of sixteen industrialized nations in spending on elementary and secondary school students.

A second problem with Reaganomics also appeared. The president argued that his tax cuts would leave wealthy Americans with money that they could invest in productive enterprises. Instead, these Americans spent their new money on personal goods. Investment in the nation's factories and service sectors remained relatively flat. Between 1972 and 1989, Americans spent about 12 percent of their GNP on plant and equipment—the goods that produced new jobs and higher real income. Japan spent an average of 17 percent of its GNP on investment, and in 1989 that figure rose to 23 percent. The difference between American and Japanese investment figures helped explain why the Japanese seemed about to replace Americans as the most productive people in the world.

A third problem of Reaganomics was that Americans demanded more from their government than they were willing to pay in taxes. Reagan had promised to cut government spending, but, bowing to voters' demands, he and Congress instead increased it. Such "entitlement" programs as Social Security and Medicaid benefits nearly doubled in the 1980s. Government subsidies for American farmers rose from nearly $5 billion in 1979 to $26 billion in the late 1980s. Military spending doubled to $300 billion during the decade. The overall government budget, which Reagan had pledged to balance, was in the red by $100 billion or more every year by the end of his presidency. The U.S. national debt doubled to nearly $3 trillion.

In 1986 alone, Americans spent $150 billion more than they produced. Private borrowing and indebtedness approached $9 trillion, twice the level of 1980. Much of that spending, moreover, went to foreign producers. Americans bought shiploads of Toyotas, Walkmans, BMWs, and machine tools from abroad. In 1981, the United States had a favorable balance in its overall foreign trade. But between 1984 and 1989, it bought from $100 billion to $150 billion more each year from overseas than it sold.

Such spending led to the fourth problem of Reaganomics: to cover the gap between what they spent and what they produced, Americans borrowed from foreigners—especially the British, Canadians, Japanese, and Germans. In 1981 the United States had been the world's largest creditor, the globe's main source of money. By 1986 the nation had suddenly become the world's largest debtor. Because of its spending spree, it owed others a half-trillion dollars by the end of the 1980s. It would be "our children," as one economist wrote, who would have to pay off the 1980s debts or else sell off U.S. properties "our kids would otherwise have inherited." Many such properties still existed, he noted with sarcasm, "There's Fifth Avenue in New York, and the whole state of Oregon. Why not liquidate some of those assets and live it up a little longer?" It was not entirely a joke. Japanese investors stunned Americans by purchasing a controlling interest in Rockefeller Center in New York City. Democratic senator

Daniel Patrick Moynihan of New York feared that the 1980s would be remembered as the decade when Americans "borrowed a trillion dollars from the Japanese and threw a party."

Americans received other jolts. On the single day of October 19, 1987, the New York Stock Exchange's main economic indicator, the Dow-Jones average of thirty industrial stocks, dropped a historic 508 points. A half-trillion dollars of wealth disappeared in a matter of hours. As the market sank, Wall Street firms fired 15,000 employees, including many newly hired recent college graduates. Fraud and corruption through stock-rigging were discovered. Former cultural heroes such as Ivan Boesky and Michael Milken were sentenced to jail for financial frauds, while Donald Trump lost much of his financial empire. Stocks rose to new heights in 1990, then fell sharply again.

During 1988, Americans began to learn of the single largest economic failure in their history. More than a thousand savings-and-loan banks (S&Ls), in which millions of Americans had deposited their savings—and from which millions more had borrowed to buy property—went bankrupt. The disaster began in the early 1980s when many government regulations (some dating from the New Deal) were lifted by Reagan's deregulation program. S&L owners raised interest rates to attract depositors, and then put the money in risky, get-rich-quick real estate ventures. When real estate slumped in the Southwest in the mid-1980s and then in the Northeast, the banks lost billions of dollars. Individual depositors, luckily, were insured by the U.S. government for up to $100,000 per savings account. But that insurance had to be paid by taxpayers who would have to provide $500 billion (or $5,000 per household) over the next forty years to bail out the S&L industry.

By 1990, Americans had less control over their own economic future than at any time in the twentieth century. Foreigners held one-third of all U.S. savings and investments. In addition, Americans' dependence on imported foreign oil, after dropping in the early 1980s, rose to historic highs in 1990. Americans were the most energy-guzzling people in the world. The Japanese, who had begun radical energy-saving measures after the 1973 oil crisis, were two-and-one-half times more energy-efficient than Americans. This meant that the Japanese could produce two-and-one-half times more goods per unit of energy than Americans. The business executive who chaired the U.S. Presidential Council on Competitiveness concluded, "America is losing its ability to compete in world markets."

AMERICANS AND THE EMERGING WORLD: THE REAGAN DOCTRINE TO IRANAMOK

Having run in 1984 on the sunny campaign slogan that "It's Morning in America," the president announced in his 1985 State of the Union address that freedom "is the universal right of all God's children." Therefore, "we must stand by all our democratic allies. And we must not break faith with those who are risking their lives—on every continent, from Afghanistan to Nicaragua—to defy Soviet-supported aggression and secure rights which have been ours from birth." This "Reagan Doctrine," as observers called it, came under attack for implying that Americans actually had the power to "secure" such rights as democracy in, say, the Middle East or poverty-stricken parts of Africa. The president nevertheless increased aid to the Afghan resistance that had been fighting a bloody war against the Soviet invaders since 1979. By 1986 the aid included ground-to-air missiles that destroyed Red Army helicopters. In 1988, as 100,000 Russian troops bogged down and took heavy casualties, Moscow officials announced their forces would be withdrawn. But a pro-Soviet regime remained in power in Afghanistan as the resistance forces fell to bitter fighting among themselves over who would lead their movement.

In two other areas, the Reagan Doctrine worked even better—but, oddly, not as Reagan himself liked. In South Africa, 5.5 million whites had long dominated 23 million blacks through the policy of segregation and military control known as apartheid. Because the white government seemed stable, was the economic powerhouse for most of Africa, and shipped valuable minerals (including uranium used in nuclear weapons) to the United States, the Reagan administration followed a policy called constructive engagement. This policy tried to reform apartheid in a slow, friendly fashion. From 1984 to 1986, however, black towns exploded against the South African police. While the white police killed 6,000 protesters, Reagan did little. But over his opposition the U.S. Congress passed a bill to cut most economic ties between the United States and South Africa. This measure was helped along when opponents of apartheid forced some U.S. colleges and state legislatures to pull their profitable investments out of South Africa. By 1989 the South African economy was badly hurt. A new white government began repealing apartheid policies and released from jail the black community's most powerful leader, Nelson Mandela, who to the world's amazement would soon become South Africa's president.

In the Philippines, meanwhile, Ferdinand Marcos, who had reigned as dictator since 1972, was overthrown and replaced through elections by Corazón Aquino (wife of the murdered opposition leader Benigno Aquino). She came to power with the help of pressure from the U.S. Department of State (who feared that instability could increase communist rebels' power in the Philippines) and despite Reagan's support for his good friend Marcos. The Reagan Doctrine was working, but not always with the help of Reagan.

It turned out that he was somewhat more involved in making Middle East policy, but it erupted into his gravest crisis. Since his 1980 campaign, Reagan had promised he would never negotiate with terrorists who held American hostages. He took an especially tough public line against the fundamentalist Islamic regime in Iran that had overthrown the pro-U.S. shah in 1979. By 1985, Iran was fighting neighboring Iraq in one of the bloodiest and most brutal of twentieth-century wars. The Iranians needed military help. Pro-Iranian groups in the Middle East had seized American hostages, including at least one CIA agent. Pressured both by his close friend William Casey (the CIA director) and by Israel (which greatly feared Iraq's growing military capacity), Reagan secretly agreed to send weapons to Iran in return for the release of hostages. He made the decision over the strong objections of Secretary of State George Shultz and Defense Secretary Caspar Weinberger. After several hostages were freed, the White House lied by asserting that "no deal was made and that our position on no concessions to terrorists has not changed."

Casey had used a White House military aide, Lieutenant Colonel Oliver North, to help arrange the secret deal. A superpatriot who believed the Reagan Doctrine must be carried out at all costs, North had fought in Vietnam and swore that Americans must never again lose such a conflict. He was obsessed with the fear, however, that the Vietnam disaster was being rerun in Central America. There the Sandinistas controlled Nicaragua with help from Cuba and the Soviet Union (as well as many West European democracies). The Sandinistas had consolidated their power in 1984 by winning a national election, which Reagan refused to recognize as valid, and by militarily defeating the U.S.-supported Contra rebels. In Washington, Congress viewed the Contras not only as losers, but also as gross violators of human rights. Congress made illegal further U.S. government aid to the Contras. North then led an effort that obtained funds, from private U.S. citizens, for more than $22 million worth of military supplies for the Contras. In late 1986, however, the Justice Department discovered that North, with the approval of Casey and of North's superiors in the National Security Council, had broken the law by selling weapons to Iran and then sending the proceeds to the Contras.

Reagan denied any crimes and applauded North as "a national hero." But special investigations revealed that the laws no doubt had been broken, especially as North tried to cover up by lying to congressional committees and destroying and falsifying government documents. The president apparently knew little about the deals. Investigations showed the seventy-five-year-old chief executive to be an uninvolved, not very knowledgeable president who devoted most of his time to speeches and television appearances. As the true story of "Iranamok" (as the scandal was soon tagged) emerged, Reagan admitted mistakes had been made, but denied he knew of the illegal diversion of funds to the Contras. Several of North's associates were indicted for the crimes, but although he was convicted for obstructing Congress and destroying documents, his convictions were reversed in 1990 on technical legal grounds. North, Casey, and their Iran-Contra episode dragged Reagan into the lowest point of his presidency in 1987, just as the nation was celebrating its 200th anniversary of constitutional government.

THE COURT AND THE CONSTITUTION:
BORK AND THE BICENTENNIAL

In 1987, the celebration of the Constitution's bicentennial coincided with a bitter debate over President Reagan's nomination of Robert H. Bork as an associate justice of the Supreme Court. Relatively little controversy had surrounded Reagan's earlier appointments of Justices Sandra Day O'Connor and Antonin Scalia or the choice of William Rehnquist to replace retiring Warren Burger as chief justice in 1986. But the circumstances of the Bork nomination were unusual. As the replacement for Justice Lewis Powell, a moderate who had often cast the deciding vote in crucial 5-to-4 decisions, Bork could swing the Court in a new direction. No one doubted what direction that would be. Throughout a distinguished career as a law professor at Yale, as U.S. solicitor general, and as a circuit court judge, Bork had attacked the Supreme Court's liberal rulings. He had argued that, in weighing a statute's constitutionality, judges merely had to decide whether it accorded with the "original intent" of the Founders, a view that perfectly suited Attorney General Edwin Meese and other conservatives.

During much of the 1980s, the Burger Court, with some notable exceptions, had handed down liberal rulings that frustrated the Reagan administration's social agenda. For example, the Court ruled in *City of Akron v. Akron Center for Reproductive Health* (1983) that local ordinances making it difficult for women to obtain first- and second-trimester abortions were unconstitutional. Speaking for a majority of six, Justice Powell affirmed the *Roe v. Wade* precedent and described the right of privacy as a "long-recognized and essential element of personal liberty." In 1985, in *Wallace v. Jaffree*, the Court struck down an Alabama statute providing for a minute of silence in the public schools "for meditation or voluntary prayer." In a concurring opinion, Justice O'Connor declared that the Constitution prohibited "making adherence to a religion relevant in any way to a person's standing in the political community." In other decisions, the Court ruled that a Louisiana statute that required teachers to

Chief Justice William Rehnquist *(right)* and Anthony M. Kennedy, the nation's
104th Supreme Court justice, walk down the stairs at the Supreme Court building
in Washington, February 18, 1988. *(James Colburn/AFP/Getty Images)*

give "creation science" equal time with the theory of evolution was an improper attempt to
inject religion into the public schools, maintained the exclusionary rule (a ban on introducing
illegally seized material into evidence), and supported an increasingly strict equal protection
standard for women.

Those who supported Robert Bork, and those who opposed him, recognized that his confirmation could move the Court sharply to the right. He had condemned the case that helped
establish the right of privacy as "an unprincipled decision" and added that *Roe v. Wade* was
"an unconstitutional decision." Terming himself an "originalist" judge, who would always
be guided by "the intentions of those who framed and ratified our Constitution," Bork said
he would have no difficulty overturning a "non-originalist precedent." So it is not surprising that his nomination sparked a vitriolic debate. From the standpoint of one conservative
evangelical organization, Bork's elevation to the Court was "our last chance . . . to ensure
future decades will bring morality, godliness and justice back into focus." Liberal Democrats

like Senator Edward M. "Ted" Kennedy of Massachusetts countered that "Bork's America is a land where women would be forced into back-alley abortions, [and] blacks would sit at segregated lunch counters." In September, when the Senate Judiciary Committee considered the nomination, both sides organized extensive lobbying campaigns that included dramatic and sometimes misleading newspaper and television advertisements.

Eventually, the Judiciary Committee recommended against approval, and in October the Senate defeated the nomination by a vote of 58 to 42. Attorney General Meese thundered that Bork was a victim of "gutter politics," the president blamed the defeat on a "lynch mob," and Bork himself said he had been "tarred, feathered, and ridden out of town on a rail." But while political considerations certainly played a role in the defeat, many senators, including conservative Democrats and moderate Republicans, had concluded that Bork's brand of conservatism did, indeed, place him outside the mainstream. Eventually, President Reagan nominated Anthony Kennedy, an outspoken but less abrasive conservative, who soothed Senate sensibilities by speaking of a Constitution with a capacity for growth and of framers who had "made a covenant with the future." The Senate quickly confirmed the new nominee.

By 1988, therefore, the Supreme Court had begun to take on a more conservative cast. Nothing more clearly illustrated this than the Court's attitude toward abortion. In *Webster v. Reproductive Health Care Services*, decided in July 1989, a five-member majority upheld a Missouri statute containing twenty provisions designed to curb a woman's right to choice. Physicians, before consenting to abortions, were supposed to perform tests (of weight, size, and lung capacity) to determine whether a fetus they thought was more than twenty weeks old was "viable"; no viable fetus was to be aborted except to preserve the pregnant woman's life or health. Four justices indicated they were prepared to overturn *Roe v. Wade*, but Justice O'Connor, although voting with the majority, did not believe the Missouri statute required the Court to reconsider that precedent. Speaking for the majority, Chief Justice Rehnquist held that the various state legislatures should set policies on abortion. The Supreme Court's goal, he said, "is not to remove inexorably 'politically divisive' issues from the ambit of the legislative process." In a scathing dissent, Justice Harry Blackmun charged that the decision would precipitate "a constitutional crisis," foment "disregard for the law," and dangerously enhance "the coercive and brooding influence of the state."

In other areas, however, even this more conservative Court adhered to liberal precedents. Perhaps the most controversial case concerned flag burning. In 1989, in *Texas v. Johnson*, Justices Scalia and Kennedy joined three liberal colleagues in holding that flag burning conveyed an "overtly political" message and therefore merited constitutional protection. The "bedrock principle" underlying the First Amendment, Justice William Brennan declared, was that government could not "prohibit the expression of an idea simply because society finds the idea itself offensive or disagreeable." Congress, seeking to get around the decision, passed a Flag Protection Act in 1989, but it too was ruled unconstitutional in 1990 in *United States v. Eichman.*

With Justice Brennan's retirement in 1990 and his replacement by President George Bush's first nominee, Justice David Souter, it seemed that the Court might move in a more conservative direction, yet the justices' inclination to adhere to precedent, and the existence of a consensus in behalf of certain rights, worked against any dramatic turnabout. Prior decisions protecting freedom of speech and religion and outlawing racial and sexual discrimination enjoyed support across the judicial spectrum. Moreover, the Court had begun to consider a new range of

Abortion advocates rally outside the U.S. Supreme Court, June 1989. *(Michael Jenkins/Congressional Quarterly/Getty Images)*

problems—the right to die, for example, and surrogate parenthood—that did not easily fit the liberal-conservative categorization. Still another new issue was the environment. As concern with environmental health and safety grew in the 1980s, so did the number of cases brought before the courts by environmental activists.

EARTH DAY AND THE ENVIRONMENT

When Ronald Reagan was first elected president, a National Broadcasting Company news analyst predicted "the end of the environmental movement." Given Reagan's views, the prediction did not seem unreasonable. As governor of California, he had opposed the expansion of Redwood National Park with the comment, "a tree is a tree. How many more do you need to look at?" He also remarked that a study had shown "that 80 percent of air pollution comes not from chimneys and auto exhaust pipes, but from plants and trees." Convinced that environmentalists were "radical extremists," the Reagan administration, according to one historian, "launched a massive assault on two decades of environmental programs."

In the course of those two decades, the environmental movement had successfully educated people about threats to the land, air, and water. Responding to a growing public awareness, Congress passed the National Environmental Policy Act in 1970 and then a series of laws designed to limit environmental hazards, protect wilderness areas, and preserve endangered species. Supported by such organizations as the Sierra Club and the Wilderness Society,

THE FITNESS CRAZE

Over 25,000 runners cross the Verrazano-Narrows Bridge at the start of the 1993 New York City Marathon. *(Bob Strong/AFP/Getty Images)*

In 1988 *Esquire* magazine told the story of a forty-one-year-old Seattle venture capitalist who had never made a sustained effort to keep himself in shape. Recently separated from his wife and facing "some tough business challenges," he suffered from high blood pressure and could "barely summon up the energy to get through the day." But his situation changed when he began an eight-week program to increase energy developed by a local consulting firm. Walking with weights, pursuing a course of aerobic exercise, doing push-ups and stretches, and changing his diet, he lost body fat, lowered his cholesterol, and boosted his strength and flexibility. At the end of the program his coworkers reported "a startling shift in his ability to come up with innovative ideas" and "to follow through on his commitments."

The experience of the Seattle investor was part of a physical fitness vogue that gained momentum in the 1970s, when jogging and running became popular. Running, its advocates claimed, increased longevity, prolonged youthfulness, staved off heart disease, built up endurance, reduced minor ills, and induced exhilaration. Doubters cited a list of hazards, such as strained knees, stress fractures, bone bruises, and inflamed tendons, but the benefits of running, enthusiasts contended, outweighed the risks. By 1977, the Road Runners Club, a national runners' organization, boasted 125 local chapters. Big-city marathons attracted hundreds of thousands of competitors. Of a dozen runners' magazines, the leader, *Runner's World*, claimed a circulation of 165,000.

By the 1980s the passion for fitness had generated a new institution, the health club. A descendant of the neighborhood gym, the one-time hangout of weight lifters and bodybuilders, the health club catered to a larger and more upscale clientele. In 1980, there were about 10,000 such clubs; a decade later, twice as many. Full-fledged health clubs provided squash and racquetball courts, jogging tracks, lap pools, whirlpools, steam rooms, saunas, scuba classes, weight training, and nutrition counseling. They contained fitness machinery, such as treadmills, cycling machines, stair-climbers, and weight-lifting apparatus. Health clubs also offered classes in physical conditioning—calisthenics, yoga, stretching, self-defense, and aerobics. Following the commands of energetic instructors, students of aerobics leaped and gyrated to tapes of disco and rock music, played at high volume and sped up to 150 beats a minute. The health club doctrine of "no pain, no gain" could cause problems. A California survey of 1,200 participants in aerobic classes reported that 43 percent had suffered minor injuries—as had 76 percent of their instructors. *Newsweek* advised readers to avoid cut-rate chain clubs, seek instructors with degrees in exercise physiology, or join deluxe establishments, where members received electrocardiograms, cholesterol analyses, and personalized programs prescribed by cardiologists. By the end of the decade sophisticated clubs offered courses in self-esteem and stress management.

The fitness craze also invaded the home, via the videocassette recorder and fitness tapes. Between 1983 and 1986, actress Jane Fonda's videotapes sold more than 900,000 copies worldwide. The profits of home exercise extended to the makers of exercise machinery. According to the National Sporting Goods Association, consumers spent $1.58 billion on home-workout equipment in the single year 1987. Retailers sold more than 1 million stationary bikes and as many rowers; hundreds of thousands of treadmills, stair climbers, cross-country trainers, and weight benches; and 586,000 home gyms—machines that provided complete workouts and cost up to $2,495.

By the start of the 1990s, the big spender had replaced the humble jogger. Physical fitness was a major industry. No facet of the industry made more impressive progress than athletic footwear: the simple sneaker had developed into a wardrobe of "athletic shoes" for specialized purposes. By 1990, the nation had a $5 billion athletic footwear business. As the attributes and prices of the shoes increased, so did the profits of their producers. Between 1984 and 1990, the revenues of Reebok International, the largest manufacturer of athletic footwear after Nike, increased 2,760 percent. The company's chairperson became the best-compensated chief executive, in terms of salary and bonus, of any publicly owned American corporation. His annual income skyrocketed from $1.2 million in 1984 to $14.6 million five years later, before he took a voluntary pay cut.

As the Cold War thawed and opportunities arose for business ventures in the Soviet Union, athletic footwear gained access to new markets. In 1990, just before the collapse of the USSR, a Long Island corporation signed an agreement with a Soviet firm for the manufacture of equipment and the training of 600 Russian workers, who would then make 50 million pairs of shoes over a ten-year period. The major item to be produced, not surprisingly, was an inexpensive "canvas-and-leather jogger shoe."

Web Links

www.nycmarathon.org/
The official website of the New York City marathon, including a history of the race.

www.baa.org/
The official website of the Boston marathon, including photos, videos, and stories.

most of the legislation won broad, bipartisan approval. Moreover, the Supreme Court generally granted conservationists standing, thereby enabling them to bring suits against business concerns responsible for pollution and against government agencies that failed to enforce the new laws. "Ecology," commented a California Democrat, "has become the political substitute for the word 'mother.'"

Public concern focused first on the need to maintain forests, parks, wildlife refuges, and open spaces, then on the dangers of air and water pollution, and, by the mid-1970s, on the importance of energy conservation and the cleaning up of hazardous wastes. Widespread publicity surrounding tragic incidents stimulated that concern. In 1978, for example, it was discovered that residents near the Love Canal in Erie County, New York, an area used as a chemical junkyard, were experiencing abnormally high rates of cancer, miscarriages, and birth defects. President Carter designated the Love Canal an emergency area. In 1979, an accident at the Three Mile Island power plant in Pennsylvania revealed the danger posed by radioactive material in nuclear reactors. By 1980, many Americans recognized the crucial importance of energy conservation, pollution control, and recycling. Barry Commoner, a leading environmentalist, warned that the continuation of older, wasteful policies "will destroy the capability of the environment to support a reasonably civilized human society."

However, programs to protect the environment conflicted with the incoming Reagan administration's determination to cut federal spending, reduce federal control, and promote private enterprise. With these goals in mind, Reagan sought to eliminate the Council on Environmental Quality, slashed funding for the Environmental Protection Agency, and placed such crucial agencies as the Bureau of Land Management, the Occupational Safety and Health Administration, and the National Park Service in the hands of administrators who had little sympathy for environmental concerns. James Watt, the new secretary of the interior, had championed the "Sagebrush Rebellion," an attempt to turn acreage in the national forests over to the states and permit private development. Anne Gorsuch, who headed the Environmental Protection Agency, favored permissive policies in policing pollution. By 1982, Congressman Morris Udall, an Arizona Democrat, could comment that Watt and Gorsuch "have done for the environment what Bonnie and Clyde did for banks."

In time, however, Reagan's "antienvironmental revolution" failed. Membership in national environmental groups soared from 4 million to 7 million in the 1980s and so did the organizations' political effectiveness. Congress frequently blocked efforts to undermine protective policies. Many states created their own, highly effective enforcement programs. Some of the most ardent antienvironmentalists were forced to resign and were replaced by administrators who more nearly reflected the national consensus. Reagan reluctantly approved environmental laws that added more acreage to the National Wilderness Preservation System in the forty-eight contiguous states than had been added under any previous president. Twenty-nine new wildlife refuges were established, and 200 plants and animals were added to the nation's list of endangered species. Measurable progress was also made in removing hazardous wastes from landfills, eliminating lead from gasoline, and protecting the ozone layer by reducing the use of chlorofluorocarbons. Environmentalists had turned back a frontal assault. As Carl Pope, a Sierra Club official, noted, "By the middle of Reagan's second term his administration's new initiatives were far closer to the mainstream than to the privatized, deregulated world the president's pre-inauguration team had laid out."

A factory worker in the union hall of Sheet Metal Workers Local 459 in a small town about to be hard-hit by the closing of a profitable manufacturing plant. *(Grey Villet/Time Life Pictures/Getty Images)*

WOMEN, THE WORKPLACE, AND THE FAMILY

For women wage earners of the 1980s, the campaign for equality involved the workplace. By mid-decade, 55 percent of women had joined the labor force, where they held about 45 percent of the jobs. Since 1980, notably, women had filled four out of five new jobs. Major concerns included wage inequities, prospects for advancement, and the integration of paid work with family life.

Some issues reflected the rapid increase in the number of working mothers. By the end of the 1980s, 68 percent of women with children were employed. Most working parents of preschoolers left them with relatives or private caretakers or in informal, unlicensed child care arrangements. One-quarter of young children attended day care centers. Still, day care remained a minimum-wage industry, with low-paid personnel and high turnover, which usually offered only custodial care; "quality care" entailed expense. Surveys reported that working women's major goals were "helping balance work and family" and "getting government funding for programs such as child-care and maternity leave."

Pregnant workers faced special problems. The federal disability law of 1978 barred discrimination against prospective mothers; a California law went further. It required unpaid leave of several months for pregnant women, who would regain their original jobs on return. In 1987, the Supreme Court upheld the California measure in *California Savings and Loan Association v. Guerra.* But the case evoked a furor about "preferential treatment." The National

Organization for Women (NOW), for instance, criticized the California law. To regard women under law as a different class of workers, NOW contended, would foster sexist stereotypes and increase discrimination against women. One solution seemed to be "parental" leave, available to either parent. By the end of the 1980s, seven states had passed parental leave laws. In 1990, President Bush vetoed a "family leave" bill that would have offered unpaid leave to workers with family obligations. Although he favored the policy, the president claimed, it should be voluntary and not obligatory on the part of employers.

Other issues involved wage differentials between male and female workers. By the end of the 1980s, the average earnings of full-time women workers were 70 percent those of men, and young women earned yet higher proportions of male wages. Still, discrepancies remained and experts offered many possible explanations: women were predominant among new entrants to the job market; they had more interruptions in their work careers; they were less likely to work in unionized sectors; if they had families, they may have preferred convenient or flexible work to higher pay; or they may have met discriminatory treatment. A lobbyist for the Women's Equity Action League blamed wage differentials on "sex discrimination, the old boys' network, and massive stereotyping of women's work." Despite women's entry into higher-paid occupations, most women of the 1980s faced a segregated job market. Three out of five held pink-collar jobs, and as a Census Bureau official explained, "Working in an occupation that has a high proportion of women has a negative effect on earnings."

The segregated job market fostered the demand for "pay equity" or "comparable worth"—an effort to raise pay levels in occupations in which women predominated. A clerical worker, pay equity advocates contended, should receive the same pay as a truck driver working for the same employer. The premise of pay equity was that the "worth" of a job could be rationally determined, based on such factors as skill, training, effort, and responsibility. Critics contended that the concept took no notice of "market forces," or the demand for certain types of workers. Supporters, too, voiced qualifications. A study published in the *Harvard Law Review* contended that comparable worth, though desirable, defied implementation by the courts and would have only a negligible impact on women's wages. A study of pay equity among public employees in Minnesota suggested that it remedied low wages but increased managerial power. Yet for feminists, pay equity retained appeal. It would affect large numbers of ordinary wage earners rather than those professionals who had thus far been the main beneficiaries of feminist breakthroughs.

A third issue concerned opportunities for advancement. Attention centered on the business world. By the mid-1980s, 30 percent of managerial personnel were women. But studies of women executives revealed "ambivalence" and "business burnout"; success in the higher ranks of business or the professions seemed to exact a price in personal life. In 1989, Felice Schwartz, president of a research group that focused on women in business, urged in the *Harvard Business Review* that women who chose to fulfill family obligations might join a slower work track that peaked at middle management. The "mommy track" evoked a storm of protest. One critic charged that it would "perpetuate a cycle in which generations of women have been depreciated, divided, and weakened." Schwartz replied that she was urging employers to "create policies that help mothers balance career and family responsibilities" and "eliminate barriers to productivity and advancement."

The changing structure of the economy itself posed problems for women workers. Since 1970, the rise of service industries and the impact of advanced technology had created many jobs for women. But new options entailed new liabilities: computers had both increased female employment and transformed the nature of office work. They may have also devalued the labor of clerical employees, for whom repetitive data-processing tasks resembled piecework. "Automation is producing the sweatshops of the 1980s," an official of a secretarial union declared. Part-time work presented problems, too. As women surged into the labor market, employers relied increasingly on temporary or part-time workers. Less costly to employers, such "contingent" workers lacked the benefits guaranteed to full-time employees. Women's need for flexible jobs could create a class of second-class workers.

Although married women constituted the majority of new employees, another group of women workers had steadily grown. Between 1970 and the mid-1980s, the numbers of women living alone increased by 73 percent, the rate of separation and divorce increased by 80 percent, and the number of women heading households increased by 84 percent. In 1986, 45 percent of women workers were single or formerly married, and many were heads of households with families to maintain. The decline of the "traditional" family increased women workers' need for a "family wage." Advocates of equity for women workers therefore faced a variety of considerations. Any acceptance in law or custom of gender distinctions might foster discrimination against women workers and leave them at a competitive disadvantage. On the other hand, insistence on absolute equality could limit the options for "flexible work" and "balance" that many women wage earners demanded.

AIDS, DRUGS, AND PRIVACY

Concern with two more immediate problems—the AIDS (acquired immune deficiency syndrome) epidemic and the growing use of crack cocaine—also came to shape public policy in the 1980s. The two problems resembled each other in certain ways: both were unknown in 1980 but had become focal points of public attention by the early 1990s; both involved issues of personal conduct that gave rise to moral judgments; both had a racial dimension; and both led to a debate over testing that posed profound questions about freedom, privacy, and social control. Moreover, women who contracted AIDS and those who used crack often gave birth to children who suffered from severe disorders or who were doomed.

In 1981, the first cases of AIDS were diagnosed among gay men. Caused by a slow-acting virus, the disease was spread through contaminated blood or semen. Since transmission usually occurred through anal intercourse or the use of shared hypodermic needles, AIDS chiefly affected homosexual males and intravenous drug users. But the disease also claimed other victims: heterosexuals who had unprotected sexual relations with carriers of the virus; patients who received transfusions of contaminated blood; newborns who were infected with the virus through their mothers' placentas; and, in a very few instances, physicians, nurses, and other health care workers who were exposed accidentally.

By 1983, 1,000 cases of AIDS had been diagnosed in the United States; by 1985, 9,000 cases; by 1990, 150,000 cases; and by 1996, nearly 515,000 cases. By then the disease had claimed the lives of 320,000 Americans. Males accounted for approximately 85 percent of those who contracted the disease, women for approximately 13 percent, and children under the age of thirteen for less than 2 percent. AIDS exacted a disproportionate toll among racial and ethnic minorities: 50 percent of the victims were whites, but 33 percent were African-Americans and 17 percent were Hispanics. Since persons infected with HIV (human immunodeficiency virus) usually remain asymptomatic for many years, many thousands more were certain to develop AIDS.

Because the illness could not be discussed without frankly mentioning sexual practices that had always been regarded as taboo, it took several years for AIDS to enter the public's consciousness. By the mid-1980s, however, the subject had become ubiquitous. In July 1985, *Life* magazine ran a cover story titled "Now No One Is Safe from AIDS"; in 1986, Surgeon General C. Everett Koop called for AIDS education "at the earliest grade possible"; in 1987, half a million people marched on Washington to demand gay rights and increased AIDS funding; in 1988, President Reagan signed a bill designating October as AIDS Awareness/ Prevention Month.

Eventually, Surgeon General Koop unveiled a national advertising campaign designed to promote the use of condoms to fight AIDS. Angry conservatives denounced Koop's approach, grumbling that it would encourage young people to have illicit sex and that it "tacitly endorses the moral position of those who consider homosexuality an acceptable alternative life-style." Despite such complaints, by 1990 the nation experienced what one writer dubbed "condomania": "safe sex" Valentine's Day cards, with enclosed condoms, soon appeared on the shelves of greeting card stores, a major university hosted a "Condom Olympics," and sales of prophylactics skyrocketed.

One of the most controversial issues associated with the disease was testing for HIV. The advantages of testing were obvious: people who were infected with the virus, but still asymptomatic would be able to conduct their lives, inform their partners, and plan their futures accordingly. Yet, as gay rights activists pointed out, testing could invade individuals' privacy and make it easier to enforce discriminatory measures. "Will test results be used to identify the sexual orientation of millions of Americans?" one gay newspaper asked. "Will a list of names be made? How can such information be kept confidential? Who will be able to keep this list out of the hands of insurance companies?" Nevertheless, public opinion polls revealed high levels of support for mandatory testing, and by 1987 the government had introduced such programs for all military personnel, reservists, and new recruits; for immigrants and illegal aliens applying for amnesty; for patients seeking admission to Veterans Administration hospitals; for inmates in federal prisons; and for applicants to the Peace Corps, Job Corps, and Foreign Service programs.

One of the few problems Americans ranked in importance even above AIDS was drugs. The two were linked, of course, since intravenous drug use was one way of spreading the deadly virus. But concern with drugs soon focused on a new form of cocaine, crack, that began to be sold in 1985. Soaking cocaine and baking soda in water, and then applying heat, produced crystals, called crack that could then be crushed and smoked. Crack was relatively cheap (selling for $5 or $10 a vial) and therefore readily available. As one expert explained, the onset of the drug's impact is "a matter of six to eight seconds, and the intense, orgasmlike high or rush lasts for perhaps two minutes, followed by a kind of afterglow that lasts ten to twenty minutes." Crack users experienced a physical addiction as well as an overpowering psychological dependence.

While cocaine use was widespread in the 1980s—22 million Americans said they had tried the drug, and 6 million used it regularly—crack, more than any other form of the drug, created chronic, compulsive users. To obtain money to support their habit, many users committed violent crimes: in 1989, for example, one-quarter of all convicted prison and jail inmates had

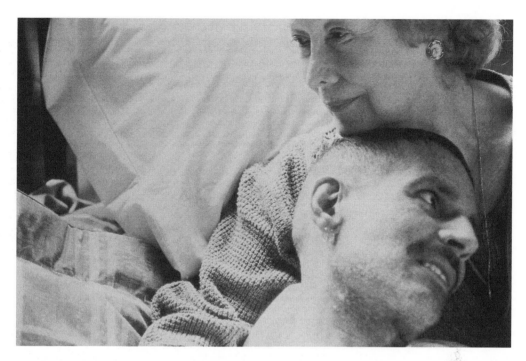

A mother embraces her son, who has AIDS. *(Bruce Ayres/Stone/Getty Images)*

used crack or cocaine in the month before their offense. Crack addicts were also prone not only to hurting others but also themselves: cocaine-related hospital emergency admissions jumped from 4,300 in 1982 to 46,000 in 1988. It was estimated that from 30,000 to 50,000 "crack babies" were born each year, 7,000 in New York City alone. Writing in the *New York Times* in 1990, Anna Quindlen described a neonatal intensive care unit: "Babies born months too soon; babies born weighing little more than a hardcover book; babies that look like wizened old men in the last stages of a terminal illness, wrinkled skin clinging to chicken bones; babies who do not cry because their mouths and noses are full of tubes."

Politicians outdid each other in taking a tough stand on drugs. President Reagan pledged, "to do what is necessary to end the drug menace" and "to cripple the power of the mob in America." In 1988, Congress passed a harsh Anti-Drug Abuse Act, which imposed stiff fines for the possession of illegal drugs, even if only for personal use; sanctioned pretrial detention and mandatory life sentences for some offenders; authorized urine testing of civil service and other workers; and provided for bus boardings, roadblocks, and other dragnet enforcement techniques. The war on drugs required an enormous increase in law enforcement personnel and, therefore, in expenditures. Federal spending on drug enforcement rose accordingly: from $1.5 billion in 1981, to $6.7 billion in 1989, to $11.9 billion in 1992.

Because crack was relatively cheap and widely available in the inner cities, it had an especially ravaging effect on African-Americans. This racial aspect led to a heated debate when Congress imposed harsher penalties for crack than for powder cocaine offenders. The government argued that such penalties were warranted because of crack's "greater abuse and dependency potential, its marketing in inexpensive quantities that makes it accessible to youth and those in a lower socioeconomic status, its association with violent crime, and its contribution to the deterioration of neighborhoods and communities." But the Reverend Jesse L. Jackson, citing statistics to show that while most crack users were white, most of those incarcerated in federal prisons for crack use were black, condemned the disparity in penalties. Echoing his view, the American Civil Liberties Union claimed that sentencing differentials "are highly inequitable against African-Americans, and represent a national drug policy tinged with racism."

The war on drugs scored some important victories, which could be measured by arrests and convictions of drug dealers, seizures of their supplies, and forfeitures of their assets. From 1984 to 1992, arrests by state and local police for the sale or manufacture of drugs doubled, while arrests for possession increased by 40 percent. The public favored stiff penalties for drug dealers and the testing of workers in dangerous or sensitive jobs. But all the punitive measures did not prevent even more cocaine from entering the United States. Moreover, as the number of drug-related convictions rose, judges imposed longer sentences and parole became more difficult to obtain, the prisons filled to the bursting point, and the cost of maintaining them became burdensome. President Reagan's goal of a "drug-free America" remained elusive.

BUSH VERSUS DUKAKIS: 1988

As the 1988 election approached, the nation faced a backlog of problems. The budget deficit and trade deficit, the epidemics of drugs and AIDS, the S&L economic debacle, the neglect of the environment, and the long-term decline of American industry—all seemed to play into the Democrats' hands. So did the "sleaze factor" that had characterized the Reagan years. Scores of administration officials had been convicted of misconduct in office or awaited trial, as did the leading figures in the Iran-Contra scandal. Astoundingly, none of these issues dominated the 1988 presidential race. Instead, the campaign itself took precedence. The "sound bite" on the nightly television news, the political commercial with a startling "visual," and "negative campaigning" became the most prominent features of the election.

At the Democratic convention in Atlanta, Massachusetts governor Michael Dukakis captured the nomination. His major rival in the primaries had been Jesse Jackson, who won both the black vote and a larger share of white votes than he had in his 1984 campaign. Dukakis chose as his running mate Texas senator Lloyd Bentsen, a conservative Democrat who had many years earlier defeated the Republican presidential candidate, Vice President George H.W. Bush, in a Texas Senate race. Bentsen, it was expected, would appeal to southerners and to party members who found Dukakis too liberal. The Democrats launched their attack on Bush with a rush of enthusiasm. Keynote speaker Ann Richards, the state treasurer of Texas, mocked the vice president's upper-class upbringing and proclivity for inept remarks. "Poor George," she declared. "He was born with a silver foot in his mouth." When the convention ended, public opinion polls gave the Democrats an overwhelming seventeen-point lead.

The Republican nominee had to overcome a liability called the "wimp factor," or a tendency to seem weak and ineffective. Bush also had to shed his eight-year record as Reagan's shadow and establish an independent identity. His acceptance speech, composed by former Reagan speechwriter Peggy Noonan, suggested that he might do both. To sever himself from his predecessor, Bush urged a "kinder, gentler America." Borrowing a popular phrase from a Clint Eastwood movie—"Read my lips"—he promised "no new taxes." Expressing interest in the young, he vowed to become the "education president." Ignoring the economic crises that the Reagan years had precipitated, Bush urged Americans to develop private agencies of voluntary benevolence, "a thousand points of light." Peggy Noonan's phrases and the vice president's effective delivery were undercut only by the nominee's choice of running mate. Bush selected Senator Dan Quayle of Indiana, who seemed likely to be a docile henchman, as Bush had been for Reagan, and whose youthful looks, Republicans hoped, would sway the women's vote. Quayle at once proved a liability. Unprepared and inarticulate, he was unable to field reporters' questions. Moreover, the press reported that he had probably used family connections to gain admission to his state's National Guard in 1969 and thereby avoid combat service in Vietnam. For the rest of the campaign, the Republicans surrounded Quayle with an entourage of advisers, separated him from Bush, and kept him out of the limelight.

George Bush quickly proved an effective and professional campaigner. Ignoring the budget crisis and the Iran-Contra scandal, he capitalized on the positive: the nation enjoyed a period of peace, low inflation, and better relations with the Soviet Union. Simultaneously, his campaign team seized the offensive. Dukakis, the Republicans charged, was weak on crime, defense, and patriotism. Bush attacked Dukakis for vetoing a bill requiring Massachusetts schoolchildren to recite the Pledge of Allegiance. The Supreme Court had declared such laws unconstitutional, the Democratic nominee explained, but his negative ratings rose. As a follow-up, Bush visited a flag factory. He then assaulted Dukakis as soft on criminals. Republicans ran television commercials about a black man who had committed rape and murder while on release from a Massachusetts prison on a furlough program. Negative campaigning was under way and affected state races as well. New Jersey voters viewed television spots that depicted the rival gubernatorial candidates as liars: each was shown with a nose that grew like Pinocchio's.

Spurning the very notion of negative campaigning, Michael Dukakis refused to reply to the Bush assaults. Instead, he posed in a tank to indicate his interest in a strong defense, promised "good jobs at good wages," stressed his managerial know-how, and pointed to the economic "Massachusetts Miracle." Nor did he attack the failures or philosophy of the Reagan administration. The election was not about "ideology," Dukakis claimed, but about "competence." Running-mate Lloyd Bentsen, an experienced and astute campaigner, presented a reassuring image. The nominee himself seemed moody, awkward, defensive, and unable to find an effective campaign theme. Only in the last few weeks of the contest did he mobilize a counterattack, refute the Republican negative charges as "lies" and garbage," and defend his role as a "liberal," a word that the Republicans had used as a term of opprobrium. But this effort came too late. The Democrats had been forced to wage a defensive fight and had never controlled the campaign agenda.

On Election Day, the Republicans won 54 percent of the popular vote for president to the Democrats' 46 percent, and an electoral college victory of 426 to 112. The Bush-Quayle ticket had carried forty states, including the entire South and almost all the western half of the nation. The Democrats fared better in the contest for president than they had in their four losing races since 1968. They also retained control of the House and the Senate, gained seats in both, and won majorities in most state legislatures. Still, in presidential races, the Democratic Party apparently faced an uphill road. Democrats had won 88 percent of black votes for president, but only four out of ten white votes. They had not regained the once solid South, now solidly Republican, nor the support of blue-collar voters, who had defected to the Republicans in the Reagan years. The traditional Democratic coalition seemed to have vanished. Most troubling was the impact of negative campaigning. As an Ohio pollster for a Democratic candidate commented, "The issues mean less and less, and the ads mean more and more." And in 1988, campaign ads had conveyed distorted messages that played on voters' fears.

CULTURE WARS AND THE BUSH ADMINISTRATION

To a remarkable degree, public attention in the late 1980s and early 1990s focused on what sociologists termed "culture wars." Some of the conflicts were of long-standing duration, such as those between pro-choice and right-to-life groups, between supporters and opponents of prayer in the public schools, and between advocates of teaching "creation science" to schoolchildren and critics who claimed the subject was not a science at all but rather religion masquerading as science. But a host of new issues arose that revealed deeply rooted cultural divisions just as clearly. In 1988, for example, Universal Studios released *The Last Temptation of Christ*, directed by Martin Scorsese, a film depicting Jesus as afflicted by doubt and subject to lust, pride, anger, and the fear of death. While a sympathetic reviewer termed it "one of the most serious, literate, complex, and deeply felt religious films ever made," conservative Catholics and evangelicals, such as the Reverend Jerry Falwell, denounced the film as "utter blasphemy of the worst degree."

In this contentious atmosphere, it was not surprising that the National Endowment for the Arts (NEA), which funded a wide range of cultural activities, became a lightning rod for criticism. In 1989, the NEA came under fire for indirectly funding the work of photographers Andres Serrano and Robert Mapplethorpe. Serrano had photographed a crucifix in a jar of urine and entitled the work "Piss Christ." Some of Mapplethorpe's photographs were explicitly homoerotic, and another one turned the image of the Virgin Mary into a tie rack. To admirers of the avant-garde, these works fulfilled an artist's responsibility to explore "the forbidden frontiers of human experience." But to critics, they were simply "morally reprehensible trash." Congress responded by slashing the NEA's budget and making it clear to the agency that certain kinds of art should not be funded.

Although George Bush had successfully exploited these kinds of cultural divisions in his 1988 election campaign, he showed little inclination, once ensconced in the White House, to exploit them any further. An instinctively cautious politician with a risk-averse temperament, Bush, unlike Ronald Reagan, distrusted change and disliked domestic crusades. Nor did he enjoy his predecessor's ardent support among conservative ideologues in the Republican Party. Much better informed about government than Reagan ever was and therefore more willing to speak to the press, Bush nevertheless sought a relatively low profile, at least in domestic affairs. As his director of communications once said, "The president does not see himself at the center of national attention."

His personal style shaped the way Bush dealt with a Congress that remained under Democratic control throughout his administration. The president seldom proposed bold domestic programs. Instead, he relied on his veto power to check congressional initiatives. By May 1992, he had vetoed twenty-eight bills, and the Democrats had never been able to muster the two-thirds vote in both houses necessary to override. But Bush's strategy paid few political dividends. When, in the summer of 1990, he accepted a tax increase in order to induce Congress to pass an acceptable budget, he was blamed for going back on a campaign promise even though he succeeded in implementing spending controls. When he vetoed a highly popular family and medical leave bill, he alienated a large number of voters who thought the measure made good sense, and this time his veto was overridden. Moreover, he received virtually no credit for the significant Americans with Disabilities Act of 1990, which prohibited discrimination against people with disabilities in employment, public services, transportation, and public accommodations. It required employers to make reasonable accommodations for workers who had a physical or mental impairment, who had a record of such impairment, or who were regarded by others as having such an impairment (for example, a disfiguring scar).

As president, however, George Bush presided over a dramatically expanded federal establishment. The average annual growth in domestic spending during his years in office was $29 billion, five times the rate under Ronald Reagan. In part, the increased expenditures were simply a legacy of the Reagan years: interest on the national debt amounted to $286 billion a year by 1992, and the bailout of savings and loan institutions cost $300 billion from 1989 to 1991. The spending also reflected the president's support for programs like Head Start, AIDS research, and environmental protection, including proposals to reduce acid rain, halt the destruction of the wetlands, end the contamination of groundwater, and ban the ocean dumping of medical wastes.

Recognizing that some of his policies had alienated conservative Republicans, the president sought to regain their favor by appointing a conservative ideologue to the Supreme Court. His selection of David Souter in 1990 had not served that purpose. But in 1991, when Justice Thurgood Marshall resigned, Bush nominated forty-three-year-old Judge Clarence Thomas, an African-American who, although lacking in significant judicial experience, was a darling of the far right. As chair of the Equal Employment Opportunity Commission (EEOC) during the Reagan years, Thomas had come out against affirmative action. But his nomination proved unexpectedly controversial when law professor Anita Hill, a former employee of Thomas's at the EEOC, claimed that he had sexually harassed her. During televised hearings of the Senate Judiciary Committee, Hill said Thomas had pressured her for dates and described sexually explicit acts he had viewed on pornographic films. Thomas denied her allegations and denounced the proceedings as "a high-tech lynching for uppity blacks." In October, the Senate finally voted to confirm Thomas by a vote of 52 to 48, the fewest number of votes any successful nominee to the Court had ever received.

The hearings went far toward solidifying a gender gap that was destined to have far-reaching political implications. Polls revealed that women were far more likely to believe Hill's story than were men, and senators (and the EEOC) were inundated with letters from women who said they had experienced similar types of harassment. Coinciding with the so-called Tailhook scandal, in which navy officers were found to have behaved improperly toward female officers at a convention, and with evidence that Senator Robert Packwood of Oregon had for many years harassed women who worked for him, the Thomas hearings raised the nation's consciousness about an issue that had too often been hushed up, minimized, or ignored.

In domestic affairs, George Bush had sought, with only partial success, to preserve the status quo. The president's view of Congress was expressed by John Sununu, his chief domestic aide, in November 1990. Speaking to a conservative group in Washington, DC, Sununu said that the administration had already obtained what it wanted from Congress and nothing more was needed: "In fact, if Congress wants to come together, adjourn, and leave, it's all right with us. We don't need them." It was in foreign affairs that George Bush—resembling no one so much as Richard Nixon—wished to leave his mark. And it was in foreign policy that he became the beneficiary of an unanticipated windfall: the sudden termination of the Cold War.

President Reagan and Soviet leader Mikhail Gorbachev in Red Square, Moscow, 1988. *(Courtesy, Ronald Reagan Library)*

THE END OF THE "EVIL EMPIRE"—
AND OF THE COLD WAR

As George Bush entered the White House, the Cold War was changing more radically than it had in forty-five years. No change was more important than the surprising crumbling of Communist Party control inside the Soviet Union and the rapid collapse of the communist bloc abroad. The Soviet revolution, which had spanned, and shaped, so much of the twentieth century seemed—to the astonishment of everyone—suddenly to be totally collapsing.

The person who presided over this historic upheaval, Mikhail Gorbachev, had led the Soviet Union since 1985. A devout communist and brilliant politician who became the youngest leader of the nation since Stalin rose to power in the 1920s, Gorbachev was also well educated. He had studied agriculture and the law and had traveled in the West. He realized that the Soviet economic system had slowed to the point of stagnation in the 1970s, lagged a generation behind the West's technology (especially in computers), and was increasingly unable to put food on the table or up-to-date weapons in the field.

He proclaimed a policy of perestroika (economic restructuring) that was to be pushed ahead by glasnost (political openness). Russians found themselves freer than at any time since 1917. But the economy continued to rot away. Gorbachev blamed Communist Party bureaucrats who clung to "the old ways." He moved to replace them with a new government based on a Congress of People's Deputies, many of whom were chosen in surprisingly open elections in which Communist Party members suffered embarrassing defeats. Gorbachev now headed both a new government and a disintegrating Communist Party.

When these measures did not help the economy, he took the next step in 1989. He refused to spend more resources on controlling a sullen, unproductive communist Eastern Europe. Without full support from Moscow, the governments crumbled, first in Poland and Czechoslovakia, then in East Germany, Bulgaria, and Romania. Most dramatically, on November 9, 1989, a hated symbol of the Cold War—the cement and barbed-wire wall that had separated West and East Berlin since 1961—was dismantled by the communists. East and West Germans flooded across the former barrier as two Germanys began once again to become one.

In an about-face that seemed nearly as remarkable as Gorbachev's, Ronald Reagan held four major summit conferences with the Soviet leader in just three years. The two leaders signed agreements that opened scientific and cultural exchanges, promised to reduce strategic arms and conventional forces, and pledged cooperation to clean up the environment. They even signed a treaty to destroy, for the first time, an entire family of nuclear missiles each had placed in Europe. Visiting and enjoying Moscow in the springtime of 1988, Reagan was asked about his earlier remark that the Soviets were an "evil empire." He replied, "I was talking about another empire." After taking power in early 1989, President George H.W. Bush held two summits with Gorbachev in which they agreed to speed up arms reductions and the opening of U.S.-Soviet trade.

Many U.S. corporations were already moving into the Soviet Union, despite such obstacles as the lack of a Russian banking system and a badly trained labor force. McDonald's opened a huge fast-food outlet close to Red Square in Moscow, H.J. Heinz sold baby food, Philip Morris shipped billions of cigarettes, Pepsi-Cola sold more than 9 million bottles of soft drink annually, and Coca-Cola prepared to challenge Pepsi for the entire former communist bloc by building a bottling operation in France that produced three-and-a-half cases of Coke each second. It was the West Germans, however, who led the drive into the East European market. They eased the way for Gorbachev's agreement for unification of East and West Germany in 1990 by agreeing to send nearly $15 billion to help revive the Soviet economy.

Gorbachev's "new thinking," as he termed it, set off not merely ripples but political tidal waves outside Europe. Communist-supported regimes in Africa, Southeast Asia, and the Middle East undertook major policy changes to find replacements for lost Soviet support. Even Cuba, where Fidel Castro had won his own revolution in 1959 with little Russian help, suffered badly when Gorbachev threatened to reduce his $5 billion annual aid, then criticized Castro for clinging to old ways of thinking. The Sandinista government of Nicaragua also felt the waves. During the middle 1980s the Sandinistas had received more than $500 million in aid each year from the Soviets, primarily to fight the U.S.-supported Contras. In 1987, however, the president of neighboring Costa Rica, Oscar Arias Sanchez, proposed a plan to bring peace and elections to Central American battlefields. Arias won the Nobel Peace Prize for his efforts, although U.S. officials greeted the plan with open hostility; they believed the Sandinistas understood only direct military force. Nicaragua nevertheless went along with much of the Arias plan and held elections in early 1990. To the Sandinistas' (and nearly everyone else's) surprise, a loose anti-Sandinista coalition led by Violetta Chamorro won. Gorbachev told the Sandinistas to abide by the results. Chamorro became president. Unfortunately, the Arias plan did not work in El Salvador, where another Central American revolution had taken 75,000 lives since 1979.

THE PERSIAN GULF WAR

With the Soviet military withdrawing from Latin America and Eastern Europe, Bush found himself heading the world's only remaining superpower. Not reluctant to use force, he deployed it twice within eighteen months. In December 1989, the president sent 27,000 troops into Panama to capture dictator Manuel Antonio Noriega and install a pro-U.S. regime. Noriega, whose power had been created through his work with the CIA and other U.S. agencies, had after 1984 refused to help the United States fight the Sandinistas. He also had enriched himself through the drug trade. U.S. forces finally captured Noriega, but did so at the cost of at least 500 (mostly civilian) lives. The drug trade through Panama, moreover, continued to flourish.

Then in August 1990, Iraq's dictator, Saddam Hussein, invaded the neighboring, oil-rich kingdom of Kuwait and threatened to strike at Saudi Arabia, long a close U.S. friend, whose desert sands covered one-quarter of the world's known oil. Bush moved more than 400,000 military personnel into the region to prevent an invasion of Saudi Arabia and to pressure Saddam to leave Kuwait. Unlike the case in Panama, where he acted without regard to the United Nations or world opinion, the president obtained support from the United Nations, from a cooperative Gorbachev, and from several Islamic nations in the Middle East who feared Iraq's power and ambitions.

On January 16, 1991, Americans entered their largest war since the Vietnam conflict when President Bush ordered U.S. and allied planes to attack the capital, Baghdad, and other targets in Iraq. The planes also began round-the-clock bombing of Iraqi troops who occupied Kuwait. The assault was led by guided missiles and by hundreds of B-52 aircraft, each of which carried forty to fifty tons of explosives.

The war was important historically for a number of reasons. First, after an intensive debate, Congress narrowly passed a resolution in January 1991 that authorized Bush to use military force against Iraq. It marked the first time since 1941, a half-century earlier, that the presidency followed a semblance of constitutional procedures by seeking the equivalent of a congressional declaration of war. Second, the United States relied extensively on new, high-technology weapons. Most notable was the Patriot antimissile weapon that destroyed low-flying Iraqi missiles. A number of the Iraqi projectiles nevertheless evaded the Patriots and killed civilians in Israel and Saudi Arabia. Third, Americans were able to follow much of the war twenty-four hours a day, especially on the CNN cable-news network, which became famous for its live, on-the-spot coverage. Even Saddam Hussein watched CNN. But television and newspaper reporters were tightly controlled by the U.S. military, which heavily censored

President and Mrs. Bush greet troops and have Thanksgiving Day dinner with the First Division Marine Command Post, Saudi Arabia, 1990. *(George Bush Presidential Library)*

the news Americans received. Military officials continued to believe—quite mistakenly—that biased, anti-U.S. media coverage had led to the defeat in Vietnam. This time Americans were to see only what U.S. officials wanted them to see. Throughout the conflict, even after scores of American lives had been lost, few bodies and little bloodshed from the war were shown on television—a medium that otherwise displayed considerable killing and gore in its regular, prime-time programs.

U.S. foreign policy was not primarily motivated by a concern for "democracy," although most Americans liked to believe it was. Freeing Kuwait of Iraqi troops meant restoring a feudal, nondemocratic regime to power in that small kingdom, and because of the heavy censorship, the American people were not well informed about the realities of war. In early 1991, the United States was spending upward of $1 billion a day and sending its forces into battle for two main objectives: to keep Middle Eastern oil in friendly hands and to destroy Saddam's military power before the dictator could gain control of the region's affairs through force—perhaps, in the not distant future, even through nuclear weapons.

On February 23, 1991, Bush sent the 700,000 ground troops of the U.S.-directed coalition into action. Within a hundred hours they overwhelmed the Iraqis and a truce was arranged. The president's supporters reveled in their triumph. Bush's approval ratings of over 90 percent were unmatched in the history of the polls. Grateful Americans, having covered front yards with yellow ribbons to remember their soldiers, welcomed them home with festivities unmatched since 1945. Pundits again discussed "the unipolar world" of a Pax Americana. The president

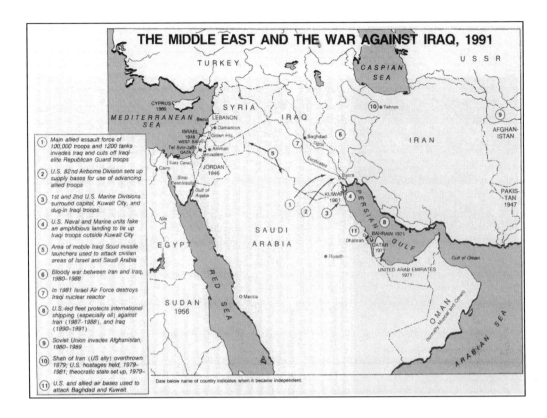

proclaimed that Americans had finally "kicked" the "Vietnam syndrome"—that is, they were no longer reluctant to trust their military to use massive force. Only 120 Americans died in action after fear had spread that thousands would be killed.

Critics, however, were not silenced. Their three main charges had as much to do with the deeper history of the twentieth century as with the hours of fighting in 1991. First, they revealed that Reagan and Bush had helped create Saddam's power by selling him weapons throughout the 1980s when he was at war with the Americans' archenemy, Iran. The two presidents, moreover, even secretly tolerated Saddam's terrorism against Americans and Israelis so that the anti-Iran policy could be continued. Foolish U.S. policy, critics insisted, had helped bring about the war. Second, critics charged that, instead of achieving his goal of destroying Saddam, Bush used such an enormous amount of firepower to obtain a quick victory that he caused "near-apocalyptic" damage (to use the United Nations' phrase) and possibly the death of 50,000 people in Iraq. Smoke from Kuwait's oil wells, set afire by the Iraqis, transformed day to night, and that cataclysm, combined with the overwhelming military destruction, turned the region into a gigantic ecological disaster. Later evaluations, moreover, concluded that probably 70 percent of U.S. bombs (including so-called smart bombs that supposedly could be guided to targets) missed their objectives. Third, Bush did not send U.S. armies into Baghdad to destroy Saddam. The president and especially his Middle East allies (such as Saudi Arabia) feared that removing Saddam would throw Iraq into chaos and endanger the entire region's stability. Bush consequently hoped the Iraqis themselves would overthrow their now-defeated dictator. But when the ethnic Kurds (who had long suffered at the dictator's hands) rose up, they were brutally beaten down by the Iraqis. Thousands of Kurds died of starvation, cold, and disease despite a too-late, too-little, U.S. relief effort.

TO THE END OF THE CENTURY

Amid the threats of such dangerous disorder, debates erupted over the question of what shape the 1990s and the early twenty-first century would take. Heated discussion focused on Francis Fukuyama's essay, "The End of History," published in the summer 1989 issue of *The National Interest*. A member of Bush's State Department at the time, Fukuyama argued that communism's failure and liberal capitalist democracy's triumph meant an end to the ideological wars that had torn apart the twentieth century. He admitted that sharp conflicts could occur over religion and environmental issues, especially in the less industrialized areas. For the industrialized world that Fukuyama cared about, however, a new—although not necessarily better—era was dawning. People, he feared, would now spend time wallowing in consumer goods and gulping down fast foods rather than fighting for great causes. "The end of history will be a very sad time," Fukuyama concluded.

A year after his essay appeared, the beginning of the new decade lacked neither excitement nor great causes. In trying to restructure, Mikhail Gorbachev lifted sixty-year-long Stalinist controls off the Soviet people. Divided among a hundred nationalities and impoverished by the breakdown of the economic system, the Soviets fell to fighting each other. Major battles erupted between ethnic groups; homeless and starving people were evident for the first time since World War II. Russia, the largest by far of the fifteen Soviet republics, threatened to leave the Soviet Union and become an independent nation despite Gorbachev's heated opposition. If the Soviet Union spun out of control, all of world affairs would become dangerously unpredictable, not least because the fate of the Red Army's 30,000 nuclear warheads would be at stake.

Gorbachev won the 1990 Nobel Peace Prize for allowing the East European peoples to vote democratic governments into power. But by 1991 the Soviet Union was disintegrating economically and politically. Gorbachev was desperately cooperating with the military and secret police to maintain order and preserve the communist nation. He failed. On December 25, 1991, bells in Moscow's Red Square rang out to announce the end of the Soviet Union, the birth of a non-communist Russia, and the replacement of Gorbachev by the more democratic Boris Yeltsin. The Cold War was over.

The power vacuum created by the Soviet breakdown was quickly being filled. Twelve European nations pledged they would form a European community without internal tariffs or other obstacles to the movement of trade, people, or money. By the year 2000, the 350 million people in the community could form the West's richest market. It would be a Europe that could act more independently of Washington and exclude American goods. In the middle of the new Europe lay a new, united Germany. Gorbachev, who now talked about "our common European home," sought to join the new Europe. The American relationship to this Europe was not clear. Since 1949 the key U.S. tie to Western Europe had been through the military might of the North Atlantic Treaty Organization (NATO). With the Soviet military threat disappearing, economics, not NATO, could shape the future.

On the other side of the world, Japan was becoming the world's richest nation. It was also becoming the center of an East Asian region that, as a top U.S. official declared in 1988, "could become the world's largest source of credit" and "the world's technological leader." By the late 1970s, for the first time in its history, the United States had more trade with the Pacific Rim countries than with Europe. How the United States could compete for these rich markets, or even maintain control of its own home market in the face of Asian competition, promised to be daily questions for Americans in the twenty-first century.

Reagan and Bush had an answer, indeed a historic answer, to these economic threats posed by the Europeans and Japanese. In 1988 Reagan signed a pact with Canada providing that in ten years the two nations would create a giant free-trade community. Already the leading American trade partner ($200 billion annually), Canada now saw its trade jump with its southern neighbor another $12 billion in 1989 to 1990. Investment capital moved rapidly in both directions. In 1990 Mexico, reversing its historic opposition, declared it also wanted to form a common market with the United States. Despite bitter opposition from American labor unions, textile manufacturers, and environmentalists (who feared low-wage Mexican competition that showed relatively little concern for environmental standards), Bush pledged to build this U.S.–Canada–Mexico free-trade community by the mid-1990s.

Some experts feared that given its rapid population increase and growing environmental problems, the globe was a ticking time bomb. Between World War II and the 1990s, world population shot up from 2.5 billion to 4.5 billion, with a projected 8 billion to 9 billion in the early twenty-first century. (It had taken 1 million years to produce the first billion, but only 120 years for the second, 32 years for the third, and 15 years for the fourth.) In Africa and the Middle East especially, growing populations, economic inequality, and political frustrations produced a surge of religious Islamic fundamentalism that posed new questions for Americans. They first had faced that challenge during the 1979 Iranian revolution. By the 1990s, Islam, which compares with Christianity as an expansive, proselytizing religion, had in its more radical form become a force in a half-dozen other nations.

Surging populations wiped out huge chunks of the earth's resources, especially rain forests necessary to cool and purify the globe. Scientific knowledge existed to meet this challenge, although science also offered problems of its own, especially in the field of biotechnology—the new industry that by combining discoveries in biology and technology gave scientists almost godlike power over human life. For three centuries researchers had known that cells form the foundation blocks of life, but not until 1951 did California researchers discover the spiral shape of the protein molecules that make up most of a cell. Two British scientists then took the crucial step of finding the specific molecules in the cell that carry genetic information (hair and eye color, height, and other individual characteristics) from one generation to the next. Once it was understood how genes were made up—that is, in long chains of deoxyribonucleic acid, or DNA—and how the long chains worked, the genes could be manipulated. "Gene machines" could even synthesize different parts of the chain.

Within thirty years, this international scientific effort produced genetic engineering that could, for example, transplant genes into a patient's cells to make the patient immune to certain diseases. Such research developed new medicines, seeds, and foods, even animals. Scientists created new species of grain that were immune to insect pests, needed little water, and miraculously gathered nitrogen from the air (thus making fertilizers unnecessary).

But playing with nature's basic tool posed great, even unknown, dangers. One laboratory used genetic engineering to produce a bacterium that could prevent a potato crop from being destroyed by frost. A judge, however, refused to allow the bacterium to be spread because no one knew what else it might do once it was released into the air. An uproar ensued when a biotechnological report noted the possibility of creating a disease-resistant person "which has only in part human attributes." Leading Protestant, Jewish, and Roman Catholic leaders warned that unless such work was closely controlled, biotechnology could lead to the horrors seen in Nazi Germany's attempts to create a supposedly "racially pure" society. Eventually, the U.S. National Institutes of Health issued national guidelines for the splicing of genes.

Whether Americans looked at their own overstretched economy, the crisis in the Middle East, the growing inequality of their society, the new challenges of a united Europe and a rising Japan, or the explosive secrets of science and technology, it was clear they confronted some of the greatest challenges of their 200-year history as an independent people. The question was not whether history, as twentieth-century Americans had known it, had come to an "end" (for in crucial areas it was clearly only beginning). The question was whether Americans could learn from their history to deal with the awesome challenges of the twenty-first century. Bill Clinton now entered the White House to lead Americans as they tried to answer that question in the new post–Cold War era.

CHAPTER EIGHTEEN

1993–2000
The Road to the Twenty-First Century

President Clinton waves during his presidential campaign, 1996. *(William J. Clinton Presidential Library and Museum)*

Americans in the twentieth century witnessed three eras of social reforms: Woodrow Wilson's New Freedom, Franklin D. Roosevelt's New Deal, and Lyndon B. Johnson's Great Society. To many, it seemed that Bill Clinton's election, following twelve years of Republican rule, would inaugurate a fourth such era. But after the new administration failed to win popular backing for its chief initiative—health care reform—and after the Republicans swept the midterm elections, Clinton moved rapidly toward the political center and even adopted policies, such as a balanced budget, that had long been a staple of conservative thought. At century's end, however, American life was being shaped not only by partisan politics, but also, and even more crucially, by ongoing changes in the world economy, by rapid technological innovation, by new patterns of immigration, by women's influence in the public sphere, and by the nature of the nation's commitments abroad.

"A DIFFERENT KIND OF DEMOCRAT": THE MEDIA AND THE ELECTION OF 1992

When Bill Clinton entered the Democratic primaries in 1992, he presented himself as a "different kind of Democrat." A member of the Democratic Leadership Council, formed to support moderate policies, Clinton sought to shift the party's image away from traditional liberal concerns, such as aid to the poor. He appealed to the middle class. His campaign planks included higher taxes for the richest Americans, more funds for infrastructure (roads and bridges), a national health care system, and welfare reform. He promised new jobs, supported protection of the environment, and urged voters to "have the courage to vote for change." Above all, the Democratic nominee recognized the voters' concern about economic issues. At Clinton headquarters in Little Rock, Arkansas, the staff posted reminders of campaign themes: "Changes vs. More of the Same" and "It's the Economy, Stupid."

George H.W. Bush began his bid for reelection with apparent advantages. The president strove to regain the great popularity he had enjoyed in the immediate wake of the Gulf War, to reenact his 1988 victory, and to capitalize on his experience in foreign affairs, an area in which Clinton seemed weak. Both nominees, however, faced unexpected problems.

The presidential race drew a third candidate: billionaire executive Ross Perot, founder of a data-processing firm. Unhindered by campaign finance law, which limited contributions from wealthy supporters, Perot spent $60 million of his own money and became omnipresent on radio and television. Reiterating the need to reduce the national deficit, the Texas businessman and his Reform Party reached out to voters disaffected from both major parties.

While Perot rallied supporters nationwide, the difficulties of the Bush and Clinton campaigns mounted. The Republicans' focus on foreign affairs backfired: voters resented that Bush had broken his pledge not to raise taxes ("Read my lips: No new taxes"). Strident and divisive speeches at the Republican convention, which centered on "family values," alienated suburban women who had previously voted Republican. In addition, the president seemed unable to communicate effectively with the electorate. Clinton ran into obstacles, too. Rumors of marital difficulties had plagued him since the primaries, when a former girlfriend, Gennifer Flowers, revealed a long-term relationship. Moreover, concern arose over how the Democratic nominee had managed to avoid military service during the Vietnam War.

The election results reflected the candidates' liabilities. Perot captured a hefty 19 percent of the popular vote, the largest third-party showing since 1912, when Theodore Roosevelt won

Billionaire businessman Ross Perot during a self-financed TV ad/program promoting his run for president in 1992. Perot was the most successful third-party candidate since 1912. *(Ted Thai/Time Life Pictures/Getty Images)*

27 percent. Clinton won a huge electoral college triumph (370 to 188) but only 43 percent of the popular vote to Bush's 38 percent. The Clinton plurality represented the smallest winning percentage since that of Woodrow Wilson in 1912 (almost 42 percent). The Democrats, however, held both houses of Congress, where African-Americans, Hispanics, and women almost doubled their numbers. In the wake of the Senate hearings on the Supreme Court nomination of Clarence Thomas, where Anita Hill faced an all-male judiciary committee, many women had mobilized to support women candidates. The new Congress found six women in the Senate and forty-seven in the House, up from twenty-eight. The press dubbed 1992 "The Year of the Women."

In the election's wake, analysts reviewed the Republican defeat. Why had Bush lost? First, the Clinton team had forced the Republicans to run a negative campaign. The Bush campaign staff had failed to read the electorate's mood, to recognize the public's concern with economic issues, or to heed a steady stream of polls that suggested objections to the way the president handled the economy. Consequently, the Republicans had never articulated a domestic agenda. Second, Bush had proved a less effective candidate than Republicans anticipated. He made many gaffes, such as confessing unfamiliarity with a supermarket cash register and calling Clinton and his popular running mate, Al Gore, "crazies" and "bozos." Third, although Perot made incursions among both Democrats and Republicans, it was likely, as exit polls suggested, that he took more votes from Bush than from Clinton.

But perhaps the most distinctive feature of the campaign, one that abetted the Republican loss, was the new role that the media played. The presidential race of 1992 was the most media-driven campaign in American history. Perot, for instance, had announced his candidacy on a popular cable television program, had appeared on many talk shows, and had run infomercials, thirty-minute television advertisements for himself. Clinton, too, had proved an adept television personality. He had played his saxophone on a late-night comedian's show, appealed to young voters on music television, performed with aplomb at televised "town meetings" in targeted states, and excelled in three televised debates that reached 88 million people. The Clinton campaign, analysts agreed, had used the media in effective ways. Its focus on pop culture deflected attention from mainstream press coverage, which tended to dwell on Clinton's problems—that is, on unflattering controversies about his character or patriotism.

Clinton's triumph was a turning point. The new chief executive, born in 1946, was the first member of the baby boom generation (those born between 1946 and 1964) to become president. His victory, however, as the press observed, embodied a paradox. According to the conventional wisdom, voters held politicians and "politics as usual" in contempt. Still, they had elected a man distinguished by political savvy, skilled in political tactics, and driven by political ambition. As he entered office, without a ringing mandate, Bill Clinton faced the task of leading a nation drastically transformed by a global economic revolution.

THE WORLD OF MULTINATIONALS—AND MILITIAS

The years 1989 to 1991 marked the end of the superpower rivalry between the United States and the Soviet Union, but the Cold War era had actually begun to ebb in the early 1970s. It was then that the Soviet economy and political system became notably bankrupt, while the American economy and society, driven by a technological revolution, entered a different historic era.

Beginning in the 1970s, a giant wave of capital and trade began to wash over the world. The sources of this trade and capital were chiefly the United States and Japan. This was the third such wave of movement abroad by U.S. multinational corporations (that is, corporations headquartered in the United States, but producing goods, and often having subsidiary units, in many foreign nations). The first wave had begun after the Civil War (post–1865) when new, highly competitive manufacturers such as Standard Oil set up overseas operations. The second occurred in the 1950s when a rebuilt Europe attracted many United States companies that dominated such basic industries as autos (where General Motors reigned) and chemicals (led by DuPont).

The third wave, however, differed from the first two. To begin with, it was formed less by manufacturing or raw material companies than by new technology (computers), services (insurance and accounting), and retailing (McDonald's and Wal-Mart). The 1970s thus began a postindustrial era. Moreover, the new wave was moved less by goods (such as oil or autos) than by capital—that is, by enormous flows of money searching for profitable investment in nearly every corner of the globe. By the 1990s, some $1.3 trillion moved through the world's financial center, New York City, each *day*. That incredible sum revealed another characteristic of the new wave: it was so huge and moved across global computer systems so rapidly that governments had little control over it. Indeed, in 1992, fast-moving speculators nearly brought down Great Britain's entire financial system when, believing the British currency overvalued, they dropped its value in a matter of hours with overwhelming amounts of money.

This crisis revealed how the world had changed. The modern nation-state had dominated world affairs since it first appeared in the seventeenth century, but now increasingly found itself at the mercy of wealthy capitalists who moved across nations' borders with the ease and speed of the fastest computers.

This movement meant that U.S. jobs were sometimes lost to the new plants and investments abroad. By the mid-1990s, American firms employed 5.5 million people overseas, 80 percent of them in manufacturing plants. This loss was offset to a degree by British, Dutch, and Japanese capitalists who invested in the United States. The state of North Carolina, for example, had sixty Japanese companies. Japanese auto plants in Tennessee, Indiana, and elsewhere employed tens of thousands of Americans. Good manufacturing jobs were nevertheless lost in the United States, especially to Latin American and Asian countries—regions that increasingly replaced Europe as the target for investors. After all, these were the regions most needing the new technology. "Half the world's population has never made a phone call," one investor observed. So U.S. firms led by AT&T rushed into China, Mexico, and elsewhere to obtain rich contracts for developing communication systems. The world's hundred largest multinationals controlled about one-third of the globe's direct foreign investment.

Aside from those who lost their jobs, other losers appeared as well in the post–1970s era. Africa was largely bypassed by the third wave. That continent was too poor, too torn by violence, too lacking in infrastructure (highways, dependable government) to attract desperately needed capital. Except for mineral-rich South Africa (where the black majority finally obtained power after 1991) and parts of northern Africa, poverty only led to more poverty over the vast continent. Losers also included many law-abiding citizens. Global crime, made possible by fast-moving mobs linked by technology, took a shocking $750 billion annually from the world economy. About two-thirds of that amount came from the illegal drug trade. Americans with out-of-control drug habits handed as much as $100 billion annually to these criminals.

Political leaders tried to keep up with this revolution by forming new regional organizations. These regional blocs were designed to attract investment and trade, but also—the designers hoped—to provide ground rules and regulations to protect the public. The European Common Market of the 1950s was the model. By the 1990s, it had evolved into the European Union (EU). The EU aimed at what it called a "single internal market" throughout much of Europe, but also worked to lessen the political hostility between France and Germany that had led to two world wars. In the Far East, the Asia Pacific Economic Cooperation (APEC) group brought together Asians and Americans to work out economic ties and, as well, to lower the risk of conflict.

One of the most important of these groups was the North American Free Trade Association (NAFTA). Its origins went back to dreams in the 1850s and the 1910s of uniting the U.S. and Canadian markets, although Americans were usually far more enthusiastic than were wary Canadians who feared the power of their southern neighbor. In 1988, the two countries signed a treaty triggering a ten-year transition period to complete free trade. Mexico, under severe economic pressures, then asked to enter NAFTA. In 1993–1994, a treaty was worked out. The U.S. Senate approved the pact only after an all-out fight. American labor opposed the treaty out of fear that jobs would move to cheaper Mexican plants. Environmentalists worried that

Western businesses in Tokyo, 1998. *(Gilles Mingasson/Liaison/Getty Images)*

strong U.S. laws to protect the environment would give way to weaker Mexican standards. President Bill Clinton, with solid Republican support, nevertheless pushed the NAFTA pact through the Senate. The result was the world's largest common market in terms of population (420 million) and production (more than $8 trillion each year).

The first years of NAFTA did not produce massive movements of jobs in either direction. Unfortunately, neither did NAFTA improve labor and environmental standards significantly. As the number of industrial and power plants in northern Mexico grew, they spewed smoke and chemicals into Texas and elsewhere along the common border. Many Canadians meanwhile rebelled against NAFTA. They believed Canada was being flooded with U.S. goods and—worse—with such cultural products as banal television programs made in Hollywood.

From 1979, when the new technology was taking hold, to 1995, more than 43 million jobs were lost in the United States. The peak occurred in 1992, when 3.4 million disappeared. Between 1991 and 1994, just five companies (IBM, AT&T, General Motors, Sears, and GTE) laid off 325,000 workers. These firms claimed that only such drastic cuts could allow them to compete in the heated global marketplace. The firings became especially difficult to explain, however, when it was revealed that the average chief executive in a U.S. corporation took home $224 for every $1 taken home by an average factory worker. (In Germany, the ratio was $14 to $1.) The rich were getting richer, the poor poorer, in relative terms. And not only were less-skilled workers hit hard. In the 1980s and 1990s, the rate of layoffs doubled for college-educated workers. The number of jobs did increase from 90 million in 1979 to 117 million in 1995, but many were low paying. In the early 1990s, the median pay for a worker who had lost a full-time job fell $85 a week—from $507 in the old job to $422 in the new. Some Americans said, as the popular film *Network* noted, "we're mad as hell and we're not going to take it anymore." Organized labor, however, could do little to help. Representing 30 percent of U.S. workers in the early 1970s, labor unions in the 1990s held less than 18 percent of the workforce.

When compared with other industrial societies, U.S. culture is notoriously violent. That violence can intensify when the society is beset by economic change of global dimensions. At the extremes, so-called militias appeared, especially in the Midwest and Rocky Mountain states. These groups were prepared to use force if necessary to defend their own culture, which was often racist and authoritarian. A small militia group bombed the Oklahoma City federal building in 1995. The crime killed 169 people. The killer, Timothy McVeigh, had earlier publicly written, "We have no proverbial tea to dump [as in the 1770s]; should we instead sink a ship full of Japanese imports?"

Such rebellion, resembling the economic change itself, broke out on a worldwide stage. In the Middle East, Africa, and South Asia, for example, religious fundamentalists used violence as they attempted to keep out Western culture and politics. In Mexico, the indigenous people of the Chiapas region rose up against their government. Their cause was considerably more justified than the cause of the U.S. militias. For generations, the Mexican government had systematically oppressed the Chiapas population. The rebels now proclaimed that NAFTA and the resulting flow of U.S. agricultural products into their country signed "the death certificate for the indigenous people of Mexico. We rose up in arms to respond." The rebels successfully used computer links to rally international support and to pressure Mexico City officials to compromise.

In the United States, those who developed the new technology and headed the multinational corporations that sold it grew wealthy. Bill Gates, the young head of Microsoft, was among the globe's richest persons with a net worth of over $20 billion. Many of Gates's associates in technology-related firms were the Rockefellers and Carnegies of their generation. Those who suffered from the new technology lost out and at times even turned to violence.

THE NEW IMMIGRATION AND ITS IMPACT

Even as the United States felt the effects of this far-reaching economic change, new patterns of immigration reshaped the nation. The Immigration Reform Act of 1965 abolished quotas based on race or national origins that had favored northern Europeans but imposed the first limits on immigration from the Western Hemisphere. According to the law, 170,000 immigrants could enter annually from the Eastern Hemisphere and 120,000 from the Western Hemisphere. Close relatives of immigrants already here would be exempt from quotas. Over the next three decades, the new policy transformed immigration to the United States, sometimes in unexpected ways: legal immigration exceeded the limits Congress had imposed, immigrants from Asia and Latin America quickly surpassed in number those who came from Europe, and illegal immigration soared. By the mid-1980s, at least 4 million undocumented immigrants had arrived in the United States (see Chapter 16).

Subsequent immigration statutes modified the 1965 law but left the basic pattern intact. In 1986, the Immigration Reform and Control Act (the Simpson-Rodino Act) outlawed the hiring of illegal aliens, penalized employers who did so, strengthened immigration controls on the southern border, and offered amnesty to immigrants who could prove that they had lived in the United States since January 1, 1982. About 3 million illegal residents won amnesty under the law. A 1990 law, the most generous of the post–World War II era, made it possible for over 800,000 immigrants to enter the United States each year. Combined with other provisions, such as those that granted asylum, this meant that legal immigration to the United States in the 1990s soared; illegal entrants multiplied, too.

Who were the new immigrants? Since 1960, about 45 percent came from the Western Hemisphere and 30 percent from Asia. Some fled repression or political turmoil in their lands of origin. Most sought economic opportunity and higher living standards. Since 1975, Asians—from China, Taiwan, Hong Kong, Vietnam, Cambodia, Japan, the Philippines, and South Korea—accounted for over 40 percent of total immigration. In the 1980s alone, the Asian-American population grew by 80 percent. Hispanic immigrants, the fastest growing group of newcomers, arrived in yet greater numbers. Between 1970 and 1990, the number of Hispanics in the United States almost tripled. Much Hispanic immigration, especially in the Southwest, reflected poor conditions in Mexico, where unemployment was high and per capita income low. The collapse of world oil prices in the 1980s made Mexico's chronic poverty worse. Then, between late 1994 and early 1995, when the Mexican government vastly devalued the currency, more jobs vanished and motives for immigration increased. Mexico's economic woes also fueled illegal immigration. The largest numbers of undocumented entrants in the 1990s came from Mexico, El Salvador, Guatemala, and Haiti, as well as from Canada, Poland, China, and Ireland. Illegal immigrants often worked without protection of law under harsh conditions in manual labor, in garment sweatshops, or as agricultural or household workers.

New immigrants had the greatest impact in places where they congregated. In the 1990s, over 70 percent of immigrants, legal and illegal, lived in six states: California, Texas, Florida, Illinois, New York, and New Jersey. In 1993, the foreign-born accounted for 27 percent of New York City dwellers, 45 percent of Miami area residents, and one out of every three residents of the Los Angeles–Long Beach metropolitan area. California's growth alone suggests the impact of the new immigration. The population of the state leaped by 6 million in the 1980s, 37 percent due to immigration, mainly from Mexico, Central America, and Asia. In the early 1990s, over a third of the immigrants to the United States went to California. By 1996, California was home to half of the nation's foreign-born.

When protests against the new immigration emerged in the 1990s, states with the largest concentrations of newcomers, such as California and Florida, led the way. Official protests mirrored widespread ambivalence about or hostility to the new immigration. An example was California's Proposition 187 (1994), which cut off all educational and non-emergency health benefits to immigrants and their children. Public opinion polls in the early 1990s suggested that over 60 percent of respondents wanted immigration decreased. The Civil Rights Commission reported growing numbers of bias episodes, such as black boycotts of Korean-owned grocery stores in New York in the 1980s and an interethnic riot in Los Angeles in 1992. Organizations opposed to immigration arose; other pressure groups promoted laws to make English the official language, a measure adopted in twenty-two states, including California. In 1993 and 1994, when tens of thousands of Haitian and Cuban refugees fled their homelands to seek asylum in the United States, concern about immigration mounted further.

The debate over the new immigration in the 1990s echoed past debates. Defenders of liberal immigration policies argued variously that America had always been a nation of immigrants,

BASKETBALL
FROM NAISMITH TO NIKE

George Mikan *(right)* and the champion Minneapolis Lakers, 1949. *(NBA Photos/NBAE/Getty Images)*

It began with one teacher and eighteen overactive students in a Massachusetts gymnasium and ended with millions of customers around the world.

In 1891, as Americans turned sports crazy, thirty-one-year-old James Naismith single-handedly invented the game of basketball. His superior at Springfield College in Massachusetts begged him to find something for bored students to play between football and baseball seasons. Naismith, borrowing from games played in his Canadian childhood, came up with the idea of throwing a soccer-type ball through a bottomless peach basket (handy from a nearby orchard) set ten feet high. That was the height of the college's gymnasium balconies to which the basket could be most easily attached. Naismith insisted on no violence. There was to be no tackling, little contact (or "fouling"), no hard throwing of the ball (hence the ten-feet-high baskets required a lob).

Within a week, Naismith's gym class was playing before fascinated crowds. In 1892, women first played the game at nearby Smith College. By 1901, the *Basketball Guide for Women* observed that females took to the game at "a time of great unrest in regard to the status of women." Contrary to Naismith's hope, however, the nonstop action and a rule that players could chase a ball out-of-bounds quickly made it a rough sport—so rough that high wire cages were built to confine the players and protect the spectators (hence the "cage game").

As early as 1896, professional basketball appeared when Trenton, New Jersey, players were paid $15. But the game grew most popular in city gyms and playgrounds where the YMCA promoted it. Jane Addams's Hull House had one of Chicago's most popular teams. The dribbling of the ball was probably first used to score points on a Philadelphia playground. Before that, only passing had been used. After 1920, an annual national championship was held, as small colleges (e.g., Wabash College of Indiana) and larger schools (e.g., the Big Ten and City College of New York) became famous for their hardwood skills. Pro teams, especially the all-white New York Celtics and the all-black New York Renaissance Five and Harlem Globetrotters, played before large crowds as they barnstormed across the country. In 1940, television first covered a college game from New York City's Madison Square Garden. That year, *Time* magazine reported that basketball, with its 70,000 teams, was followed by more Americans than any other sport.

Michael Jordan slam-dunks, 2001. *(Erik Perel/AFP/ Getty Images)*

The game, linked to the new medium of television, was poised for even greater popularity. The appearance of talented giants, such as DePaul University's six-foot-ten George Mikan (voted the best player of the 1891–1950 era); the introduction of the twenty-four-second clock (forcing teams to shoot in twenty-four seconds instead of just holding the ball); and the breaking of the racial barrier in 1951, when African-Americans began playing more regularly in the pros—all these changes drew increased numbers of fans. The University of Kentucky dominated the postwar era until the white-players-only philosophy of its coach, Adolph Rupp, made the team less competitive than the University of Cincinnati or—above all—UCLA, where John Wooden coached such legendary black players as Lew Alcindor (Kareem Abdul-Jabbar) and Sidney Wicks. In 1968, UCLA and Houston played before 53,000 fans and the then largest television audience in sports history, 30 million.

The U.S. Congress played a central role. In 1972, it passed Title IX of the Education Act, which required colleges to provide similar resources for men's and women's sports.

Women's basketball became popular as rule changes sped up the game and stars such as Carol "Blaze" Blazejowski of Montclair State College of New Jersey and Cheryl Miller of the University of Southern California (later a noted television announcer) appeared. The U.S. women's team took the Olympic gold medal in 1984.

But professional basketball was in trouble by the early 1980s—the victim of sliding attendance, too much violence, high ticket prices, and competing sports attractions. The National Basketball Association (NBA), however, developed into one of the best-known sports organizations in the world when it began using global television, made possible by the new space satellites, to promote its players and products.

This global medium was ready-made for Michael Jordan, who in 1983 moved from the University of North Carolina team to the professional Chicago Bulls. He became perhaps the world's most popular (and many said basketball's best ever) athlete. In the early 1990s, Chinese schoolchildren voted one of their political leaders the greatest person of the twentieth-century—and ranked Jordan second. They knew Jordan because of his worldwide advertisements for Nike shoes and the global marketing of the NBA.

In 1996, *Time* named Nike's founder, Phil Knight, one of "America's 25 most influential people." In 1964, Knight's new company had made $3,240. In 1996, Nike's revenue hit $6.5 billion. The company controlled one-quarter of the globe's sports-shoe sales. A turning point came in 1984 when Jordan endorsed Nike products. Advertising, it has been said, was the leading art form of the American Century. Knight and Jordan took it to new heights as Nike's swoosh symbol and Jordan's personality and championship seasons with the Bulls became basketball's best-known products. In 1996, Jordan signed a contract with the Bulls that paid him $30 million a year, but he was earning even more from his endorsements.

Critics, however, condemned Nike's advertising (such as the slogan, "Just Do It") because, they claimed, it led children to attack each other to steal sports shoes and jackets. The critics also noted that Knight moved Nike production into Southeast Asia to exploit some of the world's cheapest labor and worst working conditions. He responded that production was often done with subcontractors over whom Nike had little supervision and that, in any case, "Our business practices are no different from those of our competitors."

A century after James Naismith invented basketball, the game, like the United States itself, was a global happening, a worldwide, moneymaking machine. In the post–Cold War world of the 1990s, the U.S. power that affected billions of people's lives each day was less the military than it was the culture of sports and the economics of sports marketing.

Web Links

www.hoophall.com/
The website of the Naismith Memorial Basketball Hall of Fame in Springfield, Massachusetts.

www.wbhof.com/
The website of the Women's Basketball Hall of Fame in Knoxville, Tennessee.

that immigration revitalized the economy, that the taxes immigrants paid exceeded the costs that they incurred, that newcomers took jobs that others disparaged, that they contributed their education and skills to American enterprise, and that they had become scapegoats for other causes of economic distress, such as foreign competition and technological change. Critics of immigration policy contended that legislators since the 1960s had underestimated the size and consequences of the new immigration, that its hazards outweighed its benefits, and that cultural and economic considerations made continuing current immigration policy unwise.

According to the cultural argument, high rates of immigration would erode America's common culture. Foes of immigration voiced concern that large numbers of third world immigrants, language differences, and cultural diversity would divide Americans and slow assimilation. The economic argument involved two facets of immigration's impact. According to one part of the economic argument, high rates of immigration increased competition for jobs, caused unemployment, depressed wages, curbed the power of labor, widened the gap between rich and poor, and especially harmed those with low rank in the labor market. Another facet of the economic argument involved suspected abuse by immigrants of social and economic services. Critics claimed that immigrants, especially illegal aliens, received more in benefits (welfare, food stamps, schools, medical care, Social Security) than they paid in taxes. Consequently, as California's governor argued in 1994, state and local governments had to assume the burden of these costs. Overall, factors that fostered the critical response to immigration in the 1980s and 1990s included the unforeseen consequences of federal immigration laws since 1965; recent episodes of economic hardship, such as in California in the early 1990s; and incidents that evoked fear of foreign criminals, such as the ties of undocumented immigrants to the bombing of the New York World Trade Center in 1993. Other factors were concerns about fraudulent asylum claims, border problems, illegal entrants, and the ethnic diversity of the new immigration.

Proposals to curb immigration in the 1990s included limiting the number of immigrants to as few as 200,000 a year, more severe clamps on illegal immigration, restriction of legal immigration to those with skills, discarding the family reunification policy, and a five-year moratorium, followed by cuts in admissions. In 1996 the Clinton administration, with bipartisan support, increased the budget of the Immigration and Naturalization Service, the number of agents in the border patrol, and the rate of deportation of illegal immigrants. Still, immigration policy seemed resistant to more drastic change. The debate continued over the impact of new immigration and the question of whether current immigration rates should be maintained, modified, or ended.

BILL CLINTON AND THE END OF LIBERALISM

As Bill Clinton entered the White House in January 1993, one columnist observed that the new president offered an "ambitious, expansive, romantic vision . . . a national rebirth, a revival of hope." Clinton had encouraged such expectations when he told the Democratic National Convention in July 1992 "a president ought to be a powerful force for progress." But as a self-styled "New Democrat," Clinton was always more concerned with "renewal" than "reform," and his personal style was more naturally suited to conciliation than to conflict. After a number of initiatives failed during his first two years in office and after the Republicans chalked up massive gains in the midterm elections of 1994, the president rapidly moved to occupy the political middle ground. By January 1996, he could proclaim, "the era of big government is over."

For the most part, Clinton's successes in 1993 and 1994 came when he received bipartisan support, as in the case of the NAFTA pact. Gun control was another area in which Republican votes proved essential. The Brady bill—named for Ronald Reagan's press secretary, James Brady, who had been severely wounded in an assassination attempt on Reagan in 1981 and had then with his wife Sara spearheaded a crusade for effective gun control—was finally enacted in 1993. It provided for a five-day waiting period to allow a background check before anyone purchasing a handgun could take possession of the weapon. Clinton's two Supreme Court nominees, Ruth Bader Ginsburg and Stephen Breyer, also had impeccable credentials and received overwhelming support from senators of both parties. But two other proposals of the new administration triggered angry opposition, chiefly from Republicans, but also from members of the president's own party.

The first concerned the issue of whether gay men and women should have a right to serve in the military. During the 1992 campaign, Clinton had promised to issue an executive order to remove the long-standing ban on the grounds that "patriotic Americans should have the right to serve the country as a member of the armed forces, without regard to sexual or affectional orientation." But the president's proposal was doomed from the start: conservative religious groups opposed any policy that legitimated or sanctioned homosexuality, and the Joint Chiefs of Staff defended the ban as necessary to preserve discipline and morale. In September Clinton finally agreed to a compromise. Under the so-called don't ask, don't tell policy, gays could serve in the military so long as they did not reveal their sexual orientation or engage in sexual conduct or behave in ways that would indicate they were homosexuals, such as reading gay magazines, frequenting gay bars, or participating in gay pride marches. The nine-month-long controversy cost the president public support, and the outcome angered gay-rights groups, which felt he had turned his back on a campaign pledge.

No sooner had this issue been resolved than Clinton produced his ill-fated plan to reform the nation's health insurance system. He had made health care a central theme of his campaign, tapping into a widespread feeling that the nation faced a crisis. Health care accounted for one in every seven dollars spent in the United States. Costs were rising rapidly each year, much more rapidly than the rate of inflation; many people had inadequate health insurance coverage or no coverage at all. In September 1993, the president offered a proposal based on a report of a task force that had been headed by his wife, Hillary Rodham Clinton. Health care, he maintained, like Social Security, should be safe and available to all, a "comprehensive package of benefits over the course of an entire lifetime." More concretely, Clinton endorsed the idea of "managed competition within a budget": employers would have to offer managed care insurance plans to employees; a nonprofit health alliance would serve as a clearinghouse for all the plans in a given region and would negotiate rates with all health care providers, thereby helping to control costs.

Fully 60 percent of the American people approved Clinton's plan, leading the *Congressional Quarterly* to report that "for the first time in years, it seemed as if Congress was filled with a sense of the possibility of enacting a piece of sweeping social legislation." But public and legislative support began to erode almost immediately. The plan was inordinately complex— the bill Clinton sent to Congress was 1,342 pages long—and it involved more government control than its sponsors were prepared to admit. Private insurance companies launched an advertising campaign revolving around the homey characters "Harry and Louise," designed to show that Clinton's plan would not only be costly but would also deny patients their choice of physicians. Republicans in Congress portrayed the plan as an example of big, intrusive government, while Democrats, who had not been consulted in drafting the measure, had little incentive to support it.

The hostile response to Clinton's health care proposal bore out the fears of some of his advisers. Donna Shalala, the secretary of health and human services, had warned that the administration's program "will turn off liberals and conservatives; no one will be enthusiastic. All the interest groups will be mad—the doctors, the hospitals, the labs. You're building on all the negatives." By September 1994, a year after its unveiling, Clinton's program was, by common consent, dead. The president's inability to mobilize a constituency in behalf of the measure or to sell it to Democratic members of Congress contributed to a sense that the administration was inept. Even worse, Clinton had given his Republican opponents exactly the kind of ammunition they wanted for the midterm elections.

In 1994, Newt Gingrich of Georgia, who had served in the House of Representatives since 1978, emerged as the master Republican strategist. Gingrich proposed that Republican congressional candidates sign a "Contract with America," consisting of ten items that could be enacted within a hundred days if the party carried Congress, and published it in *TV Guide* in order to reach the broadest possible audience. The stated goal of the contract was to bring an end to "government that is too big, too intrusive, and too easy with the public's money." Most of the proposals were traditional conservative fare—a balanced budget amendment, tougher anticrime laws, a diversion of funds from summer youth employment programs to prison construction, cuts in welfare, including a "tough two-years-and-out provision with work requirements to promote individual responsibility," a capital gains tax break, and incentives for small business. The measures were given such benign titles as Fiscal Responsibility Act, Personal Responsibility Act, Family Reinforcement Act, and American Dream Restoration Act.

What the contract omitted was as significant as what it included. There was no mention at all of two controversial issues that had been part of the conservative agenda since the Reagan years: prayer in the public schools and abortion. To take a stand on those issues, one Republican strategist said, would "cloud the clarity of our message." To appease religious conservatives, the contract spoke generally of electing a Congress "that respects the values and shares the faith of the American family" and supported a $500 per child tax credit. Although less than one-third of voters said they had even heard of the Contract with America by Election Day, Gingrich had largely succeeded in nationalizing the midterm elections and making them a referendum on Clinton's first two years.

The results of the 1994 elections exceeded Gingrich's expectations. The Republicans swept Congress, winning fifty-two seats in the House and eight in the Senate. They picked up still another Senate seat when an Alabama Democrat switched parties, resulting in a 53–47 majority in that chamber. They controlled the House by a comfortable 230–204 margin (there was one Independent) and quickly moved to elect Newt Gingrich as Speaker. The Republicans also elected eleven new governors, giving them control of governors' mansions in thirty states, including eight of the nine largest states. In 1994, not a single incumbent Republican governor, senator, or member of the House was beaten. The Democrats, on the other hand, saw such prominent figures as Governor Ann Richards in Texas and Governor Mario Cuomo in New York go down to defeat.

It did not take President Clinton long to adjust to the new political situation. He quickly recruited an adviser, Richard Morris, who had assisted him in Arkansas many years before and who had helped run Texas Republican Trent Lott's successful Senate campaign in 1994. Clinton had to "coopt the more popular parts of the G.O.P. agenda," Morris said, and thereby "return to traditional Democratic issues of a kind that have strong middle-class appeal, such as education and the environment." Morris proposed that Clinton follow a policy of "triangulation," as he called it, allying himself with Democrats on some issues and Republicans on others, but never allowing himself to become hostage to either. For a president badly shaken by the 1994 elections—so shaken indeed that in April 1995 he was insisting, somewhat plaintively, that "the president is relevant here"—the strategy Morris proposed was highly attractive.

The policies Clinton embraced faithfully reflected Morris's advice. The president proposed a "Middle-Class Bill of Rights," for example, which would allow tax deductions for education and training after high school and permit tax-free withdrawals from individual retirement accounts for education, medical costs, the purchase of a first home, and caring for a parent. Clinton came out for a balanced budget. He proposed tough new laws to fight crime. He denounced excessive television violence and endorsed a v-chip that would enable parents to control what TV shows their children could watch. He called for finding more room for religion (although not prayer) in the public schools. He condemned cigarette companies that attracted minors through cleverly designed advertising campaigns. In July 1995, the president emphasized the value of civility and the need to "move beyond division and resentment to common ground."

The issue of affirmative action, however, was potentially far more explosive and far less amenable to the new White House strategy. Ever since 1978, when the Supreme Court had accepted its constitutionality in the Bakke case, a debate had raged over the effectiveness and fairness of affirmative action. Clinton enjoyed overwhelming backing from African-Americans, but Morris's strategy clearly implied that he would have to attract the support of whites who felt victimized by "goals," "quotas," "minority set-asides," and the like. Then, on June 12, 1995, the Supreme Court handed down a landmark decision permitting the continuation of federal affirmative action programs but only under tough, new guidelines. *Adarand Construction v. Pena* involved a construction company that lost a federal contract to a minority-owned "disadvantaged" business even though it had submitted a low bid. The Supreme Court accepted the racial classifications underlying affirmative action programs but allowed courts to review them under a "strict scrutiny" standard. The decision went far toward resolving the president's dilemma. In July 1995, Clinton announced that he was ordering a review of all federal affirmative action programs to see if they conformed to the Court's new standard. In general, he said, such programs remained "a moral imperative, a Constitutional mandate, and a legal necessity." With respect to affirmative action, he said, his goal was "mend it; don't end it."

The crucial test of the new White House strategy occurred in 1996 when Congress passed a bill that revamped the nation's welfare system. At the time, direct federal welfare expenditures amounted to only $12.5 billion a year, about 1 percent of federal spending. A majority of welfare families were headed by women and most of the funding went to support children. Nevertheless, politicians in both parties were determined to cut welfare costs, although Republicans favored more drastic cuts than Democrats. The bill that finally emerged from Congress cut benefits more sharply than Clinton had wanted. Proponents of welfare reform said the measure would reduce the welfare rolls, end long-term dependence, move people into jobs, and save $60 billion over six years. Opponents predicted an increase in poverty, homelessness, and hunger. The Urban Institute thought the measure was "a Trojan horse designed to dismantle the welfare state that has existed for the past sixty years."

Clinton decided to sign the measure, largely to deprive Republicans of a 1996 campaign issue. The Welfare Reform Act of 1996 reversed sixty years of federal policy. The existing program, Aid to Families with Dependent Children, was eliminated and replaced by block grants to the states: annual lump sum payments, known as Temporary Assistance for Needy Families, were to be made, but those payments would be capped rather than being adjusted to meet the need. The states would be permitted to establish their own requirements for recipients. Welfare payments would not be made to unmarried teenage mothers. Families could receive aid for a maximum of five years (although states could exempt up to 20 percent of the poor to account for emergencies). Adults who received welfare could be required to work in exchange. No aid was to be given to aliens, even to legal aliens. Unemployed adults could receive food stamps for only three months in any three-year period unless they had children under the age of eighteen.

As the president became more conservative, Republicans grew more frustrated. In November 1995, a budget impasse between the White House and the House Republican majority, chiefly involving a dispute over how deeply to cut Medicare and Medicaid benefits, led to a six-day shutdown of the federal government. Many people who were hurt and inconvenienced by the closing blamed Newt Gingrich and his followers for the fiasco. Even after Clinton accepted a compromise in which he agreed to pursue policies leading to a balanced budget by the year 2002, he could plausibly maintain that he had protected popular entitlement programs from a Republican onslaught. "There will never be a time when government can do anything for people they won't do for themselves," Clinton told the Democratic National Committee in 1995. He restated this theme in his 1996 State of the Union message: "We know big government does not have all the answers. We know there's not a program for every problem." What was needed instead, he asserted, was "a relentless search for common ground."

So far, that search had led Clinton in a conservative direction, and the search was still in its early stages. The president would further improve his standing with the public before the 1996 election by supporting the right of public schools to require students to wear uniforms as a means of ensuring discipline, by signing an executive order denying federal contracts to businesses that hired illegal aliens, and by inducing the television networks to agree to expand educational programming for children. The Clinton administration's pattern in domestic policy—early reverses and a consequent decline in popularity, followed by later victories and an accompanying rise in the polls—would be replicated in foreign policy.

CLINTON'S FOREIGN POLICIES: REVERSES . . .

In the 1992 elections, Americans had viewed foreign policy issues as important but not decisive. Bill Clinton, nevertheless, went out of his way to attack President George H.W. Bush on these issues. Clinton effectively leveled a barrage of charges against him: (1) the Persian Gulf War was not a great success because Iraq's dictator, Saddam Hussein, remained entrenched in power; (2) Bush coddled Chinese communist leaders for the sake of keeping China open to U.S. goods, even as those leaders brutalized political dissenters; (3) U.S. policy toward Haiti, where the army had driven out an elected president, Jean-Bertrand Aristide, in 1991,

President Bill Clinton and his wife, Hillary, at the Million Mom March, May 2000. The march called for strict control of handguns. *(Dirck Halstead/Liaison/Getty Images)*

had favored the military thugs, mistreated Aristide, and immorally sent back home Haitians who tried to find refuge in the United States; (4) Bush paid too little attention to the United Nations (UN), which, Clinton claimed, Americans would increasingly have to work with in the complex post–Cold War world.

In the early months of his own presidency, however, Clinton failed to reverse Bush's policies. Surprisingly, he even seemed to adopt them as his own. In regard to the Chinese, Clinton threatened to restrict trade unless the communists treated their dissenters better. When Beijing officials nevertheless continued to crack down on dissent, Clinton backed down. By 1995, he no longer linked trade and human rights in his China policies. The bottomless market of 1.5 billion Chinese was too important, in his view, to sacrifice it to principles of human rights, especially as Japanese, Europeans, and others rushed to beat American business into that market. As for Haiti, Clinton not only failed to restore President Aristide to power in 1993, but an even more embarrassing event occurred. Clinton sent the warship, *Harlan County*, to warn the Haitian military to behave. A small mob appeared on the Haitian dock, threatening to fight anyone who landed from the *Harlan County*, and the ship retreated in disgrace.

Why had Clinton so reversed himself and thrown U.S. foreign policy into such confusion? One reason was that he had little experience in overseas affairs. He spent the overwhelming part of his time on domestic economic problems. A second reason stemmed from the inability of the president and his advisers to find a coherent foreign policy strategy. During the Cold War, the strategy had been simple and direct: contain communism. Now, after the Cold War,

U.S. officials tried to use several strategies to replace containment, but none worked. Thus, Clinton, whose political antennae were extraordinarily sensitive and far-reaching, was too often left at the mercy of television and other media that blew American public opinion back and forth—with the president in pursuit.

An example was his approach to Somalia. During the Cold War, this impoverished but strategically located East African nation had been fought over by Americans and Russians. Both superpowers pumped in money and arms in order to gain influence. When the Cold War ended, both quickly lost interest in Somalia. Washington's view changed, however, in late 1992 when American television showed starvation and terrorism sweeping over the country as rival clans fought bitterly. In December 1992, President Bush, with Clinton's support, sent in 25,000 troops to feed the starving. The troops' night landing was spectacularly covered by Cable News Network and other television networks. Americans were on a mission of compassion. But in mid-1993, Clinton changed the mission. He decided Somalians could be helped only when one uncooperative clan leader, Mohammed Farah Aidid, was captured. Farah Aideed, however, proved elusive. In the autumn of 1993, his forces killed eighteen Americans, and then dragged several of the bodies through the dust—again as television cameras rolled. By early 1994, Clinton had pulled out the troops. He had tried not merely to feed, but to change, Somalia. Neither U.S. power nor, especially, American public opinion was up to that task.

As the 1994 congressional elections approached, the president's foreign policies were in disarray. Perhaps the most dangerous stumble came in Yugoslavia. In 1991–1992, that nation came apart as Croatia and Bosnia tried to separate from the dominant Serbian state. Serbians responded with force. Both sides, especially the Serbians, began "ethnic cleansing"—that is, killing masses of civilians (often after brutally raping the women) on the other side. Most Americans wanted no part of this conflict. Of special importance, the U.S. military wanted to keep its distance. A "Powell Doctrine," named after the chair of the military Joint Chiefs, General Colin Powell, promised "no more Vietnams." According to this doctrine, U.S. troops would intervene abroad only when they knew that American interests were at stake; when the president assured them they could use their full conventional force to fight, if necessary; when the military was given a date not just for entering, but for exiting, a conflict; and when the American people fully supported the operation. None of these preconditions existed in Yugoslavia. When Powell had allowed the troops to enter Somalia without these preconditions, tragedy resulted. So Clinton told Europeans they were responsible for defusing the Yugoslav conflict. The Europeans, however, turned out to be even more divided and reluctant than were the Americans. The war and the bloody ethnic cleansing threatened to spread.

. . . TO VICTORIES

Then, in 1994, Clinton's policies began to enjoy some successes. Understanding his political weakness, the president gave more personal attention to overseas crises. That attention grew after the Republican triumph in the 1994 congressional elections. Many Americans knew too little about foreign affairs, but they wanted their president to be an effective world leader, and Clinton could no longer afford to flunk this test. Moreover, General Colin Powell retired. The new military leaders were less haunted by Vietnam. They were willing to deploy troops in limited, open-ended operations—although they continued to insist that, if necessary, the troops could use all conventional power necessary to protect themselves from future Farah Aideeds or terrorists.

An initial success occurred in Haiti. Aristide, the president thrown out by the military, was a former Roman Catholic priest who condemned the exploitation of Haitians by the military and their rich civilian supporters. He wanted to end the nation's ranking as the poorest country in the entire hemisphere. But first Aristide had to regain power. He received crucial help from African-American leaders, especially Randall Robinson of the Trans-Africa organization in Washington, DC, who went on a widely publicized hunger strike aimed at forcing Clinton to restore Aristide's authority. Finally, in September 1994, Clinton moved U.S. forces toward Haiti and threatened to destroy the military thugs unless they left the country. They did so, taking, unfortunately, millions of dollars with them. As U.S. troops moved into the Caribbean nation, Aristide returned to power, the threat of Haitian refugees flooding into the United States stopped, and little was to be heard of the issue in the 1996 election campaign.

Another success followed in Yugoslavia. Here Clinton was helped by Croatian military victories that checked Serbian forces. In truth, both sides were exhausted by three years of blood-soaked war. Clinton dispatched Richard Holbrooke, his new assistant secretary of state for Europe, to broker a peace. Holbrooke did so, first with a truce in Yugoslavia, then at a late 1995 meeting in Dayton, Ohio, where tentative territorial settlements were worked out. Clinton then committed 20,000 U.S. troops as part of a North Atlantic Treaty Organization (NATO) and United Nations force to oversee the Dayton Accords. Critics warned that the Somalia tragedy would be repeated. But Yugoslavia remained calm. The peace largely held, the president paraded American power (as Europeans followed along), and again the issue did not haunt Clinton in the 1996 campaign.

He also profited politically, perhaps unfairly so, from historic peace accords hammered out between longtime enemies Israel and the Palestinians. Indeed, the Middle East peace process moved along farther and faster between 1993 and 1996 than at any time during the previous decade. The Palestinian Liberation Organization (PLO) obtained from Israeli prime minister Yitzhak Rabin a promise of self-rule on the West Bank of the Jordan River and in the Gaza Strip—both areas long and bitterly fought over. In return, Rabin received important security guarantees from the PLO. Clinton officiated at a spectacular White House signing in September 1993 and again when the peace process moved forward in September 1995. But Rabin was assassinated in November 1995. Israel's opposition party, Likud, came to power after condemning parts of the peace process as a sellout of Israeli security. Palestinians and Israelis lost their lives in renewed violence. In 1996, Clinton sent emissaries to try to pump life back into the peace talks. Since the bulk of U.S. foreign aid went to Israel and to Egypt (an ally of the PLO), the president had considerable leverage. By early 1997, parts of the agreement were restored. The conflict between Israel and the PLO continued, sometimes violently, but Clinton benefited from the perception that his officials played a vital role in keeping the peace process alive.

One of the president's most important (if less visible) successes came in dealing with the other former superpower. Boris Yeltsin, Russia's leader, suffered from heart disease, growing political opposition, and an economy riddled with out-of-control inflation and corruption. Yeltsin, moreover, tragically involved Russia in its own Vietnam when in 1994 he tried to use military force to prevent the Muslim enclave of Chechnya from leaving the Russian Federation. As they had for 1,000 years, the Chechens fought back violently against a bankrupt,

U.S. Secretary of State Madeleine Albright, 1998. *(NATO photos)*

dispirited Russian army that was falling apart. As Yeltsin's public opinion support fell to an unbelievably low 5 percent, observers speculated whether the communists or reactionary nationalists would replace him in the 1996 presidential election. Clinton, however, continued supporting Yeltsin. He had little choice, given the unacceptable alternatives of communism or anti-Western nationalism. The United States funneled millions of dollars to help Yeltsin, and then shaped the International Monetary Fund's decision to give a $10 billion credit line to prop up Russia's economy. In 1996, Yeltsin won Russia's first-ever democratic presidential election.

Another policy toward the former Soviet Union also seemed to be working: patiently pressuring, and even paying, Ukraine, Belarus, and Russia itself to dismantle nuclear weapons. Ukraine and Belarus gave up their nuclear weapons, while Russia cut back more than half to about 20,000. Negotiations began in 1997 to reduce further the U.S. and Russian nuclear arsenals. In 1994 the Clinton administration (with help from China) also successfully pressured communist North Korea to agree to freeze its nuclear weapons program in return for badly needed economic aid.

Clinton had promised in 1992 to cut $60 billion over five years from the nearly $300 billion U.S. defense budget. Instead, he kept it at about the $260 billion-a-year level, far higher than many experts had thought it would be after the end of the Cold War. Both the president and Congress (which added billions of dollars to Pentagon budget requests) declared that a flourishing arms industry was necessary to keep thousands of Americans employed. By 1995, moreover, Clinton depended on the military not only for economic benefits, but to carry out his diplomacy. In Bosnia, the Middle East, Japan (where 47,000 U.S. military personnel were stationed to maintain security for the most important U.S. ally in Asia), and in the Taiwan Straits (where Clinton mobilized a war fleet in 1996 to warn China to stay away from Taiwan), the president deployed U.S. forces.

Since 1994, he had acted, often without the United Nations but with military force. In 1997, Clinton prepared for a historic extension of this military power: expanding the most successful alliance, NATO, into Eastern Europe. The nearly fifty-year-old alliance (see page 245) was widely credited with containing Soviet power in Europe. Now with Eastern Europe free of Russian forces, the inclusion of Poland, Hungary, and the Czech Republic in NATO would tie those nations into the West while blunting any future Russian expansion. Their inclusion also allowed the United States, which dominated NATO, to gain more political influence and arms sales in Eastern Europe. Critics, however, warned with compelling evidence that Russia would not look kindly on this military powerhouse moving so close to its borders. Critics also wondered whether Americans would, in a crisis, want their sons and daughters to die for, say, interests in Hungary. Americans were discovering that the end of the Cold War did not mean the end of foreign policies that could threaten their vital interests, even their lives.

The drive to expand NATO was led by Madeleine Albright, whom Clinton named secretary of state in 1997. She became the first woman to hold the cabinet's premier position. Born in Czechoslovakia, Albright fully backed NATO expansion. While ambassador to the United Nations (1993–1996), she had become more critical of that organization and supported unilateral uses of U.S. forces.

Another central theme of Clinton's policy, as noted above, was his determination to open global markets to U.S. products. He had no choice: in the trading of goods (wheat, paper products, computer software) and the investment of money (Exxon, Pizza Hut, PepsiCo), Americans led the world and depended on world markets for their prosperity. The Clinton administration signed more than 200 agreements between 1993 and 1997 to open these markets. The president, over fierce opposition from labor unions that were key parts of his own Democratic Party, pushed through legislation in 1994 to meld the United States, Mexico, and Canada into a vast free trade area. U.S. officials downplayed China's horrible record on human rights so American firms would not be shut out of the Chinese market, which, experts believed, could overtake the United States and become the world's largest economy by the year 2020.

The Clinton foreign policies thus finally came to revolve around the unilateral use of U.S. military force and intense pressure to open global markets for the benefit of U.S. business. Both policies had deep, if not always blood-free, roots in the American Century.

GENDER, LAW, AND POLITICS

By the end of the 1980s, the women's movement had shifted its focus to workplace issues, such as affirmative action and pay equity and to persistent questions about women and public policy. Could legislation ensure equality if structural equality persisted in the family and workforce? Were policies that addressed sexual difference needed to provide equal opportunity? Or would any consideration of difference by courts or legislatures impose more problems than it solved? Three issues of the early 1990s—family leave, sexual harassment, and the gender gap in voting patterns—evoked these questions.

Family leave policy developed out of the Pregnancy Disability Act of 1978 and controversy that arose over *California Savings & Loan v. Guerra* (1987), which upheld a state law providing unpaid leave and job security for pregnant workers. But to regard women as a different class of workers, some feminists had argued, would only perpetuate sex discrimination. The solution was a broader, gender-neutral policy, one not limited to pregnant workers, such as parental leave or family leave. In 1990, President Bush had vetoed a family leave bill that would have offered unpaid leave to workers with family obligations. President Clinton, however, signed a similar bill as soon as he took office in 1993. The new law enabled workers to take four months unpaid leave for their own disabilities or to care for family members, such as new infants, sick spouses, or aged parents. Demands for maternity leave plus feminist pressure for equal treatment had spurred a new broad-based policy that affected all workers. Of course, the new law provided only meager benefits to recipients, far less than the paid maternity leaves available to pregnant workers in European states.

Sexual harassment policy had also taken root in the 1980s, after a campaign by lawyer Catharine MacKinnon to make sexual harassment a form of sex discrimination and thus barred by Title VII of the 1964 Civil Rights Act. According to the Equal Employment Opportunity Commission (EEOC) in 1980, sexual harassment meant "unwelcome verbal or physical conduct" that (1) made sex a precondition of advancement, (2) interfered with an individual's job performance, or (3) created an "intimidating, hostile, or offensive working environment." The Supreme Court endorsed both the concept of harassment as sex discrimination and the "hostile environment" test in *Meritor Savings Bank v. Vinson* (1986), a landmark case brought by a bank employee against a supervisor.

Anita Hill's allegations of sexual harassment against Clarence Thomas during the Senate hearings on his nomination to the Supreme Court in 1991 unleashed a torrent of complaints. By September 1992, the EEOC reported a 50 percent surge in harassment complaints since the hearings. Reported incidents of harassment abounded. Assaults on women at a convention of the Tailhook Association, a group of naval aviators, led to the resignation of the secretary of the navy and other upheavals. Sexual harassment charges fell upon public officials, including two senators. Employers made new efforts to sensitize workers to the nature of harassment and its consequences. According to the civil rights law of 1991, employers were now liable for up to $300,000 to victims of job discrimination, including sexual harassment.

The criteria for sexual harassment, however, especially the "hostile environment" provision, proved controversial because, in practice, the crime was defined neither by the perpetrator's intent nor by the conduct in question but by the victim's response to it. In 1991, in *Ellison v. Brady,* a federal appeals court set a slightly broader standard: harassment was what a "reasonable woman" found offensive. This definition seemed to recognize objections to the common legal standard "reasonable person," which, some feminists contended, did not reflect women's sense of vulnerability in the workplace. But feminist objections to "reasonable woman" also developed. A standard that accepted female difference in any form, some feminists argued, imposed a false unity on all women. In a 1993 sexual harassment case, *Harris v. Forklift Systems*, the Supreme Court endorsed the gender-neutral standard. A "hostile environment," said the Court, was one that a "reasonable person" would find hostile, abusive, or detrimental to job performance. The distinction between the two legal definitions, both of which mustered feminist support and critiques, represented a quandary.

The gender gap in voting behavior, meanwhile, elicited other questions about difference. Early in the century, suffragists had implied that, once enfranchised, women would vote as a bloc to support reform—such as good government, peace, temperance, and protection of children and families. But the bloc did not materialize; women seemed to vote independently, just as men did. Around 1980, however, when voters considered candidates for president, pollsters found a 5 to 9 percentage point difference between men and women. What issues caused the difference? Analysts agreed on only one facet of the gender gap: women voters (more than men) believed in activist government and the social safety net. They liked candidates who would protect Medicare, Social Security, and a system of provision for those in need. Beyond that, various hypotheses emerged. Did women share an economic perspective that differed from that of men? Were they more likely to support the Democratic Party because of their precarious vocational status and concentration in lower-income jobs? Did the care that they assumed for homes, children, and the aged affect their political vision? Or was the gender gap, in fact, caused by men, who, as writer Barbara Ehrenreich charged, lived "in a state of radical disconnection" from women and children?

Overall, research suggested mainly what the gender gap was *not*. It was not, for instance, determined by positions on abortion rights—although swing voters often turned out to be pro-choice women. It did not reflect higher standards of character, because women voters seemed more concerned with policy issues than with personality. Nor did the gender gap necessarily determine the outcome of elections. Still, voting behavior consistently suggested that women had greater confidence than men in the state's capacity to help people and more concern about reduction in services for the young, old, or poor. And this gap could affect elections, as was the case in 1996.

THE ELECTION OF 1996

In 1992, a flagging economy and a wave of discontent had fueled a Democratic victory. Four years later, the major parties' roles were reversed. Cast as challengers, the Republicans nominated Robert Dole, long-time Kansas senator, majority leader of the Senate, and a decorated World War II veteran. Dole began the race laden with liabilities. He had been sabotaged by fellow Republicans in the primaries. Plagued by the Democratic minority in the Senate, he had resigned to become "citizen" Dole, thus losing his major source of power and prestige. To compound Dole's problems, Republican strategists imposed a new campaign theme—tax cuts—that contradicted the candidate's previous assertions and deficit reduction goals. Finally, Dole was handicapped by a gloomy persona, a staccato speaking style, and his age, seventy-two. To younger voters, he seemed a relic of a bygone era.

Clinton started his fight for reelection with handicaps, too. His major initiative for health reform had drastically failed, he had suffered a crushing defeat in the midterm congressional elections of 1994, and he faced a long string of charges. As the campaign began, four independent counsels were examining the Clintons' role in Whitewater (a speculative Arkansas real estate deal), their efforts to influence the former secretary of agriculture, the business dealings of the former commerce secretary, and the honesty of the housing secretary. The Clintons also faced questions about the administration's gathering of FBI files on prominent Republicans, missing records, dismissals of employees from the travel office, and withholding of documents from government investigators. Hillary Rodham Clinton, subdued since the demise of health care reform, was at the center of most of the charges and investigations. Days before the election, a new issue arose: whether the White House condoned or aided the solicitation of questionable political contributions by a long-time Clinton friend and ally of Indonesian business interests.

Despite these handicaps, the Clinton campaign seized the initiative. A sex scandal forced presidential adviser Richard Morris to resign on the day that the Democratic Party nominated Clinton, but the strategy Morris had set in place succeeded. Defending the strong economy, Clinton sponsored an antiterrorism bill and the Welfare Reform Act of 1996. An aggressive Democratic campaign forced the Republicans to endorse popular middle-class entitlement programs, such as Social Security, Medicare, and veterans' benefits.

The Democrats turned apparent disaster into political capital: Clinton became the first Democratic president since Franklin Roosevelt to win reelection. Third-party candidate Ross Perot drew half the percentage of votes that he had in 1992. Clinton won 49 percent of the popular vote to Dole's 41 percent and another electoral landslide.

Why did Clinton win? First, voters were unlikely to unseat a president in times of peace and prosperity. Second, the president had developed a masterful ability to elude his problems. Shocked by the 1994 defeat in the midterm elections, he had been forced to return to his "New Democrat" roots; he had been able to appropriate Republican issues, to make inroads among suburbanites and Perot voters, and to carve out a position that appealed to independents. "He was stealing the center, creating the center," said campaign aide George Stephanopoulos. Third, Dole was injured by his tax reduction plank, which seven out of ten voters found unbelievable. Clinton, in contrast, defused his opponents' charges about "character" by redefining the term. "I think you can demonstrate character most effectively by what you fight for and for whom you fight," he told a television interviewer.

And, finally, there was the gender gap. A colossal twenty-point gender gap in early campaign polls had simmered down to a more modest but still stunning 11 percent gap in the popular vote. The women's vote put Clinton over the top. The president won 54 percent of women's votes to Dole's 38 percent and only 43 percent of men's votes to Dole's 44 percent. If only men had voted, in short, Dole might well have eked out a narrow victory. According to the exit polls, significantly, six out of ten women who worked supported Clinton. So did young women; among voters under age 30, Clinton had a 17 percent advantage over Dole.

Clinton assumed office as the twentieth century's last president with several challenges ahead. He faced a divided Congress as Republicans retained control of both houses. He had to keep Medicare and Social Security solvent, overhaul campaign finance law, establish a foreign policy record, eliminate the deficit, balance the budget, and subdue divisive issues, such as immigration and affirmative action. He would also have to confront ongoing investigations, including Whitewater, the travel office, the FBI files, and the Democratic Party's fund-raising relationship with foreign donors. His final term brought unexpected problems.

CLINTON'S SECOND TERM

Scandal plagued Bill Clinton's second term. Its roots lay in earlier events. In 1994, Attorney General Janet Reno had appointed an independent counsel (a special prosecutor) to investigate charges about the roles of Bill and Hillary Clinton in Whitewater, a shady Arkansas real estate venture of the 1980s. As of August 1994, independent counsel Kenneth Starr, a Republican, headed the Whitewater investigation. Also in 1994, an Arkansas state employee, Paula Corbin Jones, had filed a civil lawsuit against Bill Clinton. Jones claimed that on May 8, 1991, while he was governor of Arkansas, Bill Clinton had propositioned her in a Little Rock hotel room and that the proposition constituted sexual harassment.

Investigation of Whitewater and allegations of sexual misconduct soon converged. In May 1997, the Supreme Court unanimously rejected Clinton's request to delay the Paula Jones lawsuit until he left office. A federal district court in April 1998 dismissed the case; Jones at first filed an appeal and then settled out of court. But while the case was in progress, lawyers for Jones, who hoped to prove a pattern of sexual harassment by Clinton, called for testimony from the president and from a list of women rumored to have had relationships with him. The list included Monica Lewinsky, a former White House intern. Thus Jones's sexual harassment suit first brought Lewinsky's name to public notice.

Lewinsky and the president each signed affidavits in the Paula Jones case denying a sexual relationship. Hillary Clinton, facing the media, claimed that "a vast right-wing conspiracy" fostered Jones's accusations. Attention to Monica Lewinsky skyrocketed. On January 12, 1998, a confidante of Lewinsky, Linda Tripp, who had secretly recorded conversations with the former intern, released tapes in which Lewinsky described intimate relations with the president that had occurred in the White House from November 1995 to March 1997. Lewinsky had been twenty-two when the relationship began. The tapes gave Starr new ammunition. In January 1998, a grand jury authorized Starr to explore Tripp's charges that Clinton lied under oath in the Paula Jones trial and had urged Lewinsky to lie under oath, too. In testimony before a grand jury, Clinton again denied having sexual relations with Lewinsky. He issued similar denials to his wife, family, staff, cabinet, and members of Congress. In a televised news conference, Clinton yet again declared that he "did not have sexual relations with that woman, Ms. Lewinsky."

These denials were evasive, as new disclosures soon revealed. In August 1998, after the independent counsel had threatened her with jail and promised immunity, Lewinsky admitted an affair with Clinton to Starr's grand jury. On August 17, in his videotaped testimony before the grand jury, Clinton conceded "conduct that was wrong" and in a national address that night admitted to engaging in an "inappropriate relationship" with intern Lewinsky. He had not, he claimed, acted illegally. Moreover, he charged, politics had motivated Starr's charges. But Clinton's new statements meant that his previous assertions had been false. His admission empowered independent counsel Starr.

In September 1998, Starr delivered a report accusing the president of perjury to the House of Representatives. In December, the House, split along partisan lines—and dominated since 1994 by Republicans—sent the Senate two articles of impeachment. The articles accused Clinton of lying under oath and obstructing justice. Clinton's foes claimed that he had disgraced his office; his defenders asserted that he had not committed offenses that justified impeachment. The public agreed. Despite the astounding revelations, the president retained widespread—indeed rising—support. In the Senate, Republicans held fifty-five seats but needed a two-thirds vote to convict. On February 12, 1998, the Senate rejected the articles of impeachment against Clinton.

The second president to be impeached (the first had been Andrew Johnson in 1868), Clinton thus escaped conviction and remained in office (as had Johnson). But the impeachment crisis undercut his second term and his reputation. Irony followed irony. Sexual harassment law, a feminist advance that rested upon Title VII of the Civil Rights Act of 1964, a type of law only recently (in the 1980s) endorsed by the Supreme Court, had led indirectly to the impeachment of a president who strongly supported equal rights for women. Indeed, President Clinton in 1994 had signed the law enabling Paula Jones's attorneys to present evidence of "similar acts of sexual harassment" in a civil case and thus to request the testimony of Monica Lewinsky. Nevertheless, the president had veered toward self-destruction. Though exceptionally gifted, politically savvy, aided by skilled personnel, and favored by a booming economy, President Clinton had squandered his advantages, compromised his integrity, and undermined his administration. One result: he could no longer pursue a domestic agenda. Foreign policy was another story.

CLINTON IN A FRAGMENTING WORLD

Bill Clinton was the first president in fifty years who did not face the terrible challenges of the post-1945 Cold War. But this was not necessarily a stroke of good luck. The Cold War, at least, neatly divided the globe between leading capitalist and communist powers. Nearly every nation had to choose which side it was on. Each superpower, the United States and the Soviet Union, meanwhile attempted to control and stabilize its part of the Cold War world—not least because any sudden unpredictability (as in the 1962 Cuban missile crisis) could unleash an earth-ending nuclear war.

This world transformed during Clinton's presidency. A communist Russia no longer existed. Indeed, Russia began fragmenting: Georgia, Ukraine, the three Baltic States (Estonia, Latvia, and Lithuania), as well as five oil-rich Central Asian countries declared their independence.

The United States emerged as the sole superpower. But it could not stop the fragmenting. Yugoslavia fell apart along ethnic lines. Murderous encounters threatened to spread across southeastern Europe. Civil wars accelerated in parts of Asia. Canada nearly came apart as the French-influenced province of Quebec came close to declaring independence. And even Scotland prepared to separate itself from England's three-centuries-long control.

The newest and by far the most dangerous (and radical) form of 1990s fragmentation appeared in the form of terrorism. These new groups were startling: they had no allegiances at all to any state. For some 350 years, modern nation-states had been the bricks that formed the world's political structure. Until the 1990s, terrorists had close ties to a few such states as Libya and Iran. After 1990, however, terrorist groups had little connection to any state. The best known, al-Qaeda, led by Osama bin Laden, exemplified the new movement. (The name "al-Qaeda" translates from the Arabic as "the base.") The organization had been formed in the late 1980s when bin Laden helped Americans defeat the Soviet invasion of Afghanistan. In other words, the Ronald Reagan administration initially supported and supplied al-Qaeda.

After the United States and its allies defeated Iraq in the 1991 war, Washington officials stationed U.S. troops in Saudi Arabia. Bin Laden and many of his followers were from Saudi Arabia. As the leader of a movement shaped and motivated by a radical Islamic faith, he blisteringly attacked the "infidel" Americans for stationing their soldiers in his homeland near some of Islam's most holy sites. Al-Qaeda vowed to destroy the Saudi monarchy, Israel, and U.S. supremacy, much as al-Qaeda had helped defeat the Soviet invasion of Afghanistan in the 1980s. The world would then be ready, bin Laden believed, for the return of an Islamic caliph—the type of religious leader of 500 years earlier, a supposed direct descendant of Muhammad, the founder of Islam (570–632.) The caliph would then restore religious rule and purity to an all-powerful Islamic world.

The first major al-Qaeda action against the United States was the 1993 bombing of New York City's 110-story World Trade Center. The attack took six lives, but did little structural damage. Bin Laden, who had been expelled from Saudi Arabia (but probably managed to take hundreds of millions of his family's wealth with him), operated out of Sudan. Three years later, in 1996, he and his three wives, along with hundreds of followers, found refuge in Afghanistan, now controlled by fellow fundamentalist Muslims—the Taliban. In 1998, bin Laden issued a fatwa (a religious decree): "to kill Americans and their allies, civilian and military, is an individual duty for every Muslim who can do it in any country in which it is possible to do it." That same year, al-Qaeda bombed two U.S. embassies in Africa, killing more than 200 people, although few Americans.

Clinton responded with two U.S. attacks. One aimed to kill bin Laden at a base in Afghanistan. He apparently had left only shortly before. A second U.S. attack targeted Sudan, where al-Qaeda's chemical weapons were supposedly being made. It did little damage. Bin Laden threatened to launch "millennium attacks" as the calendar turned toward 2000. In October 2000, al-Qaeda suicide bombers attacked the USS *Cole*, docked in Yemen. They gained worldwide attention by killing seventeen American sailors.

Repeatedly claiming that terrorism was a top foreign policy priority, Clinton tightened U.S. security. Just before January 1, 2000, a terrorist who planned to bomb the Los Angeles airport was captured as he entered the United States from Canada. But while the Clinton administration had sounded the alarm, neither it nor its allies knew how to destroy al-Qaeda.

Fragmentation continued in Yugoslavia during 1999. The country's province of Kosovo held a majority of Albanian Muslims and a minority of Christian Orthodox Serbs. The Serbs controlled Yugoslavia. Through the 1980s and 1990s, Kosovo Albanians had increasingly demanded independence. In 1998–1999 the Serbs brutally retaliated, conducting mass killings in marketplaces and receiving wide television coverage. As the violence threatened to spread outside Yugoslavia, Clinton and his NATO allies decided they had to respond. NATO, the military alliance established in 1949 to protect the West from the Soviet Union, had never gone to battle against the Soviets. But in the 1990s the alliance was suddenly sent into wars to stop fragmentation in Eastern Europe. Clinton and NATO launched a major bombing campaign of Serbian outposts. The president was determined not to send in ground troops, who, he feared, might become mired down in another Vietnam-like situation. The bombings killed thousands of people. Russia stepped in to tell its historic allies, the Serbs, to give up and negotiate the crisis. The Yugoslav government backed off, UN and NATO forces entered Kosovo, and the province moved fitfully toward independence over the next decade.

President Clinton, obviously, was not reluctant to use force, whether in Kosovo, Africa, Afghanistan, or Haiti. But he preferred to try to reunite a fragmenting world through the bonds of trade and U.S. investment. In 1995, the United States helped create a new international institution, the World Trade Organization (WTO). It replaced the General Agreements on Tariffs and Trade begun in 1944. The 135-nation WTO set rules for a rapidly accelerating global trade, but its membership did not include the world's fastest growing economy—China. Chinese human rights abuses and communist-controlled economic policies were unacceptable to the WTO.

Clinton, however, smoothed the way for China's entry by rapidly building U.S. trade with, and investment in, China. By 2000, Americans had invested more than $24 billion, as General Motors, Microsoft, Dell, and General Electric, among many other corporations, rushed into a booming market nearly five times larger in population than the American. Since the 1840s

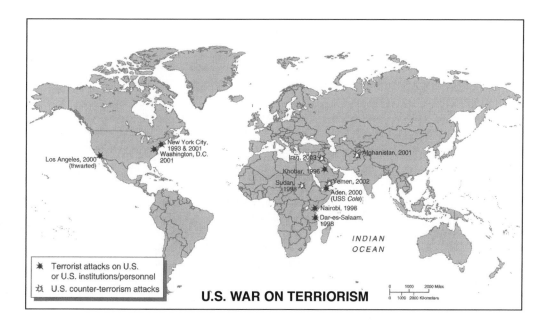

U.S. WAR ON TERRORISM

and especially the 1890s, the vision (too often the mere myth) of the supposed "Great China Market" had bedazzled—and deluded—U.S. profit-seekers. Now, as the twenty-first century dawned, the vision finally seemed to be realized—and in a communist-controlled China. Clinton also reversed the long U.S. opposition toward Vietnam. In 1995 he recognized that communist regime. By 2000 U.S. corporations, led by Coca-Cola, were selling ever-larger amounts of capitalist goods to the Vietnamese.

The major economic crisis in Clinton's second term struck in Russia. Rampant crime, corrupt politics, and the rapid movement of currency out of the country to safe Swiss bank accounts made money disappear and also made impossible any profits for Western investment. Panic struck international exchanges in 1998. Led by Secretary of the Treasury Robert Rubin, who had earlier brought similar crises in Mexico (1995) and Southeast Asia (1997) under control, the United States and international agencies rushed dollars into Russia. The Russians in turn promised to reform their decaying economy. The reforms never appeared, but the recovery did begin thanks to the outside help and, more important, ever-higher world prices for Russian-produced oil. Those oil prices were driven rapidly upward after 2000 by increasing numbers of American gas-guzzling vehicles and China's accelerating demand for its multiplying number of factories and cars.

In 1996, Clinton had successfully run for reelection by promising to build a "road to the twenty-first century." By 2000, the international portions of that road rested on two pillars. The first consisted of military interventions in Kosovo, Africa, and elsewhere; in the post–Cold War decade after 1991, Presidents Bush and Clinton deployed U.S. troops more often than presidents had over a similar period between 1945 and 1991. Dealing with fragmentation militarily cost a high price. Clinton's second pillar was a massive economic offensive that aimed to tie the post-1991 world together with golden economic links. Whether these two pillars were enough to stabilize the fragmenting globe remained an open question. Fragmentation, notably in the form of the new terrorism, continued to haunt Americans.

CHAPTER NINETEEN

9/11
Causes and Consequences

Smoke billows over New York City after the terrorist attack on September 11, 2001. *(Library of Congress)*

The terrorist attacks on September 11, 2001, which caused the deaths of 3,000 Americans, including 400 police and firefighters, dramatically transformed the nation's politics, economy, law, and foreign policy. In the wake of the tragedy, George W. Bush, the first president in more than a century to have been elected with fewer popular votes than his opponent, suddenly saw his approval ratings soar. Republicans exploited the fear of terrorism to cement their control of Congress in the election of 2002 and to reelect the president in 2004. That same fear led Congress to adopt sweeping restrictions on civil liberties with little public protest. For a time, the Supreme Court set some limits on the government's restriction of individual rights, but the appointment of two highly conservative justices suggested that the Court might not continue to play that role. Above all, the fear of terrorism provided a rationale for the president to launch an invasion of Afghanistan in 2001 and then, in 2003, to attack Iraq. After more than four years of conflict, with U.S. military deaths approaching 4,000 and with Iraq in shambles, U.S. public opinion turned sharply against the Bush administration's policies. In 2006, Democrats recaptured control of both houses of Congress. By mid-2007, 60 percent of Americans thought the United States should not have invaded Iraq, and President Bush's approval rating sank to below 30 percent. Seventy-two percent of Americans, more than at any time in the past quarter-century, told pollsters, "Generally things in this country are seriously off on the wrong track."

THE SUPREME COURT CHOOSES A PRESIDENT

In the presidential election of 2000, Republican candidate George Bush received half a million fewer votes than Democratic candidate Al Gore. The vote count in Florida, however, seemed to show that Bush had carried that state, with its twenty-five electoral votes, by a razor-thin margin of 527 votes out of 5,825,000 votes cast, providing him with a 271–267 electoral college majority. A recount was warranted, said Democrats, because of irregularities in the polling process. Although the Florida Supreme Court agreed to the recount, the U.S. Supreme Court ruled against it. The decision in *Bush v. Gore* was by the narrowest possible vote: 5 to 4. For the first time since 1888 a candidate with the smaller total of popular votes was elected president; whether Bush should also have received fewer electoral votes remained a matter of dispute.

During the campaign, the Republican and Democratic nominees had clashed on a wide range of domestic issues. On abortion rights, Gore endorsed the Supreme Court's 1973 *Roe v. Wade* ruling, while Bush opposed abortion except in cases of rape, incest, or when necessary to save the woman's life. Gore defended affirmative action programs, while Bush opposed racially preferential quotas. Gore backed the use of the Social Security surplus to keep the system solvent, while Bush proposed partial privatization. It was on environmental issues, however, that the deepest differences emerged. Gore opposed oil and gas exploration in the Alaskan National Wildlife Refuge and supported the Kyoto global warming agreement; on both issues, Bush took diametrically opposed positions.

The outcome was crucially affected by the candidacy of Ralph Nader, whose Green Party campaign was based, ironically, on the claim that Republicans and Democrats were indistinguishable. Nader's party had its own agenda: it favored universal health care, affordable housing, free education through college, a shift in the tax burden from individuals to corporations, and campaign finance reform. Yet since Nader knew he had no chance of winning, he had to

U.S. Supreme Court justices Antonin Scalia, Clarence Thomas, and Ruth Bader Ginsburg
(left to right) arrive for the funeral services of Chief Justice William Rehnquist on September 6, 2005.
(Win McNamee/Getty Images)

persuade potential supporters that a vote for him would not be "wasted," and so of necessity he argued that there were no meaningful differences between Republicans and Democrats. While he reserved his choicest barbs for Bush—calling him "a giant corporation masquerading as a human being"—he also argued that Democrats, too, were beholden to large corporate interests, "so it won't matter who wins." Nader received only 3 percent of the national vote, but his 97,400 votes in Florida far exceeded Bush's margin of victory. Most election analysts believed that Nader took more votes from Gore than from Bush, thereby playing a decisive role in the Republican triumph.

The votes cast for Nader were not the only ones cast for a minor party that helped determine the outcome in Florida. Patrick J. Buchanan, who had wrested control of the Reform Party from its founder, Ross Perot, won 17,400 votes in that state. Many of those votes were cast by people attracted by his archconservative platform, which criticized "hyphenated Americans" for weakening Anglo-Saxon culture. Buchanan opposed gay rights, condemned abortion as a "culture of death," called for ending all racial, gender, and ethnic entitlements, opposed gun control, and favored protectionism over free trade. But a substantial number of Buchanan ballots appear to have been cast by mistake. Florida used a "butterfly ballot": Gore's name appeared second on the ballot, but voting for him required punching the third hole; punching the second hole registered a vote for Buchanan. Since Buchanan received several thousand votes in districts with a heavy concentration of elderly Jewish voters, to whom his program had little appeal, it appeared likely that a significant number of votes intended for Gore were erroneously cast for Buchanan.

Given the problems in counting the ballots, it was inevitable that the controversy would wind up in court. The Democrats first appealed to the Florida Supreme Court, asking for a recount in four critical counties, including Palm Beach and Miami-Dade. On December 8, the Florida court ordered such a recount, but the next day the U.S. Supreme Court, by a 5–4 vote, ordered a halt, pending a final resolution of the case. The Court's per curiam opinion was announced by Justice Antonin Scalia, who asserted that "the counting of votes that are of questionable legality" threatened "irreparable harm to petitioner"—that is, George W. Bush—"and to the country, by casting a cloud upon what he claims to be the legitimacy of his election." Justice John Paul Stevens, speaking for the dissenters, said, "Preventing the recount from being completed will inevitably cast a cloud on the legitimacy of the election." He added that the Florida court's ruling "reflects the basic principle, inherent in our Constitution and our democracy, that every legal vote should be counted."

On December 12, the Supreme Court handed down its final ruling. One key issue was whether the Florida court, in ordering a recount, had violated the Fourteenth Amendment's equal protection clause. Bush claimed that it had, because there was no statewide standard for each county board to use to determine which ballots were legal; that is, similarly marked ballots might be counted in one county, but not in another. Gore, however, insisted that there was indeed a sufficiently clear statewide standard, the "intent of the voter." On the question of whether the Supreme Court should approve the "remedy" Bush sought—stopping the recount—the justices divided strictly along ideological lines. The five most conservative justices (Anthony Kennedy, Sandra Day O'Connor, William Rehnquist, Antonin Scalia, and Clarence Thomas) ruled in favor of Bush; the four most liberal (Stephen Breyer, Ruth Bader Ginsburg, David Souter, and John Paul Stevens) dissented.

Although a number of prominent legal scholars defended the Supreme Court's ruling, its seemingly partisan character also led to sharp criticism. More than 500 law professors took out a full-page ad in the *New York Times* declaring that the justices had acted as "political proponents for candidate Bush, not as judges. . . . By taking power from the voters, the Supreme Court has tarnished its own legitimacy." More surprisingly, two of the justices' dissenting opinions were uncharacteristically harsh. Justice Stevens wrote, "Although we may never know with complete certainty the identity of the winner of this year's Presidential election, the identity of the loser is perfectly clear. It is the Nation's confidence in the judge as an impartial guardian of the rule of law." While it is customary for a justice in the minority to say, "I respectfully dissent," Justice Ginsburg concluded her opinion more starkly: "I dissent."

Despite having received only a minority of the popular vote and despite division over the Supreme Court's ruling, President Bush did not experience any crisis of legitimacy. Although the Republicans lost seats in the 2000 congressional elections—two in the House and four in the Senate—they retained control of both chambers. In the Senate, now divided evenly between the two parties, Vice President Richard Cheney could cast the deciding vote; Republicans thus retained all committee chairmanships. Moreover, public opinion polls indicated a rise in the number of those who approved the job the president was doing: from only 46 percent when he took office in January to 59 percent by July. By the spring of 2001, when asked whether they considered Bush "to have been legitimately elected as president," 62 percent of those surveyed answered affirmatively.

During the campaign and in his first months in the White House, Bush called for a domestic program of "compassionate conservatism." He took the phrase from University of Texas professor Marvin Olasky, who asserted that "local, faith-based charitable agencies and churches" had been more successful in addressing the problems of poverty than government-run welfare programs. In 2000, Olasky published a book titled *Compassionate Conservatism* that quoted one of Bush's campaign promises: "In every instance where my administration sees a responsibility to help people, we will look first to faith-based organizations, charities and community groups that have shown their ability to save and change lives." To critics, government aid to faith-based organizations violated the principle of separation of church and state, and Olasky's emphasis on the moral shortcomings of those in need undermined support for federal antipoverty programs. Yet spokesmen for the Bush administration insisted, "compassionate conservatism serves as a true bridge from the era of big government as a way to solve social problems to a new era in which we will have a full and healthy trust in the people of this nation to govern themselves."

Armed with this belief, as well as control of Congress, Bush set forth, and implemented, an ambitious agenda. He launched a "faith-based initiative" to promote a partnership between government and religious social service providers, to permit the federal government to fund charities run by religious institutions, and to allow those institutions to use such funds to build or renovate places of worship and to hire staff members based on their religious beliefs. The president also won passage of the No Child Left Behind Act, designed to close the achievement gap between poor and rich school districts, measure student performance, provide options to parents with students in low-performing schools, and direct more federal funding to low-income schools. Congress paid no mind to critics who alleged that the focus on "high-stakes testing" and quantitative outcomes was ill conceived. Redeeming a campaign pledge, President Bush withdrew U.S. support for the pending Kyoto Protocol that sought to impose mandatory targets for reducing "greenhouse gas" emissions, that is, carbon dioxide emitted in the burning of fossil fuels. Asserting that the scientific evidence regarding climate change was suspect, Bush claimed the treaty would have an adverse effect on jobs and economic growth.

But the centerpiece of the Bush administration's legislative program was enactment of a massive tax cut. In June 2001, Congress passed a bill that would cost the government $1.35 trillion over eleven years; it not only cut individual tax rates but also repealed the inheritance tax. Additional tax cuts followed in 2002 and 2003. As a result of the tax cuts, said the Brookings Institution, taxes on the wealthiest 1 percent of Americans would fall by 17 percent by 2110; for the remaining 99 percent of taxpayers, the average reduction would be 5 percent. The decline in government revenues would shortly contribute to an abrupt reversal in the nation's fiscal position. From 1998 to 2001, the United States had enjoyed annual budget surpluses. But in 2002, it ran a deficit of $158 billion. In 2003, the deficit climbed to $375 billion. The cause, however, was not chiefly the tax cuts or even the rising costs associated with Medicare and other entitlements but rather the vast increase in military spending following the attack on the World Trade Center on September 11, 2001, the war in Afghanistan, and the invasion of Iraq in March 2003.

9/11 AND THE INVASIONS OF AFGHANISTAN AND IRAQ: 2001–2004

John Kennedy observed that presidents who win elections by slim margins should not advocate radically new foreign policies. George W. Bush had no use for Kennedy's advice. Unlike Bill Clinton, he intended to have a tough foreign policy aimed at neutralizing any possible challenge (China was seen as the greatest threat) to U.S. supremacy.

He chose key advisers known as neoconservatives (often called neocons, for short, mainly by their critics). Led by Defense Department officials Paul Wolfowitz and Douglas Feith and top members of the National Security Council (NSC), the neoconservatives, like Bush, condemned Clinton for not sufficiently building and using the U.S. military, for not acting unilaterally when longtime allies, such as Europeans, doubted American decisions, and for not promoting democracy as a cure-all for such war-wracked areas as the Middle East.

Vice President Cheney and Defense Secretary Donald Rumsfeld had doubts about spreading democracy, but they were hawks who otherwise agreed with the neoconservatives. Condoleezza Rice, head of the NSC, had been Bush's closest adviser in 2000 but was pushed to the side by Cheney, Rumsfeld, and the neoconservatives. Secretary of State Colin Powell was, according to polls, the most trusted and popular leader in the United States. Having fought in Vietnam and climbed to the highest ranks of both the U.S. Army and the federal government of any African-American in history, Powell had little faith that Americans could intervene effectively to create democracies in places such as the Middle East. Given his Vietnam experiences, he also opposed using U.S. troops in warfare unless a large set of preconditions was met by the president, Congress, and the American people. These preconditions were known as the Powell Doctrine (see page 433). The hawks in the administration mistrusted Powell's highly cautious approach to foreign policy, and, especially, to sending the U.S. military into battle.

But Powell won the administration's first foreign affairs success. In spring of 2001, a Chinese fighter plane tailing a U.S. EP3 Reconnaissance aircraft off China's coast collided with the EP3. The Chinese pilot was killed; the twenty-four U.S. crew members, who were tracking Chinese movements along the coast, crash-landed and were captured. A major crisis erupted until Powell worded an apology that released the prisoners and ended the crisis. Conservative newspaper editors and officials blasted him for a supposed "humiliation" inflicted by a nation they believed was becoming America's number one enemy.

The Bush administration paid less attention to the danger President Clinton had ranked number one: terrorism. On at least three occasions between April and early September 2001, top intelligence officials warned Rice and the president that terrorists, including Osama bin Laden's al-Qaeda, might attack the United States. Nothing was done. On the bright, sun-drenched morning of September 11, two large passenger jets, hijacked by al-Qaeda terrorists, crashed into the two 110-story World Trade Center buildings in New York City. A similar jet was seized in flight by al-Qaeda members and flown at 300 miles per hour into the Pentagon in Washington. A fourth captured jet appeared headed for the Capitol in Washington but crashed in a Pennsylvania field after heroic passengers tried to retake the plane. More than 2,800 people died in the attacks. Of the nineteen al-Qaeda members who committed suicide in the crashes, fifteen were from Saudi Arabia, bin Laden's home and for a half-century a close ally and provider of oil for the United States. China and Russia, which for years had fought Islamic insurgencies within their own countries, were among the first nations to offer Bush support in tracking down and destroying al-Qaeda.

President Bush demanded that the Islamic Taliban regime in Afghanistan hand over bin Laden and his top officials. The Taliban, whose religious fanaticism had led it to outlaw singing, schooling for females, and shaving, among other repressions, had gained control of Afghanistan in the 1990s and provided al-Qaeda refuge since 1996. When the Taliban refused, the United States—aided by most of its close NATO allies and key Afghan groups that hated the Taliban—invaded Afghanistan in October 2001. By late November, the Taliban were driven out. Bin Laden and his aides, who had once been nearly surrounded, escaped across the Pakistan border into a dense mountainous region where locals protected them. Bush made light of the escape and claimed al-Qaeda's days were numbered. But allowing bin Laden and his top advisers to escape turned into a tragedy—especially when al-Qaeda members launched murderous terrorism in Europe, Southeast Asia, and the Middle East after 2003.

In late 2001, the president turned his focus on Iraq. This shift puzzled observers. Iraq's dictator, Saddam Hussein, had never been definitively linked to the 9/11 attacks on the United States or to al-Qaeda. He was a highly secular ruler, thus a natural enemy of the al-Qaeda religious fundamentalists. Although he ruled over a predominantly Shiite nation, Saddam was a Sunni. The Sunnis are a minority in Iraq, but make up 90 percent of all Muslims. (Islam had divided into Sunni and Shiite branches soon after the Prophet Muhammad's death in 632. Shiites believed his successor had to be directly descended by bloodlines from the Prophet. Sunnis did not. Wars erupted between the two groups; but over the past several centuries, sectarian conflict between Sunni and Shiite was rare—until the U.S. invasion of Iraq disturbed the balance.) Wolfowitz and other hawks had long hoped to overthrow Saddam. Saddam had been aligned with the United States against Iran during the 1980s. The relationship soured when the Iraqi ruler invaded Kuwait, triggering the 1991 Gulf War, and encouraged (and paid) Palestinians to attack Israel, the closest U.S. partner in the region. After the Gulf War, United Nations (UN) inspectors discovered and destroyed a massive Iraqi program to develop biological and nuclear weapons.

Powell had declared in early 2001 that Saddam did not have "any significant capability with respect to weapons of mass destruction," so he was stunned after 9/11 when Wolfowitz and Rumsfeld demanded meetings to discuss invading Iraq. Bush first wanted to get Afghanistan out of the way, but then sided with the hawks. President George H.W. Bush had refused to invade Iraq and remove Saddam in the 1991 war out of fear of the chaos that could follow, but as early as November 2001, President George W. Bush ordered Rumsfeld to update plans for invading Iraq.

In his January 2002 State of the Union address, Bush declared that Iraq, Iran, and communist North Korea composed an "axis of evil," apparently in part because all three seemed bent on building weapons of mass destruction (WMD). At Powell's insistence and over objections from Cheney, who wanted nothing to do with the United Nations, Bush went to the UN in the autumn to ask for inspection of Saddam's suspected WMD. The inspectors found none. Cheney, Rumsfeld, and other U.S. officials argued that the dictator was simply hiding them, but when the UN asked for help in locating the supposed WMD sites, the American leaders provided no specific, helpful information.

In his January 2003 State of the Union address, Bush said that Saddam had sought enriched uranium from Africa for making nuclear weapons. (This claim had earlier been disproved

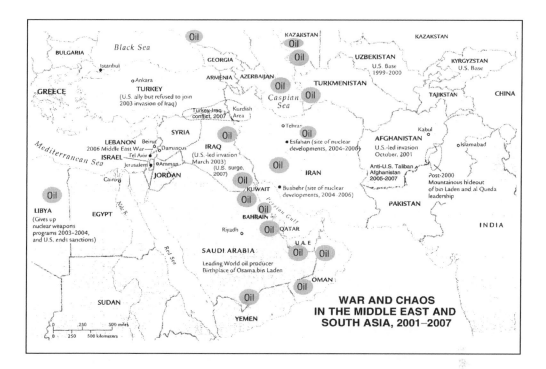

WAR AND CHAOS
IN THE MIDDLE EAST AND
SOUTH ASIA, 2001–2007

by Ambassador Joseph Wilson's secret mission to Niger, and State Department intelligence declared the documents supporting Bush's claim were clearly "forgeries," as they indeed turned out to be.) In February, Powell gave a three-and-a-half-hour speech to the UN charging that Saddam had WMD and implying the dictator was allied with al-Qaeda. Ever "the loyal soldier," as one aide called him, Powell had joined the war party. The effect was electric. The major American newspapers, columnists, and television commentators, led by Fox News Network, the *New York Times*, and the *Washington Post*, applauded Powell and fully endorsed an invasion, while condemning those who opposed it as unpatriotic.

The Bush and Powell charges against Iraq turned out to be largely untrue. Key parts of Powell's speech were based on the testimony of "Curveball," an Iraqi defector who told German intelligence that he had seen Saddam's WMD. The Germans refused to allow U.S. agents to question Curveball because, they said, he was a "drunk" and not to be believed. (After Powell left office in 2005, he admitted his UN speech was based on what turned out to be false evidence and was a "blot on my record.") Meanwhile, as war approached, Cheney announced on television that U.S. soldiers would be "greeted as liberators" by Iraqis. Wolfowitz declared that Iraq would become a democratic model for the entire Middle East. Rumsfeld assured Americans that the war "certainly isn't going to last" any more than "five weeks, or five months."

U.S. intelligence reports in 2002 had directly warned that a U.S. invasion of Iraq, a country famous over the centuries for bitterly fighting invaders, would lead to violent conflict and opportunities for al-Qaeda to spread terrorism. These reports were ignored. Indeed, in 2002 the White House had secretly set up the White House Iraq Group (WHIG): top officials who planned how to sell the war to Americans by spreading propaganda—or what one member

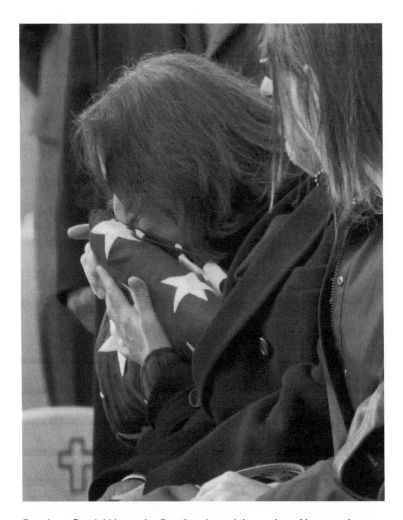

Penelope Gavriel kisses the flag that draped the casket of her son, Lance Corporal Dimitrios Gavriel, during funeral services at Arlington National Cemetery on December 2, 2004. Dimitrios Gavriel, from Haverhill, Massachusetts, died on November 19 while fighting in Al Anbar Province in Iraq. *(Win McNamee/Getty Images)*

called taking "literary license"—and playing up information about Iraq's supposed WMD. Many U.S. television and newspaper reporters uncritically believed WHIG's case for war.

Deeply angered and fearful because of the 9/11 attacks, Americans were now, with the help of leading television networks and newspapers, being transformed into all-out supporters of war against Iraq. British prime minister Tony Blair agreed with Bush's decision to invade, although the majority of his nation's citizens opposed the war. The major opposition came from former European allies of the United States, especially French president Jacques Chirac, who just before the invasion declared—correctly—that Saddam had no WMD and that the attack was unjustified. China and Russia, once strongly on Bush's side in tracking down terrorists, also opposed the invasion. Nevertheless, U.S. troops, supported by Britain and, largely symbolically, by thirty-seven other, mostly small nations, attacked Iraq on March 19, 2003. On April 9 they entered Baghdad, where looting had already begun. On May 1, Bush, dressed in *Top Gun*-style fighter pilot's uniform, landed in a jet on an aircraft carrier off San Diego, California. He proudly announced the end of the Iraq war under a huge sign reading "MISSION ACCOMPLISHED."

But the mission had only begun. Iraq's museums contained priceless artifacts of this region where civilization began. Unprotected, the museums were looted of these riches. When Rumsfeld was asked about the looting and violence, he replied, "Stuff happens," and wondered, "how many vases can they have?" The one institution he and Bush ordered U.S. troops to protect was the oil ministry: Iraq had the world's second-largest reserve of oil. Wolfowitz, who liked to note that Iraq floated on a "sea of oil," and other officials argued that these oil exports—not U.S. taxpayers—would easily pay the war's expenses. Instead, sabotage and growing resistance drastically cut oil production. Before the invasion, a top American budget official had predicted the conflict would not cost more than $1.7 billion. By the end of 2003, however, U.S. taxpayers were already paying more than $20 billion.

In mid-2003 Bush unfortunately responded to the growing violence by exclaiming, "Bring 'em on!" As the number of American lives lost stretched into the hundreds, U.S. officials reported that no WMD had been found in Iraq. The president's major reason for starting the war was thus found not to exist. Meanwhile, American soldiers complained that, despite the $450 billion U.S. defense budget, they had not been given adequate protection against snipers and roadside bombs. One infantryman asked Rumsfeld directly, "Why do we soldiers have to dig through local landfills for pieces of scrap metal . . . to uparmor our vehicles?" The defense secretary had no answer. Al-Qaeda, which did not exist in Iraq before the war, set up training bases in western Iraq, from which terrorists fanned out into the rest of the country, other Middle East nations, and Europe.

The invasion quickly turned into tragedy. The UN, which Vice President Cheney and the neocons disliked and disparaged, refused to answer Bush's pleas for help. The UN, after all, had from the start considered the invasion unnecessary and dangerous. Longtime European allies wanted nothing to do with the occupation of Iraq, although they did commit troops and resources to Afghanistan. Lost lives and costs spiraled upward. The question became whether American voters would make Bush pay in the 2004 presidential election.

THE CONSTITUTION, THE COURT, AND DOMESTIC TERRORISM

War invariably leads to a limitation of individual liberty in the name of national security. Whose liberties are curtailed, however, and to what extent, depends on the nature and duration of the war, the perceived threat to domestic security, the outlook of those in positions of power, and, in the United States, the judgments of the Supreme Court. The war on terrorism, launched in the aftermath of the destruction of the World Trade Center, differed from previous wars because terrorism was itself simply a tactic employed by many militant groups, not a nation that could actually be defeated and then brought to the peace table to sign a treaty. A new kind of war posed a new kind of threat to civil liberties. In the past, wartime restrictions on freedom were viewed as temporary and were lifted when the war ended, but the conflict that began in 2001 could have no such outcome. The creation of a permanent cabinet-level

Department of Homeland Security in 2002 only signaled that fears regarding the nation's security would also be permanent.

The wars that the United States waged in Afghanistan and then in Iraq were the first lengthy wars to be fought by an all-volunteer military. The absence of a draft muted opposition to the war. At the same time, it removed the chief justification for restricting freedom of speech: the fear that criticism of the war would interfere with raising an army. Although some opponents of American policy were subjected to informal pressures, a few even losing their jobs, the government did not seek to prosecute them as it had in past conflicts. President Bush and his attorney general, John Ashcroft, condemned critics of the Iraq war for "sending mixed signals to our troops and the enemy" and providing "ammunition to America's enemies," but those critics were never the targets of the crackdown on civil liberties.

Instead, the administration sought new authority to conduct undercover surveillance of radical Islamist political and religious groups, to engage in wiretapping and electronic eavesdropping, to gain access to Internet and e-mail communications, and to conduct clandestine physical searches of suspect organizations and reviews of their financial records. Nothing more clearly revealed the implications of the war on terrorism for civil liberties, individual rights, and the rule of law than four controversial initiatives taken in the aftermath of 9/11: the incarceration of more than a thousand resident aliens, the imprisonment of hundreds of foreign nationals at the Guantanamo Naval Base in Cuba, congressional passage of the Patriot Act, and the decision to use military tribunals, rather than civilian courts, in certain cases involving "enemy combatants."

Within weeks after the 9/11 attack, the government rounded up more than a thousand resident aliens, nearly all of them Muslims. Some of them were in the United States lawfully, others illegally. Although not charged with committing any crimes, they were placed in indefinite detention, denied access to lawyers or judicial review, and given no chance to prove their innocence. Their names were not even made public. Some of them were subjected to physical and mental abuse, confined in cells in which fluorescent lights glared twenty-four hours a day. According to a report issued by the inspector general of the Department of Justice, guards at the Brooklyn Detention Center "inappropriately used strip searches to intimidate and punish detainees . . . slammed them into walls, inappropriately twisted and bent detainees' arms, hands, wrists, and fingers, and caused them unnecessary physical pain." One detainee alleged that during the mistreatment "the officers sometimes said, 'Welcome to America.'"

Similar conditions also existed at Guantanamo Bay, where the government held more than 600 men, terrorists, it claimed, who had aided al-Qaeda. Some of them had been captured in Afghanistan by American forces, while others had been turned over to American authorities by other governments. Neither put on trial nor given access to attorneys, many of the Guantanamo internees endured solitary confinement and endless interrogation. In an effort to avoid judicial review, the Bush administration claimed that the detainees were not prisoners of war or enemy combatants but "unlawful combatants" and therefore not entitled to file habeas corpus petitions testing the legality of their detention. Since Guantanamo is not under U.S. sovereignty, the administration asserted, the prisoners had no standing before American courts.

The Guantanamo Bay naval station was a legal no-man's-land. The United States had occupied the forty-five-square-mile territory since the Spanish-American War. Agreements made with Cuba in 1903 and 1934 reserved "ultimate sovereignty" over the base to Cuba, while leaving it under U.S. control. Because Cuba technically had sovereignty, the Bush administra-

A detainee is escorted by military police at the maximum security prison at Guantanamo Naval Base in Cuba, August 26, 2004. By 2007 at least four prisoners had committed suicide at Guantanamo, and global human rights organizations condemned the United States for holding prisoners more than five years without bringing them to trial. *(Mark Wilson/Getty Images)*

tion claimed that Guantanamo was foreign soil and therefore beyond the reach of American justice. This claim ignored the fact of U.S. control. "The detainees did not accidentally fall outside of the jurisdiction of the federal courts because they ended up on Guantanamo," one human rights attorney pointed out. "Rather, they were brought to Guantanamo for the very purpose of being kept beyond the jurisdiction of the courts."

In June 2004, the Supreme Court rejected the government's contention, ruling by a 6-to-3 majority in favor of Shafiq Rasul, a British subject of Pakistani descent, who managed to obtain counsel and challenge his confinement. The opinion, by Justice John Paul Stevens, noted that Rasul had never been tried or convicted but had nevertheless been imprisoned for more than two years in territory over which the United States had jurisdiction. The federal courts, Stevens added, had to be able to determine the legality of executive action. In order to avoid the "potentially indefinite detention of individuals who claim to be wholly innocent of wrongdoing," Stevens said, "aliens held at the base, no less than American citizens, are entitled to invoke the federal courts' authority." One of the dissenters, Justice Antonin Scalia, complained that the Court was engaging in "judicial adventurism."

Unlike Shafiq Rasul, Yaser Hamdi was an American citizen, born in Louisiana, but he too was seized in Afghanistan and sent to Guantanamo. Once the authorities discovered his citizenship, he was moved to a naval base in Norfolk, Virginia, and held, incommunicado, as an enemy combatant. Yet as a citizen he was entitled to habeas corpus, and his father, a native of Saudi Arabia, was able to file a petition on his behalf. When his case reached the Supreme

Court in June 2004, the justices ruled in his favor. Justice Sandra Day O'Connor wrote the plurality opinion, which held that due process required that a citizen held in U.S. territory as an enemy combatant must have an opportunity to contest the basis for detention before a neutral decision maker, for otherwise "Hamdi's detention could last for the rest of his life." Justices Scalia and Stevens added that "the very core of liberty" has always been "freedom from indefinite imprisonment at the will of the Executive." Only Justice Clarence Thomas dissented on the grounds that the Court lacked "the expertise and capacity to second-guess" the president. Shortly thereafter Hamdi agreed to surrender his citizenship and leave the United States for Saudi Arabia, his father's homeland, and the government dropped further charges.

The centerpiece of the Bush administration's war on terrorism was the Patriot Act, which Congress passed with overwhelming bipartisan support just six weeks after 9/11. With Attorney General Ashcroft warning of further, imminent terrorist attacks, senators and congressmen rushed to pass the measure (the vote in the Senate was 98–1; in the House, 357–66) although few had taken the time to read it. The act created the new crime of "domestic terrorism." It clothed the Central Intelligence Agency with authority to conduct surveillance in the United States. It vastly expanded the government's power to investigate citizens without a need to show probable cause; to conduct those searches surreptitiously on a showing of "reasonable necessity"; to establish telephone and Internet surveillance; to gain access to student, medical, and financial records; to obtain bookstore and library records; and to arrest noncitizens and hold them indefinitely if the attorney general believed they constituted a "reasonable threat to national security." Where the act contained provisions for judicial oversight of any of these activities, the oversight was minimal.

Although justified as a weapon in the war on terrorism, the Patriot Act appears to have been a blunt instrument at best. Despite President Bush's assertion in June 2005 that "federal terrorism investigations have resulted in charges against more than 400 suspects, and more than half of those charged have been convicted," critics noted that the Justice Department's list of prosecutions showed that only thirty-nine people had been convicted of crimes related to terrorism or national security. A *Washington Post* investigation revealed that most of those convictions were for "relatively minor crimes such as making false statements and violating immigration law—and had nothing to do with terrorism." Even so, early in 2006 Congress voted to renew the Patriot Act, modifying its provisions only slightly in deference to several Republican senators who thought added protection for civil liberties was required.

Of all the measures the Bush administration proposed in its war on domestic terrorism, none had more far-reaching consequences than its attempt to place citizens on trial not in civilian courts but before military commissions, where convictions are much more easily obtained. Military tribunals are led by a presiding officer usually designated by the Secretary of Defense, are composed of three to seven officers who act as judges and jurors, require only a two-thirds majority to convict (except in the case of a death sentence), and may be conducted in secret. Many of the usual protections afforded defendants are absent: the prosecution may introduce hearsay or coerced evidence and even evidence that is not made known to the defense. Decisions made by military tribunals cannot be appealed to the Supreme Court, but only to the president. This was the system under which, in 2002, Secretary of Defense Donald Rumsfeld endeavored to try an American citizen, Jose Padilla.

He was arrested in Chicago in May 2002 as he was returning from Pakistan, charged with plotting a dirty bomb attack, and declared an enemy combatant by the Department of Defense.

Placed in a navy brig in South Carolina, he was denied access to an attorney for nearly two years. Finally, in 2004, the Supreme Court heard Padilla's case, which raised the question of whether the government had unreviewable power to imprison an American citizen. By a narrow 5-to-4 ruling, the Court dodged the issue on a technicality. Speaking for the majority, Chief Justice William Rehnquist held that Padilla's suit should have been directed not at Secretary of Defense Donald Rumsfeld, but rather at the commander of the naval brig, and would therefore need to be refiled. In his dissent, Justice Stevens wrote, "At stake in this case is nothing less than the essence of a free society. Even more important than the method of electing the people's rulers and their successors is the character of the constraints imposed on the Executive by the rule of law. . . . For if this Nation is to remain true to the ideals symbolized by its flag, it must not wield the tools of tyrants even to resist an assault by the forces of tyranny."

Recognizing that it was likely to lose if the Supreme Court reheard the case, the government abruptly moved to preempt a decision: it transferred Padilla from military to civilian custody and filed a criminal indictment that dropped any mention of a plot to use a dirty bomb but instead charged that Padilla had conspired to send money abroad to assist a "global jihad." Whether he would be able to stand trial, however, even in a civilian court, remained in doubt. His attorneys claimed that his prolonged isolation, compounded by mistreatment and sensory deprivation, had caused post-traumatic stress disorder, making him unfit to assist in his own defense. For its part, the Pentagon insisted, "Padilla's conditions of confinement were humane and designed to ensure his safety and security." There was no disputing his lawyer's assertion that during conferences, "he often exhibits facial tics, unusual eye movements and contortions of his body. . . . The contortions are particularly poignant since he is usually manacled and bound by a belly chain when he has meetings with counsel."

In December 2001, when the curtailment of civil liberties was still in an early stage, Attorney General John Ashcroft sharply criticized those who challenged the constitutionality of the administration's tactics. Testifying at a Senate hearing, he said, "To those who scare peace-loving people with phantoms of lost liberty, my message is this: your tactics only aid terrorists, for they erode our national unity and diminish our resolve. They give ammunition to America's enemies, and pause to America's friends." Most Americans, however, came to consider the loss of liberty more than a mere phantom.

BUSH REELECTED: 2004

Democrats vied for their party's nomination in 2004. Governor Howard Dean of Vermont leaped ahead of his rivals. Dean recruited thousands of "Deaniacs" on the Internet; he ran "meetups" with supporters, blog discussions, and online letter-writing campaigns. Independent political groups such as MoveOn.com had already used the Internet with skill, but Dean was the first presidential candidate to do so. Drawing big crowds, he raised millions of dollars more than other Democrats. In mid-December, he won the endorsement of Al Gore, the winner of the popular vote in 2000. Reaching 45 percent in Democratic polls, Dean dwarfed his foes. Senator John Kerry, of Massachusetts, fell to 10 percent; his staff members left for new jobs, his message meandered, and he had to take out a personal loan on his home to keep his campaign afloat.

Then, suddenly, Dean's success as front-runner backfired. Gore's endorsement imperiled Dean's role as a Washington outsider, attacks from rivals mounted, and Dean unnerved potential supporters by brash assertions—for example, that the United States was no safer with Saddam Hussein in custody than it was before. Vaulting the hurdles he had previously faced, John Kerry won the Iowa caucuses and then the primary vote in New Hampshire. By March, Kerry had clinched the Democratic nomination. Dean's stunning primary race had challenged his foes to improve their campaigns and swayed many voters who ultimately endorsed Kerry.

While Democrats battled, President George W. Bush, who faced no opposition among Republicans, easily secured renomination. Raising large sums of money, Bush began to attack Kerry even before the Democratic convention. Polls seesawed. Kerry gained a boost from his party's convention, where Barack Obama, Illinois candidate for the Senate, gave the keynote address, and from his selection of a running mate, John Edwards; he outdid Bush at the three presidential debates. But voters lacked certainty about Kerry, whom Republicans relentlessly berated. A group called Swift Boat Veterans for Truth accused Kerry of lying about his war record in Vietnam and fraudulently receiving medals for his war wounds. Though false, the charges damaged the Democratic candidate.

George Bush won 286 electoral votes compared to 254 for Kerry, and most of the popular vote, 50.8 percent, compared to Kerry's 48.3 percent. For the first time in sixteen years, a president had won a majority of the popular vote. The Republicans also retained the House and the Senate. Kerry had come close: if Ohio, a major swing state, had gone his way, he would have won the presidency. On the other hand, the Republicans had created a new majority. In states that allowed party registration, Republicans outnumbered Democrats. Republicans also held a majority of governorships and state legislator positions. Finally, President Bush beat John Kerry by 22 percent among white middle-class voters—one-third of the electorate. To the president, whose electoral college edge in 2000 had rested upon a 5-to-4 Supreme Court decision, 2004 represented a genuine mandate. "I've got the will of the people at my back," Bush declared, "and that's what I intend to tell Congress."

Why did Bush win? Though an incumbent, Bush bore a load of liabilities, including unending military conflict abroad, a controversial education policy, the mountainous federal debt, and mediocre job ratings. Kerry had greater strength in domestic issues: health care, Social Security, the environment, and the economy; in five Gallup polls of October 2004, respondents favored Kerry over Bush on economic issues. But other factors favored Bush. The electorate voiced divided opinion on the war in Iraq, a conflict that Republicans carefully linked—to the advantage of Bush—to the war against terror. The terrorism issue empowered the president. When considering the war against terror, according to Gallup polls in October 2004, respondents favored Bush over Kerry 56 percent to 40 percent. Also, said pollsters, more people saw themselves as conservative than liberal; they viewed Bush as a candidate who shared their values. Finally, Bush profited from effective Republican TV ads and from the backlash against referenda in eleven states on gay marriage.

In his second term, President Bush pushed plans to cut federal programs. He urged partial privatization of Social Security; under his proposal, workers might shift some of their Social Security funds to private investment accounts. Democrats decried the plan as an effort to undercut New Deal entitlement programs. The public agreed; most Americans objected to assuming the risk of stock portfolios and to the consequent loss of security. The plan sank. In 2006, a Medicare drug plan passed by the Republican Congress in 2003 took effect. Complex and meager, the plan confused senior citizens. Critics charged that it aided drug and insur-

President Bush declares victory in the 2004 election. *(Mark Wilson/Getty Images)*

ance companies more than retirees. The president's second-term domestic agenda failed to evoke public support.

The administration's most grievous policy failure came from an unexpected source. In August 2005, Hurricane Katrina swept through parts of Alabama, Mississippi, and Louisiana. As many as 1,800 residents died. The city of New Orleans, much of it below sea level, bore the worst damage. Levees (embankments to prevent flooding) had until then protected the city from the waters of the Gulf of Mexico and from Lake Pontchartrain. But real estate development around New Orleans had diminished marshland that absorbed water; poor levee maintenance hurt the city, too. When Katrina struck, low-lying areas, in which African-Americans lived, suffered most. Wind, rain, and storm surges weakened levees; water flooded homes, cars, and roads; many drowned or died awaiting rescue. Nursing home residents perished; schools, churches, and hospitals closed. Buses hauled some survivors to adjacent states.

Others congregated in the city's overfull Superdome Stadium, where emergency services failed. Katrina was the most destructive natural calamity in recent history.

In disaster's face, all levels of government floundered. City government capsized; state officials were ineffective. The head of the Federal Emergency Management Agency (FEMA), Michael Brown, a political appointee with no relevant expertise, could not exert control; the hapless official soon resigned. The head of the new Department of Homeland Security, formed in 2002, of which FEMA was now a part, traveled elsewhere when the storm struck. Distribution of emergency relief funds ran into fraud; government-purchased mobile homes sat empty; streets remained sodden and abandoned. The federal government neither coped with the crisis as it occurred nor generated plans to help afflicted parts of New Orleans afterward. The storm's impact on the city persisted. A year later, the population of New Orleans was no more than 40 percent what it had been before the storm. More than two years later, a study showed that the poorest families affected by Katrina had suffered further loss of income, chronic disease, rising mental health problems, and increased dependence on public assistance. Katrina's devastation also made New Orleans more dangerous. Crime rates rose, the city's criminal justice system faltered, and the city topped the nation's homicide charts. The Bush administration's flawed response to Katrina fed a growing chorus of opposition.

ECONOMIC INEQUALITY

Disparity of wealth between the rich and everyone else soared at the start of the twenty-first century. Between 1990 and 2004, real household income rose 57 percent for the top 1 percent of earners, 85 percent for the top 0.1 percent, and 112 percent for the top 0.01 percent. In the bottom 90 percent of households, in contrast, real income rose only 2 percent. Whatever standards researchers employed, the trend was the same. Two economists who examined tax returns in 2006 reported explosive growth among the highest-earning 1 percent of taxpayers, whose share of income doubled since 1980. Within that group the share for the top 0.1 percent tripled and that for the top 0.01 percent quadrupled. The rich got richer, in short, and the very rich got much, much richer. According to the Federal Reserve in 2007, the top 1 percent of households owned more than half the nation's stocks and controlled over $16 trillion in wealth—more than the bottom 90 percent.

The gulf between the pay of top executives and that of ordinary wage earners underlined the scope of wealth disparity. At the start of 2007, the chief executive of Home Depot received $210 million for giving up his job. The chief officer at Morgan Stanley got stock and options worth more than $40 million for the past year and his counterpart at Goldman Sachs over $53 million. Wal-Mart's chief executive in 2005 earned $15 million in cash, stock, and options, an amount equal to about 850 times the pay of Wal-Mart's average "associate" or salesperson. Leading Wall Street firms paid bonuses for 2006 that averaged in the hundreds of thousands; the highest sums went to well-paid managers. Waiting lists increased for yachts, luxury cars, and other expensive items.

As executive pay grew, the wages of ordinary employees stagnated. Although productivity in the nonfarm sector rose 18 percent in the first six years of the twenty-first century, weekly wages adjusted for inflation rose only 1 percent. Gains in productivity, *New York Times* columnist Bob Herbert suggested, went to pay chief executives—whose high remuneration shortchanged ordinary employees. As pay disparity increased, savings rates dropped, pension funds sank, debt increased, more people filed for bankruptcy, and, for many Americans, economic security faded. Writer Barbara Ehrenreich, who in 2001 described her stint at the bottom of the service economy as a Wal-Mart sales associate, revealed that low-level workers faced "a culture of extreme inequality" and acute distress. "You get old pretty fast here," she wrote. "What you don't necessarily realize when you start selling your time by the hour is that what you're actually selling is your life."

Many workers in the lower ranks of the service sector, like the Wal-Mart sales associates, fell into the bottom 40 percent of wage-earning families who earned too little to pay taxes and instead received money from the federal government under the earned-income tax credit, a policy to benefit low-income employed parents. Some earners of low wages joined the statistical ranks of the poor, those whose income fell under the poverty threshold of just under $20,000 for a family of four in 2005. After four years of consecutive hikes, the poverty rate stabilized that year at 12.6 percent of the population, though the rate of poverty varied by ethnicity: 24.9 percent of African-Americans were poor, 21.8 percent of Hispanics, and 8.3 percent of non-Hispanic whites.

What caused rising disparity of wealth? One reason was the decline of the manufacturing sector. In 1975, manufacturing accounted for 28 percent of the economy and the finance industry for 18 percent. Two decades later, the proportions were reversed; the finance industry accounted for 27 percent of the economy in 1995 and manufacturing for only 22 percent. Decline in manufacturing took away jobs and cut pay for those who retained them. New technology replaced employees in manufacturing and other fields. Immigration, on the rise throughout the industrial world, provided new competition for jobs. At the same time, traditional buffers such as labor unions lost bargaining power. At the start of the twenty-first century, unions claimed only 13 percent of employees, compared to 35 percent in the mid-twentieth century. When unions lost clout—and when few workplace regulations curbed management decision-making—employers chipped away at real wages.

Globalization also contributed to dwindling jobs, shrinking pay, and mounting disparity of wealth. Some multinational companies reaped benefits from the global economy (see Chapter 18). Others, facing new competitors around the world, cut production, sliced benefits, fired workers, and outsourced work in order to stay afloat. Employees confronted increasing competition for jobs: cheap imports from China deprived garment workers of jobs; call centers in India cut back white-collar work. In some industries, such as auto production, workers paid for management's mistakes. American carmakers of the 1980s underestimated Japanese competition and in the 1990s focused too heavily on sport-utility vehicles; failures of executive decision making led to the closing of assembly plants and to the firing of thousands of trained auto workers. Unskilled workers had yet fewer prospects. Globalization, wrote *Business Week* in 2004, had "thrown the least skilled into head-on competition for pennies on the dollar."

Overall, economists stressed, the global economy accentuated the divide between college-trained employees and less-trained counterparts. "The educated do well," said a Harvard Business School professor. "And those who aren't do worse and worse." Skilled practitioners in competitive and professional fields, however, faced a form of wealth disparity, too: "Winner-take-all" markets meant that small differences in performance led to huge differences in reward, not only in sports and entertainment, where a star system had long prevailed, but in law, medicine, banking, journalism, fashion, publishing, corporate management, and academic life. A small initial advantage with a personnel-hiring committee, for instance, could

THE 300 MILLIONTH AMERICAN

At 7:46 AM on October 17, 2006, the Digital Population clock at Census Bureau headquarters in Maryland announced the arrival of the 300 millionth American. Many vied for the distinction. Contenders included the son of Mexican-American immigrants, born in Queens, New York, the most diverse county in the nation; the son of Asian-Americans, born in San Francisco; the son of Latin Americans, born in Los Angeles; and, in Manhattan, the daughter of Americans of Dominican, Jamaican, and Puerto Rican heritage. The 300 millionth member of the population could have also been an immigrant at an airport somewhere in the United States. The 200 millionth American had been counted barely forty years before, in 1967.

Those born at the start of the twenty-first century were more likely than counterparts in earlier generations to be nonwhite, foreign-born, or children of newcomers. Between 1980 and 2000, 17 million legal immigrants had entered the United States, along with millions of undocumented newcomers; the census in 2000 estimated that 10.2 million illegal immigrants were in residence. Hispanics that year constituted more than half of the foreign-born, and Asians just over one-quarter. Demographers expected Asian-Americans to have the most rapid rate of growth in the next three decades, and Hispanic-Americans to account for the largest numbers of new Americans. California suggested future population trends. Non-Hispanic whites in California in 1999 dropped to below half the state population; four out of ten Californians did not speak English at home. On May 1, 2006, massive rallies across the nation spoke to immigrants' concerns about proposed measures to tighten immigration law. Marchers voiced demands for immigrant rights and for amnesty for the undocumented.

As immigration changed the ethnic composition of the population, other factors changed family life. Americans married later than at mid-century and not as often. One-third of men and one-quarter of women over fifteen in 2000 had never married; families led by married couples made up 53 percent of all families, compared to 74 percent in 1960. The number of two-parent families among households with children kept falling, and the number of families headed by single parents kept climbing. By 2000, single parents headed 27 percent of all families with children under eighteen. In 1950 births to unmarried mothers accounted for only 4 percent of all births, but by 2000 for one-third of all births. Demographers attributed the rise of single motherhood to late marriage, changing beliefs about the necessity of marriage, and women's participation in the workforce. By the start of the twenty-first century, only one in five American married couples had just a single breadwinner working outside the home. In families with children under six, barely one-third had nonworking mothers.

As the new century began, new patterns emerged. In 2005, for the first time, over half of women lived without a spouse, up from 35 percent in 1950 and 49 percent in 2000. Marriage rates had declined equally among men and women since 1960, researchers stated, but, because women lived longer, single women always outnumbered single men. Most women eventually married, but, on average, Americans now spent half their lives outside marriage. "Commitment aversion" among men in their twenties and thirties spread across class lines. However, demographers found a "marriage gap" between college-educated women—who were more likely to marry—and non–college-educated women. This gap reversed a pattern of the early twentieth century, when women who attended college married at lower

(David McNew/Getty Images)

rates than women in general. "Educated women used to have a difficult time," according to demographers. "Now they're most desired." Those who dropped out of high school, one researcher suggested, "probably have a higher propensity to drop out of marriage." Another posited, "economic resources are conducive to stable marriage." Population statistics, like statistics on income, reflected disparity of wealth among Americans.

Web Links

www.census.gov/2010census/data/
A population profile of the United States.

www.census.gov/population/www/popclockus.html
A United States and world population clock.

mean an insurmountable lead for the chosen candidate and enduring losses for competitors. "Winner-take-all markets have increased the disparity between rich and poor," economists Robert H. Frank and Philip J. Cook wrote in 1995. They also fostered wasteful patterns of investment and consumption and "have molded our culture and discourse in ways many of us find deeply troubling."

The Bush administration fostered disparity of wealth with a tax policy that favored the well off. In his first term, George W. Bush pushed through Congress tax cuts that reached all taxpayers but provided the greatest benefits, through tax cuts on investment income and steady reduction of estate taxes, to the top 1 percent of income earners (with an average income of $1.25 million a year in 2004)—those who pay 36.7 percent of federal income tax. According to Republican plans, the estate tax on inherited wealth was to be phased out by the start of 2010. Bush and his supporters wanted to extend the tax cuts enacted in the president's first term. If this happened, it would affect the national treasury just as baby boomers, born between 1946 and 1960, begin to retire. Tax cuts—and the mounting federal deficits that Bush incurred—can be time bombs.

Economists clashed over whether disparity of wealth has value. Some claimed that it does: it provides an incentive for people to work extra hard in order to come out on top. Economic growth, some analysts pointed out, had been faster recently in nations where the share of income going to the wealthy has increased sharply and workers' share of the gross national product has dropped (though in Europe wealth is less polarized than in the United States). Other economists noted that if the top earners monopolize the rewards of economic growth, the rest might find little reason to make an effort. Harvard economist Richard Freeman used a golf reference to make this point: "If Tiger [Woods] won everything, nobody would want to play." Analysts suggested that disparity of wealth was unlikely to fade anytime soon. "The rich are likely to keep getting richer," observed a global strategist at Citigroup, Ajay Kapur, in the *Wall Street Journal* in 2007, "and enjoy an even greater share of the wealth pie over the coming years."

Is vast disparity of wealth an inevitable part of a growing economy? History suggests otherwise. In the 1920s, when wages failed to keep pace with productivity, the gap between rich and poor widened, debt grew, and economic instability ensued. In the prosperous postwar years, between 1947 and 1970, in contrast, the U.S. economy grew quickly and distribution of rewards was much more egalitarian than it is today. If disparity of wealth grows, what effect will it have? Some worry that vastly uneven distribution of wealth, plus expanding foreign debt, high rates of consumption, big federal deficits, lack of fuel efficiency, and underperforming school systems could compromise U.S. competitiveness. Disparity in wealth distribution, columnist Bob Herbert contends, "is an insidious disease eating away at the structure of society and undermining its future." A better scenario: a greater tax burden on the highest earners, plus universal access to good education and health care, could curb the damage that disparity of wealth imposes and at the same time boost the economy. In the words of economists Frank and Cook, "many of the same policies that promote equality also promote economic growth."

TRANSFORMING THE SUPREME COURT

On September 3, 2005, five days after Hurricane Katrina devastated New Orleans, Chief Justice William Rehnquist died. For a beleaguered President Bush, whose popularity sank because of his inept response to Katrina, the Supreme Court vacancy provided a perfect chance to reshape constitutional law even as he lost influence over other aspects of domestic policy. Because Associate Justice Sandra Day O'Connor had already announced her intention to resign, the president had, in fact, two appointments. Having already nominated John Roberts, a staunch conservative, to replace O'Connor, Bush decided instead to make Roberts chief justice and soon thereafter nominated his friend and White House legal counsel, Harriet Miers, to take O'Connor's seat. When right-wing groups rebelled, arguing that Miers could not be trusted to follow a strictly conservative path, the administration persuaded her to withdraw. Bush replaced her with Samuel Alito, an appellate judge with a reliably conservative track record. The Republican-controlled Senate confirmed him early in 2006, largely on a party-line vote.

Alito's appointment, even more than Roberts's, promised to tilt the Court to the right since O'Connor had often been the fifth or swing vote when the justices were otherwise evenly divided. That was often the case, because several justices—notably O'Connor, David Souter, Anthony Kennedy, and John Paul Stevens—although appointed by Republican presidents, often handed down liberal rulings. Conservative frustration with the Supreme Court had mounted since 2000, especially over its decisions in the areas of abortion, criminal justice, gay rights, separation of church and state, and affirmative action.

In the most recent abortion-rights case, *Stenberg v. Carhart*, decided in 2000, Justice O'Connor cast the fifth and deciding vote against a Nebraska statute criminalizing the performance of "partial birth abortions." In fact, the Nebraska statute outlawed the most common medical procedure in second-trimester abortions and did not provide for an exception when a woman's health was threatened by her pregnancy. Indeed, it provided only a narrow exception when her life was at risk. Justice Stephen Breyer, writing the majority opinion, focused on the absence of those exceptions and also noted that the law placed an "'undue burden' on a woman's right to terminate her pregnancy before viability." Justice O'Connor wrote a separate concurring opinion. Three of the dissenting justices—Antonin Scalia, William Rehnquist, and Clarence Thomas—did not think that abortion was constitutionally protected, while the fourth, Anthony Kennedy, did not think that Nebraska had placed an undue burden on a woman seeking an abortion. "The political processes of the State are not to be foreclosed from enacting laws to promote the life of the unborn and to ensure respect for all human life and its potential," he asserted.

It was, however, Justice Kennedy who cast the deciding vote in a case, originating in Kentucky, that declared that the Constitution barred imposing the death penalty on a person under the age of eighteen (but over fifteen). In 1989, when the Court had upheld just such a state law, Justice Kennedy had joined the opinion. But in 2005, in *Roper v. Simmons*, he announced that he had changed his mind. Citing the Court's long-standing willingness to adapt the law to the "evolving standards of decency that mark the progress of a maturing society," Kennedy noted that "the overwhelming weight of international opinion" condemned the juvenile death penalty and that a new consensus against it had emerged in the United States. He also claimed that even a heinous crime committed by a young person, whose personality was still being formed, was not necessarily "evidence of irretrievably depraved character."

Justice Kennedy also delivered the majority opinion in *Lawrence v. Texas* (2003), which overturned state laws criminalizing homosexuality. The vote was 6 to 3, with Justice O'Connor writing a separate concurrence. As in the matter of the juvenile death penalty, the Court explicitly reversed a relatively recent precedent, in this instance *Bowers v. Hardwick* (1986). Kennedy's opening words eloquently stated his view:

> Liberty protects the person from unwarranted government intrusions into a dwelling or other private places. In our tradition the State is not omnipresent in the home. And there are other spheres of our lives and existence, outside the home, where the State should not be a dominant presence. Freedom extends beyond spatial bounds. Liberty presumes an autonomy of self that includes freedom of thought, belief, expression, and certain intimate conduct.

Referring to gay Americans, Kennedy said, "The State cannot demean their existence or control their destiny by making their private sexual conduct a crime. Their right to liberty under the Due Process Clause gives them the full right to engage in their conduct without intervention of the government." In her concurring opinion, O'Connor wrote, "A law branding one class of persons as criminal solely based on the State's moral disapproval of that class and the conduct associated with that class runs contrary to the values of the Constitution and the Equal Protection Clause, under any standard of review."

In its most significant decision in the area of religion, the Court once again accepted the liberal position, and once again Justice O'Connor cast the deciding vote. *McCreary County v. ACLU* (2005) held that counties in Kentucky could not post copies of the Ten Commandments in courthouses. Justice David Souter emphasized that the government must adhere to a "principle of neutrality": "the government may not favor one religion over another, or religion over irreligion, religious choice being the prerogative of individuals under the Free Exercise Clause." The alternative, he pointed out, was "the civic divisiveness that follows when the government weighs in on one side of religious debate." Endorsing this view, Justice O'Connor added that the principles of the First Amendment "embody an idea that was once considered radical: Free people are entitled to free and diverse thoughts, which government ought neither to constrain nor to direct." Writing for the minority, Justice Antonin Scalia asserted that "the acknowledgment of the contribution that religion in general, and the Ten Commandments in particular, have made to our Nation's legal and governmental heritage is surely no more of a step towards establishment of religion than was the practice of legislative prayer" that the Court had approved in the past.

Affirmative action was yet another controversial area in which the Court adhered to a liberal precedent. In *Gratz v. Bollinger* (2003) the justices overturned, by a vote of 6 to 3, a preferential admissions policy for undergraduates at the University of Michigan, but in a companion case they narrowly accepted a race-conscious admissions policy at the University's law school. In that decision, *Grutter v. Bollinger*, Justice O'Connor yet again cast the crucial vote. Closely tracking Justice Lewis Powell's opinion in the Bakke case (1978), Justice O'Connor asserted that "student body diversity is a compelling state interest that can justify the use of race in university admissions." Diversity promoted cross-racial understanding, she reasoned, and helped break down racial stereotypes. Four justices dissented, including William Rehnquist, who termed the law school's policy "a naked effort to achieve racial balancing," and Clarence Thomas, who stated, "the majority has placed its *imprimatur* on a practice that can only weaken the principle of equality embodied in the Declaration of Independence and the Equal Protection Clause."

Because Justice O'Connor's vote had proven decisive in the affirmative action, religious freedom, and abortion rights cases, it appeared likely that the Court, with Justice Alito serving in her place, would eventually rule differently. Yet it was in the areas of civil liberties and national security that Alito, along with Chief Justice Roberts, was likely to have the greatest impact. In June 2006 the Supreme Court had ruled in *Hamdan v. Rumsfeld* that the military commissions created by the Bush administration to try detainees at Guantanamo Bay violated the Universal Code of Military Justice and the 1949 Geneva Convention. The justices divided 5 to 3, with Chief Justice Roberts recusing himself because he had already rendered a decision when the case arose before the court of appeals. The majority, however, did not decide whether the president possessed the constitutional power to convene military commissions, but only that such commissions had not been authorized by statute. Consequently, the administration pressed for new "antiterror" legislation and Congress responded in September by passing the Military Commissions Act, which was sure to provoke a constitutional challenge.

Sweeping in scope, the measure provided for trying terrorist suspects for war crimes before special military tribunals. It stripped detainees of the right of habeas corpus and gave the president power to detain indefinitely not only foreign nationals but also citizens whom he declared enemy combatants and whom he deemed to have aided terrorist groups. It authorized the use of secret and coerced evidence. Finally, the act gave government officials immunity for past war crimes, such as torturing detainees. In his concurring opinion in *Hamdan*, Justice Kennedy noted that "Congress, not the court, is the branch in the better position to undertake the sensitive task of establishing a principle not inconsistent with the national interest or international justice." As challenges to the act worked their way to the Supreme Court, it remained to be seen how the justices would strike a balance between judicial oversight in protecting individual liberties and deference to the president and Congress during time of war. They would, in truth, have to decide, in the words of one constitutional scholar, whether or not the Military Commissions Act of 2006 "essentially revokes over 200 years of American principles and values."

THE GROWING CRISIS OVER GLOBAL WARMING

In mid-2007, the once thick polar ice cap around the Arctic Circle had, for the first time in recorded history, sufficiently melted so that ships could sail through passageways around the North Pole. Russia immediately planted a flag to claim its right to the rich oil and gas reserves known to lie below the melting ice cap. Canada, Denmark, Finland, Norway, and the United States, among others, then staked their own claims to the same beds of petroleum. By melting ice caps thousands of years old, global warming had triggered an international confrontation.

During the 1970s and after, scientists increasingly noted rising temperatures around the globe. They agreed that 1998 and 2005, and perhaps 2007, were the warmest years on record since temperatures had begun to be tracked in the 1800s. Overall, the earth's atmosphere had warmed by 1.4 degrees Fahrenheit, compared with pre–nineteenth-century levels. The United Nations Intergovernmental Panel on Climate Change (IPCC) warned in 2007 that if temperatures continued to rise and reached (as many predicted they would) 1.8 to 3.6 degrees Fahrenheit above 1980 levels, environmental catastrophes would include placing 20 to 30 percent of all species on earth "at increasing risk of extinction," destroying many coral reefs on which fish depend, and producing sharply increased numbers of victims from "heat waves, floods, and droughts."

Leading scientific organizations concluded that these pending disasters were caused by greenhouse gases produced by fossil fuel (coal, petroleum), which are increasingly trapped in, and warms, the atmosphere. In 1997, 172 nations responded to this crisis by ratifying the

Kyoto Protocol. This agreement, sponsored by the UN's IPCC, required the signatories to reduce their emissions of carbon dioxide and other greenhouse gases by set amounts before 2012, when the Protocol was to expire. The two largest producers of greenhouse gases, the United States and China, refused to sign the Protocol. The U.S. opponents of the pact, which included the world's largest oil company, ExxonMobil, argued that the scientific evidence was inconclusive, and that if the Americans signed while the Chinese did not, the U.S. economy would be at a great disadvantage (by having to spend dollars on cleaning up the gases Americans produced) when competing with China. The United States, after all, produced more greenhouse gases than any other country. The Chinese gladly used the U.S. refusal to sign as an excuse for also not signing the Protocol.

President Clinton did not send the agreement to the U.S. Senate for ratification because he believed opposition to it was too great. After 2001, President George W. Bush actively opposed the Protocol. A close Bush ally in the private sector, the American Enterprise Institute, received funding from ExxonMobil and other oil companies as it attacked the IPCC's work and offered funds to researchers who would undermine the argument that emissions from coal and oil caused global warming.

As the debate raged on, however, temperatures and drought intensified. The U.S. Geological Survey warned that the warmer temperatures melting the Arctic ice cap threatened to kill two-thirds of the world's polar bears by 2050. Melting icebergs and Arctic ice could raise ocean levels until flooding threatened coastal American and European, as well other global, cities. The increased heat naturally intensified storms. In 2007, East Texas faced a storm whose winds suddenly rose from 35 mph to hurricane-force 85 mph in just 18 hours. Hurricane specialists noted, "no tropical cyclone in the historical record has ever reached this intensity at a faster rate near landfall." Intense storms and flooding made millions homeless in Africa and Asia. Sir John Holmes, head of the UN's emergency relief effort on those continents, declared, "We are seeing the effects of climate change. . . . The flooding in Africa just now [2007] is the worst anyone can remember."

Near the end of his second term in office, President Bush and his scientific advisers admitted that dangerous climate change was occurring and that it was linked to the production of greenhouse gases through humans' use of coal and oil. But Bush continued to reject the Kyoto Protocol's schedule for reduction of the gases. He instead offered only vague voluntary efforts to reduce the emissions. China followed the president's policy. Meanwhile, the UN's IPCC won the 2007 Nobel Prize for Peace and shared it with former Vice President Al Gore, whose film, *An Inconvenient Truth*, had dramatically depicted the growing climate dangers to global audiences. Gore's film had earlier won an Oscar award from Hollywood. When announcing the Prize for Peace, the Nobel committee warned, "Extensive climate changes may alter and threaten the living conditions of much of mankind. . . . There may be increased danger of violent conflicts and wars, within and between states."

THE "LAST THROES" OF TERRORISM?
U.S. FOREIGN POLICY AFTER 2003

By 2004, the Bush administration's problems in handling the growing economic inequality, the Patriot Act, and the captured prisoners, mirrored the president's multiplying foreign policy failures in Iraq and Afghanistan. Saddam Hussein had finally been found in a filthy underground hideout in late 2003, and then hanged by an Iraqi court in December 2006. But Saddam's capture did nothing to slow the accelerating anti-American revolt in Iraq.

Unable to control the growing insurgency, Defense Secretary Rumsfeld nevertheless insisted on keeping U.S. troop levels low (about 100,000) in the hope of avoiding another Vietnam-type entanglement—and in the false hope that the Iraqis would quickly overcome their deep internal divisions and govern themselves. Instead, the Sunnis, who, though a minority, had grown used to governing Iraq under Saddam's rule, and the Shiites killed each other in ever-larger numbers. At least 24,000 Iraqis died in 2005 from the fighting, and the number probably increased by at least 50 percent in 2006. It is necessary to say "probably" because as a U.S. commander said, "We don't do body counts." Body counts had spurred antiwar activism during the Vietnam War, so Bush determined they would be ignored in Iraq; photos could not be taken of U.S. soldiers' coffins as they returned to the United States.

Nor did the administration want publicity for the mutilated, limbless soldiers who, thanks to modern medicine's miracles, survived. In 2006 and 2007, the *Washington Post* shook the government by describing the low budgets, staff shortages, and dirty, ill-equipped, and vermin-infested rooms of Washington's Walter Reed Hospital, where many of these soldiers were cared for. The condemnation of "government," made popular by talk-radio hosts, Ronald Reagan, and George W. Bush, had produced a government that could not handle Hurricane Katrina's devastation or care for the maimed U.S. soldiers returning from Bush's war on terror.

Vigorously pushing his goal of spreading democracy across the globe, the president agreed to hold an Iraqi national election in early 2005, although he knew that the country had no democratic tradition and that the majority Shiites would win—as they did. Angry Sunnis boycotted the election, and then intensified their war against the Shiites and the United States. Vice President Cheney was unmoved. "I think they're in the last throes, if you will, of the insurgency," he told television's Larry King in mid-2005. The vicious civil war between Sunni and Shiite instead accelerated, with U.S. troops trapped between the two factions. In February 2006, bombs destroyed the Shiite Golden Mosque in the city of Samarra. The bombers were probably al-Qaeda members (who are Sunnis) seeking to strike a blow against the "heretical" Shiites and to fuel sectarian strife. The Shiites struck back and Sunnis responded in kind. Nearly a hundred civilians were killed each day in the first half of 2006 by suicide bombers and assassination teams. American troops suffered a death toll that in early 2007 surpassed 3,500, hundreds more than the number of deaths caused by the 9/11 attacks. To escape the violence, some 2 million Iraqis, including physicians, teachers, and other middle-class professionals, fled to neighboring nations. As a result, schools and hospital services virtually disappeared. Almost 2 million more Iraqis, out of the country's total population of 28 million, were displaced within Iraq. (This was the equivalent of roughly 43 million Americans leaving their homes to seek refuge elsewhere.)

The Bush administration trusted private U.S. firms to rebuild Iraq. But a special U.S. inspector general, Stuart W. Bowen, reported in early 2007 that Rumsfeld's Defense Department had no strategy for rebuilding either the Iraqi government or the economic infrastructure, and that since 2003 the Bush administration had not come up with a plan to restore the increasingly devastated society. Billions of taxpayers' dollars had disappeared or otherwise been wasted because of contracts given to U.S. corporations without any competitive bids or effective oversight. A secret report from the U.S. Embassy in Baghdad said in 2007, "Iraq is not capable of even rudimentary enforcement of anticorruption laws." In the Iraqi oil fields, it was estimated that between 100,000 and 300,000 barrels—the equivalent of $5 million to $15 million—were lost to corruption and smuggling *every day.*

As a consequence, the World Health Organization reported in 2007 that 80 percent of Iraqis lacked access to "sanitation" (meaning toilets); 70 percent did not have regular access to clean water. Diarrhea and respiratory infections accounted for two-thirds of the deaths of children under five, and at least one of every five children was chronically malnourished. Electricity was available only a few hours a day in many cities. Not surprisingly, Lieutenant General Peter Chiarelli, commander of U.S. ground forces, declared in 2006, "People who were on the fence or supported us" in the past "have in fact decided to strike out against us." In 2007, Retired Lieutenant General Ricardo Sanchez, who commanded U.S. forces in Iraq during 2003–2004, declared the Bush war plan "catastrophically flawed" and that the United States was "living a nightmare with no end in sight."

Afghanistan was also sliding into civil war and chaos. An elected government chosen by the United States exerted control mostly in the northern parts of the nation. The southern portions were increasingly contested by the Taliban, which had supposedly been driven out in the U.S.-led invasion in 2001. The Taliban had rebuilt itself in the mountainous border region between Afghanistan and Pakistan, where it was greatly helped by Osama bin Laden and al-Qaeda. Some 24,000 U.S. troops, aided by 21,000 NATO (especially British, Canadian, and Dutch) forces, tried to stop the Taliban. When in power before 2001, the Taliban had attempted to destroy Afghanistan's famous poppy crop, which had provided much of the world with opium. But in 2007 Afghans, who could find no other profitable crop, raised 50 percent more poppies than in 2005 and provided 93 percent of the globe's opium for drug users. The crop now enriched the Taliban, fueled corruption, and undercut the pro-U.S. government that was helplessly trying to deal with the poppies. The UN reported that in 2007 violence increased 25 percent over 2006, making 2007 the bloodiest year since the U.S. invasion of 2001.

U.S. mistakes in late 2001 had allowed bin Laden and his top aides to escape from Afghanistan. They quickly decentralized authority within al-Qaeda, but held significant control over the organization. The chaos in Iraq gave al-Qaeda the opportunity to set up training bases in the country's western sections. From there, terrorists fanned out across the Middle East and Europe. In 2006, approximately 14,000 terrorist attacks (by both al-Qaeda and other groups) occurred globally, killing more than 20,000 people. These figures marked a 25 percent increase in the number of attacks and a 40 percent increase in deaths over 2005. The United States had fortunately been spared, but the Middle East, South Asia, and Europe did not escape. A 2003 bombing in Istanbul, Turkey, killed 57 people. In 2004, train bombings in Madrid, Spain, took 191 lives. A 2005 attack on the transport system killed 52 people in London, England.

Bush's antiterrorism policies had other high costs. The U.S. military was so overstretched that, for example, waivers were given for the first time to violent criminal offenders so they could join the depleted troop units. In Washington, Cheney's chief of staff and closest adviser, Lewis "Scooter" Libby, was convicted on felony counts and sentenced to jail for lying about the administration's efforts to manipulate and control information about Saddam Hussein's supposed WMD program.

Other foreign policies also suffered. In 2002 Bush had called North Korea, Iraq, and Iran an "axis of evil." In 2004, it was revealed that the North Korean communists were reestablishing their nuclear weapons program. Bush at first refused to negotiate with such an "evil" regime. In 2006, North Korea began to test its weapons. The president then hurriedly allowed

China and Russia to join the United States in negotiating a delicate, tentative deal in which the North Koreans would stop their nuclear program in return for massive economic help and security assurances.

The other member of the "axis of evil," Iran, meanwhile emerged as the dominant power in the Middle East. The United States had not recognized the Islamic Shiite regime since it had seized power in 1979. Bush refused to talk with its leaders even after the Iranians began working closely with their fellow Shiites who gained power in Iraq. By late 2006, however, the president desperately needed Iranian cooperation in Iraq—and to stop, somehow, Iran's rapidly growing nuclear weapons program, which threatened the entire region. In 2007, for the first time in nearly three decades, the United States undertook negotiations with this member of the "axis of evil."

In 2000, Bush had promised to improve relations with Latin America, the area he probably knew best. But after 9/11, the region fell off his priority list. The president simply hoped that opening more free enterprise economic relationships would be enough. It was not. The closest and most important U.S. ally in the region, Mexico, fell into deep economic problems, which led millions of Mexican laborers to enter the United States illegally to find work. Meanwhile, the criminal drug trade and its accompanying violence raged along the U.S.-Mexican border. More than 2,000 people, including police and antidrug agents, lost their lives as Mexican crime groups tried to eliminate each other and seize the rich profits of supplying dependent American drug users.

Further south, a major challenge to U.S. influence appeared. General Hugo Chavez won the Venezuelan presidential election in 1999. Taking advantage of the nation's oil, which provided one of every six gallons of gas Americans used, Chavez set up an increasingly autocratic regime, moved away from the United States and its free trade policies, and became a close friend of China and Castro's Cuba. In 2002, an attempt to overthrow Chavez failed, despite some U.S. support for the rebels. Chavez cracked down on television and other media to ensure he would remain president indefinitely. He moved quickly to replace U.S. oil producers, such as ExxonMobil and Chevron, with Chinese and Brazilian oil firms. Chavez also crafted new ties with regimes in Bolivia, Ecuador, and Nicaragua, among others, which became increasingly sympathetic to his policies and less friendly with the United States.

Overall, relations between the United States and Latin America had soured considerably since 9/11. So had Bush's relations with other longtime American allies. Even Prime Minister Tony Blair of Great Britain, after ten years in office, was forced from power in 2007 because he had been too supportive of Bush's policies, especially in Iraq, for British voters' tastes.

CONCLUSION: THE WORLD AFTER 9/11

In November 2006, Democrats tried to frame the congressional elections as a vote on Bush's foreign policies. In the 2002 and 2004 balloting, the president's top political adviser, Karl Rove ("Bush's Brain," as he was called), had successfully used the issue of terrorism to win Republican victories. In 2006, Rove's strategy backfired. With al-Qaeda cells growing and Iraq in near chaos, the Democrats regained control of the House of Representatives, after twelve years, by gaining thirty seats. They (barely) won back the Senate by taking six seats.

For the first time in American history, a party—in this case, the Democrats— did not lose a single seat in either the House or the Senate in a national election. This stunning result, polls indicated, was clearly caused by Bush's failures in Iraq. His approval rating was in the 30–35 percent range, the lowest since Harry Truman's during the Korean War and a sharp drop from Bush's nearly 90 percent approval rating immediately after the 9/11 attacks. Vice President Cheney's approval rating had sunk to an astounding low of 25 percent.

U.S. elections are usually determined by economic conditions, not foreign policy. In 2006, the stock markets moved to record highs. The overall economy seemed good. As this chapter has emphasized, however, economic inequality increased dangerously. Globalization accelerated the inequality. Those with capital could easily move it across national borders to find profitable investment, but American workers could not move with the capital to China or even Mexico. Despite the $12 trillion gross national product (by far the world's largest), glaring problems of inequality seemed only to be growing—not diminishing as they had between 1930 and 1950. In addition, controversy over the recent Supreme Court decisions on such issues as abortion and equal pay contributed to the Democrats' success.

Surveying the results of the 2006 elections, Bush admitted that his Iraqi policies were heading "to a slow failure." He came up with a policy of "a surge": sending 21,000 or more troops to Iraq to join the 130,000 already there so together they could try to restore some order. By this time war costs approached $1 trillion. These costs helped create a federal budget deficit of about $200 billion each year. Americans depended on the rest of the world to loan them $2 billion each day so they could deal with their trade and budget deficits, keep interest rates low, and live the life of consumerism many of them assumed was their natural right. Meanwhile, Republican and Democratic leaders alike increasingly agreed that U.S. troops would have to remain in Iraq and probably in Afghanistan indefinitely in order to fight a reviving al-Qaeda, counter Iran's growing regional power, and protect U.S. access to Iraq's rich oil fields.

After the end of the Cold War in 1991, Americans spoke confidently about their role as the world's last remaining superpower, proud and unchallenged. Before and especially after 9/11, however, America's power and its political, economic, military, and moral authority began to dissipate at an accelerating pace. The new world order raised a new question: Would there be another American Century?

CHAPTER TWENTY

2007–2012

Obama—"America is a Place Where All Things Are Possible" (Sometimes)

Barack and Michelle Obama watch the January 2009 Inaugural Parade from the viewing stand in front of the White House, Washington, DC. *(Carol M. Highsmith Archive, Library of Congress)*

The answer to the question posed at the end of the last chapter ("Would there be another American Century?") was attempted by President Barack Obama in 2010. He informed an Iowa audience, "There's no reason the twenty-first century is not going to be the American Century just like the twentieth-century was." During the economic, political, and foreign-policy crises that struck the United States after 2007, however, a number of books bearing such titles as *The End of the American Century* provided more pessimistic insights into the nation's future. At home, women, despite having taken giant strides in the workplace since the 1950s, continued to struggle to reach parity with men's incomes and ranking in corporate America. School testing came under attack for narrowing students' interests and stunting their imagination. Supreme Court decisions seemed to many critics to be determined by a conserva-tive majority that threatened to take the nation backward on such issues as affirmative action, gun control, and the financing of political campaigns. The seemingly contradictory combina-tion of bitter political factionalism and strict party allegiance made it nearly impossible to form the compromises necessary for the functioning of the country's legislative system. In foreign affairs, U.S. troops departed from long, bloody wars fought in Iraq and Afghanistan, having achieved few of the original American objectives and leaving behind areas wracked by revolutions and corruption. China, meanwhile, verged on overtaking the United States as the globe's greatest economic power, while Americans already owed the Chinese some $2 trillion of debt. Whether President Obama was a true prophet or a false prophet about the coming of another American Century depended on how the nation dealt with these and other challenges both at home and overseas.

THE GREAT RECESSION, 2007–?

In early 2009, the outgoing Bush administration left historic and disastrous policies for the incoming Obama White House to deal with, including two of the nation's longest and least successful wars in Iraq and Afghanistan. But the most complex and threatening legacy (no-tably in regard to Obama's reelection chances in 2012) was a severe economic downturn. It had begun in late 2007, peaked in 2008–2009 with more than 10 percent of U.S. workers unemployed, and lingered on into 2012 with over 8 percent, or about 12.8 million, remaining out of work. The 2007 downturn had become the Great Recession. It was the worst economic slide to afflict Americans since the Great Depression of the 1930s.

The causes of the catastrophe were many, including weakening, heavily indebted economies in Europe (particularly Italy, Spain, and Greece) that had earlier gone on a spending binge that finally created financial crises. These crises threatened to take down the entire European Union structure of twenty-seven countries. Historically, these nations had been the Ameri-cans' largest markets. China now rapidly moved to become an ever more important trading partner of the United States and also the largest foreign purchaser (some $2 trillion worth) of U.S. governmental debt. The Chinese financed much of Washington's budget deficits. The deficits added up until by 2012 they equaled the gross national product of the United States itself—some $14 trillion. Never in modern American history had another country held such influence over the U.S. Treasury.

China was on course to replace the United States as the globe's number one economic power by 2020. In 2010, however, the Chinese economy began to slow from its 10 percent annual increase to 7 percent. Although still at least twice the U.S. and European rate of annual increase, this lessened rate of growth was a warning signal that the Chinese might not become the hoped-for market for either American producers or U.S. government bonds.

The trigger that set off the Great Recession, however, was pulled in the United States itself. Since 2001, when President Bill Clinton left office after several years of balanced (and often surplus) budgets, both the U.S. government and individual Americans had lived on foreign borrowing (as from China) and credit card debt, which had skyrocketed from $238 billion in 1989 to $962 billion in 2008. Many Americans, especially the 80 percent of income earners in the middle class and lower, lost increasing amounts of their share of the nation's wealth to the upper 20 percent and especially to the top 1 percent who now held a stunning 40 percent of that wealth. From the New Deal to the early 1970s, the middle class had earned an ever-larger share of the economic pie. From a gross national product of $1 trillion in 1970 to more than $14 trillion in 2012, that pie grew spectacularly larger, but the bottom 80 percent of American income earners received an ever-smaller slice.

They maintained their lifestyle by increasing their credit card debt and taking advantage of attractive mortgage interest rates to buy homes. These homes could then be used as collateral for yet more borrowing. After all, the thinking went, U.S. home prices had risen ever higher since the end of World War II. Any downturns had been brief. Most homeowners, however, did not know what was actually happening to their mortgages. Local banks encouraged mortgages because they could then be sold to larger institutions for a good profit. By 2005, the larger institutions were turning them into "derivatives"—packages of mortgages (some good, some bad), commodities (some good, some bad), and national currencies (some rising, some falling). These complex packages were supposed to be a form of insurance against falling home prices. But by late 2007, housing prices stalled; U.S. homebuilders had overbuilt. Such popular areas as Las Vegas, along with large parts of California and Florida, were faced with neighborhoods of either empty houses or homes whose value was rapidly sinking below the mortgage amounts that the owners owed the banks. As home values plummeted in late 2007 to 2008, heavily involved banks (notably the giant Bank of America) and investment houses that held many mortgages in the form of increasingly worthless derivatives faced a crisis. A major, frightening collapse occurred when the distinguished investment firm of Lehman Brothers suddenly disappeared in September 2008. As credit dried up and companies began to lay off personnel, thousands of Americans, unable to pay mortgages on homes that were rapidly losing their value, simply moved out of the houses and no longer paid anything on their mortgages.

By 2010, the median income of U.S. households (that is, the midpoint of all household income, with half of all incomes above and half below) had dropped to $49,112, about the same figure as in 1996. Nearly fifteen years of American middle-class income increases had been wiped out since 2007. Government regulators and the independent Federal Reserve Board (FRB), under its chairs Alan Greenspan and then, after 2006, Ben Bernanke, at first did little. Greenspan had constantly played down the danger. In 2009–2011, long after he left power, he admitted that not recognizing what he termed this "once-in-a-century type of event" had been a great mistake on his part. He had earlier fondly noted that one of his heroes was Ayn Rand, whose popular novels and movies (including *Atlas Shrugged* and *The Fountainhead*) had preached the need for unfettered free enterprise and the evil of state power, including regulatory power. In 2009, however, Greenspan too late admitted amid the darkening economic gloom that he now saw "no alternative to a set of heightened federal regulatory rules for banks and other financial institutions."

By then, President Obama and congressional Democrats were trying to stop the downturn with several major pieces of emergency legislation. The first was the American Recovery and Reinvestment Act (ARRA), which passed Congress and was signed into law by Obama in February 2009. It followed the traditional path (after 1933) of trying to stimulate the depressed economy by pumping in large sums of money, in this instance roughly $800 billion over the next ten years. Billions were spent to help the unemployed, including additional food stamps and health care. Some near-bankrupt states could not, or would not, any longer pay such costs. Most notably, Congress appropriated billions to build badly needed infrastructure (crumbling roads and bridges especially), as well as new mass transit, such as modern fast-train systems in California and Florida. Some of the intended recipients at the state level, including Florida's Republican governor, refused to take the money from a Democratic president and Congress to build infrastructure. Large ARRA sums also aimed to help students from kindergarten through college. Pell grants for needy college students, for example, received $14 billion so that long-successful program could continue with slightly higher amounts. Various areas of scientific research received more than $7 billion.

Republican senators Tom Coburn of Oklahoma and John McCain of Arizona attacked ARRA for including some 200 "wasteful projects." Their amounts involved less than 2 percent of the bill, others did not consider the projects "wasteful," and both senators admitted the legislation would act as a stimulus. ARRA passed the House 246–183, with every Republican and seven Democrats voting against, and then the Senate 60–38, with all Democrats and only three Republicans in favor. Obama was determined to work on a bipartisan basis with Republicans. As one critic observed, the president unfortunately seemed to believe that "'partisan' equaled 'parochial,' or even 'corrupt.'" Obama therefore made important compromises with Republicans, who nevertheless in the end overwhelmingly opposed the bill.

The president's unfounded faith that he could find bipartisan support, the Republicans' refusal to cooperate with his attempts to stimulate the economy, and the rapidly growing federal budget deficit combined to kill efforts to pass another major stimulus package, even as the economy slowed and many millions of Americans remained unemployed. As Republican Senate Leader Mitch McConnell of Kentucky candidly admitted in a newspaper interview, "The simple most important thing we want to achieve is for President Obama to be a one-term president." It was a notable statement, one that directly disavowed the bipartisanship that had marked both parties' willingness to work with various presidents over the years to deal with economic downturns.

The second historic piece of legislation, signed by Obama on July 21, 2010, was the Dodd-Frank Wall Street Reform and Consumer Protection Act. Stung by Wall Street's mishandling of the mortgage market, Democratic senator Christopher Dodd of Connecticut and representative Barney Frank of Massachusetts, along with their supporters, were angered by the increased absence of needed governmental supervision and regulation since the 1970s. A highly instructive example involved the New Deal's Glass-Steagall Act of 1933. This historic legislation had ended the practice of commercial banks recklessly using their depositors' money in order to become investment banks that invested that money in the stock market. Millions of Americans had, as a result, lost their life savings after 1929 when the stock market collapsed. After 1933, commercial banks and their depositors were to be rigidly separated from investment banks. The separation worked well. It lasted, with modifications, for sixty-six years—until 1998–1999, when banker Sanford Weill led a $200 million lobbying drive in Congress to repeal the Glass-Steagall Act so Weill's new Citigroup (the world's largest financial services corporation) and other mammoth banking institutions could be free to invest depositors' money in the stock market and other speculative markets. The other markets included the derivatives, which increasingly used the highly questionable mortgage packages. With the support of President Clinton and Secretary of the Treasury Robert Rubin (who later became a top official in Citigroup), Congress repealed Glass-Steagall in 1999. In 2008–2009, as the collapse of stock prices and particularly the mortgage market threatened to ruin some of the largest banks, including Citigroup, Obama and Congress saved them by pouring billions of dollars into the system. The amount included a $45 billion bailout to save tottering Citigroup. In 2012, Sanford Weill admitted that "what we should probably do is go and split up investment banking from [commercial] banking"—that is, reinstall a version of the Glass-Steagall Act.

The Dodd-Frank legislation was not able to go quite that far, although several powerful financial institutions, on their own, did finally split off investment banking from commercial banking in order, among other objectives, to attract fearful depositors. Dodd-Frank nevertheless became the most sweeping and important legislation to attempt to control American finance since the 1930s. It created nearly 250 new regulations. Several were particularly important to the average American. (1) The law tightened and made more comprehensive federal regulation of financial markets, including for the first time forcing the trading of derivatives to be more open, transparent, and accountable. (2) Dodd-Frank set up a new Bureau of Consumer Financial Protection to protect consumers, for example, from the manipulation of mortgages that had caused many to lose their homes after 2007 and to ensure that finance laws for ordinary Americans were "fair, transparent, and competitive." (3) The Financial Stability Oversight Council was created to monitor and regulate risky operations of both large banks and certain nonbank corporations. These were the kinds of highly speculative operations that had helped set off the Great Recession. (4) To attempt to control corporate boards of directors who sometimes wildly overpaid top company officials, even at the common shareholders' expense, the boards would have to follow new standards, including fuller disclosure of their decisions. These and other provisions created an uproar of protest from both businesses affected and Republicans who vowed to repeal much of Dodd-Frank once they gained control of the White House and Congress.

THE GREAT RECESSION: AN END TO AN AMERICAN DREAM?

The Dodd-Frank legislation tried to change fundamentally how the American economy, especially its financial institutions, operated and how hundreds of millions of consumers were protected. Many hoped-for results were not immediate. Some provisions were not to take effect until 2014 or after. The Bush-Obama stimulus packages, however, changed too little, too slowly. Obama's advisers initially believed, with most other expert observers, that the economy was shrinking at the rate of 3.8 percent per year. The actual rate of the downturn turned out to be an astounding 9 percent. The 2009 Obama stimulus package of nearly $800 million was too small to reverse such a drop. Republicans, with a few Democrats, barred another stimulus from consideration. They were determined to block many of Obama's programs: between 2009 and 2012, the minority Senate Republicans began more filibusters (nonstop speaking on the Senate floor to paralyze meaningful debate and prevent voting) than had occurred during the 1950s, 1960s, and 1970s combined.

By 2010, it was becoming clear that unemployment would not sink below 7 percent over the next two years. But the lack of another stimulus package was not the only problem. A more fundamental change had occurred. As one journalist phrased this problem, in the 1930s building "the Hoover Dam put 5,000 Americans to work with shovels. A comparable project today would require only a few hundred workers with heavy [high-tech] equipment . . . Ultimately the stimulus [bill of 2009] was a 2.5 million-job solution to an 8 million-job problem."

That conclusion raised the question of whether the government could quickly help the other 5.5 million left unemployed. When the Pew Research Center asked Democratic voters whether "it is the responsibility of the government to take care of people who can't take care of themselves," the response remained fairly even between 1987 and 2012 with 75 to 79 percent approving the statement. But Republican voters' approval of that statement dropped from 62 to 40 percent over those years, with much of the fall occurring after 2007. "Americans' values and basic beliefs are more polarized along partisan lines than at any point in the past 25 years," the Pew study concluded.

Some of that response was based on ignorance. When Cornell University political scientist Suzanne Mettler asked a selected sample of 1,400 Americans whether they used a government social program, only 43 percent said that they did. When Mettler then read off a list of twenty-one such programs, including those providing student loans and Medicare, 96 percent had to admit that they indeed had used government aid.

As many of these programs were not expanded, or faced actual reductions, as a result of the growing budget deficits and demands for balanced budgets, Americans had to adjust their lifestyles. Marriage rates dropped and age at marriage rose. By late 2011, barely half of all U.S. adults were married. In 1962, 72 percent of all adults over age 18 were married, but in 2011 only 50 percent had taken such vows. The median age for brides (26.5 years) and grooms (28.7) had reached a record high. Nearly half (49 percent) of U.S. adults ages 18 to 34 said in 2012 that because of the depressed economy, they had taken a job they did not want in order to pay their bills. About 25 percent of that same group declared they had to quit living on their own and move back in with their parents.

Americans, famous historically for "lighting out for the territory" in the West, to use Mark Twain's famous phrase, were also becoming much less mobile. In 1985, 20 percent moved during the calendar year. Between 2010 and 2011, fewer than 12 percent changed residences, the lowest rate since the census began keeping track of such movements in 1948. Barely 7 percent of 20- to 24-year-olds moved, in part because their high unemployment rate and tight bank credit during the recession sharply cut young Americans' ability to obtain mortgages or other loans.

The post-2007 Great Recession sharply affected the middle and lower classes more than it did wealthier Americans. The top 1 percent of American earners (their average income was a little over $1 million) enjoyed an increase of 11.6 percent in their income. The bottom 99 percent of earners' increase was essentially flat. The downturn accelerated a post-1970 trend that made the rich richer and the rest relatively poorer. This trend climaxed in 2010 as 93 percent of the new income created in the United States that year ($288 billion) went to the top 1 percent of taxpayers. That the very rich enjoyed such an advantage was not surprising given that much of the new wealth was created in the high technology and financial sectors (not manufacturing or retail, which used more wage labor). But the radical gap in the difference between the rich and everybody else was surprising. Particularly noticeable was the number of households living on less than $2 per person per day in 2012—a rate the U.S. Census Bureau termed "extreme poverty." That number more than doubled between 1996 and 2011 to some 1.46 million homes. The number of children in such homes also doubled to 2.8 million.

These poverty rates were rising in the world's richest nation. Minority groups, especially Hispanics and African-Americans, especially suffered. The Pew Research Center's analysis of government data revealed that between 2005 and the worst downturn in 2009, median household wealth declined 16 percent for whites, but fell 66 percent for Hispanics and 53 percent for blacks. As a result, Pew concluded, "the typical black household had just $5,677 in wealth (assets minus debts) in 2009, the typical Hispanic household had $6,325 in wealth, and the typical white household had $113,149."

There seemed to be much less chance than in earlier years to escape such poverty. Another Pew Research Center study concluded in 2011 that upward economic mobility, so much a part of the American Dream, had become an illusion for most people: 65 percent of those born in the bottom fifth of income earners now remained in the bottom two-fifths. Those in Denmark and even Great Britain, with its well-known class boundaries, enjoyed more upward mobility than did Americans. Overall, as an economist pointed out, "This is truly a lost decade. We think of America as a place where every generation is doing better" than the last one, "but we're looking at a period when the median family is in worse shape than it was in the 1990s."

OBAMA WINS: THE ELECTION OF 2008

The presidential campaign of 2008 took shape against a backdrop of financial turmoil. Among Democrats, New York senator and former first lady Hillary Clinton held a big lead in opinion polls. The presidency, said Clinton, remained "the highest and hardest glass ceiling in America." Her main rival, Illinois senator Barack Obama, the Democratic keynoter in 2004, had served in the Senate for only two years; he faced an uphill fight. Trailing the front-runners was former North Carolina senator and 2004 candidate for vice president, John Edwards, who suspended his campaign at the end of January 2008. Through months of primaries, Democrats weighed whether to endorse the party's first woman nominee or its first African-American nominee. Clinton enjoyed name recognition, though her family connection drew mixed responses. Obama overcame initial mistrust among black voters, many of whom had been firmly in Clinton's camp. His critique of U.S. involvement in Iraq increased his standing in opinion polls. Finally, he raised funds, inspired young supporters, and gave stirring speeches that stressed unity and change. "We are one people, and our time for change has come," Obama declared after winning the Iowa primary. By early June he had eked out enough delegates to prevail, though only by a narrow margin. Hillary Clinton's strong showing proved that gender no longer impeded presidential bids. Still, Obama turned elsewhere for a running mate. He chose Delaware senator Joe Biden, long familiar to voters and experienced in foreign affairs.

Republican candidates faced greater hurdles than Democrats: whoever won the party's nomination would be saddled with the record of President George W. Bush—that is, low approval ratings, an unpopular war, and a floundering economy. However, candidates crowded the Republican field. Longtime Arizona senator John McCain, who had lost the Republican nomination to Bush in 2000, had to appeal to right-wing evangelical voters, who preferred his rival, Arkansas governor Mike Huckabee. Massachusetts governor Mitt Romney sought the nomination, too, as did New York City's former mayor Rudolph Giuliani. To win, Mc-

Cain claimed to espouse conservative values, played down his previous role as a "maverick," and capitalized on his patriotic record (he had been a prisoner of war for five years in North Vietnam). He also coped effectively with the problem of age (he was 71). "I'm not the youngest candidate," McCain told a Wisconsin crowd, "but I am the most experienced." But as nominee, McCain ran into problems again. He lacked affinity for economic issues, which surged to the front of voters' concerns, and never assuaged distrust on the right. To cater to the party's conservative wing, McCain chose as his running mate Alaska governor Sarah Palin, whose verve energized the Republican base at the party convention. But doubts arose about her competence. Lacking familiarity with public policy, notably foreign policy, she seemed unready for the national stage. A disastrous interview with CBS anchor Katie Couric, in which Palin could not identify Supreme Court decisions with which she claimed to disagree, reinforced her liabilities.

The Obama campaign met unexpected hazards, too, including bad publicity involving the minister of Obama's family church in Chicago, the Reverend Jeremiah Wright, who had issued inflammatory statements. But Obama survived that debacle and held advantages. His campaign made few mistakes. His upbeat if vague rhetoric about change, hope, and bipartisan goals appealed to voters; many independents veered toward the Democrats. Donations also favored the Democrats. The Obama campaign was the first presidential campaign to completely drop the public finance system that had started in the 1970s; an outstanding fund-raising effort drew $764.8 million, far more than Republicans attracted. In addition, the Democrats turned to "new media"—innovative web-based and cell-phone technology—to reach volunteers, convey information about campaign events, and raise money. Supporters, in turn, used websites, blogs, social networking sites, video-viewing sites, and podcasts to share political views. New media further involved young voters, most of whom endorsed the Democrats. Finally, the nation's imperiled economy provided an advantage. For the first time in history, a financial crisis interrupted a political campaign. In September 2008, global markets fell: the investment bank Lehman Brothers collapsed, stocks lost 40 percent of their value, pension funds plummeted, and the federal government lunged to save a failing financial system. As the economy sank, the fortunes of Democrats rose: the crash of 2008 damaged McCain and other Republicans by underlining the need for "change."

Obama won an electoral majority (365 to 173) and more than 53 percent of the popular vote. He captured pivotal swing states—Florida, Ohio, Pennsylvania, Michigan, Colorado, and some previously Republican states (Virginia and North Carolina). Black turnout surged; the black percentage of the electorate in 2008 leaped from 11 to 13 percent. Obama won 95 percent of the African-American vote and 44 percent of the white vote. The 2008 results showed that race did not bar winning the presidency. Democrats also won majorities in both House and Senate. Many factors fused to foster Obama's victory. Economic crisis proved a benefit for the Democrats. New media and innovative technology supported the Democrats' vast volunteer and fund-raising efforts. Finally, Democrats won by default. Republicans could neither overcome nor sever themselves from the disappointing two-term legacy of Bush/Cheney.

"America is a place where all things are possible," Barack Obama told the nation on election night. His early life supported such a statement. The new president was born in 1961 in Hawaii to parents in insecure circumstances. His father was a graduate student in economics from Kenya, to which he would soon return. Obama's mother, whose family came from Kansas, was then in college; she later became an anthropologist. Obama grew up with her in

Indonesia and then with his maternal grandparents in Hawaii. He attended Occidental College and transferred to Columbia. After Harvard Law School, he became a community organizer in Chicago, where he met his wife, Michelle, also a Harvard-trained lawyer. He began his political rise in 1996 with election to the state senate in Illinois. His inauguration as president in 2009 marked a moment of pride for African-Americans, who thronged to Washington to see it. Obama started his term of office amid immense good will and with a Democratic congress. But the new administration had cause for concern. The United States was a divided nation; partisan antagonism remained strong. Most important, the departing Republicans left behind a mountain of debt and a tottering economy.

A "NEW, NEW DEAL": BARACK OBAMA'S DOMESTIC POLICY

It was perhaps inevitable, in the days following his 2008 electoral victory, that Barack Obama would be compared with Franklin D. Roosevelt. "What Barack Obama can learn from F.D.R.—and what Democrats need to do," was the lead story in *Time* magazine. Yet while Obama surely faced daunting economic problems, the political environment in which he operated could hardly have been more unlike that of the 1930s. FDR took office after more than three years of a devastating economic decline that had driven the unemployment rate to 25 percent; by contrast, the jobless figure stood at 7.8 percent when Obama took office, and the recession was still in an early stage. In 1933, the crisis atmosphere had led many Republicans to support early New Deal recovery measures, but Obama's efforts to spur recovery met with inflexible partisan opposition.

In 2009, the devastating downturn that had begun in the last months of the Bush administration worsened. More than 1 million workers lost their jobs in the last four months of 2008, but nearly 3 million more lost theirs during 2009, Obama's first year in office. By December 2009 nearly 10 percent of American workers were unemployed, and the number remained at about that level during all of 2010. The jobless statistics, if anything, understated the extent of the suffering, for they did not include men and women who had given up looking for work in despair, those who had found only part-time work, or those who had jobs they disliked but were afraid to leave. By December 2011, nearly three years after Obama took office, 13.1 million workers remained unemployed, an additional 8.1 million were "involuntary part-time workers," and 2.6 million more wanted jobs but had given up looking for work. The number of workers remaining jobless for six months or more, one writer noted, "soared to levels not seen since the Great Depression."

The slump affected millions of Americans but exacted the highest toll on racial and ethnic minorities. By mid-2011, the unemployment rate among African-Americans—16.1 percent— was more than double that among whites—7.9 percent—and substantially higher than the rate—11.3 percent—among Latinos. Even some of the president's most ardent supporters, such as California representative Maxine Waters, a member of the Congressional Black Caucus, began to voice criticism: "We're supportive of the president, but we're getting tired," she said. "We're getting tired . . . We want to give him every opportunity, but our people are hurting. The unemployment is unconscionable. We don't know what the strategy is."

To combat economic decline, the Obama administration supported an economic stimulus package that provided for $787 billion of spending along with tax cuts over ten years. In addition to numerous tax breaks for businesses, the measure authorized spending on infrastructure (especially for "green investments"), an expansion of unemployment benefits and food stamps, subsidies for individuals to purchase health insurance after they had lost their jobs, and substantial aid to states. The law also reduced taxes for nearly everyone, bringing tax rates to their lowest levels in sixty years. The cuts, the president asserted, were designed "to help middle class families weather the storm, to jumpstart our economy, and to bring the fundamentals of the American Dream—making an honest living, earning an education, owning a home, and raising a family—back within reach for millions of Americans."

It took a painfully long time for the stimulus to have an effect but, eventually, it did. The rate of joblessness finally began to decline late in 2011, falling to 8.5 percent by January 2012. In fact, more new jobs were created in Barack Obama's first term than during the previous eight years under George W. Bush. While the stimulus did not restore prosperity, it did, as one writer said, "put a bottom under the free-fall" and "prevented a spiral downward that could have led to the Second Great Depression." And the stimulus was only one of a number of the administration's economic initiatives: others included the bailouts of General Motors, Chrysler, and major banking institutions, programs that had begun under the Bush administration and were implemented, and expanded, by Obama.

The most important achievement of the Obama administration—and surely the most controversial—was the enactment, in March 2010, of comprehensive health care reform. Known as the Patient Protection and Affordable Care Act, the measure reformed aspects of the private health insurance industry, increased insurance coverage for preexisting conditions, expanded access to insurance to over 30 million Americans, and boosted medical spending. The "individual mandate" provision required that everyone who was not covered by either a private or public health insurance plan would have to purchase a private insurance policy or pay a penalty (unless exempted for reasons of religion or financial hardship). Health insurance exchanges in every state would offer a marketplace where people could compare premiums and purchase insurance, and a government subsidy would be provided for low-income families. The measure, as political scientist Theda Skocpol noted, "draws resources from the privileged to spread access to affordable health insurance to most of the U.S. citizenry."

The bill narrowly passed the House by a margin of 219–212, with 34 Democrats and every Republican voting in opposition. In the Senate, Republicans appeared to have just enough votes—41—to kill the measure by a filibuster, but the Democrats resorted to "reconciliation," a procedure requiring only a simple majority, which both parties had previously used to pass temporary tax cuts. Ironically, since that procedure meant that the votes of the most conservative Democrats were no longer essential, the final bill contained some extraordinarily liberal provisions that would not have been included had Republicans agreed to negotiate rather than simply opposed the measure. In the end, the measure passed the Senate by a vote of 56–43. According to the Congressional Budget Office, the legislation would reduce the number of uninsured persons by 32 million, yet still leave 23 million uninsured by 2019 when all its provisions will have taken effect. The measure also promised to cut the federal deficit by more than $140 billion over the first decade and by over a trillion dollars over the second.

During the congressional debate, Republican opponents of the measure, as well as supporters of the newly founded Tea Party, made dire predictions, including claims that the bill would lead to the creation of "death panels," a charge first made by former Alaska governor Sarah Palin, who contended that the legislation would permit bureaucrats to decide whether elderly or ill Americans were worthy of receiving medical care. And once the bill became law, its constitutionality was immediately challenged in federal court. Opponents claimed, among other things, that fining individuals for failing to buy insurance was not within the scope of Congress's taxing powers and that the measure violated state sovereignty. More than two dozen states backed a joint lawsuit to challenge the individual mandate provision.

The Obama administration could also point to other significant accomplishments. Some were achieved through executive orders: the president reversed the Bush administration's policy that banned federal grants to international groups that provided abortion services or counseling, and he lifted restrictions on federal funding of embryonic stem cell research. In addition, the president signed the Lilly Ledbetter Fair Pay Act of 2009, which revised the statute of limitations for filing pay discrimination lawsuits. He expanded health care for millions of children; and he signed a law substantially raising the federal tax on cigarettes. Obama won approval for a law that ended the role of private banks in making federally insured student loans, thereby realizing a considerable savings. He also signed the Dodd-Frank Wall Street Reform and Consumer Protection Act, which overhauled the financial system and protected consumers from unfair loan and credit practices. Finally, the administration won repeal of "don't ask, don't tell," thereby allowing gays to serve openly in the military. Since 1993, when the policy had been introduced, more than 13,000 gay service personnel had been discharged. Signing the bill, the president declared, "As of today, patriotic Americans in uniform will no longer have to lie about who they are in order to serve the country they love."

Despite this record, many of Obama's most important objectives remained unfulfilled, blocked by partisan wrangling, Republican intransigence, and Democratic discord. One of those goals, in the president's words, was "comprehensive immigration reform" to cope with the problem posed by the 10.8 million illegal immigrants estimated to be in the country. Bills to address the problem, however, bogged down in Congress. What instead emerged, aside from legislation to patrol the borders more strictly, were measures passed by various states, led by Arizona, requiring police officers to check the documents of anybody they stopped if they had a "reasonable suspicion" that the person was here illegally. Another goal of the administration—to reduce dependence on foreign oil by converting from fossil fuel to clean energy—also was stalled. Although the House of Representatives, in June 2009, narrowly passed a comprehensive energy and climate change bill, it died in the Senate, derailed by the economic downturn, the debate over health care, and a resurgent conservative movement.

The slow pace of the economic recovery, the controversy over health care reform, and the stalled legislative agenda all contributed to Democratic losses in the 2010 midterm elections. Only 82.5 million voters went to the polls, compared to 131.3 million in the 2008 presidential election, and the electorate, relatively older, whiter, and more affluent, was also relatively more conservative. Republicans, often with Tea Party support, gained six seats in the Senate and sixty-three in the House of Representatives (the largest change since 1948), taking control of that body. Nearly two out of three voters named the economy as the single most important issue and they voted heavily Republican. As the president admitted, his prospects for election to a second term depended largely on the direction the economy would take during the remainder of 2012.

THE ROBERTS COURT

In 2007, before his election, Barack Obama observed that Supreme Court justices could interpret the Constitution in different ways: "one way is a cramped and narrow way in which the Constitution and the courts essentially become the rubber stamps of the powerful in society. And then there's another vision of the court that says that the courts are the refuge of the powerless." As Obama saw it, the Court's role, in large part, was "to protect people who may be vulnerable in the political process, the outsider, the minority, those who are vulnerable, those who don't have a lot of clout." During his first term, Obama appointed two justices—Sonia Sotomayor and Elena Kagan—but the Court, led by Chief Justice John Roberts, nevertheless adopted a staunchly conservative position on most issues. In 2006, President Bush had chosen Samuel Alito to replace Sandra Day O'Connor, thus shifting the Court's balance substantially to the right. Roberts and Alito, along with Justices Antonin Scalia and Clarence Thomas, only had to win the support of Justice Anthony Kennedy to form a reliably conservative, if narrow, five-member majority.

That is in fact what happened as the justices, in several crucial decisions—each by a vote of 5 to 4—gave the police new authority, dismantled affirmative action, approved laws banning partial-birth abortions, overturned state gun control laws, authorized the use of tax revenues to support religious schools, and, perhaps most important, gutted campaign finance reform. In each of these cases the Court was sharply divided, and in each the five conservative justices formed the needed majority. The Supreme Court, one observer pointed out, "became the most conservative one in living memory."

Hudson v. Michigan (2006) was particularly significant because Justice O'Connor, present when the Court first heard the case, had been replaced by Justice Alito when it was reheard and decided. At issue was whether evidence had to be suppressed if the police, in entering a home, failed to follow the "knock-and-announce" rule. Justice O'Connor had signified her possible doubts about the constitutionality of such a search by asking, "Is there no policy protecting the homeowner a little bit and the sanctity of the home from this immediate entry?" But in June 2009, Justice Alito cast the fifth and deciding vote to uphold the validity of the police entry. Justice Scalia's opinion held that evidence seized in the search, unlike evidence seized in a warrantless search, was admissible. In his dissenting opinion, Justice Stephen Breyer argued that the Court's failure to apply the exclusionary rule to knock-and-announce violations would remove an important deterrent to unlawful government behavior.

In 2007, the Court reconsidered the use of affirmative action to achieve public school integration in *Parents Involved in Community Schools v. Seattle School District No. 1*. Unlike the landmark case of *Brown v. Board of Education*, which in 1954 had produced a unanimous opinion, *Parents Involved* found the justices evenly divided, with Justice Kennedy, "concurring in part and concurring in the judgment," casting the fifth, deciding vote for the majority. The decision, written by Chief Justice Roberts, prohibited the assignment of students to public schools solely to achieve racial integration and declined to recognize racial balancing as a compelling state interest. Racial diversity, he asserted, was not a goal that could justify the use of race in selecting students for admission to public high schools; consequently, a school district that normally permitted a student to choose his or her high school violated the equal protection clause by denying the student admission because of race in an effort to achieve a desired racial balance. The Constitution's guarantee of equal protection, Roberts said, required that "the Government must treat citizens as individuals, not as simply components of a racial, religious, sexual, or national class . . . The way to stop discrimination on the basis of race is to stop discriminating on the basis of race." Justice Kennedy's concurring opinion held that while race-conscious means could be used to achieve diversity, the schools in this case had not tailored their plans in a sufficiently narrow way. "Race may be one component of that diversity, but other demographic factors, plus special talents and needs, should also be considered." So he agreed with Roberts that the school had not presented a "compelling state interest" that would justify the assignment of students on the basis of race. "It is not often in the law that so few have so quickly changed so much," Justice Breyer wrote in dissent. He termed the ruling a radical step that would break the "promise" of *Brown* and deprive schools of an essential tool to combat segregation. It was a decision, he wrote, "that the Court and the Nation will come to regret."

The Court's about-face on the issue of late-term abortions, sometimes called "partial-birth abortions," was equally striking. The procedure was usually performed during the second trimester. In 2000, by a narrow 5–4 vote, the Court had overturned a Nebraska statute that outlawed the practice. But in 2003 Congress prohibited the procedure, and in 2007 the Court, in *Gonzalez v. Carhart*, upheld the statute. What had changed was the makeup of the court: Justice Alito, who had replaced Justice O'Connor, now cast the deciding vote to uphold the measure. Justice Kennedy's majority opinion argued that the case differed from the earlier one because the Partial-Birth Abortion Ban Act defined the banned procedure more explicitly. But his opinion was chiefly notable for how it characterized women: "Respect for human life finds an ultimate expression in the bond of love the mother has for her child. The Act recognizes this reality . . . While we find no reliable data to measure the phenomenon, it seems unexceptionable to conclude some women come to regret their choice to abort the infant life they once created and sustained." In dissent, Justice Ruth Bader Ginsburg termed the decision "alarming," arguing that it departed from established abortion jurisprudence, which held that the lack of a health exception "jeopardizes women's health and places doctors in an untenable position." She thought that the claim that the statute "furthers any legitimate governmental interest is, quite simply, irrational."

Perhaps no decision was more representative of the Roberts Court's conservative jurisprudence than *District of Columbia v. Heller*, which held that the Second Amendment protected an individual's right to possess guns for such purposes as self-defense within the home. (The justices did not decide whether the ruling curbed state as well as federal gun laws, but in 2010 they decided that it did.) Writing for the majority, Justice Scalia said individuals had the right to possess guns and to use them for lawful purposes, such as self-defense within the home, but added that laws prohibiting possession by felons and the mentally ill, or barring firearms in school, were legitimate. In his dissent, Justice John Paul Stevens said that the phrase in the Second Amendment—"to keep and bear arms"—referred to those serving in state militias, not to all citizens. Stevens added, "The Court would have us believe that over 200 years ago, the Framers made a choice to limit the tools available to elected officials wishing to regulate civilian uses of weapons . . . I could not possibly conclude that the Framers made such a choice."

The conservative outlook that prevailed in cases involving criminal law, abortion, affirmative action, and gun control was also evident in the area of state-church relations. In 2011, in *Arizona Christian School Tuition Organization v. Winn*, the justices upheld a state tax credit for those who donated to organizations that subsidized religious schools; the schools, in turn, provided scholarships to students. Speaking for the majority, Justice Kennedy ruled that taxpayers lacked "standing" to challenge the program because they themselves were not harmed by it. Justice Kagan dissented on the grounds that "cash grants and targeted tax breaks are means of accomplishing the same governmental objective—to provide financial support to select individuals or organizations" and therefore amounted to an illegal establishment of religion.

Of all the rulings by the Court, none would have greater impact on American politics than *Citizens United v. Federal Election Commission.* Decided in January 2010, again by a 5–4 vote, it held that the First Amendment prohibited the government from limiting spending for political purposes by corporations and unions. The Court thereby struck down key provisions of the McCain-Feingold Act that prohibited those groups from broadcasting "electioneering communications." Justice Kennedy's majority opinion held that, "If the First Amendment has any force, it prohibits Congress from fining or jailing citizens, or associations of citizens, for simply engaging in political speech." He further asserted, "Political speech must prevail against laws that would suppress it, whether by design or inadvertence." The dissent, by Justice Stevens, argued that the Court's ruling "threatens to undermine the integrity of elected institutions across the Nation" and amounted to "a rejection of the common sense of the American people, who have recognized a need to prevent corporations from undermining self-government since the founding, and who have fought against the distinctive corrupting potential of corporate electioneering since the days of Theodore Roosevelt."

As expected, President Obama criticized the decision, although it was surprising that he did so in his 2010 State of the Union message, in the presence of the justices. "I don't think American elections should be bankrolled by America's most powerful interests, or worse, by foreign entities," the president asserted, while Justice Alito, who had voted with the majority, appeared to mouth the words, "not true, not true." The decision, with few exceptions, was hailed by conservatives but condemned by most liberals, who complained that "we are facing a second Gilded Age where American democracy is for sale to the highest corporate bidder." In the 2010 congressional elections, spending by the candidates, the political parties, and outside groups amounted to an unprecedented $4 billion.

None of the decisions of the Roberts Court, however, would have a more far-reaching effect on the American people than its ruling on the Obama administration's health care law. In March 2012, after twenty-six states and countless organizations had asked the justices to strike down the act, the Court heard five and one-half hours of oral argument. The question was whether Congress had overstepped its powers by requiring all Americans to buy health insurance by 2014 or pay a penalty, a provision known as the "individual mandate." Given the even division between liberals and conservatives on the Court, it seemed that Justice Kennedy might cast the deciding vote, but in fact it was Chief Justice Roberts who provided the fifth vote to uphold the law.

Although he rejected the Obama administration's argument that the law should be sustained either under the Constitution's commerce clause or the "necessary and proper" clause, Roberts believed that the mandate fell within Congress's power to "lay and collect taxes." The law simply imposed a tax on those without medical insurance; the mandate did not require anyone to buy insurance but merely made going without coverage "just another thing the Government taxes, like buying gasoline or earning income." At the same time, the chief justice rejected provisions of the measure that expanded Medicaid to meet the health care needs of those with an income below 133 percent of the poverty level. Those provisions, he said, were not part

People line up after receiving tickets to view arguments at the U.S. Supreme Court, March 27, 2012, in Washington, DC. The Supreme Court dealt with the heart of President Barack Obama's signature health care reform law by taking up its most dismissive requirement—that Americans maintain insurance or be fined. *(Brendan Smialowski/AFP/Getty Images)*

of "a program to care for the neediest among us, but rather an element of a comprehensive national plan to provide universal health insurance coverage."

Justice Ginsburg's concurring opinion for the liberal members of the Court sharply criticized the chief justice's narrow view of the commerce clause. That view, she claimed, "makes scant sense and is stunningly retrogressive," yet she naturally supported his conclusion that the measure was constitutional. For justices Scalia, Kennedy, Alito, and Thomas, however, the majority opinion amounted to "a vast judicial overreaching. It creates a debilitated, inoperable version of health-care regulation that Congress did not enact and the public does not expect . . . The fragmentation of power produced by the structure of our Government is central to liberty, and when we destroy it, we place liberty at peril." Partly because the dissenters referred to Justice Ginsburg's concurrence as a "dissent," many observers speculated that the chief justice had originally been inclined to strike down the law but had then switched sides, thereby making the most important social reform enacted in a generation "constitutional" by the narrowest possible margin.

WOMEN IN ASCENT

"This downturn—the recession combined with the weak recovery—has . . . been far tougher on men than women," journalist David Leonhardt wrote in 2011; few disagreed. Recession hit hardest in sectors of the economy where men were concentrated—in construction, steel mills, auto plants, and manufacturing. Men lost jobs in greater proportions than women and sustained more permanent loss. Women seemed less vulnerable. Throughout the recession, their paychecks inched closer to those of men and their contributions to family income increased. Financial crisis underlined larger trends in women's employment. Women were still clustered in low-paying jobs, but their share of the work force continually grew; they constituted (briefly) over half of workers in 2009 and 2010. Even before recession struck, women's income compared to men's steadily rose. Finally, shifts in the economy favored white-collar fields and service industries in which women worked; the job categories they entered were those expected to expand.

Women's progress in the economy had been gradual. Federal policies since the 1960s had made an impact. Title VII of the Civil Rights Act of 1964, which barred discrimination on the basis of race, sex, color, religion, or national origin, could not ensure equality but offered a channel through which grievance could flow. The Family and Medical Leave Act of 1993, which provided short periods of unpaid leave and job retention in organizations with over fifty employees, responded to working parents' demands. Such policies at least impeded discriminatory practices. A few recent Supreme Court decisions, in contrast, thwarted women's ambition. *Ledbetter v. Goodyear Tire and Rubber* (2007) rejected Lilly Ledbetter's antidiscrimination suit because she had not filed charges against her employer within 180 days of her first complaint. Congress in 2009 passed an act to make filing charges slightly more feasible. In 2011 the Supreme Court denied class action status to a decade-long antidiscrimination suit on behalf of 1.5 million current and former Wal-Mart employees by raising the bar for class action cases. Still, even with setbacks, women's economic progress had been unrelenting. Much of the long-term change reflected women's rising aspirations—their planning, focus, and tenacity.

Women's role in the military suggests the impact of gradual change. Women's proportion of the military rose steadily from 2 percent in 1973 (the start of an all-volunteer force) to 14 percent in 2010. Their role in combat rose, too. The armed services barred women from serving in ground units where combat was the primary mission (such as the infantry and special operations). But women moved into situations that involved combat anyway. They flew in combat aircraft and served on ships that entered combat. War in Iraq and Afghanistan had a marked impact; conflict against guerrilla insurgents after 9/11, a military analyst wrote, "blurs the distinction between front-line and rear areas." Surveys of veterans suggest that policy changes plus more than a decade of conflict since 2001 increased women's combat exposure. Among post-9/11 veterans, 30 percent of women had served in combat, compared to 57 percent of men. Statistical differences between women and men in the military persisted. Among women in 2010, a larger share (almost one-third) were African-American, compared to men (16 percent). A smaller proportion of women in the military married; among these, most wed fellow service members. Women veterans more zealously criticized the U.S. role in Iraq and Afghanistan. But equal proportions of men and women became officers. In 2012 the Marines began integrating women into their frontline units, though not into infantry.

Incremental change characterized women's progress in the workforce in general. The proportion of women age 25 to 54 at work or seeking work kept rising, from 35 percent in 1950 to 75 percent in 2010, and 80 percent among college-educated women. Employment rose especially among mothers of school-age children. What women did in the workforce shifted too. Women made special progress in the professions. By 2010 they were more than half of managers and professionals (including teachers) and dominated a variety of professional fields. They held majorities, for instance, among veterinarians and psychologists, optometrists and pharmacists. Among doctors, women practitioners held majorities in a range of specialties, from pediatrics and dermatology to medical genetics. In professions and other vocations, women moved into expanding sectors. They dominated job categories expected to grow the most in the near future, such as teaching, health care, nursing, accounting, marketing, social services, and food services. Their income kept climbing. In 1979, among full-time workers, women earned only 63 percent of men's income. In 2010, they earned 81.2 percent of men's pay; among younger women (age 25 to 34), 91 percent.

By 2010 a new economic trend emerged: among married couples, increasing numbers of women earned more than their spouses. In 1970 only 4 percent of working wives did so, but by the early twenty-first century, almost one-fourth. The recession boosted the percentages even more. According to journalist Liza Mundy's 2012 book, *The Richer Sex*, the percentage of households in which the wife out-earned the husband every year was going up. Rising income was most pronounced among college-educated wives. The change was one of two unplanned role reversals. First, as two out of five children were born to households headed by women, more women than men were now the main breadwinners in all households with children. Second, as sociologists noted, the rise of the high-earner wife might reshape courtship and the marriage market. Or, as a representative for the Pew Research center stated with circumspection in 2010, "With the rise of well-paid working wives, the economic gains of marriage have been a greater benefit to men."

Women's advance in higher education greatly abetted their shifting economic role. By 2010 a greater proportion of women than men graduated from high school (72 percent to 65 percent); men earned fewer college degrees and took longer to receive them. On most campuses women outnumbered men. The transformation began in the 1970s when women's expectations suddenly rose; their applications to college and professional school soared. In 1980 women became half of college students and four years later a majority of graduate students. Public policy helped too. The Women's Educational Equity Act of 1972 (Title IX) barred sex discrimination in academic and athletic programs in schools, colleges, and universities that received federal aid. The Supreme Court decision in the Virginia Military Institute case, *U.S. v. Virginia* (1996), made equal educational opportunity a guiding principle. By 2012, women received almost three out of every five bachelor of arts degrees (and two-thirds among African-Americans); they constituted three out of five graduate students and half of graduates in law and medicine. The trend in education transcended class structure. In 2010, among families in which parents had not attended college, daughters more than sons were likely to attain college degrees; the less a family earned, the greater the gap between women and men in college enrollment. Students offered varied perspectives. "The girls care more about their GPA and the way they look on paper," a North Carolina student (male) told a reporter. "The men don't seem to hustle as much," a woman student in Washington, DC, commented. "I don't think the guys' willingness to work and succeed has changed," she explained. "It's more that the women have stepped up."

Feminists debated the significance of women's recent advances in the workforce and education. Clearly, over the past half-century, women's drive and determination had made crucial dents in what had once been men's entitlements; women had modified what analysts

SCHOOL WARS

Critics have always carped about failing public schools, and the twenty-first century has proved no exception. Complaints surged in the wake of the No Child Left Behind (NCLB) law of 2002, when the administration of George W. Bush linked federal funding to annual tests of student skills. Student scores in math and reading determined whether a school succeeded or failed. If scores sank, the law set forth a series of remedial steps to boost school performance; in the most extreme instance, after five years of school failure, the state had to close the school, replace it, or take it over and run it. Critics charged that NCLB reliance on standardized tests forced teachers to focus on a narrow set of skills—to "teach to the test"—instead of providing a rich curriculum.

The Obama presidency brought only a degree of change. Guided by Secretary of Education Arne Duncan, the new administration retained testing demands but modified NCLB by granting waivers to several states. Within four years, such waivers reached more than half the states. In 2009 the Obama administration introduced Race to the Top, a plan to spur innovation and reform. The plan awarded funding—up to a total of $4.3 billion—to selected states. The program of competitive grants sought to assess, in the federal government's words, "whether a state is ready to do what works." Requirements addressed adopting learning standards, recruiting teachers and principals, measuring student and teacher success, using computers in classrooms, promoting charter schools, and turning around low-performing schools. States with the winning plans received "award buckets,"

At least some of these students, graduating from Pittsburgh University, will leave college encumbered with debt. *(KitAy)*

size-dependent on school enrollment. Critics challenged the value of proposed reforms as well as the mode of choosing winners. Above all, critics declared, the unending focus on testing crushed creativity and stunted learning.

Charter schools, a central component of Race to the Top, stirred special controversy. Charter schools are state-approved alternatives to public schools, established variously by parents, teachers, nonprofit groups, or business ventures. Free to students, such schools received public funds but escaped some of the rules imposed on public schools; for instance, they could hire nonunionized staff. Student chose whether or not to attend charter schools. When the number of applicants exceeded the places available, charter schools ran lotteries. The documentary film *Waiting for "Superman,"* by Davis Guggenheim, followed five children whose families sought to avoid failing public schools by entering lotteries for charter school admission. Would charter schools force public schools to compete and improve, as their advocates claimed, or, as critics charged, were such schools a way to undercut public education with a nonunionized substitute? To critics, charter schools epitomized the insidious growth of privatization; many charter schools were for-profit schools—private businesses that operated at public expense. Nor did charter schools invariably surpass public schools, as their supporters argued. Rather, their effectiveness varied. A national study of charter schools in 2009 concluded that 17 percent were superior to comparable public schools, 37 percent were worse, and the rest about the same.

Debates over teaching—teacher standards, teacher training, merit pay schemes, and teachers' unions—arose as well. A focus of controversy was Teach For America (TFA), a nonprofit group founded in 1990 by Princeton graduate Wendy Kopp. In its first twenty years, TFA placed more than 20,000 teaching corps members in school positions nationwide. College seniors and recent graduates competed for selective places in the corps; each corps member signed on for two years in assigned schools—typically low-income, disadvantaged schools in urban or rural communities—where they received regular salaries and benefits. Their goal was to make a positive impact on students and become leaders in the cause of educational equity. Usually uncertified, TFA members attended a summer institute to prepare for their stints. Some stayed on in the schools where they served their terms, some moved on to jobs in other schools, and some shifted to other vocations. About two-thirds of former corps members, said TFA, remained in the educational field. Criticism mounted among teachers and their unions, which envisioned teacher layoffs and displacement by TFA corps members. Teachers colleges, which assailed the brief preparation and lack of experience among TFA teachers, questioned TFA's "elitist" assumption that young corps members, with their short stints and rapid turnover, could surpass the classroom performance of professional teachers. Some studies, in contrast, reported positive effects on students scored under TFA participants and a high appreciation rate among principals and school districts.

As new disputes over schools and teachers arose, one issue that had formerly dominated educational discussion simmered in the background: school desegregation had failed to occur. Research showed that African-American youngsters educated in integrated schools fared better in life than counterparts and shared their advantages with their children. But only a portion of black or Hispanic schoolchildren in the twenty-first century escaped segregated education. According to social scientist Gary Orfield and the UCLA Civil Rights Project, achievement gaps between white and African-American students had narrowed in the 1980s but persisted thereafter as school integration faltered. In the 1990s, federal courts had stopped overseeing school desegregation plans. In 2007, the Supreme Court ruled that a school district could not impose an integration plan that distinguished children by race.

As a result, twenty-first century schools were more segregated than schools in the mid-twentieth century. Among African-American and Hispanic populations, two out of five children attended "intensely segregated" schools in which nonwhites constituted more than 90 percent of the students. As always, school segregation reflected residential segregation. Schools in low-income communities remained unequal in funding, curriculum, teacher qualifications, and graduation rates. According to the UCLA project, recent school reform programs had not dented school segregation or its impact. No Child Left Behind failed to narrow the achievement gap between successful schools and underperforming schools. Charter schools, promoted by Race to the Top, were "vastly more segregated" than regular public schools: Seven out of ten black charter school students attended schools with extremely low numbers of white students. Hence, ironically, charter schools increased school segregation, or, as a UCLA report stated, "Charter Schools' Political Success Is a Civil Rights Failure."

Higher education, finally, retained a crucial place as a focus of debate. As recession-plagued states cut back on funds for state colleges and community colleges, some potential students turned to for-profit colleges and vocational schools, whose numbers soared. The growth of for-profit institutions had taken hold in the 1990s: Congress in 1992 provided that up to 90 percent of students enrolled at a for-profit institution could obtain federal subsidies and loans to pay their costs. Managers of for-profits thus found a way to channel federal funds to themselves: they recruited low-income students, those who might obtain federal funds, with promises of jobs after graduation. For-profit schools claimed to reach students who lacked other educational opportunity and to offer them entry to middle-class lives. But students at for-profit institutions graduated far less often than other students. Many, who either dropped out before graduation or failed to find jobs that paid well enough to repay their loans, faced substantial long-term debt. They also defaulted on their loans. Students at for-profit colleges, who by 2012 constituted 11 percent of all college students, received one-fourth of federal student loans and grants and were responsible for almost half of all student loan defaults. The problem of crippling debt did not end with students at for-profits; it surged among all college students, of whom more than nine out of ten borrowed to pay their higher education costs. Since the 1980s, tuition at four-year colleges had been rising faster than family income. Loans came from relatives, private lenders, and the federal government. Average debt among degree-earners in 2011 was $13,000, but some graduates owed almost $50,000. By now college debt had become a way of life. Its extent reflected both the unprecedented cost of higher education and a national reluctance to invest in human capital.

Web Links

www.charterschoolcenter.org
The website of the National Charter School Resource Center, with resources "to build top-notch charter schools."

www.vanderbilt.edu/schoolchoice/
The website of the National Center on School Choice.

viewed retrospectively as "a lifelong affirmative-action program for men." Still, some sets of statistics showed a slowing of economic gains, pockets of rising gender segregation in employment, and persistent inequalities. "What we are seeing is a convergence in economic fortunes, not female ascendance," scholar Stephanie Coontz observed in a *New York Times* article of 2012. Which of women's achievements would prove ephemeral and which enduring remained unknown. For the near future, however, women would enter the workforce with higher educational qualifications than men.

THE WORLD AS A POOL TABLE

In 1991, the Cold War between the United States and the Soviet Union had abruptly ended. Instead of a globe dominated by the two predictable superpowers, it instead became fragmented and unpredictable as new nations suddenly appeared. United Nations membership, for example, leaped from 166 to 192 by 2012. The Soviet Union itself split into a dozen independent countries. The ultimate splintering occurred for Americans on September 11, 2001, when they were attacked not by another nation, but by al-Qaeda terrorists based in no particular country. In this unpredictable, post-1991 world, groups with no national or geographical base could suddenly kill 2,800 Americans and involve the United States in a decade-long series of wars. The world suddenly resembled a pool table after the balls were struck by the cue ball and went off wildly in many directions.

President George W. Bush had hoped that his invasions of Afghanistan and Iraq would not only destroy terrorist bases, but trigger a restructuring of those areas that would result in democratic governments and U.S. access to their mineral wealth, especially Iraq's great oil reserves. A restructuring indeed began, but not the kind Bush favored. By 2012, the invasions had turned into two of the longest, costliest wars in American history, with more than 5,000 U.S. soldiers dead and nearly $2 trillion consumed. Much of that money disappeared abroad even as bitter debates raged in Congress over whether Washington could afford to help millions of unemployed Americans and bankrupt homeowners who were victims of the post-2007 Great Recession.

U.S. secretary of defense Robert M. Gates served under both Bush and President Barack Obama. When Gates spoke to West Point cadets just before he retired in 2011, he declared, "In my opinion, any future defense secretary who advises the president to again send a big American land army into Asia or into the Middle East or Africa should 'have his head examined.'" President Obama had opposed the invasion of Iraq in 2003 and in that respect seemed not to need such an examination.

As they evolved during his presidency, however, Obama's foreign policies proved to be more complex. Running for president, he had pledged that if elected he would withdraw U.S. troops from Iraq. But once in the White House he showed his determination to use military power by rapidly raising the number of troops in Afghanistan as part of a "surge" intended to destroy the anti-U.S. Taliban forces. The Taliban, which had controlled the Afghan government during the 1990s and been driven out by American-led forces in 2001, had regrouped and, by 2012, reclaimed large parts of southern and eastern Afghanistan. Facing this growing threat, as well as the dangers appearing in Iraq and elsewhere in the Middle East, Obama did not devise an overall strategy to deal with the entire pool table (as did, for example, President Harry Truman in 1947 when he devised "containment" globally to stop communist threats—

see Chapter 11). Obama instead seemed to have a checklist of problems he hoped to deal with individually. As the president's director of national intelligence, Admiral Dennis Blair, phrased it, "There quickly developed what I thought of as the top-10 list of individual issues that needed to be worked—Iran, a treaty with Russia, the South China Sea, the Middle East peace process. Never did there seem to be an idea of a strategy—where do we want to be, what's important, and how do we get there." Blair emphasized that Obama's policies seemed to be shaped above all by the president's reading of domestic policies: "Domestic political considerations were ground in very early, very early."

In this context, Hillary Clinton was a superb choice to be Obama's secretary of state. A popular, powerful New York senator who had been Obama's chief challenger in the 2008 Democratic presidential primaries, she knew domestic policies thoroughly. As first lady during her husband's presidency and later as a senator from New York, she had traveled widely and dealt with thorny diplomatic problems—including her decision to support Bush's invasion of Iraq in 2003 while Obama was opposing it. Clinton nevertheless resembled the president in having a "top-10 list" of foreign policy problems with few connections, rather than devising an overall strategy with distinct priorities.

The Obama-Clinton policies consequently responded in sharply differing ways to the crises that erupted between 2009 and 2012. Although Obama made clear he would get U.S. forces out of Iraq, he quickly dispatched 33,000 more troops to deal with the Taliban opposition in Afghanistan. Even when he was awarded the Nobel Prize for Peace in 2009, the president emphasized that in some foreign problems, a quickly sought peace was not the answer: "A non-violent movement could not have halted Hitler's armies. Negotiations cannot convince al-Qaeda's leaders to lay down their arms. To say that force is sometimes necessary is not a call to cynicism—it is a recognition of history, the imperfections of man, and the limits of reason." Many listeners were surprised to hear such words commemorating a peace prize. Obama's intention to rely on force in certain situations, however, was clear. He differed from Bush not in his reluctance to use the U.S. military, but in his reluctance to use it without the cooperation of American allies and, if possible, the United Nations.

The long U.S. war in Iraq became a case study of Obama's policies. In 2002, he had opposed the impending invasion with the words, "I'm not opposed to all wars. I'm opposed to dumb wars." After entering the White House, he pledged to pull the last U.S. combat troops out of Iraq (so the military could focus on Afghanistan and China's rising power) and did so in December 2011. Many of those troops, however, were placed in neighboring Kuwait, just in case Iraq came apart and terrorists (or Iranians) tried to move in. But his hand had also been forced by Iraqi officials, led by Prime Minister Nouri al-Maliki, who wanted the Americans to leave as quickly as possible. When the last U.S. troops departed in somber ceremonies on December 18, 2011, seats were reserved for the top two Iraqi leaders. Neither showed up. Obama, like Bush, had hoped a number of U.S. troops could remain to help maintain order in Iraq. Americans had built the world's largest embassy building in Baghdad to direct and maintain a deep U.S. involvement.

Instead, Maliki, having gained power in U.S.-supported elections, wanted no U.S. troops in his country. As a Shiia Muslim, he felt closer to the Shiia regime of neighboring Iran, a longtime U.S. enemy. He also moved to destroy hopes that the U.S. intervention in 2003 could lead to American oil companies enjoying access in 2010–2011 to what was now the world's fourth-largest oil reserves. Maliki's government granted twelve licenses for such

American Casualties in Afghanistan War Through January 2012 (in thousands)

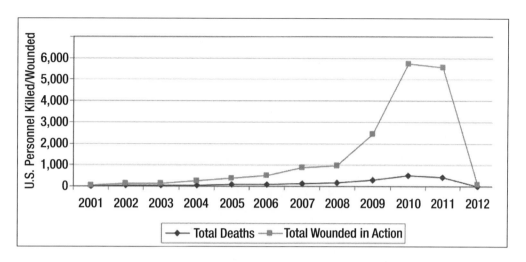

access. China, Russia, and South Korea were among the lucky recipients, but only one U.S. company, Exxon Mobil, received Maliki's blessing. ExxonMobil did gain additional rights to oil in northern Iraq, where the semi-autonomous Kurdish government had control. Maliki's government quickly declared the Kurdish grant illegal. The prime minister was having his own problems. He could not form a government for months in 2011 because of vicious infighting among the three main religious groups—Sunnis (the minority who had controlled Iraq before the U.S. invasion), Shiites (Maliki's faith), and Kurds (who, scattered throughout Iraq and Turkey, had been determined for centuries to form their own nation at the expense of both Iraq and Turkey).

This was a recipe for chaos, which promptly erupted as the U.S. troops were leaving. Sunni insurgents and al-Qaeda terrorists repeatedly attacked Maliki's government and killed hundreds of Iraqis in attempts to divide and seize parts of the country. Maliki's Shiia group fell into such bitter infighting that he could not form a government for months. Iraq's 700,000-strong security forces, built with the help of U.S. training and equipment, could not stop widespread bombings and assassinations. As Maliki moved closer to Iran, many in the United States asked why Americans had sacrificed lives and money for nearly a decade. Dali, a popular Iraqi singer who had left Iraq before 2003 and now returned late in 2011, was stunned by what she found: "I can feel how Iraq has changed now, and how it is sad. All of Iraq is sad." On the U.S. side, Vali Nasr, a former senior State Department official, voiced a widely held view: "The larger legacy of Iraq was that the U.S. military cannot shape outcomes."

As President Obama ordered U.S. troops out of Iraq, he rapidly ratcheted up the effort in Afghanistan while urging his NATO allies to join him. Few cooperated. They believed, and a majority of Americans agreed, that the war in Afghanistan could not be won. The conflict swallowed resources badly needed elsewhere, particularly to contain Iran's nuclear ambitions and China's accelerating economic and military offensives. The president was nevertheless determined to fight a successful counterinsurgency war to win, whatever that word meant, in Afghanistan.

Deaths of Coalition Partners in Afghanistan

Country	Number of deaths in 2011	Total number of deaths
Australia	12	32
Belgium		1
Canada	4	158
Czech Republic	1	3
Denmark	3	42
Estonia	1	9
Finland	1	2
France	24	78
Georgia	4	9
Germany	7	52
Hungary	2	6
Italy	9	44
Jordan	1	1
Latvia		4
Lithuania		1
Netherlands		25
New Zealand	2	4
Norway	1	10
Poland	12	36
Portugal		2
Romania	2	19
South Korea		1
Spain	4	34
Sweden		4
Turkey		2
United Kingdom	44	395
Total	134	974

A counterinsurgency strategy aimed at two objectives: militarily defeating the growing Taliban insurgency, and creating an effective Afghan government on both the national and local levels that could provide services and protection for the Afghan people, thus destroying their belief (or fear) that joining the Taliban was the only way to attain order. Obama's policies could achieve neither objective. In early 2009, he found 47,000 U.S. troops in Afghanistan, sent 27,000 more, and then in late 2009 another 33,000. They fought valiantly but could not destroy the growing Taliban forces or limit the rampant corruption of President Hamid Karzai's government. An estimated $10 million per day was smuggled out of the country in 2009, with much of it, along with massive amounts of money earned by Afghans growing poppies to produce opium, funneled to the Taliban. Between 2001 and mid-2012, Karzai's government did not prosecute even one high-level corruption case.

One thousand U.S. troops died in Afghanistan fighting between 2001 and 2008. Over just the next twenty-seven months of 2009 into 2011, another thousand lost their lives. The fatalities did not stop there: more U.S. active-duty and reserve troops committed suicide in 2010 (278) than died in Afghan combat. Meanwhile, an estimated 22,000 Afghan civilians perished as the fighting accelerated between 2007 and 2011.

By June 2011, Obama quietly decided his counterinsurgency strategy had failed. He began to pull out U.S. troops while declaring that their combat mission would end in 2014. The war was going so badly that Secretary of Defense Leon Panetta declared in 2012 that the mission would end in 2013, a year earlier than scheduled, and all U.S. troops would be withdrawn by late 2014.

Many Afghans, especially soldiers and local rulers, were parochial, uneducated, and—from centuries of bitter experience—fearful and mistrustful of foreign troops, whom they privately condemned as "foreign occupiers." So-called Green on Blue attacks, by Afghanistan's troops on U.S. soldiers who often had trained and fought beside them, rapidly increased in both number and the lists of American dead. Meanwhile, the Taliban, sometimes disguised in U.S. military uniforms, accelerated their attacks. In September 2012, they killed two U.S. Marines and destroyed eight jet fighters. It was the Marine squadron's worst loss of aircraft since 1941, when Japanese forces had reduced its planes to rubble after the Pearl Harbor attack.

Not surprisingly, a few U.S. soldiers could not endure such pressures. In early 2012, one left his base, walked a mile into a village, and opened fire on its inhabitants, killing sixteen, most of them women and children. Anthony Cordesman, a distinguished military analyst, observed that "If you get two 18-year-olds from two different cultures and put them in New York, you get a gang fight. What you have left [in Afghanistan] are two very different cultures with very different values. They treat each other with contempt." Another perspective was offered by a U.S. soldier, Michael Farwell, who served sixteen months in Afghanistan. When his unit received letters from American grade-school students addressed to Marines in Iraq (the wrong war), he said, "We all laugh[ed] about how no one really cares. All the 'support the troops' stuff is bumper sticker deep." Except, of course, for the soldiers and their families. But they represented less than 1 percent of the American population. Obama could move troops in and out of Afghanistan with few Americans seeming to know or care. His major critics were Republican leaders, including Senator John McCain, who attacked the president for not sending more forces into the war.

Obama gained considerable protection against such criticism when he ordered a top-secret Navy Seal team to helicopter into Pakistan and attack a compound where the president suspected Osama bin Laden was hiding. In minutes on May 2, 2010, the Navy Seals flew into Pakistan air space, entered the compound, killed bin Laden, and transported his body and suitcases of valuable documents, which revealed many al-Qaeda personnel and plans, to a safe location. Bin Laden's body was quickly buried at sea. President Obama had not been certain bin Laden was in the compound, and given that several of the president's top officials had advised him not to attempt the highly dangerous operation, Obama emerged as a hero for going ahead with

A senior airman in the U.S. Air Force holds a folded American flag while a coffin in the background returns home the remains of a colleague killed in the Middle East. The George W. Bush administration initially would not allow Americans to see such photos, fearing that they would help trigger anti-war movements, as they did during the Vietnam War. *(Photo © Nicholas A. Price)*

the mission. Bin Laden's death weakened al-Qaeda's central operations, but those had become much less important than the scattered, largely independent al-Qaeda cells that were small, but growing in dozens of countries, especially in the Middle East and eastern Africa.

The president's success was not popular in Pakistan. The Navy Seals had penetrated its air space without informing the Pakistanis, whom the Americans did not trust—and with reason, given that bin Laden's compound was just blocks from Pakistani government facilities. Parts of Pakistan's government, particularly its vaunted Inter-Services Intelligence spy agency, had for years been suspected of working with al-Qaeda and anti-U.S. elements in neighboring Afghanistan who, after all, might survive and come to power after the Americans left. Pakistan's volatile politics turned even more anti-American. The government temporarily closed the road on which American troops depended to truck tons of supplies each day into Afghanistan. The Pakistani government, with its more than 100 nuclear weapons, became weaker and gravely endangered by insurgent, anti-U.S. factions. The on-and-off, thirty-year Afghan war cast darker shadows than most Americans realized.

THE "ARAB SPRING"—AND SOME IMPLICATIONS

Thus, in South Asia, two post-2001 allies, Afghanistan and Pakistan, seemed to be turning away from the United States. In the Middle East, anti-American opinion also rose, but in a

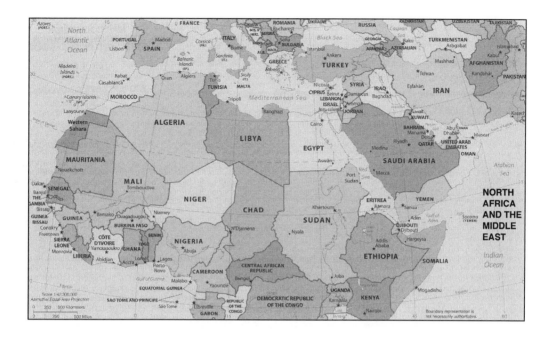

different form. That opinion became only part of larger movements that were determined to destroy long-standing authoritarian regimes, a number of which Washington had supported and supplied. The uprisings began in late 2010 in Tunisia when a fruit vendor burned himself to death in protest against police corruption. In February 2011, they suddenly spread to the leading Middle East nation when massive protests erupted in Egypt against the thirty-year dictatorial rule of Hosni Mubarak, a valued friend of the United States since Ronald Reagan's presidency. Within eighteen days, Mubarak resigned. The 2012 elections brought to power the Muslim Brotherhood, whose religious influence and charity work spanned much of the Middle East. It was viewed by many as anti-American and anti-Israeli, although when it gained power in Egypt, its leaders declared their intention to work with both Washington and Tel Aviv. It was nevertheless clear that the Middle East was fundamentally changing, and the American position weakened, with Mubarak's sudden overthrow.

Smaller nations in the region went through a similar "Arab Spring," producing various results. Tunisia's rulers were removed in 2010, while those in Libya and Yemen, as well as Egypt, followed in 2011. Uprisings also occurred in Bahrain, Algeria, and Kuwait. In Syria, a long, bloody uprising against a half-century-long dictatorship threatened to lead to confrontation between, on the one side, the United States and Europe, which supported the uprising, and, on the other, Russia and China, which had long benefited militarily and economically by backing the dictatorship. U.S. officials, understanding that after the 2003 invasion of Iraq their country was deeply unpopular in much of the Middle East, decided to keep a low profile, particularly after discovering that Washington had little, if any, leverage in controlling the outbreaks. The closest U.S. ally in the region, Israel, felt endangered by the overthrow of longtime friends, particularly Mubarak, and the diminishing of U.S. authority.

Iran moved to the center of American and Israeli concerns. Possessing the world's second-largest natural gas reserves and the third-largest petroleum reserves, Iran had been controlled since 1979 by a Shiia regime viewed by both Washington and Tel Aviv officials as an enemy—especially after the Iranians continued to develop nuclear power capabilities that they said were for peaceful (electrical) purposes, while Israel, the United States, and some Europeans feared the facilities ultimately aimed to create nuclear weapons. Obama imposed tough economic sanctions that badly hurt Iranian banks and oil exports, but in 2011–2012 he would not bend to Israel's repeated demands that military action was required to destroy Iran's possible bomb-making capability.

China's role in both Iran and Syria was notable. Beijing depended almost entirely on foreign oil. Its petroleum concessions in Iran, as well as mineral rights in Syria, led the Chinese to support both besieged governments. China passed Japan to become the world's number two economic power (measured by the two nations' gross national products), second only to the United States. Experts estimated that the Chinese would seize the top ranking from the Americans by 2020, possibly 2018. That success was being protected by growing military (especially naval) forces fueled by rapidly rising military budgets that in 2012 helped launch the first Chinese aircraft carrier. Beijing clashed diplomatically with its neighbors over claims, including petroleum rights, in seas to the east and south of China, and it was rapidly building a navy to back its claims.

Soon those claims extended even to the so-called backyard of the United States—Latin America. Brazil was the continent's greatest economic and political power, a power vastly strengthened by its discovery of immense offshore oil and gas fields. Brazil had long been an economic and military partner of the United States, but by 2011 China had won giant mineral and other concessions to replace the Americans as Brazil's top economic partner. That partnership was, rather ironically, greatly helped by the United States finally surrendering in 1999 its eighty-five-year-old Panama Canal to the Panamanians. To the surprise of Americans who believed Panama's government weak and inept, that government successfully undertook a multi-billion-dollar effort to enlarge the canal. In 2012, only 40 percent of the world's ships were small enough to use the canal. When the expanded canal opens in 2014, it will be able to take 70 percent of those ships—including huge transports moving between China and Latin America's eastern ports, especially those in Brazil.

Obama responded with a widely publicized shift in U.S. policy. He and Secretary of State Clinton signaled in 2010–2011 that the United States was pulling out of Iraq and Afghanistan in part to shift those forces to the containment of Chinese ambitions in Asia and elsewhere. The United States signed new agreements to give military aid to Australia and the Philippines and to place American naval units and some soldiers in both nations. The post-9/11 world was changing. U.S. interests were endangered not only by spreading terrorist cells, but by China's mushrooming military and economic might.

A highly significant result of the wars in the Middle East and South Asia was President Obama's deployment of a new, deadly, and somewhat mysterious weapon that could be used almost magically against terrorist leaders traveling in automobiles or against an enemy's cities. Drones, or unmanned aerial vehicles (UAVs), were controlled by operators thousands of miles away in the United States. The deadly drones, carrying a range of high-tech surveillance equipment and/or explosive materials, could be as small as an insect or as large as a traditional jet plane. They were cheap. And they proved deadly. Flying quietly over parts of the Middle East, Afghanistan, Pakistan, and east Africa, the UAVs located (usually in cars and buildings), then killed, nearly half of the top thirty al-Qaeda terrorist leaders. Tragically, some of the attacks also destroyed innocent men, women, and children. World opinion condemned the drone campaigns. In seventeen of twenty countries, most of whom were long-time U.S. allies, more than half of those polled disapproved of the drone attacks, largely because of the often inescapable civilian casualties.

The American people were about to become directly involved. In 2012, some drones already flew over the United States to locate crimes or to help with flood relief and immigration control. In less than twenty years, the U.S. government estimated, some 30,000 drones would be watching Americans. Critics claimed these drones would violate the Constitution's Fourth Amendment protecting Americans from unreasonable search and seizures. The respected American Civil Liberties Union warned that unless policy was quickly changed, the country would be subject to the "routine aerial surveillance of American life."

In 1991, Americans had emerged victorious from the Cold War and hoped for a long, enjoyable vacation from the burdens of foreign affairs. The explosive fragmentation of world politics that began during the 1990s, and then the 9/11 attacks, destroyed such hopes. By the end of Obama's first term, Americans had discovered that the global economic downturn, growing terrorism, Iranian nuclear development, China's rapidly rising power, Latin America's movement away from Washington's authority, and the drones' deadly threat at home as well as abroad—all of these were necessarily reshaping the hopes of Obama and most Americans for another American Century.

THE 2012 ELECTIONS: OBAMA, ROMNEY—AND HURRICANE SANDY

President Obama began his 2012 reelection campaign with several foreign policy accomplishments (withdrawal of U.S. troops, finally, from the long wars in Iraq and Afghanistan, as well as the assassination of Osama bin Laden) and legislative victories that increased the scope of badly needed health insurance and, through the Dodd-Frank legislation, toughened regulation of Wall Street—although not a single Wall Street figure had been brought to trial for the financial scandals that caused the economic crisis. That crisis created an unemployment rate of nearly 8 percent from 2008 until the last week of the 2012 campaign, a level that had destroyed earlier presidents' hopes for a second term. This economic backdrop for the election was noted by the head of the largest U.S. bond firm: "This is the first American generation that's seriously at risk of doing less well than [its] parents."

Fortunately for Obama, it was also to be a historic election for other reasons, including the roles played by women, ethnic groups, younger voters, and multibillionaires. Amid the economic crises, the country was fundamentally changing. For the first time, a member of the Mormon religion was nominated by a major party for the presidency. Born to money and power, Mitt Romney became a quarter-billionaire himself when in the 1980s he became head of Bain Capital, which bought failing companies, restructured them (at times by laying off workers, moving the firms abroad, or loading them with debt), then profitably selling the results. Romney invariably made money as he became a successful symbol of late twentieth-century American finance capitalism.

In 1994, he entered his father's other realm, politics. The son did not start small but ran against powerful Massachusetts senator Edward Kennedy by proclaiming himself a "progressive Republican" and supporting abortion rights, suggesting a comprehensive state health welfare plan, and promising to outdo Kennedy in advancing gay rights. Romney lost, but next made an international name for himself by taking over the failing 2002 Olympic Games in Salt Lake City and turning them into one of the most successful Olympics in modern history. Two years later he won the Massachusetts governorship. His signature success was a widely applauded state health care law, the first with an individual mandate (meaning that all persons who could afford health care insurance would purchase a minimally comprehensive policy). It became a model for Obama's 2010 national health care law.

In 2007, Romney entered the Republican presidential race. It seemed to be a culture shock: coming from one of the most liberal states, he found himself in a party under the control of social conservatives. Romney promptly tried to distance himself from his own past by condemning *Roe v. Wade* as well as gay marriage. Opponents quickly labeled him a "flip-flopper." He lost the nomination to Senator John McCain, but as the party turned increasingly to the right, notably with the emergence in 2009 of the Tea Party faction (ultraconservatives who bitterly opposed Obama's health care law, government spending to lift the nation out of the recession, higher taxes, and many other federal programs), Romney turned with it. Even then, in early 2012 he suffered primary losses in key states before finally emerging as the winner in a weak group of Republican opponents.

Nor was he helped when in midsummer 2012 he tried to demonstrate his ability to handle foreign policy issues by visiting the Olympic Games in London and then making a highly publicized trip to Israel. Romney made embarrassing statements in both places. In London, for example, he declared that the British were not properly prepared to handle the Olympics. Prime Minister David Cameron, justifiably proud of Britain's preparations, tartly responded that the games were of course easier to run when they were held "in the middle of nowhere."

The official Republican Party platform opposed abortion rights, even in cases of rape or incest; rejected any legal recognition of same-sex civilian unions and marriage; proposed a tough series of anti-immigration (and anti-immigrant) laws; condemned "social experimentation" in the military, including allowing women to serve in combat zones; and pledged no tax increases, "with exceptions for only war and national emergencies." One Platform Committee member called it "the most conservative platform in modern history." The Democratic Party platform rejected each of these Republican planks.

Trailing Obama in public opinion polls, Romney dramatically turned his campaign around in the first of three debates in early October when he moved to a centrist position on many issues. Obama had apparently not taken his opponent seriously. That quickly changed. The president's next two debate appearances were successful. Meanwhile, his reelection organization outmaneuvered Romney's in key battleground states (notably Ohio, Michigan, Pennsylvania, Colorado, Wisconsin, and Florida), where the election would be determined. In Ohio and Michigan, moreover, Obama and a Democratic Congress had saved the all-important auto industry with billions of dollars in aid during 2009–2010. Romney, on the other hand, had written a newspaper column arguing that such government help was unhealthy and that the car plants should be allowed to fail. He later made it worse by declaring that at Bain Capital he liked "being able to fire people."

Perhaps Romney faced his most serious setback when a film emerged in which he was seen telling (he thought privately) a group of wealthy supporters that 47 percent of Americans paid no income tax, but "believe they are victims" who also "believe the government has a responsibility to care for them." The statement ignored the nearly two-thirds of Americans who did pay payroll taxes, while many more also paid state, local, sales, gas, and property taxes. *Los Angeles Times* surveys found that many in the 47 percent bracket who had intended to vote Republican now believed Romney had "contempt for half the population."

His remarks exemplified the major Republican theme of opposing spending programs to fight the economic downturn in order to cut the federal debt and individual taxes, especially the taxes of the wealthiest 2 percent, the supposed job-creators. As this debate raged, Hurricane Sandy struck just a week before the November 6 election—unfortunately for Romney and tragically for millions who lived along the East Coast. One of the two or three worst storms ever to hit the eastern United States, Sandy killed over a hundred people, caused at least $20 billion in property damage, and cut electrical power for some 8.5 million people, many for several weeks or longer. Their responses to Sandy revealed important differences between Obama and Romney. The president quickly mobilized the Federal Emergency Management Agency (FEMA) to pour dollars and personnel into the rescue effort. Romney had declared the agency should be disbanded so states and private companies could handle the relief efforts. FEMA had instead been rebuilt, notably by the Obama administration, and now became a lifesaver.

Many weather experts claimed that the strength of Hurricane Sandy was an ominous result of the warming of the climate over the previous twenty years. New York governor Andrew Cuomo believed that Americans were now facing every two years the kind of flood that formerly hit once every 100 years. The role, if any, government should play in dealing with this dangerous climatic change was an explosive political subject. Most Democrats demanded government action to counter the danger, but many Republicans disagreed. For his part, Obama did not even emphasize the subject during his first term until the week between Sandy's appearance and the 2012 election. A CBS News analysis concluded that "the longer he runs for president, the more doubts" Romney expressed about "the science behind global climate change." After Sandy hit them, however, many voters no longer had such doubts.

On November 6, Obama received 60.5 million votes, Romney 57.7 million, while the president won the decisive Electoral College count 332 to 206. In the Senate, the Democrats gained two seats while two independents decided to caucus with the Democrats, giving them a 55-45 majority. In the House of Representatives, Republicans held on to their majority, 234–201, but the Democrats had gained eight seats and had polled a million more votes nationally than did Republican candidates. Republican state leaders had tried to reduce voting by pro-Democratic minority groups, particularly in Ohio, Pennsylvania, and Florida, by demanding new types of voter identification. But their efforts failed, and these swing states supported Obama while Democrats picked up congressional seats. Notably, several Tea Party–sponsored Senate candidates in Iowa and Indiana, who had been running well ahead of their Democratic opponents, lost after making erroneous, negative statements about abortion rights.

The makeup of the Democratic vote was at points historic. The new Congress had a record number of women: twenty senators and at least eighty-one representatives. Three of the four new female senators, and sixteen of the nineteen new female congressional members, were Democrats. New Hampshire became the first state to send only women to the U.S. Senate and House. Romney won the white vote 59 percent to 39 percent. But as it had since 1992, white voters' portion of the turnout again declined. In all, 55 percent of women voted for Obama, while only 44 percent voted for Romney. Although men preferred Romney by a margin of

52 to 45 percent, women made up more than half—54 percent—of the electorate, and so the gender gap amounted to an astonishing 18 percent. Four African-Americans, ten Latinos, and six Asian-Americans were newly elected to Congress. All were Democrats. In addition, the first nontheist, the first Hindu, and the first Buddhist senator (Mazie Hirano from Hawaii) won congressional seats. Again, all were Democrats. Wisconsin Democrat Tammy Baldwin became the first openly gay person elected to the Senate. Congress also became younger, and for the first time four Democratic candidates born in the 1980s won election. These included Joseph Kennedy III of Massachusetts, whose great-uncle was President John F. Kennedy. Fifty-five percent of their fellow Millennials (those born after 1980) voted Democratic.

On the other hand, the Pew Research Center found that lower-income and less-educated whites, as well as the so-called Silent Generation (those over age seventy), moved increasingly to the Republicans. Middle-income whites, who had split evenly in 2008, voted Republican in 2012 by 17 points. These groups, however, could not match the Democratic support. Nor did they receive sufficient help from the Christian Right, whose organizations had appeared as a potential force during Ronald Reagan's presidency. By 2012, they had faded. Younger voters were less religious; pollsters called one-fifth of Americans "nones" because they had no religious affiliation. A leader of the Southern Baptists lamented that "millions of American evangelicals are absolutely shocked" by the election. "It's not that our message—we think abortion is wrong, we think same sex marriage is wrong—didn't get out. It did get out. . . . An increasingly secularized America understands our positions and has rejected them."

Opponents of same-sex marriage had never lost a statewide referendum, but won thirty-two times. In 2012, however, they lost four referenda, clearing the way for gay marriage in Minnesota, Maine, Maryland, and Washington. On this and other questions, particularly those involving the presidency and Congress, wealthy conservatives had mustered nearly $500 million for their new Super PACs (political action committees), made possible for the first time in 2010 by federal court decisions, to support their causes and candidates. Although the Democrats raised only about $200 million in similar Super PACs, they nevertheless swamped key states with campaign offices and personnel to ensure that their supporters voted. In Ohio, for example, Obama's campaign had set up 100 more such offices than did Romney's. Winning in the twenty-first century, as in the eighteenth century, required a continuing focus on grassroots, get-out-the-vote politics, while wealthy contributors canceled each other out or finally bored media viewers to distraction.

The election seemed to be a natural conclusion to the previous dozen years. Obama was rewarded in part for finally beginning, after several missteps, to pull U.S. troops out of the bloody, unprofitable wars begun a decade earlier. In several respects, such as his evolving view of gay rights, the president represented and spoke for the growing minority groups that played a historic role in the 2012 elections. Some of this was not new in the nation's history. Germans, Irish, Poles, Hungarians, Jews, and many other immigrants had acquired significant political (and cultural) influence since the 1890s. At the same time, the election graphically demonstrated that the wealthiest Americans, despite their Super PACs, were unable to shape the outcome. Meanwhile, in the aftermath of the 2012 contest, many of the nation's citizens continued to debate whether the coming years would, in fact, constitute an "American Century."

Guide to Further Reading

Beisner, Robert L., ed. *American Foreign Relations Since 1600: A Guide to the Literature.* 2nd ed. 2 vols. Santa Barbara, CA: ABC-CLIO, 2003. This guide is available and updated online.

Norton, Mary Beth, and Pamela Gerarde, eds. *The American Historical Association's Guide to Historical Literature.* 3rd ed. New York: Oxford University Press, 1995.

http://historymatters.gmu.edu
Created by the American Social History Project/Center for Media and Learning/Graduate Center of the City University of New York. This site provides a gateway to Web resources, listing more than 1,000 annotated Web sites on American history, and includes 1,000 primary documents and images.

www.blackpast.org/?q=african-american-history-bibliography/
A bibliography of African-American history.

www.cnr.berkeley.edu/departments/espm/env-hist/us-hist.html
A bibliography of environmental history.

www.digitalhistory.uh.edu
Developed by the University of Houston, the Chicago Historical Society, the Museum of Fine Arts in Houston, the National Park Service, and the Gilder Lehrman Institute of American History, this Web site provides a wealth of information about writings on all aspects of American history.

www.digitalhistory.uh.edu/modules/mex_am/bibliography1.html
A bibliography of Mexican-American history.

www.library.yale.edu/rsc/american
A selected bibliography of new works in American history arranged by topic as well as by historical period.

The following *Columbia Guides* are especially useful for specific topics. These titles can be found at **www.columbia.edu/cu/cup/catalog/date/CGAH.HTM:**

Carolyn Merchant, editor, *The Columbia Guide to American Environmental History.*

Robert L. Harris, Jr., and Rosalyn Terborg-Penn, editors, *The Columbia Guide to African American History Since 1939.*

Catherine Clinton and Christine Lunardini, editors, *The Columbia Guide to American Women in the Nineteenth Century.*

Timothy J. Meagher, editor, *The Columbia Guide to Irish American History.*

Gary Y. Okihiro, editor, *The Columbia Guide to Asian American History.*

Michael Kort, editor, *The Columbia Guide to Hiroshima and the Bomb.*

David Farber and Beth Bailey, editors, *The Columbia Guide to America in the 1960s.*

David L. Anderson, editor, *The Columbia Guide to the Vietnam War.*

Index

About the Authors

Walter LaFeber is the Andrew Tisch and James Tisch University Professor Emeritus at Cornell University. His publications include *The New Empire: An Interpretation of American Expansion, 1865–1898* (1963, 1998); *America, Russia, and the Cold War, 1945–2006* (10th ed., 2007); *The Deadly Bet: LBJ, Vietnam, and the 1968 Election* (2005); *The American Age: U.S. Foreign Policy Since 1750* (2nd ed., 1994); and *Inevitable Revolutions: The United States and Central America* (2nd ed., 1991). He is a Stephen H. Weiss Presidential Teaching Fellow at Cornell.

Richard Polenberg is the Marie Underhill Noll Professor Emeritus of American History at Cornell University. He is the author of *Reorganizing Roosevelt's Government, 1936–1939* (1966); *War and Society: The United States, 1941–1945* (1972); *One Nation Divisible: Class, Race, and Ethnicity in the United States Since 1938* (1980); *Fighting Faiths: The Abrams Case, the Supreme Court, and Free Speech* (1987); and *The World of Benjamin Cardozo* (1997). He is the editor of *America at War: The Home Front, 1941–1945* (1968); *Radicalism and Reform in the New Deal* (1972); and *The Era of Franklin D. Roosevelt, 1933–1945* (2000). He is a recipient of the Clark Award for Distinguished Teaching and is a Stephen H. Weiss Presidential Teaching Fellow at Cornell.

Nancy Woloch is the author of *Women and the American Experience* (4th ed., 2006) and *Muller v. Oregon: A Brief History with Documents* (1996); coauthor of *The Enduring Vision: A History of the American People* (6th ed., 2008); and editor of *Early American Women: A Documentary History, 1600–1900* (2nd ed., 2002). She teaches history at Barnard College, Columbia University.